FROM GOVERNMENT TO GOVERNANCE

Foundation The Hague Joint Conferences on International Law gratefully acknowledges the indispensable financial support of the following organisations and companies in connection with the Sixth Hague Joint Conference:

Main Sponsor

Gemeente Den Haag

Sponsors

ABN.AMRO
Algemene Loterij Nederland
De Brauw Blackstone Westbroek
Gravin van Bylandt Stichting
Clifford Chance
Fonds 1818
Stichting Geld- en Effectenhandel
Ministerie van Justitie
Stichting Levi Lassen

FOUNDATION THE HAGUE JOINT CONFERENCES
ON INTERNATIONAL LAW

FROM GOVERNMENT TO GOVERNANCE

The Growing Impact of Non-State Actors on the International and European Legal System

Proceedings of the Sixth Hague Joint Conference held in
The Hague, The Netherlands
3 – 5 July 2003

Edited by:

WYBO P. HEERE

T·M·C·ASSER PRESS
The Hague

Published by T.M.C.ASSER PRESS
P.O.Box 16163, 2500 BD The Hague, The Netherlands
www.asserpress.nl

T.M.C.ASSER PRESS English language books are distributed exclusively by:

Cambridge University Press, The Edinburgh Building, Shaftesbury Road,
Cambridge CB2 2RU, UK,
or
for customers in the USA, Canada and Mexico:
Cambridge University Press, 40 West 20th Street, New York, NY 10011-4211, USA
www.cambridge.org

ISBN 978-90-6704-177-5

The Foundation Hague Joint Conferences on International Law was founded in 1999. Its objective is to further the study of issues of international law through activities organised in the city of The Hague, the Netherlands. The Foundation aims to achieve this objective by means of seminars, conferences, scientific meetings and all other activities that may contribute to the Foundation's objective.

The organizations that have set up the Foundation Hague Joint Conferences on International Law are:

1. The Nederlandse Vereniging voor Internationaal Recht (Netherlands Society of International Law);
2. The Stichting Promotie Den Haag en Omstreken/VVV;
3. The American Society of International Law;
4. Stichting T.M.C. Asser Instituut, Institute for Private and Public International Law, International Commercial Arbitration and European Law.

PREFACE

On behalf of the Stichting 'The Hague Joint Conferences on International Law' I express my gratitude for the publication of the proceedings of the Hague Joint Conference 2003. It was a milestone to have this conference again in The Hague, the first of its kind that was organized under the auspices of the 'Foundation The Hague Joint Conferences on International Law' which was established in 1999 to secure the continuation of the Joint Conferences in the future.

The central theme 'From government to governance' gave an excellent opportunity to elaborate the role of State- and non-State actors in a wide area of international law. International law in an era of international terrorism is more important than it ever has been. State- and non-State actors need each other more than ever to succeed in a world-wide peaceful coexistence.

We appreciated it very much that Piet Hein Donner, Minister of Justice of the Kingdom of the Netherlands, opened the conference, and Peter H. Kooijmans, member of the International Court of Justice, made an address related to the role of non-State actors and international dispute settlement. Furthermore, Thomas Buergenthal, also a member of the International Court of Justice, gave an inspiring dinner speech, while the thought-provoking farewell address was delivered by President Shi of the International Court of Justice.

We enjoyed the arrival and participation of so many persons during the conference at the Kurhaus Hotel in Scheveningen on 3-5 July 2003, debating about the various themes, such as international organisations – governmental and non-governmental – and good governance, multinational business and corporate governance, public and private international law and responding to international terrorism.

I express my deep gratitude to Anne-Marie Slaughter, president of the American Society of International Law and to Nico Schrijver, President of the Netherlands Society of International Law. Thanks also go to the staff of the American Society of International Law and to the T.M.C. Asser Instituut, to Ige Dekker and Dorinda Dallmeyer, the program-directors.

We are grateful to our sponsors and contributors who helped to ensure a secure financial base for the Sixth Hague Joint Conference, in particular the Municipality of The Hague giving hospitality to many international and European institutions and without the generous support of which the Conference would not have been realised.

We look forward to the Seventh Hague Joint Conference which has been scheduled for 30 June until 2 July 2005.

The Hague, April 200

REIN JAN HOEKSTRA
Chairman
Foundation The Hague Joint Conferences on International Law

Contents

Preface
Rein Jan Hoekstra ... V

Introduction
Anne-Marie Slaughter and Nico J. Schrijver ... XIII

Editor's Note ... XV

Opening Session

Welcoming Address
Address by Theo van Boven ... 3

Opening of the Conference
Address by Piet Hein Donner, Minister of Justice of the Kingdom of the Netherlands ... 7

International Organizations as Law-Makers
Address by José Alvarez ... 11

The Role of Non-State Actors and International Dispute Settlement
Address by Peter H. Kooijmans, Judge of the International Court of Justice ... 21

International Organizations – Governmental and Non-Governmental – and Good Governance

International Organizations as Autonomous Subjects in the International and European Legal System ... 31
Chairs: Niels Blokker and Ramses Wessel
Contributions by:
Nigel D. White ... 31
Pieter-Jan Kuijper ... 39
Charles N. Brower ... 44
Rolf Einar Fife ... 51
Discussion ... 55

Accountability and Control of International Governmental Organizations – Principles and Procedures of "Good Governance" 60
Chair: Anne-Marie Slaughter
Contributions by:
Bimal N. Patel 60
Charlotte Ku 66
Daniel D. Bradlow 73
Laurence Boisson de Chazournes 76
Alfred E. Kellermann 83
Discussion 93

Legitimacy, Recognition, Democratic Control, Transparency and Accountability of Non-Governmental Organizations 95
Chair: Deirdre M. Curtin
Contributions by:
Siegfried Wiessner 95
Stephan Hobe 101
Peter J. Spiro 108
Math Noortmann 113
Discussion 120

Review of Application of Principles of Good Governance by International Organizations in Practice 123
Chair: Theodor Meron
Contributions by:
Theodor Meron 123
John King Gamble and Amanda Grolemund 124
Rick Lawson 130
Philippe Lortie 134
Christa Meindersma 145
Hans Thoolen 154
Ralph Wilde 164
Discussion 170

MULTINATIONAL BUSINESS AND CORPORATE GOVERNANCE – PUBLIC AND PRIVATE INTERNATIONAL LAW

Corporate Governance – The Role of Internal or External Codes of Conduct 175
Chair: René van Rooij
Contributions by:
Lucy F. Reed and Hannah R. Garry 176
Willem van Genugten 187
Michel Nussbaumer 194
Jaap Winter 197
Discussion 200

Corporate Responsibility for Human Rights and Environmental Damage – Issues of Transnational Litigation Including International Jurisdiction 202
Chair: Georg Berrisch
Contributions by:
Malgosia Fitzmaurice 202
Pieter H.F. Bekker 209
Harold H. Koh 216
André Nollkaemper 224
Andrew Clapham 227
Michael K. Addo 238
Discussion 239

Using Treaty Cooperation to Improve Capital Flows: The Hague Conference Convention on Securitization 244
Chair: Christophe Bernasconi
Contributions by:
Sir Roy Goode 244
Joyce Hansen 249
Discussion 257

Dinner Speech 258
Address by Judge Thomas Buergenthal, Judge of the International Court of Justice

RESPONDING TO INTERNATIONAL TERRORISM

Challenge of International Terrorism to the International Security System – Designing Responses Within the UN Charter and Treaty Frameworks for Regional Security 265
Chair: Jan Wouters
Contributions by:
Michael Byers 265
Vera Gowlland-Debbas 273
Marcelo G. Kohen 288
Mary Ellen O'Connell 294
Discussion 297

Concerted Actions to Combat Terrorism and the International Financial and Economic Legal System 301
Chair: August Reinisch
Contributions by:
Axel Marschik 301
Albert Straver 310
Himamauli Das 317
Willy Bruggeman 322
Marcel M.T.A. Brus 328
Discussion 334

International Terrorism and International and European Criminal Law 339
Chair: Harry H.G. Post
Contributions by:
Andrea Gioia 339
Leila Nadya Sadat 348
William J. Fenrick 354
Jordan J. Paust 360
Christopher C. Joyner 369
Monica den Boer 379
Discussion 387

SUMMING-UP: A CONCLUDING DEBATE

The Structure of the International and European Legal System and its Values 391
Chair: Dorinda Dallmeyer and Ige F. Dekker
Contributions by:
Sean D. Murphy 391
Theo Raaijmakers 395
Anne-Marie Slaughter 407
Discussion 417

Closing of the Conference
Address by Judge Shi Jiuyong 425

APPENDIX

Round Table Utrecht 1-3 July 2003
'GOVERNANCE AND INTERNATIONAL LEGAL THEORY'
Chair: Wouter G. Werner

Introduction 433

Capitulations of Political Governance in the WTO:
An Alternative Narrative of International Judicialization
Tomer Broude 435

John Rawls on Constitutionalism and the Charter of Fundamental
Rights of the European Union
Paul de Hert 443

Globalization and Global Governance: A Conceptual Analysis
Roland Pierik 454

Anything New under the Sun? The Political Struggle behind the
Legal Debate on International Terrorism
Jörg Friedrichs and Raphael Muturi 463

Irrational Governance: The Use of Force
Nicholas Tsagourias 472

The World Summit on Sustainable Development: Turning Point in Global Governance
Joyeeta Gupta and Nicolien van der Grijp 479

Binding Decisions of International Organizations and their Legitimacy: No Love at First Sight?
Nikolaos Lavranos 490

Best Practices Concerning Corporate Governance – Codes of Conduct: An Alternative Instrument for National Legislation and International Treaties?
Herman Voogsgeerd 494

Tracing the Sources of Non-State Actor Regulation: The Setting of Global Technical Standards in Cyberspace as an Example
J.P. Mifsud Bonnici and C.N.J. de Vey Mestdagh 503

Programm Committee and Officers 517

List of Abbreviations 519

Index of Names 527

Subject Index 529

Introduction

As the presidents of the American and Netherlands Societies of International Law we welcome very much this publication of the proceedings of our Hague Joint Conference 2003. We are grateful that, after a brief interruption, our societies could resume the rhythm of joint conferences. We believe that it is of the utmost importance that American and European international lawyers meet and interact on both sides of the Atlantic. We are also proud that many practitioners and academics from other parts of our globe found their way to our joint conference. A total of nearly 300 persons from 25 countries participated in the conference, which took place in The Hague on 3-5 July 2003.

The central topic of the 2003 ASIL-NVIR conference was a timely one: 'From Government to Governance.' We are increasingly aware that the making, the application and even the enforcement of international law is no longer confined to national States. A rapidly growing number of non-State actors do play a role. These actors are rather heterogeneous. Their role, representativeness and thus legitimacy greatly differ. However, they have in common that they challenge basic assumptions on which international law and international relations have been based. These challenges include the gradual replacement of traditional diplomatic relations by networks of national government officials interacting with one another across borders. These government networks are in turn often embedded in larger 'global policy networks' that involve a wide variety of non-State actors – NGOs, corporations, individual experts, and intergovernmental organizations. New forms of accountability for these non-State actors are also emerging.

The 2003 Hague Joint Conference was our first conference after the horrifying September 11th attacks on the United States, which shocked all of us deeply. As an international law community we have a responsibility to meet in a dignified way the challenges the post-September 11th world poses to international law in terms of combating international terrorism as well as its root causes. We believe our two societies and their biannual conferences provide a very useful platform for dialogue on how to meet these challenges.

Finally, we would like to put on record our sincere appreciation for the tireless joint efforts of the two programme directors Dorinda G. Dallmeyer (ASIL) and Ige F. Dekker (NVIR) in putting together such an intellectually stimulating conference, to the *Foundation The Hague Joint Conferences on International Law*, led by Mr Hoekstra of the Netherlands Council of State for the effective relaunching of the project of our joint conference, to the T.M.C. Asser Institute for so ably organizing the conference, to the staff of the American Society for the unfailing support it provided and to the City of the Hague for providing a financially solid basis to embark on this venture. With the kind help of so many hands our two societies have a wealth of human capital at their disposal to help build a firm foundation for future co-operation. We look forward to seeing you at the next Hague Joint Conference.

ANNE-MARIE SLAUGHTER
President
American Society of International Law

NICO SCHRIJVER
President
Netherlands Society of International Law

Washington DC/The Hague, April 2004

Editor's Note

The Sixth Hague Joint Conference, organized by the *Foundation The Hague Joint Conferences on International Law* in narrow collaboration with the American Society of International Law, the Nederlandse Vereniging voor Internationaal Recht and the T.M.C. Asser Instituut took place on 3-4 July 2004. The theme was 'From Government to Governance? The growing impact of non-State actors on the international and European legal system'.

The meeting was very successful with a great number of panels dealing with a wide range of topical issues in international law. A satisfying number of participants from the United States and Europe participated in the Conference and the variety of their opinions made discussions worth listening to.

A number of young post-graduate students assisted me in the writing of panel reports and the collecting of papers and reports. Unfortunately, some of the papers never reached us and wherever this was the case, you will find 'No paper received' in the Proceedings. Once again, many texts had to be shortened because they exceeded the maximum permitted page quote. Several authors shortened their papers at my request, for others I had to do the work. I am satisfied with the final result of the Proceedings: there is enough difference of opinion between the contributions, so it is worthwhile to formulate your own opinion and compare it with the papers as presented to you in this publication.

At the end of the Conference, information was received that a small preparatory conference took place in Utrecht on 1-3 July on the theme of 'Governance and international legal theory'. The Governing Board of the Foundation decided to include the pre-Conference in the present Proceedings and you will find them following the reports of the main Conference.

As always I could rely on the professional support of the T.M.C. Asser Institute, and my thanks go to Inge van Dun-van den Bosch and Marjolijn Bastiaans.

Conferences are an excellent way to meet colleagues and to exchange opinions on new, sometimes conflicting, issues. May all those who assisted at the Sixth Hague Joint Conference remember it with pleasure, and may the reader who was not there realize that he/she should be there next time.

Utrecht, April 2004

Wybo P. Heere
Senior Lecturer in Public International law
University of Utrecht

OPENING SESSION

Welcoming Address

by Theo van Boven*

Excellencies, Ladies and Gentlemen,

It is my pleasure to welcome you on behalf of the four sponsoring and organizing organizations:

- The American Society of International Law
- The Nederlandse Vereniging voor Internationaal Recht
- The Foundation The Hague Joint Conferences on International Law
- The T.M.C. Asser Institute; Institute for Private and Public International Law, International Commercial Arbitration and European Law.

I am very pleased indeed that this 2003 Hague Joint Conference on Contemporary Issues of International Law is resuming a tradition that was initiated in the early summer of 1990 and that actually started in July 1991 by the joint endeavours of the American Society of International Law and the Nederlandse Vereniging voor Internationaal Recht under the general heading: 'Contemporary International Law Issues: Sharing Pan-European and American Perspectives'.

In the introduction to the Proceedings of the 1991 Joint Conference the then Presidents of the Nederlandse Vereniging and of the American Society stated that in organizing the conference they anticipated a number of difficult substantive and logistical issues but that they could not know that the invasion of Kuwait in August 1990 and the subsequent Gulf War would intervene and threaten their enterprise until only a few months before the actual date.

In fact, since the first Joint Conference was held in 1991, up till this year's sixth Hague Joint Conference twelve years later, extraordinary events and developments took place. These events and developments did not so much threaten the continuation of the Hague Joint Conferences but they did touch upon some of the very foundations of international law. They provide in these days even stronger arguments than in 1991 to engage ourselves as international lawyers from the United States and from Europe in a constant dialogue and appraisal. Such dialogue may have a transatlantic setting but not in a sense of dividing us on the two sides of the ocean but rather in a common endeavour to support and defend the concepts and values we all share.

It is also appropriate to recall that since 1991 the city of The Hague asserted itself as what is called 'the legal capital of the world'. As the already venerable seat of such prominent judicial and academic institutions as the International Court of Justice, the Permanent Court of Arbitration, the Hague Conference on International Private Law

* Nederlandse Vereniging voor Internationaal Recht.

and the Hague Academy of International Law, The Hague was also chosen in recent years to be the host of the International Criminal Tribunal for the Former Yugoslavia and the International Criminal Court. Efforts to pursue peaceful settlement of disputes between States and to seek and meet out justice in reaction to the most serious crimes of concern to the international community are marked by the stature of The Hague as a city of peace and justice. It was also in this spirit that a large group of dedicated organisations, institutions and personalities launched in 1999, at the centenary of the First Hague Peace Conference, the Hague Appeal for Peace comprising an ambitious agenda for a future based on human dignity.

As international lawyers we are facing questions of our roles and responsibilities in a world that is struck by violence, repression and poverty affecting large numbers of people in all continents. Such questions of roles and responsibilities were implicit in an anecdote which I came across some time ago and which may be known to many of you. When Robin Cook, a former British foreign secretary, told the then United States Secretary of State Madeleine Albright that he had 'problems with his lawyers' over using force against Yugoslavia without Security Council approval, Albright responded: 'Get new lawyers'. In this short welcoming statement I will not enter into the substantive issue that was at stake in the conversation between Cook and Albright. Neither will I address the issue whether new lawyers are expected to defend new land that may be distinct from prevailing legal prescriptions and perceptions. The only question I want to touch upon is what purposes lawyers and in particular international lawyers are called upon to serve.

This sixth Hague Joint Conference is structured around the evolving feature and reality in international law and international relations of the growing impact of non-State actors and their status and their relationship with the classical and primary subjects in the international and European legal order, namely sovereign States. The underlying *problématique* in its broadest sense is well captured by the intriguing phrase 'From Government to Governance?', I venture to say that this phrase is not meant as indicating a process of shifting from systems of 'Government' to other forms of authority under the heading of 'Governance'. Rather I see it as a process towards attaching qualitative requirements to State actors and non-State actors alike for the sake of their own legitimacy.

One of the most elaborate statements in support of governance or rather good governance – the two terms are not necessarily identical – was included in a resolution on human rights, democracy and development adopted under Netherlands presidency as early as in November 1991 by the Council and Member States of the European Community (now European Union). The resolution spelled out at some length what should be understood by the policy notion of good governance:

'While sovereign States have the right to institute their own administrative structures and establish their own constitutional arrangements, equitable development can only effectively and sustainably be achieved if a number of general principles of government are adhered to: sensible economic and social policies, democratic decision-making, adequate governmental transparency and financial accountability, creation of a market-friendly environment for development, measures to combat corruption, as well as respect for the rule of law, human rights, and freedom of the press and expression'.

The text just referred to bears the imprint of the last decade of the twentieth century and it applies primarily to domestic State structures, but the principles it enunciates remain nonetheless a vital and present-day postulate for all actors that exercise political and moral authority in international relations. The ultimate test for the validity of such authority is that it promotes and protects human dignity and human welfare. I am confident that our deliberations at this Conference will be guided by the same perspectives.

Opening of the Conference

by His Excellency P.H. Donner
Minister of Justice of The Netherlands

Excellencies, Ladies and Gentlemen,

Next month, on the 24th of August, it will be 105 years ago that Czar Nicolas II of Russia issued his call to the nations to join in a conference dedicated to the problems of world peace and the limitation of armaments. An initiative which led to the first Hague Peace Conference of 1899; a landmark event in different respects. The conference started the emergence of The Hague as a forum for international law and international judicial bodies. The 1899 Hague conference has also been the start of a long series of conferences and meetings on international law here in The Hague, of which the present 6th Joint Conference is but the most recent. From its inception in 1991 the Joint Conference has brought together people from all over the world, who share a common belief in the core values of peace, freedom, democracy, stability and the rule of law. It has proven to be a platform for a transatlantic dialogue on international law that though at times critical, has always been constructive. I am convinced that this 6th Joint Conference will continue that tradition and it is therefore my pleasure to welcome you all at its opening.

The theme of this year's conference: 'From government to governance' reflects the growing awareness that international law is in transition. The observer of the current state of international law is confronted with a number of trends for which 'proliferation' seems to be the most adequate catchword: proliferation of legal subjects, of international organisations, of international judicial institutions, of multilateral treaties, supervisory mechanisms, working groups and international legal norms.

International relations in the 20th century are stigmatised by two world wars, numerous lesser conflicts, unprecedented atrocities and the rise and fall of a bipolar world. But in the shadow of these major developments and in the wake of their disappearance, we see the growth of an ever wider and ever more intricate network of treaties and organisations dealing with an ever wider set of issues and social problems. Improved means of communication and transport, new technological developments, an unprecedented growth of international trade and increasing flows of migration, have laid the foundation for an interdependent, multicultural and ever smaller world. In it national States are no longer capable of dealing effectively with a growing number of transnational problems, and national law does not provide any longer a sufficient institutional framework for social and economic intercourse.

In this process many regional and multilateral organisations have gradually filled in areas that traditionally belonged to the exclusive domain of national governments. It is estimated that next to the 191 Member-States of the UN, the world hosts hundreds of international organisations. Estimations range from 450 to 700 international organisations, depending on the definition. If we multiply these numbers by 50 –

which is a modest estimate of the number of working groups per international organisation – we get the number of groups of civil servants in which political decision making is prepared. Consequently, the concept of the nation State as the sole actor in international law is slowly disappearing. New actors have entered the scene.

The progressive 'individualization' of international law is another feature of its development in the last half century. States are no longer the exclusive subjects of international law. Individuals can invoke a growing number of rights and international norms, either in their national courts or in an increasing number of international supervising or judicial bodies. The reverse is also true. Since the recent establishment of the International Criminal Court, individuals, suspected of having committed crimes against humanity, can now be brought to justice, both in national and in international courts.

What we observe in fact through the rapid accumulation and proliferation of actors, norms, organisations and judicial institutions, is the slow emergence of a real international legal order in which multilateralism prevails and government power is constrained by widely accepted legal norms. It is a continuation of the gradual development of international law. But at the same time it is a fundamental transition in a process that started in 1648 with the Peace Conference of Westphalia, which gave birth to the modern international State system. A system that was at its start predominantly characterised by power politics, but that slowly evolved into the European inter-State system based on such fundamental notions as sovereign equality, independence and territorial integrity. Eventually the Vienna Congress of 1815 laid the foundation, not only for a more stable European system but also for a century characterised by a growth in international conferences and multilateral treaties. A century that also saw the rise of the first international organizations, like the Berne General Post Union. A century that finally culminated in the initiative of Czar Nicholas II to convoke an international conference dedicated to problems of world peace and disarmament. Henceforth, the principles of arbitration and pacific settlement of disputes had definitively penetrated into international practice, thus underlining the increased significance of the rule of law in international affairs.

After the disruption by two subsequent world wars, of this slow growth of an international order it was taken up again in the multilateralism that emerged from these wars. A process that started out as an answer to the weakness of individual States, but then became a channel for regional coexistence which has since matured into a vessel needed to foster international cooperation and which is now evolving into an international legal order in which multilateralism prevails over unilateralism, diplomacy over sanctions and the peaceful settlement of disputes over war.

But, as I said earlier, it is an order that is at the same time characterised by a proliferation of international legal norms, organisations and fora. A proliferation that reflects a certain degree of maturity but at the same time risks to create new problems. Permit me to highlight four of them:

First, the existence of hundreds of international organisations may lead to a needless and even counterproductive competition between organisations, resulting in a hazy picture of overlapping competences and uncoordinated action.

Second, the proliferation of international organisations leads to unfamiliarity, resulting in a gap between these organisations and the citizens and the institutions in the constituent States. A development that raises issues of accountability and democratic legitimacy.

Third, the practice of repeated incorporation of international norms of a similar nature in varying instruments – bilateral, regional and global treaties, resolutions, declarations etc. – may strengthen their coercive nature, but hardly adds to the transparency of the international legal order. On the contrary, the resulting patchwork in which an international norm may be dressed, fundamental as it may be, runs the risk of creating confusion instead of legal certainty.

Finally, international law is not only applied by national courts, but by a growing number of international judicial institutions. Obviously, national and international courts will try to respect and –if possible– even incorporate each other's rulings. But mechanisms to ensure mutual coherence between international judicial fora are largely lacking. As a consequence the risk of diverging interpretations in international law is increasing.

From the long-term perspective of history these are just mid-term challenges. The same holds true for other questions, such as enforcement and the adaptation of public international law to the phenomenon of international organisations. Challenges that provide as many clues as to the possible future developments. Because the present phase of proliferation will eventually have to be followed by a phase of consolidation and condensation of rules, norms and institutions, into a consistent and comprehensive body of legal rules. The number of international organisations will have to be reduced in order to provide international society with a more practical executive power. The judiciary will eventually have to evolve into a coherent organisation of courts.

It is tempting to speculate about future developments and the emerging structure of the international legal order. But temptations are there to be resisted. Speculation is not really productive. History provides us with certain parallels to the present development. There are for example some striking similarities with the evolution of political society during the Middle Ages. But one thing is sure: history never repeats itself. An aspect devoutly to be wished for, because if one thing is clear from history it is the fact that these processes in the past have never succeeded without war and the application of force. That is the challenge for the present and the future; to succeed where others have failed – without war.

Which brings me to one last aspect: the need for power to enforce the emerging international legal order. Law in itself will not be sufficient. As Pascal remarked in his Pensées: 'It is right to follow the right, but it is necessary to follow the mighty. Right without might is helpless, might without right is tyrannical.' It appears to be an acute dilemma with which the international legal order is at present confronted, as some States appear to be withdrawing with impunity from international obligations. At the same time we must realise that the fact that in the present world only very few States have the power to withdraw unilaterally from the international system, is in itself proof of the coercive force of that system. Moreover, the issue of power will have to be dealt with by the international society, because as Pascal remarked: 'Right without might is challenged, ... Might without right is denounced. We must therefore combine right and might, and to that end make right into might and might into right.' (Or in French: 'Il faut donc mettre ensemble la justice et la force, et pour cela: faire que ce qui est juste soit fort ou que ce qui est fort soit juste'). In that respect we need not despair. In the end law, international law is but the institutionalisation of good faith. Good faith of which a famous countryman of mine – Grotius – said: 'it is not only the principal hold by which all governments are bound together, but it is the keystone by which the larger society of nations is united. Destroy this, and you destroy the intercourse of mankind.' And no State, not even the mightiest one, is able in the long run to withdraw from that intercourse.

Ladies and Gentlemen,

At the dawn of the twenty-first century, international law faces many challenges. The creeping erosion of State sovereignty has brought a post-territorial world in sight. The main challenge – and our shared responsibility – is to create, improve and maintain an international society that is characterized by peaceful coexistence, interdependence and justice; individually and between States. A stable international legal order presupposes an international society in which the perspective of peace, freedom and prosperity can be shared. An adequate international legal order is a necessary but insufficient condition to achieve these goals. Regional stability, sustainable development, global security, the fight against poverty and access to fundamental resources, such as water, are equally important, if not more so.

Let me finish by wishing that this conference will prove to be one worthy of the long tradition of meetings and conferences on international law in the Netherlands. I hope that the Dutch and the American Society of International Law will continue their cooperation for many years to come, and I wish you a successful conference.

International Organizations as Law-Makers

José E. Alvarez*

Goodmorning, Ladies and Gentlemen. Welcome to the panel on Transnational Norms of Criminal Procedure.

Frankenstein's monster, as we all know, changed his maker, Dr. Frankenstein. In the same way, the creatures fashioned by international lawyers – inter-governmental organizations such as those of the UN system – are changing us. Inter-governmental organizations (or IOs) have changed our sources of law, the substantive content of our law, as well as the actors that make it. And, as my reference to Frankenstein suggests, IOs pose new risks and challenges.

IOs and the sources of law

From the beginning, IOs have made it easier to conclude multilateral treaties. Political scientists and economists have told us why IOs have become effective treaty machines. IOs are sites for iterated cooperation; vehicles for the pooling of information, expertise, and resources; for reducing transactions costs, uncertainty, and free riders; and for facilitating path dependencies.[1]

From a more lawyerly perspective, IOs have been responsible for three central innovations in treaty making:

(1) UN-styled treaty making conferences with divisions between plenary and specialized discussions, formal and informal, consensus-decision-making, and groupings of States to facilitate the nesting of issues
(2) Initial draft texts done by experts like the International Law Commission or UNCITRAL, whose academic competence is counter-balanced with the political savvy of other bodies, like UN General Assembly's Sixth Committee.
(3) Managerial regimes – as in trade, human rights, the environment and even tobacco control – whose regular meetings permit continuous legislation vastly different from the one-off law-making efforts of the pre-UN era.[2]

As even positivists now accept, IOs have also transformed customary international law.[3] Historical surveys of the practice and reaction of bilateral sets of States across decades are now passé. No one has the patience to comb through laborious diplomatic exchanges to discover whether custom exists. IOs have given us shortcuts to find custom that trouble legal historians. Increasingly we rely on IOs' legislative treaties to

* Professor of Law, Columbia Law School. Text of Keynote Address, presented at The Hague, 4 July 2001.

1 See generally, Kenneth W. Abbott and Duncan Snidal, *Why States Act through Formal International Organizations*, 42 J. Conflict Resolution 3 (1998).

2 See generally, Jose E. Alvarez, *The New Treaty Makers*, 25 Boston College Int'l and Comp. L. Rev. 213 (2002).

3 See, e.g., Bruno Simma and Andreas L. Paulus, *The Responsibility of Individuals for Human Rights Abuses in Internal Conflicts: A Positivist View*, 93 AJIL 302 (1999).

suggest custom binding even on non-parties, on General Assembly resolutions, on the practice of IO organs or their secretariats, and even on the occasional principle proclaimed at a UN conference (such as the precautionary principle). We also find custom and general principles of law in another product of institutions: in the judgments issued by a proliferating number of international dispute settlers – now embracing some 200 international judges across some 50 judicial or quasi-judicial venues.[4]

IOs also produce lots of post-modern or post-positivist norms, outside the three traditional sources of international law. IOs generate enormous quantities of 'soft law' and some of it hardens (if not in pedigree at least in effect) as a result of other organizational processes. To the regret of positivists, the result is that it is often difficult to tell the difference between black letter law **that is** and the law that **ought to be.** In fact some soft law, produced either by inter-governmental bodies or even private associations, such as codes for marketing foodstuffs or packaging goods or the World Bank's Guidelines, are more effectively enforced than are some "hard" treaties – as in hands of WTO panelists or the World Bank's Inspection Panel. If, to the horror of scholars like Prosper Weil, modern "norm cascades" enjoy a spectrum of binding force, IOs must be given the requisite credit or blame.[5]

Although we still do not know if IOs have increased the **quality** (and not just the **quantity**) of law, we do know that they have helped to transform how States comply. IOs have fashioned creative enforcement mechanisms that help to make up for the absence of a global police force or a single court with compulsory jurisdiction. IOs are important elements to the models for compliance that we have: the managerial model of Chayes and Chayes, the harder edged enforcement approaches of neo-realists like George Downs, the consensual approaches of European positivists, Thomas Franck's legitimacy, Slaughter and Moravcsik's liberal theory, or Harold Koh's transnational legal process.[6] IOs help explain why the modern State behaves under all of these theories. They supply the needed forms of transparency, dispute settlement, or capacity building vital to managerial regimes. They sometime provide the hard sanctions sought by those with more realist inclinations (whether through Security Council sanctions or WTO licensed trade retaliation). They extend the time-line of positivists' consent so that it now includes, for example, the practice of an ILO Commission of Inquiry or even political organs like the Security Council. They provide the pedigreed multilateral legitimacy for Franck's "compliance pull" – as do fact-finding bodies within technocratic organizations; and are often the target, or the product, of liberals' interest group politics – as is clear from the stakeholder driven-agenda of the WTO's Committee on Trade and Environment.[7] Institutional human rights bodies – from in-

4 See Cesare P.R. Romano, *The Proliferation of International Judicial Bodies: The Pieces of the Puzzle*, 31 N.Y.U. J. INT'L L. & POL. 709 (1999).

5 Compare Prosper Weil, *Towards Relative Normativity in International Law*, 77 AJIL 413 (1983)(objecting to relative normativity) to Martha Finnemore and Kathryn Sikkink, *International Norm Dynamics and Political Change*, 52 INT'L ORG. 887 (1998)(describing the cascade and impact of soft law).

6 For a description of compliance theories, see Kal Raustiala and Anne-Marie Slaughter, *International Law, International Relations and Compliance*, in HANDBOOK OF INTERNATIONAL RELATIONS (Beth A.Simmons, et al., eds., 2002), at 538.

7 For a description of the politics of the WTO's Committee on Trade and the Environment, see Gregory C. Shaffer, *The World Trade Organization Under Challenge: Democracy and The Law and Politics of the WTO's Treatment of Trade and Environment Matters*, 25 HARV. ENVIRON. L. REV. 1 (2001).

ternational criminal courts to commissions – are among the interactive forums in which human rights norms emerge and are internalized as domestic law in the transnational legal process.

IOs AND THE CHANGING CONTENT OF INTERNATIONAL LAW

IOs have also helped to transform the substantive content of international law. Some of these changes are obvious. The sheer diversity of subject matter that characterizes IOs is reflected in the diversity of modern treaties and custom. IOs have been instrumental promulgators of human rights, with still unknown implications for the now challenged notion (from the *Lotus* case) that States remain free to do whatever is not explicitly prohibited. On-going legislative enterprises (from those created under the European Convention on Human Rights to those undertaken under protocols in the ozone regime) deepen international cooperation and make international law more responsive both to rapid technological change and to the demands of non-State actors.

But it is not just that IOs have reduced the gaps in international law. IOs have created rules that would have been unimaginable without them. IOs have led to new kinds of international duties that presuppose an institutional reaction: duties to report; duties to warn; duties to negotiate multilaterally prior to taking unilateral action; and duties to negotiate in good faith. These duties have changed what States expect from each other, leading to arguments, for example, that the United States had a duty to continue to negotiate at Kyoto or to negotiate multilaterally prior to undertaking unilateral measures to protect sea turtles.[8] IOs supply the "international community" that lead to concepts premised on a hierarchy of values. It is not accidental that the notion of *jus cogens* and *erga omnes* obligations came to fruition only in the post-WW II age of institutions. The continuous iteration of IO practice, as both the Trusteeship Council and the General Assembly, has also given greater precision to vague principles such as "self-determination" and "sovereign equality." We now know that at a minimum self-determination means the right not to be a colony and to exercise some control over one's natural resources. Sovereign equality means at least the equal right to participate in international negotiations and, in the context of particular IOs, may entitle States to many more procedural rights. As is clear from the World Court's interpretations of the UN Charter, IOs have also inspired teleological canons of treaty interpretation, particularly in the course of Advisory Opinions. The use of limiting *travaux préparatoires* has given way to expansive canons of interpretation such as the "principle of effectiveness".

IOs AND RELEVANT ACTORS

As the first type of "international legal person" apart from States ever recognized, IOs have generated a "participant revolution" in the making of international law. Although we now tend to see IOs and NGOs as potential adversaries or competitors, we should not forget that international organizations have made NGOs the powerful agents and enforcers that they are today. They have given NGOs the participation

[8] See generally, Pierre-Marie Dupuy, *The Place and Role of Unilateralism in Contemporary International Law*, 11 EJIL 19 (2000).

rights which make it credible for many of them to credibly claim to represent "international civil society." And to the extent some individuals and corporations have rights and even sometimes duties under international law, this too is at least partly the direct access granted such entities before some institutionalized dispute settlers.[9]

IOs also reproduce. They generate a multitude of quasi-autonomous bodies, such as those charged with monitoring arms control regimes.[10] We now have so many plausible "international legal persons" that we are no longer sure what that term implies. MOPs or "meetings of the parties" under various environmental framework conventions talk and act like IOs: they conclude treaties and seem to enjoy "implied powers" even though they were never formally established as international organizations or as independent legal persons.[11] And even when States choose to avoid the expense and bureaucratic nightmares of a full-fledged inter-governmental organization, they can't help borrowing elements from IOs – such as privileges and immunities based on international institutional law, the secretariats of established IOs, or institutionalized dispute settlement.[12] Even those transnational networks of government regulators that some have suggested are displacing traditional intergovernmental organizations, such as the Basle Committee on Banking Supervision, operate in the shadow of IOs or in conjunction with them.

Perhaps most significantly, IOs have helped to transform what continue to be the principal actors: namely States. This is so not only because the majority of States today would not exist but for the decolonization efforts of the UN, but also because IOs have transformed how we recognize when States exist. IO membership has always been significant to those for whom recognition as a State is not a foregone conclusion from the component parts of the former Yugoslavia to today's advocates for a Palestinian State.

But even for those not insecure in their statehood, IOs have transformed what it means to be modern sovereign. As the Chayes have pointed out, the single greatest determinant of sovereignty today is probably not what remains of "internal" or "domestic" jurisdiction but the *status* of States, as determined by the degree to which they participate in IOs and are able to take advantage of its privileges.[13] Most States find that it is impossible to fulfill the modern expectations of their populations without the tangible assistance of the WHO, the IMF, or even the WMO. And even powerful States like the United States and China find that they cannot fulfill all of their goals without the assistance of IOs.

IOs have also gotten *inside* the State, transforming the way governments organize themselves and what they think lies in their national interest. IOs have also convinced States that they need independent labor unions to conform to the ILO's expectations

9 For a description of the differing impact of dispute settlers open only to State claimants as opposed to those that are open to individuals and corporations, see Robert O. Keohane, Andrew Moravcsik, and Anne-Marie Slaughter, *Legalized Dispute Settlement: Interstate and Transnational*, 54 INT'L ORG. 401 (2000).

10 See Paul Szasz, *The Complexification of the United Nations System*, MAX PLANCK UNYB 3 (1999).

11 See, e.g., Robin R. Churchill and Geir Ulfstein, *Autonomous Institutional Arrangements in Multilateral Environmental Agreements: A Little-Noticed Phenomenon In International Law*, 94 AJIL 623 (2000).

12 Thus, many of the over 2000 bilateral investment treaties that form the backbone of an emerging global regime for foreign investment rely on the dispute settlement facilities of the World Bank, namely the International Centre for the Settlement of Investment Disputes (ICSID).

13 See Abram and Antonia Chayes, THE NEW SOVEREIGNTY at 27 (1995).

of tripartite membership, modern ministries of health and education compatible with the expectations of the WHO and UNESCO, civil aviation authorities that can comply with ICAO Standards and Recommended Practices, regulatory enforcement capabilities consistent with the demands of UN Sanctions Committees, and domestic courts capable of protecting rights like those in the TRIPs Agreement. In some cases, States have been able to build such internal institutions only after technical assistance provided by IOs.

And the existence of rival or complimentary institutional structures at the global level has changed how States' internal government branches and agencies behave or interact. The existence of international courts, for example, has altered the content of national judicial conversations and led to "trans-judicial communications", and not only within Europe.[14] IOs have affected the nature of federal/state relations throughout Europe and even, to some extent, within the United States. While IOs are often associated with a relative increase in the power of executive branches, some IOs have constrained the powers of both executives and legislatures. Given what WTO dispute settlers have said about section 301 of the U.S. Trade Act, for example, both the U.S. executive branch and its Congress face some constraints on the use of unilateral trade sanctions.[15]

For all these reasons, we international lawyers are justly proud of these creatures of our creativity. IOs, after all, are our primary vehicles for transforming international law from rudimentary framework for bilateral barter to systems of governance premised on multilateral cooperation.[16] IOs provide greater opportunities for all States, regardless of wealth or power, to participate in the formation of law. The making of international law in the age of international organizations is now open to non-European States that would have been dismissed as "uncivilized" in the 19th century and to an ever increasing number of non-State actors, from NGOs to MNCs. Thanks largely to institutionalization, the late Jonathan Charney was able to proclaim that we now have something new: truly "universal" international law.[17] IOs have produced *more* law, more democratically and transparently, and, given all our compliance efforts, presumably, to more effect. Who could ask for anything more?

It turns out that many of us do ask for more. The rise of IOs has transformed us as scholars. More of us are working on issues comparable to those which have preoccupied others working on institutions, in national law or in non-legal fields. We are discovering the challenges and risks that accompany institutionalization. We are discovering the need to justify the proper level of regulation (the market?, the State?, the region?, the world?), as well as the appropriate venue (court or regulatory process?, specialized technocratic forum or politicized, but possibly more legitimate, plenary body? International, regional, domestic, or "hybrid" court?). We are asking questions familiar to our constitutional and procedural law colleagues: What makes for an accountable judiciary? When does a court engage in judicial review over another political organ? What checks exist on interstitial judicial law-making or on forum shopping?

14 See, e.g., Anne-Marie Slaughter, *Judicial Globalization,* 40 VA. J. INT'L L. 1103 (2000).

15 See the WTO panel decision in United States-Sections 301-310 of the TRADE ACT OF 1974, WT/DS152/R, 22 December 1999.

16 See generally, Bruno Simma, *From Bilateral to Community Interest in International Law,* VI RECUEIL DES COURS 217 (1994).

17 See Jonathan I. Charney, *Universal International Law,* 87 AJIL 529 (1993).

We are also asking questions familiar to our friends in administrative law: Is there a doctrine of improper delegation? Is there room for notice and comment? Can this process be made more transparent and yet remain efficacious?

We are engaged in a second generation of inquiries with respect to IO law-making. As the generation 'present at the creation' gradually passes from the scene, the rest of us confront complaints of looming "democratic deficits" and competing visions of "constitutionalism."[18] We are also increasingly concerned with how IO law-making relates to power in all its forms – ideological, economic, hegemonic. I will address these challenges at a bit more depth.[19]

The ideological concerns are of various kinds. IOs' continuing inabilities to fulfill the promise of equal participation of men and women and complaints that they merely replicate at the global level the gendered practices of nation States, have helped to inspire critiques that IOs replicate patriarchy. The gender inequities or blindspots within institutions like the international civil service, the International Law Commission, or arbitral institutions are seen as partly responsible for the gendered gaps in international humanitarian law, the legal regulation of peacekeepers, the rules governing international assistance and refugees – and the international processes for establishing all of these.[20] IOs promulgate and give effect to "human" (but not always "women's") rights. IO law-making all too often falls into the same problematic public/private dichotomies evident in national law: At both the international and national levels States claim that they can't or won't prevent horrors such as female infanticide, bride burning, genital mutilation, trafficking in women, or "private" violence against women. At both the international and national levels, sex discrimination claims face defenses based on "culture" more often than other claims for equal treatment. Despite progress made within some institutions – as through the persistent efforts of female judges and others within the *ad hoc* war crimes tribunals – there is concern that IO law-making continues to ignore the legitimate concerns of one half of the world's population.

A second, not unrelated, set of concerns arises from the fear that, particularly since the end of the Cold War, IOs have been enablers of the "Washington Consensus." For critics from the global South, IOs have become primarily, if not exclusively, agents for the ideology of the free market, for deregulation and other U.S.-centric structural reforms, and for the promotion of only those civil and political rights and forms of "democratic" governance associated with Western liberal States. Fears that the WTO is the agent of "predatory economic globalization" have generated debates about the goals of the Doha Round, about whether and when to admit *amicus* briefs, and about the domain of WTO dispute settlement. Comparable North/South divisions arise with respect to the "mission creep" evident in the operations of the IMF or the World Bank and with respect to the continued marginalization of claims to economic and social rights within all global institutions.

Many fear that the systems for global and regional governance that we have favor economic over social values. There is also concern that to the extent our IOs focus on

18 See, e.g., Eric Stein, *International Integration and Democracy: No Love at First Sight*, 95 AJIL 489 (2001).

19 For one recent attempt to address all three of these concerns, see Ugo Mattei, *Globalization and Empire: A Theory of Imperial Law: A Study on U.S. Hegemony and the Latin Resistance*, 10 IND. J. GLOBAL LEG. STUD. 383 (2003).

20 See generally, Hilary Charlesworth and Christine Chinkin, THE BOUNDARIES OF INTERNATIONAL LAW (2000), and especially Chapter 6, at 171-200.

economic or social issues, they favor the interests of the West and North. We worry more about protecting intellectual property or reducing child labor and less so about the elimination of agricultural and textile subsidies or establishing genuinely effective rights to housing, health and food. Some believe that IOs now do a better job of protecting the rights of free traders and foreign investors than of ordinary people they employ or adversely affect. The world appears to lack a social architecture to rival the WTO's powerful tools for case by case law-making, the IMF's powerful economic inducements for regulatory uniformity, or the NAFTA's or the Luxembourg Court's models for enforcement through private rights of action. Some even see a dark side to the proliferation of international courts since this replicates globally Americans' tendency to rely on adjudication over other forms of public regulation.[21]

Finally, there is fear that some IOs, especially those which can only act with the consent of the United States such as the Security Council, are subject to capture by the Hegemon. I will focus on the Council to suggest that despite the recent debacle over Iraq, it is not absurd to worry about an "Imperial" Security Council.

Since 9/11, the United States has successfully used the Council to pursue its war on terrorism through financial sanctions and other forms of criminalization,[22] to secure a license to use self-defense,[23] to recognize its powers as Iraq's occupier,[24] and to carve out an exception to the International Criminal Court's (ICC's) jurisdiction.[25] While all of these actions are probably legal under the UN Charter, each evinces troubling features.

The Security Council now releases periodic lists of alleged terrorists or those who materially assist them. Individuals are identified by the Council's 1267 Sanctions Committee as associated with Al Qaeda or the Taliban, usually at the request of executive agencies in the United States or its allies. All the assets of these individuals are, under binding Chapter VII order, frozen.[26] At the same time, the Council's Counter-Terrorism Committee (or CTC) is engaged in examining what States have been doing to comply with the many other counter-terrorism demands imposed on States under Council Resolution 1373. The goals of the CTC are to provide technical assistance to States to be sure that they take effective action against terrorism. The Council hopes to use its CTC to endorse a global template for national counter-terrorism legislation. According to officials in the Bush Administration, the goal is to export to the world the U.S. Patriots Act.

As might be expected, human rights advocates in particular have expressed qualms about the Council's contribution to the war on terrorism. Although the Council's actions here directly impact on individuals,[27] its non-transparent procedures for "de-listing" individuals remain dependent on the willingness of the State which initial-

[21] See, e.g., Mattei, *supra* note 20; Jane Jenson and Boaventura de Sousa Santos, ed., GLOBALIZING INSTITUTIONS (2000).

[22] S.C. Res. 1373 (28 September 2001); S.C. Res. 1390 (28 January 2002).

[23] S.C. Res. 1368 (12 September 2001); S.C. Res. 1373 (28 September 2001).

[24] S.C. Res. 1483 (22 May 2003).

[25] S.C. Res. 1422 (12 July 2002).

[26] While humanitarian carveouts from the effect of these sanctions are possible, the Sanctions Committee reserves the right to object to these within 48 hours. See S.C. Res 1452 (20 December 2002).

[27] See, e.g., Paul C. Szasz, *Note and Comment: The Security Council Starts Legislating*, 96 AJIL 901 (2002).

ly targets an individual for sanction to admit its mistake. Judicial challenges by individuals who have been publicly stigmatized as terrorists and whose assets are frozen have so far proven to be unavailing in national courts. To date, the Council appears bent on inflicting what is tantamount to a criminal financial sanction without itself defining what the relevant crimes are, without benefit of due process, and while imposing the burden of proving innocence on those whom it chooses to punish. At the same time, the reports States have filed to the CTC concerning their own efforts to root out "saboteurs and terrorists"(as Cuba's 143 page report puts it) have provided a boon to opportunists around the globe. Thanks to the CTC, long standing human rights violators such as China, Egypt, and Cuba have an effective new defense for their actions against political opponents: "the Council made me do it."[28]

It is also not clear whether the CTC's own legal harmonization efforts will be any more sensitive to human rights since it has so far rejected demands that it have a human rights specialist among its seven principal experts. As might be expected given the CTC's limited expertise and interests, States reporting to it have not been asked whether their counter-terrorism laws comport with their other obligations, including human rights treaties. Human rights critics of U.S. actions in its territory and in Guantánamo since 9/11 are not comforted by the prospect that the Council's template for global counter-terrorist legislation might be based on U.S. models.

Two Council resolutions, issued in the immediate wake of 9/11 and in the midst of U.S. threats to take military action in Afghanistan and wherever else Al Qaeda operates, appear to endorse an expanding concept of individual and collective self-defense that accepts (1) that an attack by a non-State actor may constitute an "armed attack"; (2) that acquiescence in such action by the non-State actor's home State may permit defensive military action against both non-State actor and harboring State; and (3) that such defensive action remains permissible even after an armed attack occurs and even if the threat of renewed attack remains highly uncertain. As with the Council's counter-terrorism actions, these Council actions appear, at first glance, to be perfect examples of the Council working as intended. At last, the "until" phrase in Article 51 of the Charter is getting some use: the Council is itself legitimizing a particular instance of self-defense. Yet, given U.S. warnings that it will not distinguish between terrorists and governments who fail to cooperate with the U.S. and U.S. threats to take preemptive force against both, there are understandable qualms about what the Council's endorsement of self-defense means and about how this open-ended, self-judging license will be interpreted by the licensee.

Council Resolution 1483, which affirms the United States' and the United Kingdom's powers over occupied Iraq, is yet another Janus-faced resolution. From one perspective the Council is merely affirming the obligations an occupying power owes under international humanitarian law. From another perspective, that resolution comes close to endorsing, *post hoc*, U.S. and U.K. arguments that they remain free to use force unilaterally when the Council refuses to act multilaterally, even when their self-defense is not triggered. While Resolution 1483 does not explicitly approve of the military invasion of Iraq, presumably one does not hand over what looks like a new kind

[28] But see S.C. Res. 1456, annex (20 January 2003)(non-binding "declaration" stating that States must ensure that their counter-terrorism measures are in accordance with international law, including human rights, refugee and humanitarian law).

of trusteeship to an aggressor. Quite apart from the troubling possibility that this and future Council actions regarding Iraq might eventually be treated as precedents for enforced "regime change" for illiberal States, Resolution 1483 pretty much gives Iraq's new occupiers carte blanche without imposing troublesome requirements such as demanding an accounting of war dead or insisting on UN involvement for the criminal accountability that it envisions for members of Hussein's regime. The resolution also does not suggest the possibility of an independent assessment of whether anyone, apart from the former Iraqi regime, might be found to be in violation of the laws of war, including the laws of occupation.

S.C. Res. 1422, of 12 July 2002 requests the ICC not to commence any prosecution directed at any acts or omissions relating to a UN "established or authorized" operation involving persons from a State that is not a party to the ICC. This looks like the kind of "request" anticipated by the Rome Statute's Article 16 but this Council "request" is backed up by a binding order to States, adopted under Chapter VII, that they take no action inconsistent with this request. And although the exception from ICC jurisdiction was stated to last for only a 12 month period, the Council expressed its intent to renew its request and indeed did so a few weeks ago. The Council's temporary "request" is starting to look like a permanent order to the ICC. It is not clear what was the triggering "threat to the international peace" that prompted this extraordinary action. The possibility that either the United States' threat not to contribute troops to UN peacekeeping or that the possibility that some UN peacekeeper might one day find himself before the ICC may itself constitute a "threat" to the international peace seems bizarre. Despite the lop-sided votes within the Council in favor of this exception, this action appears to respond primarily to U.S. unilateral threat and to its perverse perceptions of what constitutes a multilateral one. It is also not clear what the exemptions for UN "established or authorized" operations are. If the Council has exempted from ICC jurisdiction any and all military operations, including U.S. actions against terrorists that, like those in Afghanistan in 2001, receive the Council's blessing, Resolution 1422 and its anticipated annual extensions may authorize, through the back door, precisely the kind of blanket exception from ICC jurisdiction that the United States unsuccessfully sought to achieve for itself during negotiations for the Rome Statute.

As these recent actions suggest, despite the Security Council's recent paralysis over Iraq, it may yet emerge as the Hegemon's best little helper or junior partner. We may applaud all or most of what the Council is doing in these cases, yet it is hard to avoid seeing how nicely all these resolutions fit within Detlev Vagt's description of hegemonic international law.[29] This is Council-generated "universal international law" very different from Charney's original conception. This is *ostensibly* multilateral law that is unilateral in many of its effects. Aspects of these resolutions severely undervalue the formal equality of States, substitute dictate and blackmail for genuine dialogue and cooperation, devalue or ignore reciprocal obligations on the Hegemon, regard Hegemonic breach as seed for new custom or new treaty interpretation, and encourage the Hegemon's projection of force or intervention in others' internal affairs. All of these resolutions are characterized by indeterminacy or vagueness that accrue to the benefit

29 Detlev Vagts, *Hegemonic International Law*, 95 AJIL 843 (2001).

of the Hegemon and its allies. Most avoid entangling the Hegemon in other international obligations and, on the contrary, enhance its opportunities for self-judging interpretation within a forum that, as we all know, has few, if any, checks on its own freedom of action. And two of these resolutions – 1373 and 1422 – appear intended to displace what Bruno Simma once called the "vehicle par excellence of community interest" namely the multilateral treaty.[30] Resolution 1373 selectively enforces, on the world, some (but by no means all) of the provisions from the International Convention on the Suppression of Terrorist Financing.[31] Resolution 1422 does not displace as much as amend an existing treaty, namely the Rome Statute, providing what may become a permanent, anomalous exception never contemplated by its drafters.

To be sure, most IOs are not likely to become agents of global hegemonic law. Few of them pose the risks that Mary Shelley's benevolent monster posed. But the Security Council example suggests the need for continued vigilance lest IOs become figleaves for the equally benevolent (?) Hegemon.

Conclusion

As is suggested by my survey of the risks posed by IO law-making, we need to approach this subject – as we do Frankenstein's monster – with our eyes open, attentive to the possibility that all forms of regulation – national and international – can be abused and may need some kind of check. Context-specific inquiries may reveal that even IOs with universal membership do not always further principles of sovereign equality or reciprocity; that gaps in IO regulation and enforcement may reflect ideological preferences and not merely practical difficulties; that there is a price to be paid for more "efficient" forms of "universal" legislation that make it unnecessary to endure arduous treaty negotiations; that overly flexible interpretations of IO charters might be just as dangerous as rigid textualism; and that reliance on institutional practice to progressively develop the law may not always constitute "progress" or be politically "progressive." Looking carefully at both the promise and the risks of IO law-making suggests – finally – that we need to worry about not only *whether* the Hegemon goes to institutions like the UN but about what it does when it gets there.

30 Simma, *supra* note 16 (Recueil des Cours), at 323.

31 Omitted were, for example, that Convention's explicit recognition of the rights due those accused of terrorism or extradited on that basis or the Convention's recognition, through its reliance on the ability to bring interpretative disputes to the ICJ, of the need for impartial judicial review. See *International Convention on the Suppression of the Financing of Terrorism*, 39 ILM 270 (2000).

The Role of Non-State Actors and International Dispute Settlement

Peter H. Kooijmans*

At first sight it seems rather odd – if not somewhat incongruous – to invite a person, who is Judge in a Court before which according to its Statute only States can be Parties, to give a keynote address on the role of non-State actors and international dispute settlement.

It is true, of course, that the Statute of the International Court of Justice and the United Nations Charter authorize the Court to give Advisory Opinions at the request of a number of international organizations and that this Court is stated to be the principal judicial organ of the United Nations, itself an IGO and therefore a non-State actor. But nevertheless the International Court of Justice remains, in particular since the Permanent Court of Arbitration opened facilities for dispute settlement between States and non-State Parties, more than any other legalized settlement mechanism the judicial institution par excellence for the settlement of inter-State disputes.

The question may be asked – and is actually raised from time to time – whether this does not push the International Court of Justice to the margin of international dispute settlement if not of the legal order itself. International dispute resolution has expanded enormously in the last half century, and a real proliferation of judicial and quasi-judicial tribunals, panels or similar institutions has taken place. Many of these mechanisms reflect an increase of the number of actors on the international scene, a phenomenon which is often characterized as globalisation. Gone are the days when international litigation was invariably either inter-State dispute settlement or commercial arbitration with a sparse mixture of the two in the case of State contracts. The post-World War II mechanisms give access to a great variety of non-State actors, be it individuals, corporations, business firms, minorities and indigenous peoples, non-governmental organizations and inter-governmental organizations. Although they are usually established by inter-State agreement, the role of the State as gatekeeper to the facilities provided is steadily decreasing. Even where States are nominally still in control of the legal process, like, e.g., in the WTO, in practice it is business which is the driving force behind the formal Parties, as is convincingly shown by Keohane, Moravcsik and Slaughter[1]).

Is the State slowly but incessantly losing its dominant place on the international playing field? Do transnational processes of interaction, does global net-working push aside the State to a place where it is only one unit next to many trans- or sub-national social organizations without any longer being able as the exclusive territorial unit to

* Peter H. Kooijmans, Judge, International Court of Justice.

1 R.O. Keohane, A. Moravcsik and A.-M. Slaughter, 'Legalized Dispute Resolution: Interstate and Transnational' in 54 *International Organisation* (2000) p. 462.

have a decisive grip on what is going on? 'The steady concentration of power in the hands of States that began in 1648 with the Peace of Westphalia is over', writes Jessica T. Matthews,[2] but she cautiously adds 'at least for a while'. Will government (until recently a State monopoly) be gradually sidetracked by governance, whatever may be understood by that concept? 'But governance without government is governance without power', Slaughter says. And she adds: 'Transgovernmental networks allow governments to benefit from the flexibility and decentralization of non-State actors . . .. These globe-spanning networks will strengthen the State as the *primary* player in the international system' [emphasis added].[3]

What does this confusing picture of the 21st century world mean for international dispute settlement?

Let me first say that the existence of non-State actors (I am not yet speaking of their role) is very much noticeable even in traditional inter-State dispute settlement, which certainly no longer is restricted to the old text-book cases of territorial border-disputes or delimitation of maritime areas although such disputes still form part of the Court's docket. But that docket also reflects the increasing diversity of international relations which transcends State-boundaries, even if access to the Court for non-State actors will for the foreseeable future remain barred. Although after eighty years a face-lift would not be wasted upon the Court's Statute, the fact that it is an integral part of the Charter condemns it to the same state of textual stupor as the Charter itself, compelling a State to the cumbersome procedure of filing applications against ten States (with all their diverse acceptances of the Court's jurisdiction) instead of against one IGO. But the winds of change do not leave the Court untouched.

Let us take, for instance, the most recent case initiated by Congo-Brazzaville against France. That case started with a complaint filed with a French prosecutor by a number of human rights organizations, NGOs therefore. The complaint contained accusations of crimes against humanity and of torture allegedly committed in the Congo against Congolese nationals by a number of high Congolese officials, amongst whom the President of the Republic and the Minister of the Interior.

The facts are similar to those of a number of criminal investigations started in Belgium against foreign dignitaries, one of which (the case against the Foreign Minister of Congo-Kinshasa, Mr. Yerodia) was considered by the International Court of Justice, and which are initiated on the basis of a law which has recently given rise to the explicit displeasure of the United States Secretary of Defense. Let me add, however, that the scope of the French law is not as broad as that of the Belgian law.

The case was brought by Congo-Brazzaville because an initial investigation was started during which, *inter alia*, the Congolese President was asked to provide evidence.

The case, although brought as an inter-State dispute, has a high transnational character. It reflects the intense networking between human rights NGOs. But also the Congo's submissions transcend the traditional inter-State patterns and touch global values. The Congo not only alleges that France violated the immunity of its Head of State (a typical inter-State issue) but also the principle that a State may not exercise

2 Jessica T. Matthews, 'Power Shift', 76 *Foreign Affairs* (1997) January/February, p. 50.

3 Anne-Marie Slaughter, 'The Real New World Order' in 76 *Foreign Affairs* (1997) September/October, p. 195.

its authority on the territory of another State by unilaterally attributing to itself universal jurisdiction in criminal matters. This latter element was dropped by the Parties in the *Yerodia* case and passed over by the Court – unjustly so in the opinion of two of my colleagues and myself.

The second interesting aspect of the case is that France, normally a jealous and rather reluctant gate-keeper as far as the Court's jurisdiction is concerned, accepted for this specific case the Court's jurisdiction on the basis of a provision of the Rules of Court which had never been used before (Art. 38.5 Rules of Court). It thus allowed the Court to give its view on an issue which goes far beyond the strict bilateral relations between the two countries.

The third element that deserves attention is that the Court will never even touch the question whether the allegations brought against the Congolese dignitaries are or are not well-founded. But its decision may be of crucial importance for the question what is in the remit of national criminal instances as far as the prosecution of criminal acts committed elsewhere are concerned.

Similarly, in another case recently submitted to the Court (the *Avena* case, *Mexico* v. *United States of America*), the Court will never say whether the 51 Mexican nationals, on whose behalf Mexico sought interim-measures of protection, were rightly or wrongly sentenced to death nor whether these sentences may eventually be executed. But it will have to decide whether the review and reconsideration, to which foreign nationals whose right to consular assistance has not been respected are entitled, is, as it is now practised by the United States, appropriate and meaningful. But this decision will have an impact which vastly surpasses the immediate effect for the two Parties to the dispute, as is already evidenced by the Mexican Application itself since this is based upon a previous decision of the Court in another case to which Mexico was not a party, namely the *LaGrand* case.

Is the International Court of Justice developing itself to a genuine World Court, willy-nilly maybe? So much is certain, the Court has to stay strictly within the limits of its Statute and of a system of jurisdiction that is based on State consent. But within these limits it is increasingly confronted with issues which are not strictly of inter-party relevance and do not have merely effect on bilateral relations between States, as, for instance, is the case with judgments regarding territorial issues where the Court interprets and applies the customary rules of territorial acquisition.

In a properly restrained way the Court seems to recognize the global values which are invoked by non-State actors like humanitarian organizations. In this respect it deserves mentioning that even in cases where the Court found that it had no *prima facie* jurisdiction and therefore had to dismiss a request for provisional measures, it nevertheless reminded the parties – if the case concerned the use of force – of their duty to comply with their obligations under international law, in particular humanitarian law and to prevent violations thereof. In a remarkable declaration, annexed to the Order of the Court in the case of the Democratic Republic of the Congo against Rwanda, Judge Buergenthal criticized this practice, since in his view the Court then deals with matters it has no jurisdiction to address once it has found that it has no *prima facie* jurisdiction. Although from a formal point of view Judge Buergenthal seems to have the Statute on his side, I venture to disagree with him. The Court is not only the guardian of the Statute but – as the principal judicial organ of the United Nations –

also the guardian of the values this Organization stands for, in particular if these values have crystallized into binding legal norms.

Of course there is always the risk that such hortatory reminders develop into a mantra but even then the Court would be remiss if it abdicated from this function now that it has assumed it.

I turn now to the role non-State actors play or should play in international legal proceedings themselves. I have already observed that under a number of arrangements certain categories of non-State actors have been given direct access. This goes true in particular for individuals and sometimes also NGOs under human rights instruments, even if these instruments initially did not provide the supervisory bodies concerned with the competence to entertain cases brought by non-State actors unless the State concerned had previously expressed its consent, but first and foremost entrusted them with the task of monitoring the Contracting Parties' compliance with their treaty-obligations (the United Nations-system) or to deal with traditional State-to-State complaints about non-compliance (the European system).

This situation has dramatically changed over the years and the right of access under human rights instruments has considerably broadened.

To these bodies, which are competent to deal with claims of individuals (or groups) to have their rights respected by States in the jurisdiction of which they find themselves, have now been added judicial bodies which deal with the conduct of individuals who have acted in violation of highly important norms of international law. Although for the initial phases, before the proceedings themselves can start, the role of States is still crucial, the State-actor is conspicuously absent when it comes to the trial itself; the Prosecutor does not represent a State, he does not even represent the community of States, he speaks for mankind. And the accused is dealt with in his individual capacity even if he often will have committed the alleged acts as a State-agent. International criminal proceedings in all probability are the only ones that have a purely and genuinely transnational character but maybe for that reason they can no longer be considered to be part of international dispute settlement.

For similar reasons I will not deal with the European Court of Justice either since this Court has developed itself into a true supra-national (which is not the same as transnational) judicial body.

There are other instruments which provide non-State actors with direct access (I only mention ICSID), but maybe access is not the most important issue in a world where the borders between inter-national (in the sense of inter-State) and transnational get inevitably blurred. If non-State actors play nowadays an increasingly important role in the identification of global values and the development of the body of law which reflects these values, should not their voice be heard also when disputes concerning these norms and values are settled?

To come back to my own Court – a forgivable sin I hope – the Court deals or has to deal with transnational issues like the principle of universality in criminal jurisdiction, it deals with the legal position of global human rights monitors (Mazilu and Cumaraswamy), it deals with the right of peoples to self-determination (East-Timor), it deals with environmental issues (Gabčíkovo-Nagymaros), it deals with the survival of mankind (the legality of nuclear weapons), but does one hear in the Peace Palace, apart from the voices of the State Parties or (exceptionally) of inter-governmental organisations, also the voice of civil society, of the global village?

The International Court of Justice has been criticized for being unduly restrictive in its practice with regard to information provided by non-State actors. I quote Dinah Shelton. After having observed with appreciation that the International Court of Justice is aware of the impact that its decisions and pronouncements can have beyond the Parties and the narrow issues before it, she writes: 'In these circumstances it would seem to be appropriate, or even essential due process, for the Court to ensure that, in cases where the broad public interest may be affected by its decision, some method of participation is provided'. And she continues that, as the International Court of Justice moves into new areas of global public concern, it is crucial that the Court hears from all relevant interests. And not without pathos she claims that 'justice requires that non-governmental organisations representing the public interest have the opportunity to submit information and arguments to the Court', as is already possible in the case of most other international tribunals.[4] A similar suggestion was made by Christine Chinkin during the Colloquium held on the occasion of the Court's 50th Anniversary. To illustrate the usefulness of *amicus curiae* briefs she referred to the Tribunal for the Former Yugoslavia, which had accepted and considered *amicus* briefs on specified areas of concern upon which there are divergent views.[5] And warningly she adds: 'The contribution of the International Court of Justice as 'principal judicial organ of the United Nations' to global governance should take into account its own relationship with civil society'.[6]

It cannot be denied that the International Court of Justice, with one exception in an advisory proceeding in 1950, has been less than lukewarm with regard to the submission of *amicus* briefs. Although the Statute allows for information provided by organizations, this is for contentious proceedings restricted to 'public international organizations' (Art. 34, 2); Article 66, 2 dealing with advisory proceedings is less strict, since it only speaks of 'international organizations' *tout court*, but in practice it has been applied as having the same meaning as in Article 34, 2. In a letter to Professor Michael Reisman, of 6 November 1970, the Court's Registrar expressed the belief 'that the Court would be unwilling to open the floodgates to what might be a vast amount of proffered assistance'.[7]

The floodgate argument certainly is not an easy pretext. If one takes into account that in the *Nuclear Weapons* case 42 States (about one quarter of the United Nations membership at that time) filed written documents under Article 66, 2, one can only speculate about which percentage of the infinitely greater number of NGOs would have felt compelled to do so, if they had been given the opportunity. Moreover, just as the Court is not completely dependent upon factual evidence provided by the Parties, but can also attach a certain amount of weight to public knowledge,[8] it has also knowledge of legal appreciations which are not necessarily those of the Parties; it is not living in an ivory tower. But this can, or rather should, not be the end of the story.

4 Dinah Shelton, 'The Participation of Non-Governmental Organisations in International Judicial Proceedings', 88 *American Journal of International Law* (1994) pp. 641-642.

5 Conny Peck and Roy S. Lee, eds., *Increasing the Effectiveness of the International Court of Justice* (The Hague: Nijhoff 1997) p. 54.

6 Ibid., p. 55.

7 *1970 International Court of Justice, Pleadings (Legal Consequences)* Vol. II, p. 639.

8 *Military and Paramilitary Activities* (*Nicaragua* v. *United States of America*) *I.C.J. Reports 1986* p. 40, para. 63.

Another argument which is sometimes raised against a more liberal attitude towards information provided by non-State Parties is that it might make States, on whose consent the Court is dependent for carrying out its function, more reluctant to submit disputes to it. States would be averse from having NGOs, even in an indirect way, getting involved in a bilateral dispute, in particular if the views presented are not to their liking. That argument certainly should not be taken lightly, although it would not apply to advisory proceedings. But Shelton is right when she says that in the case of human rights tribunals, where the *amici* usually do not express support of the defendant State's position but are opposed to it, there has hardly been any opposition by States against the admission of *amicus* briefs.

It will be dependent upon a thoughtful, balanced and selective system whether a floodgate effect can be avoided and a useful effect on the Court's functioning can be realized. The con's have to be weighed against the pro's, but I would like to mention one particularly weighty pro: the relationship of the Court, not only as the principal judicial organ of the United Nations (as Chinkin said), but also as an inter-State dispute resolver, with civil society, which was once described by the Secretary-General of the United Nations as 'an essential dimension of public life at all levels and in all parts of the world'.

It is often said that decisions of the International Court of Justice get hardly any attention in the media, at least outside the territory of the State Parties involved in a case, this in contrast with decisions of human rights tribunals and criminal tribunals. One reason for this scant attention undoubtedly is that cases before the International Court of Justice usually lack 'the human factor'. But closer attention would certainly have been appropriate in all those cases where the decision transcends the narrow interests of the Parties to the dispute. It is often only at a later stage that this wider importance of the decision is duly appreciated. But this lack of attention may be due to the fact that the views of the 'world at large', whose interests are nevertheless involved, cannot be communicated to the Court and, consequently, are not communicated to the media either.

I believe that this relationship with civil society is vital, not in order to bolster up the Court's public relations, but to strengthen its capacity to carry out its function as an institution which was established long ago to settle inter-State disputes, but is also the principal judicial organ of the United Nations.

And now I come back to what I said in the beginning. I hope I have made clear that the fact that the International Court of Justice is primarily an inter-State court has not pushed it in a globalized world to the margins of the international legal order. First, because in settling inter-State disputes and advising United Nations organisations it deals increasingly with transnational law and with global values. But, second, because it is in my view a gross simplification to draw a picture of a slow but unstoppable retreat of the State in order to make place for a network of transnational arrangements.

True, in a shrinking and increasingly interdependent world society, the State can no longer carry out the function traditionally attributed to it; its ability to do so is considerably curtailed. Each State no longer is the centre of its own world; the nation-State's monopoly over internal sovereignty, its exclusive territorial sovereignty, has come to an end and now only exists in name. But the State has remained the main organizational unit in today's world and has to adapt in order to be able to meet today's challenges and to protect civil society against dangers coming from transnational criminal networks,[9] even if it cannot do so alone. Jessica Matthews observed that controlling globalized crime – and the same can be said of that modern plague terrorism – will require States to pool their efforts and to establish unprecedented cooperation with the private sector. And Philip Alston states that there is an urgent need to revisit the distinction that is reflected in international law between the public and private domains (which is certainly not the same as that between public and private law) and he raises the question whether existing doctrines and institutional arrangements are adequate to deal with the complexities and realities of a globalized world.[10]

My conclusion can be brief:
International dispute settlement procedures should open up to non-State actors (as has already been done in a number of cases), not in order to change their character, but in order to enable them to reflect adequately the body of law they have to apply in a globalized world. The relevant question should not be 'if' or 'when', but 'how'.

[9] See Alex P. Schmid, 'Non-State Actors: Organized Crime, Human Rights NGOs and the United Nations', in T.C. van Boven, et al., *The Legitimacy of the United Nations: Towards an Enhanced Legal Status of Non-State Actors* (Utrecht: Studie- en Informatiecentrum Mensenrechten 1997) p. 125.

[10] Philip Alston, 'The Myopia of the Handmaidens: International Lawyers and Globalization', *European Journal of International Law* (1997) p. 448.

INTERNATIONAL ORGANIZATIONS – GOVERNMENTAL AND NON-GOVERNMENTAL – AND GOOD GOVERNANCE

International Organizations as Autonomous Subjects in the International and European Legal System

The panel was convened by its Chairs, Niels Blokker* and Ramses Wessel**.

Remarks by Nigel D. White***

Discerning separate will

Introduction

What signifies that an international organization is an autonomous actor on the international plane? Historically the debate has been about the existence of separate will or *volonté distincte*, and traditionally the conundrum has been "[h]ow … can an international organization, 'made' by States which have no superiors in international law, be independent of the will of its members?".[1]

Schermers and Blokker suggest that an organization must have at least one organ with a *will* of its own.[2] Will is often expressed by international lawyers as the possession of international legal personality, though it can more widely be expressed as the transference of will by the founding States to an organization or the restrictions on the will of Member States by an organization.[3] The concepts of international legal personality and that of separate will are conflated to a large extent. Though the former is a much more legalistic concept than the latter, for international law, the existence of separate will is largely encapsulated by the concept of international legal personality. An organization with certain elements is presumed to have international legal personality.[4] Those elements vary between writers, with some emphasising permanency, separate purposes, and distinct powers, as well as organ(s);[5] while others include organ(s), membership and *decision*-making.[6] It is interesting to note that *law*-making may be included in the latter element, though traditionally it is seen as an issue of competence or powers. Having said that, of course an organization that has law-making competence on the international stage must first of all have international legal personality. While the *existence* of separate will is embodied in the concept of international legal personality, the *extent* of separate will is to be found in the nature of those elements: for instance in the presence of majority voting in the organs; the width of purposes; the intrusiveness of powers; the nature of decision-making; and the depth of member-

* Ministry of Foreign Affairs, the Netherlands.
** University of Twente, Utrecht University.
*** Professor of International Organisations, School of Law, The University of Nottingham, UK.

ship. These are reflective of the fundamental legal nature of the organization, which may tend towards the contractual or the constitutional.[7]

INTERNATIONAL LEGAL PERSONALITY

Of course the founding States of an organization have the initial choice to confer upon the organization separate will. They can do this by expressly granting the organization international legal personality, though this is still relatively rare. However, express grant without giving the organization the equipment necessary to express its separate will is of limited relevance, though the organization remains legally distinct from its Member States. The founding States can more effectively bestow separate will by establishing some or all of the elements mentioned above. Sometimes the lack of express grant in the treaty can be reflective of a failure to achieve consensus in the negotiations on the issue of personality/will. Once created, though, and in the absence of clear intent to the contrary, an organization possessing these elements has personality.

Organizations without personality – the G7 for instance – can be said to have a separate existence but not separate will at least in a legal sense. True, the G7's communiqués reflect the collective view of seven States but, without separate will, such communiqués do not have legal status as G7 decisions *per se*. Without separate will the G7 certainly has no law-making power. Regular G7 meetings indicate its separate existence, but States have not transferred any of their will to the G7, or given the G7 the elements that would enable it to develop a will of its own. Thus "for an international entity to be regarded as existing separately from its Member States, the entity must have a decision-making organ that is able to produce a 'corporate' will, as opposed to a mere 'aggregate' of the wills of the Member States".[8] Nevertheless, the impact of certain fora lacking formal personality should not be underestimated. As Blokker notes "G8 consensus was crucial in the spring of 1999 to 'solve' the Kosovo crisis".[9]

Contrast this with a decision of the Security Council, even one adopted by the unanimous vote of all 15 members. This is a reflection of the will of the Security Council, not the combined view or even combined will of the members of that body. The separate personality of the UN establishes the will of the organization as a whole, though in the case of the Security Council there is a concentration of will, enabling it, for example, to take mandatory decisions imposing non-military measures binding on the whole membership. The Court in the *Reparation* case was inaccurate in stating that the UN had a large measure of personality,[10] personality is after all either present or not. The Court was possibly referring to the fact that the Charter confers a large measure of separate independent will on the UN, more in certain organs than in others. Personality is the starting point for legal analysis, after that the extent of an organization's will is to be found not just in the capacities or competences (powers) of the organization, but perhaps more profoundly in its fundamental legal nature. Legal powers are a significant element in any analysis of this nature and these may be conferred expressly or impliedly by Member States, or may be developed and deployed by the organization itself. The competence to legislate to create international criminal tribunals or to legislate to combat terrorism, for instance, can hardly be said to have been the intention of the founding States, in reality they are a creation of the Security Council itself, a product of its separate will.

Recognizing that international organizations possessing certain features have objective personality, even if phrased as a presumption, does not mean that they inherently have the same rights and duties as States. Personality is the starting point, once it is present organizations may have similar competences to States, though normally they have far less, but in other rare instances they can have more. Those competences may be conferred expressly, or impliedly, though sometimes, they are the product of the will of the organization itself. Of course that will must be exercised within the legal framework of the constituent document, but those documents are notoriously open textured allowing for organic growth by the organization itself, disembodied from the will of each Member State.

Fundamental legal nature

The extent of institutional will, above and beyond the presence of personality, is evidenced by the legal nature of an international organization. International organizations based on contractual foundations, where the Member States remain to all intents and purposes the masters of the treaty,[11] may have separate will in the sense above, but the extent of it, and the possibility of its future development, are very limited. Other organizations based on constitutional foundations often possess, or have the potential to develop, significant separate wills. Constitutions have their foundation in an original contractual agreement between the partners, but thereafter the partners cease to be masters of the treaty but become subject to it. A constitution not only constitutes a political order and established political institutions, it regulates that order in terms of the competences of different institutions, in terms of the relations between institutions and the subjects of the order, and between the subjects themselves.[12] Once constitutions are established, they become living instruments, through a combination of "usage", "authoritative interpretation" (by political and legal organs) and by "formal amendment".[13]

Of course there are various strengths of constitutions, some may command more respect and loyalty by States and, on occasions, individuals, than others.[14] The stronger the constitution the greater the separate will of the organization. The driving force in such organizations is not so much the doctrine of powers, but the practice of the organization, which creates "customary constitutional law" that gradually fills in the legal framework created by the constitutive document.[15] "We have, then, the merger of treaty and custom into the life of the" organization.[16] That legal development by practice regarded by the organs of the organization as normative is a product of the separate will of the organization, as opposed to the doctrines of express and implied powers which aver to the intention of the (founding) members.

While not suggesting that the legal nature or character of an organization is a better method of discerning the extent of separate will or autonomy than the orthodoxy that looks at the issues of capacities and competences, it is posited here as a development of it. It is useful to recount some of the historical discourse on this matter.

Attempts have been made, mainly since the adoption of the League of Nations' Covenant in 1919 to suggest that there is a considerable distinction to be drawn between ordinary "contractual" bilateral or multilateral treaties and "constitutional" multilateral treaties. Such a suggestion was quite a radical departure from the view dominant in the nineteenth century that international law was in essence private law between consenting States acting as equals, rather than any form of public law.[17] The fine balance in the debate can be seen as far back as 1919 when Max Huber stated of the legal character of the League of Nations Covenant that it was "neither contractual nor constitutional".[18]

McNair, writing in 1930, was less cautious about the constitutional nature of the Covenant stating that "the society of States has not yet got a complete Constitution, but it has a great deal of Constitutional Law", including not only the Covenant but also other foundational treaties. He concluded by stating that "it seems to me that these constitutional treaties ... create a kind of public law transcending in kind and not merely in degree the ordinary agreements between States".[19]

Though debate still continues in the post-1945 era, it is difficult not to accept Allott's suggestion that "the exercise of public power in intergovernmental organizations may be explained and justified at the level of international society in terms of a theory of constitutionalism".[20] As stated there are varying strengths of constitutions. Some may simply be constitutions in a formal sense of "establish[ing] and regulat[ing] the main organs of government, their constitution and powers".[21] Others may be constitutions in a more fundamental sense. Raz has defined these as having the elements of not only being constitutive, but also stable, written, superior, justiciable, entrenched, and an expression of a common ideology.[22] Arguably for more profound constitutions there is an additional need for loyalty and identity, but Raz shows that these elements are not necessary to have a constitution in a more profound sense than simply a constitutive document. In this sense, the fundamental treaties and documents of many international organizations can be seen as constitutions in a deeper sense.

There are certainly problems in characterising the UN Charter as a constitution in any absolute or developed sense,[23] particularly when issues of loyalty or identity are considered, though it may be so in certain weak or failed States where the UN (through the World Food Programme, for instance) is owed more loyalty than the government. However, at least formally, the UN system is not simply governed by a series of treaties, but is governed by a complex constitution, with the UN Charter at its heart. Of course, this does not lead automatically to government, but to governance whereby laws are made and applied and legal claims adjudicated.[24] Such a view may seem to go against the decision of the International Court in the *WHO Opinion* when the Court seemed to view the UN system in a purely "sectoral" sense.[25] This would signify that the UN Charter may be a constitution in a stronger sense than the constituent treaties of the agencies. However, the Court's vision of the UN system is arguably deficient, the agencies after all are charged with achieving UN purposes that are found in the Charter, and many refer in their constituent treaties to the values of the UN Charter, principally peace and security. In this sense the treaties form part of a constitutional hierarchy.

A constitution in a weak sense signifies a constitution that is not different legally from the basic rules governing a sports club, both constitute an organization. However, the UN Charter together with the treaties of the agencies make a complex constitution which has moved towards the stronger sense of constitution defined by Crawford – "a constitution which constitutes a society and not just an organization – a constitution which is basal and not only bureaucratic".[26]

Other organizations too are governed by constitutions though the strength of the constitution varies. The European Union has a constitution in the stronger sense. Its increasing commitment to issues of social justice as well as purely market matters, combined with an increasing incorporation of human rights, have reinforced this move towards greater constitutionalism. However, the foundational documents have not yet provoked sufficient allegiance in European citizens to have replaced, or competed with, their allegiance to nation States. This signifies that it certainly has not achieved the status of a constitution in the strongest sense. Although the European Court of Justice, for instance, has significantly enhanced the constitutional order of the European Community, by developing concepts such as "direct effect, supremacy and preemption",[27] it is still significant that major changes in the political and legal order are implemented by a contractual process of all Member States negotiating and agreeing on a significantly amended treaty. It is arguable that contractual revisions are necessary in cases of processes where creating a legal and political order or polity remain unfinished.[28] With the EU hovering somewhere between inter-governmentalism and supranationalism, between confederation and federation, and between State interest and democracy, the EU legal order remains somewhat short of a constitution in the strongest sense. Nevertheless, the EC "has developed from a legal relationship binding upon the States *qua* States, to an integrated legal order that confers rights and obligations on private parties, and one in which the controls on the exercise of public power are similar in nature to those found in nation States".[29] It has a constitution, although it does not yet have one document labelled as such.

At the time of agreeing upon the creation of any international organization, States are sitting down together and making a contract either in a contractual or in a constitutional sense. In many instances the latter sense prevails simply because the contract constitutes an organization. The question though is whether the entity created by that contract can take on a life of its own, acting independently of the States. This can be done by, for instance, preferring majority voting to unanimity. Although most organizations are based, in varying degrees, on the constitutional model, others seem more firmly based, in a continuing sense, on a contract. This is, or should be, the case, with defence organizations, where there is a clear contractual exchange, namely reciprocal protection. The founding treaty of the leading defensive organization, NATO, the North Atlantic Treaty of 1949, uses the term "parties" to the treaty as opposed to "members", and any decisions are to be made by the parties acting together, not by an institution created by them. The only body created by the treaty is the Council, which, according to Article 9, "considers matters concerning the implementation of the treaty". The Council has the authority to set up subsidiary bodies and it is upon this provision that a complex military organization has been established.

Despite this institutional aspect, there does not appear to be within the treaty any scope for a profound move away from the original contract. The contract made between State parties to the treaty in 1949 is contained in Article 5 whereby each State is provided with defence in return for contributing to the defence of others. However, even though the text forming the basis of NATO appears limited, NATO's reinvention as a collective security organization with the end of the Cold War has been supported by attempts to tie its activities in Bosnia from 1994 and Kosovo in 1999, to the 1949 Treaty. This is done by emphasizing the purposes of the treaty which in the preamble are widely phrased by the parties to be safeguarding the "freedom, common heritage and civilisation of their peoples, founded on the principles of democracy, liberty and the rule of law". In the Alliance's Strategic Concept document of 1999, NATO heads of State and government agreed that these wide purposes gave NATO competence to conduct, by consensus, what are called "non-Article 5" operations to enhance the security of the Euro-Atlantic Area. The Concept states at one point that "NATO forces must maintain the ability to provide for collective defence while conducting effective non-Article 5 crisis response operations". The considerable stretching of its military competence beyond the defensive to the offensive certainly indicates a constitutional approach to interpretation, although it may be argued to have gone beyond the limits of that approach by violating the essence of NATO – namely that it is a defensive organization.

There are strong arguments for saying that NATO members ought to make a new contract instead of trying to layer constitutional interpretations upon what clearly remains a contract. The 1949 treaty was not drafted as a type of "super" contract, that is a document that can evolve into a constitution. Furthermore, the precision achieved in the original contract has been lost by these ambiguously phrased assertions of greater competence. The whole essence of the contract, providing for certainty and clear mutual advantage for the parties, has been lost. Even if there is a new deal, it, like the existing treaty regime, must conform with the principles of international law particularly those restricting non-defensive uses of force.

In general contracts are narrowly interpreted by relying primarily on a textual approach. Although the Vienna Convention on the Law of Treaties of 1969 (in Article 31) can be said to recognize without distinction all three approaches (textual, purposive and practical), it is submitted here that the weight given to each does vary with the type of treaty. However, the significance of the distinction between a contractual paradigm and a constitutional one is not simply confined to the question of interpretation. In general in a contractual-type treaty the parties are clearly in charge. Their sovereignty is not to be undermined, unless they have expressly consented to it by the treaty. Logically this signifies that if an organization's founding document remains contractual the organization and its organs perform functions that are expressly delegated to those organs in the treaty. They should not do more than this. The goals and purposes of the organization should not be read as defining the limits of the organization's competence. The organization's competence is defined by the express powers granted in the body of the treaty. Change to the treaty is normally achieved through the formal amendment process, and it should be unanimous – a "consensual" approach to amendment. That arguably is the theory, though the practice of NATO may suggest that it may not be as black-and-white as this.

An organization with a constitutional base, however, signifies that although States may control the creation of the organization, once created it can develop significant separate will. Although State representatives sit in the organs, the fact of majority rule, and the interpretation of the mandates of organs by individuals working for the organization, signify that it is no longer in the control of each State. The establishment of a constitutional order signifies the importance of the values of the constitution – found in the Preamble and opening articles. These, legally speaking, are the guiding lights, the legal framework within which the organization can grow. Thus the practice of the various organs as a means of developing and protecting these values becomes important, as does the implication of powers, though not expressly granted, to achieve the aims of the organization.[30] The text becomes less important, but there are still clear legal limits as set by the constitution. Thus the treaty is a living instrument – it evolves and develops – thereby enabling it to keep up with developments in the international order. Normally there is no need to go through the formal amendment process, except for certain institutional or fundamental changes. Even then the formal amendment process normally allows for revision by a majority, "legislative" amendment in effect, binding on all the members.

Conclusion

An independent will located within a constitutional framework will often find expression in the form of legal output, so that there are many organizational legal orders (UN law, ICAO law, ILO law, IAEA law for example) and some more developed institutional legal systems (EU law). Indeed, this was not anticipated in the immediate post-war period when it was envisaged, for instance, that the specialized agencies would be "forum organizations"[31] with little law-making or indeed operational competence. The growth of legal orders and the increasing operational activities of organizations have meant increasingly overlapping competences, so that, in the case of the specialized agencies, for instance, the system is no longer one of discrete sectorial competences as originally envisaged in 1945.[32]

Though the legal output of organizations is not formally seen as a separate source of international law, it does contribute to the creation of legal regimes. Such a regime can be defined as a "set of implicit or explicit principles, norms, rules and decision-making procedures around which actors' expectations converge in a given area of international relations".[33] It follows that State behaviour is not only to be evaluated by reference to treaty or custom. Although there is no current international legislature, the effect of law-making by organizations should not be underestimated. Organizations "make international law less through affirmative 'international legislation' than by relatively informal operations, directives and initiatives. When international institutions make this kind of law they are acting less as persons, and more as communities. The institution does not 'make' the legal rules or norms, it facilitates the creation of the regime by being the center of the community".[34] Legal personality is thus seen not as central to the issue of separate will, it is simply the starting point of an analysis that must look beyond that debate to discern the presence of a sense of community existing within a fluid constitutional framework.

Notes

1 D.J. Bederman, 'The Souls of International Organizations: Legal Personality and the Lighthouse at Cape Spartel', 36 *Virginia JIL* (1996) 275 at 357.

2 H. Schermers and N.M. Blokker, *International Institutional Law*, 3rd edn. (1995) 29.

3 States are often resistant to the latter view. See the recent criticism by the UK Minister on the draft EU Constitution: "It is not the constitution that grants competences, but the Member States, through the constitution". R. Watson, 'Giscard's Plan for Europe Swamped by Amendments', *The Times*, 25 February 2003, 16.

4 C.F. Amerasinghe, *Principles of the Institutional Law of International Organizations* (1996) 89-90; J. Klabbers, 'Presumptive Personality: The European Union in International Law', in M. Koskenniemi, ed., *International Legal Aspects of the European Union* (1998) 243-9.

5 I. Brownlie, *Principles of Public International Law*, 5th edn. (1998) 679-80. See further Amerasinghe, *Principles*, 83; R. Higgins, *Problems and Process: International Law and How We Use It* (1994) 47.

6 R.A. Wessel, 'Revisiting the International Legal Status of the EU', 5 *European FAR* (2000) 507 at 517.

7 International law draws a distinction between legal personality on the one hand, which is either present or not, and capacities and competences (powers) on the other which are variable in nature, though this tends to narrowly equate the extent of separate will to the extent of powers. See P.H.F. Bekker, *The Legal Position of*

Intergovernmental Organizations (1994) 51-85.

8 Wessel, 'Revisiting', 517.

9 N.M. Blokker, 'Proliferation of International Organizations: An Exploratory Introduction', in N.M. Blokker and H.G. Schermers, eds., *Proliferation of International Organizations: Legal Issues* (2001) 1 at 6.

10 1949 *ICJ Rep.*, 174 at 179.

11 A.D. McNair, 'The Functions and Different Legal Characters of Treaties', XI *British YBIL* (1930) 100 at 105.

12 B. Fassbender, 'The United Nations Charter as Constitution of the International Community', 36 *Columbia JTL* (1998) 529 at 536. This paper does not cover the democratic deficit in international organizations – for discussion see S.M. Marks, *The Riddle of all Constitutions* (2000).

13 H. Abromeit and T. Hitzel-Cassagnes, 'Constitutional Changes and Contractual Revision: Principles and Procedures', 5 *European LJ* (1999) 23 at 24-25, 28-32.

14 P. Craig, 'Constitutions, Constitutionalism, and the European Union', 7 *European LJ* (2001) 25 at 125.

15 Pollux, 'The Interpretation of the Charter', 23 *British YBIL* (1946) 54 at 54.

16 Bederman, 'Souls', 358.

17 Allott argues that this continued in the 20th century where "the controllers of the national public realm [acted] in relation to each other like unconstitutional monarchs". P. Allott, 'Intergovernmental Societies and the Idea of Constitutionalism', in J.-M. Coicaud and V. Heiskanen, eds., *The Legitimacy of International Organizations* (2001) 69 at 92.

18 Cited in A Zimmern, *The League of Nations and the Rule of Law, 1918-1935* (1969) 290-1.

19 McNair, 'Functions', 112.

20 Allott, 'Intergovernmental', 70.

21 P. Craig, 'Constitutions', 126.

22 J. Raz, 'On Authority and Interpretation of Constitutions: Some Preliminaries', in L. Alexander, ed., *Constitutionalism* (1998) 152-3.

23 G. Arangio-Ruiz, 'The "Federal Analogy" and UN Charter Interpretation: A Crucial Issue', 8 *EJIL* (1997) 9. But see R. Bernhardt, 'On Article 103', in B. Simma, ed., *The Charter of the United Nations: A Commentary*, 2nd edn. (2002) 1295; C. Tomuschat, *The United Nations at Fifty: A Legal Perspective* (1995) ix; P.-M. Dupuy, 'The Constitutional Dimension of the Charter of the United Nations Revisited', 1 *Max Planck Yearbook of UN Law* (1997) 20.

24 Fassbender, 'United Nations', 574.

25 *Legality of the Use by a State of Nuclear Weapons in Armed Conflict* [hereinafter *WHO Opinion*], *ICJ Rep.* (1996) 66 at 80.

26 J. Crawford, 'The Charter of the United Nations as a Constitution', in H. Fox, ed., *The Changing Constitution of the United Nations* (1997) 8.

27 Craig, 'Constitutions', 129.

28 Abromeit and Hitzel-Cassagnes, 'Constitutional Change', 40.

29 Craig, 'Constitutions', 128.

30 J.E. Alvarez, 'Constitutional Interpretation in International Organizations', in Coicaud and Heiskanen, eds., *Legitimacy*, 104 at 136-7 – "The IO interpretative enterprise is not driven, as it would be in the context of a contract, by an effort to give effect to the parties' 'original intention', and even the plain meaning of the charter's text may only be the beginning of the interpretative exercise". Further, "[i]nstitutional practice is readily transformed into 'precedent' to be cited in support later, as needed, out of deference to consistency and stability. The silence of members in the face of institutional practice is usually treated, fairly or unfairly, as acquiescence".

31 P. Taylor, in P. Taylor and A. Groom, *The United Nations at the Millennium* (2000) 103.

32 But see *WHO Opinion*, 80. However, there is something of a recent change of perception that suggests that the progressive growth of international organizations has been brought to a halt, reversed even – see J. Klabbers, in Coicaud and Heiskanen, eds., *Legitimacy*, 243, 246. See further Blokker, 'Proliferation', 1-11.

33 S. Krasner, 'Structural Causes and Regime Consequences: Regimes as Intervening Variables', 36 *International Organization* (1982) 184 at 186.

34 Bederman, 'Souls', 372.

Remarks by Pieter-Jan Kuijper*

Will the European Union ever be a normal partner in international negotiations?

The Single Personality of the European Union and the disappearance of "mixity"

1. Introduction

Even after over fifty years of existence and ever increased transfer of powers from the Member States to first the European Community and then the European Union, the participation of the Community/Union in international negotiations and international treaty-making, is still not easy. Its role is enormously increased, but its participation is never simple or accepted without special measures.

There are three reasons for that: one external and two internal to the Community/Union. First of all, the Community/Union as an international organization is not admitted as full member to international negotiation fora or assemblies of international organizations, which have a statute which provides only for States as members or full participants. Secondly, if the Community/Union is admitted to such negotiation fora or assemblies of international organizations, it is often confronted with the consequences of the division of powers between the Community and the Member States in the field of external relations. This is so-called "classical" mixity and it entails consequences which sometimes have a debilitating effect on the Community's capacity to negotiate "normally". Finally, since the latest modifications in the Union treaty, which equipped the Union with treaty-making power, a new phenomenon is on the rise: the so-called cross-pillar mixity, i.e. negotiations about international agreements which fall both under the Community and the Union treaty.

These three phenomena will be briefly discussed below, in particular as to how they form barriers to "normal" participation of the Community/Union in international negotiations and what will be the consequences of the creation of a Union with a single personality as foreseen in the Convention draft of a Union Treaty.

2. Not a Member or full participant in negotiating bodies

The Community/Union is not a full member of most worldwide international organizations and, therefore, often not a full participant in international negotiating bodies. Its full membership in FAO is an exception.[1] A good example is formed by the recently concluded negotiations for the so-called Tobacco Convention. Participation in that conference was based on Membership in the WHO and the Community is only an observer in that organization. Although the Community had enacted internal law, the Tobacco publicity directive, so as to give itself a large measure of competence with respect to the subject of the Tobacco Conference, it remained quite difficult for the Community, because of its status as a mere observer, to participate effectively in the negotiations. Negotiating as an observer means negotiating from the sidelines. The

* Principal Legal Adviser for External Relations, European Commission and Visiting Professor of European Law, University of Amsterdam. The views expressed are purely personal.

Commission, the representative of the Community in the negotiations, sometimes almost took the position of a quasi-outsider, comparable to the way NGO s tried to influence negotiations. It organized so-called Community consultations before meetings, in order to press the Member States to toe the line of the Community position. It sometimes participated in discussions as member of the Delegation of the Member State holding the Presidency of the EC Council of Ministers, in order not to be condemned to always speaking last as observer.

It is obvious, therefore, that lack of full membership or full participation status of the Community can be a considerable handicap for the Community in international negotiations.

3. "Classical" mixity

Even where the Community finally succeeds in acquiring membership or participant status, such as in the FAO or very recently in the Codex Alimentarius, its participation is often far from simple. This is the result of the fact that, even in organizations that seem to be active in areas that are traditionally a realm of Community activity, such as agriculture, the transfer of powers from the Member States to the Community is upon precise analysis not complete and hence the Community must team up with its Member States in order to cover the whole field covered by the organization or negotiations in question. This is what is called in Community parlance: "classical" mixity.

Even though in theory third States should perhaps accept that the Community and its Member States together can assume all obligations that might result from the negotiations in question,[2] in reality third States are not that easily convinced that this is the case, whilst Member States like to show to third States that their presence in the organization or negotiating forum is not merely ceremonial.

The consequence of this are the well-known declarations of competence, which the Community makes when acceding to international organizations, such as the FAO, or to international agreements, such as the Third UN Convention on the Law of the Sea. The recent accession of the European Community to the Codex Alimentarius Commission is based on the same model.

It is well-known that such declarations, especially if they, as is the case in the FAO, also require declarations about who will have the right to speak and to vote during a meeting, on the different agenda points, the Community or the Member States can be extremely cumbersome. Sometimes they are also accompanied by internal arrangements decided by the Council on how the latter declarations will be made through consultations with Member States on the spot and/or, in case of conflict, by referring back to Coreper or the Council in Brussels, and by which majorities this will be decided.[3]

Again, it is easy to see that such complications of "classical" mixity may lead to diminished input and effectiveness of the Community, when participating in international negotiations.

Only in an organization like the WTO, were "mixity", such as it is, is very minimal and *de facto* Member States never speak in the meetings of the organization except about nominations and budgetary matters, the EC participates in the most effective way possible. Even then, there are nearly daily meetings with the Member States in order to clear Community positions to be taken in the various meetings that take place every day at the WTO. But this kind of co-ordination is hardly any worse than inter-departmental co-ordination for some unitary States Members of the WTO.

4. The Community and the Union: the rise of "cross-pillar" mixity

The Treaty of Maastricht created the European Union, this strange hybrid entity which at the same time embraces, and stands apart of, the European Community. It embraces the Community to the extent that it introduces a number of general clauses which also cover Community law (Articles 1-7 and 46-53 TEU), but it stands apart from the Community to the extent that it governs the Common Foreign and Security Policy (CFSP, Articles 11-28) and the policy in the realm of Justice and Home Affairs (JHA, Articles 29-45), also called the second and third pillar respectively. In these two domains the "Community method" does not apply, the method of co-operation is purely intergovernmental, decision-making is mostly by unanimity, the legal acts are of a different nature than in the Community realm and do not enjoy supremacy over national law, and the Court of Justice has no jurisdiction at all (in CFSP) or only to a limited extent (in JHA). Accordingly the Community domain is protected from "pollution" by the intergovernmentalism of the CFSP in particular (see Article 47 TEU).

Though the Union Treaty does not contain a provision on the legal personality of the Union, the Treaty of Amsterdam provided for a treaty-making capacity within these domains (Articles 24 and 38 of the Union Treaty). Such treaties are concluded by the Council, but it is not clear on the basis of the text alone whether they are so on behalf of the Union or of the collectivity of the Member States. Although the Treaty of Nice, entered into force on 1 March 2003, may have slightly reinforced the cause of those who believe there is a treaty-making capacity of the Union contained in Article 24, it is primarily the Council itself, by concluding a considerable number of agreements under Article 24 TEU in the name of the Union, which has created a practice which may amount to recognition of the Union's international legal personality by quite a number of third States, notably the Balkan States and countries of central and Eastern Europe, but also the United States. (It is somewhat ironic to note that such practice can only acquire a certain legal force because there is no jurisdictional control by the Court of Justice in the CFSP area).[4]

At any rate, this new-found treaty-making power of the Union has led to a new phenomenon, which may be called "cross-pillar" mixity. That is to say that provisions in a projected treaty that relate to political and security co-operation, and also to police and judicial co-operation in the field of anti-terrorism, which in the past used to be seen as being within Member States' power and hence as giving rise to classical mixity, are now seen to fall under the scope of CFSP (second pillar) and JHA (third pillar) co-operation and hence as falling under the treaty-making power of Article 24 (and 38) TEU. This gives rise to new complications, since the largest part of the agreement is likely to fall under Community competence in the field of trade (Article 133 TEC) or transport (Article 71) and others, and hence should be concluded under Community treaty-making procedures (Article 300 TEC). Presently the negotiation of the trade agreement with Iran and the free-trade agreement with the Gulf Co-operation Council, which both should include provisions on political co-operation and possibly terrorism, cause these problems, as does the projected agreement with Switzerland on its participation in the Schengen system. This means conflicting negotiation methods under different negotiators – the Commission under the EC Treaty and the Presidency under the Union Treaty. It means different methods of conclusion and of provisional application of the agreement, as well as different roles for the European Parliament in treaty-making – in the Union procedure Council unanimity is required and there is no parliamentary influence whatsoever, whilst under Community law qualified majority in the Council and, depending on the subject matter, parliamentary advice or consent is necessary.

Normally, under Community law the more onerous procedure would have to be applied, but in this case – quite apart from the difficulty of deciding which one is the most onerous – that is not possible because of the Community-procedure-protection clause (Article 47 TEU): Article 24 TEU and its procedure could not possibly be applied to the Community-side of the agreement.

Hence there is the need to conclude two separate agreements, one under Article 24 TEU and the other under Article 300 TEC. Obviously this will again create complications in international negotiations. Instead of having to explain to partners in a negotiation that both the Community and the Member States need to be party to an agreement for reasons related to the division of powers between them, it would now need to be explained that two international organizations need to participate in the discussion, each represented by a different chief negotiator and that two agreements need to be concluded. Not exactly an improvement over "classical" mixity, this new "cross-pillar" mixity.

One might, of course, consider not to bother our treaty partners too much with these problems and conclude *one* agreement with *two* organizations, the Union and the Community, as partners on the European side. The agreement would be concluded through two approval decisions, one based on Article 24 TEU, the other on Article 300 TEC. These decisions should specify which parts of the international agreement falls under its jurisdiction and which (CFSP) part does not. Nevertheless such a double approval procedure might be of doubtful legality in the light of Article 47 TEU, since failure to reach unanimity under Article 24 TEU could doom an agreement for the Community aspects of which the requisite qualified majority could be reached.

5. The consequence of a Union with a single personality

After having considered the new complications and legal uncertainties of "cross-pillar" mixity, which are just as bad if not worse than those of "classical" mixity, one would hope that the idea of a single Union, replacing the three pillars, as broached in the European Convention, might bring the solution to all these woes and lead to a single Union negotiating more effectively with its partners.

The answer to this hope will depend very much on the kind of Union treaty that will come out of the Convention and the subsequent Intergovernmental Conference. Will it be a true single Union treaty with a unified method of negotiating and concluding international agreements (with perhaps varying majorities in the Council and EP involvement, depending on different types of agreement) and a jurisdiction of the Court, which covers all aspects of Union law, although perhaps with varying intensity? Or will it be a Union treaty in which the "intergovernmental" method in foreign policy and defence will continue to co-exist with the "Community" method, and the jurisdiction of the court will remain restricted to the area covered by the latter? In that case the "protection" of the Community method against the intergovernmental method will probably need to continue, with all the complications resulting from it.

It would seem, unfortunately, that the Convention has followed the second model.[5]

There will be one Union, with one (international) legal personality (Article I.6).

There remains, however, a clear distinction between the CFSP on the one hand and the other external policies, on the other hand. Article III-222 of the Convention draft makes a clear distinction between treaty approval procedure for CFSP and for Community domains. And the CFSP is clearly excepted from the ECJ's jurisdiction over external relations (Article III-282); only sanctions measures against natural or legal persons can be reviewed for their legality. Given these continuing sharp distinctions between the domain of the Common Foreign and Security Policy, including Defence Policy, and the Community domain, it is not surprising that a clause comparable to Article 47 TEU can be found in the Convention draft (Article III-209). The firewall will still need to be there.

There can thus be little doubt that all the negative consequences and complications (resulting from all three factors mentioned above) for the effectiveness and cohesion of the Union's participation in international negotiations will continue to apply. Unless at least some improvements can be found in the new institutional structure proposed by the Convention which will counteract the persisting negative aspects.

Two elements from the Convention draft might be of interest here: the single personality of the Union as such and the suggested function of Minister of Foreign Affairs of the Union. One can only speculate on how these elements might influence the future negotiation practice of the single Union. But the matter may not become much simpler once the Union becomes a single entity with a single external representative, who can receive the proverbial telephone calls from Mr. Kissinger and his present-day successor, Ms. Rice. Once the Union negotiates an agreement covering both CFSP and other areas, the firewall provision may need to be respected, which may mean that, at least internally, parts of one and the same agreement need to follow different paths of decision-making. However, if one part of the agreement, on CFSP, needs unanimity in the Council and no parliamentary scrutiny at all, but the other part, on Community matters needs only qualified majority in the Council combined with Parliamentary consent, it would seem inevitable that Council unanimity will also govern the Community part and parliamentary consent the CFSP part of the agreement. This would be difficult to reconcile with the firewall provision (Article III-209) and would be subject to the jurisdiction of the Court.

Some further reflection would seem to be necessary here.

Notes

1 On FAO membership see Rachel Frid, 'The European Community, A Member of a Specialized Agency of the United Nations', *EJIL* (1993) pp. 239-255.

2 See Ruling 1/78 (Euratom Treaty) 1978 *ECJ Reports* 2151, point 9.

3 Such internal agreements, even when informal, are enforceable, see Case C-25/94 *Commission* v. *Council*, 1996 *ECJ Reports* 1969.

4 Case 327/91, *France* v. *Commission*, 1994 *ECJ Reports* 3641, point 36, in which the Court declared that "mere practice" in the field of treaty-making cannot override the provisions of the Community treaty. Since the Union Treaty is outside the jurisdiction of the Court, its provisions can be overridden by "mere practice."

5 The last version of the new Union Treaty to come out of the Convention bears doc. no. CONV.850/03. The article references are with respect to that text.

Remarks by Charles N. Brower*

The interaction of international organizations and arbitral tribunals in the development of transnational commercial law

I. Introduction: Traditional sources of transnational commercial law

Parties to international investment and other commercial transactions, State-owned entities and private ones alike, increasingly prefer to settle their disputes through international arbitration – i.e., neutrally, impartially and fairly, hence outside of any national court system, according to law and with final and binding effect. This preference for "denationalized justice" often extends beyond the *fora* for the resolution of such disputes to include, as well, privatization of the applicable *rules of decision*.[1]

International organizations have long played an important role in formulating such neutral legal principles. The Hague Conference on Private International Law, for instance, has worked since 1893 to unify, through multilateral conventions, rules of private law (whether substantive or choice-of-law rules) in numerous fields.[2] The United Nations General Assembly likewise plays an important role, and indeed is charged by Article 13 of the UN Charter with "encouraging the progressive development of international law and its codification." The General Assembly established the United Nations Commission on International Trade Law (UNCITRAL) in 1966 to further "the progressive harmonization and unification of the law of international trade."[3] To that end, UNCITRAL has promulgated model laws (such as the 1985 Model Law on International Commercial Arbitration, which has inspired arbitration legislation in thirty-five countries as well as in Hong Kong, Macao, Scotland and five US states[4]) and has drafted numerous treaties (such as the 1980 Convention on Contracts for the International Sale of Goods ("Vienna Sales Convention"), to which 62 States currently are party).[5] Although these model laws and conventions are devised and promulgated by international organizations, their substantive provisions achieve force of law only through their ratification and implementation by States. As such, uniformity of the underlying rights and obligations hinges on States' compatible understanding and incorporation of those provisions, which are not easily achieved.

In addition, non-governmental organizations such as the Grain and Feed Trade Association and the International Chamber of Commerce (ICC) have proven important in, for example, standardization of many rules and procedures for parties engaged in various types of international trade and commerce.[6] While standard forms promulgated by these organizations do not purport to constitute complete or autonomous legal regimes, their wide incorporation into contracts ensures the easy resolution of recurring issues in international commerce and trade and thereby staves off disputes.

* Judge of the Iran-United States Claims Tribunal, Member of 20 Essex Street Chambers (London) and Special Counsel to White & Case, LLP; formerly, Acting Legal Adviser, United States Department of State, Deputy Special Counsellor to the President of the United States, President of the American Society of International Law and Chair of the Institute for Transnational Arbitration.
The author acknowledges with deep appreciation the invaluable assistance in the preparation of this paper rendered by Jeremy K. Sharpe, his Legal Assistant at the Iran-United States Claims Tribunal and a Member of the New York Bar.

Finally, international tribunals such as the Iran-United States Claims Tribunal ("Tribunal") have been at the forefront of promoting neutral principles of transnational law. The 1981 Claims Settlement Declaration establishing the Tribunal provides in Article V that "[t]he Tribunal shall decide all cases on the basis of respect for law, applying such choice of law rules and principles of commercial and international law as the Tribunal determines to be applicable, taking into account relevant usages of the trade, contract provisions and changed circumstances."[7] The Tribunal itself recognized from its beginning that

> [i]t is difficult to conceive of a choice of law provision that would give the Tribunal greater freedom in determining case by case the law relevant to the issues before it. Such freedom is consistent with, and perhaps almost essential to, the scope of the tasks confronting the Tribunal, which include not only claims of a commercial nature, . . . but also claims involving alleged expropriations or other public acts, claims between the two Governments, certain claims between banking institutions and issues of interpretation and implementation of the Algiers Declarations.[8]

Because the Tribunal largely has avoided to the extent possible applying the laws of either Iran or the United States, it has had ample opportunity over the past two decades to apply and develop transnational law from numerous sources, including treaties, custom and general principles of commercial law, or the *lex mercatoria.*

II. A NEW APPROACH: THE "CREEPING CODIFICATION" OF *LEX MERCATORIA*

Recent years, however, have witnessed a fundamentally different kind of law-making, which Professor Klaus Peter Berger has termed the "creeping codification of the *lex mercatoria*,"[9] *i.e.*, the development of a body of "privatized" principles, standards and rules of transnational commercial law. The novelty of this approach is the rendering, divorced from State control, of "draft" or "model" international law that transforms concepts of *lex mercatoria* into concrete, accessible and pragmatic principles for use by parties, courts and arbitrators. At a time when international conventions are increasingly difficult to negotiate and bring into force on any subject,[10] the informal codification of uniform, neutral rules of transnational law represents a welcome and potentially important trend.

The most important such development is the Principles of International Commercial Contracts ("UNIDROIT Principles"),[11] issued in 1994 by the International Institute for the Unification of Private Law,[12] which has been characterized as "a totally new approach to international trade law." [13] The UNIDROIT Principles are neither model clauses, nor contract forms, nor international trade terms, nor international legislation adopted by States through international agreements. As one arbitral tribunal has noted, the UNIDROIT Principles are

> a restatement of international legal principles applicable to international commercial contracts made by a distinguished group of international experts coming from all prevailing legal systems of the world, without the intervention of States or governments, both circumstances redounding to the high quality and neutrality of the product and its ability to reflect the present stage of consensus on international legal rules and principles governing international contractual obligations in the world, primarily on the basis of their fairness and appropriateness for international commercial transactions falling within their purview. . . .[14]

The UNIDROIT Principles are similar in their concept and genesis to the *Restatements* of the American Law Institute. The UNIDROIT Principles' 119 "black-letter" articles are accompanied by commentary and examples, to guide users from disparate legal traditions. Furthermore, the draftsmen of the UNIDROIT Principles – legal scholars, practitioners, judges and civil servants expert in contract, comparative and international commercial law – acted in their private capacities and not as representatives of their respective governments or of any commercial interests.

In one important respect, however, the UNIDROIT Principles differ from the *Restatements*: while the *Restatements* ostensibly "attempt to state and clarify *existing* law,"[15] the UNIDROIT Principles consciously, and progressively, seek in many instances to state the *best*, neutral law applicable for drafting and interpreting international commercial contracts, regardless of whether those Principles constitute extant *lex mercatoria*.[16] Thus, they expressly lay claim to being either "common to existing national legal systems" or those rules deemed "best adapted to the special requirements of international commercial transactions."[17] As such, they are *pre-statements* of the law that evolve into the law by their progressive use in international commercial contracts and application by national courts and arbitral tribunals.[18]

UNIDROIT's Governing Council itself has underscored that the UNIDROIT Principles "do not involve the endorsement of Governments" and "are not a binding instrument," [19] rather in contravention of Article 14 of UNIDROIT's Statute, which provides that its "Governing Council shall present drafts adopted to governments, solicit their input and convene diplomatic conferences to examine the drafts."[20] It is precisely because many governments reportedly would have refused to consent to the UNIDROIT Principles as a restatement of international contract law,[21] however, that they were promulgated as "draft" law. This informal approach obviated the need to receive States' imprimatur and avoided further rounds of debate, delay and compromise that inevitably would have been required to obtain governmental assent.[22] Indeed, given the UNIDROIT Principles' broad subject matter and avowedly universal ambit, it is questionable whether even a significant portion of the now roughly 200 independent States could have reached any meaningful consensus at all.

The conclusion is obvious: The conscious exclusion of governments as such from any formal role in this extensive codification of transnational commercial law has greatly enhanced its progressive development and application, if not indeed made it possible at all.

III. Use of the UNIDROIT Principles in International Arbitration

Unsurprisingly, the creeping codification of the *lex mercatoria*, as exemplified by the UNIDROIT Principles, is extensively evident in the context of international arbitration, a forum in which adjudicators arguably have more freedom to apply transnational law than do judges in national courts. Indeed, arbitration is the crucible in which the UNIDROIT Principles are themselves being tested.

Arbitrators have invoked the UNIDROIT Principles in a variety of contexts. First, they frequently have been used to interpret or supplement uniform law instruments, notably the Vienna Sales Convention. Indeed, one ICC tribunal cited the UNIDROIT Principles as "perfectly suited" to resolve the disputed termination of an exclusive distributorship contract under the Vienna Sales Convention. The Tribunal held that Article 1.8 of the UNIDROIT Principles ("The parties are bound by any usage to which they have agreed and by any practices which they have established between themselves") extended the comparable article of the Vienna Sales Convention (9.1) to all international commercial contracts.[23]

Second, the UNIDROIT Principles have been used to "provide a solution to an issue raised when it proves impossible to establish the relevant rule of the applicable law" "and a solution can be found in the Principles."[24] Thus, the UNIDROIT Principles have been applied in an *ad hoc* arbitration in New Zealand in which the applicable national law was deemed to be "in a somewhat unsettled state," as well as to fill lacunae and resolve ambiguities in the law of a former Soviet State transitioning to a market economy.[25] This application of the UNIDROIT Principles may prove particularly important, given that the vast majority of arbitration cases involve contracts designating a national law as the governing law[26] and such law often fails the particular needs of international commerce.

Third, the UNIDROIT Principles have been used to demonstrate the compatibility of the applicable national law with neutral international principles. Indeed, cases abound in which arbitral tribunals (and even a few national courts[27]) have relied on the UNIDROIT Principles to underscore the compatibility of the applicable national law with international legal precepts.[28]

Finally, the UNIDROIT Principles often have been applied when parties have agreed that their contract be governed by general principles of law or the *lex mercatoria*.[29] Arbitrators have found the Principles particularly useful in providing accessible, concrete rules to implement the broad legal references often employed by drafting parties. Arbitrators thus have invoked the UNIDROIT Principles where contracts have called for the application of "generally accepted principles of international commercial law,"[30] "international practices,"[31] "rules of natural justice,"[32] "general principles of equity,"[33] and even "Anglo-Saxon principles of law."[34] Significantly, national courts appear unwilling to set aside awards on grounds that arbitral tribunals have applied the UNIDROIT Principles as *lex mercatoria*,[35] and in fact the United Nations Convention on the Recognition and Enforcement of Foreign Arbitral Awards provides no support for States' failure to recognize and enforce such arbitral awards.[36]

IV. Conclusion

International organizations have long striven to facilitate an autonomous law of international commerce through promulgation of uniform laws, trade terms and contract forms. Arbitral tribunals have encouraged this development through their recognition and application of these sources. Today, however, we are witnessing a dynamic shift in the evolution of transnational commercial law, through the creeping codification of the *lex mercatoria* by such means as "draft" principles of transnational commercial law. Three aspects of this process bear noting.

First, the process stands traditional, positivist law-making on its head,[37] eschewing State-backed codification in favor of private efforts – albeit at times under the umbrella of international organizations. Indeed, this is but one manifestation of the global retreat of State authority and the privatization of functions that previously had been the sole province of governments. It must be remembered, however, that these developments are made possible only by States' acceptance and facilitation of party autonomy, which enables contracting parties to stipulate the law governing their rights and duties.

Second, the process may lead to better and more transparent application of transnational commercial law. No longer must arbitrators who apply *lex mercatoria* draw from a grab bag of unwritten rules; they may now identify the source of the applicable transnational law. In resolving international commercial disputes involving parties from disparate legal and cultural traditions, the use of concrete, neutral, pragmatic principles can only lead to greater certainty, predictability and fairness.

Third, the process is not fixed, immutable and static, but is tentative, flexible and adaptable. Indeed, the authors of the UNIDROIT Principles deliberately sought to make them "sufficiently flexible to take account of the constantly changing circumstances brought about by the technological and economic developments affecting cross-border trade practice."[38] Accordingly, principles that fail to serve the interests of international commerce will be cast off, and new principles will be, and are being,[39] devised as needed.

To borrow from Lord Mustill, the UNIDROIT Principles exist for one purpose only: "to serve the commercial man".[40] The UNIDROIT Principles will not fail merely because they lack governmental blessing, nor will they succeed merely as the darling of international legal scholars. Rather, if the UNIDROIT principles do accomplish their ambitious task, it will be because they bridge a gap between the overly general *lex mercatoria* and insufficiently neutral national laws. If successful, the UNIDROIT Principles may well portend a viable new species of international lawmaking.

Notes

[1] See Charles N. Brower, 'The Privatization of Rules of Decision in International Commercial Arbitration', in Robert Briner, et al., eds., *Law of International Business and Dispute Settlement in the 21st Century: Liber Amicorum Karl-Heinz Böckstiegel* (2001) p. 111.

[2] The Hague Conference on Private International Law convened its first session in 1893 at the initiative of T.M.C. Asser and became a permanent international organization in 1955, upon entry into force of its Statute. See <http://www.hcch.net/e/conventions/text01e.html>.

[3] *Establishment of the United Nations Commission on International Trade Law*, G.A. Res. 2205, UN GAOR, 21st Sess., Supp. No. 16, at 99 (1966), available at <http://www.uncitral.org>.

[4] UNCITRAL Model Law on International Commercial Arbitration (1985), available at <http://www.uncitral.org/en-index.htm>. Other UNCITRAL model laws include the Model Law on International Commercial Conciliation (2002); Model Law on Cross-Border Insolvency (1997); Model Law on Electronic Commerce (1996); Model Law on Procurement of Goods, Construction and Services (1994); and Model Law on International Credit Transfers (1992). See *idem.*

In the United States, for over a century, the National Conference of Commissioners on Uniform State Laws has worked similarly, drafting over 200 proposals for uniform and model laws, including the Uniform Commercial Code. See <http://www.nccusl.org>.

[5] United Nations Convention on Contracts for the International Sale of Goods, 10 April 1980, UN Doc. A/Conf. 97/18, with Annex, reprinted in 19 *ILM* 668 (1980). Other UNCITRAL conventions include the United Nations Convention on the Assignment of Receivables in International Trade (2001); United Nations Convention on Independent Guarantees and Stand-by Letters of Credit (1995); United Nations Convention on Liability of Operators of Transport Terminals in International Trade (1991); United Nations Convention on International Bills of Exchange and International Promissory Notes (1988); and United Nations Convention on the Carriage of Goods by Sea (1978).

[6] See, e.g., Michael C. Rowe, 'The Contribution of the ICC to the Development of International Trade Law', in Norbert Horn & Clive M. Schmitthoff, eds., *The Transnational Law of International Commercial Transactions* (1982).

7 Declaration of the Government of the Democratic and Popular Republic of Algeria Concerning the Settlement of Claims by the Government of the United States of America and the Government of the Islamic Republic of Iran, 19 January 1981, reprinted in 1 *Iran-U.S. Cl. Trib. Rep.* 9, 11.
8 *CMI Int'l, Inc.* and *Ministry of Roads and Trans.*, Award No. 99-245-2 (27 December 1983), reprinted in 4 *Iran-U.S. Cl. Trib. Rep.* 263, 267-68.
9 See Klaus Peter Berger, *The Creeping Codification of the Lex Mercatoria* (1999) p. 233.
10 See Vera Gowlland-Debbas, ed., *Multilateral Treaty-Making: The Current Status of Challenges to and Reforms Needed in the International Legislative Process* (2000) (discussing, at the 1998 Forum Geneva, contemporary difficulties of multilateral treaty-making).
11 International Institute for the Unification of Private Law, *Principles of International Commercial Contracts* (1994), available at <http://www.unilex.info>. The UNIDROIT Principles are divided into seven chapters: General Provisions, Formation, Validity, Interpretation, Content, Performance and Non-Performance.
The Principles of European Contract Law, developed by a Commission headed by Danish Professor Ole Lando, provide a similar example (in form and substance) of this trend.
12 The International Institute for the Unification of Private Law (UNIDROIT) is an independent intergovernmental organization. UNIDROIT originally was established in 1926 as an auxiliary organ of the League of Nations and, following the League's demise, was reestablished in 1940 on the basis of its Statute. See <http://www.unidroit.org/english/presentation/main.htm>.
13 Michael Joachim Bonell, 'The UNIDROIT Principles of International Commercial Contracts: Why? What? How?', 69 *Tul. L. Rev.* (1995) pp. 1121, 1122.
14 Partial Award in ICC Case No. 7110, June 1995, reprinted in part in 10 *ICC Int'l Ct. Arb. Bull.* (1999) pp. 39, 49.
15 *Restatement (Second) of the Foreign Relations Law of the United States*, (1965) at xi [emphasis added]. The 1987 *Restatement (Third) of the Foreign Relations Law of the United States* sustained criticism, even prior to its completion, that it does not always reflect existing law, but promotes the authors' views of what the law ought to be. See 'The Draft Restatement of the Foreign Relations Law of the United States', 76 *Am. Soc'y Int'l L. Proc.* (1982) p. 184.
16 See Bonell, *supra* note 13, at p. 1129 ("[W]hat was decisive was not just which rule was adopted by the majority of jurisdictions, but rather which of the rules under consideration had the most persuasive value or appeared to be particularly well-suited for cross-border transactions or both.").
17 UNIDROIT Principles, *supra* note 11, at p. 3 (cmt. 4.a to Preamble).
18 See Klaus Peter Berger, 'The New Law Merchant and the Global Marketplace: A 21st Century View of Transnational Commercial Law', in Klaus Peter Berger, ed., *The Practice of Transnational Law* (2001) pp 1, 13.
19 Introduction to UNIDROIT Principles, *supra* note 11, at ix.
20 See <http://www.unidroit.org>.
21 Hilmar Raeschke-Kessler, 'Should an Arbitrator in an International Arbitration Procedure Apply the UNIDROIT Principles?', in *UNIDROIT Principles for International Commercial Contracts: A New Lex Mercatoria?* (1995) pp. 167, 169-70.
22 The Vienna Sales Convention, for example, required twelve years to develop within UNCITRAL, which followed twenty-two years of preparatory work by UNIDROIT. See John A. Spanogle, Jr., 'The Arrival of International Private Law', 25 *Geo. Wash. J. Int'l L. & Econ.* (1991) pp. 477, 488.
23 See Final Award in ICC Case No. 8817, December 1997, reprinted in part in 10 *ICC Int'l Ct. Arb. Bull.* (1999) pp. 75, 77.
24 UNIDROIT Principles, *supra* note 11, at pp. 1, 11 (Preamble, para. 3; cmt. to Preamble, sec. 5).
25 See Karl-Heinz Böckstiegel, 'The Application of the UNIDROIT Principles to Contracts Involving States or Intergovernmental Organizations', UNIDROIT Principles of International Commercial Contracts: Reflections on Their Use in International Arbitration, *ICC Int'l Ct. Arb. Bull.* pp 51, 54 (Special Supp. 2002) [hereinafter UNIDROIT Principles of International Commercial Contracts].
26 See Julian D.M. Lew, 'The UNIDROIT Principles as Lex Contractus Chosen by the Parties and Without an Explicit Choice-of-Law Clause: The Perspective of Counsel', in *UNIDROIT Principles of International Commercial Contracts*, *supra* note 25, at pp. 85, 86 (citing "statistics show[ing] that around 80% of matters that come to ICC arbitration have a predetermined choice-of-law provision" designating the law of one State).
27 See, e.g., *Hughes Aircraft Sys. Int'l* v. *Airservices Australia* (1997) 76 *FCR* p. 151 (citing the UNIDROIT Principles for their recognition that the duty of good faith and fair dealing is a fundamental principle in international commercial contracts); see also <http://www.unilex.info> (citing national courts' reliance on the UNIDROIT Principles in France, The Netherlands and New Zealand).

[28] See <http://www.unilex.info> (citing cases).
[29] UNIDROIT Principles, *supra* note 11, at p. 1 (Preamble, para. 3).
[30] See Böckstiegel, *supra* note 25, at p. 54.
[31] See Final Award in ICC Case No. 10114, March 2000, reprinted in part in 12 *ICC Int'l Ct. Arb. Bull.* (2001) pp. 100.
[32] See Partial Award in ICC Case No. 7110, June 1995, reprinted in part in 10 *ICC Int'l Ct. Arb. Bull.* pp. 39, 48-49 (1999) (concluding "that the reasonable intention of the parties regarding the substantive law applicable to the Contracts was to have all of them governed by general legal rules and principles in matter[s] of international contractual obligations such as those arising out of the Contracts, which, though not necessarily enshrined in any specific national legal system, are specially adapted to the needs of international transactions like the Contracts and enjoy wide international consensus"— as "primarily reflected by . . . the UNIDROIT Principles").
[33] See Final Award in ICC Case No. 9797, July 2000, reprinted in part in 12 *ICC Int'l Ct. Arb. Bull.* (2001) pp. 88, 89 (declaring UNIDROIT Principles "a reliable source of international commercial law in international arbitration[,] for they contain in essence a restatement of those '*principes directeurs*' that have enjoyed universal acceptance and, moreover, are at the heart of those most fundamental notions which have consistently been applied in arbitral practice") [citation and internal quotation omitted].
[34] See London Court of International Arbitration Award, 1995, cited at <http://www.unilex.info>.
[35] See, e.g., *Ministry of Defense and Support for the Armed Forces of the Islamic Republic of Iran* v. *Cubic Defense Systems, Inc.*, 29 F. Supp.2d 1168, 1173 (S.D. Cal. 1998) (holding that the arbitral "[t]ribunal's reference to and application of the UNIDROIT Principles and principles such as good faith and fair dealing [did] not violate Article V(1)(c)" of the New York Convention); see also Michael Joachim Bonell, 'UNIDROIT Principles: A Significant Recognition by a United States District Court', 1999 *Unif. L. Rev.* p. 651.
[36] The limited defenses to the recognition and enforcement of foreign arbitral awards under the New York Convention are: incapacity, improper notice or inability to present one's case, improper composition of the tribunal, non-arbitrability of the subject matter, or the award is not yet binding, deals with matters beyond the parties' submission to arbitrate or is contrary to public policy. United Nations Convention on the Recognition and Enforcement of Foreign Arbitral Awards, opened for signature 10 June 1958, art. V, 21 U.S.T. 2517, 330 U.N.T.S. 3.
[37] Contrast this kind of lawmaking with Justice Holmes's positivist pronouncement that "law in the sense of which courts speak of it today does not exist without some definite authority behind it" and the "only authority is the state." *Black and White Taxicab & Trans. Co.* v. *Brown and Yellow Taxicab & Trans. Co.*, 276 U.S. 518, 533, 535 (1928) (Holmes, J., dissenting).
[38] Bonell, *supra* note 13, at p. 1134. The UNIDROIT Principles' openness to usages – whether those established by parties or general trade usages – is an essential component of that flexibility.
[39] Indeed, UNIDROIT is currently drafting a second edition of the Principles, the new topics of which will include agency, limitation of actions, assignment of contracts, contracts for the benefit of a third party, set-off and waiver. See Hilmar Raeschke-Kessler, 'The UNIDROIT Principles in Contemporary Contract Practice', in *UNIDROIT Principles of International Commercial Contracts*, *supra* note 25, at pp. 99, 100.
[40] "Commercial arbitration exists for one purpose only: to serve the commercial man." Rt. Hon. Lord Justice Mustill, 'The New Lex Mercatoria: The First Twenty-five Years', 4 *Arb. Int'l* (1988) p. 86.

Remarks by Rolf Einar Fife*

The role of international organizations in international treaty-making

Some reflections on the negotiations on the International Criminal Court (ICC)

The entry into force in July 2002 of the 1998 Rome Statute for the International Criminal Court stands as a milestone in the development of international law.[1] The establishment of the Court in The Hague marked the attainment of a long-term objective that engaged States and non-State actors. The objective of a treaty-based global criminal court had been identified several decades ago as a priority at the United Nations. Pledges were made in the wake of the Nuremberg and Tokyo trials (1945-46) and were also reflected in Article 6 of the 1948 Genocide Convention.

This paper briefly sketches some reflections on the contributions and limitations of non-State actors, in particular international organizations, in the context of the multilateral treaty negotiations between States which led to the establishment of the Court.

1. A bird's eye view of the treaty-making process

It would be far from the truth to state that these negotiations built on the shifting sands of sudden, fashionable and untested new ideas. Nor were the negotiations carried out hastily and without due preparation, thrusting previously unknown legal norms upon Governments. Moreover, while non-State actors clearly had an important impact on States engaged in treaty-making, they did not challenge the role of States as negotiators and treaty-makers.

The negotiation process was time consuming and mobilized considerable resources. It was combined with the convergence and then confluence of broad values and interests within the international community, which it would be easy to underestimate. Aspirations for an international criminal jurisdiction for the worst international crimes, in the absence of functioning national systems, were hardly new. Layers of legal bricks and normative mortar had already been laid. They constituted rock-solid foundations for a focus on a limited catalogue of universally condemned crimes. Near universal acceptance of key instruments of international humanitarian law had led to broad agreement on the individual criminal responsibility for a catalogue, soon to be nicknamed the "core crimes". For long, while individual responsibility was a fact, the international response to enforce it was not.

The negotiation process proper could be divided into four main phases:

(1) the preparation of a draft Statute by the International Law Commission (1992-1994), based on a request to this expert body from the United Nations

* Director General, Department of Legal Affairs, Royal Ministry of Foreign Affairs, Norway. The author headed the Norwegian delegations in the negotiations on the International Criminal Court throughout the negotiation process. The author is solely responsible for this presentation, which does not constitute a statement of the Government of Norway.

General Assembly and input from States in debates in the Assembly's Sixth Committee,

(2) the deliberations, compilation and consolidation of alternative proposals from States, first in an Ad Hoc Committee and then in a Preparatory Committee under the General Assembly (1995-1998),

(3) the Rome Diplomatic Conference (15 June-17 July 1998), resulting in the adoption of the Rome Statute, and

(4) the ensuing negotiation in the Preparatory Commission of crucial additional instruments, including the Elements of Crimes and the Rules of Procedure and Evidence (1999-2002). All additional instruments negotiated after the Rome Diplomatic Conference were adopted without a vote, with the participation also of States who had not voted in favour of the Statute.[2]

In addition, a fifth stage might be added to the above time line. This is the phase of implementation and internalization of the Statute in national systems, where non-State actors also play an active role. [3]

This timeline only sketches a formal negotiating structure. The sequence of the separate phases provides a framework for analyzing a linear development. On that basis, it will be apparent that the process developed from an open-ended and broad gathering of proposals, via slow consolidation of options, over to the identification of solutions and drafting which could command the broadest international support. Thereafter, additional instruments were negotiated, which in certain cases provided increased clarity about the articulation of certain principles, rules or procedures. All these stages were separate, with transparent and agreed negotiating mandates.

Such a linear perspective needs, however, to be supplemented by an understanding of the diversity of contributions to the treaty-making process from various, and at times competing, interests within the international community. Several strands appear, which involved non-State actors. These strands often had a direct impact or indirect influence on the process.

2. Various strands which influenced the negotiation process – with an emphasis on contributions through or by international organizations

2.1 The United Nations General Assembly provided the initial debating forum and negotiating arena. Its mandate includes, in accordance with Article 13 of the Charter, initiation of studies and making of "recommendations for the purpose of encouraging the progressive development of international law and its codification", through its subsidiary body the International Law Commission. After having considered comments from Governments in the Sixth Committee of the General Assembly, the Commission submitted to States a revised draft Statute, which constituted the basis for their negotiations as from 1994.

2.2 Decisive impetus was given to the work of the International Law Commission, when the United Nations Security Council established the International Criminal Tribunal for the former Yugoslavia (ICTY), through Resolution 827 (1993). The establishment of this subsidiary body of the Security Council, pursuant to Chapter VII of the Charter after the determination of a threat against international peace and security, marked a watershed. It signified to the General Assembly and the International Law Commission that it could be politically and legally feasible to establish a permanent international criminal jurisdiction for serious violations of international humanitarian law. Additional impetus was added by the establishment of the International Criminal Tribunal for Rwanda (ICTR) in 1994. The action of the Security Council also demonstrated the close relationship between international peace and security and the prevention and suppression of cultures of impunity for mass atrocities.

2.3 Throughout the ensuing treaty negotiations, the rapidly expanding case law of the ICTY and the ICTR, as well as their practical administrative experience, provided both catalyzing illustrations and building-blocks for the rules of the ICC. With regard to these contributions, it is fair to speak of a direct and rapidly evolving normative influence of the United Nations through the two *ad hoc* tribunals, to the negotiations.

2.4 The permanent staff members of international organizations also played an important role. First, it would be easy to overlook the discrete, yet essential operational role of the United Nations Secretariat, through the Office of Legal Affairs (OLA). Competent officials provided, in addition to conference and other administrative services, assistance in drafting of key documentation. Officials of the *ad hoc* tribunals provided neutral, yet essential factual information about rules and activities of their institutions. Their presence was unassuming and unimposing, but ensured the constant availability of institutional memory and practical experience. More than one debate risked bogging down to a total halt due to theoretical cleavages and opposed views based on different national legal traditions. Many were brought back into focus, thanks largely to informal information provided upon request from experts from the two tribunals, which shed light on how one had managed to bridge differences there.

2.5 It has been asserted that international organizations are a "focused and intensified arena of public justification".[4] Moreover, it has been demonstrated how they also can serve as "magnifiers of concern, facilitators of argument and builders of capacity".[5]

The various negotiating bodies under the General Assembly of the United Nations, as well as the Rome Diplomatic Conference itself, enabled a constant inter-disciplinary gathering and cross-fertilization of national delegates and observers from civil society. Participation of international and criminal lawyers, military and civil experts contributed to in-depth consideration of definitions of crimes and other issues. They made it possible to conduct intensive exchanges between various legal systems, whether civil law, common law, Chinese, Islamic law, etc. At best, they were a paradise for comparative lawyers and bridge builders. At worst, the slow pace in clarifying misunderstandings, was taxing. This did nothing to diminish the satisfaction ultimately felt when broad agreement emerged on common language.

The negotiating bodies were also, and primarily, a transparent meeting place for major powers as well as small States, industrialized and developing States. The establishment of trust funds by the General Assembly of the United Nations enabled participation of experts also from the least developed countries. The negotiating bodies also provided opportunities for representatives of all States, and in particular States with small delegations, to develop new insights or expertise. They also made it possible for States to form coalitions. This they did, including through the constantly expanding Like Minded Group (LMG) of States supportive of a fair, independent and credible Court.

2.6 These arenas may have permitted, moreover, the development of what in international relations theory have been described as *epistemic communities*[6]and *transgovernmental networks*[7]. Representatives and experts from various national bureaucracies rubbed shoulders, often over several years, in an increasingly common search for answers and solutions. In this, they were also aided by experts of non-governmental organizations, academic experts and competent officials of staffs of international organizations. These transnational links between experts across the divide of various national systems contributed substantially to institutional learning.

Expert advice was provided by non-governmental organizations efficiently organized under the umbrella of the NGO-Coalition for the International Criminal Court. Among other prominent examples of non-State actors and organizations which provided expert advice, particular mention could be made of as diverse examples as the International Committee of the Red Cross (ICRC) and Interpol.

2.7 After the adoption of the Statute, regional organizations have played an active role in supporting the establishment of the Court and providing assistance to States with regard to implementation into national laws. The European Union developed common positions on the ICC and contributed, *inter alia*, to advice about matters related to implementation. The Council of Europe has also provided an important forum for exchanges of views and information on such matters. This approach is in keeping with the priority stated in the first preambulary paragraph of the Statute of the Council of Europe ("Convinced that the pursuit of peace based upon justice and international cooperation is vital for the preservation of human society and civilisation").

2.8 Contributions of international staffs of international organizations are clearly limited by the requirements of neutrality and objectivity incumbent on them, as well as by the need to preserve the full legitimacy and respect for the independent mandate of the organization concerned. In the case of the ICC negotiations, the expertise of international officials proved extremely useful, particularly when they acted, with tact and judgment as they did, as repositories of institutional knowledge and experience.

3. An attempt to summarize

The negotiations on the International Criminal Court did not call into question the primordial role of States in international law-making. Any rumours about the demise or ailments of the Grotian or Westphalian systems are highly exaggerated, on the basis of these negotiations and the resulting Statute. Increasing complexity and interdependence in international society, combined with the recognition of the upgrowth of other subjects of international law or actors, have largely removed a monopoly of States in influencing international treaty negotiations. However, States retained the key role.

The contributions of non-State actors and States are necessarily of a different nature, and may be complementary. The preparation of national negotiating positions and strategies requires mobilization and involvement of various competent national authorities (i.e. within Justice and Defence affairs), internal negotiation and clarification of positions. In democratic systems this is also based on unequalled accountability.

In guise of concluding remarks, it is submitted that international organizations had an important impact on the treaty-making process which led to the establishment of the ICC. They notably made essential normative contributions, played a necessary operational role and provided a constituent element in the upgrowth of transnational "epistemic communities".

NOTES

1 Rome Statute for the International Criminal Court, U.N. Doc. A/CONF.183/9* (1998), available at <http://www.un.org/law/icc/statute/romefra.htm> [hereinafter Statute]. The Statute was adopted at the United Nations Diplomatic Conference of Plenipotentiaries on the establishment of an International Criminal Court by a vote of 120 in favour, 7 against and 21 abstentions. According to Article 126 of the Statute 60 ratifications were required for it to enter into force. As of 5 September 2003, 139 States had signed the Statute and 92 had ratified or acceded to it.

2 On the drafting histories of successive phases, as seen by some key participants, see in particular, Roy S. Lee, ed., *The International Criminal Court, The making of the Rome Statute, Issues, Negotiations, Results* (Kluwer Law International 1999); Roy S. Lee, ed., *The International Criminal Court, Elements of Crimes and Rules of Procedure and Evidence* (Transnational Publishers 2001); *Twenty-fifth memorial issue, The Eve of the International Criminal Court: Preparations and Commentary*, 25 *Fordham Int l. J.* (2002). For comprehensive commentaries of the Statute, see Antonio Cassese, Paola Gaeta, John R.W.D. Jones, *The Rome Statute of the International Criminal Court: A Commentary* (Oxford University Press 2002); Otto Triffterer, ed., *Commentary on the Rome Statute of the International Criminal Court* (Baden Baden, Nomos Verlagsgesellschaft 1999).

3 A further development of these points is contained in Rolf Einar Fife, 'The International Criminal Court: Whence It Came, Where It Goes', *Nordic J. Of Int l L.* (2000) pp. 63-85. Translated into Russian 'Mezjdunarodnyj Ugolovnyj Sud', 1 *Moscow J. Of Int l L.* (2001) pp. 60-87.

4 Abram Chayes, *The Cuban Missile Crisis: International Crises and the Rule of Law* (Lanham, Md. Uni. Press of America 1987) p. 104, also quoted in Abram Chayes and Antonia Handler Chayes, *The New Sovereignty, Compliance with International Regulatory Mechanisms* (Harvard Uni. Press 1995) p. 125.

5 Peter Haas, Robert O. Keohane, Marc S. Levy, eds., *Institutions for the Earth Sources of Effective International Environmental Protection* (Cambridge, MIT Press 1993) p. 409, quoted in Chayes and Chayes, *The New Sovereignty, supra.*

6 Peter M. Haas, 'Introduction: Epistemic Communities and International Policy Coordination', 46 *International Organization* (1992) 1.

7 Anne-Marie Slaughter, 'The Real New World Order', 76 *Foreign Affairs* (1997) 183-197, at 193; Anne-Marie Slaughter, 'Government networks: the heart of liberal democratic order', in Gregory H. Fox and Brad R. Roth, eds., *Democratic governance and international law* (Cambridge University Press 2000) p. 199.

DISCUSSION

The opening question of the discussion concerned the emerging hierarchy in international law-making over the last years, including norms of *jus cogens.*[1] What is the role of international organizations involved in the development of this rising hierarchy in the international legal order, which in a sense represents the core of the international value system?

Two points were made in this regard. The first concerns the Iran-US Claims Tribunal.[2] This institution is unique both in deciding issues of public international law as we know it, as well as issues of private law or of what Judge Brower refers to as rules of decisions in the commercial area. An interesting lack of hierarchy of tribunals exists and the Iran-US Claims Tribunal gives an example thereof. Federal judges from the United States have been astonished by this lack of hierarchy.

Awards of the Iran-US Claims Tribunal have, more than once, been subjected to the scrutiny of courts in the United States when they were called upon to enforce awards of the Tribunal in favor of the Islamic Republic of Iran. An example concerns a case where a US District Court, confirmed by a 2 to 1 majority in the US Court of Appeals for the Second Circuit, declined to enforce an Award of the Tribunal claimed under the New York Convention.[3] That Court concluded that the American party against whom the Award was issued had not had a proper opportunity to present its case as required by the New York Convention. In response, the Islamic Republic of Iran instituted proceedings at the Iran-US Claims Tribunal where it argued a breach of the Algiers Accords[4] by virtue of the United States judicial system not having enforced an Award of the Tribunal. The Tribunal, by majority vote, ruled that the United States was in violation of the Accords on the grounds argued.

This practice of national courts judging decisions of International Tribunals could also be seen in the courts of British Columbia with respect to the North American Free Trade Agreement,[5] in particular with regard to Chapter 11 on Arbitral Awards of international arbitral Tribunals. International Tribunals on the other hand have incidentally called decisions of national courts to account under that same Chapter 11 of NAFTA.

A second point in this regard was made in the light of the experiences of the European Community.[6] The Community has had much difficulty with the final creation of a hierarchy within its own law: this hierarchy has been problematic for the Community ever since 1945. As a result, it does not seem to worry about this hierarchy at a larger scale. The Community seems to be in a fix as its powers do not go as far as for example certain United Nations Security Council Resolutions concerning international trade with "the enemy." Such Resolutions seem to justify the stigmatization of certain process and the denial of their right to due process or remedies. On the other hand, they do allow the establishment of actions like the freezing of assets and transfer thereof to the Iraqi development funds. The European Community has no power to take such measures: its law prevents the Community from changing its property regime in Member States in any way. There have been instances where States, which often lack legal possibility or capacity to implement such provisions in an easy manner, have waited until these laws are implemented at the Community level, thereby relying on and profiting from the direct applicability of laws. This practice, which results in a shift of the burden to the Community and its Court of Justice, gives some practitioners reasons to be somewhat skeptical about the ways to treat issues of *jus cogens* and hierarchy in international law.

A second issue raised during the discussion concerns the different demands, claims and expectations of the various actors in international law. It was asked whether the dichotomy between "the State" and non-State actors is not partly unrealistic? Are some non-State actors, like multinational corporations, able to influence, even control, some State elites and to participate directly and indirectly in shaping law? If so, is participation by NGOs at international conferences sometimes merely the participation of other non-State actors who may not be able to directly influence or control "the State"? Is participation ultimately often more "democratic"?[7]

It was noted that authors are aware of the fact that State actors as such are under great influence of non-State actors at times. In the example of the WTO Secretariat, it was quite clear that certain States initiated particular cases as a result of great internal pressure.[8] This, as well as a reference to events taking place during the negotiations of the Tobacco Convention,[9] could arguably – and perhaps provocatively – be a basis for a partial understanding of the undemocratic aspect of the European Community.

With regard to the remark from the floor that we are not speaking about the role of international organizations influencing the States which are the State actors, it was added that this, being a matter of internal politics, is clear.[10] We all understand that the international involvement of NGOs certainly is matched by and in fact emanates from a much earlier activity on the part of NGOs in various countries within their national systems.

A third question from the floor was: "how can the European Union effectively negotiate as a member of an international organization on matters perhaps falling within or outside the competence of the Union itself?"[11] Does the negotiation method laid down in the Union's Treaty not depend on the degree of external competence of the Union, which can hardly be a negotiating player in issues outside its competence?

The question was interpreted as a statement that it is inconceivable that the Community or the Union ever negotiates outside its own competence.[12] Since that competence will never truly encompass the plenitude of powers of States, there will always be a certain handicap, and one is utopian to state that this handicap does not exist. Even if this were the case, utopia is there to be striven after and the reduction of the handicap in international negotiations, at least as seen from Brussels, is quite relevant in certain situations.

The topics under discussion raise interesting problems about the status of individuals within the system that were described in this panel.[13] The concept of legal personality and the existence of separate will enable to informally distinguish an organization from State members and from individuals. However, the extensive separate will reflected in deeper constitutionalization of organizations, maybe the individual's loyalty or their internal aspects, as borrowed from Hart's ideas, can shift from States' organizations. It is very important to apply Hart's test of loyalty and identity to members of the international civil service as that is done to citizens of States.

A fourth issue raised from the audience concerned the fact that "reflection needs to be undertaken on the interaction between all the actors and how they affect the process of governance when for instance a State representative becomes an international organizational official or an NGO representative and vice-versa."[14] Practice shows that it is often difficult to negotiate with a balanced point of view when different interests are at stake.

In Washington, the situation where an individual may at the same time be involved in an international organization, successively in an NGO and then in some other capacity, is referred to as the "revolving door."[15] The United States has a tradition where people go into and out of government and through universities, international organizations and private practice and so forth with a freedom and regularity which is largely unknown in the rest of the world. Judge sees great potential in this tradition, as it enables people to learn and understand the perspectives of other individual. As long as regulations exist to prevent serious conflicts of interest to this regard, this movement is only to the advantage of everyone involved.

The fifth question posed concerned the flexibility of the UNIDROIT Principles.[16] Do the cases mentioned by Judge Brower not reflect a somewhat too flexible attitude? Considering that we are looking for legal certainty, are these not "free and wild" applications of the UNIDROIT Principles? Has UNIDROIT foreseen the need for a body to monitor these applications?

One must keep in mind that Judge Brower's view derives from a judicial perspective. That aside, the monitoring indicated might be appropriate for the practice as it has recently been developing. Conceivably, this will be done by UNIDROIT but it is unclear what its plans are in this regard. The "market place" can have a corrective effect: this will either appear from a general satisfaction, and if not, solutions will eventually be found through a different system to deal with monitoring.

Finally, the term "epistemic" community as used by Mr. Fife was elaborated upon.[17] International organizations as well as States and NGOs have their institutional interests, and international organizations are clearly motivated by certain values and interests as well. If our aim is to strengthen the international legal order, an aim that seems to follow from the panel's speakers this morning, one of the challenges we might face is the fact that we have to work towards integration and use a common language in order to strengthen these common interests and values.

In practice knowledge is required to influence treaty-making and the development of international law. This applies both to the representation of a major power as well as that of a small State. Knowledge can be an equalizer: even the smallest power can have an enormous amount of influence in multilateral parliamentary settings through using this knowledge. We need networks in order to update our knowledge and in order to speak the same language.

*Reporter: Ms. W. Henning**

* University of Amsterdam.

Notes

1 Question posed by Dr. Habil Erika de Wet of the Amsterdam Center for International Law, addressed to Pieter-Jan Kuijper of the European Commission and Judge Charles N. Brower of the Iran-US Claims Tribunal.

2 Point made by Charles N. Brower.

3 Convention on the Recognition and Enforcement of Foreign Arbitral Awards of 10 June 1958 ("the New York Convention"), reprinted in 330 *U.N.T.S.* 38 (1959).

4 Claims Settlement Agreement of 19 January 1981 (the "Algiers Accords"), reprinted in 20 *ILM* 223 (1981).

5 North American Free Trade Agreement of 8 December 1993, ("NAFTA"), reprinted in 32 *ILM* 289 (1993).

6 Point made by Pieter-Jan Kuijper.

7 Question posed by Jordan Paust of the University of Houston Law Center.

8 Answer by Pieter-Jan Kuijper.

9 World Health Organization's Framework Convention for Tobacco Control (Intergovernmental Negotiat-

ing Body on the WHO Framework Convention on Tobacco Control): Draft WHO Framework Convention on Tobacco Control, A/FCTC/INB6/5 (3 March 2003).

10 Charles N. Brower.

11 Question posed by Roy Goode of Oxford University, addressed to Pieter-Jan Kuijper.

12 Pieter-Jan Kuijper.

13 Nigel White of the University of Nottingham.

14 Question posed by Tanya Vella of UNESCO Culture Sector, France.

15 Charles N. Brower.

16 By Bert Barnhoorn of the T.M.C. Asser Institute, posed to Judge Brower.

17 By Bert Barnhoorn of the T.M.C. Asser Institute, posed to Rolf Einar Fife of the Ministry of Foreign Affairs in Oslo.

Accountability And Control Of International Governmental Organizations – Principles And Procedures Of "Good Governance"

The panel was convened by its Chair, Anne-Marie Slaughter*.

Introductory remarks by Anne-Marie Slaughter

Professor Slaughter opened the panel and explained how the accountability and control of international governmental organizations can be framed as the question who guards the guardians on the international level. She identified four mechanisms of accountability in this regard. First, there is the possibility of self-regulation by IGOs, for which the World Bank Inspection Panel may serve as an example. Second, control can be exercised by a separate international organization, for example a tribunal such as the ICJ. Third, non-governmental organizations can function as self-appointed guardians of IGOs. Finally, while so far limited in practice, national government institutions like courts can in principle hold IGOs accountable. After this introduction, she turned the floor over to Mr. Patel.

Remarks by Bimal N. Patel**

Principles and procedures of "Good Governance" in the implementation of the Chemical Weapons Convention and the role of the OPCW

The Organization for the Prohibition of Chemical Weapons (OPCW) is an intergovernmental organization with an independent legal personality deriving its authority from the Chemical Weapons Convention (CWC) – a multilateral treaty. The headquarters of the Organization are in this city and in fact not very far from where we are sitting.

Good governance conveys the idea of purposefulness and effectiveness of the governing institution and transparency and accountability in the accomplishment of the goals and objectives. Not only this refers to the moral rectitude of the authorities but also implies the existence of a system based on the active participation of all actors involved in the political process. Therefore, good governance is now being heralded as

* Princeton University; ASIL.

** Bimal N. Patel, PhD candidate (International Law), University of Nijmegen; staff member, Organisation for the Prohibition of Chemical Weapons, The Hague, the Netherlands. The views are expressed in the personal capacity of the author.

an emerging international law issue in such a way that it could take the shape of an *erga omnes* obligation.

Nowadays, we are witnessing a trend with a kind of shopping list of ingredients for good governance – accountability, transparency, non-corruption, rule of law, etc. These concepts are themselves colossal and have hardly been subjected to proper analysis in the light of the actual process of governance. In the time I have, I shall enumerate the principles, procedures and other elements of good governance as they manifest themselves in the implementation of the CWC.

In the context of the OPCW, good governance may mean the exercise of political, legal, financial and administrative power to achieve the goals and objectives of the CWC – chemical weapons disarmament, non-proliferation, universality, security through confidence-building, and economic and technological development through the peaceful uses of chemistry.

Let me stipulate some important features with regard to the mandate of the OPCW and the CWC:

1. The OPCW is mandated to prohibit the development, production, stockpiling, and use of chemical weapons and accomplish their destruction;
2. It obliges each Member State to harmonize its laws in conformity with the CWC;
3. The implementation of the CWC affects world trade in chemicals and the security of States Parties;
4. The CWC requires States Parties (military and industry sectors alike) to submit sensitive and confidential business and military information;
5. The activities of natural and legal persons belonging to States Parties are also regulated by the CWC; and
6. To achieve these objectives of the CWC, the Organization is endowed, among other things, with an independent international and municipal legal personality, human and financial resources, etc.

In other words, the OPCW can be seen as an institution of global governance seeking to facilitate the harmonization of national policies in the area of CWC.

The OPCW has 153 Member States, twenty-five States have signed but not yet ratified whereas 16 States have neither signed nor ratified the Convention.

Structure of the OPCW and Interaction among All Actors

The purpose-oriented and -focused governance of the OPCW is inseparable from democratization. It means consensus-building and extending democratic principles and methods to the day-to-day business. Democratization in the OPCW also means recognizing that all States, large and small, CW possessor and non-possessor, must have a say in the decisions related to the issues of the Convention. In addition to being a healthy principle, the rule of democracy has become a categorical imperative in order to achieve the goals of the Convention.

The OPCW structure has a mechanism to ensure democratic process in decision-making. It has three main organs: the Conference of the States Parties, the Executive Council (EC) and the Technical Secretariat. We can see that in addition to the mechanism of the Conference of States Parties where each State Party can express its will, the EC provides a forum in which all regions can make their voice heard through their representative Member States in the EC, endowed with a fixed number of seats from all the geographic regions. This process indeed creates the political and legal stability necessary to achieve the decisions in a harmonious manner. While decisions can easily be taken through the voting mechanism, consensus-building, albeit slow and at times frustrating, satisfies the concerns of all, big and small. This provides a level playing field and encourages greater transparency and compliance.

Democracy in international institutions can be realized only on the basis of a constitution which provides stability by instituting the separation of powers among its organs. The CWC has drawn a clear line between the powers and competence of these two political organs. Barring a handful of occasions, all decisions in the CSP and the EC have been taken by consensus which shows to a great degree, unity of mind and purpose among the States Parties.

The Technical Secretariat is a technical and professional organ and performs tasks and functions mandated by the two political organs.

The chemical industry plays an important role in facilitating an effective implementation of the CWC at the international and national levels. Participation of the chemical industry is crucial for the success of the Convention. Thus, by ensuring broader participation, the OPCW can count on the necessary support of the international community to enhance its effectiveness and its credibility.

Declarations and information

Good governance requires transparency of information so that each and every State Party is aware of how the Convention is being implemented in the other States Parties. Declarations, regular reporting mechanisms, such as the verification of implementation reports, and regular updates by the Secretariat fulfill this role. The CWC requires a series of systematic and detailed declarations on CW and the chemical industry which is a point of departure for the implementation of key obligations under it. The Technical Secretariat verifies this information and reports to the policy-making organs of the OPCW. The CWC allows access of all States Parties to the initial and annual declarations of other States Parties. Thus, each State Party, in principle, is able to see what has been declared by all other States Parties.

Declarations play a crucial role in bringing to the surface the situation leading to liability and/or responsibility of a State Party or the OPCW. It is a vital monitoring tool and aims to enhance the transparency and confidence-building measures among the States Parties. The OPCW experience shows that there has not been any serious cause of concern leading to a breach by any State Party under the CWC. Emerging declaration-related issues are not buried but discussed and debated until they are resolved and decisions are taken. This approach has led to increased confidence and harmonious decision-making, without acrimony, in a healthy environment.

Verification

The verification regime of the CWC is comprehensive and intrusive, in certain circumstances, and thus unprecedented in the arms control regimes. The Convention provides for routine inspections and challenge inspections as well as investigations of alleged use of chemical weapons. The verification regime ensures that information declared by the States Parties is verified and the crucial tasks of verifying the destruction of CW and destruction or conversion for non-prohibited purposes of the chemical weapons production facilities are carried out in conformity with the Convention. Here one can observe various elements of good governance in operation: all CW and chemical industry mandated verification activities are governed by the explicitly agreed-upon operational rules and procedures and facility agreements; secondly, verification activities are carried out in a transparent manner. Issues arising from the inspections are generally resolved through mutual dialogue and there have been very few instances where issues had to be brought before the Member States.

Another pillar of good governance has been the application of the Convention in a non-discriminatory manner to all Member States. No distinction is made in the application of various obligations. As a result, all States Parties have made a determined attempt to conform to disarmament timelines, as stipulated in the CWC. However, during the implementation of the CWC, practical difficulties faced by Member States have been taken into consideration, for example, extension of timelines to destroy CW stockpile, efficiency in verification measures, optimization of verification costs, etc. The experience of CW destruction shows that although significant stockpiles of CW have yet to be destroyed, the cooperation of the States Parties as shown by their declaration of and their commitment to destroy stockpiles, has remained excellent. This flexibility, without compromising on underlying CWC principles is another indicator of the ability of the Organization to move with the times. As a result, co-operation amongst members has been excellent. The assistance provided by the United States of America, the United Kingdom of Great Britain and Northern Ireland, the European Union and the Russian Federation in the destruction of its CW is a good example of solidarity.

Furthermore, there has not been any significant accident involving personnel, either of the Technical Secretariat or any State Party, which demonstrates that health and safety principles and measures required by the Convention and its bye-laws have been implemented in an effective manner. Nor has there been any significant breach of the confidentiality regime as can be seen in the reports of the Director-General. As one can imagine, the implementation of the Convention requires the handling of enormous amounts of confidential military and business information. Special procedures have been adopted by both the States Parties and the Technical Secretariat with regard to the security of confidential information. The periodic auditing of such systems and procedures has reinforced confidence of the State Parties in the ability of the Technical Secretariat to handle confidential information.

We can say that all actors involved in the implementation have embraced a pragmatic and practical approach to all issues arising out of the application and interpretation of the provisions of the Convention and this approach has been instrumental in the successful implementation of the Convention thus far. It has remained very interesting to see how the legal and political diplomatic machineries of the Member States, in combination with the expertise of the Technical Secretariat, have resolved a number of difficult issues.

Challenge inspections

Another important element of good governance in the CWC is the possibility of launching a challenge inspection when a particular problem can not be resolved through routine verification or through consultation and cooperation. Full compliance with the CWC as well as confidence on part of all States Parties to the CWC that all other States Parties are fully complying with their undertakings, is a key to the successful implementation of the CWC. This mechanism is aimed at maintaining or restoring confidence in the Convention at critical moments. This mechanism further allows the challenged State Party to demonstrate its compliance with the Convention. While each State Party has a right to request a challenge inspection, any abuse of the right to request a challenge inspection is considered as non-compliance on the part of the requesting State Party and can be dealt with accordingly.

Restriction on chemicals – non-proliferation

One of the important pillars of the CWC is the non-proliferation of chemical weapons. The Convention provides a detailed mechanism to find and deal with any breach of non-proliferation regime of the CWC. It restricts the transfer and use of certain chemicals according to their potential to pose a threat to, or to damage the object and purpose of the CWC. Certain types of chemicals cannot be traded outside the OPCW community, and thus, non-Member States with a high dependence on these chemicals may face economic problems.

To implement the non-proliferation principle of the Convention, the States Parties provide detailed information on imports and exports of chemicals, the Technical Secretariat checks all declared information and provides necessary information to the policy-making organs. If there is any discrepancy or cause of concern, the Technical Secretariat and the concerned State Party or the States Parties themselves, as the case be, undertake clarification and consultation with a view to reach a resolution of the problem. Enactment of national implementation measures can facilitate this task.

National implementation measures

The CWC requires each State Party to enact national implementation measures to carry out its obligations at the national level, in accordance with the national constitutional procedures. The CWC requires States Parties to prohibit natural or legal persons under its jurisdiction from undertaking any activity prohibited to a State Party, to enact penal legislation (which may provide administrative or criminal penalties or both), to cooperate and afford appropriate legal assistance to the OPCW, to assign highest priority to ensuring the safety of people and to protecting the environment in implementing the CWC. In order to facilitate smooth communication between the OPCW and a State Party on one hand and between a State Party and other States Parties on the other, the Convention requires States Parties to designate a national authority. Last but not least, the Convention requires States Parties to cooperate with the Organization in the exercise of its functions and to provide assistance to the Technical Secretariat.

ASSISTANCE AND PROTECTION

This tool accords a right to States Parties to protect themselves against the use or threat of use of CW and obliges all States Parties to contribute to the assistance and protection programs and tools so that the Organisation can coordinate and deliver protection when needed.

The OPCW is mandated to mobilize, deliver and coordinate the necessary assistance and protection against CW. The Technical Secretariat maintains a data bank, provides experts' advices within the resources available. While the EC can take the decision with regard to dispatching emergency assistance, the Technical Secretariat will carry out this task on the ground. There has not been any instance of a request for assistance by any State Party. The resolve of solidarity and cooperation between all members will be instrumental in meeting the challenges in future.

ECONOMIC AND TECHNOLOGICAL DEVELOPMENT

This is another important pillar of the Convention. One can immediately think of the so-called Peace Dividend: when a State Party gives up its arsenals of chemical weapons and undertakes the obligations of the Convention, it may wish to also gain certain benefits in return.

The Convention aims to promote economic and technological development among States Parties through various means. Furthermore, the Convention requires that measures taken to implement the Convention in no way hamper the economic and technological development of the States Parties, and each State Party has a right to participate in the exchange of chemicals, equipment / information to the fullest possible extent.

DISPUTE SETTLEMENT

As one can imagine, the implementation of a comprehensive and delicate verification regime can entail disputes/disagreements. To resolve these, the CWC has various mechanisms. Although the Convention has not visualized any centralized and dedicated dispute settlement machinery, as in the case of WTO, its decentralized approach emphasizes the prevention of disputes. Provisions on dispute settlement include, among others, a provision to seek an advisory opinion from the International Court of Justice, the recommendation of collective measures in conformity with international law, and the possibility to bring the issue to the attention of the UN General Assembly and UN Security Council in case of particular gravity.

So far, there has been no significant dispute among any of the Member States or between any of the organs of the Organization.

CONCLUDING REMARKS

The CWC envisages the functioning of the Organization in an accountable manner and is remarkably specific to guide the understanding on various issues of accountability.

Purpose-oriented and focused governance requires the ability to assess where we stand in a historical perspective and to foresee the major challenges that lie ahead. The reports of the Director-General and the Member States allow the OPCW to assess where it is standing in a historical perspective and to foresee the major challenges ahead, such as an accelerated pace of CW destruction and the boosting of international economic assistance to the destruction programs in the Russian Federation, the optimization of verification costs, and the achievement of a universal adherence to the Convention.

In view of its effectiveness and credibility and its capacity to deal with horrendous weapons of mass destruction, the OPCW has been called upon to play a role in the global campaign against terrorism. Pursuant to Security Council Resolution 1456 of 20 January 2003 which recognizes that international organizations should evaluate the ways in which they can enhance their effectiveness in this area, the Security Council directed its appeal to the OPCW which is at the forefront of CW destruction and non-proliferation.

It can be said that the leadership of the Organization has enabled the international community to witness how indispensable the OPCW is in ensuring the implementation of the only universal and non-discriminatory disarmament instrument. There is no doubt that the effective functioning of the OPCW provides a strong stimulus to other arms control and disarmament regimes too, notably, to the Biological Weapons Convention.

We all recognize that good governance is not a luxury but a vital necessity and that each international organization is obliged to perform its mandates in respect both of substance and procedure, in an accountable manner. The OPCW is well positioned to serve as an instrument of good governance, due to its impressive record on universality within the short period of its existence and its normative and operational capacity and achievement records. As an instrument of good governance, the OPCW benefits from the synergy of experience and expertise of its Member States and in addition, serves as a repository of knowledge for good governance at the national level.

Remarks by Charlotte Ku*

Accountability and capacity when using military forces in international operations

The evolving United Nations security system

An often neglected, but important question about the accountability of international organizations is that of the accountability required by democratic governments when their military forces are used in international operations. Historically, accountability to citizens for the use of military forces was a central component of the struggle to establish democratic forms of government. But how specifically do these governments

* The American Society of International Law, 2223 Massachusetts Avenue, NW, Washington, DC 20008, USA. <cku@asil.org>. I wish to acknowledge the invaluable research assistance of Zachary Clopton and Ronald T. Alcala in the preparation of this paper.

maintain accountability when their soldiers take part in international operations decided upon and mandated by international organizations? What happens to this accountability when the mandate is changed? How are the elected representatives of participating States held accountable either for any harm that may befall soldiers taking part in these operations or for the conduct of their soldiers? The issue is important because of the number and complexity of international military operations now taking place and the important contributions in manpower and materiel that democracies make to those operations.[1]

Although the United Nations Charter went farther than the League of Nations Covenant in establishing a system of collective security, its relatively clear vision of how military forces would be used was altered almost from the outset. Article 43 agreements, that would have designated Member State troops for UN operations, were never completed, and the UN Security Council has never had military forces at its call. The result has been that Member States decide on a case-by-case basis whether to contribute their military forces to particular UN operations, what forces to contribute, under what conditions, and for what purpose.[2] Where this approach is seen as only partially satisfying the requirements of regulating the use of force is where action relies on the military might of one particular State, creating a situation where "the action is essentially unilateral with multilateral imprimatur."[3]

Despite these shortcomings in the UN security system, military forces of democratic States were used 78 times for a broad range of purposes under UN authorization from 1946 to 2002 and once under a NATO mandate.[4] Table 1 below places the 79 cases into five broad categories. These categories are based on: the mandate of the operation, the rules of engagement given to the military forces, whether or not they enter the territory of the State where they operate with the consent of that State, and the number and types of military personnel involved.[5]

> *Monitoring and observation* involves the positioning of troops, military observers and related personnel on one or both sides of a line between entities that are or have been engaged in, or where there is a threat of, armed conflict, with the primary objective of preventing (renewed) hostilities. The observers are stationed with the consent of the host country and are impartial. They carry no arms.
>
> *Traditional Peacekeeping* involves unarmed or lightly armed military contingents in the monitoring, supervision, and verification of cease-fire, withdrawal, buffer zone, and related agreements, with the consent of the parties. It requires consent of the host country and impartiality; the use of military force, other than in personal or small unit self-defense, is incompatible with the concept.
>
> *Peacekeeping plus State-building* supplements traditional peacekeeping with activities such as election monitoring or organization, human rights protection, and civil administration functions or assistance during transition to independence or democracy.
>
> *Force to Ensure Compliance with International Mandates* involves the use of force to ensure the safety of peacekeepers, enable them to carry out a mandate that is being frustrated, and protect international legal principles. Military forces engaged in such operations usually also perform State-building tasks.
>
> *Enforcement* involves the use of military forces to maintain or restore peace in a conflict or major security crisis. The classic enforcement operation responds to an attack on the territorial integrity of a State. By definition, enforcement does not require the consent of the State deemed to be a threat to the peace.

Table 1: Uses of Military Forces under the Auspices of the UN and NATO[6]

	Period	
Forms of Use of Military Forces	**1946-1989**	**1990-2002**
Monitoring and Observation	9 (45%)	9 (15%)
Traditional Peacekeeping	5 (25%)	2 (3%)
Peacekeeping plus State-Building	3 (15%)	25 (41%)
Force to Ensure Compliance	2 (10%)	22 (39%)
Enforcement	1 (5%)	1 (1.6%)
Total	20 (100%)	59 (100%)

As Table 1 shows, military forces were used under UN and NATO auspices more frequently in the decade starting in 1990 than in the preceding four decades. Prior to 1990, military actions were either unilateral or within the regional security frameworks of the Organization of American States or the Warsaw Pact. From 1946-89, the UN was called on to undertake actions where neither the USSR nor the USA could hope to do more than contain each other's influence, with the exception of the Middle East, where its role emerged out of the Palestine mandate of the League of Nations. UN-commanded operations were deployed 17 times from 1945-89, but 38 times from 1990-2002.

Table 1 also shows that the nature of UN missions using military forces changed in the two periods. Monitoring and observation missions constituted 45% of deployments in the first period, and only 15.2% in the second. In sharp contrast to the Cold War period, when missions in the first four categories were deployed only with the consent of the host State, many operations in the 1990s did not have the consent of the host State, were more intrusive, and were involved in intra-State conflicts. The more intrusive an operation is, the higher the cost and risk to those undertaking it. The higher the risk, the more contributing States will need to justify the risk to their soldiers.[7]

In addition to thwarting cross-border aggression in Korea and Kuwait, the case for which the doctrine of collective security and the UN security system was designed, UN operations have included several purposes that were not anticipated when the League Covenant and UN Charter were signed. Among these were maintaining cease-fire agreements, preventing genocide and serious violations of human rights, and restoring a democratically elected government. Another unanticipated development was the need to address intra-State conflicts. Between 1945 and 2002, twenty-one of the twenty-seven operations (78%) authorized by the Security Council under Chapter VII of the Charter involved intra-State conflicts.

Reconciling international mandates and operational capacity

A closer look at the 79 operations summarized above shows that these operations address only 33 conflicts – a reminder that many conflicts last a long time and that a single UN-authorized mission might remain in an area through several phases of a conflict.[8] UN estimates are that UN peace operations "addressed no more than one third of the conflict situations of the 1990s."[9] Of the 79 operations authorized either by the United Nations or NATO, 15 (18.9%), remain active today, including the United Nations Truce Supervision Organization (UNTSO) deployed in 1948 to supervise the truce between Arabs and Israelis.[10]

Table 2 confirms what the UN Panel on Peace Operations noted, that "the United Nations does not wage war."[11] It also shows that the closer an operation is to war, the more the UN relies on single powerful States or coalitions of the willing. In these cases, the accountability problem may be less to the citizens and national authorities, than to the international organizations and Member States that authorized a particular operation. This occurs because of the delegation that effectively occurs when a State or group of States is authorized to take certain action, but where oversight over the action taken is inconsistent or non-existent.[12] Perhaps one of the most controversial existing delegations is that resulting from Security Council Resolution 688 and the protection of the safe havens for Iraq's Kurdish population.[13]

Table 2: UN Command by Form of Use of Military Forces

Forms of Use of Military Forces	Total Number	Under UN Command
Monitoring & Observation	18	18 (100%)
Traditional Peacekeeping	7	7 (100%)
Peacekeeping plus State-Building	28	28 (100%)
Force to Ensure Compliance	24	2 (8%)including one co-led by the UN and the US
Enforcement	2	0 (0%)
Total	79	55 (70%)

Although mission creep can be a problem for nationally mandated and commanded operations, it certainly is for internationally mandated and commanded forces. For international operations, the issue of mission creep is most likely to arise within the category of peacekeeping plus State-building. These are operations deployed in areas where there is little or no effective government in place, or where the government itself is responsible for the breakdown of order that required an international response. The International Commission on Intervention and State Sovereignty explains how this might occur.

> Mandates are often adjusted incrementally in reaction to new demands during the course of an intervention, and this may well be inevitable given the special nature of interventions for human protection purposes where much depends upon the attitude and level of cooperation received from the targeted State. While the initial mandate may reflect a preoccupation with human protection, political and security concerns sooner or later predominate. The more limited the initial vision in relation to the real problem at hand, the more likely that mission creep will take place.

> Somalia is a clear example where the initial response to insecurity and famine was not also accompanied by sufficient support to achieve long-term solutions. The follow-on UN operation (UNOSOM II) included ambitious security and political tasks but without commensurate means to realize them. However, the mandate should define in clear language what the aims of the intervention in the various phases of it would be and it should spell out that the desired end state is the restoration of good governance and the rule of law.[14]

Accumulated experience of using military forces under international auspices now reveals that the authorizing institution, the receiving State/s and the contributing State/s need to maintain accountability at critical points along the decision-making and operational continuum. Authorization may be required more than once depending on circumstances. The mandate, capacity, and objectives need to be congruent to ensure operational success. Operational failure will discredit the authorizing institution, possibly exacerbate a conflict, and can cost the lives of soldiers and materiel of contributing States. The importance of crafting a mission precisely cannot be overemphasized. As we see in the concerns of contributing States over mission creep following UN involvement in Somalia, any misalignment of these factors can have long-term consequences for future operations. If international institutions are to remain in a position to carry out peace operations, it is important that their decisions are credible and feasible.

Yet, we see the difficulty in maintaining the proper balance between the required level of force, the objectives of the international community, and the capacity of those willing to contribute to an operation. Maintaining the balance can be complicated by changing conditions in the field, the length of time required to carry out an operation, and the availability of the needed resources. Where the international institution must rely on national contributions, appropriate troops, supplies, and transport may not always be available. The withdrawal, for example, of the Indian contingent to UNEF I in 1967 on the eve of the Six Days War effectively ended that operation.

Setting up credible operations begins with a mandate that is clear and informed by intelligence with a realistic assessment of troop capabilities required by the mission. As the Brahimi Report noted: "…no amount of good intentions can substitute for the fundamental ability to project credible force if complex peacekeeping, in particular, is to succeed."[15] Since there will be multiple layers of civilian and military authority, blame shifting will occur if the response is inadequate or fails. As the most widely recognized source of authorization for the use of military forces, the UN Security Council is the most important institutional organ in the area of international peace and security. Yet, the Security Council's proceedings are frequently not transparent. Those who do not participate in its deliberations cannot be certain about the grounds for decisions that are taken or not taken. This was particularly a problem with respect to the transformation of the mandates of UNPROFOR and UNOSOM II. It was also a problem with respect to the United Nations Observer Mission in Uganda-Rwanda (UNOMUR), when in the face of increased killing, the Security Council refused to expand the mission and instead reduced its size. Lack of transparency confounds democratic accountability by limiting possibilities for understanding the bases and purposes of UN-authorized military operations. This precludes informed national debate prior to the commitment of troops. The Security Council's lack of transparency is further complicated by the rotating membership of the Council so that over the life of a mission, the Member States authorizing the operation could change.

As mandates shift, political conditions on the ground can change and the level of consent provided an international operation may also erode. As the International Commission on Intervention and State Sovereignty notes, "consent is rarely absolute and often evaporates."[16] The more narrowly conceived the mandate, the more likely it will shift, confounding desires of contributing States to have clear and specific mandates. Consent by the parties and by the contributing States may then have to be reaffirmed as operations continue. Changing conditions may require capabilities that are different from those initially deployed or thought to be necessary. This was, for example, the problem encountered by the Dutch battalion in Srebrenica in 1995.

Conclusion: Reconciling political responsibility and operational necessity

The UN is only as effective as its members provide it the means to be. However, for the UN to have its needs met requires that it be able to identify those needs in ways to which Member States can respond. One primary consideration must be the requirement of democratic governments to meet standards of accountability, both internationally and nationally. The decades since the founding of the UN have shown that there are few clear-cut cases that fit directly into the Charter's initial definition of threat to the peace. And when such a case comes to the UN Security Council, action may still be blocked by a veto if it is perceived to be against the interests of one of the Council's five permanent members.

The UN system also faces a challenge of implementation, since many States can be involved in making a decision to take action, but the number of States able to implement decisions requiring the threat or use of force may be far smaller. For example, the 19 NATO countries account for over 60% of the world's military expenditures, with over 4 million personnel in their armed forces. China, Russia, and India represent other significant military powers. Sixty-seven percent of the world's military expenditures are made by democracies, but only 29% of the world's armed forces come from democracies or emerging democracies.[17] For operations that require long-range force projection and sustainment, there are only a few States whose armed forces have such capabilities. The latitude these States demand when carrying out operations is another aspect of current UN practice that requires assessment.

Despite these challenges, the UN has been involved in more than 70 operations using military forces for a variety of functions. More than five decades of UN experience suggest that the UN's capacity to perform can vary greatly depending on the form of the operation. In operations where a cease-fire is in place and where parties to a dispute agree to an international presence, the UN can perform well. Once operations depart from a consent-based mandate, the UN may become less effective in commanding forces and better serves as a policy body to guide the objectives of an operation and to monitor compliance with international humanitarian law and other international standards.

But even within traditional consent-based peacekeeping operations, UN commanded operations may be complicated if missions are ill-defined and equipped or asked to meet impossible objectives. These operations may be further complicated by the length of missions, their changing character that can put contributor State troops in harm's way or make them part of the conflict. And when operations move from consent-based to non-consent based, adequate consideration needs to be given to whether those already deployed are able to carry out the new mission and if not, to make plans for their safe removal. Where strong military power is required for a mission, the UN functions by delegation with less than 15% of operations classified as force to ensure compliance or enforcement commanded by the UN. In these cases, delegated operations can exceed the intended mandates with little recourse.

The UN or any international institution therefore needs to be able to address national authorities with the purposes of a mission; the rules of engagement; and other relevant practical considerations that allow a State to make a decision as to whether it will commit troops to an operation. This might mean that international institutions may not be able to respond to crises if they cannot find the appropriate troops to carry out a mission. However, to deploy forces on the basis of wishful thinking has proven costly in the long term. In light of these complicated conditions, part of the UN's decision-making system is also to determine when no action can be taken under its auspices.

All concerned need a deeper understanding of responsibility and accountability: those making the decisions, those contributing to the operation, and those who are to be the beneficiaries. This may require exercising accountability in different ways and at different times, but procedures should collectively provide the information and the transparency required of general good government. This may require working more than one single framework to include national considerations and also regional ones, where appropriate.

Recent events with regard to the lack of UN Security Council authorization for the US-led war in Iraq made these questions salient. But the political questions cannot be answered without considering the UN's operational role and where its contribution to the maintenance and restoration of peace and security can be greatest. This includes conflict prevention and addressing the multifaceted sources of conflict in a State. The UN also can contribute by building on its vast body of experience in reconstruction and State building. The international security system is a malleable one. It is important that both institutions and their Member States make informed assessments of their capabilities not only to make decisions, but also to implement them. If not, the ability of international institutions to respond to the security challenges of the future will be further eroded.

Notes

1 See *The Military Balance* published annually by The International Institute for Strategic Studies (London, Arundel House) for a review of military expenditures.

2 Jules Lobel and Michael Ratner, 'Bypassing the Security Council: Ambiguous Authorizations to Use Force, Cease-fires and the Iraqi Inspection Regime', 93 *American Journal of International Law* 1 (1999) 124-54.

3 Lori Fisler Damrosch, 'The Role of the Great Powers in United Nations Peace-Keeping', 18 *Yale Journal of International Law* (1993) p. 430.

4 These operations may have included forces from States that do not have democratic governments, but democracies are the focus of this essay and so have been singled out for attention.

5 See Charlotte Ku and Harold K. Jacobson, *Democratic Accountability and the Use of Force in International Law* (Cambridge, Cambridge University Press 2003) pp. 19-25. This categorization draws heavily on the concepts developed in Gareth Evans, *Cooperating for Peace: The Global Agenda for the 1990s and Beyond* (St. Leonards, Allen and Unwin 1993). It is related to but different from the categorization developed by Boutros Boutros-Ghali in his *An Agenda for Peace* (United Nations 1992). More broadly, it draws on the wide literature concerning peacekeeping, including: Paul F. Diehl, *International Peacekeeping* (Baltimore, MD, The Johns

Hopkins University Press 1993); William J. Durch, ed., *UN Peacekeeping, American Policy, and the Uncivil Wars of the 1990s* (New York, NY, St. Martins Press 1996); Ramesh Thakur and Carlyle A. Thayer, eds., *A Crisis in Expectations: UN Peacekeeping in the 1990s* (Boulder, CO, Westview 1995); and, James S. Sutterlin, *The United Nations and the Maintenance of International Security: A Challenge to be Met* (Westport, CT, Praeger 1995).

6 Updated from Charlotte Ku and Harold K. Jacobson, *Democratic Accountability and the Use of Force in International Law* (Cambridge, Cambridge University Press 2003) p. 24.

7 UN Doc. A/55/305, SC/2000/800, 'Report of the Panel on United Nations Peace Operations' (21 August 2000) para. 19, pp. 3-4.

8 Depending on how one counts, the UN and NATO authorized the deployment of military forces in about half of the inter-State conflicts and a third of the intra-State conflicts recorded from 1946 to 2000. See Meredith Reid Sarkees, 'The Correlates of War Data on War: An Update to 1997' 18(1) *Conflict Management and Peace Science* (2001) pp. 123-44.

9 UN Doc. A/55/305, SC/2000/800, 'Report of the Panel on United Nations Peace Operations' (21 August 2000) para. 29, p. 5.

10 See UN Security Council Resolution 50 (29 May 1948).

11 UN Doc. A/55/305, SC/2000/800, 'Report of the Panel on United Nations Peace Operations' (21 August 2000) para. 53, p. 10.

12 For examples of the problem of delegation and a theoretical discussion, see Danesh Sarooshi, *The United Nations and the Development of Collective Security: The Delegation of the UN Security Council of its Chapter VII Powers* (Oxford, Oxford University Press 1999).

13 For a discussion of related issues, see Frederic L. Kirgis, 'The Legal Background on the Use of Force to Induce Iraq to Comply with Security Council Resolutions', *ASIL Insight* (1997) <http://www.asil.org/insigh12.htm>.

14 *The Responsibility to Protect*, Report of the International Commission on Intervention and State Sovereignty (International Development Research Centre 2001) p. 60.

15 UN Doc. A/55/305, SC/2000/800, 'Report of the Panel on United Nations Peace Operations' (21 August 2000) p. viii.

16 *The Responsibility to Protect: Research, Bibliography, Background*, Supplementary Volume to the Report of the International Commission on Intervention and State Sovereignty (International Development Research Centre 2001) p. 181.

17 See Charlotte Ku and Harold K. Jacobson, *Democratic Accountability and the Use of Force in International Law* (Cambridge, Cambridge University Press 2003) p. 30 and *The Military Balance* published annually by The International Institute for Strategic Studies (London, Arundel House).

Remarks by Daniel D. Bradlow*

The Governance of the International Financial Institutions: The Need for Reform

My presentation focuses on a case of pathological governance: the International Monetary Fund (IMF). This pathology manifests itself in the lack of IMF accountability to key stakeholders and the seemingly politicized nature of IMF decision-making. This is a serious problem only for the IMF's developing country Member States (consumer States) and civil society. It is not a problem for rich Member States, particularly the G8.

I will first discuss the governance problems in the IMF. Thereafter I will discuss four legal issues that arise from the governance problem. All four issues can be relatively easily resolved within the existing governance arrangements of the IMF. Their reso-

* Professor of Law and Director, International Legal Studies Program, American University Washington College of Law, Washington D.C.

lution would positively affect IMF accountability and would reduce the perception of politicized decision-making in the IMF.

I. Diagnosis of IMF's governance problems

The IMF's governance problems have both structural and functional causes. The structural problems are caused by the fact that its membership has increased from 39 Member States in 1946 to 184 Member States today. While it's Executive Board has only grown from 12 to 24 members.

The composition of the Executive Board exacerbates this problem. Of the 24 Executive Directors (EDs), 8 represent single States, of which 6 are G8 countries. The remaining 176 Member States are divided into constituencies that are represented by 16 EDs. This means that the average size of a constituency increased from about 5 to about 11 Member States from 1946 to the present. In addition, depending on the year, 6-7 of the 16 EDs come from rich countries. This means that 12-13 of the 24 EDs come from rich countries.

The representational imbalance in the Board is exacerbated by the IMF's voting structure. Each member's vote consists of 250 basic votes plus an additional number of votes that is based on its quota. The basic vote has declined since 1946 from 11.3% of the total vote to about 2.2%. Even though the Board usually operates on the basis of consensus, the votes are important because the consensus is shaped in the 'shadow' of the votes.

The structural characteristics of the Board enhance the rich countries', particularly the G8, ability to concentrate on the issues and countries of most interest to them and to develop the expertise and institutional memory to be effective in shaping IMF policy and operations. The EDs of the consumer States, on the other hand, are subjected to too many competing demands to be effective advocates for their constituents' specific programmatic interests and their general concerns about IMF policies.

Thus, the structural evolution of the IMF has resulted in increased rich country domination of the institution, even as the likelihood that they will use the services of the IMF has decreased.

There have been three important developments in the functioning of the IMF. The first is the phenomenon of mission creep, which has seen the IMF evolve from a monetary institution with a clear mandate into a macro-economically focused development financing institution with an ill-defined mandate. Second, the group of Member States that actually use the IMF's services has shrunk from all its Member States to only its developing country Member States. Third, IMF programs and the conditions attached thereto have become more complex.

These developments have had two consequences. First, the IMF now plays a key role in policy-making in its consumer Member States. This has increased the importance of the IMF's own policies, which in turn has increased the G8's influence in the IMF. Second, these developments have adversely affected the ability of the IMF's EDs to understand and evaluate IMF operations. This means its ability to hold staff and management accountable has declined.

The net effect of this evolution is that the IMF is increasingly under the control of two unaccountable groups: the G8, and the IMF staff and management.

II. Four legal issues

1. Administrative procedures

The IMF has nothing comparable to the World Bank's Operational Manual, which contains the Bank's operational policies and procedures. Thus, there are no publicly available documents that describe either how the IMF conducts its operations or the responsibilities of staff in these operations. This makes it difficult for both the EDs and other stakeholders to hold IMF staff and management accountable for their conduct during IMF operations.

The solution to this problem is for the IMF to develop formal operational policies and procedures, including formal rulemaking procedures. To its credit the IMF has begun to take some tentative steps in this direction.[1] Unfortunately, the IMF used informal rulemaking procedures in drafting these documents.

2. The principle of uniformity

Uniformity, which is one of the IMF's key operating principles, means that all IMF Member States have the same rights and responsibilities and that the IMF will not discriminate among its Member States based on their wealth, size, level of development, or importance in the international monetary system. Thus, unlike the World Bank, the WTO or the United Nations, the IMF does not differentiate between its Member States.

The principle of uniformity made sense when the IMF functioned purely as a monetary institution and all its Member States, in fact, were utilizing its services. It does not make sense when its services are only being utilized by developing country Member States. If the IMF could differentiate between categories of its Member States it could, for example, use its general resources to fund financing facilities that are explicitly meant only for certain Member States. This would avoid the politicized fundraising that accompanied the creation of the Poverty Reduction and Growth Facility (PRGF) and its predecessors. It would also create space for more creative approaches to its governance problems. For example, it would allow the IMF to follow the example of institutions like the Global Environmental Facility, and offer its poorer Member States more opportunity to participate in decision-making.

3. The IMF's 'Political Prohibition'

The Articles of Agreement require the IMF in its operations to pay due regard to social and political conditions in its Member States. The IMF has historically interpreted this requirement as prohibiting it from being influenced by political considerations in its dealings with its Member States.

This interpretation may have made sense when the IMF's operations were limited to monetary issues. However, it is neither prudent nor principled for a macro-economically focused institution to pretend that it is not be influenced by social and political considerations. The only function that the current interpretation serves is to obscure what political considerations the IMF does view as relevant to its operations, what principles it applies in making these judgments and what process it follows in reaching these decisions.

This lack of clarity also leaves undefined the outer limits of the IMF's specialized economic mandate. The lack of clear principles establishing how the IMF should incorporate 'political' issues like human rights into its calculations makes its decisions in this regard appear arbitrary and influenced by the interests of its richer Member States.

4. Legal nature of the IMF's standby arrangement

For many years the IMF has maintained that the standby arrangement through which it provides much of its financing is not a legal contract. This means that a Member State that does not meet the performance criteria or other requirements of the standby arrangement will not incur any legal liability. Until recently, the IMF also relied, in part, on this characterization to avoid publicizing the Member State's Letter of Intent.

The IMF's formalist position had a certain utilitarian value when the IMF functioned as the manager of the par value system, and the conditions attached to its financing included a change in the par value of the currency. The same considerations do not apply to its current operations.

The IMF's position is problematic for two reasons. First, if the arrangements were treated as international agreements they would be registered with the United Nations. Consequently, the IMF could require, rather than – as it currently does – encourage, Member States to publish their Letters of Intent.

Second, as IMF transactions become more complex, there is a greater need for these arrangements to be subjected to predictable principles of interpretation. The reason is that it is now possible for disagreements to arise about what constitutes sufficient compliance with the conditions of the agreement to justify allowing the country to obtain the next tranche of the funds. The lack of obviously applicable rules of interpretation renders the transactions amenable to *ad hoc* and arbitrary interpretation. This reduces our ability to hold either the Member State or the IMF accountable for the execution and interpretation of these Arrangements.

Note

1 See, International Monetary Fund, *Guidelines on Conditionality*, 2002, available at <http://www.imf.org/External/np/pdr/cond/2002/eng/guid/092302.pdf>; International Monetary Fund, *Operational Guidance on the New Conditionality Guidelines*, available at <http://www.imf.org/External/np/pdr/cond/2003/eng/050803.htm>.

Remarks by Laurence Boisson de Chazournes*

Accountability, rule of law and ICJ advisory opinions

Introduction

The concept of accountability stands for answerability for the performance of an actor towards others.[1] Two kinds of accountability can be distinguished: an internal ac-

* Professor and Head of Department, Department of Public International Law and International Organization, University of Geneva.

countability and an external one. In the case of international organizations, the internal system of accountability refers to the structure of accountability within them, i.e., towards the Member States. The external accountability focuses on accountability towards the international community at large (which includes States, international organizations, non-governmental organizations (NGOs) and other non-State actors). Accountability for the respect for the rule of law falls within both types of accountability: internal and external.

Application of the rule of law contributes to better accountability towards others in increasing the legitimacy of the decision-making process within an international organization. It provides for objective standards and rules and helps reaching agreed positions among members of an organization. It thus detracts from subjective assessment and unilateralism in favor of a third-party evaluation.

At a time when international organizations are increasingly placed in the turmoil of identifying agreed policy positions on a number of highly controversial issues such as the struggle against international terrorism, the legality of the use of force, the challenges posed by global environmental problems or the elimination of weapons of mass destruction, it is all the more important to assess the means of identifying the legal principles which can or could resolve such issues.

Advisory opinions and more specifically the ones rendered by the International Court of Justice (ICJ), is one means among others to this end. They constitute a channel through which legal considerations may find their way into the international debate. In rendering these opinions, the Court contributes to the clarification of the applicable law and in so doing helps to prevent uncertainties, tensions and disputes from arising within the organization and outside the organization. Advisory opinions provide for legal parameters, which then contribute to assessing the conduct of an organization. They contribute to making the legal "rules of the game" less controversial.

Up until now, the vast majority of the advisory opinions given by the Court have essentially dealt with issues of a constitutional nature. They, however, can also play an important role in identifying the law and policy issues which are of interest to an international organization.

Noteworthy is the fact that better legal certainty goes hand-in-hand with increased legalization of the international discourse, which is taking place in world politics. It is perhaps the legal discourse being engaged in, and applied to, non-State actors that is the most striking in this context. An example can be found in the increased submission by civil society of *amicus* briefs to Courts and tribunals as a means of having their opinions heard when legal proceedings are instituted.[2]

For international organizations and their organs to be able to have legal issues clarified, and by the same token to increase their internal and external accountability, an important issue to be dealt with is access to the ICJ. It is also important to analyze the way advisory proceedings are conducted, and more specifically the involvement of States, international organizations and non-State actors in these proceedings. Openness and inclusiveness criteria contribute to the legitimacy of the identification process of the rule of law.

I. The request for an ICJ advisory opinion

Article 65 of the ICJ Statute provides that the Court may give an advisory opinion "on any legal question at the request of whatever body may be authorised by or in accordance with the Charter of the United Nations to make such a request". The Charter of the United Nations in its Article 96 states that "The General Assembly or the Security Council may request the International Court of Justice to give an advisory opinion on any legal question. Other organs of the United Nations and specialized agencies, which may at any time be so authorized by the General Assembly, may also request advisory opinions of the Court on legal questions arising within the scope of their activities".

In practice, in addition to the two UN principal organs foreseen by the Charter, other organs have been granted this privilege: they are the Economic and Social Council, the Trusteeship Council and the Interim Committee of the General Assembly. All specialized agencies with the exception of the Universal Postal Union have been granted this possibility.[3]

It is interesting to note that most of the requests have emanated from the General Assembly or from other plenary bodies of specialized agencies, which comprehend almost all States of the international community. In such circumstances, one cannot but note "a general presumption that the request reflects a profound concern of the international community requiring a judicial answer".[4] In a context of profound questioning, not to say search for identity, with respect to the means for promoting common interests, it is hoped that the international organizations' plenary organs become even more active. Examples are numerous where there is a need for increased legal clarity and certainty.

The possibility to request advisory opinions granted to specialized agencies was given at a time when the creation of an international organization was a novelty.[5] The organizations whose creation was foreseen in the 1940s were universal and were supposed to be part of a system. Indeed, according to the ICJ, "[...] the Charter of the United Nations laid the basis of a "system" designed to organize international co-operation in a coherent fashion by bringing the United Nations, invested with powers of general scope, into relationship with various autonomous and complementary organizations, invested with sectorial powers. The exercise of these powers by the organizations belonging to the "United Nations system" is co-ordinated, notably, by the relationship agreements concluded between the United Nations and each of the specialized agencies [...]."[6] It was as yet inconceivable that most of the organizations to be created thereafter would not be part of the UN system as conceived in 1945.

It is true that cooperation with regional organizations had also been foreseen by the UN Charter in the area of peace and security issues. The eligible organizations were those with jurisdiction in dispute-settlement and enforcement matters. However, these organizations were not granted the right to request advisory opinions.

This point is to be borne in mind, as direct access to the ICJ is currently the privilege of a very small number of international organizations. The possibility of extending access to advisory opinions to international institutions other than the ones already granted that right, would be a means to promote respect for the rule of law. It would also contribute to increasing consistency in the interpretation of core principles of international law in a world with numerous actors, institutions and dispute-settlement procedures.

International organizations are important *fora* for promoting respect for the rule of law as well as for involving all concerned actors, by enabling them to have a say in the decision-making process. This is all the more true in a context of multiplication of international organizations, whether they are universal or regional. Their functions might overlap or create uncertainty as to the legality of the actions to be taken. One can think, for example, of the recent developments in the area of collective security with NATO, OSCE and the EU as well as other regional organizations, being increasingly active in a field where, traditionally, the Security Council was the sole "maître du jeu". One way to strengthen respect for the rule of law would be for international organizations to be able to submit legal questions to the ICJ. Not being specialized agencies in the meaning of the UN Charter, one could envisage that their requests be conveyed by the General Assembly, the Security Council or any one of the specialized agencies.

Noteworthy in this context, is the path followed by the 1993 Chemical Weapons Convention which provides that "The Conference and the Executive Council are separately empowered, subject to authorization from the General Assembly of the United Nations, to request the International Court of Justice to give an advisory opinion on any legal question arising within the scope of the activities of the Organization. An agreement between the Organization and the United Nations shall be concluded for this purpose [...]".[7]

One could also consider the possibility of amending the Statute of the ICJ so as to enable these organizations established beyond the United Nations circle to make such requests directly.[8]

II. About the openness and inclusiveness of the ICJ advisory process

Having dealt with the issue of the institutions entitled to request an advisory opinion, it is then interesting to assess the current openness of the ICJ Advisory proceedings when such a request has been brought. Openness and inclusiveness are seen as ways to contribute to increasing the legitimacy of the procedure as well as the chances that the identified rule of law by the ICJ finds application. The public character of the advisory opinions proceedings is also a means to this end by helping to avoid contests and tensions.

In the context of advisory proceedings, Article 66(2) of the ICJ Statute provides that "The Registrar shall also, by means of a special and direct communication, notify any State entitled to appear before the Court or international organization considered by the Court, or, should it not be sitting, by the President, as likely to be able to furnish information on the question, that the Court will be prepared to receive, within a time limit to be fixed by the President, written statements, or to hear, at a public sitting to be held for the purpose, oral statements relating to the question". All Member States of an organization that has brought a request have the right to make oral and written statements in the course of the procedure by means of a "special and direct communication." They can thus express their views. This was widely exemplified by the requests on the legality of nuclear weapons brought by the WHO and the General Assembly. Forty-two States participated in the written phase of the pleadings, the largest number ever to join in proceedings before the Court. Among the participants to the written stage, four of the five declared nuclear weapons States participated, as did one "threshold" nuclear weapons State, NATO members as well as many developing countries that had not previously contributed to proceedings before the ICJ. During the oral proceedings, twenty-two States participated.[9]

In advisory proceedings the Court can request and receive submissions from "international organizations" considered by the Court as likely to be able to provide information on the question. This is the case with the organization that has brought a request before the ICJ. Other international organizations and institutions that are competent in the fields dealt with by a request, can also submit written statements and make oral comments before the Court. They can be universal or regional organizations, specialized agencies or non-specialized agencies, organs of the UN or otherwise. Such was the case with the International Labour Organization, the Organization of American States and the UN Secretary General in the context of the request brought by the General Assembly on Reservations to the Convention on Genocide.[10] The Organization of African Unity did the same at the oral stage in the *Namibia* case.[11] The UN Secretary-General, for his part, made communications in the *Mazilu*[12] and *Cumaraswamy*[13] cases.

The participation of all interested and concerned organizations in advisory proceedings is all the more important in an era of increased interdependence where issues become linked to each other and need to be looked at in a more holistic manner.

A question arises as to the proper means for identifying an international organization in the context of a request for an advisory opinion. So far, the Court has limited the scope of Article 66 (2) of the ICJ Statute by interpreting the notion of "international organizations" as referring to "inter-governmental organizations". One should, however, note the difference in wording between Article 66 (2) and Article 34 (2). Article 34 (2) refers to "public international organizations"[14] and Article 66 (2) is not limited by the adjective "public". In addition in Article 66 (4), which allows States and organizations to comment on the submissions by other States and organizations, the word organization is used without any further specification that it is limited to international organizations.[15]

If one were to consider that advisory proceedings are only open to international organizations as understood by international treaty practice, as for example the 1986 Vienna Convention on the Law of Treaties between States and International Organizations or between International Organizations, there might be difficulties as some international institutions do not fit within a definition based on the unique involvement of States in the creation of an organization through a constitutive treaty-type instrument.[16]

One might think for instance of the institutions established under multilateral environmental treaties (MEAs), known as "Conference of the Parties" or "Meeting of the Parties"[17] whose creation as international organizations was not foreseen by the parties to the MEAs, but which overtime gained such standing. There are also cases of institutions where international organizations, States and NGOs are acting in partnership such as for example the Global Initiative Alliance for Vaccines and Immunization (GAVI). And what about the International Red Cross Committee (ICRC) whose legal standing in the international order makes it a subject of international law? Should the openness of the advisory process be further strengthened so as to allow for broader participation? But what should be the criteria for allowing access to the ICJ?

Notwithstanding the existing possibilities for international organizations' involvement before the Court, in practice their participation has been very limited. While international organizations have on occasion been requested to provide information to the Court, particularly in relation to advisory proceedings, they have rarely sought to become involved on their own initiative.[18]

The openness of the advisory proceedings also raises the issue of access given to non-State actors. With the exception of the International League for the Rights of Man which was accorded permission to make a written statement to the Court in the *South West Africa* case,[19] but failed to do so,[20] NGOs have been firmly excluded from the proceedings.

It is interesting to note that since the *South West Africa* opinion, the Court and the Registrar have made it clear that the right to provide information in advisory or contentious proceedings under either Article 34 or 66 of the Statute is limited to international organizations.[21] The only pathway for NGOs – or other members of the international civil society – intervention before the Court is for their statements to be joined to States' communications.[22]

International law, however, is no longer a field in which States have an absolute monopoly of interest and action. This complexity of the world "stage" brings transformations in the decision-making process.[23] This was vividly evidenced through the requests for advisory opinions on the legality of resorting to nuclear weapons. They have raised concerns with respect to the legitimacy of the process for requesting advisory opinions because of the intervention of non-State actors. This was even commented upon by Judge Guillaume in his Separate Opinion in the 1996 Advisory Opinion on the Legality of the Threat or Use of Nuclear Weapons requested by the General Assembly, when he said:

> "I am sure that the pressure brought to bear [by the NGOs who in the last analysis initiated the request] did not influence the Court's deliberations, but I wondered whether, in such circumstances, the requests for opinions could still be regarded as coming from the Assemblies which have adopted them or whether, piercing the veil, the Court should not have dismissed them as inadmissible. However, I dare to hope that Governments and inter-governmental institutions still retain sufficient independence of decision to resist the powerful pressure groups which besiege them today with the support of the mass media. *I also note that none of the States which appeared before the Court raised such an objection* [emphasis added]. In the circumstances I did not believe that the Court should uphold it *proprio motu*."[24]

Insights from past practice are interesting to take into account, as the majority of the requests transmitted by the Council to the Permanent Court of Justice were not in substantial terms requests of the Council. They were actually submitted at the instance of States or of an international organization other than the League of Nations.[25] In the 14th Annual Report of the Permanent Court, sixteen such requests are identified. Six are identified as deriving from the ILO. And interestingly enough, the Court's report lists among the international organizations interested in the case not only the ILO but various non-governmental organizations as well. These were the International Confederation of Christian Trade Unions and the Netherlands General Confederation of Trade Unions[26]. It would seem that this practice could be revived.

Conclusion: Rule of law and accountability

There are many global policy issues under discussion where the question of the applicable law is one of the core questions. There is, in other words, a quest for legal answers to public policy concerns. The United Nations, its specialized agencies, as well as other institutions, confront such issues on a daily basis in the course of their activities. Advisory opinions while providing an answer to legal questions can also be seen as a means for improving accountability. The promotion of the rule of law is a means to this end as it sets criteria against which practices can be assessed. In addition, the contribution of the courts to legal queries, especially if it emanates from advisory opinions, has certain advantages, notably that it may reduce the influence of the most politically powerful States.[27] All States are able to express their views in advisory proceedings and this contributes to a levelling of the playing field. Furthermore, increased participation of international organizations in, as well as access for NGOs to, advisory proceedings would make the process more inclusive and contribute to shaping in judicial terms the changes that are taking place in the international decision-making process. States are no more the only actors involved in law-criteria and law-application functions. Others are claiming such privilege, and more specifically non-State actors. There is however a lack of formal and substantial criteria for their involvement in international arenas. Their participation in advisory proceedings would contribute to identifying these criteria.

NOTES

1 See I.F.I. Shihata, *The World Bank Inspection Panel: In Practice*, 2nd edn. (Oxford, Oxford University Press 2000) pp. 237-240.

2 L. Boisson de Chazournes and M.M. Mbengue, 'The Amici Curiae and the WTO Dispute Settlement System: The Doors are Open', in *The Law and Practice of International Courts and Tribunals* (Forthcoming 2003).

3 C. Romano, 'International Organizations and the International Judicial Process: An Overview', in L. Boisson de Chazournes, et al., eds., *International Organizations and International Dispute Settlement: Trends and Prospects* (New York, Transnational Publishers 2002) p. 20. In 56 years of existence, the ICJ has rendered 23 opinions. By comparison, 98 contentious cases have been submitted.

4 Ch. Tomuschat, 'International Law: Ensuring the Survival of Mankind on the Eve of a New Century. General Course on Public International Law', 281 *RCADI* (1999) p. 86.

5 See, for example, the statement made by the ICJ with respect to the legal personality of the United Nations in *Reparation for Injuries suffered in the Service of the United Nations*, Advisory Opinion of 11 April 1949, *ICJ Reports* 1949, p. 182: "The Court is here faced with a new situation. The question to which it gives rise can only be solved by realizing that the situation is dominated by the provisions of the Charter considered in the light of the principles of international law [...]".

6 *Legality of the Threat or Use of Nuclear Weapons*, Advisory Opinion, *ICJ Reports* 1996, para. 26.

7 Article XIV, para. 5.

8 In this sense, see G. Abi-Saab, 'Fragmentation or Unification: Some Concluding Remarks' to the Symposium "the Proliferation of International Tribunals: Piecing Together the Puzzle", 31:4 *NYU Journal of International Law and Politics* (1999) pp. 928-929.

9 L. Boisson de Chazournes and Ph. Sands, 'Introduction' in L. Boisson de Chazournes and Ph. Sands, eds., *International Law, the International Court of Justice and Nuclear Weapons* (Cambridge, Cambridge University Press 1999) pp. 5-6; Th. FRANCK 'Fairness and the General Assembly Advisory Opinion' in L. Boisson de Chazournes and Ph. Sands, eds., ibid., pp. 511-519.

10 See *Reservations to the Convention on Genocide, Advisory opinion, ICJ Reports* 1951, p.18.

11 *Legal Consequences For States Of the Continued Presence Of South Africa In Namibia (South West Africa) Notwithstanding Security Council Resolution 276 (1970), ICJ Reports* 1971, para. 11.

12 *Applicability of Article VI, Section 22 of the Convention on Privileges and Immunities of the United Nations, ICJ Reports* 1989, para. 5.

13 *Difference Relating To Immunity From Legal Process Of A Special Rapporteur Of The Commission On Human Rights, ICJ Reports* 1999, para. 5.

14 "The Court, subject to and in conformity with its Rules, may request of public international organizations information relevant to cases before it, and shall receive such information presented by such organizations on their own initiative".

15 R. MacKenzie and Ch. Chinkin, 'Intergovernmental Organizations as "Friends of the Court', in *International Organizations and International Dispute Settlement: Trends and Prospects*, op. cit., pp. 140-141.
16 On the issue of the definition of an international organization, see *First report on responsibility of international organizations* by Mr. Giorgio Gaja, Special Rapporteur, Doc. *A/CN.4/532*, paras. 12-34.
17 See R.R. Churchill and G. Ulfstein, 'Autonomous Institutional Arrangements in Multilateral Environmental Agreements: A Little-Noticed Phenomenon in International Law', 94 *American Journal of International Law* (2000) p. 623.
18 R. Mackenzie and Ch. Chinkin, op. cit., p. 159.
19 *International Status of South West Africa*, Advisory Opinion of 11 July 1950, *ICJ Reports* 1950.
20 See R. Clark, 'The International League for Human Rights and South West Africa 1947-57: The Human Rights Non-Governmental Organization as Catalyst in the International Legal Process', 3 *Human Rights Quarterly* (1981) p. 101.
21 R. MacKenzie and Ch. Chinkin, op. cit., p. 140.
22 For example, a resident of the Marshall Islands described what has happened following the series of hydrogen bomb tests conducted in the 1950s during the proceedings on the *Legality of the Threat or Use of Nuclear Weapons*.
23 The negotiations of the Rome Statute establishing the International Criminal Court or the negotiations of the Ottawa Convention on the elimination of landmines have revealed the increased role of non-State actors in the creation of international law.
24 *Legality of the Threat or Use of Nuclear Weapons*, Advisory Opinion, *ICJ Reports* 1996, p. 288.
25 S.M. Schwebel, 'Was the Capacity to Request an Advisory Opinion Wider in the Permanent International Court of Justice than it is in the International Court of Justice?', LXII *BYIL* (1991) p. 81.
26 See, e.g., *Nomination of the Workers' Delegate to the International Labour Conference; International Labour Organization and Personal Work of the Employer and Employment of Women in the Night*. See Fourteenth Annual Report of the Permanent Court of International Justice (15 June 1937-15 June 1938), PCIJ Series E, N° 14, pp. 72-75.
27 J. Charney, 'International Law-Making – Article 38 of the ICJ Statute Reconsidered', in J. Delbrück, ed., *New Trends in International Lawmaking – International "Legislation" in the Public Interest* (Berlin, Duncker & Humbolt 1997) p. 182.

REMARKS BY ALFRED E. KELLERMANN*

THE GROWING IMPACT OF THE PRINCIPLES OF GOOD GOVERNANCE IN STRENGTHENING THE APPLICATION OF THE RULE OF LAW IN EUROPEAN CONTEXT

INTRODUCTION

The term "good governance" does as yet not have a clearly defined legal definition in any system of law. In the European context, the term embodies a range of traditional legal and non-legal concepts and applies as well as to governmental organizations as well as to private organizations.

In this paper we will especially focus on the monitoring by European Institutions of compliance with good governance by its institutions and the Member States. Compliance by business and corporate organizations with these principles of good governance, which is nowadays a hot item not only in the USA (Enron, Worldcom) but also in the Netherlands (Worldonline, Ahold) will be dealt with under the session of Corporate Governance.

* T.M.C. Asser Institute, the Netherlands.

What is "bad governance"? A contrario not complying with the principles of good governance! From a lawyer's viewpoint, we may consider principles of governance as *soft law*, which contains rules that are not legally binding whereas the rules of the European Community law are *hard law*, legally binding and enforceable before national and supra-national courts. The principles of good governance apply to all levels of government (public international organizations and national governments).

To monitor the compliance by the European institutions, the Member States and the decentralized authorities with the European rule of law, which is hard law, is the responsibility of the European Commission, the national courts and finally the European Court of Justice. The European Court of Justice (ECJ) guarantees respect for the rule of law. This topic is, however, not the objective of this conference report. In this contribution we will mainly focus on the monitoring of the principles of good governance which are non-binding and do not aim at detailed prescriptions for national legislation. Their purpose is to serve as a reference point. These principles can be applied by policy makers like the European Institutions, Governments of the Member States, regional and local authorities, civil society and business.

Recently, in the opening of the Draft Articles of the Constitutional Treaty, from the European Convention of Brussels of 26 February 2003, the Convention addressed matters relating to the Constitution's nature, values, objectives and competences, for which exercise reference was made to the Declaration of the Laeken European Council. The Laeken European Council called on the Convention to consider "how the division of competence can be made more transparent", one of the principles of good governance and "how to ensure that a redefined division of competence" is maintained, which regards openness, effectiveness and accountability, which are the other criteria for good governance, as mentioned in the White Paper of European Governance.[1]

The decision of the European Commission to step up dialogue with associations of regional and local authorities is another recent example of the Commission's commitment in the White paper on European Governance. Indeed, it is at regional and local level that European policies produce their effects or are applied. Regional and local authorities should be given the opportunity to express their views, through their associations, before the formal decision-making processes are set in motion. After enlargement, the European Union will comprise some 250 regions and 100.000 local authorities.

The Commission has suggested to the Convention on the Future of the Union[2] that an article on good governance should be incorporated into the future Constitution. An article of this kind would provide an additional guarantee to local and regional authorities on their increased involvement in deliberations before the adoption of legislative proposals that concern them. When the Commission adopted its Report on European Governance[3] it confirmed this commitment.

Before the recent Laeken Declaration and the Brussels Convention and the Decision of the European Commission of 28 March 2003 to step up the dialogue with associations of regional and local authorities, three interesting cases and reports were published in which principles of good governance, code of conduct and standards of behaviour in the EU context and international legal rules where more or less debated. These three reports and documents show the growing impact of principles of good governance in the European society. Therefore we have selected them for a summary report, analysis and discussion in the following text.

I. Report of 8 September 2000 by *Mahrtti Ahtisaari, Jochen Frowein and Marcelino Oreja.*
The commitment of the Austrian Government to the common European values, in particular concerning the rights of minorities, refugees and immigrants.

II. Report of the Committee of Independent Experts 15 March 1999.
Members: *Andre Middelhoek (Chairman), Mrs Inga-Britt Ahlenius, Mr Juan Antonio Carrillo Salcedo, Mr Pierre Lelong, Mr Walter van Gerven.*
The allegations regarding Fraud, Mismanagement and Nepotism in the European Commission

III. The White Paper from the European Commission on European Governance of 25 July 2001.

I. MONITORING THE COMPLIANCE OF THE AUSTRIAN GOVERNMENT WITH "COMMON EUROPEAN VALUES"

The question was discussed if Austria did comply with "common European values". However, what interpretation and definition has to be given to the common European values? Do they include the human rights and fundamental freedoms as well as the rights of minorities, refugees and immigrants? Do they include principles of good governance, as far as they are not legally binding? An answer to these questions was necessary in the Austrian case. The above-mentioned Report of 8 September 2000 concluded that there are several legally binding but also non-binding documents, which enshrine the positive obligation of European States to protect and promote human rights and fundamental freedoms, pluralist democracy and the rule of law.

The binding treaties are in particular the *European Union Treaty (EU)* and *the European Convention on Human Rights (ECHR)* mentioned expressly in Article 6 para. 2 of the EU Treaty.

Further *The Framework Convention for the Protection of National Minorities and the Convention relating to the Status of Refugees.*

In its Article 6, para.1, the *EU Treaty* expressly declares that "the Union is based on the principles of freedom, democracy, respect for human rights and fundamental freedoms, and the rule of law, principles common to all Member States." We may therefore conclude that the commitment to the protection and promotion of human rights constitutes a legal obligation on the part of the EU Member States. The case law developed by the organs set up under the European Convention on Human Rights is also of particular importance in this regard.

Common European values

a) **Standards concerning human rights and fundamental freedoms**
The European Convention for the Protection of Human Rights and Fundamental Freedoms (ECHR), signed in 1950, expresses in its preamble that the governments of European countries, which are likeminded and have a common heritage of political traditions, ideals, freedom and the rule of law, take the first steps for the collective enforcement of certain of the rights stated in *the Universal Declaration of the United Nations* of 1948. All Member States of the Union have ratified the Convention. Of particular importance in the present context is the clear guarantee of non-discrimination

in the enjoyment of the rights and freedoms set forth in the Convention which is expressed in Article 14. According to that Article the rights and freedoms of the Convention shall be secured without discrimination on any grounds such as sex, race, colour, language, religion, political or other opinion, national or social origin, association with a national minority, property, birth or other status.

Non-discrimination is also a fundamental principle in European Union Law. Article 13 of the *EC Treaty* as amended by the *Amsterdam Treaty* gives a mandate to the Council to take measures against discrimination on the basis of sex, racial or ethnic origin, religion or belief, disability, age or sexual orientation. A directive has been adopted on 29 June 2000, and must be implemented in all Member States before July 2003. This Directive sets substantive standards, which have to be followed in accordance with its objectives by all national authorities. In the new Draft Charter of Fundamental Rights of 28 July 2000, Article 21 prohibits discrimination based on sex, race, colour, ethnic or social origin, genetic features, language, religion, political or other opinions, membership of a national minority, property, birth, disability, age or sexual orientation.

Austria has ratified the *European Convention on Human Rights* in 1958 and is the only country in which the Convention enjoys full constitutional rank. On the basis of a specific constitutional legislation of 1964, the European Convention on Human Rights became part of Austrian constitutional law.

b*)* **Standards concerning the rights of national minorities**

In 1995 the Council of Europe adopted the *Framework Convention for the Protection of National Minorities,* which is an important standard with regard to minority protection of the European Union Member States. The Convention entered into force for Austria on 1 July 1998. According to Article 6 the parties shall encourage a spirit of tolerance and intercultural dialogue and take effective measures to promote mutual respect, understanding and cooperation among all persons living on their territory, irrespective of those persons' ethnic, cultural, linguistic or religious identity, in particular in the fields of education, culture and the media. The parties expressly undertake to take appropriate measures to protect persons who may be subject to threats or acts of discrimination, hostility or violence as a result of their ethnic, cultural, linguistic or religious identity.

The Convention has been ratified by 32 States, among them nine Member States of the European Union.

c) **Standards concerning the rights of refugees**

All EU Member States are bound by the *Geneva Convention on Refugees* of 1951 and the amending Protocol of 1967. According to Art. 33 of the Geneva Convention no contracting State shall expel or return ("refouler") a refugee in any manner whatsoever to the frontiers of territories where his life or freedom would be threatened on account of his race, religion, nationality, membership of a particular social group or political opinion. *The Dublin Convention* of 1990 has confirmed these principles within the Community system, establishing the criteria to be applied for the determination of the State responsible for asylum applications lodged in one of the Member States. In the *new EU Charter of Fundamental Rights* Article 18 proclaims the right of asylum on the basis of the *Geneva Convention of 1951 and the Amending Protocol of 1967.*

The European Court of Human Rights has clarified that Article 3 of *the European Convention on Human Rights* prohibits Member States of the Convention from extraditing or deporting persons to countries where they would be exposed to inhuman treatment. The same principle is laid down in Article 19 para. 2 of the *EU Charter of Fundamental Rights.*

d) **Standards concerning the rights of immigrants**

With the coming into force of the *Treaty of Amsterdam*, the European Community has expressly recognized in Art. 13 that discrimination on the ground of race, ethnic origin or religion among others is against the ground values of the Community system. The first legislative measure adopted in accordance with this provision is the *Directive against discrimination of 29 June 2000,* which came into force on 19 July 2000.

Recommendations for a follow-up of the report

1) The development of a mechanism within the EU to monitor and evaluate the commitment and performance of individual Member States with respect to the common European values. A follow-up of this report was the introduction of preventive and monitoring procedures as drafted into Article 7 (1) and (2) of the EU Treaty of Nice.
2) A system of prevention should be put in place which would react through information and educational measures to any forms of direct or indirect discrimination or xenophobia: the creation of a Human Rights Office within the Council, reporting to the European Council and the establishment of a full EU Agency on Human Rights.

II. Monitoring the compliance of the European Commission with rules of good governance

The emergence of principles of good governance regarding the political responsibility and accountability of the European Commission towards the European Parliament has been analyzed in two reports which the *Committee of Independent Experts* designated by the EP to examine allegations of fraud, mismanagement and nepotism in the European Commission, has made public on 15 March 1999, respectively 10 September 1999. These allegations may be considered as "bad governance".

The monitoring procedure started with the adoption of a resolution by the European parliament at its plenary sitting of 14 January 1999. Paragraph 1 of this resolution on improving the financial management of the European Commission reads:

> "Calls for a committee of independent experts to be convened under the auspices of the Parliament and the Commission with a mandate to examine the way in which the Commission detects and deals with fraud, mismanagement and nepotism including a fundamental review of Commission practices in the awarding of all financial contracts, to report by 15 March (1999) on their assessment in the first instance on the College of Commissioners;"

According to a note adopted on 27 January 1999 the European Parliament's Conference of Presidents: The first report could seek to establish to what extent the Commission, as a body, or Commissioners individually, bear specific responsibility for the recent examples of fraud, mismanagement or nepotism raised in Parliamentary discussions, or in the allegations which have arisen in those discussions. On 23 March 1999 the European Parliament adopted a second resolution confirming the mandate of the Committee in the following terms:

> "Looks forward to the second paper by the Committee of Independent Experts containing a more wide-ranging review of the Commission's culture, practices and procedures and in particular its concrete recommendations for strengthening these procedures and any other appropriate reforms to be considered by Commission and Parliament ……………".

After having focused in its first report on the collective responsibility of the Commissioners (which provoked the resignation of the Santer-Commission) the Committee analyzed in Chapter 7 of its second report of 10 September 1999 the issue of accountability and (personal and political) responsibility of Commissioners in connection with their duties of integrity in public life and of leadership and sound management as members of the Executive branch of the European Community.

In its second report of 10 September 1999 on Reform of the Commission the Committee presents an analysis of current practice and proposals for tackling mismanagement, irregularities and fraud.

The Committee of Independent Experts made the following 90 Recommendations, which de facto refer to many principles of good governance:

15 recommendations concerning improving contracting management.
19 recommendations concerning improving the control of expenditures of structural agricultural funds.
18 recommendations concerning improving the personal responsibility for authorizations by a professional and independent Internal Audit Service.
8 recommendations concerning the appointment of an independent European Public Prosecutor (EPP) and creation in each member State of a National Prosecutors Office for European Offences (POEO).
13 recommendations concerning improving personnel management.
17 recommendations concerning codes of conduct for the Commission. The attribution of responsibilities and a chain of delegation between the Commission, single Commissioners and the departments.

In this report the Committee of Independent Experts is also referring to the code of conduct adopted by the OECD on 23 April 1998 "Principles for Managing Ethics in Public Service", as an illustrative example.

The code of conduct prepared by the Commission rightly takes the Treaty articles concerning the Commission (see TEC Article 213) as a legal basis, making particular reference to the independence enjoyed by the members of the Commission, who are required to discharge their duties in the general interest of the Community. It continues to state:

> "In the performance of their duties they must neither seek nor take instructions from any government or from any other body. The general interest also requires that in their official and private lives Commissioners should behave in a manner that is in keeping with the dignity of their office."

This example shows that non-binding principles of good governance have often their legal basis in the rule of law.

III. The scope of the White Paper on European governance

Reasons to reform European governance

European integration has delivered fifty years of stability, peace and economic prosperity. It has helped to raise standards of living, built an internal market and strengthened the Union's voice in the world. It has achieved results, which would not have been possible by individual Member States acting on their own. It has attracted a succession of applications for membership and in a few years time it will expand on a continental scale. It has also served as a model for regional integration across the world.

These results have been achieved by democratic means. The Union is built on the rule of law; it can draw on the Charter of fundamental rights, and it has a double democratic mandate through a Parliament representing EU citizens and a Council representing the elected governments of the Member States.

The decreasing turnout in the European Parliament elections and the Irish "No" vote also serve to show the widening gulf between the European Union and the people it serves:

* There is a perceived inability of the Union to act effectively where a clear case exists, for instance, unemployment, food safety scares, crime, the conflicts on the EU' s borders and its role in the world.
* Where the Union does act effectively, it rarely gets proper credit for its actions. People do not see that improvements in their rights and quality of life actually come from European rather than national decisions. But at the same time, they expect the Union to act as effectively and visibly as their national governments.
* By the same token, Member States do not communicate well about what the Union is doing and what they are doing in the Union. "Brussels" is too easily blamed by Member States for difficult decisions that they themselves have agreed or even requested.
* Finally, many people do not know the difference between the Institutions. They do not understand who takes the decisions that affect them and do not feel the Institutions act as an effective channel for their views and concerns.

In early 2000 the Commission decided to launch the reform of European governance[4] as a strategic objective – well in advance of the Nice European Council.

Each of the five principles of good governance is important for establishing more democratic governance. They underpin democracy and the rule of law in the Member States, but they apply to all levels of government – global, European, national, regional and local.

* *Openness.* The Institutions should work in a more open manner. Together with the Member States, they should actively communicate about what the EU does and the decisions it takes. They should use language that is accessible and understandable for the general public. This is of particular importance in order to improve the confidence in complex institutions.

* *Participation.* The quality, relevance and effectiveness of EU policies depend on ensuring wide participation throughout the policy chain – from conception to implementation. Improved participation is likely to create more confidence in the end result and in the Institutions which deliver policies. Participation crucially depends on central governments following an inclusive approach when developing and implementing EU policies.
* *Accountability.* Roles in the legislative and executive processes need to be clearer. Each of the EU Institutions must explain and take responsibility for what it does in Europe. But there is also a need for greater clarity and responsibility from Member States and all those involved in developing and implementing EU policy at whatever level.
* *Effectiveness.* Policies must be effective and timely, delivering what is needed on the basis of clear objectives, an evaluation of future impact and, where available, of past experience. Effectiveness also depends on implementing EU policies in a proportionate manner and on taking decisions at the most appropriate level.
* *Coherence.* Policies and action must be coherent and easily understood. The need for coherence in the Union is increasing: the range of tasks has grown; enlargement will increase diversity; challenges such as climate and demographic change cross the boundaries of the sectoral policies on which the Union has been built; regional and local authorities are increasingly involved in EU policies. Coherence requires political leadership and a strong responsibility on the part of the Institutions to ensure a consistent approach within a complex system.

Each principle is important by itself. But they cannot be achieved through separate actions. Policies can no longer be effective unless they are prepared, implemented and enforced in a more inclusive way.

The application of these five principles reinforces those of

* *proportionality and subsidiarity.* From the conception of policy to its implementation, the choice of the level at which action is taken (from EU to local) and the selection of the instruments used must be in proportion to the objectives pursued. This means that before launching an initiative, it is essential to check systematically

– if public action is really necessary,
– if the European level is the most appropriate one, and
– if the measures chosen are proportionate to those objectives.

The Union is changing as well. Its agenda extends to foreign policy and defence, migration and the fight against crime. It is expanding to include new members. It will no longer be judged solely by its ability to remove barriers to trade or to complete an internal market; its legitimacy today depends on involvement and participation.

Proposals for change

The proposals for change in the White Paper are divided into four sections.

A first section focuses on improving involvement in shaping and implementing EU policy.

Action Point – Adopt before the end of 2001 minimum standards for consultation and publish them in a code of conduct that sets minimum standards. According to the European Commission creating a culture of consultation cannot be achieved by legal rules which would create excessive rigidity and risk slowing the adoption of particular policies.

A second section aims at improving the quality and enforcement of EU policies.

Action Point – Improving the quality of regulation, its effectiveness and simplicity of regulatory acts.

The Commission will present an Action Plan for Better regulation to the Laeken European Council; within that framework it will promote greater use of different policy tools, (regulations, "framework directives", guidelines, recommendations). The creation of further autonomous EU regulatory agencies in clearly defined areas will improve the way rules are applied and enforced across the Union. The Commission will define in 2002 the criteria for the creation of new regulatory agencies, respecting the balance of powers between the Institutions.

A third section calls for a stronger link between European governance and the role of the Union in the world.

Action Point – Improve the dialogue with governmental and non-governmental actors of third countries when developing policy proposals with an international dimension. Propose a review of the Union's international representation under the existing Treaties in order to speak more often with a single voice.

A fourth section examines the role of the Institutions.

Action Point – The Commission will bring forward at the next Intergovernmental Conference proposals to refocus executive responsibility on the Commission, while streamlining the control by Council and the European Parliament over how the Commission uses its executive powers.

Finally the White Paper presents suggestions to improve the functioning of the Community Legal order. The Union is based on the Rule of Law. Monitoring the application of Community law is an essential task for the Commission. The Commission will therefore pursue infringements with vigour. In dividing powers between the legislature and the executive and the Union needs clear principles identifying how competence is shared between the Union and its Member States.

IV. Final Remarks

Governance, according to the European Governance White paper, is a political concept and means rules, processes and behavior that affect the way in which powers are exercised as regards the five principles: *openness, participation, accountability, effectiveness and coherence*. The rules are non-binding and do not aim at detailed prescriptions for national legislation. The principles underpin democracy and the rule of law, but apply to all levels of government as well as business and corporate organizations. However there are differences in the character of these principles. Some principles are laid down in binding laws and conventions. Others are just "soft law" and therefore not enforceable before courts.

The rules of good governance may be implemented by codes of conduct and standards of behavior.

In his Guest editorial: The Commission White Paper on Governance in the EU, Christian Joerges[5] concludes that the White Paper in its final version is a non-win text:

"In a somewhat abstract formulation: Europe's legitimacy problem in fact necessitated a dual analytical and normative effort. Reformers, when resorting to the language of governance, have focused on the analytical side and have resorted to the toolkits of political science. They have failed, however, properly to explain how their rhetoric might be normatively compatible with Europe's commitment to law-mediated legitimacy, i.e. the rule of law and constitutional governance."

The European governance principles are generally based on the principles of the rule of Public law (European law especially), whereas the OECD Corporate governance principles are based especially on principles of Private law (especially company law).
By referring repeatedly to the Union legal order and implementation of Community law, the White Paper, implicitly recognizes that without the rule of law, good governance is not effective. But on the other hand practice has shown that without good governance, the rule of law is not effective! These points are clear as a bell!

The Action Points of the White Paper on European Governance focus as well on legislation as on principles of governance, principles which are only regulated in non-binding codes of conduct etc. Improving the Quality of Legislation still remains one of the priorities.[6]

According to the Commission the effectiveness of European policies will be improved by a combination of legislation with non-legislative and self-regulatory solutions. The solutions of the Commission to divide powers between the legislature and executive as well as establishing clear principles how competence is shared between the Union and its Member States may be an improvement of the actual situation as soon as there are found effective solutions for the monitoring of these divisions of competence. The creation of regulatory agencies may be helpful, but risk the creation of a bureaucratic government. We prefer that the interpretation of these powers will be given by the existing institutions: national courts, national parliaments and national governments, in the second instance by European institutions (European Parliament, Council, Commission) and in last instance by the European Court of Justice.

Our Final Conclusion is that a combination of governance with legislation is necessary to make governance effective. Principles of good governance otherwise lack, as a consequence, legal procedures of enforcement for realization of good governance. However there are exceptions.
Principles of good governance may also be effective if there are social or economic sanctions. The principles of corporate governance of the OECD for example need no legal sanction or legal penalty to be complied with. If business organizations do not comply with these principles the sanction or penalty has not a legal character but rather an economic character. The EBRD will not invest money in such companies.

Looking finally in a more broad perspective after reading the respective conference reports and listening to all discussions during this Hague Joint Conference, I must conclude that the principles of good governance and corporate governance deal with more or less identical issues and objectives. The application of criteria as openness, participation, accountability, effectiveness are applied as well as in good governance guidelines as well as in corporate governance instructions. These criteria are focusing to improve the management of organizations be it business or government organizations. In my opinion there is theoretically and in principle no difference between good governance and corporate governance. These principles could equally be applied for the EC Institutions, the IMF and OPCW as well as for Multi National Business Organizations.

I conclude with a personal note.
As I was appointed last year as a Team Leader of an EU Tacis Project in Moscow on the approximation of Russian legislation to EU Standards and as a consequence therefore living in Moscow, I discovered that the principles of Good Governance such as openness and participation are also influencing the Russian Administration. Some examples:
Friday 20 June 2003 President Vladimir Putin forwarded information in the annual Press Conference and answered many questions of journalists at a Press Conference, which lasted nearly three hours.
Another example is the official Website of Putin: <www.kremlin.ru>.
"As an integral member of the global community, Russia considers the Internet to be an indispensable tool in the modern times for fast and easy access to information", says a greeting signed by Putin in a Section of the site called 'A Word to the visitors' (*Moscow Times*, Wednesday 25 June 2003, p. 8).

NOTES

1 COM (2001)428 final, 25 July 2001.
2 DN:IP/03/448, 28 March 2003.
3 COM (2002) 705 final, 11 December 2002.
4 "Governance" means rules, processes and behavior that affect the way in which powers are exercised at European level, particularly as regards openness, participation, accountability, effectiveness and coherence.
5 39 *Common Market Law Review* (2002) pp. 441-445.
6 See Alfred E. Kellermann, et al, eds., *Improving the Quality of Legislation in Europe* (The Hague, T.M.C. Asser Instituut, Kluwer Law International 1998).

DISCUSSION

VADIM SAVELYEV (Law Department of the State Duma, Russian Federation) stated that the recent military operation in Iraq was carried out in violation of the UN Charter and asked whether the ICJ's power to issue advisory opinions is the only possible response of international law at this time or if there are other legitimate ways to react to such violations.

ELLE PAWELSKI (Leyden University) invited the panel to comment on the effectiveness of self-regulation, which she called an unsatisfying mechanism of accountability but sometimes the best possible option.

BERT BARNHOORN (T.M.C. Asser Institute) asked Prof. Bradlow what kind of mechanism could improve accountability within the IMF. He asked Mr. Patel to explain what sort of problems the otherwise smoothly operating OPCW had experienced and how these were solved.

RENÉ SMITS (University of Amsterdam) complimented Prof. Bradlow on his critical presentation and in particular on his expression that consensus in the IMF is being 'shaped in the shadow of what the votes would be.' He disagreed, however, with the statement that the G7 members take decisions without being affected by them, as their reserves are used to fund IMF lending operations and asked whether this situation did not alter the picture just sketched by Prof. Bradlow. Finally, he remarked that in the case of the Economic and Monetary Union, the IMF fails to acknowledge the exclusive EU competence in monetary affairs but instead still allows the eurozone's Member States to play the tune.

LAURENCE BOISSON DE CHAZOURNES agreed that the Iraqi crisis was a traumatic experience that brought great problems in assessing the legality of the resort to force. This prompted the question what ways are available to determine the rule of law and indeed an Advisory Opinion by the ICJ is one of them. The fact that only a simple majority in the General Assembly suffices to request an Advisory Opinion makes it a very open process for States. It can provide both an internal and an external means of accountability for international organizations and its potentialities should be more explored.

DANIEL BRADLOW acknowledged the fact that G7 reserves are used to fund IMF operations but noted that only a very small portion of G7 reserves are used for IMF purposes. He maintained that in the more important sense of the policies and structural adjustments implemented by the IMF, G7 members remain unaffected. He also noted that for his expression of consensus being 'shaped in the shadow of what the votes would be' he was indebted to Ronald Gilson and Robert Mnookin, who coined the term 'bargaining in the shadow of the law.'

In response to Mr. Barnhoorn, he noted that the IMF had a few years ago established an independent evaluation office which functions like the Operations Evaluation Department of the World Bank. It reviews operations post-hoc in a transparent manner. However, the functioning of a self-regulating accountability mechanism in the IMF is severely complicated by the absence of Operational Rules and Procedures, the adoption of which is thus one of the most important changes needed.

BIMAL PATEL explained that in the OPCW Member States made use of voting mechanisms a couple of times only, such as the appointment of the external auditor and the tenure of the first Director-General, but that in general the Chemical Weapons Convention worked so well because of successful consensus building.

CHARLOTTE KU stressed that the effectiveness of self-regulation could only be assessed over time. While she agreed that the war in Iraq was undertaken illegally in the absence of Security Council authorization, she felt a similar situation in the future would meet different reactions, including in the USA domestically. The effectiveness of self-regulation and control should therefore not be too easily discarded and note should be taken of future episodes in this regard. The interaction of national and international processes currently taking place gains in sophistication and strenghthens the overall system of accountability and responsibility.

ANNE-MARIE SLAUGHTER added that experience in the private commercial sector had shown that self-regulation works best when reputation matters and there is a network that provides consequences to violating norms. She then ended the meeting.

*Reporter: Ward Ferdinandusse**

* University of Amsterdam.

Legitimacy, Recognition, Democratic Control, Transparency and Accountability of Non-Governmental Organisations

The panel was convened by its Chair, Deirdre Curtin.*

Remarks by Siegfried Wiessner**

Legitimacy and accountability of NGOs: A policy-oriented perspective

In Washington, you know you are a serious player when The American Enterprise Institute and The Federalist Society join hands in not only holding a conference, but creating a website on you. <www.ngowatch.org> has just become the newest denizen of our virtual universe. Gone are the days when NGOs were exemplified by the idealistic students channeled by Peter Benenson into writing polite letters to dictators around the world imploring them to let their victims go. Today's NGOs have grown to a $1 trillion industry, riding the global wave of privatization of services, and have become major channels, if not the most important conduit, of governmental aid to developing countries and other flashpoints of need. Even more threatening to established holders of power is their surprising success in the political field: for one, without them, the International Criminal Court would not be set up in this city, as we speak. The idealists of yesterday have not only mushroomed, according to some estimates of reliable institutions there are now 40,000 of them, operating, and thus creating moving targets, in changing coalitions and Internet-based networks around the planet. They are no longer mere irritants to the major decision-makers in the global social process; they no longer only meddle in the corridors of power. They have arrived.

Power is a jealously guarded thing. Macchiavelli's Prince could tell you a story or two on how to achieve and maintain it. So are the other seven things humans want out of life: wealth, affection, well-being, enlightenment, respect, rectitude, and skills. NGO's should not be surprised that they have come under increasing scrutiny as they scale the fortress of entrenched international (and domestic) decision-making structures. The Empire will strike back, and try to shake the cardinal stock in trade of the self-styled vanguards of 'global civic-mindedness' (Wapner): their credibility. Just as experienced trial lawyers will spare no effort to discredit, on personal grounds, a witness who saw their client-killer in the act. But this is only part of the story. Some NGOs have brought it on themselves: through horror stories of fiscal mismanagement, nepotism, and internecine warfare. Severe irregularities in contracting, includ-

* Utrecht University.

** Professor of Law and Director, Graduate Program in Intercultural Human Rights, St. Thomas University School of Law, Miami, Florida.

ing allegations of kickbacks, have tarnished their image. Another issue of concern raised is the absence, in many of them, of internal democratic structures of authority. And, finally, the age-old question: *quis custodiet custodes*? If you hold others to account, should not you be held accountable as well? Should NGOs be entitled to hide behind the veil of private action, while public actors have to perform in the sunshine of everybody's scrutiny?

To the credit of NGOs, many have asked these questions themselves. In fact, they have entered an era of 'unprecedented self-questioning' (ID 21). A careful response to these complex questions needs to start from the proper location of NGOs in the global social process, in particular, the process of authoritative and controlling decision commonly designated as law.

There is no question that NGOs are actors in the social process. Many studies expertly define them (Spiro, Hobe, social scientists, etc.), and describe their role. There is an issue, however, as to whether NGOs are relevant actors in the law, in particular, international law. As discussed elsewhere, law is not properly defined as a bundle of rules, independent from their creators and the circumstances of their creation. Not only in the view of policy-oriented jurisprudence, but today predominantly so, law is a dynamic concept, a process with a past and a future, a process of decision. A decision is a policy statement, and the decisions of law emanate from persons with authority and control intent. Often, this concept of decision is reduced to its crystallization in a statute or a convention, i.e. a prescription (e.g. 'if you commit genocide, you are subject to the jurisdiction of the International Criminal Court'), or the application thereof (e.g. the conviction and sentencing of a person alleged to have committed this crime). It is much more helpful, as Reisman and others have done, to unpack the concept of decision, and to discern the seven phases of a decision of law, in order to properly locate the function of any actor involved in this process. Policy-oriented jurisprudence provides a refined way of thinking about processes of decision-making. It conceives of decision processes in terms of the functions they perform. These functions include the gathering of intelligence, the promotion of preferences, the prescribing of authoritative policy or lawmaking, the invocation of prescriptions, the application of prescriptions, their termination, and the appraisal of the aggregate performance of a community's decision processes in terms of community goals.

The function of NGOs in the *research* aspect of finding a solution to social problems, and moreover, their *promotion* of a preferred solution based on that analysis, is too large to be overlooked. The coalition to ban landmines provides just one example for the essential role NGOs play in this crucial field of preparing prescription. Often the final signature under a prescriptive document (here: the Ottawa Convention to Ban Landmines) is but a formality which would never have come to pass without the diligent analysis and dedicated lobbying, conventional and unconventional, of pertinent NGOs. Still, according to voices of traditional international law, this signature, a move of the hand, is the only act that matters ('legally speaking'). *Prescription* itself is largely reserved to entrenched actors, the traditional nation-States, even though a more realistic assessment of the creation of expectations of lawful behavior will have to take into account more supple avenues such as the passing of best practices codes by private actors, voluntary restraint undertakings, and so on – the phenomenon often described as 'soft law', *one* concession of traditionalists to reality. Even there, NGOs have entered the field, as other authors have documented. The *invocation* of prescriptions in cases of perceived violations is another stronghold of NGO action. Without such invocation (especially of human rights norms), there would be little application and enforcement, taking the lifeblood out of the prescriptions enunciated by governments. The act of *application*, by courts or other bodies, is ever more subject to NGO participation (from the admission of NGO complaints in various intergovernmental human rights systems to the acceptance of NGO *amicus* briefs in WTO dispute settlement process, to mention but a few such avenues). Obviously, NGOs are also involved in constant *appraisal* of existing norms and try to compare them to a preferred outcome, which sometimes results in the *termination* of a suboptimal norm.

Having thus located NGOs, *grosso modo*, in the process of international law, we can proceed to take a closer look at the demands made of them, i.e. the claims that they establish their legitimacy to justify their recognition, set up processes of internal democratic control, and respond to the clamor for accountability and transparency. I will address these issues in the order they were presented.

Legitimacy

In our secular age, it is taken as an article of faith that power, especially political power, can only be 'legitimized' by reference to the will of the people. And, since every human being is essentially valued the same, the majority of the expressions of the will of the people counts. That is why, it is argued, in any political community, the will of the majority of the people need to prevail.

Some of these assumptions are questionable. The will of the majority does not necessarily lead to good results, or wise decisions. But, so in essence Winston Churchill's argument goes, democracy is the 'second-best of all forms of government,' acceptable only because of our failure to know a better one. As Max Weber has demonstrated, as recently amplified by Jost Delbrück in the context of NGOs, there were, and are, other models of legitimacy such as tradition, religion, and charisma.

To ask 'democratic legitimacy' of NGOs in the sense of them reflecting 'the will of the people,' however, runs against their *raison d'être*. In most cases, they have been founded precisely in order to counter the will of the majority. The consequence, however, is this: the majority may accept NGOs as voices in the cacophony of (international and domestic) society, but, since they are not elected by the community at large, they may be legitimately excluded from decision-making for the community at large.

Defenders of NGOs have attacked this line of reasoning by pointing out the lack, or dearth, of popular input, or representation of the true will of the people in modern mass democracies (referring, *inter alia,* to the inordinate amounts of money needed to launch a successful political campaign – the McCain critique –, or the shrewd manipulation of consciousnesses of the masses of politically undereducated people – the 'false consciousness' or *panem et circenses* point). The argument goes: since you (the government) are not truly representative of the will of the people, we (the NGOs) do not need to be either.

This argument does not properly address the concern about legitimacy of any organization. For one, one imperfection does not excuse another. Second, and more importantly, the argument does not take into account the function of NGOs which should drive the assessment of their legitimacy.

NGOs are best understood as associations of people who organize themselves to achieve a particular political end. More profoundly, they articulate, and combine to a pointed political force, the needs and aspirations of individual human beings with respect to a discrete policy issue. Those needs and aspirations, or things humans value, ergo 'values,' have conveniently been described as power, wealth, well-being, affection, enlightenment, skill, respect, and rectitude (with no particular order between them). Law, or governmental decision, effectuates distributions of these values in society. An ideal legal order maximizes access by all to all these things humans desire.

The legitimacy of an NGO in such a dynamic process of social life is tied to the authenticity of its mission, not the strength of its numbers. If the goal is not, as Bentham would have it, 'the greatest happiness of the greatest number,' but access to all values by all, the essential contribution of NGOs is the authentic expression of sincerely held beliefs that represent to the decision-maker in any relevant community a value preference that he/she should take into account when trying to arrive at a solution to the societal problem at issue that approximates the public order of human dignity. The most successful NGOs would be those that make the argument of their preferred solution as representing the common interest of the community most effectively and persuasively.

If authenticity of aspiration in a pluralistic society is thus the touchstone of legitimacy, a good argument can be made for the proposition that NGOs that are founded in order to disguise the real motives of their founders, or are only established to generate wealth or other hidden benefits for their leaders and administrators, would be considered illegitimate. Others, tiny as they might be, are proper amplifications of otherwise isolated and ignored 'voices in the wilderness.'

Ultimately, the effectiveness of any social organization committed to policy changes in an open society, especially one that has only limited resources and/or access to the media, depends on its sincerity and credibility: it needs to be authentic. Legitimacy is achieved, not conferred; and it is promoted by openness on essential facts such as mission, source of funding, activities and impact of the organization.

Recognition

The issue of recognition would arise at both a formal and an informal level. Formally, NGOs strive for recognition at the United Nations or other intergovernmental level; domestically, they have to meet certain requirements for incorporation, tax-exempt status, etc. which allow them to function in a particular state, country and beyond. The legal prescriptions in this area as they relate to recognition requirements for NGOs at international and domestic levels have been criticized and reformed; they need to allow for the representation of authentic voices in the decision-making processes of both arenas.

Informally, recognition within a given community depends on the credibility mentioned above. It generates acceptance or rejection by other members of the community, including those expected to make controlling decisions, i.e. law. Its authenticity *vel non* regarding the representation of certain interests or societal claims makes or breaks an NGO.

Internal Democratic Control

The issue here is the internal structuring of the organization. With the exception of Amnesty International and few others, democracy within an NGO is limited to voting with the pocketbook: if members disagree with a decision from the top, they will not try to dislodge the leaders, but simply stop paying their dues. Dissent is remedied by exiting from the organization (Spiro). Some organizations are not even membership-based such as a foundation or a trust. A corporation would not be controlled by the democratic principle of 'one shareholder, one vote'; obviously, weighted voting governs decision-making in this structure.

In light of the cardinal function of NGOs as representatives of interests in society, large or small, internal democratic control would seem to carry less weight than other concerns. Ralph Nader, for example, would appear to have exactly the same impact upon decision-making processes whether he is the elected representative of an organization or not. The same, however, might not be true for leaders of other organizations. Whether membership-based organizations have their members elect their leaders, or allow dissenting members only the exit option, appears therefore to be more a matter of expediency than a matter of legitimacy.

Transparency and Accountability

The strongest point of the NGO critique is the often-encountered absence, or dearth, of transparency and accountability. There are many arguments in favor of organizational openness and responsibility. The obvious ones are the prevention of fraud and financial mismanagement, as mentioned above. This is a major goal for public order. If an NGO receives public monies, e.g. from USAID, the misuse of it through excessive administrative expenses, cost overruns by subcontractors, etc. diverts funds urgently needed for other programs essential to the community at large. If the abuse is of a criminal nature, the security of a community is at stake, and criminal accountability of the offenders is a needed response.

Beyond the misuse of money, the openness about sources of funding, in particular, and the NGO's mission, activities and expenses would check the *de facto* power of NGOs as much as reporting requirements on lobbyists in the legislative process do. In addition to these advantages to the general public, the benefits of transparency and accountability should be clear to the NGOs themselves. As stated above, the stock in trade of NGOs is their credibility. The sources and use of their entrusted funds should be known to the public, to actual and prospective donors. Such openness ultimately results in more effective championing of causes and endorsements of candidates for public office.

Done right, it also has a chance of significantly improving the organization. Internal evaluations, in particular, spotlight what the organization is doing, how it is doing it, with what impact, etc. Of particular use in this context appears to be Fowler's distinction between output, outcomes and impact. Also, a SWOT analysis could be a helpful method of assessment. These processes could and should be used to highlight problems, streamline internal procedures and ensure compliance with the stated mission.

The downside of strict requirements regarding transparency and accountability is the over-bureaucratization of the effort, the racing from one planning retreat to the other, the development of a cottage industry of evaluators. Also, it is not always easy to measure the impact, as exemplified in, say, an evaluation of NGOs set up to enhance the rule of law in certain countries or regions. When I had the chance of monitoring the American Bar Association's Central and Eastern European Law Initiative, for example, we had to use qualitative rather than quantitative data to gauge the true impact of CEELI's expert assessments of pending legislation in the target countries. Also, the over-formalization of procedures in response to evaluations may leave the organization less flexible when responding to new situations and demands. In addition, there are certain areas that should not be discussed in the sunshine, such as privacy issues of employees, issues of national security, if applicable, etc.

An argument might be made that NGOs should not be subject to the same transparency and accountability regime as government officials, since, after all, they do not make laws, and do not hold similar power over individuals. This argument of asymmetry of power is blunted, however, by reference to, say, the corporate sector, where best practices codes and regimes of voluntary self-restraint have been instituted successfully at both domestic and international levels,

The issue, then, is not whether transparency and accountability of NGOs are needed or desirable. They clearly are. The true issue concerns the ways these goals are achieved. Who does the evaluation: is it internal, external, or conducted both from the inside and the outside? Who is it that the NGOs are reporting to? Beyond the government, the internal revenue services of various countries, and the donors, openness on major data regarding the organization should exist toward the public at large. The modern means of communication, in particular the Internet, should be used effectively for that purpose. Ideally, an annual report on the institution's mission, its activities, sources of funding, its expenses, impacts and plans for the future should be published on the worldwide web.

As to power and inclusion of NGOs in formal processes of domestic and international decision-making, the prevailing debate on the 'international legal subjecthood' of NGOs, limited or not, appears to be singularly unhelpful. Its sterility should be replaced by a functional analysis of areas in which such claims of participation are particularly apposite. In the context of indigenous peoples, I could well imagine, say, the newly-established Permanent Forum on Indigenous Issues, composed, in equal number, by government representatives and representatives of indigenous communities, to provide major benefits for world public order by acquiring the power to address, and decide, conflicts resulting from treaties between States and indigenous peoples.

A final point: the obligation of transparency and accountability upon an actor should be directly proportional to the degree of inclusive influence that it has. This is a principle that should not only apply to NGOs, but also to States and all other categories of actors. Power, public or private, needs to be checked as intensely as it imposes itself.

Conclusion

NGOs perform their function best by not only aggressively and authentically promoting the causes for which they have been established, but by opening themselves up to constant self- and outside scrutiny. Credibility is their major stock in trade. Public trust is gained and maintained by self-critical reporting, not only about successes, but also about failures and the paths chosen to overcome them. Best practices codes or framework conventions could be used to specify these critical requirements of transparency and accountability. Democratic legitimacy appears to be less of a concern, since the amount of support, financial or numerical, for the particular cause championed by the NGO does not necessarily indicate its fitness as a solution maximizing access by all to all the things humans desire, the touchstone of a just public order.

So let us watch NGOs, on websites, if need be, and support their causes if they are truly the voice of the people and bring us a step closer to the goal of a world order of human dignity.

Remarks by Stephan Hobe*

Legitimicy, recognition, democratic control, transparency and accountabilty of Non-Governmental Organisations

I. Introduction – The reshaping of the international system in the era of globalisation and its consequences for international law

It is almost commonplace to state that the international system is undergoing fundamental changes at the transition from the 20th to the 21st century and that the main reason for these fundamental changes is the phenomenon of globalisation.[1] Globalisation, understood as a process of denationalisation, is mainly characterised by the technology-based capacity of international transactions to bypass State control. Be it financial transactions, be it the merger of multinational enterprises, or be it huge streams of information and a transborder mobility of populations of an unknown range, the common denominator is always that the State-based vision on which the old Westphalian system was based, is about to be fundamentally changed. New actors enter the international scene among which transnational corporations and particularly non-governmental organisations play – as will be shown in this paper – an ever increasing role. And it is quite obvious that these fundamental changes have also important repercussions on the structure of international law that, based on the Westphalian system, has very much relied on an almost undoubted control function and law-making capacity of States. The entrance of new actors of a private nature into the international system brings about obvious new problems concerning the access of other actors besides the nation State in general and by this fact particularly the problem of the legitimacy of public authority. In the traditional system, democracy as the exercise of the people's will was the means to legitimise public authority. This was naturally the case within States but also – to a much more limited extent – within international organisations. Today, however, we face a system in which public functions are performed by States,

* Chair for Public International Law, European Law, International and European Economic Law, Jean Monnet Professor, Director of the Institute of Air and Space Law and of the Law Centre for European and International Cooperation at the University of Cologne.

international and supranational organisations, that are supplemented by the increasingly important activities of non-State actors. All these actors become involved in law-making and in the enforcement of and securing compliance with international law.

With regard to these new phenomena, the quite traditional strategies of legitimising public authority must necessarily be transferred to the transnational activities wielding public authority within the multi-layered system of governance.

In this paper, the attempt will be made to answer some of these questions and particularly the question of the legitimicy of actions of NGOs in the exercise of public authority in a system of global governance. This requires an investigation that starts out by first looking into the particular role of non-governmental organisations (*infra* II.), then looks into some specific problems of legitimacy, recognition, and transparency of NGOs (*infra* III.) before the specific problem of accountability of acts of non-governmental organisations is addressed (*infra* IV.). This shall allow for some final conclusions (*infra* V.) as to the function of non-governmental organisations in the multi-layered system of governance.

II. The particular role of Non-Governmental Organisations

1. The problem of an official definition of a NGO

There is no official definition on an NGO. However, State practice and particularly the practice of the United Nations and its organs (ECOSOC) have established some definitional elements.[2]

Generally, NGOs are defined as private associations, founded by natural or legal persons on a private and not-international legal basis. NGOs aim at achieving ideal goals at the international plane. Thereby, the practice of the United Nations also accepts such organisations as non-governmental that show some participation of governments as long as this does not amount to a dominating influence of the States. The organisations must have a certain organisational structure and have their own headquarters. Only those NGOs fall under the definition that are not profit-oriented. Insofar as economic involvement of NGOs is not excluded, one should accept that the main line of their activities is non-profit-oriented. Finally, the organisations must be committed to legally acceptable goals, so that, for example, the Mafia cannot by definition be denominated as an NGO.

2. The different roles of NGOs

NGOs play an important role in a variety of fields. Those encompass, *inter alia*, humanitarian, social and technical aid, the cultural sector, sports, acitvities of the churches and the protection of the environment. Among the more prominent NGOs are, for example, the International Pen Club, Amnesty International and Greenpeace. Apart from these different fields of activity, it is very interesting to observe that their specific activities can be divided into two parts. On the one hand, they are acting on their own if, for example, Amnesty International or Greenpeace campaign against grave violations of human rights or a presumed distortion of the environment. Of particular interest are, however, the activities of non-governmental organisations if it comes to international law-making and law enforcement. One should mention in this regard that based on Article 71 of the UN Charta, the ECOSOC has provided for procedures by which certain NGOs possess the status of observers and have the right not only to attend open meetings of the ECOSOC and of its sub-organs, but also to make written and oral contributions to the deliberations of the respective organs. A similar status is provided for by other UN family organisations and by the Council of Europe. In such a function, NGOs advise the organs of international organisations, but they sometimes even go further which is interestingly reflected by the fact that some of the major universal conferences of the United Nations have also made use of the expertise of NGOs that act as advocates of the public interest of the international community (e.g. Rio, Cairo, Beijing, Vienna).

Particularly in the field of international protection of human rights, the will of NGOs has been developed. Even its law provides for NGO participation. They possess, for example, standing before international human rights courts and before other human rights monitoring bodies, *inter alia* under the protocol additional to the UN Covenant on Civil and Political Rights, the European and the American Human Rights Conventions. Their expertise in the course of their monitoring activities is increasingly made use of by international tribunals, such as the Tribunal on Former Yugoslavia (Rule 74 of the Tribunal's Rules of Procedure), by inviting relevant NGOs as *amici curiae.* Similar monitoring and implementation functions are accorded to NGOs in international conventions concerning environmental protection: This is the case for the so-called Ramsar Convention on Wetlands of International Importance especially as Waterfowl Habitat, the Washington Convention on International Trade in Endangered Species of Wild Fauna and Flora and the Convention to Combat Desertification in those Countries Experiencing Serious Drought and/or Desertification. Moreover, NGOs have played an important role in the evolution of so-called framework conventions. Framework conventions are multilateral conventions which determine only basic principles of intended State conduct. Very often the detailed regulations are left to the later adoption of amending protocols. In cases of highly technical regulations, the regulatory function is even delegated to expert committees or technical institutions being NGOs. The reason for this procedure is that framework conventions of this kind require a higher degree of expertise for the elaboration of the detailed regulations. Moreover, because of the rapidly changing scientific findings they need to be amended relatively frequently. Given the fact that the amending protocols frequently enter into force through a simplified procedure, the regular input by the NGO-experts can well be characterised as being dominant. In short, NGOs supplement and sometimes even substitute the implementation of public tasks incumbent on State parties to the respective conventions. One can make the point that in some instances, e.g. with regard to the Desertification Convention, NGOs are even acting for the implementation of the main goals of the conventions because as grassroot organisations they help to provide the specific network in the particular country suffering from desertification that helps fulfilling the task of the Convention. The different and sometimes very important roles of NGOs make it growingly doubtful whether one can still regard them as entities without any legal subjectivity under international law. Rather, one should make a distinction: Insofar as NGOs are acting particularly within the legal framework of an organ of an international governmental organisation, like is the case for example in the field of protection of human rights, they are incorporated in the exercise of public authority. At least in these cases, their legal subjectivity cannot be totally negated; rather a limited subjectivity under international law on a case to case basis seems to be the appropriate description of that legal status under international law.

III. Specific problems

Among a variety of interesting aspects this paper will now deal with three specific problems. First, the question shall be asked whether or not recognition is required, second the concepts of legitimacy, transparency, and democratic control are looked at and finally and in a more detailed way the problem of accountability will be discussed.

As to the requirement of recognition, we have already seen in the previous section that a de facto recognition takes always place insofar as non-governmental organisations are taking part in the exercise of public authority.[3] In other words, if there is an official request by an international governmental organisation for NGO participation in the official work of the organisation or the organ, a favourable answer to this official request amounts to the recognition of the NGO of exercising public authority. On the other hand, in all those cases where NGOs, e.g. in campaigns for the protection of human rights or for the preservation of the environment act as an "agent of the public interest"[4], even direct protest action against governments which officially exercise public authority can hardly be connected with any kind of official recognition.

The other problem areas under consideration, particularly transparency and democratic control that eventually may contribute to the legitimacy of the acts of NGOs are very much open to discussion. Here precise requirements are much more difficult to establish.

There can be no doubt that NGOs very rarely possess any democratic mandate and that they are in many cases internally not democratically structured. Moreover, even closely connected to this democratic deficit, their internal transparency does in some cases not amount to the kind of transparency they often forcefully ask for. But it is quite questionable whether or not one can and should apply in these cases the criteria of democracy, transparency, and legitimacy as they are used with regard to government, i.e. in the State-internal system. One must always be aware that NGOs act on the international plane, i.e. by way of compliance control, human rights monitoring, and in the field of implementation of environmental law. If one observes for example the activities of intergovernmental organisations one should ask the question in how far criteria like the democracy principle are fulfilled there. We still have, e.g., a widespread discussion if it comes to the democratic deficit of the European Union – an organisation that undoubtedly exercises public authority – and insofar it seems to be a general consensus that democracy cannot be fulfilled to a hundred per cent comparable to the State-internal system. Therefore, applying the criteria that are often used, when for example the democratic deficit of the European Union or of other international intergovernmental organisations is under review, it seems preferable to strengthen participatory surrogates for democratic legitimacy and other means of legitimacy such as efficiency, transparency, accountability and ex post acceptance of public acts. Therefore, transparency in general and accountability in particular as being closely related to the democratic model are also valid as independent criteria of legitimacy if it comes to judging the deficit in fullfilling the democracy principle by NGOs. Consequently, it shall be particularly stressed that, on the one hand, as much transparency as possible is necessary in order to strengthen legitimacy of the work of international non-governmental organisations. On the other hand, as today's international system shall be subject to some form of global governance as a set of pluralistic arrangements by which States, international organisations, international regimes, non-governmental organisations, citizen movements, and markets combine to regulate or govern aspects of global affairs,[5] this pluralistic model comes down to a need of surrogating the democracy principle not only by a necessary demand for greatest transparency of all actors, but also by some kind of accountability for the acts of all actors. Because of the specific problems involved here the criteria for accountability will be addressed in the following separate section.

IV. The specific problem of accountability of acts of NGOs

The concept of accountability is broader than just the legal concepts of liability or responsibility. Besides being responsible for an act in the legal sense, accountability means and encompasses political, administrative, and various informal, non-legal mechanisms by which someone may be held answerable for something.[6] Any invocation of liability or responsibility normally finds its basis in adjudicative means. Besides these means there are, however, various degrees of binding results to be reached by alternative forms of dispute settlement, be it by way of arbitration, mediation, or conciliation or be it by non-compliance procedures, inspection panels, and ombudsman institutions. Particularly the *Brent Spar* incident of 1995 can be taken as an interesting example.[7] Some environmental NGOs, most prominently Greenpeace, had claimed that the dumping of oil from a platform by Shell into the North Sea posed a serious ecological threat to the region. Despite the company's assurances to the contrary, Greenpeace demanded a costly alternative of disposing of the oil platform. The action caused widespread attention including boycott actions against products of Shell. Subsequently, it turned out that most of the NGOs' allegations were incorrect. Shell did not recover the additional costs incurred. Although in this case one can even ask whether or not any kind of legal responsibility of Greenpeace would have effectively brought positive results for the oil company that had suffered serious damage, particularly because of the additional consumers' boycott initiated by Greenpeace concerning the products of the Shell company, it is important to reflect the possible legal consequences of these false allegations. In this respect, it has been asked whether or not legal means like a court injunction enjoining NGOs from making false allegations would be a Pyrrhic victory for the affected companies. Nevertheless possible legal consequences will be discussed in the following.

If one first applies the broader approach of accountability, the establishment of internal accountability mechanisms, like for example inspection panels that have already been set up by the World Bank and other regional development banks, might be one step to get control over NGOs actions. But as the *Brent Spar* example makes evident, it is quite questionable whether such tool can be successful at all.

Therefore in the perspective of this paper, some international legal consequences in terms of responsibility shall be discussed. In principle, four possibilities seem to exist:[8]

First, one could think of the elevation of NGOs to the status of subjects of international law in order to make them directly responsible for violations of the law. But in the case of NGOs this seems not to be very realistic since there is a number of 5.000 to 10.000 NGOs that actually play a certain role. And it is in fact very difficult to grant a legal status to NGOs in respect of all their actions, since, as we have seen before, the kind of necessary recognition can be granted only in cases of some kind of "official" incorporation of NGOs in the work of intergovernmental organizations. Therefore, it seems to be more successful to carefully implement an accreditation policy in terms of allowing only such NGOs to cooperate with UN organs that give a certain guarantee for constructive work with the UN organs. [9]

A second option could be to attribute acts of NGOs to a State that then could be treated as being responsible under international law for acts of the NGO. A possible starting point must be the necessity of a genuine link of the NGO to a State that could normally be provided by the headquarters of an NGO. The concept of de facto organ[10] could be the legal concept under which the attribution of such acts to a State could be envisaged. Article 8 of the Draft Principles on State Responsibility reads: "The conduct of a person or group of persons shall be considered an act of a State under international law if the person or group of persons is in fact acting on the instructions of, or under the direction or control of, that State in carrying out the conduct." But here, of course, it is open to discussion what precisely "control" means. It could arguably be the effective control of the government in the sense of the ICJ's judgement in the *Nicaragua* case[11] or its overall control in the sense of the *Tadić* judgement of the Yugoslav Tribunal.[12]

The third option would promote the enlargement of the validity of human rights also for non-State actors. Here we can observe a certain development in this direction. E.g., more and more transnational corporations accept to be measured against human rights standards with respect to their work. They themselves accept for example the prohibition of slavery or child work as being an important part of their business strategy.

In the same direction goes, as the fourth option, an extension of the validity of human rights with the effect that international law obligations also apply to private actors. This third-party effect of human rights (so-called *Drittwirkung*) could very much be promoted if States would start to translate international human rights into national law obligations for corporations or other international organisations asking them to pursue a certain conduct. In this respect in more recent times, victims of human rights violations have started to institute legal proceedings before national courts, particularly in the United States, alleging various human rights violations committed by transnational corporations.

All options are very difficult to implement in practice. It seems that per se responsibility of NGOs in cases of their official participatory activities could be an appropriate solution. Moreover, in cases of actions arising from the free will of NGOs as "agents of the public interest" an accountability by treating them as de facto organs of the State where they are headquartered could be a solution for this kind of action, based on the understanding that "overall control" is required as control criteria for de facto organs in the sense of Article 8 of the ILC Draft Rules on State Responsibility.

In sum, however, all four options just mentioned are open to discussion if one is of the opinion that non-legal means of accountability in the broader sense of the meaning of this concept are not sufficient and that, therefore, some kind of legal responsibility is required.

V. Conclusion

This paper started out by describing the current effects of the era of globalisation on the development of international law. This law is about to be challenged as profoundly as was the case in previous times when one could observe the first change of paradigm from a mere law of coexistence to a law of cooperation.[13] But the law of cooperation is still very much based on inter-State relationships by the traditional cooperation in intergovernmental organisations. However, in the era of globalisation new actors have arrived at the international legal sphere, actors that reside in the private field like, most prominently, non-governmental organisations and transnational corporations. This indicates also a certain change from State government and inter-State government to governance as a system whereby interested players interact in solving problems, and, on the global level, a pluralistically organized global governance.[14] Hence, in the future, international law has to find answers and has to address the question in how far the actions of non-State actors shall be addressed under international law. Traditionally, the State-centred system of international law-making did not award any law-making function to non-State actors nor did it address the question of accountability or responsibility of non-State actors.[15] This period of time will, however, come to an end. It is one of the most pressing contemporary issues to accept the at least partial law-making function of non-governmental organisations and, on the other hand, look for consequences with regard to their accountability. If this question cannot be answered any longer in a traditional way, i.e., by attributing these acts to States in the international arena, one must look for other options mentioned above. The international system has to be based on the rule of law. We cannot afford loopholes in terms of the accountability of private actors like NGOs as this would be detrimental to the credibility of international law.

Notes

1 J. Delbrück, 'Structural Changes in the International System and its legal order', *Swiss Journal of International and European Law* (2001), 1 et seq.

2 See for the problem of definition and further problems S. Hobe, 'Der Rechtsstatus der Nichtregierungsorganisationen nach gegenwärtigem Völkerrecht', *Archiv des Völkerrechts* (1999) 152, 153 et seq.

3 Hobe, n. 2, 159 et seq.

4 See S. Hobe, 'Global Challenges to Statehood: The Increasingly Important Role of Nongovernmental Organizations', 5 *Indiana Journal of Global Legal Studies* (1997) 191, 208.

5 Commission on Global Governance, Our Global Neighbourhood (1995) 4.

6 See e.g. A. Reinisch, 'Governance Without Accountability', 44 *German Yearbook of International Law* (2001) 270, 274 with further references.

7 Description of the facts by L. Dickson and A. McCulloch, 'Shell, the Brent Spar and Greenpeace: A Doomed Tryst?', *Environmental Politics* (1996) 122 et seq.; L.D. Brown and M. Moore, 'Accountability, Strategy and International Nongovernmental Organizations', *Nonprofit and Voluntary Sector Quarterly* (2001) 569 et seq.; and Greenpeace, archiv.greenpeace.de/GP-DOK-3P/Chronik/ C12CH01.HTM.

8 Discussed by Reinisch, n. 6, 297 et seq.

9 A step into this direction is indicated by the practice of ECOSOC that by Res. 1996/31 applies stricter criteria for the accreditation of NGOs.

10 Art. 8 of the 2001 ILC Draft on State Responsibility, UNGA Res. 56/83 of 12 December 2001; see also Commentaries to the Draft Articles on Responsibility of States for internationally wrongful acts, Doc. A/56/10, Art. 8 and C. Tams, 'All's Well That Ends Well – Comments on the ILC's Articles on State Responsibility', 62

Zeitschrift für ausländisches öffentliches Recht und Völkerrecht (2002), 759 et seq., 795.

11 ICJ Reports 1986, 1, 50 et seq (section 86); 64 (section 115).

12 ICTY, Appeals Chamber, Judgement, 15 July 1999, *The Procecutor* v. *Dusko Tadić a/k/a "Dule"*, Case n° IT-94-1-A, section 116 et seq.

13 W. Friedmann, *The Changing Structure of International Law* (1964).

14 See J.A. Rosenau, 'Governance, Order and Change in World Politics', in J.N. Rosenau and E.-O. Czempiel, eds., *Governance without Government: Order and Change in World Politics* (1992) 1.

15 Description of the evolution by O. Kimminich and S. Hobe, *Einführung in das Völkerrecht*, 7th edn. (2000) 61 et seq.

Remarks by Peter J. Spiro*

Unpacking NGO accountability

In the wake of this new-found power, commentators are coming increasingly to question the legitimacy of non-governmental organizations (NGOs) and the influence they now exert at the international level. This response should come as unsurprising, given the general perception (not all that well-founded) of NGOs as working to advance progressive agendas. For those for whom national sovereignty has emerged as a rallying call, NGOs are now being lumped together with faceless bureaucrats in Geneva as the bugaboos of global governance. In this view, NGOs have mounted a sort of free-form coup against international institutions, representing nothing more than themselves.

Those who resist the assertion of NGO power are perhaps most resistant to their participation in formal international decision-making. That seems to me exactly the wrong answer to the NGO challenge. Wherever power is exercised, questions of accountability are appropriately posed. One can never assume that power will be deployed in a responsible manner; indeed, where power shifts have not yet been reflected in the decision-making architecture, one can assume the opportunity for abuse. NGOs now garner power independent of States and other entities; international law and international institutions, however, are still largely premised on a world in which States had the last word. Some who question NGO legitimacy would simply wish a return to the old world in which States aggregately held most associational power. Insofar as NGO power is beyond the control of States (and of their intergovernmental creatures), it cannot be reversed by the policymakers.

Rather, in what might be called the inclusion paradox, the accountability challenge may be better answered by formally and fully recognizing their power in international institutional architectures. Formal NGO participation in international decision-making would have the effect of outing NGO power and advancing a transparency objective. It would also hold NGOs, as repeat players, accountable to institutional bargains. NGOs now participate in international negotiations, in the hallways or through State surrogates. But because their participation is non-formal, they are free

* Professor, Hofstra University Law School, Hempstead, NY. For an elaboration of the arguments made here, see Peter J. Spiro, 'New Global Communities: Non-Governmental Organizations in International Decisonmaking Institutions', *Wash. Q.*, Winter 1995, at p. 45; Peter J. Spiro, 'New Global Potentates: Non-Governmental Organizations in an 'Unregulated' Marketplace', 18 *Cardozo L. Rev* (1996) p. 957.

subsequently to reject results not to their liking. That threatens to keep the international lawmaking process unstable at a crucial juncture in its evolution.

Unpacking accountability: To constituencies and to process

The accountability card often conflates two types of accountability, internal and external. Internal accountability confronts the agency questions of representation of memberships by necessarily limited numbers of leaders. External accountability addresses the responsiveness of organizations to larger systems of which they are a part. As deployed against NGOs, the first problem is exaggerated, and the second is better answered by elevating, not suppressing, the status of NGOs in the international context.

Internal accountability

No doubt NGO staffs have wide discretion in representing their members or other, less formal constituencies, in many cases wider than that enjoyed by governmental representatives. In the category of membership organizations, with a few notable exceptions (Amnesty International and the Sierra Club among them), the leaderships of most NGOs are not formally elected or otherwise directly answerable to individual members. Individual members are unlikely to monitor complete organizational agendas; insofar as they do engage in such monitoring, they are unlikely to take NGO leaderships to task on particular issues. NGO executive directorates have membership and other funds at their disposal, with few strings attached, and can claim to speak for thousands, sometimes millions of members who as a practical matter exercise little scrutiny of their representatives. The problem is arguably aggravated in the context of non-membership organizations

But these problematizations of internal NGO accountability seem unable to address at least two possible objections. First is that they discount the possibility of competition among NGOs as a form of discipline. Unlike citizens *vis-à-vis* States, the costs of exit for members of NGOs are relatively low. No NGO (at least as defined as an advocacy group) has a monopoly in any particular issue context. Assuming some basic level of monitoring – now often enabled by the mainstream media – one can simply let a membership lapse in the wake of a disagreement with an NGO's policy or tactics, and turn those dollars or other forms of commitment over to another group instead. If nothing else, a group that is ineffective or unresponsive will lose members and other sources of support; in no model where choice is available will a loser sustain support over the long-term.

The second response to charges of internal unaccountability highlights the fetishization of other forms of associations. In other words, compared to what? In this context the democratic State is implicitly idealized on the accountability metric, above all by virtue of periodic elections. But the franchise is itself a crude tool for keeping governmental authorities in line. This is true even in the legislative context, where multiple issues will afford representatives wide discretion, even against collective constituent preferences. This phenomenon will be more characteristic of the foreign policy realm. Here, the relevant decision-maker is typically the executive branch, and particular foreign policy decisions, on anything but the most grave issues of national security, are unlikely to be scrutinized by the average voter (leaving aside the large numbers who do not bother to vote at all). Governments can get away with an awful lot before having to answer to their memberships, and yet of course that has supplied no argument against their participation in international institutions. Indeed, insofar as NGOs tend to be more focused in their issues orientation, their members will be in a better position to monitor and discipline leaderships than are voters with respect to governmental representation. Unlike in the NGO context, the costs of exit from States are quite high.

NGOs are perhaps more appropriately compared to corporations for accountability purposes. In the corporate context, shareholders play the role of NGO members; they may control the corporation as a formal matter, but as a practical one, they are often powerless (in the face of high monitoring costs and collective action problems) to control directors and management. That is not to say, however, that corporations are unaccountable. As with NGOs, in most cases shareholders enjoy the exit options of selling their shares, in rather the same way that NGO members can decline to renew their memberships. Accountability and agency problems are central to corporate law, but are confronted as a challenge amenable to at least incremental amelioration. That should inform a similar orientation with respect to the internal accountability of NGOs. There is surely room for enhancing the discipline of NGOs representatives. In the end, however, this is a question of international not-for-profit law. It may be something more than technical, and will in fact require creative thinking, parallel to the demands globalization poses in the corporate law context. But there is no strong argument here against the NGO participation in international institutions.

External accountability

Issues of external accountability are more submerged and challenging. The question here is how to keep NGOs accountable to the system in which they are exercising power. Before the end of the Cold War and the advent of globalization, NGOs worked through States and had little independent influence; in that context, there was no need to address the issue. Today, the problem is potentially serious. NGOs are significant independent players in the global system, and yet the system does not recognize them as such. As a result, NGOs comprise a potentially destabilizing force. They can use the system to advance their agendas, but are not answerable to the system; they can bring others to task, but have themselves been immune.

That was fine for so long as NGOs remained under the control of another entity which was held responsible for their conduct – namely, the State – but as that control has eroded, NGOs have been able to play the role of policy potentates. NGOs participate in international standards-setting in institutional settings, by influencing State parties to formal negotiations, in some cases through delegation capture. This participation is rarely formal, or at least formal participation is consistently subordinated, consistent with traditional conceptions of international law under which NGOs had no legal personality.

This lack of standing can work to NGO advantage. Because the participation in international decision-making is informal, NGOs have no obligation to respect decision-making results. They first work inside the halls of power, securing what they can in formal, institutionalized results. What they do not get on the inside, however, they can try to secure through other means, rejecting those elements of institutional bargains not to their liking. Insofar as NGOs garner independent power, that rejection can be consequential. By mobilizing consumer constituencies, most notably, NGOs can set regulatory-like standards even where formal regulation would be beyond reach. They enjoy many of the advantages of participation rights without the downside of having to abide by agreements that will inevitably reflect compromise and other interests.

This leads to what might be called the inclusion paradox. States resist enhancing the formal status of non-State actors in international decision-making for fear that it will further fuel the rise of NGOs and threaten the monopoly of States over international lawmaking. But the formal inclusion of non-State actors in international decision-making might present more of a restraint on NGO power than an accelerant. Major NGO players already effectively have a seat at the table; formal, direct participation would not add much to their influence. But it would increase their external accountability. No longer could NGOs opt out of bargains to which they had attached their names. As ongoing institutional participants, they would have a greater incentive to facilitate institutional success. Advocacy groups would no longer be able to launder their influence through pliant front-States or backroom lobbying. In that respect, formal inclusion would also elevate transparency values, as well as accountability among NGOs. Major NGO players would have to answer to their lesser counterparts were they to enjoy rights to represent broad non-State interests in international decision-making.

As a matter of international legal doctrine, the upshot would be formal legal personality for non-State actors, with the rights and responsibilities that such status entails. The former would come primarily in the form of participation rights. The modalities here may be complex and institutionally variable. Selecting participants from among potentially infinite eligible NGOs would present one notable question. In some contexts that challenge appears to have been overcome, for instance, in composing "liaison" committees between non-State and governmental forums at the world summits on women, population and development, human rights, and other subjects. The International Labor Organization, in which employers and unions are directly represented along with States, demonstrates the efficacy of formal non-State participation. Way-station possibilities include advisory committees, as already innovated by the World Bank and the OECD. In judicial-type tribunals, standing to bring suit and to participate in *amicus* capacities present logical end-points. Here the domestic models translate more easily, as gatekeeping is more easily undertaken. The European Court of Justice now accepts NGO submissions, and NGO *amicus* participation in the WTO appears inevitable.

On the responsibilities' side, one could begin to speak of international law violations by entities other than States. Symmetrical to rights of participation would be obligations to respect negotiated results. NGOs could be meaningfully held to the bargains that they entered into in standards-setting processes, so that they could not undertake extrainstitutional action to undermine such bargains. If formally accountable to the process, Greenpeace could not launch a boycott seeking to advance protective standards different from those negotiated among relevant international actors (corporations included). In this respect, formal recognition of NGOs would enhance their external accountability.

Accountability and process stability in international law

External accountability is already being innovated outside of public international institutions. Advocacy NGOs and transnational corporations have been negotiating agreements to govern corporate conduct on such issues as labor rights and environmental protection. Some of these agreements are being elaborated into refined codes of conduct, complete with comprehensive monitoring schemes. For big corporations, these arrangements are "voluntary" in name only; on the contrary, the standards they set are beginning to look like law. Corporations participate because such schemes insure the external accountability of the counterpart NGOs and enhance regime certainty. NGOs participate because it gives them unmediated power.

But the code of conduct model poses its own set of accountability concerns. NGO representation and relations between the various actors will be more difficult to monitor than in a public institutional process. The North-South divide among NGOs may be less vigilantly confronted. The risk of conflicts of interest is also magnified in the private sphere. How, for instance, will those regimes police corporate contributions to their supposed NGO guardians? In these early stages, some of these problems can be mitigated through a form of competition among private codes, as is now occurring in the labor rights context. In the long-run, however, the barriers to entry will be formidable for initiating new regimes, and this check will be effective only against sustained misfeasance.

Hence the possible virtues of migrating such standards-setting to public institutions. Public institutions focus attention, are more likely to achieve universality of coverage, should facilitate monitoring and enforcement, and are ultimately more likely to promote the legitimacy of international law. Enhanced NGO participation is a necessary condition to the stability of standards established in public institutional contexts. Of course, one could not force NGOs to participate. But if major institutions extended meaningful formal channels for participation, there would be powerful competitive incentives (in terms of attracting members and funding) for particular NGOs to sign on.

This leaves us with an answer that transcends the question posed here. The formal inclusion of non-State actors in institutional decision-making will not only advance the accountability of NGOs to the system, such inclusion will advance the system itself. Non-State power is a fact of the new world. International law will need be accountable to that power if it is to emerge the governor of global affairs into the future.

Remarks By Math Noortmann*

Who really needs Article 71? A critical approach to the relationship between NGOs and the UN

Introduction

An obscure consortium of US NGOs with the applicable acronym ABLE, successfully lobbied for the adoption of a provision in the UN Charter that would provide a legal basis for the formalization of arrangements between the United Nations and Non-Governmental Organizations.[1] While early critics wondered whether the result was a great step forward compared to the informal system of the League of Nations, NGOs soon started to apply for a consultative status under Article 71[2] of the United Nations (UN) Charter. A trend was set.

More then 50 years later, Article 71 is still considered to be the prototype provision for the relationship between the UN and Non-Governmental Organizations (NGOs). At the same time, however, it is widely acknowledged that the Article 71 system is only one possibility for arranging UN-NGO relationships. The enormous proliferation and diversification of institutional arrangements between the UN (institutions) and NGOs alone justifies the question: "who really needs Article 71".[3] In this paper, however, I am not interested in identifying and comparing alternative institutional solutions or in "review[ing] existing institutional arrangements and operational practices in the UN system and provid[ing] suggestions for enhancing the participation of non-governmental organizations in all areas of the United Nations system".[4]

The question should focus on the identification of the motives or interests of the stakeholders.... *who* really needs Article 71? The United Nations organization itself is in apparent need of legitimacy, constituency, information and operational assistance, but does this justify the co-optation of NGOs into a formal arrangement? NGOs that seem to be on a collective search for international status and money, conference passes and access to the corridors of decision-making. And last but not least, what about "we, the people"? Do we need Article 71, because it constitutes a form of public participation in the halls of international civil society?

The debate on the form of the relationship, especially the level of formalization and the content of access privileges has been determined by different perceptions on the function of NGOs and international organizations. Ideas on the form and the content of the relationship are neither shared within the NGO community nor within the UN family. Indeed, "[t]he NGO sector constitutes a very diverse institutional category with significant variations with respect to size, resources, impact, methodology, *objectives and approach to international organizations*".[5] The same observation can be made with respect to the UN; its various committees and agencies also differ with respect to the objectives and approaches to NGOs.

In this article, I will question the opinion of (neo)functionalists who consider Article 71 as a contribution to international pluralism in decision-making.[6] The formalized system of Article 71 merely co-opts NGOs into the UN system for UN rather than NGO purposes. The article addresses factors that constrain NGO participation

* Erasmus University, Rotterdam.

in the UN such as the 'screening' and 'performance review' and the rights and duties of NGOs accepted to the system. While a relationship between the formal status and position of NGOs in IOs and the former's ability to influence the latter's decision-making process is frequently assumed, the article does not seek to assess the influence or impact of NGOs in IOs' policies nor does it seek to determine whether one system of NGO participation is inherently superior or inferior to another.[7]

Formalizing institutional arrangements

The League of Nations' system is considered to be the first outstanding example of the 'informal system'. The absence of a formal provision in the League's Covenant[8] did not prevent the organization from maintaining relations with " unofficial organizations dealing with *some aspect or another* of League problems".[9] These relations were in the first years of the League's existence developed and maintained on an informal and *ad hoc* basis.[10]

By 1921, the growing number of NGOs put serious constraints on the League's informal approach, which resulted in an attempt to formalize the NGO/League relationship. On the basis of an extensive and teleological interpretation of Article 24 the League's Council adopted a resolution, which "made it possible for *the patronage of the League* to be given to *all* international bureaux".[11]

Two years later, however, the Council reversed its decision. The Council's reasoning is remarkable. The Council emphasized first of all "the value which it sets on the collaboration with unofficial organizations in the study of specific questions, and its freedom to solicit the opinions of these organizations, without prejudicing their autonomy". In the operative part of the resolution, the Council stated, " it is not desirable to risk diminishing the activity of these voluntary international organizations, the number which is fortunately increasing, by even the appearance of an official supervision."[12]

Various observers and annalists of the League's practice have speculated on the reasons for the decision. White points out that NGO proposals "upset" the established bureaucratic routine which had been developed by the League's civil servants over the years and that the political problem-oriented attitude of NGOs conflicted with the a-political diplomatic approach of the League.[13] Pickard mentions the increase in the number of NGOs and the growing difference in the private, non-governmental character of NGOs and the public, governmental character of international organizations.

It must then be questioned whether the 1923 Resolution merely stopped the process of formalization or whether it reflected a general change in attitude of the League towards NGOs?

Seary maintains that after 1923 "[a]t an informal level, the presence of NGOs was an established fact".[14] But what was the quality of this 'informal presence'? In this respect Seary, observes that "the interaction.... changed from one of NGOs supporting and contributing to the policy work of the League to one where the League was less interested in the opinions of NGOs, but more willing to provide information for and about them."[15] White also concludes that " *the early League attitude* toward the private organizations was one of *wholehearted cooperation*.... [but that i]n the latter years of the League's existence [there was] considerable dissatisfaction among INGO's regarding what they considered to have been a growing tendency of the League to withdraw from collaboration and cooperation".[16]

Whereas the 'informal system' remained 'formally' intact, the experiences of the League have influenced its attitude towards NGO participation. Did these experiences equally affect the actual *ad hoc* arrangements for access and participation? Most writers tend to answer this question in the affirmative. The *ad hoc* structure of the informal system remained the same: NGOs obtained seats on several committees of the League, they were invited as full participants to the League's meetings and conferences and they even occasionally gained voting rights.[17] The more structural arrangements for participation in Committees, which equaled the rights and privileges of Government representatives except for the right to vote, diminished and were 'virtually eliminated' in some committees.[18] Chiang Peng-hei even concludes that

> [t]he method of using NGO assessors, for example, was abolished in 1936 and in its stead a system of correspondents was established with reduced privileges. The correspondent members participated in committee work only upon invitation and *only* when that had special competence in the subject under consideration.[19]

The question is whether and to what extent these experiences and 'new' practices have entered the 'collective memory' of international organizations and influenced subsequent attempts to regulate NGO involvement. Robb's conclusion that, "the League's system of NGO representation paved the way for the more coherent and formal system [the consultative system] which was to follow" could be understood as a cynical remark.[20] Pickard, one of the early critics mentioned in the introduction, doubted from the very beginning whether 'consultation' represents a higher status for NGOs then the 'informal participation without a vote' system within the League of Nations.[21]

ARTICLE 71: FROM CO-OPTATION TO COLLABORATION

The UN officially broke with the established practice of its predecessor, by first creating a formal status for NGOs and later by developing a detailed application procedure designed to screen and assess acceptability. From a (neo)-Marxist approach, the relationship between NGOs and the UN is one that starts with co-optation and ends with collaboration.[22]

The process of co-optation is carefully worked out in ECOSOC Resolution 1996/31.[23] It's clear that NGOs do not get 'consultative' status under Article 71 for free. In order to obtain access to *some* of the meeting rooms, they have to show that they are capable of making "substantive and substantial contributions [...] to the achievement of the objectives of the United Nations", they also have to declare that "if granted consultative status [the] organization will act in accordance with the Charter of the United Nations *and* ECOSOC Resolution 1996/31".[24] On the basis of that unilateral declaration, consultative status can be withdrawn or suspended if (1) the NGO " clearly abuses its status by engaging in a pattern of acts contrary to the purposes and principles of the United Nations including unsubstantiated or politically motivated acts against member States"...or (2) "did not make any positive or effective contribution to the work of the United Nations".[25] The procedure on the withdrawal of the consultative status of Christian Solidarity International demonstrates the highly politicized decision-making process with respect to such cases.[26] Why was the status of CSI revoked? Because it invited the Sudanese rebel leader John Garant to speak as its representative in Geneva, because it bought and subsequently released slaves in Sudan or simply because in the end – as the Algerian representative put it – "NGOs had been given the message that they must abide by United Nations rules".[27] If NGOs "must abide by the United Nations rules", the relationship between 'the bureaucracy and the free spirits' is not as positive as Donini asserts.[28] Hudock has observed a trend to "cultivate informal linkages", because of the existence of constraints of formal interaction between NGOs and the UN.[29] According to the latter author, collaboration between the UN and NGOs is "in many ways…implausible", which can only be explained as a symbiotic necessity. NGO's and the UN have 'allianced' for many reasons. According to Hudock, NGOs " continue to engage with the UN […], since the relationship [] provide[s] them with resources, recognition, and in some cases the change to influence politics".[30] NGOs seem to prefer these benefits to the "danger of co-optation" by agencies, which they "provide […] with an opportunity publicly to support development efforts towards the poorest groups, while at the same time retaining policies which worsen their conditions".[31]

This observation raises the question as to why the UN needs NGOs. The answer is twofold. The UN needs NGOs to deliver service and provide information, as well as legitimacy and promotion.

With respect to the information flows we are tempted to recall Seary's observation that when the League of Nations became "less interested in the opinions of NGOs", [they became] more willing to provide information for and about them."[32] The question is whether the one-dimensional focus on information flows has been altered in the UN system. NGOs are in a clear need for access to the UN's optical disc system, access to document distribution counters, the promptness and comprehensiveness of information, and last but not least the availability of information for NGOs in less developed regions,[33] The UN seeks to obtain a "composite picture of the NGO community".[34]

According to the NGLS, "The importance of working with NGOs as an integral part of the United Nations information activities was recognized when the DPI (UN Department of Public Information [MN] was established".[35] The Resolution establishing the DPI, however, limits and qualifies "the importance of working with NGOs" to "actively assist and encourage ….[NGOs] …interested in spreading information about the UN".[36]

Is co-operation beyond Article 71 undesirable?

Scholars continue to observe that NGO participation evolves "in a most diversified way, beyond the formal framework of Article 71".[37] This development includes the informal participation of NGOs in the work of the Assembly's Main Committees, UNGA subsidiary bodies, UN Programs and conferences and even Security Council committees have occasionally granted NGOs access to their sessions in order to report on violations of sanctions. [38] According to Willets, "it is unclear whether these are isolated events or the first step down the road towards regular direct involvement in the Assembly."[39] The UN stresses that "the Consultative status with the Economic and

Social Council remains at the core of the formal relationship between the United Nations and NGOs [and that] no such arrangement has been established by the General Assembly".[40]

The UN clearly has an interest in reinforcing the Article 71 system. Why? Does the diversity in NGO status, procedures, rights and duties hamper effective NGO participation and effective utilization of NGO expertise by the UN at large? The Secretary-General's 1998 Report demonstrates, that appeals for 'streamlining and updating' the UN system should be taken seriously.[41] Can we expect a new wave of formalization? Are Article 71 procedures going to be extended to other – more informal – institutional arrangements, confining the status of NGOs to a consultative one? The fear for extended co-operation outside the Article 71 framework seems to be triggered by (1) the fear for formalizing the relationship between NGOs and the UN General Assembly and (2) the fear for a growing and unbridled network between NGOs and the UN and the increasing desire for participation of the former movement.

The discussion on the modalities of an arrangement between NGOs and the UNGA cannot but center around the observer status which according to Sybesma-Knol is "fundamentally different" from consultation. According to the latter writer, the observer status is (1) granted by the General Assembly and thus (2) entails recognition, and (3) is informal and *ad hoc*.[42] Additionally, Sybesma-Knol suggests that no clear criteria are established for granting an observer status. She expects "so dramatic an expansion of the number of requests that the General Assembly will either have its work impaired or will have to consider drastic curtailment of privileges that flow from observer status".[43] But is it really this technical argument, which prevents the UN from considering this possibility or is it the desire to formally confine NGOs to the corridors of ECOSOC?

Until 1960, the UNESCO regime was characterized by its "very close relationships....on an *ad hoc* basis and with a relatively small number of NGOs".[44] On the basis of this characterization the UNESCO regime can be defined as an 'informal' one, in the first 15 years of its existence. According to Hoggart, UNESCO had to 'formalize' the regime because "the number [of NGOs] increased significantly in the late 1950s".[45]

Hoggart endorses the presumption that a causal link exists between the number of NGOs participating in the system and the 'informal' character of the regime. At the same time he suggests that UNESCO preferred quantity to quality. The formalization process resulted in a set of *Directives Concerning UNESCO's Relations with International Non-Governmental Organizations.* NGOs became obliged to: (1) provide advice, (2) offer technical cooperation, (3) express views and opinions, and (4) assist to prepare and execute programs of activities.

The system of categorization mirrors the ECOSOC regime. However, the criteria for categorization are considered to be fundamentally different. According to Hoggart, the ECOSOC categorization is based on the activity of the NGO in question, whereas the UNESCO categorization is based on the degree of cooperation.[46] From a formal point of view, Hoggart is right. However, in the case of ECOSOC we can also observe cases of categorization, which are not exclusively based on the 'activity' of an NGO. In the UNESCO categories we also find NGOs, which cannot be considered to belong there on the basis of the degree of cooperation. In this respect, practice differs from theory in both regimes and the 'fundamental difference' is mitigated in practice.

It is interesting to note that Hoggart concludes that " [t]he 1960 Directives are detailed, helpful and precise as to the rights and duties of NGOs; indeed they are wide, liberal and enabling… [and] they have stood the test of time well and are still in force…[but] the recent increase in numbers….has put the system under stress".[47] This observation tends to the conclusion that formalization and regulation of NGO involvement is not the solution to the increase in the numbers of NGOs participating in the work of an IGO.

Conclusions; dangerous liaisons

The question as to 'who needs Article 71' is difficult to answer. The UN and NGO-community have entered a formal relationship, which not only creates opportunities but tensions as well. To the extent that the formal arrangement is designed only for a relationship between NGOs and the ECOSOC (bodies), other UN bodies and NGOs will enter into less formal relationships. The decision to enter into a less formal relationship is based on a negative consideration. However, if the duties and obligations of NGOs under the Article 71 scheme are taken into account, the possibility to enter into less formal relationships with UN bodies must be considered as a real option. The possible danger in this case is that NGOs will be (mis)used for various tasks and operational matters without a clear agreement on specific rights and duties of the parties involved in a specific project.

From a Marxist perspective, the relationship between NGOs and the UN must be seriously questioned. According to Petras and Veltmeyer, the fact that NGOs are "embedded in the world of institutions" stands in contrast with their 'basic philosophy … transform solidarity into collaboration and subordination into self-exploitation". NGO – International organizations relationships do seem to achieve the exact opposite according to the latter authors. The question whether "[W]e, the people…" do need the UN-NGO relationship and collaboration is from a Marxist perspective equally easy to answer: " [t]here is a direct relation between the growth of NGOs (so vividly demonstrated by the list of NGOs with consultative status) and the decline of living standards".[48]

Article 71 has become a symbol rather then a vehicle of progress. A reconsideration of the relationship between the UN and NGOs is required. Civil society is not served by co-opting NGOs into a bourgeois governmental or State system, but by creating independent opposition to secure the necessary checks and balances to establish a livable, just, sustainable society.

Notes

1 For a detailed account on the history of Article 71, see Chiang Pei-heng [1981] 39-49, Seary [1996] 25-27.

2 Article 71 reads: The Economic and Social Council may make suitable arrangements for consultation with non-governmental organizations, which are concerned with matters within its competence. Such arrangements may be made with international organizations and, where appropriate, with national organizations after consultation with the Member of the United Nations concerned.

3 See United Nations Non-Governmental Liaison Service (NGLS), *The NGLS Handbook*, 3rd edn. (2000).

4 See report on the 'Arrangements and practices for the interaction of non-governmental organizations in all activities of the United Nations System', UN Doc. A/53/170, 10 July 1998.

5 Report SG [1998] [italics MN].

[6] Reinalda, B., 'Private in form, Public in Purpose: NGOs in International Relations Theory', in Arts, Noortmann, Reinalda, eds., *Non-State Actors in International Relations* (Ashgate 2000) p. 19.

[7] Such a presumption can according to the present author be detected in the writings of scholars who consider the possibility that one system could function as 'a model' for NGO participation. See e.g.Virginia A. Leary, 'The ILO: A model for Non-State Participation', in Van Boven, Flinterman, et al., eds., *The Legitimacy of the United Nations: Towards an Enhanced Legal Status of Non-State Actors* (Utrecht 1997) at 61.

[8] Article 25 of the Covenant of the League of Nations reads: The Members of the League agree to encourage and promote the establishment and cooperation of duly authorised voluntary Red Cross organizations having as purpose the improvement of health, the prevention of disease and the mitigation of suffering throughout the world. Article 24 provided for the placement "under the direction of the League of all international bureaus already *established by general treaties*" [italics MN].

[9] Cited from White [1968] at 250 White, L.C., *International Non-Governmental Organizations: Their Purposes, Methods, and Accomplishments* (1968).

[10] See White [1968] at 248, Chiang Pei-heng [1981] at 85, Chiang Pei-heng, *Non-Governmental Organizations at the United Nations: Identity, Role and Function*, 1981. The League of Nations' Charter only provided for a special relationship with the 'national Red Cross organizations' (Art. 23).

[11] League of Nations Council Resolution of 27 June 1921, League of Nations, *Handbook of International Organizations* (1925) at 8 (quoted from Chiang Pei-heng [1981] at 36). [italics MN].

[12] *League of Nation's Official Journal*, 4th Year no. 8. (quoted from Chiang Pei-heng [1981] at 36).

[13] See *idem.*

[14] Seary [1997] at 22.

[15] Seary [1996] at 23.

[16] White [1968] at 252 and 254.

[17] For concrete examples see generally, Seary [1996] at 22-24, Seary, B., 'The Early History, from the Congress of Vienna to the San Francisco Conference', in P. Willetts, ed., *"The Conscience of the World"; The Influence of Non-Governmental Organizations in the UN System* (1996) at 15-30.

[18] See Seary [1996] at 23, White [1968] at 254.

[19] Chiang Peng-hei [1981] at 38.

[20] Robb [1955] at 6. Robb, Janet, Conference of Consultative Non-Governmental Organizations, Charter Review Study Group. 'Historical Background of Article 71'. Submitted to the 6th General Conference, New York 9 June 1955. (quoted from Chiang Peng-hei [1981] at 39).

[21] Pickard [1956] at 24-27, Pickard, B., The Greater United Nations, 1956, see also Chiang Pei-heng [1981] at 7.

[22] See Petras, J., and Veltmeyer H., *Globalization Unmasked, Imperialism in the 21st Century* (2001) at 128-135.

[23] ECOSOC Res. 1996/31, 49th plenary meeting 25 July 1996.

[24] See Form for Application for Consultative Status with ECOSOC, at <http://www.un.org/esa/coordination/ngo/documents.htm>.

[25] ECOSOC Resolution 1996/31, Art. 57 *sub* (a) and (c).

[26] Press Release ECOSOC/5876, 26 October 1999.

[27] *Idem.*

[28] See Donini, A., "The bureaucracy and the free spirits: stagnation and innovation in the relationship between the UN and NGOs', in 16 (3) *Third World Quarterly* at 421-438.

[29] Hudock [1999] at 50. Hudock, Ann C., *NGOs and Civil Society Democracy or Proxy?* (1999).

[30] *Idem* at 52.

[31] *Idem.*

[32] Seary [1996] at 23.

[33] See UN S-G report [1998] at paras. 77 and 78.

[34] *Idem.*

[35] NGLS Handbook 2000: 12.

[36] *Idem.* In other international organisations, the problem of disclosure of information to NGOs has been a more fundamental problem. The European Bank for Reconstruction and Development adopted a policy on Disclosure of Information only in 1996. According to Hallo, "the latest trend in the information disclosure policy of the EBRD and World Bank is to encourage involvement of local or national NGOs rather than that of the International NGO movement." See, Hallo [1996] at 73. Hallo, R et al., Multilateral Lending Institutions and Public Participation, Beyond Boundaries, in the Regional Environmental Center for Central and

Eastern Europe, The international dimension of Public Participation for the Countries of Central and Eastern Europe (1996) at 65-77.

37 Sybesma-Knol [1997] at 38.

38 See *idem,* Willetts [1996] at 53.

39 Willetts [1996] at 53. But see Sybesma-Knol [1997] at 38 who asserts that "this trend has been a rather continuous one."

40 UN-SG Report 1998, para. 8.

41 See Sybesma-Knol [1997] at 38.

42 Sybesma-Knol [1997] at 27.

43 *Idem* at 26.

44 Hoggart [1996] at 101. Hoggart Richard, 'UNESCO and NGOs: A Memoir', in P. Willetts, ed., *"The Conscience of the World": The Influence of Non-Governmental Organizations in the UN System* (1996) at 98-115.

45 *Idem.*

46 Hoggart [1996] at 102.

47 Hoggart [1996] at 101-102.

48 Petras, J., and Veltmeyer H., *Globalization Unmasked, Imperialism in the 21st Century* (2001) at 129.

REMARKS BY CAROL LYONS*

No paper received.

DISCUSSION

The convener remarked that in the drafting process of the European Constitution NGOs (as well as the European Parliament) were sidelined by the Council of Ministers.

FEMKE DE LANGE (University of Tilburg): 'How do the panel members view the fact that in spite of the 1995 Brent Spar incident, the UNECE 1998 Aarhus Convention on Access to Information, Public Participation and Access to Justice in Environmental Matters, gave NGOs explicit rights, and only required them to have the official aim of protecting the environment?'

THEO VAN BOVEN (NVIR; University of Maastricht): He remarked that the issue of accountability and responsibility of NGOs is 'very fashionable' these days, and asked for some caution in this respect. He pointed out their variety: Some of them have a private character; others, a public character; and many, in fact, work for justice and human rights as well, and they are running serious risks. As *rapporteur* on torture, he received 80 or 90% of his information from NGOs and they do so often at great risk. It is the tendency of many governments to control them, to restrict their activities and to discredit them. As responsible international lawyers, we should not play in the hands of those governments and other sectors in the international society (referring to the newly established 'NGOs Watch'). Instead of putting so much emphasis on control and on responsibility, we should also think on protection and the rights of the NGOs, and put emphasis on that aspect from the international law perspective.

AUGUST REINISCH (University of Vienna): He addressed the first three panellists on the question of the legal personality of NGOs. We should not worry so much about their accountability and responsibility, but rather about their free activity. It is not sure that legal personality under national or international law would be a viable

* University of Aberdeen.

option for NGOs accountability taking into account their structure; their disappearance, for instance, may be easy, unlike the same possibility for States.

SUSAN LEUBUSCHER (European Court of Justice): She addressed the issue of accountability of NGOs. In terms of internal accountability, the issue does not concern international law. In terms of external liability, the NGO experience is not clear, because they do not always act responsibly. In terms of environmental NGOs, she pointed out that we should look into accountability to their goals.

CYRIL FEGUE (Free University of Berlín): World politics and international relations are experiencing profound changes in which the postulate of democratisation of the international decision-making institutions is at the forefront. That democratisation is mainly conditioned by the co-optation of NGOs in the UN, the key organization. Article 71 of the UN Charter is central here. Nevertheless, the question of the legitimacy of NGOs seems not to have received the necessary attention within the global bodies. Do the conceptual underpinnings of Article 71 symbolise a clear and moral recognition of NGOs as democratic agents? Was it just a decision under civil society pressure? If so, what are the next challenges towards wider *de facto* legitimisation of NGOs as a legal enforcement of the democratisation of the decision-making process within the UN system? What will be the legal configuration of the growing phenomenon of the 'public-private partnership' in post-modern international relations?

ELLEN HEY (Erasmus University): What happens with NGOs at the international and European level, also happens in The Netherlands, where they work in a different way from ten years ago. An important difference is the existence at the national level of certain legal procedures for both, NGOs and government, where the former may be held accountable to the latter. NGOs play a very important role in human rights and environmental matters. In her opinion, the question of their legal personality is a very theoretical one.

SOPHIE VAN BIJSTERVELD (University of Tilburg): She directed two questions to Carol Lyons: Do you think the development of involvement of NGOs in international policy-making in the context of international organisations can be turned back? If not, would it then not be better simply to accept this development as a given fact, and try to deal with it both in its positive aspects (rights) and with regard to necessary constraints (conditions)?

TONY BUNYAN (Statewatch): He recalled it was put forward that States and governments should be responsible for the actions of NGOs under international law. He imagined a demonstration where hundreds of NGOs take part and protest. If governments are to be held accountable for those groups, then they will deny the right to free movement and the right to protest, and this is very dangerous for democracy.

CAROL LYONS (University of Aberdeen): She answered Mrs van Bijsterveld by saying that clearly some NGOs do a work of great value, and added that NGOs participation is a meagre excuse for democracy because the reality of such participation in challenging EU legislation by judicial review is so limited. She also considered herself cynical about the real role of NGOs and how EU institutions are manipulating them, but not about the NGOs motivations and the work they do.

MATH NOORTMANN (Erasmus University): He said 'yes', in relation to the question whether Article 71 of the UN Charter provides for some legitimacy to the number of NGOs which participate under it, but just in a legal sense. He added that NGOs also need some political legitimacy and was of the opinion that the UN is not concerned about what kind of NGOs fall under the Article 71 regime. He considers Article 71 as giving a legal status to NGOs, but not legitimacy at all.

PETER SPIRO (Hofstra University Law School): He agreed with Theo Van Boven in not playing in the hands of those governments which try to discredit NGOs activities, but added that in the face of NGOs power one cannot ignore the questions of accountability and responsibility. He also commented on August Reinisch' words, by saying that the question of how easy NGO' s may disappear is similar to the situation of corporations. Last, he concluded by saying with regard to Ellen Hey's comments that she was right, but that there is nothing wrong in trying to articulate a theoretical basis for the legal personality of NGOs.

STEPHAN HOBE (University of Cologne): On the one hand, the international system is changing in many respects; and, on the other, international law has not yet adapted to these changes. He gave the example of international lawmaking, which takes place mainly in international organizations. There, the democratic element comes in via the participation of NGOs. Some NGOs participate officially in the international legal process since they acquired legal personality, like the International Committee of the Red Cross. He admitted August Reinisch' argument about how easy NGOs may disappear and that it is difficult to do something here. Finally, he proposed to strengthen NGOs participation in international law-making and to strengthen international control mechanisms, thereby admitting, for example, NGOs to do their work and involving them in respect of the effects of their participation.

SIEGFRIED WIESSNER (St. Thomas University): He considered unhelpful the discussion about international legal personality of NGOs, because it does not relate to what happens in reality. He definitely agreed with Professor van Boven in relation to the protection to be given to NGOs, but he also was of the opinion that some of them have problems of nepotism and mismanagement and need to be watched.

Finally, the convener thanked the panellists and the floor.

*Reporter: Fabián Raimondo**

* University of Amsterdam.

Review of Application of Principles of Good Governance by International Organizations in Practice

This panel was convened by its Chair, Theodor Meron.*

Introductory remarks by Theodor Meron

International organisations, be they governmental or non-governmental, are often advocates of "good governance" for States, corporations and other entities. More rarely, however, attention is turned to their own governance structures. It seems reasonable that these organisations, especially when they are large donors, should strive to achieve the same "good governance" that they expect of the organisations and individuals with whom they interact. The EU, for example, should display accountability and democratic procedures not only to ensure that Member States and their populations have faith in its abilities as a governing and policy-making body, but also as an example to governments and institutions who are recipients under their development programmes.

Pinning down the concept of "good governance", though, is no easy task and, while we can draw up lists of items that can be included on the good governance 'shopping list', international organisations and governments adopt a wide variety of definitions, making comparison of policies, and evaluation of their application, difficult.

Nevertheless, while a 'shopping list approach' to defining governance may be less than perfect, it does at least identify a number of general areas that are worthy of scrutiny. In their remarks today, the panelists will refer to a number of topics that we can reasonably include on such a list, for example: accountability, transparency, access to information, anti-corruption, democratic procedures, rule of law, human rights, decentralization, and the advancement of women. We expect international organizations to implement policies that at least go some way towards achieving these goals and almost all organisations now have policy statements setting out how they are working towards some or all of these aims. The views of my colleagues on the panel represent a range of opinions to help us review how well international organisations are doing, if they are doing enough, or even if they are doing too much in their pursuit of "good governance".

* Judge, International Tribunal for the former Yugoslavia.

Remarks by John King Gamble and Amanda Grolemund*

Excellent governance and functional failure: An impossible juxtaposition?

A skeptical approach

As our cynical title might suggest, these remarks are skeptical: will heightened concern for good governance have any positive effect? Why settle for good governance? Should not the goal be excellent governance? Is it possible to adhere to a long list of good governance standards and still accomplish little according to the official objectives of an international organization? Put more concretely, could the FAO operate nearly flawlessly according to accountability, transparency, anti-corruption, democratic procedures, decentralization, etc.[1] and still not "raise levels of nutrition around the world, make food production and distribution more efficient, and improve the conditions of rural life."[2]

On a theoretical level, it is difficult to argue with most of the principles usually thought to be key to good governance. Do we really need to debate such self-evident principles? It is similar to the argument in the United States during the 1990s about vending machines, 300 kg, 2.5 metre tall contraptions from which college students – and professors – buy unhealthy food. If these machines malfunction and do not dispense the item purchased, college students get very angry. Some even shake the machines violently occasionally toppling them over. Do these machines need warning signs saying "DO NOT SHAKE" this 300 kg machine, it might fall over and kill you? Are principles of good governance as self-evident as the fact people should not shake vending machines? If so, much of the discussion of good governance may be a misdirected distraction from important issues.

One of the most frequently-cited aphorisms in political science and public administration comes from British poet and philosopher Alexander Pope who wrote:

> For forms of government let fools contest;
> Whate'er is best administer'd is best.
> For modes of faith let graceless zealots fight;
> His can't be wrong whose life is in the right.[3]

Pope's observation certainly is profound; no wonder Voltaire called Pope's essay "the most beautiful, the most useful, and the most sublime didactic poem ever written in any language."[4] Many IGOs have elaborate websites explaining their adherence to principles of good governance, but do these really matter much in comparison to accomplishing their mission.

Anyone living in the post-World War II era cannot help but be struck by an increasing emphasis on evaluation, assessment, total quality improvement, etc., goals that sound much like good governance. Universities in the USA want good teachers, an unassailable goal. Pennsylvania State University, one of the largest in the USA, uses

* John King Gamble, Professor of Political Science and International Law and Amanda Grolemund, Schreyer Scholar, The Behrend College, The Pennsylvania State University, Erie, PA 16563 USA telephone: 814.898.6291, e-mail: jkg2@psu.edu.

a student evaluation questionnaire for virtually every course taught. Further, there are peer reviews of teaching, alumni surveys of former students, pre and post-tenure reviews of teachers, a self-assessment program, and a huge central office charged with the improvement of teaching quality. Do these do any good? Probably they do, but at what cost? All organizations need ways to assess the effectiveness of their programs, but it can seem that organizations spend more time evaluating, assessing, explaining, etc. than actually doing their job, a situation that we call hyperbureaucratization.[5]

Vastly different kinds of organizations have been plagued by hyperbureaucratization. A recurring problem with communist political systems starting with the Soviet Union was excessive centralization and planning coupled with ultimate accountability to the Communist Party often defying commonsense and economic rationality. Civil servants in the United Kingdom today are so concerned about "excessive bureaucracy and ill-conceived government performance targets" that many are leaving their jobs.[6] Even an organization one would think has clear goals and an explicit chain of command, the United States Marine Corps, bemoans the "profound and negative effect" of "bureaucratic expansion at the tactical level."[7]

Good governance applied by international organizations, if carried too far, can produce hyperbureaucratization. The existence of hyperbureaucratization in IGOs, NGOs, universities, foreign ministries, law firms, almost any large organization, is undeniable. The Reagan and Thatcher "revolutions" of the 1980s were reactions against the perceived hyperbureaucratization of governments. The problem, of course, is to distinguish between reasonable levels of transparency, control, and accountability and these same tendencies carried to extreme, hyperbureaucratization. The 1980s saw fierce disagreements in many countries including Britain, the USA, and Canada. The governments of Prime-Ministers Thatcher and Mulroney and President Reagan thought government had become too large, inefficient, and unresponsive, hyperbureaucratized. Political opponents asserted the real reason was their fundamental dislike and distrust of government.

The neo-conservative ideologies of Reagan, Thatcher, etc. held that the marketplace was the best remedy for hyperbureaucratization. Privatize inefficient government enterprises and Adam Smith's invisible hand will produce goods and services efficiently as people "vote" with the choices made in a free market. The rapid growth of free market economies during the 1990s shows that scores of governments accepted the fact that many activities are better carried out by the private sector.

Hyperbureaucratization is facilitated by certain characteristics of organizations. Every large organization has potential turf wars, e.g., does the foreign or the defense ministry play the primary role in implementing a particular policy. Large international organizations have turf wars; they also are susceptible to problems arising from the fact they are creatures of States that voluntarily established a new entity, the IGO. As the European Union demonstrates on a daily basis, there is constant tension between those who see the principal locus of power resting with Member States themselves and those who believe power has been transferred to the organization in order to fulfill the mandate of the constituent document. Pleas for good governance in IGOs often can be traced to opposing philosophies about where the center of gravity of authority should lie. At the extreme, calls for good governance can be a subterfuge by those who dislike an organization and prefer paralysis to action.

Organizational effectiveness becomes more difficult when primary and secondary goals are intermingled. This example from the United States illustrates the point. Billions of dollars per year are provided by the national government to the 50 states to assist with the cost of building and maintaining highways. However, governments at both levels add requirements that have nothing directly to do with building the best possible roads for the lowest price per kilometer. For example, it is common to require that some percentage of the contract value be set aside for businesses owned by minorities. Further, contractors may be required to pay wages higher than those prevailing in the local area and to use materials made in the USA. These represent positive social goals but they increase cost and bureaucratic complexity. Goal co-mingling occurs in international organizations as well, e.g., in the requirement that nationals of all Member States be represented in specified numbers among the staff. These factors acting in concert create the impression of lethargy and ineffectiveness and pressure for "solutions" often cast in terms of good governance.

DEFINITIONS AND TYPOLOGIES

Given the attention it commands – witness this conference – there have been very few articles dealing directly with the idea of good governance as applied to international organizations. Further, writers seem to assume there is consensus on what "good governance" means but show considerable divergence when they try to define terms. One must begin with at least some attention to understanding "governance". Political scientist James Rosenau was one of the first to deal with the concept. He found the notion of government too limiting tied as it was to States. The broader concept of governance is more useful and will be "transcendent" starting in the late twentieth century.[8]

Francis Botchway defined governance as "the exercise of political power to manage a nation's affairs."[9] However, such a formulation seems little different from government and is not clearly expandable to encompass international organizations. Subsequently in his article, Botchway takes a more expansive view remarking that "good governance is the search for the proper role of the law, mainly via the State, for the economic and social modernization of society."[10]

From these vague and imprecise notions of "governance", "good governance" seems to have taken on a life of its own. A UNDP paper makes the amazing assertion that "it is only with good governance that we can find solutions to poverty, inequity, and insecurity."[11] This leads to the suspicion that good governance can be anything that works; Pope would be smiling.

Botchway whose article began modestly asserts:

> The 'elevation' of good governance to the position of a principle not only legitimizes its status as an inexorable and self-evident truth or standard but also grounds the emanation of constituent elements to concretize it. These elements considered important include competitive democracy, the rule of law, effective bureaucracy, discretion and decentralization.[12]

The ILA Committee on the Accountability of International Organisations has produced several important reports dealing with the subject of good governance. The most recent of these reports produced for the 2002 New Delhi Conference stated:

> The principle of good governance (or of good administration) as it is commonly understood, and which is of an evolving nature, includes the following elements: transparency in both the decision-making process and the implementation of the ensuing institutional and operational decisions; a large degree of democracy in the decision-making process; access to information open to all potentially concerned and/or affected by the decisions at stake; the well-functioning of the international civil service; sound financial management; and appropriate reporting and evaluation mechanisms.[13]

Others find a naïve superficiality in applying these principles, e.g., that they boil down to a shopping list of requirements including "accountability, transparency, anti-corruption, rule of law, advancement for women, democracy and decentralization."[14] Not only can these principles be applied arbitrarily, but they can work at cross purposes with one another. There also is the issue of how broadly applicable these principles are, e.g., if they were championed by international development institutions, do they "fit" other contexts?

Given these major reservations about the viability of the concept of good governance, it becomes even more important to ask how and where these principles might be applied. The following simple scheme suggests four possibilities:

	Focus of good governance efforts	
Type of Organization	intramural	extramural
NGOs	A	B
IGOs	C	D

The above framework illustrates that one might look at non-governmental organizations or inter-governmental organizations and for each apply principles of good governance to internal operations (intramural) or to the standards the organization demands from those entities to whom it renders services or makes demands (extramural). Of course, there is considerable seepage among the four possibilities suggested above. For example, an IGO whose internal workings are transparent, democratic and accountable is more likely to demand similar behavior from others and have credibility in doing so; this would be seepage from C to D.

Listing good governance characteristics is not difficult. Applying them is much more problematic. More than 100 years ago, Max Weber taught the world that modern, complex bureaucracies need different modes of analysis. However well-intentioned attempts to demand good governance from IGOs might be, one must remember that one size of governance standards does not fit all contexts. The concept of governance originally "meant the exercise of political power to manage a *nation's* affairs."[15] [emphasis added] Practices developed for national governments or private enterprise may not be easily transferred to IGOs. Attempts to expand good governance principles even further to non-governmental organizations pose even greater difficulties. The number, diversity, and lack of information about NGOs make them very difficult to accommodate. It has been estimated there are more than 15,000 international NGOs, defined as operating in more than two countries and financed internationally.[16] It is arguable that NGOs are so diffuse and illusive that trying to analyze them in the same way as IGOs is at least confusing and maybe impossible.

Recommendations

With more than 2000 major IGOs, it is not feasible to discuss how each has reacted to the good governance movement, but a few illustrations are needed. IGOs have responded in very diverse ways to calls for good governance. The FAO is one example. Director-General Jacques Diouf has spent enormous effort much of which has been aimed at explaining the FAO's mission:

> This practice [monthly seminars] eventually reflected in the Corporate Communication Policy and Strategy relating to externally directed activities in general and informing Permanent Representatives on key programs and achievements. The concept also became part of the overall package of reforms introduced in the Organization to enhance operating efficiency and improve certain elements of governance; more recently, it has been incorporated in the Organization's Strategic Framework as being related to one of the major comparative advantages of FAO.[17]

These efforts seem well intentioned; some even trumpet the FAO as an example of good practices. However, a more critical examination might conclude these actions amount to nothing more than clever public relations and commonsense, e.g., find leaders "with good managerial skills"[18]

The poster child for IGO excesses may well be UNESCO. *The Wall Street Journal* wrote:

> The U.N. Educational, Scientific and Cultural Organization is almost a textbook case of gross mismanagement and political failure. . . . Consensus has disappeared. The agency has been degraded, debased and nearly destroyed. Its staff is demoralized, its civil servants terrorized, its programs chaotic, its spending out of control and the simplest bookkeeping and personnel systems have become nightmares of inefficiency, favoritism and boondoggling. . .By radically increasing the ratio of support staff – such as gardeners, chauffeurs and secretaries – to professional staff, Mr. M'Bow's UNESCO appears primarily preoccupied with the sustenance and maintenance of the headquarters' bureaucracy.[19]

Mr. Federico Mayor who followed Mr. M'Bow as Director-General attempted reform but was criticized for mismanagement. Mr. Koichiro Matsuura, a Japanese diplomat elected in 1999, had a "mandate to simplify its sprawling bureaucracy and woo back Washington."[20] Soon after assuming the leadership post, he described UNESCO this way:

> It is more of a think tank. It should be measured by its programs and ideas. Thus, because people represent UNESCO's main capital, 60% of its annual $272 million budget goes to administration, and it is also vulnerable to bad management at the top.[21]

Does this represent good governance in action? None of the usual watch words is used. However, the idea that accomplishments should be measured against the nature of the mission and that attention should be paid to the portion of the budget going to administration are important principles that might well improve the operation of international organizations.

Where does this leave us? It would be unfair to dismiss the good governance movement as much ado about nothing. Tautological as it may seem, good governance is important because it is perceived to be so:

> Indeed, these institutions themselves have put good governance on the agenda because they realize the extent to which their programs need to be at least understood and perceived as legitimate not just by governments but by a wider range of actors within States"[22]

A good governance shopping list is important to understanding expectations. Professor Botchway's list is comprehensive and tracks with most others:

- accountability
- anti-corruption
- effective bureaucracy
- decentralization
- transparency
- rule of law
- advancement for women
- democracy[23]

There are problems with the list some of which may be insoluble. What happens when goals on the list work at cross purposes, e.g., decentralization and accountability?

If we must have a shopping list, it should be accompanied by another list, perhaps called "commonsense in applying good governance principles."

- Do not forget the *raison d'être* of the IGO.
- Good governance is a means, not an end.
- NGOs and IGOs are so fundamentally different that using the same modes of analysis for each is fraught with danger.[24]
- Even among the 2000 or so major IGOs, purposes are so different that trying to apply the same standards might be impossible.
- Watch out the co-mingling of primary and social purpose goals.
- Hyperbureaucratization is a systemic problem that has the potential to make good governance worse than the disease it was supposed to treat.
- Good governance standards can be applied intramurally or extramurally.

Good governance may be a necessary condition for effective IGOs; it certainly is not sufficient condition. Good governance has assumed a life of its own and hence cannot be ignored. But we must not become contesting fools believing that, when each box on a good governance checklist is filled, success has been achieved. Good governance and functional failure is not an impossible juxtaposition; it may be the path of least resistance.

Notes

1 Francis N. Botchway, 'Good Governance: The Old, The New, The Principle, and the Elements', 13 *Florida J. of Internat'l. L.* (2001) p. 161.

2 Functions cited in 'Harvesting Votes', *The Economist* (15 May 1999) at p. 49.

3 Alexander Pope, *The Works*, Vol. II, Containing the Epistles and the Satires, 'An Essay on Man' (1736) Epistle iii, p. 42, lines 301-304.

4 Cited in Edmund Fuller, *The Wall Street Journal*, 1 July 1986, at p. 1.

5 We could find only one other explicit use of the term, "hyperbureaucratization." Romanian Dan

Perjovschi, LIFE! FROM THE GROUND THE FROG'S KNEE!, Chisinau – Republic of Moldova, last modified 15 June 1998, <http://scca.soros.md/eng/projects/gioconda/perjovschid/>.

6 John Carvel, *The Guardian* (3 September 2002) at p. 18.

7 Mark Cancian, 83 *Marine Corps Gazette* (1999) p. 46.

8 James Rosenau, 'Governance, order, and change in world politics', in James Rosenau and Ernst-Otto Czempiel, eds., *Governance without Government: Order and Change in World Politics* 1 (1992).

9 Botchway, *supra* note 1.

10 *Id.* at p. 171.

11 UNDP: Governance Policy Paper (last modified January 1997) <http://magnet.undp.org/policy>, at p. 163.

12 Botchway, *supra* note 1 at p. 209.

13 The ILA Committee on the Accountability of International Organisations, 2002 New Delhi Conference, <http://www.ila-hq.org/html/layout_committee.htm at 2>.

14 UNDP, *supra* note 11 at p. 161.

15 Botchway, *supra* note 1.

16 Thomas G. Weiss and Leon Gordenker, 'Pluralizing Global Governance: Analytical Approaches and Dimensions', in Thomas G. Weiss and Leon Gordenker, eds., *NGOs, The UN, and Global Governance* (1996) p. 17.

17 Peter G. Wilson, 'Auditing, Management and Governance Enhancing Trust and Transparency', 27 *Internatl. J. of Gov't. Auditing* (2000) pp. 8-9.

18 *Id.* at p. 9.

19 James H. Scheuer, 'UNESCO's Bunker Mentality', *The Wall Street Journal* (19 November 1984) at p. 1.

20 Owen Bowcott, 'Threat of War: Mission: After 18 Years, Washington Rejoins UNESCO in Surprise Announcement: US Pledge on Human Rights and Tolerance', *The Guardian* (13 September 2002) at 1.5.

21 Alan Riding, 'A UN Agency is Revitalized by Re-entry of the US', *The New York Times* (29 September 2002) at 1.22.

22 Ngaire Woods, 'Good Governance in International Organizations', 5 *Global Governance* (1999) pp. 57-8.

23 Botchway, *supra* note 1.

24 Weiss, Gordenker, *supra* note 16, Leon Gordenker and Thomas G. Weiss, 'NGO Participation in the International Policy Process', at p. 217.

Remarks by Rick Lawson*

What I have in mind for the coming ten minutes is to draw your attention to one case only, which is now pending before the European Court of Human Rights. It is only one out of 60,000 cases, it does not involve any blood, torture; it is not dramatic. Still I believe that it is an interesting case, since it raises the issue whether Member States may be held responsible for alleged violations of human rights by an international organization of which they are members. I should add that I am a European, continental lawyer. Yet I tend to be pragmatic, and I think that rights are great, but remedies are even greater. So the reason for looking at this case is the fact that it may offer specific, concrete remedies in connection with international organizations. This case is *Senator Lines* v. *15 Member States of the European Union.*

* Prof. dr. Rick Lawson, Kirchheiner Chair, Faculty of Law, Leiden University.

In search of accountability for the conduct of international organisations: the case of *Senator Lines*

Preliminary remarks

1. The focus of this paper is *not* on the extent to which international organisations can *contribute to* the application of principles of good governance, for instance in aid receiving countries (cf. Thoolen). Instead, the emphasis will be on the reverse side of the coin: to what extent can one force international organisations to *comply with* these principles?
In doing so, I will leave the very specific situation of UN interim administrations aside (cf. Meindersma), but rather concentrate on 'ordinary' international organisations.

2. The notion of good governance is far from clear. For the purposes of this paper, attention will be confined to compliance with human rights, more precisely the (limited) set of 'classic' rights protected by the European Convention on Human Rights (1950). The main reasons for this choice: the position of the European Court of Human Rights (Strasbourg) is well-established; its case law has greatly refined the meaning of the rights and freedoms protected by the Convention; right now an essential case is pending.

The case of *Senator Lines*

3. Facts: German company complains of a breach of the right to a fair trial (Article 6 ECHR) by the Court of First Instance of the European Communities (CFI) and the European Court of Justice (ECJ). Appl. No. 56672/00, now pending before the Court's Grand Chamber.

4. Complaint against the European Union? At present not a party to the Convention. Article 34 ECHR: "The Court may receive applications from any person ... claiming to be the victim of a violation *by one of the High Contracting Parties* of the rights set forth in the Convention ...".

5. Complaint against the 15 Member States of the European Union? Can one hold the Member States collectively or individually responsible for violations of the Convention by Community institutions? Respondent States deny responsibility and argue that the EU has separate international legal personality.

6. 'Intuitive' arguments in favour of accepting 'Member State Responsibility':
(a) From the individual's perspective it would be unacceptable if violations of his basic rights remained unaddressed, merely because the perpetrator was an international body established by his own State, rather than the State itself.
(b) States should not be allowed to escape their obligations under the Convention by transferring powers to international organisations.
But is it acceptable that Member States may be held responsible for the conduct of organs of international organisations of which they are members?

MEMBER STATE RESPONSIBILITY IN GENERAL INTERNATIONAL LAW

7. The issue of MSR is controversial. In *Senator Lines*, the French government argues there is no general rule of international law whereby States members are, due solely to their membership, responsible for the conduct of an international organisation of which they are members. This appears to be true.

8. But one should be careful not to overlook that the Resolution of the *Institut de Droit International (IDI),* to which the French Government refers, is mainly concerned with liability *for the obligations of an international organisation itself.*[1] Cf. the famous case of the International Tin Council which was unable to meet its financial obligations: the question arose if and to what extent its Member States were liable to pay for the ITC's debts. The English courts replied essentially that this was not the case.

9. Can one distinguish the 'ITC scenario' from the situation where an international organisation interferes with the *obligations of its Member States*? One may think of an organisation that seeks to develop nuclear weapons whereas its Members are parties to the Non-Proliferation Treaty, or – more pertinent in *Senator Lines* – an organisation that allegedly violates the human rights which its Member States have undertaken to secure. The question is then not so much whether Member States may be held liable for the obligations of 'their' organisation, but rather whether they can hide behind the corporate veil of the organisation if it is said to violate their own obligations.

RELEVANT STRASBOURG CASE LAW

10. Cases concerning delegation of powers to private bodies (*Van der Mussele*, 1983; *Costello-Roberts*, 1993)

11. Case of *M. & Co.* (European Commission on Human Rights 1990): equivalent protection doctrine:

> [T]he transfer of powers to an international organisation is not incompatible with the Convention provided that within that organisation fundamental rights will receive an equivalent protection.

Questions:
(a) would the Convention be opposed to a transfer of powers to an organisation *in abstracto* as long as there are no problems in practice?
(b) what will the consequences be once Strasbourg finds that the transfer of powers to an organisation *was* incompatible with the Convention?

12. *Advantages* of the doctrine: respecting autonomy and independent legal personality of the organisation. Conflicts with other organisations avoided. Member States not held responsible for decisions which they, perhaps, could not prevent.

13. *Disadvantages:*
(a) focus on the general level of human rights protection within an international organisation. Apparently the possibility of incidental violations is accepted as long as the general level of human rights protection is satisfactory. This trade-off is hard to reconcile with "the object and purpose of the Convention as an instrument for the protection of individual human beings", the very essence of which is "respect for human dignity and human freedom".
(b) significant pressure to "approve" international organisations.

14. Towards a shift in the case-law? Court avoided issue in *Bankovic* (2001). But it touched upon it in the case of *Waite & Kennedy* (1999):

> where States establish international organisations in order to pursue or strengthen their co-operation in certain fields of activities, and where they attribute to these organisations certain competences and accord them immunities, there may be implications as to the protection of fundamental rights. It would be incompatible with the purpose and object of the Convention, however, if the Contracting States were thereby absolved from their responsibility under the Convention in relation to the field of activity covered by such attribution. It should be recalled that the Convention is intended to guarantee not theoretical or illusory rights, but rights that are practical and effective.

And in *Matthews* (1999) it observed:

> The Convention does not exclude the transfer of competences to international organisations provided that Convention rights continue to be "secured". Member States' responsibility therefore continues even after such a transfer.

Waite & Kennedy concerned ESA' immunity from judicial proceedings in its host State. The circumstances in *Matthews* were also exceptional. Will the Court take the next step in *Senator Lines?*

Conclusion

Rolv Ryssdal, then President of the European Court of Human Rights, observed in 1991:

> It is difficult to accept that the Contracting States of the Convention should be in a position to shed their Convention obligations simply as a consequence of transferring certain of their competences to an international organisation.

Judge Ryssdal was right. Any other conclusion would be likely to undermine public support for international cooperation at a time when more and more international organisations are established and the impact of their decisions is growing.

Note

1 "The Legal Consequences for Member States of the Non-fulfilment by International Organizations of *their Obligations* toward Third Parties" [emphasis added], in 1996 *Annuaire de l'IDI*, pp. 445-453.

Remarks by Philippe Lortie*

Review of the application of principles of good governance by international organisations in practice

General introduction

Good governance has been the preoccupation of many States such as Australia, Canada and the United Kingdom during the 1990s.[1] Espousing good governance principles such as transparency, openness, participation, co-operation, democratic control, legitimacy, effectiveness and accountability led to major governmental reforms in response to the disconnection between government programs and population needs on the one hand and governments' financial constraints on the other hand. In Canada, after years of overspending and a new liberal government in place in 1993, downsizing of resources and operations hit every department of the federal government. At first the government reduced its operation budgets by freezing salaries and by inviting a number of public servants to retire. In the light of the resulting pressures, the machinery of government was "reinvented" in order to develop systems aimed at doing more with less. As these systems did not alleviate the remaining pressures, governments conducted introspection exercises. Through SWOT[2] analysis governments identified operations and programmes to be transferred to the private sector or to be abandoned. During this long phase of downsizing, governments started using business models such as strategic plans and business plans thus embracing fully principles of good governance.

As international organisations are the creation of States, it is only logical that States' principles of good governance are now being applied to them as well. The first step towards the application of good governance by international organisations was the imposition by States of the zero nominal growth policy to the budgets of international organisations. The objective of this policy is to downsize the operation and resources of international organisations and to force introspection of their policy and work programmes while they absorb the cost of rising inflation through their frozen budgets. However, the uniform application of this policy was detrimental to the smaller organisations that were already "lean and mean"[3] and which, as a consequence, did not have the flexibility to absorb a zero nominal growth budget policy. Thus, an organisation such as the Hague Conference on Private International Law, for which the finding of additional resources became an urgent matter in the light of its expanding Work Programme, was forced to embrace the application of business models such as strategic plans. Putting together supplementary budgets to which States could voluntary contribute was also a way to by-pass the zero nominal growth budget policy. Good governance principles such as transparency, effectiveness and accountability resulting from the strategic planning of the Hague Conference were reinforced along with the principles that were already fully embraced by the organisation such as openness, participation, co-operation, democratic control and legitimacy.

* First Secretary. The views expressed in this conference paper are the views of the author and should not be attributed to the Hague Conference on Private International Law.

Part I. Overview of the Hague Conference on Private International Law

I.1. **Origin and vision of the organisation**

The Conference held its first meeting in 1893, on the initiative of T.M.C. Asser (Nobel Peace Prize 1911). It became a permanent inter-governmental organisation in 1955, upon entry into force of its Statute. The ultimate goal of the Organisation is to work for a world in which, despite the differences between legal systems, persons – individuals as well as companies – can enjoy a high degree of legal security.

I.2. **Mission of the organisation**

Personal and family or commercial situations that are connected with more than one country are commonplace in the modern world. These may be affected by differences between the legal systems in those countries. With a view to resolving these differences, States have adopted special rules known as "private international law" rules. The statutory mission of the Conference is to work for the "progressive unification" of these rules. This involves finding internationally-agreed approaches to issues such as jurisdiction of the courts, applicable law, and the recognition and enforcement of judgments in a wide range of areas, from commercial law and banking law to international civil procedure and from child protection to matters of marriage and personal status. Over the years, the Conference has, in carrying out its mission, increasingly become a centre for international judicial and administrative co-operation in the area of private law, especially in the fields of protection of the family and children, of civil procedure and commercial law.

Activities of the Conference are co-ordinated by a multinational Secretariat – the Permanent Bureau – located in The Hague. The Conference's working languages are English and French.[4] The Secretariat prepares expert meetings as well as Diplomatic Sessions, and carries out the basic research required for any subject taken up by the Conference. It also engages in various activities to support the effective implementation and operation of the Conventions.

I.2.A. *Law-making organisation*

The Organisation meets in principle every four years in Plenary Session (ordinary Diplomatic Session) to negotiate and adopt Conventions and to decide upon future work. The Conventions are prepared by Special Commissions (plenary meetings of experts or small working groups) held several times a year.

I.2.B. *Post-convention services*

Meetings of experts are also organised to review the operation of the Conventions and adopt recommendations with the object of improving the effectiveness of the Conventions and promoting consistent practices and interpretation. With the aim of harmonising the implementation of the Conventions, the Secretariat organises, assists in organising and participates in conferences and seminars held at both international and national levels to train the various persons involved in the implementation of the Conventions, including judges, Central Authority personnel and members of the legal profession. A judicial newsletter on international child protection is also published. INCADAT, the International Child Abduction Database[5] is a special initiative which provides easy access to many of the leading judicial decisions taken by national courts around the world in respect of the 1980 Hague Convention on international child abduction. The Permanent Bureau regularly publishes and maintains a Collection of Conventions together with handbooks on the operation of certain Conventions. It also edits the Proceedings of each of the Diplomatic Sessions which now encompasses an impressive collection of "Actes et documents". The Conference website[6] presents general information concerning the Hague Conference as well as detailed and updated information on the Hague Conventions: text of the Conventions, full status reports, bibliographies, information regarding the authorities designated under the Conventions on judicial and administrative co-operation, explanatory reports, etc.

I.3. Membership and States parties

With more than 60 Member States representing all continents, the Hague Conference on private international law is a global inter-governmental organisation. It is a melting pot of different legal traditions that develops and services multilateral legal instruments in response to global needs. An increasing number of non-Member States are also becoming parties to the Hague Conventions. As a result, the work of the Conference encompasses more than 118 countries around the world.

I.4. Key conventions

Between 1893 and 1904, the Conference adopted 7 Conventions, which have all been subsequently replaced by more modern instruments. Between 1951 and 2003, the Conference adopted 35 Conventions. Even when they are not ratified, the Conventions have an influence upon legal systems, in both Member and non-Member States. They also form a source of inspiration for efforts to unify private international law at the regional level, for example within the Organization of American States, the Council of Europe or the European Union.[7]

PART II. THE INSTITUTION & GOOD GOVERNANCE – DEVELOPMENT AND MANAGEMENT OF THE ORGANISATION – THE STRATEGIC PLAN OF THE HAGUE CONFERENCE

The Hague Conference has in recent years experienced an unprecedented period of growth, both in its Membership and activities. In 2002 the Member States of the Conference approved a Strategic Plan – the blueprint of the Conference for responding to the many trends that are influencing its activities – put together by its Secretariat. These trends are driven by the phenomenon of globalisation, the internationalisation of business and family life, the pace of technological change, changing public attitudes and regionalisation. More particularly, such trends are evidenced by

- new technologies resulting in an explosion of new products and services, business, knowledge sharing and accelerated communications;

- the ever increasing cross-border movement of persons, goods, services and capital;
- the pressure toward increasing the global span of the Conference;
- an increasing public interest in being informed about rights; and,
- the enlarged role of regional integration organisations, such as the European Union, in the area of private international law.

The trends have resulted in a number of pressures and changes for the organisation, including

- the growing demands from target audiences such as Member States; non-Member States Parties to Conventions; individuals associated with the different judicial systems; Central and other National Authorities; families, children and other individuals; industry and private companies; other international organisations; and the professional and academic communities;
- the increased diversity in the Membership of the Conference;
- the additional work involved in developing new Conventions for a diverse Membership; and,
- the growing burden of servicing existing Conventions.

However, over the years the resources to respond to these pressures, changes and growing demands have not been adjusted adequately.[8] The result has been a mismatch or gap between the demands made on the organisation and the resources made available to meet those demands.

The Strategic Directions making-up the Strategic Plan are largely based on good governance principles that will assist the Permanent Bureau and the Member States in continuing to adapt to the changing and growing demands on the work of the Conference. The good governance principles described thereafter provide a framework for the way in which the Conference carries out its mission and operations.

II.1. Openness – Increasing the global coverage of the organisation by increasing the membership of the organisation and the number of States parties to Hague Conventions[9]

A considered growth in the number of Member States is desirable in order to assist the Conference in affirming and responding to its global mission.[10] The Conference should place itself in a better position to respond to the growing needs of regions such as Africa, Asia and the Middle East that have traditionally had a smaller representation at the Conference. The involvement in the work of the Permanent Bureau of experts from other legal traditions in addition to the civil law and common law traditions is essential in order to develop universal norms and cross-border co-operation.

II.2. Working under constraints – Governance imposed by governments

The Organisation is funded principally by its Member States. Its budget is approved every year by the Council of Diplomatic Representatives of Member States. The Organisation also seeks and receives some voluntary funding for special projects from Member States and other sources.

II.2.A. *Being selective in relation to the projects undertaken*[11]

In an environment where the workload is increasing and the allocation of resources is not necessarily following, the Conference continues to focus equally on its two core activities – the development and review of Conventions, and the provision of unique post-Conventions services.[12] The Conference builds on its strengths that include the development and aftercare of Conventions and the establishment of co-operation mechanisms.

The Conference concentrates its work on well-defined, widely recognised and pressing problems in areas in which States have a strong interest. Conventions are the main vehicle of the Conference; recommendations, good practice guides, model laws and other non-binding instruments will be devised when appropriate.

II.2.B. *Consolidating post-Convention services*[13]

With the expansion in the number of States Parties to certain Conventions the work on post-Convention services continues to expand without an appropriate increase in the regular budget. In consolidating its post-Convention services, the Conference continues to develop partnerships with States, governmental and non-governmental organisations, academic and research institutes, and continues to concentrate its efforts on supporting activities to which it brings its unique expertise. Through partnerships, the Conference tries to do more with less of its own resources. The value of post-Convention services provided by the Secretariat is widely acknowledged by Member States. The services are designed to promote the effective implementation and operation of the Conventions, to encourage consistency in interpretation and practice under the Conventions, to address specific obstacles to the proper functioning of Conventions, as well as to maximise the number of Contracting States.

II.2.C. *Enhancing working methods and reducing costs by providing flexibility in the development process*[14]

In an environment where the legal and political issues are increasingly complex, resources are limited and the number of interested parties is constantly growing, it is essential to provide flexibility in the development of new instruments. Depending on the nature and stage of the projects, the development of different types of instruments,[15] including Conventions, may require different methods. When appropriate, the Conference conducts more regional preparatory meetings in order to facilitate the input of all interested stakeholders and, when possible, to reduce the number or length of larger meetings. Furthermore, depending on the projects, it may be opportune to utilise more expert working groups in addition to or instead of larger meetings. In order to ensure the objectivity of these alternate working methods the Conference makes certain that these undertakings are as transparent as possible through the use of public Reports.

II.3. Transparency and accountability

II.3.A. *Enhancing the management of information*[16]

The Hague Conference website, which is up-dated every day, receives more than 20,000 hits a day. In the near future, the information found on the website will be stored in a database. Thus, it will be possible to research the entire content of the site with a search engine. In addition, this may enable the automatic notification of modification of the site to any interested stakeholder. The underlying objective of tailor-made information is closer co-operation and networking.

II.3.B. *Increasing communication and co-operation with other international organisations*[17]

Increasing effective co-operation and developing useful partnerships with other organisations can result in resource savings for both States and organisations. It is the objective of the Conference to remind other organisations of the work and research already accomplished by the Conference in order to avoid duplication. In developing co-operation and partnerships with sister organisations the Conference will continue to be selective and to weigh the costs and benefits of partnerships.

II.3.C. *Matching resources and demands by making the decision-making process more transparent and informed*[18]

While the decisions on financial matters are left to the Council of Diplomatic Representatives, decisions on the Work Programme of the Conference rest with different policy organs of the Conference.[19] This system certainly has its advantages, but there is room to connect the two decision-making processes more fully. In order to help close the gap between resources and demands, the Conference is identifying the resource implications of new initiatives to be undertaken, to ensure the decision-making process is more transparent and informed.[20] By bringing together policy matters and their financial implications, the Conference endeavours to create partnerships with its Member States in order to devise alternative funding solutions such as voluntary supplementary funding and contributions in kind, for example secondment of State officials, internships and the supply of equipment. In order to facilitate this dialogue, the Special Commission on General Affairs and Policy now meets on a more regular basis to make adjustments to the Work Programme in the light of the regular and additional resources available.

Part III. Law making & good governance – Development of universally acceptable international instruments

III.1. Openness – Constituting a universal legislator / lawmaker

The involvement of experts and States from different legal traditions such as civil law, common law and Islamic law is essential in order to develop universally acceptable international instruments.

For example, the 1954 Convention on Civil Procedure, like its predecessors of 1896 and 1905, never attracted any ratification from States of common law tradition because it was mainly based on the civil law tradition of legal co-operation through official channels. With the participation of the common law countries, the Convention was revised in three stages. This led to the Conventions on Service and Evidence Abroad and on Access to Justice that have successfully accommodated the needs of both systems. The 1970 Evidence Convention reconciles differences between the common law and the civil law traditions for taking evidence. In a common law jurisdiction, the preparation of a case for trial is the private responsibility of the parties. In many civil law countries, on the other hand, the taking of evidence is part of the judicial function, and official permission is needed before evidence can be taken privately. As a consequence, civil law countries may object to direct requests for evidence from a party from a common law State, and may not permit a court official of that State to take evidence or to administer an oath on its territory. Nowadays, States of civil law tradition may declare, under the 1970 Evidence Convention, that they will allow the taking of evidence by private parties in their jurisdiction. Similarly, States of common law tradition may allow the taking of evidence in their jurisdiction by members of the judiciary from civil law States.

Certain Hague Conventions also accommodate Islamic law. Already in 1970 the Divorce Convention dealt with the recognition of divorces according to Islamic law, provided they had been obtained following judicial or other official proceedings. In the preparations of the Trust Convention special attention was given to the Islamic *waqf* (or *wakf*), which is the Islamic law equivalent of the trust, mostly used for family and charitable purposes. In the family law area, the 1996 Convention on the Protection of Children includes recognition of arrangements made by way of the Islamic law institution of *Kafala*, which is a functional equivalent of adoption that falls outside the scope of the 1993 Intercountry Adoption Convention.

It is also essential to have the participation of States with different structures such as unitary States, federal States, plura-legislative unitary States and States organised in Regional Economic Integration Organisations. It is only since the early 1970s, after Canada became a Member of the Organisation in 1968, that Hague Conventions included federal State clauses allowing the extension of the application of a Convention to territorial units on a piece-meal basis. The 1970 Divorce Convention allows its application to States like Israel where religious and civil law cohabit. Finally, the latest of the Hague Conventions, the *Convention on the Law Applicable to Certain Rights in respect of Securities held with an Intermediary* allows the accession of Regional Economic Integration Organisations.

III.2. **Participation and co-operation – The Hague Network**

In addition to the Diplomatic representations in The Netherlands, the Secretariat maintains direct contact with Member States through designated National Organs. It also develops permanent contacts with experts and delegates of the Member States, with more than 700 National and Central Authorities designated under certain Conventions, as well as with international governmental and non-governmental organisations, with professional and academic communities and the judiciary. It is through the consultation of this large network that the Permanent Bureau collects most of the information it needs in order to conduct its work.

III.3. **Legitimacy – Is this the appropriate forum?**

Legitimacy is not limited to what is allowable according to law. It is also what is reasonable and acceptable. In this respect, the Hague Conference is known for the high-quality and scientific excellence of its work, for the development of creative solutions and for its unrivalled contribution to private international law over a period of more than 110 years. Furthermore, the Hague Conference is an organisation within which world experts and delegates are committed to working together on the basis of mutual trust, support and respect.

III.4. **Democratic control**

Like in any Legislative Assembly or Parliament, the adoption of Hague Conventions or of the Work Programme is done through a majority vote. However, during the 1st Phase of the Diplomatic Conference on the Judgments project held 6-20 June 2001, the development of the Securities Convention and more recently in relation to the work on a new instrument on the international recovery of child support and other forms of family maintenance, the Conference has been working on a consensus basis. There are a number of pros and cons to both approaches and a thorough analysis of the issues would be outside the scope of this paper. In a domestic context, usually the adoption of a legal norm results in the coming into force of that norm for all. The same cannot be said about the international context because States usually have the discretion as to whether to become a Party to a Convention after it has been adopted.

Working on a consensus basis may help achieve this result on a fast track basis. In this respect, it may result into two kinds of norms or a mix of both. It may evolve either towards the smallest common denominator or towards a brand new system. In the first case, the outcome may be a legal norm less appealing than what other States will have developed on a bilateral basis or at a regional level. It will achieve universality but probably with lower standards. As to the new system, in the second case, it could either be a success or a failure; it will depend on the comfort level of the States.

On the other hand, working on the basis of votes may result in the adoption of a norm departing from the lowest common denominator; the outcome could also be a new system. In the first case, universal implementation may take longer to reach since a minority of States may have to undergo legal reforms in order to become a Party to the new Convention. But, at the end of the day, it may contribute to overall legal reforms. Nevertheless, some States, for constitutional reasons for example, may never be able to undertake the necessary legal reform to implement the Convention. Secondly, reforms could also be achieved with the help of innovations or new systems, but as was mentioned above it could result in success or failure. Striking the right balance between a consensus approach and a voting approach is not an easy task. However, one thing is certain, success stories at the Hague Conference are most of the time the result of innovations or new systems such as co-operation mechanisms.

Part IV. Implementation & good governance – Validation and assessment of the international instrument

IV.1. **Legitimacy – Is the international instrument acceptable?**

IV.1.A. *Connection with other international instruments*

The modern Hague Conventions on the international protection of children provide an example in this respect. The general norms that apply to the protection of children in cross-border situations are found in the *1989 United Nations Convention on the Rights of the Child.* These norms consist of well-known general principles such as the best interest of the child, non-discrimination, and the right of the child to be heard. The norms also include more specific principles applicable to cross-border situations, such as the right of the child to maintain continuing contact with both parents (Articles 10 and 9), general principles regulating intercountry adoption (Article 21) and the general objective of the recovery of child support from abroad (Article 27). The need for international co-operation at all levels, judicial and administrative, is referred to time and again within the UN Convention, with its frequent encouragement of bilateral and multilateral arrangements and agreements in areas such as the illicit transfer and non-return of children abroad (Article 11), intercountry adoption (Article 21), refugee children (Article 22), recovery of child support (Article 27), sexual exploitation (Article 34), and sale, trafficking and abduction (Article 35).

The three modern Hague Conventions on International Child Abduction (1980), Intercountry Adoption (1993) and International Child Protection (1996), even though one of them pre-dates the UN Convention, may be regarded as answering this call for international co-operation at the multilateral level. Negotiations towards a new Hague Convention on the international recovery of child support may also be regarded as answering this call. The purpose of the Hague Conventions is to provide the nuts and bolts for achieving cross-frontier child protection through the development of specialised legal frameworks, combined with workable systems of international co-operation both at administrative and judicial levels.

IV.1.B. *Quality of the text*

Since the official languages of the Hague Conference are French and English, the texts of Hague Conventions is drafted in French an English simultaneously in small bilingual drafting committees with the assistance of members of the Secretariat. The bilingual discussions and the simultaneous drafting of the committee are important components with regard to the substance of the instrument as they often bring-up points of misunderstanding or points which require further clarification which were not revealed during the plenary meeting of experts. In addition to being truly bilingual, since 1980 modern Hague Conventions are gender neutral.[21] Finally, in some cases resort has been made to terms that are legal tradition neutral in order to ensure wider acceptance of the texts. The term "habitual residence" used as a connecting factor is one example among others. The definition of the term "domicile" differs from one State to another and therefore the term "habitual residence" which is not defined is universally acceptable. Furthermore, the use of the term "habitual residence" as a connecting factor served as a compromise between the connecting factors of "nationality" and "domicile".

IV.1.C. *Durability of an international instrument*

Conventions are usually limited to the needs of the States that have negotiated them. As noted earlier, the 1954 Convention relating to Civil Procedure was meant for the Member States of the time which were mostly of civil law tradition. Nowadays, as the Membership of the Hague Conference comprises States from all continents and all legal traditions more recent Hague Conventions are most likely to respond to global needs and to be universally implemented. History will tell if they are durable. Furthermore, as mentioned earlier, appropriate post-Convention services such as monitoring, review and support for implementation should also help Hague Conventions to pass the test of time.

IV.2. **Effectiveness – Does the international instrument produce the results it was intended to?**

IV.2.A. *Measuring effectiveness through monitoring case law*

In the absence of a single court to give authoritative rulings on the interpretation of Hague Conventions dealing with private international law matters, achieving a reasonable level of consistency in the interpretation of the Conventions by national courts in the many States Parties remains a challenge. A prerequisite to uniform interpretation is ready access to the many judgments that have now been delivered in the different national courts in relation to the different Hague Conventions. Under the 1980 Convention on International Child Abduction, the Permanent Bureau maintains an international child abduction database (INCADAT) that contains at this point more than 500 summaries in English and French of leading decisions from around the world. Practical Handbooks published by the Permanent Bureau achieve a similar result for the Conventions of 1965 and 1970 on the Service Abroad of Documents and the Taking of Evidence Abroad Conventions.[22] In collecting these decisions, the Permanent Bureau analyses the different interpretations of the Conventions. Therefore, when the Conference reviews the practical operation of these Conventions, the Permanent Bureau with the support of questionnaires ask the States Parties questions in relation to the different interpretation and/or application trends identified. The States Parties discuss their answers to the questionnaires and Recommendations and Conclusions are then adopted with a view to a uniform interpretation and/or application.

IV.2.B. *Measuring effectiveness through gathering statistics*

Criticism and review of practice under Hague Conventions should be based on a firm foundation of facts. There is a need to gather from all States Parties reliable and comparable basic data concerning the number and nature of cases being processed, as well as certain key aspects of the national procedure. The gathering of detailed statistics and data imposes considerable additional work, however, the exercise is essential for the process of objective review of the Conventions' operation and for improving the practice.

IV.2.C. *Measuring effectiveness through cost / benefit analysis – the next step*

There is no doubt that legal certainty and security are of direct benefit to international commercial undertakings. Legal certainty and security will attract business people and investors. Furthermore, as legal certainty and security will reduce the risks associated with commercial operations, interest rates will decrease as well as the State's credit rating. The *Convention of 5 October 1961 Abolishing the Requirement of Legalisation for Foreign Public Documents*, the *Convention of 15 November 1965 on the Service Abroad of Judicial and Extrajudicial Documents* and the *Convention of 18 March 1970 on the Taking of Evidence Abroad in Civil* all apply to commercial matters and tend to enhance legal certainty and security. The impact on State's credit ratings and interests rates would only be a first step in measuring the effectiveness of these commercial related conventions. In order to convince States Parties and non-Parties of the effectiveness of these instruments it will be necessary to analyse other cost / benefit elements of these Conventions such as rapidity of process, the resulting savings for the Diplomatic services, etc.

Conclusion

The Strategic Plan of the Hague Conference having received the support of its Member States it is most likely fair to say that most of the governments of these States probably embrace the good governance principles resulting from the Strategic Plan. However, it remains to be seen if these principles are universally accepted or if they only happen to be principles the acceptance of which is limited to the Membership of the organisation.

Notes

1 The author was a Canadian federal public servant during that period.

2 SWOT stands for "Strength, Weaknesses, Opportunities and Threat".

3 PricewaterhouseCoopers, "The Hague Conference on Private International Law: Resources Deficiencies and Strategic Positioning", The Hague, May 2001, at para. [302] p. 21, 26 p.

4 In recent years, the Conference has been working occasionally in Spanish in addition to French and English for certain children related projects that attract the interest of South and Central American States.

5 <http://www.incadat.com>.

6 <http://www.hcch.net>.

7 The key Conventions deal with judicial and administrative co-operation and the international protection of children. They are: the *Convention of 5 October 1961 Abolishing the Requirement of Legalisation for Foreign Public Documents*; the *Convention of 15 November 1965 on the Service Abroad of Judicial and Extrajudicial Documents in Civil or Commercial Matters*; the *Convention of 18 March 1970 on the Taking of Evidence Abroad in Civil or Commercial Matters*; the *Convention of 25 October 1980 on International Access to Justice*; the *Convention of 25 October 1980 on the Civil Aspects of International Child Abduction*; the *Convention of 29 May 1993 on Protection of Children and Co-operation in Respect of Intercountry Adoption*; and, the *Convention of 19 October 1996 on Jurisdiction, Applicable Law, Recognition, Enforcement and Co-operation in respect of Parental Responsibility and Measures for the Protection of Children*.

8 See *supra* General Introduction.

9 See April 2002 Hague Conference Strategic Plan, available at <http://www.hcch.net>, Strategic Direction No. 1, at paras. [404]-[407].

10 In the near future, the organisation may also welcome regional integration organisations as Members. The European Community has transmitted a request to that effect to the Secretary General of the Conference in December 2002.

11 See April 2002 Hague Conference Strategic Plan, *supra*, note 9, Strategic Direction No. 2, at paras. [408]-[409].

12 Including treaty administration, monitoring and review, the provision of technical advice and assistance with training and education, the gathering and disseminating of information and promoting consistency in State practice.

13 See April 2002 Hague Conference Strategic Plan, *supra*, note 9, Strategic Direction No. 3, at paras. [410]-[412].

14 Ibid. Strategic Direction No. 3, at paras. [413]-[415].

15 As mentioned under II.2.A., *supra*, the conference may use other procedures of less binding effect, such as Recommendations and model laws. Other non-binding harmonising mechanisms include model forms and guides to good practice. Such instruments may require less resource to develop and may be easier to implement.

16 See April 2002 Hague Conference Strategic Plan, *supra*, note 9, Strategic Direction No. 8, at paras. [436]-[437].

17 Ibid. Strategic Direction No. 7, at paras. [434]-[435].

18 Ibid. Strategic Direction No. 6, at paras. [425]-[430].

19 The Diplomatic Sessions and, in between sessions, the Special Commission on General Affairs and Policy of the Conference.

20 See, for example, Preliminary Document No. 4 of March 2003 for the attention of the Special Commission of April 2003 on General Affairs and Policy of the Conference describing the planning for 2003-2005 regarding the projects concerning the children's Conventions, maintenance, adults and cohabitation.

21 See Adair Dyer, former Deputy Secretary General, "To Celebrate a Score of Years!", in "Celebrating Twenty Years: The Past and Promise of the 1980 Hague Convention on the Civil Aspects of International Child Abduction" (2000) 33:1 *NYU J. of Int'l Law and Pol.* 1, at p. 3.

22 *Les Nouvelles Conventions de La Haye*, Vol. I-V, published by the Asser Instituut, achieve a similar result for all the modern Hague Conventions until 1996.

Remarks By Christa Meindersma*

The UN Mission of Support in East-Timor is the UN mission that has stayed in East-Timor to follow up the transitional authority that administered East-Timor in the 2,5 years leading up to its independence. My intervention today is more concerned with that period of transitional authority of the United Nations.

Application of principles of good governance by international organizations in practice: United Nations transitional administrations

I. Introduction

1. In Kosovo and subsequently in East Timor – currently called Timor-Leste – the UN was requested to take on the role of government and provide an interim administration for both territories. Rather than advising governments on aspects of governance or monitoring the compliance of States with their international obligations, the UN was put in the position to administer territories in transition.[1]

* Political Officer Security Issues/Border Demarcation UNMISET; prior Legal Adviser UNMIK (1999) and UNTAET (2000-2002). The views expressed in this article are entirely the views of the author and do not necessarily reflect the views held by the United Nations.

2. In East Timor and Kosovo the UN was given a full-fledged executive, legislative and judicial mandate, in a non-self governing territory emerging from foreign occupation and in a province of a State respectively. Both mandates were established under Chapter VII of the UN Charter, following a determination by the Security Council that the situation constituted a threat to peace and security. The scope of the responsibilities deriving from these mandates was unprecedented in UN peacekeeping, particularly in East Timor, where UN administration was to prepare the territory for independence.

3. At the same time as performing *ad interim* administrative functions, in the vacuum created by the departure of prior administrative structures, civil servants and in the case of in East Timor, the destruction of all public infrastructure, the UN was to develop and establish democratic, indigenous and viable institutions of administration and governance. In both cases, this was not limited to setting up political or basic administrative structures but included the rebuilding of the entire public sector, reconstruction and operation of public utilities, ports, airports, establishing a civil service, social services, health care, education, water, sanitation, a banking and taxation system, customs, immigration, developing budgetary and currency policies, establishing a public media, and conducting elections.

II. Good governance

4. Against this backdrop, I will briefly review some aspects of the application of principles by good governance by contemporary UN territorial administrations. For purposes of this article, I understand governance to refer to the process whereby public institutions – *in casu* UN administrations- conduct public affairs and manage public resources. Good governance accomplishes this in a manner free of abuse and corruption, and with due regard to the rule of law; the true test of good governance being the degree to which it creates an environment conducive to the enjoyment of human rights. The UN Commission of Human Rights identified the key attributes of good governance as: transparency, responsibility, accountability, participation, and responsiveness to the needs and aspirations of the people.[2]

III. Challenges to UN Transitional Administration

5. Mr. Sergio Viera de Mello, Special Representative of the Secretary-General (SRSG) and Transitional Administrator (TA) in Kosovo as well as East Timor, pointedly remarked that 'for decades the UN have advised, indeed lectured Governments on how to best go about their business. Now the organization finds itself in the awkward position of being called upon to practice what it has preached.'[3]

6. While not attempting to justify potential shortcomings of contemporary UN administrations, I would like to highlight some challenges inherent in the mandates of UN transitional administrations. Obviously, there exists a duality between being the administration of a territory and simultaneously establishing an adminis-

tration for that same territory. UNMIK was mandated to provide transitional administration while establishing and overseeing the development of self-governing institutions. The first such institution was the Joint Interim Administrative Structure in Kosovo, set up in January 2000, to provide an interim administration under UN-oversight, followed by the Provisional Institutions of Self-Government in the legislative, executive and judicial fields through elections in 2001 under ultimate authority of the TA. Likewise, UNTAET was endowed with responsibility for the administration of East Timor, capacity building for self-government, the development of local institutions and the transfer to these institutions of its administrative functions.

7. Obviously, an administrative mandate initially requires the UN to devote its resources primarily to the setting up of the administration. The development of local institutions necessarily comes second, leaving the UN open to criticism that it is predominantly or exclusively focussed on its own needs. Likewise, through the mandated end-goal for the UN is to make itself redundant by decreasing the participation of the international administration while increasing self-government, this may be hard to reflect in practice at the early stages of the administration.

8. The effectiveness of the exercise of administrative functions by the UN is also dependent on the intended future status of the territory. The UN's role in East Timor was facilitated by a clear determination as to the territory's impending independence. The final status of Kosovo, however, was left undetermined and UNMIK was charged with providing an interim administration under which the people of Kosovo could enjoy substantial autonomy within the FRY as well as facilitating a process designed to determine Kosovo's future status. In implementing its mandate, UNMIK had to walk a tightrope maintaining the *status quo* while keeping the option of a change in status open and contributing actively to the process through which that change in status might be achieved. This has led some to accuse the UN of having assumed the role of the FRY government, precluding the achievement of full independence, and others to accuse it of creating conditions that will result in the separation of the territory from Yugoslavia through, for instance, the introduction of different regimes (legal, taxation), allowing Kosovo to function without reliance on Yugoslavia.

9. A legitimate question is how UN transitional administrations could exercise good governance having been endowed with absolute powers. The Security Council resolutions establishing both missions give the UN full powers to administer the territory. The Transitional Administrator, appointed by the Secretary-General, has the power to determine essential policies, adopt national laws in the form of regulations and directives, rebuild or create institutions, establish a judiciary, remove and appoint national personnel such as judges and prosecutors and has the highest command of the army, *e.g.* international peacekeeping troops. While the resolution establishing UNMIK tasks it with performing basic civilian administrative functions where and as long as required and maintaining law and order, Resolution 1272 establishing UNTAET explicitly states that the transitional ad-

ministration is empowered to exercise all legislative and executive authority, including the administration of justice and maintaining law and order. The powers are absolute – authorizing UNTAET to take all necessary measures to fulfill its mandate – and there is no separation between legislative, executive and judicial power. How can this lead to the establishment of democratic institutions of governance and a society respecting the separation of judicial, legislative and executive powers, particularly when the territory has no legacy of democracy, democratic institutions or even self-governance?

10. There is an array of other challenges to successful implementation of a UN administrative mandate including the lack of preparedness on the part of the UN to carry out the tasks entrusted to it, administrative requirements that may prevent it from working most effectively, the level of destruction of the territory, the absence of qualified local professionals, the lingering of ethnic hatred, the existence of parallel structures of government, aspirations of the inhabitants of the territory that differ from the mandate given to the UN which is based on the will of the international community and may reflect a political compromise, unfamiliarity of the local population with the UN and foreign presence, customs and preoccupations, to mention but a few.

IV. Rule of law

11. A functioning legal and judicial system based on the rule of law constitutes a cornerstone of good governance. Public confidence in the institutions that apply the law is essential to maintain the confidence of the people in the temporary UN administration as protector and guarantor of their rights. Realizing this, one of the first activities by both UN administrations was in the legal field.

12. In East Timor and Kosovo, the UN was empowered to exercise all legislative and executive authority, including the administration of justice. Resolution 1272 explicitly endows the TA with the power to 'to enact new laws and regulations and to amend, suspend or repeal existing ones.' The resolution establishing UNMIK is less explicit but subsequent regulations interpret the powers provided by the Security Council in the same broad manner. Executing his legislative powers, in both territories the TA promulgated Regulation No. 1, a constitutional-type regulation delineating the authority and powers of the administration, defining the applicable law and repealing certain existing laws. Regulations No. 1, almost identical in Kosovo and East Timor, form a bridge between the Security Council resolutions from which the UN administration's powers derive and the law of the land as promulgated by the administration. The regulations also stipulate that in the exercise of their functions, all persons undertaking public duties or holding public office shall observe internationally recognized human rights standards and declare certain treaties binding on the UN Administration.

13. In both Kosovo and East Timor, the UN declared the continuation of the law in force prior to the start of the UN administration, except insofar it conflicted with international norms. While desirable from the viewpoint of stability, the decision

to continue the application of Yugoslav law in Kosovo was controversial and after refusal by Albanian judges to apply Yugoslav law, had to be revised. In December 1999, the key date for Yugoslav law remaining in force, was changed from 24 March 1999 to 22 March 1989, the day that Yugoslavia unilaterally withdrew Kosovo's autonomy. In East Timor, where most lawyers had been trained in Indonesia, the decision to continue the laws applied prior to 25 October 1999 (Indonesian law) with similar modifications, though politically controversial, was welcomed by the legal community. However, the shortcomings of the law were such that the UN had to draft a new code of criminal procedure to guarantee the application of basic standards of fair trial and due process. In both territories, the continuation of prior law, modified by subsequent UN regulations, administrative directives – in East Timor subsequently followed by the laws of the independent country – forms a complex pyramid of applicable law that now constitutes the legal order of the territory. The ensuing situation in both territories was one of substantial legal uncertainty, exacerbated by the lack of available legal texts and access to UN regulations in both territories.

14. As to legislative procedure, the power to issue regulations, directives and executive orders is vested solely in the TA and regulations enter into force upon simple approval and signature by the TA. In East Timor, soon after the start of the mission, a National Consultative Council was established to provide an advisory mechanism on matters related to the exercise of the TA's legislative functions. In fact, though the Council was consulted on most if not all UNTAET regulations it was often ill prepared to perform this role lacking the professional expertise and organizational capacity to do so. The Kosovo Transitional Council performed a similar role and faced similar limitations. Subsequently, in both territories, parliamentary type bodies were set up to ensure more meaningful participation of the local population in the legislative process.

15. In both East Timor and Kosovo, the UN had to establish a judiciary from scratch, given the vacuum created by the departure of those who held these positions prior to UN administration and the destruction of judicial infrastructure. The arrest and detention of persons suspected of having committed serious crimes or having engaged in post-conflict criminality demanded the immediate establishment of judicial structures to review the legality of detention and provide some semblance of respect for the rule of law by the administration. Experience in both Kosovo and East Timor has revealed, however, that it is very difficult to quickly establish functioning judicial structures in post-conflict situations. One complication is that institutions are not developed in a logical sequential manner based on an overall plan approved by representatives of the local population but in an *ad hoc* fashion responding to immediate needs. In reality, there is a need to do all at once: determine the applicable law, devise and set up a court system, prosecution and defence capacity, identify, train and appoint judges, lawyers and prosecutors, set up a prison system and police, and manage detention facilities. The lack of qualified local judges, prosecutors, defence lawyers and law and order personnel in East Timor, and the hatred towards Serbs in Kosovo complicated the establishment of an independent and impartial judiciary. The resulting situa-

tion in both East Timor and Kosovo a few years later is a continuing lack of systems of credible justice.

16. The ICTY has jurisdiction to prosecute war crimes and crimes against humanity committed in Kosovo. In East Timor, a two-tier system of justice was devised with special panels in the Dili district and appellate courts, comprised of international and East Timorese judges with jurisdiction modeled on the ICC Statute. In Jakarta, special human rights courts were set up by Presidential decree with narrowly circumscribed jurisdiction for some atrocities that occurred in 1999 in East Timor applying Indonesian law. A memorandum of understanding for legal, judicial and human rights cooperation signed between Indonesia and East Timor in 2000, regulated the 'transfer' of suspects and accused. However, despite requests for transfer of Indonesian persons indicted by the courts in Dili, no accused were transferred. The trials of certain accused in Jakarta, though some appeals are still pending, have so far not been able to bring to justice those held responsible.

17. An interesting feature of UNTAET was the TA's assumption of treaty-making powers, beyond agreements regulating the receipt of development grants from foreign donors. During UNTAET tenure, a number of 'arrangements' were concluded between UNTAET, on behalf of the East Timor Public/Transitional Administration, and Indonesia on such topics as setting up a Joint Border Committee, establishing a bus service between the enclave of Oecussi and the remainder of East Timor, establishing postal links between East Timor and Indonesia, the transfer of Indonesian rupiah to Indonesia and pension payments to former civil servants of Indonesian military and police. The validity of some arrangements has been extended after independence as between Indonesia and Timor-Leste. As such the Joint Border Committee has been functioning and continued the negotiations started prior to independence, including on crucial matters such as the demarcation of the international boundary between Indonesia and Timor-Leste. In the absence of an agreed border, the UN military (PKF) concluded an arrangement with the Indonesian military (TNI) defining a Tactical Coordination Line in lieu of a border which even today separates the jurisdiction of border control agencies on both sides.

V. Participation

18. The UN Secretary-General has emphasized that better governance means greater participation, coupled with accountability. The resolutions establishing UNMIK and UNTAET emphasize local participation and consultation without giving specific guidance as to how such participation should be effected. Resolution 1272 simply dictates that UNTAET needs 'to consult and cooperate closely with the East Timorese people in order to carry out its mandate effectively with a view to the development of local democratic institutions.' The resolution establishing UNMIK is silent on the matter. UNTAET Regulation No. 1 reiterates that the TA shall consult and cooperate closely with representatives of the East Timorese people in the exercise of his functions.

19. A number of complexities emerge when attempting to effectuate meaningful participation of the local population from the initial stages of the transitional administration's mandate. In the absence of elections and elected representatives, cooperation with local people can have a significant impact on political developments. The choice of local interlocutors may increase the political profile of certain persons or entities or (be seen to) favor or strengthen a political party or interest at the expense of others. The local persons the UN engages with may not always represent the population and may reflect traditional (non-democratically elected) structures, and may exclude certain groups, such as, for instance, women. It has been questioned whether power sharing under these circumstances is the most effective way to achieve democracy and good governance.[4] On the other hand, participation of local representatives provides the requisite legitimacy to what is essentially a foreign administration and may enhance the recognition and sustainability of local institutions of self-government set up by the UN administration. Participation of local representatives also ensures a sense of ownership of crucial decisions that have to be taken early in the transitional administration but that have implications beyond the immediate administration. Decisions as to the legal, financial and border control systems are but examples of this.

20. In Kosovo, the original Kosovo Transitional Council with a consultative role was integrated into a Joint Interim Administrative Structure in 2000 to share provisional administrative management with the UN. The Interim Administrative Structure consisted of an Interim Transitional Council whose membership comprised representatives of the political forces in Kosovo and UNMIK and Administrative Departments jointly led by an UNMIK and Kosovo head of department, performing provisional administrative tasks and making policy recommendations. Its aim was to incorporate the existing parallel structures, such as the provisional Government and Presidency of Kosovo. The TA retained legislative and executive authority while the Interim Administrative Council had the power to propose amendments to applicable law, initiate new regulations and propose policy guidelines. In May 2001, after negotiations involving representatives of society, UNMIK promulgated a Constitutional Framework for Provisional Self-Government in Kosovo. The framework established provisional institutions of self-government in the legislative, executive and judicial fields, including an Assembly, Presidency, Government and Ministries, as well as a court structure comprising a Supreme Court, district courts and municipal courts. The framework confirmed the right of persons to file complaints with the office of the ombudsperson and the independence of several commissions including a banking and payments' authority and election commission.

21. Local participation in East Timor was initially effected through the National Consultative Council, set up in December 1999, comprised of representatives of the National Council of East Timorese Resistance (CNRT), political groups outside the CNRT, the church and UNTAET officials, appointed by the TA. The Council was envisaged to be the 'primary mechanism through which representa-

tives of the people of East Timor shall actively participate in the decision-making process during the period of the UNTAET, and through which the views, concerns and interests of the East Timorese people will be represented.' It functioned under ultimate authority and chairmanship of the TA who retained legislative powers. The National Consultative Council was replaced by the National Council in July 2000, a body with provisional parliamentary competencies such as the power to require the appearance of 'Cabinet Officers' to answer questions regarding their functions and to initiate, modify and recommend regulations. Members of the National Council represented a wider spectrum of interest groups including political parties, religious groups, women, youth, NGO society, professional associations and the districts. The final decision-making power remained vested in the TA who chaired the Cabinet meetings. The National Council functioned in tandem with a Cabinet made up of Cabinet Officers appointed by the TA, with the power to formulate policies and programs for the government, supervise the East Timor Administration, recommend regulations to the National Council, and after adoption by the Council, to the TA for approval and promulgation.

VI. Accountability

22. Questions of accountability are more acute given the broad powers afforded to the TA under transitional administration mandates, the lack of separation between legislative, judicial and executive powers, and the lack of in-built checks and balances. The Secretary-General directed UNMIK to be guided by internationally recognized human rights as the basis for the exercise of its authority. However, other than the elaboration in Regulation No. 1, no mechanism was established to ensure compliance with human rights norms was set up. In fact, human rights monitoring mechanisms established by the UN Commission on Human Rights, have entertained complaints by individuals from territories under UN administration. For example, the UN Special Rapporteur on Torture has reported on complaints received from individuals in Kosovo.[5]

23. The sweeping powers given to the TA raise questions of individual accountability as well as accountability of the UN administration as a whole. The establishment of a non-UN oversight body in Kosovo, made up of countries with representation in the territory and regional organizations, provides an interesting example of a mechanism to remedy the lack of systems of accountability. A UN administration is first and foremost a subsidiary organ of the Security Council from where its powers derive and to whom the Secretary-General reports. Mission staff are UN staff to whom a distinct set of rules and regulations apply including functional immunity. The military component reports to national command centers and take their operational orders from the Force Commander. Consequently, the entity that governs the territory is not directly accountable to the people it administers nor for that matter has it been elected or otherwise chosen by the people in the territory it is administering. The governmental authority is not based on an expression of the will of the people, though in the case of UNTAET, a period of transition under the authority of the UN formed part of the choice for indepen-

dence under the popular consultation and therefore it may be argued that UN administration was based to some extent on an expression of the will of the people concerned.

24. In a functioning democracy, remedies such as an independent and impartial court and an ombudsman may be available to address grievances of persons disadvantaged by actions of persons exercising public functions. Under UN administrations, accountability structures have a dual function, in relation to alleged abuse of authority by members of the interim administration, as well as regards members of emerging local administrative structures. Moreover, implementation of adequate accountability mechanisms for staff of UN territorial administrations assumes added importance in that its actions lay the foundations for the practice of future indigenous institutions.

25. In Kosovo, an Ombudsperson was established in 2000 with the power to investigate complaints from any person or entity concerning actions constituting an abuse of authority by the interim civil administration and emerging local or central institutions. However, the Ombudsperson has subsequently criticized the 'blanket lack of accountability afforded by UNMIK to KFOR and civilian personnel which paved the way for immunity of the state.'[6] In East Timor, a regulation to establish an Ombudsperson's Office which could entertain complaints against UNTAET officials was drafted but not adopted and the Ombudsperson's Office did not function.

26. The absence of adequate accountability mechanisms for UN staff is not specific to UN territorial administrations but has caused concern in peacekeeping missions around the world. In East Timor, in a number of cases of alleged criminal acts committed by UN staff, the Secretary-General clarified that immunity does not apply to acts committed outside the performance of official duties and proceedings before local courts were in fact initiated. In Kosovo, a regulation clarified the immunities and privileges of members of KFOR and UNMIK. However, in practice there is no transparent and satisfactory mechanism to address alleged abuse by officials in UN transitional administrations. Likewise, establishing accountability mechanisms for indigenous structures set up under the UN mandate, such as the police, has not always been given the necessary priority.

VII. Concluding remarks

27. Designs for UN territorial administrations do not include mechanisms that ensure the UN's observance of principles of good governance such as accountability, local participation and the rule of law. The dual functions of UN territorial administrations as organs of the United Nations and administration of the territory complicate this further. The application of principles of good governance by UN administrations assumes added importance as institutions set up by the UN become permanent features of the territory and the UN regulations will effectively remain applicable for some period after the UN administration leaves.

NOTES

1 UN Security Council Resolutions 1244 (June 1999) and 1272 (October 1999).
2 UN Commission for Human Rights, Res. E/CN.4/RES.2000/64.
3 'How Not to Run a Country: Lessons for the UN from Kosovo and East Timor,' (conference paper 2001) p. 1.
4 Jarat Chopra, 'Building State Failure in East Timor', 33/5 *Development and Change* (2002) pp. 979-1000.
5 Report of the UN Special Rapporteur on Torture, E/CN.4/2002/76/Add.1, 14 March 2002, p. 361, paras. 1819-1820.
6 *Special Report No. 1 on the Compatibility of Recognized International Standards of UNMIK Regulation No. 2000/47 on the Status, Privileges and Immunities for KFOR and UNMIK and Their Personnel in Kosovo (18 August 2000) and on The Implementation of the Above Regulation*, Ombudsperson Institution in Kosovo, cited in *The Democratic Republic of Timor-Leste, A new police service: A new beginning*, (Amnesty International, ASA 57/001/2003, section 6.1).

REMARKS BY HANS THOOLEN*

APPLICATION OF PRINCIPLES OF GOOD GOVERNANCE BY INTERNATIONAL ORGANIZATIONS[1]

1. GOVERNANCE AND GOOD GOVERNANCE: MOSTLY A *'TARTE à LA CRèME'*

If 'good governance' is hailed by the Secretary-General of the UN as "perhaps the single most important factor in eradicating poverty and promoting development",[2] one would assume that the term is widely understood and that substituting it by other terms such as "democracy", "human rights", "social justice" or "peace" would render the phrase above meaningless. Alas, no so much precision exists yet.

A group of experts from different EU countries recently agreed to the following elaborate definition of 'governance': "the rules, processes, and behaviour by which interests are articulated, resources are managed, and power is exercised in society. It involves the rules that define the competencies of public authorities, the rules that translate social interests and preferences into public decision-making authority, and the rules that organise market activity. It involves the legislative, executive and judicial functions of government, the interest articulation functions of political parties, trade unions, pressure groups and social movements, and the educational functions of media, schools and universities".[3]

The same group could find each other in the following description of '**good** governance': governance that promotes social cohesion, sustainable economic development and the protection of human rights. Effective realisation of these goals requires, *inter alia*, relations between State and society that are governed by the rule of law; civil society and media sectors that are free to organise and articulate public interests; State institutions that are transparent, democratically accountable and capable of ensuring the effective implementation of laws and policies; and respect for internationally-recognised human rights reflected in legislation and in the behaviour of State officials.

On its website, the World Bank uses similar language but focuses on the governmental aspect: "We define governance as the traditions and institutions by which au-

* Martin Ennals Foundation, Crete.

thority in a country is exercised for the common good. This includes (i) the process by which those in authority are selected, monitored and replaced, (ii) the capacity of the government to effectively manage its resources and implement sound policies, and (iii) the respect of citizens and the State for the institutions that govern economic and social interactions among them." In fact, most international organisations have their own definitions, including or stressing particular aspects, ranging from the 'legitimacy of government' to 'building tolerance'.[4]

The term 'good governance' is basically a catch-all for assistance policies that (1) relate to *governance* (e.g. institution building, capacity building, participation, accountability) and (2) purport to lead to a *better* situation for the country as a whole and vulnerable groups in particular.

As international organisations never pursue '*bad* governance' in relation to recipient governments, the opposite of 'good governance' is even less defined.[5] However, governments do sometimes pursue bad governance, which raises the ugly question of intervening politically, withdrawing aid or conditioning it.[6] Until now the good-governance discourse has been able to evade this thorny issue but this could change in the future.

Taking position on human rights, democracy and even good governance can create tension for international organisations. The World Bank had a spat over it back in 1991, when its President addressed the OAU General Assembly about the importance of freedom of people to participate in development, of freedom of speech and freedom from arbitrary arrest and torture, while at the same time its Vice-President for Africa claimed that development could – at least for a while – do without democracy.[7] Such views have not died out as a recent op-ed by Marina Ottaway shows. She argues, rather cohesively from the point of view of advancing governance, that Africa has a 'governance deficit' (weak administrative agencies) that needs to be addressed with priority, if need be before limited resources are spent on democracy.[8] But she does not rely on the World Bank's previous excuse that its Articles of Agreement preclude it from 'political' considerations.[9]

Still, publicly assessing the behaviour of recipient governments, in particular when it is done by international organisations, remains problematic. The United Nations Development Programme (UNDP) had its share of controversy over efforts to try and rank countries according to freedom and human rights indexes in the early nineties. The use of the term 'governance' in connection with its human development concept has been less controversial, but this may have been helped by the lack of definition as admitted by UNDP itself in a 1997 policy paper: "The challenge for all societies is to create a system of governance that promotes, supports and sustains human development – especially for the poorest ands most marginalized. But the search for a clearly articulated concept of governance has just begun".[10] Some of the key elements of good governance were already listed, such as: transparency, accountability and participation by all, in particular the most vulnerable. Good governance should also be effective, equitable, promoting the rule of law and [*a year later*] … 'integrate respect for human rights'.[11] UNDP is clearly the international organisation that has most operationalised the concept 'governance', but it has done so with regard to 'democratic governance' rather than 'good governance'.

In addition to international organisations (which are the focus of this paper), most bilateral donors also use the magical term 'good governance'. In fact they have often preceded the international organisations in this respect and some have been actively pushing international organisations in the direction of more good governance. Many continue to cooperate closely with international organisations and are funding their good governance programme and projects. However, most bilateral donors themselves use good governance as a broad concept that includes democracy and human rights, and simply list the trinity without making distinctions. Many have special departments and/or budgets that include 'good governance',[12] while the Development Assistance Committee of the OECD has had for years an Ad Hoc Group on Participatory Development and Good Governance. However, when comparing only four Northern donors in 1996, Crawford[13] concluded that the implementation of good governance varied considerably and even more than with regard to human rights and democratisation.

Given the circumstance that bilateral donors generally embrace 'good governance', it comes as no surprise that the European Commission has a fairly elaborate policy for good-governance related assistance work. A soon to be published 'Handbook on Governance' (the result of a long process of consultation and networking among the various EuropAid departments and other DGs in the EC) tries to bring together all the issues of good governance, from design to implementation. Total spending in the broad area of human rights, democracy and good governance is still not easy to identify, but is well over 500 million.[14]

An interesting illustration of the wide stretch of good governance can be found in a recent paper[15] arguing that the Organisation for Security and Cooperation in Europe should have a comprehensive concept of good governance. It describes good governance sweepingly as "governance which delivers effectively and efficiently what the population wants, above all prosperity and security." The seven broadly-formulated key components of such good governance[16] are all considered *essential* components and all need to be achieved *simultaneously* as "failure to meet any of the targets is likely to mean that work on strengthening good governance in other areas is wasted".

A telling illustration of good governance 'popularity' is that the New Partnership for Africa's Development (NEPAD) has frequently and explicitly embraced good governance language.[17] In its wake, the African Union elaborated the pledges of democracy, good governance and human rights. The latter two categories are given distinct colours by specifying that 'good governance' entails: an "accountable, efficient and effective civil service", "effective functioning of parliaments [...], anti-corruption bodies", and "the independence of the judiciary", while 'human rights' entails: "vibrant civil society organisations", "cooperation with the UN High Commissioner for Human Rights" and "responsible free expression".[18] In addition there is an African Peer Review Mechanism established that, on the basis of voluntary accession, will review performance in these and other areas.

Non-governmental organisations – in particular those involved in development – are also at ease with 'good governance' but tend to add more wishes as the following example demonstrates [emphasis added]: "Good governance is a process by which governments *and people together* identify shared values, needs and challenges,....with *shared* responsibility for outcomes that are responsive, gender-sensitive and broad-based." For good measure, the meeting added that this can only "occur within a context of *peace and stability*...and presupposes the *elimination of poverty*" and that an "underlying premise for good governance is that it requires a *legitimate government*".[19]

So, it should not be surprising that the term 'good governance' has now entered into the daily parlance of many organizations,[20] the media and politicians.[21] It is clear that the term 'good governance' has been enthusiastically but uncritically endorsed by many actors and that the lack of clarity is not seen as an obstacle. To the contrary, its open-endedness may, in fact, help to explain its popularity.

2. Good governance: 'human rights' through the backdoor?

Rightly Margot Picken points out that the international discourse on human rights has been 'enriched' by terminological innovations of unclear meaning… "Safe havens, civil society, empowerment, democratisation, governance, humanitarian, rule of law are examples of terms that have entered into international use since 1989, primarily through the Unites States. They have been influential in reorganizing the international agenda, but could divert from, rather than support, a human rights approach."[22] With the exception of the term 'the rule of law' which was introduced long before 1989,[23] the writer makes a good point, especially when contrasting it with human rights which have been 'tied down" at least to some extent and have been given common definition and meaning, although even then many people and States ignore this or deliberately 'hijack' the term for other uses.

Could it be that that 'good governance' is basically an effort by Governments of all stripes – both donors and recipients – to evade the use of the more precise and therefore more controversial terminology of internationally recognised human rights; and that weaker actors, such as international governmental and non-governmental organisations decided to make the best of it rather than to fight this obfuscation head-on?

Or could it be – more charitably – that human rights are seen as minimum standards, limited in scope and content, while good governance is more open-ended and better able to accommodate claims that are legitimate yet exceed the minimum standards of human rights? Several articles in a recent volume by the Raoul Wallenberg Institute[24] make the argument that human rights and good governance are inter-related concepts that develop along parallel tracks and that building bridges between the two is the best way to ensure both policy coherence and a higher level of implementation of human rights.

Whatever the relation between the two concepts may be, it is clear that at least the donors do see them as intimately linked and often merge them in their assistance policies. So do many international organisations, especially those that provide assistance. Therefore, a closer look at two of them may be justified: the Office of the High Commissioner for Human Rights (OHCHR) and the United Nations Development Programme (UNDP).

a. **OHCHR and good governance**

From the side of the OHCHR, good governance language is used increasingly, but predictably directly linked to human rights: "Governance is the process whereby public institutions conduct public affairs, manage public resources and guarantee the realization of human rights. *Good* governance accomplishes this in a manner essentially free of abuse and corruption, and with due regard for the rule of law. **The true test of good governance is the degree to which it delivers on the promise of human rights: civil, cultural, economic, political and social rights**" [emphasis added].[25]

Its website shows a concerted effort to 'recuperate' the good governance concept for human rights work, with titles such as:

- Good governance at the international level
- Good governance at the national level
- OHCHR and good governance
- Assistance for good governance.[26]

This concept of good governance has been 'clarified' by the Commission on Human Rights,[27] which identifies the key attributes of good governance as: transparency, responsibility, accountability, participation, and responsiveness. The same Resolution expressly links good governance to an enabling environment conducive to the enjoyment of human rights and "prompting growth and sustainable human development."

At a recent session of the Human Rights Committee, the treaty body dealing with civil and political (!) rights, the OHCHR used the following phrase [emphasis added]: "Given the experience of the Committee and the United Nations in general, the human rights cause must be advanced through the following strategies. **First,** good governance was crucial to protect and ensure human rights. Secondly, the rule of law was essential..."[28]

The 2002 Commission on Human Rights requested the OHCHR to make a compilation of practical examples of activities that have been effective in promoting good governance. The report presented in 2003,[29] is disappointing in the number of replies (nine governmental, seven international bodies and two NGOs) and illustrating the lack of definitional agreement. It is a hotchpotch of national reports *(e.g. our Constitution of 1962 proclaims that sovereignty resides in the people…)* and institutional achievements (a *programme for rehabilitation of disabled people*) that are grouped around governance, but are in fact a random sample of development aid related to human rights.[30]

Another problem is that the 'human rights assistance programme' of the OHCHR – in spite of recent increases in its fund for technical assistance - remains in absolute terms a tiny player when it comes to human rights related assistance; far more is spent through bilateral channels or through regional organisations[31]. Efforts to increase the field presence of the OHCHR have yielded some results but many of these offices are in crisis areas where normal 'good governance' work is hardly possible (usually monitoring is the prime justification for such offices). It would seem that a better solution is to seek systematic cooperation and even integration with UNDP, which has already an elaborate system of field offices and whose 'good governance' (human rights) programmes dwarf the resources of the OHCHR.

b. UNDP and democratic governance

In its 2002 report UNDP states clearly that "from the human development perspective, good governance is democratic governance" and that democratic governance means the following:

- People's human rights and freedoms are respected, allowing them to live with dignity
- People have a say in decisions that affect their lives
- People can hold decision-makers accountable
- Inclusive and fair rules, institutions and practices that govern social interactions
- Women are equal partners with men in private and public spheres of life and decision-making
- People are free from discrimination
- The needs of future generations are reflected in current policies
- Economic and social policies aim at eradicating poverty and expanding the choices that all people have in their lives."[32]

UNDP's concrete work in democratic governance is summarised into the following six categories, with a few concrete examples provided to give an indication of the size of the projects:

- *Legislatures* (example: 2,5 million US$ for Capacity Development Support to the Cambodian Parliament, 2001-2005)
- *Electoral Systems and Processes* (example: 3,7 million US$ support for the Constituent Assembly process in East Timor, 2001-2002)
- *Access to Justice and Human Rights* (example: 8,3 million US$ for the Consolidation of the Rule of Law for Conflict Reduction in Haiti, 2001-2003)
- *Access to Information* (example: 5,3 million US$ for development of the media in Mozambique – through UNESCO, 2001-2004)
- *Decentralization and Local Governance* (example: 5,1 million US$ in Cambodia to strengthen participatory local development management, 2001-2005)
- *Public Administration and Civil Service Reform.*

To enhance UNDP's ability to promote democratic governance and establish interaction with other actors, the Oslo Governance Centre was officially opened on 5 March 2002. It will focus on four policy areas within the area of Democratic Governance: Access to Justice, Civil Society, Human Rights and Conflict Prevention. UNDP also established a Thematic Trust Fund for Democratic Governance. This fund enables donors to provide additional, multi-year contributions for work in that UNDP practice area. The indicative target figure for the period 2001-2003 was 100 million US$.

Assessing what is happening in practice should not be impossible as much of what UNDP does becomes ultimately available in publications or on websites. The problems are that: (1) much of the democratic governance work is recent and the multi-year projects are often running into the mid of this decade; (2) evaluations are couched in diplomatic language, come out late, and (3) the reporting is part of a complex, multi-faceted system that does not allow easy identification of the amounts spent on democratic governance.[33]

c. **The Case for convergence**

It is nowadays widely accepted that human rights constitute a broad category, including not only civil and political rights but also social, economic and cultural rights. Moreover, many would add collective rights, such as self-determination and minority and indigenous rights. Even if some individuals and NGOs do not accept this wide definition or in practice focus on a subset, the international organisations, which are the subject of this article, all accept the wide definition.[34]

The OHCHR claims that it has been providing rights-based assistance to developing countries *since 1955* and that in that sense good governance (which it equates to a large extent with 'rights-based development') is nothing new. In 2002, the High Commissioner for Human Rights pointed out[35] that rights-based approaches bring the promise of more effective, more sustainable, more rational and more genuine development processes, such as:

- o Enhanced accountability by identifying specific duties and duty-bearers in the development process, making it easier to monitor progress.
- o Higher levels of empowerment, ownership, and free, meaningful and active participation.
- o Greater normative clarity and detail, provided by the international instruments and the authoritative interpretations of treaty bodies and human rights mechanisms, which define the content of development, including the requirements of, for example, health, education, and housing.
- o A more complete and rational development framework.
- o More effective and complete analysis: a human rights analysis reveals concerns of the poor themselves, including the phenomena of powerlessness and social exclusion.

On the other hand, UNDP also claims to have played a leading role in applying a rights-based approach to development. More generally, UNDP has since the end of the 90s explicitly embraced human rights. Its Executive Committee approved a policy on human rights in November 1997. A policy paper Integrating Human Rights with Sustainable Human Development was published in early 1998, followed by a lesser-known, but more precise document: "UNDP and Human Rights, Questions and Answers." It makes clear that UNDP wants to mainstream human rights, that human rights should be considered when planning or implementing *any* of UNDP's activities[36] and that human rights should be viewed as an integral element of the SHD concept. The same paper also sets honestly some limits on this role: that UNDP's traditional focus remains to achieve social and economic progress,[37] that its habit of working through the Government could lead it to play a soft rather than confrontational role[38] and that it sometimes will have to take distance from human rights NGOs.[39]

Whatever the remaining shortcomings may be in UNDP's good governance programme and approach to human rights (and certainly in the eyes of human rights activists they will loom large), the last decade has brought such a 'conversion' – and such an acceptance of the human rights language by donors and recipient countries alike - that there seems to be no justification for keeping a small, separate 'human rights assistance' programme in the OHCHR. Especially not now that consultation and cooperation between the two bodies has intensified and 'good governance' is almost equated with human rights, or at least with a rights-based approach to development. UNDP would have not have to engage in monitoring human rights violations, but should have no qualms about insisting on the use of the words 'human rights' (it is difficult to imagine any government that finds such language unacceptable but would perform well in good governance).

However, in case of a 'merger' of human rights development work in the UN, the OHCHR should keep preponderance with regard to the application of entry and exit criteria for good governance and human rights programmes (i.e. the decision on whether a country is in such a bad state of governance that starting or continuing good governance programmes would be both a mockery and impossibility – to be concrete: should at present Zimbabwe or Burma be recipients of good governance assistance?). The two organisations would also have to ensure that the 'subjective indicators of governance' (see below) become more universal and impartial.[40]

To the extent that these international organisations feel they can only work through governments or provide funding with explicit governmental consent, this should be spelled out in advance, which would allow other (bilateral) donors to increase their assistance through non-governmental channels.

3. Conditionality and Indicators, and Other Lessons Learnt

Libraries have been written about the topic Human Rights and Development (especially since the 80s) and it would serve no purpose to even try and summarize that discussion.[41] Suffice to say that many of the same arguments pop up in the 'good governance' debate but in a mitigated fashion. This mitigation is due to human rights having become less controversial but also to the perception that good governance is about more than 'only' human rights. Institution and capacity building (for human rights) fits easier in a good governance context as it demands long-term and heavy investment, while the political will of the recipient government is crucial for its success.

In the late nineties, donor countries showed considerable variance with regard to what should be *labelled* human rights assistance. Amid this confusion, it was observed by this author, governments could frivolously claim that almost all their aid was potentially supporting human rights: every activity in the social or cultural sphere could become human rights assistance (education, job training, housing), while food aid and medical assistance – in fact all humanitarian and emergency aid – could also qualify as such (right to life, right to food).[42] If this was true then for the human rights category, *a fortiori* such dangers would be even bigger with regard to the loose term 'good governance', unless it is accepted that the vague terminology was introduced for the very purpose of covering up such differences, in which case it can be called highly successful. But in that case one could cynically conclude that it is only a matter of time before military aid is labelled as human rights aid, e.g. when it is provided to implement the right to self-determination, a right laid down in both international covenants.

The number of donors in the area of human rights and democracy – all with their own motivations, policy guidelines, budgets and preferences – made coordination both necessary and difficult. It would seem to be no different for good governance. However, the most challenging inheritance from the debate on 'human rights and development aid' is the inter-related question of Conditionality and Indicators. Negative or positive conditionality cannot be wished away for the simple reason that resources are always limited and some choice will have to be made. This is problematic for the UN, and in particular UNDP, which in fact rejects conditionality as a matter of principle.[43] However, this does not solve the political problem of conditionality because public rankings, based on the work of international organisations, can used by other (bi-lateral) donors.

In 1990 UNDP started its Human Development Index (HDI), which measures not only GDP but also performance in health and education. Aware of the omission of the freedoms dimension, UNDP published a Human Freedom Index the following year and a Political Freedom Index in 1992. These were so controversial that they had to be withdrawn almost immediately. A decade later, in line with its emphasis on democratic governance, UNDP made a ranking of 173 countries, this time by Governance. It used *Objective indicators of governance* (elections, turn-out, women participation, trade union membership, number of NGOs) as well as *Subjective indicators of Governance* (such as human rights, voice and accountability, corruption, rule of law, law and order), warning all along that they are subjective and should not be taken as authoritative.

An interesting test will be the Millennium Challenge Account (MCA) set up by the USA. This potentially large increase in core development assistance (to 5 billion US$ over 3 years) is specifically "devoted to projects in nations that govern justly, invest in their people and encourage economic freedom."[44] There is a list of 16 indicators against which good performance will be measured. Only countries with scores above the median on half of the indicators will qualify, while special weight is given to the corruption indicator by stating that countries scoring below the median would be excluded from MCA funding.[45] These indicators are sourced with the World Bank (five governance indicators are the same as those used by the World Bank), the IMF, Freedom House, the Heritage Foundation and others. Although there is no reference to the governance ranking work by UNDP or to the OHCHR, this could well mark the beginning of the process that will make 'good governance' as controversial as human rights testing was in the recent past.

NOTES

1 This article deals only with the 'external' aspect of good governance by international organisation; it deals neither with the internal aspect (the application of good governance to their own functioning) nor with good governance by bilateral donors.

2 Pronounced in 1998, as quoted in the *Human Development Report 2002*, UNDP, p 51.

3 From DG DEV proposal (unpublished).

4 One recent overview is to be found in Mette Kjaer and Klavs Kinnerup, 'How Does Good Governance Relate to Human Rights?', in Hans-Otto Sano and Gudmundur Alfredsson, *Human Rights and Good Governance* (Martin Nijhoff 2002) pp 1-18.

5 Only Cuba submitted examples of 'bad governance' to the UN (see note 29 below) including disinvestments in economies of the South, predatory action by transnational corporations and the decline in ODA to the third world.

6 An interesting question in this context is whether the international organisation should in some way be held accountable for providing loans to countries with bad governance. It has been argued that when a regime is 'odious' enough, successor governments would not have to repay the debts on the basis of the reasoning that the previous regime showed such bad governance that banks and donors should not have made the loans to start with.

7 Described in Katarina Tomasevski, *Development Aid and Human Rights Revisited* (London, Pinter Publishers 1993) p. 62.

8 Marina Ottaway (Carnegy Endowment for International Peace), 'African Priorities: Democracy is not the place to start', *International Herald Tribune* of 23 June 2003.

9 Cf what the World Bank had to say about human rights in 1998: "The World Bank believes that creating the conditions for the attainment of human rights is a central and irreducible goal of development" in *Develop-*

ment and Human Rights (Washington, World Bank September 1998) p. 2.

10 UNDP Policy Paper, *Governance for sustainable human development* (New York, UNDP 1997).

11 UNDP Policy Paper, *Integrating Human Rights with Sustainable Human Development* (New York, UNDP 1998).

12 E.g., Australia, New Zealand, Sweden, Denmark, Switzerland, Norway, Chile, the Netherlands, Canada, USA.

13 Gordon Crawford, *Promoting Democracy, Human Rights and Good Governance through Development Aid, A Comparative Study of the Policies of Four Northern Donors* (Sweden, US, UK, EU). (University of Leeds 1996).

14 EC, Annual Report 2001 on EC Development Policy, p 188.

15 Food for thought paper of the EU on 'Good Governance and the Economic and Environmental Dimension', 14 May 2003, issued in Vienna by the Greek EU Presidency.

16 Peace and Security; Personal Safety (which includes respect for human rights); Business-Friendly Environment; Basic Needs; Transparency and Public Participation; a Skilled Public Service, and Eliminating Corruption.

17 Its website quotes the constituent document as saying: "It is generally acknowledged that development is impossible in the absence of true democracy, respect for human rights, peace and good governance."

18 African Union, Assembly of Heads of State and Government, 38th session, 8 July 2002 (AHG/235 (XXXVIII) Annex 1, pp. 5-6.

19 From the regional NGO consultation "Building Partnerships Towards a Common Agenda for Governance in Africa," co-sponsored by the UNDP and UN Economic Commission for Africa in Addis Ababa 23-24 May 1997.

20 Even the World Intellectual Property Organisation has couched in terms of good governance its institution- and capacity-building programme in the area of intellectual property rights management (E/CN.4/203/103 para 24).

21 A recent example is the debate on the Iraq war in British parliament on 18 March 2003, when Prime Minister Blair listed good governance as one of the things to be achieved, together with human rights and justice, in Iraq.

22 Margot Picken, 'Human Rights Policies of the 1990's: Some Hometruths', in Coomans, et.al., eds., *Rendering Justice to the Vulnerable* (Kluwer 2000) p 228.

23 It was the key notion of the International Commission of Jurists during the cold war period and is still an operational concept for this and other human rights organisations.

24 Hans-Otto Sano and Gudmundur Alfredsson, *Human Rights and Good Governance*, Martin Nijhoff, 2002.

25 From the website of the OHCHR: "What is good governance".

26 'Assistance for good governance' seems to be conducted through a new UN system-wide programmatic collaboration based on the ACC Matrix of Governance; however, this document cannot be found on the UN website and a request for a copy was not answered.

27 CHR Resolution 2000/64.

28 CCPR/C/SR.2012. 2012th meeting (Summary Record), 8 July 2002.

29 The Role of Good Governance in the Promotion of Human Rights (E/CN.4/2003/103).

30 A seminar – to be organised jointly with UNDP – was also foreseen by the same Resolution but could not be held due to a lack of financial resources.

31 Figures are almost impossible to come by due to widely varying definitions of what constitutes 'development aid' and what constitutes assistance to 'human rights and democracy'. For a more elaborate discussion of these aspects, see Ahmadi/Thoolen, 'Human Rights Funding', in Coomans, et al., eds., *Rendering Justice to the Vulnerable*, Liber Amicorum for Theo van Boven (Kluwer 2000) pp 259-275.

32 Human Development Report, 2002, UNDP, p 51.

33 E.g. in the 2001 Results Oriented Annual Report typical governance expenditure (strengthening key governance institutions) is a sub-goal under a general heading "Creation of an Enabling Environment for Sustainable Human Development" and provides only a break down by percentage.

34 The World Conference on Human Rights: "*Vienna Declaration and Programme of Action*, UN doc. A/CONF.157/23 (1993), part I, para. 8, reads: Democracy, development and respect for human rights and fundamental freedoms are interdependent and mutually reinforcing. Democracy is based on the freely expressed will of the people to determine their own political, economic, social and cultural systems and their full participation in all aspects of their lives. In the context of the above, the promotion and protection of human rights and fundamental freedoms at the national and international level should be universal and conducted without conditions attached. The international community should support the strengthening and promotion of democ-

racy, development and respect for human rights and fundamental freedoms in the entire world."

35 Opening statement to the General Assembly Special Session on Social Development, Geneva, June 2000.

36 Somewhat contradictorily, it says that there will also be a *Global Sub-Programme for Human Rights Strengthening* (HURIS) which will encourage programmes that focus on 'human rights' issues.

37 "Yes, the indivisibility of human rights must be maintained, but there certainly will be situations and particular times where practical action in the sphere of social and economic development will be the limit of what UNDP can achieve. We have reason to remember that the area of economic, social and cultural rights is the traditional area of operation for UNDP and will continue to be so."

38 "Some governments will not like to hear any mention of human rights in the context of the UNDP programme. In such situations arguing over words probably does less good than practical interventions which can reduce poverty, give children education, strengthen the rights of women, etc. And it should be remembered that these efforts help promote human rights, even if the activities are not called by that name."

39 "There will be situations when support to or cooperation with a human rights organization which is hostile to the government could undermine UNDP's cooperation with the government. In such a situation, the UNDP country office may find it in the best interest of UNDP to keep the human rights organization at arms length."

40 The 'subjective' indicators of governance used by UNDP and the World Bank are much too narrow in particular with regard to fundamental human rights, where US-based and US-biased organisations such as Freedom House and the Heritage Foundation often constitute the single source. Key NGOs with an international reputation, such as Amnesty International, Human Rights Watch, the International Federation of Human Rights, the Lawyers Committee for Human Rights and the World Organisation against Torture, produce annual and other reports that could and should be used.

41 My own modest effort is to be found in: o.c. note 31.

42 The donors' replies to a survey prepared for the Informal Experts Workshop organised by the OECD Development Centre, Paris, February 1996, were remarkably incomplete on the point of quantification of human rights assistance and, to the extent that (partial) answers were provided, they confirmed the variety of definitions. See Simia Ahmadi, 'Key Issues in Donor Practices: Human Rights and Development Assistance', in *Human Rights in Development Cooperation*, SIM Special No. 22 (Utrecht, Netherlands Institute for Human Rights 1998).

43 UNDP and Human Rights, Questions and Answers: Question 7: Is UNDP introducing conditionality? Answer: No. There may be situations, however, when the Executive Board can set special restrictions on the use of the UNDP resources because of the country's human rights record. The Country Cooperation Framework (CCF) is based on a dialogue been the government and UNDP and approved by the Executive Board. The UNDP policy on human rights does not change this process.

44 President George W. Bush, Monterrey, Mexico, 22 March 2002.

45 The main authors of the World Bank's research on indicators state that there is such a large margin of error in the indicators that one-third of the countries have a 25% chance to be mistakenly classified.

REMARKS BY RALPH WILDE*

THE ACCOUNTABILITY OF INTERNATIONAL ORGANIZATIONS AND THE CONCEPT OF 'FUNCTIONAL DUALITY'

It is increasingly argued that greater awareness is needed about the role of international organizations in general, and the UN in particular, in human rights violations. The UN

* Dr Ralph Wilde, Lecturer in Law, University College London (UCL), University of London, <ralph.wilde@ucl.ac.uk>. © Ralph Wilde 2003. Thanks are due to Edmond Rhys Jones for excellent research assistance. This paper is a revised version of part of a lecture delivered at the 2001 Annual Meeting of the American Society of International Law. See Ralph Wilde, 'The Complex Role of the Legal Adviser When International Organizations Administer Territory,' (2001) 95 *ASIL Proc.* 51.

reports on the genocide in Rwanda in 1994 and the massacre in Srebrenica in 1995 highlighted the role that the organization, alongside other actors, played in those horrific events.[1] Consequently, it has been suggested that the UN should generally be bound by the principles of international human rights law.[2] Those making such a suggestion usually consider the application of the law with the UN as the relevant legal person, arguing how the UN, according to the usual principles concerning legal personality, can itself be considered bound by international human rights law. In this paper, I would like to suggest that there is another, parallel way in which international law generally and international human rights law in particular come into play. This occurs in a special context: when international organizations exercise administrative prerogatives over territory.

Although much attention is presently focused on the challenges faced by the Coalition Provisional Authority (CPA) in Iraq, such challenges are familiar to those who have worked in field operations for international organizations in recent years. The exercise of administrative prerogatives over territory by international organizations – what I term international territorial administration (ITA) – witnessed an upsurge towards the end of the last century.[3]

In Bosnia and Herzegovina, certain governmental functions – such as the passing of laws and the dismissal of government officials – have been asserted by the Office of the High Representative (OHR), a *sui generis* entity created by the Dayton Peace Agreement and an associated Security Council Resolution.[4] In addition, certain members of key government institutions – from the Constitutional Court to the Human Rights Chamber – are foreigners appointed by international organizations.[5] In Bosnia and Herzegovina, then, we have what I term 'partial ITA': certain administrative prerogatives asserted by international organizations, operating alongside other such prerogatives exercised by local actors. An historical example of this would be the UN Mission in Cambodia in 1991 (UNTAC), which was given the authority both to carry out elections and to supervise certain governmental activities to ensure that the elections were free and fair.[6]

In Kosovo and East Timor, what I term 'plenary ITA' was implemented. From 1999, the United Nations Mission in Kosovo (UNMIK) and the United Nations Transitional Authority in East Timor (UNTAET) asserted the right to exercise full administrative prerogatives in their respective territories, although some of these prerogatives were delegated to other international entities – such as the OSCE who carries out the elections in Kosovo – and/or exercised after consultation with local actors.[7] Whereas UNTAET's mandate ended with East Timorese independence in May 2002, UNMIK's administrative role in Kosovo continues pending a settlement of the territory's final status. There are a number of historical precedents for plenary ITA, such as the UN Transitional Authority in Eastern Slavonia (UNTAES) which ran from 1996 to 1998.[8]

The second route to the application of international human rights law in the territorial administration context exists because of the distinctive nature of the activity being performed. In the administration missions, the international organizations involved do not claim sovereignty in the sense that the territories in question are their own (albeit on a temporary basis). Rather, they claim the right to administer territory, either by consent of the territorial sovereign, on the authority of the Security Council, or both. Given that the starting point for determining sovereignty under international law is to ask whether or not the actor concerned actually makes a claim to this particular entitlement, none of the territories in which ITA takes place can be considered 'international' or 'UN' territory in the sense that territorial title is enjoyed by the international organizations exercising administrative prerogatives therein.

To take the examples of Kosovo and East Timor, Kosovo is considered to be still formally a part of what is now called Serbia and Montenegro, and the enjoyment of title by that State is implicitly affirmed by the Security Council in the way it frames the United Nations' administration mandate in the territory.[9] However, the same mandate leaves Kosovo's future status open.[10] In East Timor the situation is reversed. When UNTAET was created, the intended future status of East Timor was clearly established as statehood, but the territory's status during the period of UN administration was less clear.[11] Since Indonesia had formally renounced its dubious claim to title, but East Timor had not yet declared independence, East Timor during that period was either still part of Portugal or enjoyed a form of *sui generis* legal personality as a non-State territorial entity that was to become a State within a finite period. What is clear, however, is that it was not – despite the suggestions of some commentators – UN 'sovereign' territory.[12]

In each situation of international territorial administration, therefore, two legal persons are in play. First, the international organization which enjoys legal personality in international law. Second, the relevant territorial unit, whatever its status. So with Kosovo and East Timor we are concerned with territories that form part of larger legal persons (the States of Serbia and Montenegro and Portugal, respectively) or, in the case of East Timor, possibly a *sui generis* non-State territorial entity.

One way of understanding the link between these two legal persons is to see the international organization as asserting the power to act as the territorial government. In international law, the term 'government' refers to the agent through which the legal person of the State (or a non-State/sub-State territorial entity) acts. Applying the term in this context means that the administrative acts of the United Nations in Kosovo and East Timor are or were, legally the acts of Kosovo and East Timor, at least for the duration of the United Nations' governmental powers in each place. So when UNMIK and UNTAET passed regulations in Kosovo and East Timor, these regulations were binding as the law of Kosovo and East Timor.[13] Equally, when in February 2000 UNTAET signed an agreement with the Australian Government to continue the regime exploiting the resources in the Timor Gap until independence, it did so 'on behalf of East Timor.' The agreement would seem to be binding as between East Timor (whatever its status was at the time) and Australia, rather than between the United Nations and Australia.[14]

In the usual run of things, the corporate entity performing the governmental role in the State does not have legal personality on the international legal plane in its own right. It serves only as agent for an actor which *does* enjoy such legal personality: the State. In these projects, by contrast, the body acting as the agent for one international legal person (the State or sub-State/non-State territorial entity) also enjoys international legal personality in its own right. This situation was discussed in a case before the Constitutional Court of Bosnia and Herzegovina at the end of 2000.[15]

The case arose from a decision made by OHR on 13 January 2000, imposing the 'Law on the State Border Service.'[16] Eleven members of the House of Representatives of the Parliamentary Assembly initiated proceedings before the Constitutional Court, asking the Court to evaluate the constitutionality of the law. The Court first had to decide whether the case was admissible, since the High Representative enjoys 'final authority . . . in theatre' to interpret his mandate – effectively immunity *rationae materiae* – and, moreover, is immune from suit as a legal person – immunity *rationae personae*.[17] These immunities might suggest that the case would be inadmissible before the Court.

However, in its judgment of 3 November 2000, the Court looked carefully at the character of the activity performed by OHR. It stated that OHR's role is 'not unprecedented' and in the context of previous instances of such a role being performed, remarked that:

> Though recognized as sovereign, the States concerned were placed under international supervision, and foreign authorities acted in these States, on behalf of the international community, substituting themselves for the domestic authorities. Acts by such domestic authorities were often passed in the name of the States under supervision.[18]

The court went on to say that:

> Such situation amounts to a sort of functional duality: an authority of one legal system intervenes in another legal system, thus making its functions dual. The same holds for the High Representative: he has been vested with special powers by the international community and his mandate is of an international character. In the present case, the High Representative – whose powers are not subject to review by the Constitutional Court – intervened in the legal order of Bosnia and Herzegovina substituting himself for the national authorities. In this respect, he therefore acted as an authority of Bosnia and Herzegovina and the law which he enacted is in the nature of a national law and must be regarded as a law of Bosnia and Herzegovina.[19]

Effectively, the Court said that the acts of OHR are the acts of two distinct legal persons simultaneously. On the one hand, they are the acts of OHR, which has international legal personality. On the other hand, they are governmental acts within Bosnia and Herzegovina and, as such, are the acts of the State of Bosnia and Herzegovina. While such acts could not be reviewed as acts of the High Representative because of the immunity he and his acts enjoy with respect to national law, they could be reviewed as acts of the government of Bosnia and Herzegovina, in this case as the acts of the legislature. This is not because the acts were somehow jointly performed by OHR and the locally constituted parts of the legislature – the acts in question were performed by OHR exclusively – but that the OHR performed them in its capacity as part of the government of the State.

The approach taken by the Court suggests that the distinctive nature of the activity conducted in these missions gives rise to an equally distinctive (and unusual) legal situation. As a matter of international law, the missions involve one legal person – the international actor – taking on, in whole or in part, the role of agent for another legal person – the State or non-State/sub-State territorial entity – without losing its own distinctive legal personality in the process. As a result, the international actor manifests the 'functional duality' mentioned by the Court. Its functions flow from, or give rise to, its own legal personality, and operate within, and serve as acts of, another international legal person.

The 'functional duality' of international organizations in the ITA missions is analogous to those circumstances in which a State official simultaneously engages State responsibility and his or her individual criminal responsibility. Individual State officials used not to enjoy distinct international legal personality in respect of the official acts they performed. Their acts were considered solely as acts of the State and not also the acts of the individuals personally. However, international criminal law changed this situation by creating a functional duality for individuals with respect to certain acts. Such acts, as well as engaging the international responsibility of the State (because they are official), also engage the international responsibility of the individual. Two legal persons are in play on the commission of a single act.

Moreover, because of this functional duality two different legal regimes are in play simultaneously. On the one hand, we have the law applicable to States (comprising international law) and the law applicable to State governments (comprising national law and, indirectly, the international law that applies to States). So in the Bosnia and Herzegovina case, the issue was the application of domestic constitutional law to the acts of the legislature. On the other hand, we also have the legal regime applicable to international organizations, comprising international and domestic law. Again, in the Bosnia and Herzegovina case, the Court could not even investigate what law might be relevant here, since a case relating to OHR directly would have been inadmissible. As before, the scenario of two regimes of law applying to the same activity echoes the situation for those official acts that give rise to individual criminal responsibility in international law. So in the *Pinochet* case we had alleged acts of torture that, as acts of the Chilean State, were violations of international human rights law and, as acts of Pinochet the individual, were also violations of international criminal law.[20]

Two sets of international legal standards are therefore potentially in play with respect to the same acts. So in the sphere of human rights, we have not only the international human rights law that is applicable to international organizations qua international organizations.[21] The international human rights law applicable to States can *also* be in play when a governmental role is performed. This is not because the acts performed by international actors are analogous to the acts performed by national governments – this would be relevant to the issue of the law applicable to international organizations qua international organizations – but, rather, because these acts *are* the acts of national governments. Such norms are binding, therefore, in a different sense: not on the international organization directly but on the State whose responsibility is engaged by the acts of the organization. As agents of that State UN officials must comply with the international legal norms applicable to it. Moreover, these norms, and the norms applicable to international organizations, are not just both in play – they are both in play with respect to the same acts.

As the Bosnia and Herzegovina case above suggests, the second aspect of this situation of two concurrently applicable regimes is that each administrative act is simultaneously immune, and not immune, from national jurisdiction, depending on which of the two legal persons is being focused on. If the act is being considered in its capacity as an act of an international organization, then the immunities claimed by the international organization involved would prevent jurisdiction.[22] However, if the act is being considered in its other capacity as a governmental act, then the above-mentioned immunities are inapplicable. The question then will be whether governmental acts, and the officials who perform them, are immune from jurisdiction rather than whether the acts of international actors, and the individuals who perform them, are so immune. Again, the analogue of individual criminal responsibility, as discussed in the *Pinochet* case, is instructive here. In *Pinochet*, the situation was one of exercising jurisdiction not over the State for the acts of torture involved – even if one could conceive of State criminal responsibility, the State was immune – but, rather, over the individual for the same acts. Since the assertion of jurisdiction was under this separate heading of individual responsibility, the immunities of the State were irrelevant.

The situation of 'functional duality' in international territorial administration missions requires officials on such missions to think differently about their role, and the potential standards that are applicable to it. As government officials, they need to be trained in, and appraised in accordance with, the domestic and international standards applicable to the conduct of State governance – for example administrative law on the domestic level, and international human rights law on the international level. Whatever the scope of the international human rights obligations applicable to the international organization, the full range of State obligations are also applicable when the governmental role is performed. Officials need to be aware of this latter set of obligations, and ensure that their behaviour is in conformity with them. If they do not, their acts will give rise to violations of international law, in this case violations committed by the State or non-State/sub-State unit in whose name they act.

Notes

1 See Letter dated 15 December 1999 from the Secretary-General addressed to the President of the Security Council (containing the *Report of the independent inquiry into the actions of the United Nations during the 1994 genocide in Rwanda*), UN Doc. S/1999/1257, 16 December 1999; Report of the Secretary-General pursuant to General Assembly Resolution 53/35, The fall of Srebrenica, A/54/549, 15 November 1999.

2 See Ralph Wilde, '*Quis Custodiet Ipsos Custodes?*: Why and How UNHCR Governance of "Development" Refugee Camps Should Be Subject to International Human Rights Law,' 1 *Yale Human Rights & Development Law Journal* 5 (1998) (hereinafter Wilde 1998), in relation to refugee camp administration, and Ralph Wilde 'Accountability and administration in Bosnia, Kosovo and East Timor,' (2001) 7 *ILSA Journal of International & Comparative Law* 455, in relation to territorial administration generally.

3 The factual information and the purposive analysis referred to in this chapter is set out in more detail in Ralph Wilde, 'From Danzig to East Timor and Beyond: the Role of International Territorial Administration,' (2001) 95(3) *AJIL* 583, hereinafter Wilde 2001.

4 On OHR in Bosnia and Herzegovina, see Wilde 2001, above note 3, 584n4, 584n8, 585n10, 594-6, 599-601, sources cited therein and accompanying text.

5 On the international appointments in Bosnia and Herzegovina, see Wilde 2001, above note 3, 584n9 sources cited therein and accompanying text, 597, 599.

6 On UNTAC, see Wilde 2001, above note 3, 598 and sources cited therein.

7 On UNMIK in Kosovo, see e.g. Wilde 2001, 585n11, 585n13, 593-5, 597, 598-601. On UNAMET and UNTAET in East Timor, see e.g. Wilde 2001, above note 3, 585n12, 597 (for UNAMET) 585n12, 585n13, 593, 595, 599, 600 (for UNTAET).

8 On UNTAES in Eastern Slavonia, see e.g. Wilde 2001, above note 3, 589, 590 and sources cited therein. Eastern Slavonia is part of Croatia.

9 See SC Res. 1244, para. 10 & preamble para. 10; Agreement on the Principles (Peace Plan) to Move Towards a Resolution of the Kosovo Crisis Presented to the Leadership of the Federal Republic of Yugoslavia by the President of Finland, Martti Ahtisaari, representing the European Union, and Viktor Chernomyrdin, Special Representative of the President of the Russian Federation, 3 June 1999, Contained in Letter from Germany to the President of the Security Council, 7 June 1999, para. 5.

10 SC Res. 1244, para. 11(e); see also Annex 1, para. 8

11 The intended future status of East Timor as statehood is implicit in SC Res. 1272, pmbl., para. 3.

12 For such a suggestion, see e.g. Jarat Chopra, 'The UN's Kingdom of East Timor,' (2000) 42 *Survival* 27 at 29-30.

13 UNMIK Regulation 1999/1 (as amended) contained in Regulation 2000/54, 27 September 2000, UNMIK Doc. UNMIK/REG/2000/54 (2000), §1.1, 4, and UNMIK Regulation 1999/24, 12 December 1999, UNMIK Doc. UNMIK/REG/1999/24 (1999), §1.1. For East Timor, see SC Res. 1272, paras. 1, 6, and UNTAET Regulation 1999/1, 27 November 1999, UNTAET/REG/1999/1 (1999), §1.1, 3, 4.

14 UNTAET's repeated reference to 'acting on behalf of East Timor' in its note contained in the Exchange of Notes constituting an Agreement between the Government of Australia and the United Nations Transitional Administration in East Timor (UNTAET) concerning the continued Operation of the Treaty between Australia and the Republic of Indonesia on the Zone of Cooperation in an Area between the Indonesian Province of East Timor and Northern Australia of 11 December 1989, 10 February 2000, 2000 Austl. T.S. No. 9. Note also the citation of UNTAET alongside the 'Government of Australia' rather than 'Australia' in this title.

15 See Constitutional Court of Bosnia and Herzegovina, Case U 9/00 (evaluating the Law on State Border Service), 3 November 2000, available at <http://www.ustavnisud.ba/home/en/index.html> (hereinafter Case U 9/00).

16 Office of the High Representative, Decision Imposing the Law on State Border Service, 13 January 2000, available at <www.ohr.int>.

17 See General Framework Agreement for Peace in Bosnia and Herzegovina, 14 December 1995, (1996) 35 *ILM* 75, Annex 10, Art. III, para. 4 (privileges and immunities), Art. V (final authority to interpret mandate).

18 Case U9/00, above note 15, para. 5.

19 *Id.*

20 See *Regina* v. *Bow Street Stipendiary Magistrates and Others, ex parte* Pinochet Ugarte (No. 3) [1999] 2 WLR 827, [2000] 2 AC 147.

21 As argued in Wilde 1998, above note 2.

22 For OHR immunity see above note 16. For UNMIK immunity, see UNMIK Regulation 2000/47, 18 August 2000, UNMIK Doc. UNMIK/REG/2000/47 (2000). UNTAET considered itself immune within East Timor but did not promulgate a regulation to this effect.

Discussion

Erika De Wet (University of Amsterdam): I have a question for Ms. Meindersma and Mr. Wilde, concerning the absence of an Ombudsperson in East-Timor. The case that Mr. Wilde mentioned at least had the effect that the actions of the Office of the High Representative in Bosnia-Herzegovina could be measured against international human rights standards. To my knowledge, nothing has been struck down so far, but at least it *can* have the effect that there is some kind of control over UN officials. In Kosovo, there is an Ombudsperson who has some supervision over the actions of UNMIK, if not necessarily over the civil actions of KFOR. To the best of my knowledge, nothing like this has ever been implemented in East-Timor, and I find that the UN has immense nerve in imposing so-called 'standards of good governance' on a country, such as East-Timor, while it does not even provide for an Ombudsperson, which, even though a restricted mechanism, provides for some form of independent human rights monitoring. I cannot see how there can be any legitimacy if you impose these – very good – standards on a territory without emplacing or structuring a mechanism for self-monitoring. Please correct me when these gaps in the system have been filled, but to my knowledge they are still there.

Christa Meindersma: During UNTAET, the transitional authority in East-Timor, there was an attempt to establish an Ombudsperson-institute. A regulation was drafted, but never adopted. There was an Ombudsperson, but he was not functioning. In UNMIK the situation is different: there is an Ombudsperson. There is also a regulation in Kosovo that clarifies the immunities of KFOR and the members of the transitional administration. At the moment, in the independent country of East-Timor, I have not really touched upon it, but UNMISET, the mission I am currently part of, has a very interesting mandate. It is not a transitional authority, but, as Mr. Wilde would perhaps call it, has elements of it. Still, in its mandate there are important powers that are partially, if not entirely, with the UN. For instance, the ultimate responsibility for the police still rests with the UN. This raises the issue of the accountability of international police officers. At the moment, the only mechanism is the internal professional standards review, which is a process that completely lacks transparency. It does not always achieve a satisfactory result, if any result at all. On a positive note, in a number of cases in East-Timor that clearly went beyond 'abuse of governmental authority', 'negligent exercise of authority' etc., so in cases of alleged criminal conduct by UN staff, the Secretary-General has clarified that immunity does not apply. He did not waive immunity, but said that it does not apply, since immunity is linked to the exercise of functions by UN staff. Consequently, national laws were enforced against a number of UN staff members in national courts. One such case was an alleged rape and one concerned alleged drunk driving by a UN staff member resulting in a traffic accident, causing the death of an East-Timorese person. At the moment, an 'Office of the Provedor', that includes but is not limited to the functions of an Ombudsperson, is being set up at the national level in East-Timor. A very interesting question that has not been clarified so far is to what extent that Office would have powers in relation to UNMISET personnel, when UNMISET still partially fulfills or facilitates a governmental mandate.

RALPH WILDE: Indeed there is a paradox in the idea of inculcating democracy and good governance through a mechanism which is fundamentally undemocratic, imposed on the local population and lacking the checks and balances that the UN would normally call upon States to accord in the operation of national governments. I suppose that this is partially explained by the fact that these missions were set up in emergency post-conflict situations, and that they are supposed to be temporary. That is to mitigate the, as it were, dictatorial way in which they operate. It seems to me that that is perhaps defensible in the first weeks or months of a mission, but within a year such missions should be in the position to set up domestic accountability mechanisms relative to their administrative activities. Of course, the mission in Kosovo has been there since 1999, in Bosnia-Herzegovina the High Representative has been there since 1996. I would draw your attention to cases before the Human Rights Chamber in Bosnia-Herzegovina where legislation by the High Representative is now being reviewed. Of course, the lack of domestic accountability mechanisms is replicated on the international level, where there are no adequate supervisory mechanisms for the conduct of administration by international organizations either. In my own work, I trace the parallels between these missions and the mandate in trusteeship systems. Of course, in those systems there is quite an advanced supervisory mechanism. In the trusteeship system, for instance, by the Trusteeship Council. That system was not revised in the context of East-Timor and Kosovo. One could imagine the problems with making Kosovo a trust territory, given the self-determination entitlement consequences of trust territory-status. However, there would not seem to be any problem in that regard as far as East-Timor is concerned. Yet even in the context of East-Timor a trusteeship council that could have offered an international supervisory mechanism for the conduct of the administration was not revised, which I find regrettable. I think that the Security Council offers a degree of scrutiny, but that is of course by the same body that was involved in conceiving the mandate of the mission. It falls well short of the idea of a supervisory mechanism that operates at one step removed from the actor being supervised.

TANYA VELLA (UNESCO Culture Sector): If, from your experience in Kosovo and East-Timor where the UN had a transitional administration mandate, you had to pick some basic principles of good governance applicable for transitional administrators, even in the absence of a Chapter VII, UN Charter mandate, what would they be?

My second comment pertains to the definition of global governance. In his pursuit of perpetual peace, Immanuel Kant (1795) held that the legal principles implemented within each State should ultimately lead to a global legal order that unites all people and abolishes war. He found that a 'federation of nations' could be in the self-interest of each State, based on the peaceful character of republics, the power of international trade and on the regulatory function of the public sphere (global civic society). Despite some limitations, it could be applied today.

RALPH WILDE: I cannot adequately answer your question on the principles of good governance for transitional administrators, but it really is time for an attempt to an idea of how these missions should be set up. The structures that are created in these territories, as Ms. Meindersma has pointed out, are remarkable projects of political, constitutional transformation. It is simply not enough for people to go in and try their best, drawing on their own experience and national background as a basis for creating a government and a constitution of a new State. One can appreciate the 'neo-colonial angst' that prevents the UN from coming up with a universal model that can be transplanted to any country in the world, but it seems to me that if the UN is actually in the business of creating new States in this way, there needs to be more joined-up thinking about the kind of structures that are going to be introduced in those territories.

CHRISTA MEINDERSMA: I agree with what has been said. Maybe not going as far as a 'universal model' that could be applied anywhere for the reasons mentioned, but some inbuilt checks and balances on the absolute powers given to the transitional administrations are necessary. A mechanism of accountability needs to be established for people who are put in the position to exercise those absolute powers. In the current missions, both UNMIK and UNTAET, one can look far and wide, but those checks and balances are not there. They are not inbuilt. I think that some form of checks and balances should be devised for and built in any future mission.

THEODOR MERON: Thank you very much. I would like you to join me in thanking the panelists for their splendid presentations. This session is adjourned.

*Reporter: A.W. Eikelboom**

* Amsterdam.

MULTINATIONAL BUSINESS AND CORPORATE GOVERNANCE – PUBLIC AND PRIVATE INTERNATIONAL LAW

Corporate Governance – The Role of Internal or External Codes of Conduct

The panel was convened by its Chair, René van Rooij*.

Introductory remarks by René van Rooij

Good morning Ladies and Gentlemen and welcome to the section devoted to corporate governance and the role of codes of conduct. I am working for an international oil company (Royal Dutch Shell) but I am here in a private capacity. What I observed over the years working for an international company in the field of natural resources is that the line between the public and the private sector is becoming vaguer. And that should be in itself a very interesting subject for discussion.

The speakers of today are talking about various aspects of this subject: which rules and principles apply in public and private international law in relation to behaviour of companies ('business principles') in the international arena.

The order of the speakers will be as follows. First, Lucy Reed will give a 'helicopter view' on codes of conduct (the general picture). The second speaker, Willem van Genugten, will discuss the question whether these codes and commitments contain binding rules or not. Michel Nussbaumer will do a side step into a very interesting area of Eastern Europe, and will discuss corporate governance rules that EBRD are developing for that part of the world. And, finally, Jaap Winter will talk of certain rules of corporate governance, which have been developed recently under his leadership in Europe.

Lucy Reed is a partner in an international law firm, Freshfields Bruckhaus Derringer specializing in public international law and arbitration. She has had an impressive career. She acted as an arbitrator of the Ethiopia–Eritrea claims commission. She is a member of the Executive Committee of the American Society of International Law. She has been general counsel of an international organisation dealing with North Korea, the Korean Energy Developing Organization, which is a subject of attention in the press nowadays. And formerly she was a lawyer with a Legal Advice Office of the US State Department and US agent for US-Iran claims tribunal.

* Shell, London.

Remarks by Lucy F. Reed and Hannah R. Garry*

From the aspirational to the operational: Multinational corporations, corporate codes of conduct and human rights

In our work we do regularly advice multinational clients either directly on codes of conduct, or how to deal with allegations, when they have violated laws or situations that are covered nowadays by the codes of conduct. I will make a few points about the special needs and codes in the extractive and natural resources industries. Not because my chairman is from Shell, but because it is a special sector for that purpose.

1. Introduction

International human rights law traditionally applies to the conduct of States within their respective jurisdictions. In the immediate aftermath of the atrocities of WWII, beginning with the International Bill of Rights,[1] there has been rapid development of human rights law through international conventions calling for respect and promotion of individual rights and freedoms.

While the State unquestionably remains the predominant authority within the 21st century, there has been a marked rise in the importance and influence of various non-State actors. One of the most powerful is the multinational corporation (MNC).[2] In the past decade, the number of MNCs has increased dramatically. The UN Conference on Trade and Development (UNCTAD) estimates that there are now 65,000 MNCs worldwide. More than half of the world's largest economies are corporations; for example, General Motors has a bigger economy than Denmark.[3] Post-Cold War MNCs have been a "prime mover" for globalization[4] and world economic growth, accelerating the diffusion of technology, trade and communication through cross-border investments and transactions. The same globalization phenomenon has allowed for the international media to expose MNC conduct *vis-à-vis* respect for human rights within host countries where they are investing and where they are often more powerful than the host State itself.[5] MNC investments, particularly in cash-strapped developing countries, have increasingly been politicized. Rightly or wrongly, MNCs have been associated with the complex human rights abuses often plaguing the countries where they are investing. A direct result has been a loss of credibility, consumer boycotts and increased litigation costs, especially in US courts under the Alien Tort Claims Act (ATCA), ultimately leading to lost profits for some MNCs. Furthermore, there has been increased demand for greater national and international regulation of MNCs with regard to overseas investments and respect for human rights.

In response, multilateral organizations such as the United Nations (UN) and the Organization for Economic Cooperation and Development (OECD), governments, non-governmental organizations (NGOs), and corporations themselves have drafted "codes of conduct" (Codes or Corporate Codes) regulating corporate social responsibility of MNCs, including with regard to respecting human rights norms. The prolif-

* Lucy Reed and Hannah Garry are members of the international arbitration group of Freshfields Bruckhaus Deringer LLP. This paper reflects their personal views. They thank their colleague Stéphanie Giry for her invaluable help.

eration of model corporate codes has increased dramatically in the past several years so that some MNCs are now complaining of "code fatigue" as they attempt to incorporate the latest developments.[6] In addition, there has been a greater willingness by MNCs to engage with their critics, particularly NGOs, to formulate new development initiatives for dealing with human rights abuses in the countries where they do business.[7] On the one hand, one author has hypothesized that these developments indicate "the beginning of a second human rights revolution" not pertaining to States, but to MNCs as private actors.[8] On the other hand, another author argues that the proliferation of corporate codes has failed to date to be sufficient for proving MNCs *actual* commitment to upholding human rights norms.[9]

The purpose of this paper is to present an overview of the increased attention to respect for human rights norms by MNCs in their business practice as evidenced in recently drafted corporate codes of conduct. As a case study, this paper notes efforts made within the extractive industries. As observed by one executive of a large extractive industry company, "the exploration, extraction and distribution of mineral and petroleum resources take companies to some of the 'most difficult operating environments in the world.'"[10] The complexities faced by MNCs with regard to human rights are particularly acute for those in the extractive industries whose investments are often tied to the natural resources of States with failed or weak government structures. Where human rights problems erupt due to conflict, endemic corruption, or lack of the rule of law, these MNCs cannot simply pull out their investments.

Section One briefly defines what is meant by "corporate codes of conduct," distinguishing between those which are internally and externally generated. This section also gives an historical framework for the explosion of corporate codes addressing human rights norms. Section Two compares some of the internal and external corporate codes recently drafted for and incorporated by extractive MNCs addressing human rights concerns and highlights methods for implementation including acceptance, reporting, external monitoring and internal enforcement mechanisms. Section Three presents the current debate surrounding the efficacy of voluntary, non-binding corporate codes for ensuring respect for human rights by MNCs in host countries. This section flags recommendations that have been proffered for making corporate codes more credible in the absence of a legally binding multilateral regulatory framework.

It is submitted that the recent voluntary efforts by MNCs to promote and protect human rights norms are to be applauded as a "first step" towards a new human rights revolution. Through corporate codes that make explicit reference to proactive responsibilities on the part of *private* actors to uphold human rights, MNCs are contributing to the evolution of international human rights law going beyond the simple requirement that non-State actors refrain from infringing on the rights of others. MNCs, by example, are also contributing to strengthening enforcement of human rights norms *vis-à-vis* the conduct of States. However, it is imperative that MNCs endeavor to ensure that the codes are not aspirational only; it is in their long-term business and ethical interests to take further steps that indicate genuine commitment to realization of these rights.

2. The historical development of MNC corporate codes of conduct incorporating respect for human rights

Defining corporate codes of conduct

There is no one standard definition for what constitutes a "corporate code of conduct." With that in mind, this paper adopts the following definition:

> *"Codes of conduct are statements that encompass the company's core beliefs related to its ethical practices and its responsibilities to uphold human rights, labor, and environmental standards in all its operations and the operations of its suppliers."*[11]

Codes of conduct are non-legal policy statements voluntarily adopted by corporations with a view towards socially responsible behavior in their respective business activities. Corporate codes for MNCs may be drafted internally by corporations themselves or externally by industry groups, labor organizations, NGOs, governments and intergovernmental organizations such as the UN, OECD, and the International Labor Organization (ILO). The content and form of corporate codes varies widely, ranging from the very general to the specific. With regard to internal corporate codes, The Conference Board, a non-profit business membership and research organization of over 2,500 businesses with a presence in 60 nations, has identified three typical categories:[12]

- *Compliance Codes*: directives, which give specific guidance and prohibit certain kinds of conduct.
- *Corporate Credos*: broad, general statements often made publicly (for the benefit of suppliers, customers, consumers and shareholders) which encompass a corporation's values, objectives, and commitments to its constituencies.
- *Management Philosophy Statements*: formal enunciations of the company or CEO's way of doing business.

As for external corporate codes, they range from broad aspirational declarations calling for respect for values and norms generally, to more specific documents addressing topics such as: the environment, labor rights, apartheid, and health and safety issues. While adoption of external corporate codes is also non-binding, some multilateral organizations may require adoption of a code and compliance with it in exchange for membership in that organization.

External codes of conduct

In 1974, first efforts were made towards *binding* international regulation of MNCs with regard to human rights and their investments in host countries. The UN Economic and Social Council (ECOSOC) formed the UN Commission on Transnational Corporations (TNCs) for the purpose of drafting a binding international code of conduct for TNCs. Establishment of the Commission was influenced in part by lobbying from the G-77 group of newly independent States who wanted to ensure that TNCs would neither threaten their sovereignty nor exploit them economically. Paragraph 14 of the 1990 draft code, (similar to paragraph 13 of the 1982 draft) provided that:

"14. Transnational corporations shall respect human rights and fundamental freedoms in the countries in which they operate. In their social and industrial relations, transnational corporations shall not discriminate on the basis of race, colour, sex, religion, language, social, national and ethnic origin or political or other opinion."

By 1992, negotiations for a global code of conduct failed due to the inability of the drafters to strike an acceptable balance between the obligations of MNCs to respect human rights in their business practices and the assurances of host States to provide for non-discriminatory treatment and protection of MNC investments. In 1994, the Commission was moved from the auspices of ECOSOC to UNCTAD, signaling that, post-Cold War, developing countries have suffered from an "acute shortfall of investment" and thus MNCs "are no longer seen as suspicious intruders ... but rather, as welcome and wealthy guests."[13] Consequently, talks of international regulation of MNC conduct *vis-à-vis* human rights through a binding code of conduct have fallen by the wayside in the race to attract foreign investment.

In the 1970s, in addition to efforts towards a binding global code of conduct through the UN, two other multilateral organizations developed voluntary "guidelines" regulating member MNCs primarily with regard to labor rights. In 1976, the OECD produced the Guidelines for Multinational Enterprise (OECD Guidelines). While the original OECD Guidelines did not explicitly make reference to respect for human rights in overseas investments, they did call on multinational enterprises to respect certain rights such as freedom of association and nondiscrimination in employment. In 2000, the new OECD Guidelines were issued and state more broadly that multinational enterprises should "[r]espect the human rights of those affected by their activities consistent with the host government's international obligations and commitments."[14] Under the OECD Guidelines, the Universal Declaration of Human Rights and other human rights obligations of the host government are of relevance to the MNCs; MNCs are to encourage their business partners – suppliers, contractors, subcontractors, and licensees – to also respect human rights; and MNCs are urged to increase transparency of their operations by making disclosure statements on their commitment to social responsibility to the public and those affected by their activities.[15]

In 1977, the ILO released its non-binding Tripartite Declaration of Principles for Multinationals and Social Policy. In the first paragraph of the declaration, the ILO recognized the ability of multinational enterprises to contribute "to the enjoyment of basic human rights, including freedom of association, throughout the world."[16] The declaration makes explicit reference to protection of rights such as the freedom of association, the right to collective bargaining, and freedom from discrimination in employment.[17]

At the same time that the OECD and ILO were releasing their guidelines, Reverend Leon Sullivan, a board member at General Motors, led a private international initiative to develop a corporate code of conduct specifically combating apartheid in South Africa. By 1986, nearly 200 of the 260 US corporations conducting business in South Africa adopted the "Sullivan Principles" which required non-discriminatory practices in the workplace and called for strategic investments in South African communities aimed at bringing an end to racial oppression. "Sullivan companies" were graded on their commitment to upholding the principles through public audits conducted by Arthur D. Little, a Massachusetts consulting firm. In the end, while the Sullivan principles were not enough to dismantle apartheid itself, they contributed to desegregation within South Africa and attracted global condemnation of the policy.

Following the demise of apartheid, Reverend Sullivan developed the "Global Sullivan Principles of Social Responsibility" at the request of industry leaders and with the assistance of several MNCs. Although currently on standby, these new principles call for: express support for "universal human rights," equal opportunity and freedom of association in the workplace, and cooperation with local governments and communities to improve the quality of life in host countries where MNCs are investing. Endorsers are to implement the principles through internal policies, procedures, training and reporting structures. They are also asked to publicly report their efforts towards implementation of the principles in business practice on an annual basis, which is then published on the Global Sullivan Principles website.

One of the most recent international initiatives is the UN Global Compact. In July 2000, Secretary-General Kofi Annan launched the Global Compact following his speech in January 1999 before the World Economic Forum in Davos. Annan called on the private sector "to embrace, support and enact a set of core values in the areas of human rights, labour standards, and environmental practices."[18] Today, over 700 companies, in addition to NGOs, labor organizations, and academic institutions, have pledged support for the nine principles that make up the Global Compact. Principles 1 and 2 explicitly call upon businesses to "support and respect the protection of international human rights within their sphere of influence" and to ensure that they are not complicit in human rights abuses. The UN Global Compact Office in New York works in partnership with the Office of the UN High Commissioner for Human Rights (OHCHR) in Geneva which seeks to provide information and education on human rights to MNCs; to recognize good business practices which enhance enjoyment of human rights; to support corporate codes of conduct and auditing procedures; and to ensure accountability for human rights violations by MNCs as private entities.[19] In the words of Secretary-General Annan in a speech to international business leaders in April 2002, the Global Compact is an effort by the UN (authorized by General Assembly resolution) "to gain greater relevance in the twenty-first century by showing that it can work with non-State actors, as well as States, to achieve the broad goals on which its members have agreed."

Internal codes of conduct

The proliferation of MNC internal codes of conduct has to a large extent been reactive, responding to external events involving human rights violations and accusations of alleged complicity. In the early 1990s, MNCs in the clothing and footwear industries concentrated efforts on drafting corporate codes and industry codes with regard to protection of human rights, especially labor rights, after media discoveries of forced labor and child labor in the factories of China, Southeast Asia and El Salvador. These MNCs include Levi Strauss, Sears, the Gap, Nike, Reebok and Timberland. Their corporate codes have included requirements of minimum respect for human rights by vendors; have gone beyond stipulating respect for labor rights to protection for civil and political rights such as freedom of association and expression; and have provided investment criteria for MNCs on whether or not to do business in a country with human rights problems.[20]

In 1995, international attention was focused on the extractive industries with the trial and execution of Ogoni environmental activist Ken Saro-Wiwa in Nigeria. Royal Dutch Shell came under international scrutiny when the *New York Times* investigated its joint venture with Nigeria's State oil company. The Nigerian military brutally suppressed the Ogoni people for their protests against environmental damage to their lands due to oil drilling and against the sole use of oil revenue by the corrupt Nigerian government. Shell was castigated by the international community for its alleged complicity and silence with regard to these human rights violations against the Ogoni.

These events led Shell and many of the major oil companies such as Exxon, Mobil and British Petroleum to draft human rights-specific corporate codes of conduct. These codes have been accompanied by detailed procedures for pre-investment assessment of risks of human rights abuses being committed in host countries, for training employees on human rights and for reporting on human rights abuses. For example, in 1997, Shell amended its "Shell Group Business Principles" (first published in 1976) to incorporate explicit human rights language for the first time. Shell companies are expected to promote the principles in their relationships with contractors and suppliers and in joint ventures. In 1998, Shell published its "Human Rights Management Primer" (the Primer), which seeks to introduce Shell employees to the concept of human rights and international law pertaining to respect for human rights norms. As a supplement to the Primer, Shell's "Human Rights Training Supplement," produced in collaboration with human rights NGOs, provides case scenarios of various "human rights dilemmas" and points to consider for handling them. Finally, Shell has also developed its "Group Security Standard,""Guidelines on the Use of Force," and "Rules of Engagement" for operating in complex security situations. Each year in its annual report, Shell provides detailed internal and external assessments with data tables analyzing its progress in promotion of and respect for human rights in the countries where it is operating.

3. The Drafting of Corporate Codes for the Extractive Industries Regarding Security and Human Rights

As demonstrated by past conflict in the Niger Delta, the province of Aceh in Indonesia, and Colombia, companies in the extractive and energy sectors are often confronted by complex issues relating to ensuring the safety of their investments on the one hand while respecting human rights on the other. In response, in December 2000, the US State Department and the British Foreign and Commonwealth Office initiated the "Voluntary Principles on Security and Human Rights" (the Principles). For the first time, *governments* initiated and developed principles addressing protection of human rights in collaboration with major US and British oil and mining companies such as Chevron, BP and Shell *and* with human rights NGOs including Amnesty International, Human Rights Watch and International Alert. These principles demonstrate that home governments have important economic and political stakes in ensuring that their "flag companies" in the extractive and energy sectors continue to do business in various host countries, enjoy good global reputation, and play a part in strengthening respect for human rights internationally.[21]

The principles provide specific guidance for MNCs such as recommending preliminary risk assessment for both short and long-term operations by gathering extensive background information on local conditions including political, economic, civil or social factors which may create security of investment risks; root causes, patterns and potential for violence in various regions; human rights records of public and private security forces; rule of law in the local courts for holding violators of human rights accountable; and past incidents of human rights violations related to MNCs' equipment transfers to public or private security.

In deploying local public security forces, MNCs are encouraged to do thorough background checks on human rights violations; to consult regularly with local communities about the impact of security arrangements on them; to encourage security arrangements to be open and transparent; to ensure that the type and number of public security forces deployed and the use of force is proportional to the threat; to comply with applicable laws and regulations for equipment transfers to public security forces; to encourage human rights training for public security forces; and to record, report, and actively monitor credible allegations of human rights abuses by public security in their areas of operation.

Finally, where public security is unavailable or unwilling to protect MNCs' assets, MNCs may deploy private security forces following the same general guidelines for interacting with public security. However, MNCs should also ensure that private security engages in "preventative and defensive" services *only* and not responsibilities exclusive to State military or law enforcement officials. In so doing, MNCs are encouraged to have contractual provisions in their employment contracts that allow for discipline and/or termination upon discovery of credible evidence of unlawful and abusive behavior.

In addition to the Voluntary Principles on Security and Human Rights initiative, the UN Global Compact office and OECD have conducted their own studies on the increasingly important topic of the role of the extractive industries in zones of conflict. In March 2001, the UN Global Compact launched its first policy dialogue on the issue with over 100 participants from NGOs, MNCs, the World Bank and the UN resulting in publication of two reports in April and May 2002. One key aspect of the May report is the emphasis on "pragmatic solutions" such as "revenue-sharing regimes."[22] Revenue-sharing regimes promote equitable distribution of resources among MNCs, host governments and local communities. They may include bilateral agreements with indigenous peoples (such as in Australia between Western Mining Company & Normandy Mining with the Bla'an tribe which created a local Community Development Fund financed by mining royalties) or multi-stakeholder natural resource funds (such as the Niger Delta Development Commission) which are paid for by the host government and oil companies, professionally invested and audited by a third party, and designed to support sustainable development and remediate environmental damage.[23] The report emphasizes the importance of effective transparency mechanisms and dispute resolution clauses, such as arbitration clauses, in order to create legitimate revenue-sharing regimes.[24] Finally, the Global Compact produced a how-to business guide for MNCs on managing risk and assessing human rights, humanitarian law, labor, environmental and transparency issues while operating in conflict zones.

In May 2002, the OECD Secretariat published its paper, "Multinational Enterprises in Situations of Violent Conflict and Widespread Human Rights Abuses," responding to the circumstances surrounding the Yadana pipeline in Myanmar. The report documents violence and human rights violations in the immediate vicinity of extractive MNCs' operations and provision by extractive MNCs of "large revenues" to corrupt and weak governments as both the "means" and "motive" for conflict.[25] The report also summarizes current efforts being made by extractive MNCs to combat human rights abuses through reform of internal management practice, development of guidelines for operations, and collaboration with local governments for transparency and accountability in budget processes.

4. The efficacy of MNC codes of conduct relating to respect for human rights

Given that existing corporate codes for MNCs, both internal and external, are entirely *voluntary*, the efficacy of a corporate code for changing corporate behavior and effecting positive change with regard to respect for human rights by MNCs "depends on its credibility [which] ... depends on monitoring, enforcement and transparency."[26] As noted in this article's summary of the provisions in various existing MNCs' corporate codes, the extent to which they actually give practical guidance to MNCs for respecting and protecting human rights varies. In order for MNC corporate codes to be truly credible, they must move beyond the merely aspirational to the operational.[27] The Voluntary Principles on Human Rights and Security seem to be a step in the right direction. How is credibility achieved?

First, it is important that MNCs play a primary role in the drafting of the codes while involving all possible stakeholders such as governments, NGOs, employees and local populations.[28] MNCs will be more willing to take "ownership" of their responsibilities to uphold human rights norms, while the involvement of all stakeholders helps to ensure proper implementation of the codes.[29] The codes should be drafted by top management within MNCs rather than public relations or communications offices in order to avoid the codes being seen as mere public relations.[30]

Second, it is imperative that the drafting of the MNC codes of conduct is clear and unambiguous. To that end, it is helpful for the codes to be "narrowly tailored to address substantive issues with a high level of detail."[31] This does not mean that codes should "succumb to the 'Tyranny of the Minimum;'" rather, they should seek to incorporate higher standards of ethical behavior for MNCs. The language of the codes should expressly incorporate human rights norms and inform decision-making with detailed plans of action for responding to a variety of possible scenarios where human rights abuses occur.[32] It is advisable that in-house or other legal counsel versed in international human rights law are involved in the process.

Third, MNCs need to effectively disseminate their codes of conduct among employees, suppliers, subcontractors and those protected by their provisions in order to enhance protection of human rights.[33] As a supplement to dissemination, MNCs must implement proper training programs on the codes *vis-à-vis* responsibilities of the MNC to uphold and protect human rights norms.

Fourth, MNC codes should provide for viable enforcement mechanisms. These may include public reporting on compliance with the codes; monitoring which is internal (e.g. through a committee, ombudsman, regular reporting obligation, field visits, contractual self-certification by subcontractors or hot lines (to answer questions on the guidelines or report suspected violations) and/or external (e.g. through an NGO, outside auditor, or consultant); complaint or grievance procedures for those affected by MNC business practice;[34] appropriate disciplinary measures where there is a violation of the corporate codes; and positive reinforcement for abiding by the codes such as retention of existing contracts or awarding of new contracts.[35]

With regard to disciplinary measures, broad general statements should be avoided whereby violations of the codes may merely be cause for correction. Rather, disciplinary measures should apply to the primary violator as well as others involved in the misconduct requiring specific action such as counseling, oral or written reprimands, warnings, probation or suspension without pay, demotions, reductions in salary or termination of employment.[36] Other possible measures include monetary fines or penalties, corrective action, provision of education to the violator(s) or cancellation of a contract.[37]

5. Conclusion

The existing plethora of voluntary MNC codes incorporating obligations to respect and protect human rights is a significant development in the new human rights revolution applying to private, non-State actors. "Corporate codes of conduct have extended the responsibility of the corporation from the shareholder to the communities and global marketplace where they operate."[38] Furthermore, "the idea of a corporation as a legal fiction without responsibilities [for the protection of humanity] is no more sacred or accurate than the idea of unfettered State sovereignty."[39] No longer do MNCs strictly subscribe to the argument of Nobel prize-winning economist Milton Friedman that "there is only one social responsibility of business ... to increase its profits so long as it stays within the rules of the game."[40] Studies of MNCs indicate an increased willingness to forego investment opportunities on human rights grounds.[41] In addition, "new patterns of dialogue and partnership are emerging as companies become more willing to acknowledge the need to engage" on human rights issues with NGOs and other stakeholders.[42] Overall, MNCs have recognized that proactive respect for human rights norms in their investments is in the interest of their bottom line.

However, the success of this new human rights "revolution" hinges on the MNC codes being "made real through concrete implementation strategies."[43] At present the large numbers of corporate codes, both internal and external, which address human rights issues have been criticized for being "short on specific content," "not taken seriously" within MNC organizational structure, and lacking "effective and meaningful [external] monitoring procedures" to ensure compliance.[44] In sum, as highlighted previously in this paper, if private actors such as MNCs are to voluntarily assume international legal responsibilities for individual rights through their codes of conduct, it is imperative that they demonstrate the seriousness of their intent by making their codes of conduct credible at every stage of the process from drafting, to implementation, to enforcement.

Notes

1 The "International Bill of Rights" is the common phrase used to refer to the rights and obligations contained within the 1948 Universal Declaration of Human Rights (UDHR) which were later incorporated into

binding multilateral treaties including the 1966 International Covenant on Civil and Political Rights (ICCPR), the 1966 Optional Protocol to the International Covenant on Civil and Political Rights, and the 1966 International Covenant on Economic, Social and Cultural Rights (ICESCR).

2 In this paper, we adopt the definition of a multinational corporation as "a corporation with affiliated business establishments in more than one country." *See* Barbara A. Frey, *The Legal and Ethical Responsibilities of Transnational Corporations in the Protection of International Human Rights,* 6 MINN. J. GLOBAL TRADE 153 n. 2 (Winter 1997).

3 Corporate Watch, *What's Wrong with Corporations?* (visited 9 July 2003) <http://www.corporatewatch.org.uk/pages/corporations.html#Anchor-Corporations-14210>.

4 The International Labor Organization (ILO) refers to "globalization" as "a process of growing interdependence between all people ... spurred by market liberalization and information, communication and transportation technologies." ILO, *Globalization,* at p. 1 *available at* <http://www.itcilo.it/english/actrav/telearn/global/ilo/globe/new_page.htm> (visited 16 April 2003).

5 Bennett Freeman, Maria B. Pica, Christopher N. Camponovc, *A New Approach to Corporate Responsibility: The Voluntary Principles on Security and Human Rights,* 24 HASTINGS INT'L & COMP. L. REV. 423, 424 (Spring 2001).

6 *Id.* at 425. Some of the codes which have proliferated include the UN Global Compact, the Global Sullivan Principles, the OECD Guidelines for Multinational Enterprises, the ILO Tripartite Declaration of Principles Concerning Multinational Enterprises, the ICC Charter of Sustainable Development, the Ceres Principles, and the Caux Roundtable Principles, to name a few.

7 *Id.* at 424.

8 Douglass Cassel, *Essay: International Security in the Post-Cold War Era: Can International Law Truly Effect Global Political and Economic Stability? Corporate Initiatives: A Second Human Rights Revolution?,* 19 FORDHAM INT'L L.J. 1963, 1964 (June 1996).

9 S. Prakash Sethi, *Setting Global Standards* (John Wiley & Sons, Inc., 2003).

10 OECD Secretariat, *Multinational Enterprises in Situations of Violent Conflict and Widespread Human Rights Abuses,* WORKING PAPERS ON INTERNATIONAL INVESTMENT, No. 2002/1 (May 2002) at p. 6.

11 David M. Schilling, *Making Codes of Conduct Credible, in* GLOBAL CODES OF CONDUCT 221, 224 (Oliver F. Williams, ed., 2000).

12 *See* <http://www.conference-board.org> (visited 22 June 2003) *as cited in* ILO, *Corporate Codes of Conduct,* at p. 1 *available at* <http://www.itcilo.it/english/actrav/telearn/global/ilo/code/main.htm> (visited 11 March 2003).

13 *See* Frey, *supra* note 2 at 167.

14 Article 2, OECD Guidelines for Multinational Enterprises *available at* <http://www.oecd.org> (visited 11 March 2003).

15 OECD Committee for International Investment and Multinational Enterprises, *OECD Guidelines for Multinational Enterprises: Review 2000 Commentaries,* (27 June 2000) at pp. 3-5 *available at* <http://www.oecd.org> (visited 11 March 2003).

16 International Labour Office, *Tripartite Declaration of Principles Concerning Multinationals and Social Policy,* at para. 1 (Geneva, November 1977 *as amended* November 2000) *available at* <http://www.ilo.org/public/english/employment/multi/tridecl/index.htm> (visited 11 March 2003).

17 *Id.* at Arts. 8, 21 and 42.

18 UN Global Compact Office, *The Global Compact: Report on Progress and Activities (July 2002),* at p. 3 *available at* <http://www.unglobalcompact.org> (visited 11 March 2003).

19 UN Global Compact Office, *The Global Compact and the Office of the High Commissioner for Human Rights,* at pp. 1-2, *available at* <http://www.unglobalcompact.org/content/TheNetwork/unAgencies/unAgencies_OCHR.htm> (visited 11 March 2003).

20 *See* Frey, *supra* note 2 at pp. 177-180.

21 Freeman et al., *supra* note 5 at p. 427.

22 Juliette Bennett, *The Role of the Private Sector in Zones of Conflict 2: Conflict Prevention and Revenue-Sharing Regimes,* GLOBAL COMPACT POLICY PAPER SERIES (May 2002).

23 *Id.* at pp. 1, 13, 16-17, 19.

24 *Id.* at pp. 4, 6.

25 OECD Secretariat, *supra* note 10 at pp. 3-4.

26 ILO, *Corporate Codes of Conduct, supra* note 12 at p. 2.

27 Freeman et al., *supra* note 5 at p. 435.
28 *Id.* at pp. 429-30.
29 *Id.*
30 Schilling, *supra* note 11 at p. 225.
31 Freeman et al., *supra* note 5 at p. 435.
32 *Id.* at pp. 429, 436.
33 Garth Meintjes, *An International Human Rights Perspective on Corporate Codes in* GLOBAL CODES OF CONDUCT 83, 95 (Oliver F. Williams, ed., 2000).
34 *Id.*
35 ILO, *Corporate Codes of Conduct, supra* note 12 at p. 2.
36 As provided in the Halliburton Code of Business Conduct *available at* <http://www.halliburton.com/about/3_0001.jsp> (visited 10 July 2003).
37 ILO, *Corporate Codes of Conduct, supra* note 12 at p. 2
38 Freedman et al., *supra* note 5 at p. 429.
39 Meintjes, *supra* note 33 at p. 87.
40 *Id.* at p. 86.
41 The Shell Group, *Business and Human Rights: A Management Primer*, at p. 16 *available at* <http://www.shell.com> (visited 11 March 2003).
42 Freeman et al., *supra* note 5 at p. 424.
43 Schilling, *supra* note 11 at p. 226.
44 Sethi, *supra* note 9 at p. 82.

DISCUSSION

DIMITROS VRYONIDES*: Let me play the role of devil's advocate here. Many people believe or complain that the codes of conduct are at the end of the day PR operations for many industries – either to improve tarnished public images. I can give a very concrete example. When one company sold infant formulas to many children in Africa – the public relations crises which ensued basically placed them in the corner where they had no other alternative, but to immediately develop a code of practice to alleviate what was happening to them. So the question is: is there any evidence on how the codes really work – is there any evidence that these codes really work? I have specific industry in mind where we know that the codes of conduct were developed, but self-regulation was not successful and that was the tobacco industry.

LUCY REED: I pointed out in my presentation that the code of conduct is only a voluntary norm, a step and internal compliance is important. In this respect, I recall one study, which is an old, thought a good study. The point in the study was that the major factor leading multinational companies, again in extractive industries from moving from proposal to actual project was human rights risks in the area – twenty percent withdrew from the project. Sixteen percent turned away because of the corruption in the region. So I think that this is an important factor. But I am optimistic and believe that the first step is made and there are at least codes, and now it is time to implement and monitor compliance.

RENé VAN ROOIJ: Let me give you some personal observations. Although I am not here on behalf of my company, the name of Shell has been mentioned several times. Lucy said that Shell and other companies have had these codes only recently. But in

* Dimitros Vryonides, United Nations, Switzerland.

Shell and quite a few other companies these codes have existed for many decades. The Shell code was refined about 6-7 years ago, language about human rights was included.

These codes are two-fold – they are indeed a reaction to developments in the outside world, to which companies respond. Companies are part of society in a particular country and also of the global society. The influence which companies have on the societies in which they operate, is sometimes a bit overrated. And the world around them has a huge impact on them. People do not buy their products if they are seen to behave unethically. But more importantly, something which most people do not realize, is the importance of staff morale. People will generally not wish to work for, or be a director of, a company, which behaves unethically.

Remarks by Willem van Genugten*

Companies and human rights: the binding character of voluntary codes of conduct[1]

First, let me specify the title of my presentation – it is about the involuntary character of voluntary codes of conduct. Since it is a legal conference, I will give legal arguments, I can give you four. The core is a combination of human rights and companies. It will not be about financial issues, or salaries, on which there also exist a number of voluntary codes.

1. Introduction

Codes of conduct for companies, internal as well as international ones, are always characterized as 'voluntary'. They are based on self-regulation, meaning that companies opt for standards they like and that external supervision is absent, even in cases the self-regulation is not leading to results that should be realized according to the codes of conduct themselves. The question is, however, whether codes are as voluntary as they look like at first sight. 'Voluntary' is often seen as the opposite of 'legally binding', the latter rightly associated with 'enforcement'. However, there is a huge gap between 'voluntary' on the hand and 'legally binding' on the other. How about this 'grey zone'?

2. Internal codes of conduct: contracts and promises

Internal codes of conduct deal with such issues as the absence of corruption, the intention to operate in a way which contributes to sustainable development, and the application of basic social standards, for instance in the field of child labour, forced labour and freedom from discrimination. In order to have a clear insight into the legal/semi-

* Prof.dr. Willem van Genugten, Professor of International Law at Tilburg University and Professor of Human Rights at Nijmegen University.

legal/non-legal status of these internal codes of conduct, it is first of all fruitful to make a clear distinction between generally worded (provisions in these) codes, and more specifically worded intentions. If a company states that it will insist on 'fairness on all levels of its economic activities', such a formulation might be considered valuable from a moral point of view, although even then it can be considered an 'open door' formulation, which lacks specificity. However, legally speaking it is quite useless. Suppose an employee would address a national court, complaining about a lack of fairness of his company management which did not offer him the job that was given to a less qualified colleague, the court would never accept the relevant provision in the internal code of conduct as a source of law. If, however, the code states that the company will pay specific (levels of) wages for specific types of work, or if it explicitly says that the company will not make use of child labour, thereby even specifying what it considers to be child labour, this creates controllable obligations, which can even be used within legal procedures. In that case, the relevant provision of the code of conduct can be woven into a legal defence, as a supportive argument as well as a secondary source of law. A provision like the one related to child labour, for instance, creates expectations which are legally speaking relevant, and which come close to real contractual obligations.

Other grounds than the one indicated, can also give legal effect to internal codes of conduct. One such ground relates to the rules of fair competition amongst enterprises. If a company states it will not make use of labour for which it pays less than five times the local minimum wage, and the company uses such an argument when advertising its products, rival companies have a case at the moment that it becomes clear that the 'promising company' does not keep its word. The same goes for what I would like to call 'promises to consumers'. Many internal codes of conduct are not only applicable to internal business practices in the more strict sense of the word, but also to chains of contractors, sub-contractors and even buying agents. If a company states in its internal code of conduct that it will not make use of semi-manifactured articles produced with child labour, this again raises legally relevant arguments. Suppose a toy shop sells footballs made under the conditions as described. It would definitely have a case against the company importing the balls, even if the needlework was done by the company's subcontractors. The same would go for a consumers' organisation, making use of the possibility of an *actio popularis* to complain about the company's breach of its self-created obligations. It also would have a case, which, in many ways, resembles the one following from a breach of an official written contract.

3. International codes of conduct: self-regulation with consequences

Over the years, several international codes of conduct have been adopted. One can refer to the Guidelines for Multinational Enterprises, adopted by the OECD in 1976 (and since then modified several times)[2] and to the Tripartite Declaration of Principles Concerning Multinational Enterprises and Social Policy, adopted by the International Labour Organisation (ILO) in 1977.[3] Without going into detail as to the contents of these and other international codes of conduct, one can say that they are highly relevant from the perspective of the present contribution. The ILO code, for instance, states, in relation to the issue of human rights protection: 'All the parties concerned by this Declaration (…) should respect the Universal Declaration of Human Rights and the corresponding International Covenants adopted by the General Assembly of the United Nations as well as the Constitution of the International Labour Organisation and its principles according to which freedom of expression and association are essential to sustained progress.'

In relation to such international codes of conduct, it is also often stated that they are (more or less) meaningless from a legal point of view. They are, alongside with internal codes, considered to function on a voluntary basis, to contain morally and – due to the involvement of governments – politically binding provisions, but in terms of legal coercion they are considered next to void. The arguments partly run like the ones concerning internal codes of conducts. The same goes for my counter-arguments. I will not repeat these, but add some which specifically relate to international codes of conduct.

First of all, one can say that some of the international codes have their own implementation mechanisms, which make them at least 'quasi-legally binding'. For the implementation of the OECD Guidelines, for instance, a system has been developed, consisting of, amongst others, the possibility to raise concerns about the non-implementation of the OECD Guidelines by parties concerned at the OECD Committee on International Investment and Multinational Enterprises (CIME), whose major task it is to provide clarifications on the interpretation of the Guidelines. Weak as it is from a strictly legal point of view – the OECD itself states 'that the non-binding nature of the Guidelines precludes the Committee from acting as a judicial or quasi-judicial body'[4] – the system makes the Guidelines more binding than they are normally said to be. OECD Member States cannot freely neglect the CIME clarifications and observations, as if they are expressions of a passenger coincidentally coming by in the international economic arena. The same goes for the ILO Tripartite Declaration, to which the ILO developed a system of questionnaires, asking governments for information about the implementation of the Declaration. The system is based on the ILO code itself, which in its Introduction states that 'triennial surveys are conducted to monitor the extent of the application of the Declaration by governments, employers, workers and MNEs [Multinational Enterprises]'. As to the ILO 'implementation procedures', one can, amongst (many) other things, also refer to the Organisation's Constitution, saying in Article 19, para. 6 about the binding or non-binding character of its recommendations that 'apart from bringing the Recommendation before the said competent authority or authorities, no further obligation shall rest upon the Members, except that they shall report to the Director-General of the International Labour Office, at appropriate intervals as requested by the Governing Body, the position of the law and practice in their country in regard to the matters dealt with in the Recommendation, showing the extent to which effect has been given or is proposed to be given, to the provisions of the Recommendation and such modifications of these provisions as it has been found or may be found necessary to make in adopting or applying them'. Binding in a strict legal sense? No. Binding in the broader sense, as discussed in this paper? No doubt.

Despite these 'implementation mechanisms', the legal character of both the OECD and the ILO code is – and can indeed be – disputed. The OECD itself makes the following statement on this issue: 'The [OECD] Declaration on International Investment and Multinational Enterprises [of which the Guidelines form a part, WvG] constitutes a political commitment, adopted by the Governments of the OECD countries in 1976 with the objective of facilitating direct investment among OECD Members. (...) The Guidelines are voluntary and, consequently, not legally enforceable. This, however, does not imply less commitment by OECD Governments to encourage their observance.'[5] In addition, the OECD states that the Guidelines 'carry the weight of a joint Recommendation of OECD Governments' and that they 'alongside with national laws (...) form part of the legal infrastructure which promotes responsible behaviour of MNEs.'[6] 'Not legally binding on the one hand', and belonging to 'the legal infrastructure' on the other. Is that not a grey zone?

Further evidence for their legal status, can be found in the codes themselves, in combination with the way they have been adopted, as well as the way implementation and supervision are taken care of. In general, one can say, that *States* are the producers of new international legal instruments – mainly treaties, but one should also think of the ways they contribute to the coming into existence of international customary law – and that, subsequently, States can decide to be bound by it, for instance, by ratifying the treaties they have developed. In the case of the OECD code, however, taking into consideration the involvement by employers' as well as employees' organisations, and even more in the case of the ILO code, which is made by an organisation that is famous for its tripartite structure (governments, employers and employees being represented in all the important ILO policy-making bodies), one can say that the standards have been co-developed by *the companies themselves*. The ILO code, for example, states that 'the principles [set out therein] are intended to guide the governments, the employers' and workers' organisations and the multinational enterprises in taking (...) measures', etc. In other words: the employers involved in the process of adopting the declaration, 'order' *themselves* to live up to it. We then speak about 'self-regulation', but it would be a mistake to misunderstand the word as 'without binding force' or 'without engagement', as is often done. The latter would be similar to saying that international actors in their common international arena can say and promise whatever they want, without legal or quasi-legal repercussions. Apart from the very important notion that self-regulation, without external control, might be a good, or even the best, system to make companies move towards practices that are in conformity to internationally accepted human rights standards, in the area of the OECD as well the ILO self-regulation also has a serious, quasi-legal content. In addition, one can think of both codes in even strict legal terms. See the arguments related to the specificity of the provisions and contractual obligations I gave in the section on internal codes. They are relevant *mutatis mutandis* in the case of a breach of international codes like the ones adopted by the OECD and the ILO.

4. Internal and International Codes of Conduct, and Their 'Marriage' to the ILO 'Human Rights Conventions'

Due to their activities in diverging cultural and economic contexts, (multinational) companies in many ways are concerned with issues like child and forced labour, discrimination, the freedom to establish trade unions and the right to collective bargaining. These issues are covered by the so-called 'human rights conventions' of the ILO: C.29 (1930) on Forced Labour; C.87 (1948) on Freedom of Association and Protection of the Right to Organise; C.98 (1949) on The Right to Organise and Collective Bargaining; C.100 (1951) on Equal Remuneration; C.105 (1957) on Abolition of

Forced Labour; and C.138 (1973) on Minimum Age, in 1999 partly replaced by C.182 on The Prohibition and Immediate Elimination of the Worst Forms of Child Labour.[7]

The ILO 'human rights conventions' are considered to belong to the peremptory standards of international law (*ius cogens*). Of course, companies cannot be parties to treaties. They are bound by international legal standards through the States they legally speaking belong to. In that respect, it is interesting to note that in 1998 the ILO adopted its Declaration on Fundamental Principles and Rights at Work,[8] which declares that 'all Members, even if they have not ratified the Conventions in question, have an obligation arising from the very fact of membership of the Organization, to respect, to promote and to realize, in good faith and in accordance with the Constitution, the principles concerning the fundamental rights which are the subject of those Conventions'. The adoption of the Declaration, as well as of the (light) supervisory procedure annexed to it – consisting of the publication of an annual global report on the core rights (i.e., *grosso modo* the standards incorporated in the previously mentioned 'human rights conventions') to be reviewed by the ILO Governing Body –, was broadly supported by the employers active in the tripartite International Labour Conference of the ILO. It makes the Declaration and its follow-up mechanism an interesting combination of self-regulation and (light) supervision from outside.

5. Some conclusions

Talking about co-responsibilities for companies in the field of human rights and related issues is 'in the air' again. The question is what this means in terms of international legal obligations and the consequences thereof. My answer is: inevitably a lot, in the short run (a situation which can be considered *de lege lata*, i.e., the already existing legal and quasi-legal obligations) as well as in the long(er) run, i.e. *de lege ferenda*: law that still has to come into existence. Law basically reflects (or rather: tries to reflect) dominant moral and practical conceptions, be it on the national level or on the level of the world community of States. It is not a static phenomenon, which does not adapt itself to new situations and demands. As such, it is obsolete to think that States, and to some extent individuals, are the only real subjects of international law. In that respect one can think of 'non-State actors' like companies. There is an undeniable trend to broaden the scope of international law (standards as well as supervision), and to admit as well as urge other actors than States and individuals, including companies, to enter the playing field of international law. This is basically related to the new 'division of labour' in today's world: States accompanied by the 'civil society' in setting standards and discussing implementation procedures, and the free market ideology asking States to partly (!) withdraw themselves from the scene and to make room for companies.[9] Their activities then have to be carried out with full respect for recognized human rights principles. Companies will have to act in accordance to international human rights law whether they like it – and say so in their self-regulatory voluntary codes – or not.

Doing so, companies are not free to pick and choose from international law whatever they want. International law is not a shop from which one can take whatever one likes, forgetting about the less profitable and less convenient elements. Although many parts of international law are treaty based only, meaning that the standards are only binding for those States that decide to become a party to the relevant treaties, many other parts of international law belong to the previously mentioned *ius cogens* standards, a violation of which is not allowed, not by States nor by non-State actors like companies. The discussion then is not about the question of whether the standards are binding or not, but about the question of whether the implementation and supervisory procedures are sufficient (see the proceedings op Panel B 2).

Having said that, it might be good to underline that self-regulation without external legal control might work, and often actually works. Knowing that companies are not acting in a vacuum, and are 'helped' by the international civil society and its many members, self-regulation might well lead to a situation which is in conformity to the standards discussed in this paper. But legal enforcement mechanisms are not so much meant for situations in which one is doing good. They are a last resort, in those situations where companies earn extra credits for their financial stakeholders through an officially declared human rights policy which, however, is not in conformity with international human rights standards. In such cases, companies should not be allowed to act as their own judges, but should accept external control, knowing they have nothing to fear if they have nothing to hide.

Notes

1 The article draws upon – and can be seen as an update of – the author's previous work in this field. See, *inter alia*, his 'Codes of Conduct for Multinational Enterprises: Useful Instruments or a Shield against Binding Responsibility' (with Sophie van Bijsterveld), 7 *Tilburg Foreign Law Review*, No. 2, 1998, pp. 161-177; 'Multinationale ondernemingen en de rechten van de mens', 25 *Nederlands Juristen Blad*, 2000, pp. 1231-1236; and especially: 'The Status of Transnational Corporations in International Public Law', in Asbjørn Eide, et al., eds., *Human Rights and the Oil Industry* (Antwerpen/Groningen/Oxford, Intersentia, 2000) pp. 71-89.

2 See the OECD Website: <http://www.oecd.org/daf/cmis/CIME/mneguide.htm>.

3 See the *Official Bulletin* of the ILO, 1978, Vol. LXI, Series A, No. 1.

4 See <http://www.fifoost.org/allgemein/divers/oecd_multinat_corp/node59.php>, para. 23.

5 See the previously mentioned OECD Website.

6 Ibidem.

7 As of 1 September, 2003, these Conventions were ratified by: C.29: 162 States, C.87: 142 States, C.98: 153 States, C.100: 161 States, C.105: 161 States, C.138: 130 States, and C.182: 143 States.

8 *International Legal Materials*, 1233 (1998).

9 See Willem van Genugten and Ruud Lubbers, eds., *Division of Roles in the International Economic and Legal Order; Enterprises, Governments, Trade Unions, NGO's and Human Rights* (Nijmegen, Wolf Legal Publishers, 2002).

Discussion

Susan Leubuscher*: I would like to raise an extreme question to all of this. And I imagine that it will relate to what will come up later and what will come up in the rest of the day. While we are discussing the possibly involuntary codes of conduct, while we are discussing how companies want to be ethical and how workers in the companies want to be ethical, while we are discussing that the companies must take up codes of conduct and guidelines in order to do business properly, this is all going on in public. What is going on in private, particularly in extractive industries, is making con-

* ECJ.

tracts, which are private contracts, which are being concluded between multinationals and developing countries. In these contracts, there are provisions, which, number one – allow private and public security forces without further authorisation to derogate for the period of contract, which is usually up to sixty years, from all environmental laws, from all conservation laws, which affect the property related to the project, and that property is not defined. For example, for the pipeline it is not only pipeline itself, but also all infrastructure related to the project – and that has very wide application.

In the Philippines, these contracts, which are generally for mining, cover about 20 per cent of the national territory. And they completely supersede national laws; they completely supersede international obligations, which these countries entered into. So, I guess my question is: we have been told that the companies are making a larger effort, on the other hand these contracts are private, they remain private. When NGOs asked for these contracts, they have been told that these cannot be given after they are adopted by national parliaments, nothing can be done about them anymore. If these companies are really serious, why are they not going to accept either binding regulation, since they say they want to comply with existing law, and at the same time if they want to be really serious about wanting to be part of international community, why do they not allow these contracts, which after all do become public, after they are cited in official journals in certain francophone countries to be looked at by the international community beforehand? So that these companies and these companies could be advised on what possible implications these contracts have.

WILLEM VAN GENUGTEN: If you believe in self-regulation, which I do, self-regulation is a very important instrument. But if it does not work, you might want to see to what extent you can go back to the law. Indeed, the companies do not like external control, they do not like to be checked by commissions coming along, consisting of lawyers, NGOs, trade unionists, to see what they really do to implement promises, which they gave to the outside world. It is also a game to some extent - it is not risky games for the companies to my mind. So if to answer this question – the main reason is that they are afraid of external control.

RENé VAN ROOIJ: Does any other panellists want to respond to this?

LUCY REED: I cannot comment. These are purely private contracts, to which I have been exposed. But I think one should not forget, that most of these big contracts are funded in one way or another by international lending agencies, which have due diligence, that at this point is very thorough as far as human rights record is concerned – we have just come through it in a number of investment projects for a number of our clients. Always, I have to agree, there is a big retention where the public security forces are involved, and they cannot be relied upon because of human rights abuses to the area they are brought in.

RENé VAN ROOIJ: Indeed, extracting companies often operate in countries, where sophisticated environmental laws as in Western Europe and the United States, do not exist. More often we have to invent environmental laws, and we have our own environmental standards. We also have very sophisticated internal and external assurance procedures including audit programmes. We need to do this ourselves, because the governments in most of the countries we are operating are dealing with completely different problems than the environment – they are dealing with poverty, with corruption and so on and so forth.

Remarks by Michel Nussbaumer*

From government to governance? The growing impact of non-state actors on the international and European legal system

It is my pleasure to speak at this conference today. You may see that my presentation is called "Corporate Governance as a Foundation of Capital Flows". Here I think the focus will be slightly different from the previous speakers: a little bit less about human rights and a little more about shareholder protection. The reason for this is that our Bank is a major investor in Eastern Europe and we do not normally deal with multinationals, we normally deal with small companies, medium-size or sometimes large companies, but these are local companies. And in that part of the world the problems are different too. The horror stories that you hear about corporate governance are more about shareholders deprived of their rights, being unable to register their shares rather than about child labor and slave labor.

Poor corporate governance is a risk factor that can be a serious impediment to the future smooth and successful running of an investment. Over the past few years, the European Bank for Reconstruction and Development (the "EBRD") has highlighted the need to develop measures aimed at strengthening corporate governance in its countries of operations.[1] As part of this process, the Office of the General Counsel, led by its Legal Transition Team, undertook a Corporate Governance Assessment Project (the "CG Assessment Project"), which we would like to present to the seminar.

Corporate governance sector assessment project

Background

The CG Assessment Project is part of the EBRD's efforts to promote good corporate governance in the Bank's countries of operations. As an international institution with the mandate to assist the countries whose economies are in transition, the EBRD views the promotion of good corporate governance as essential to its work.[2]

The aim of the CG Assessment Project is to gauge the status of corporate governance related laws and regulations in the Bank's countries of operations. The focus of the Project is to analyse these laws and to identify those aspects which require further development when compared to established international standards of corporate governance. The overall objective of the Project is to encourage, influence and provide guidance for existing and future development of corporate governance related legal reforms in the Bank's countries of operations.

In order to analyse and evaluate the relevant information available in each country, the Bank and its external legal consultants engaged for this Project, Lovells CIS and Ernst & Young, have devised a checklist of questions (the "Checklist") covering the key areas of issues concerning corporate governance. The questions in the Checklist were developed, based on the *Principles of Corporate Governance* published by the

* Senior Counsel, Head of Legal Transition Team, European Bank for the Reconstruction and Development.

Organisation for Economic Co-operation and Development ("OECD"), which are briefly described below.[3]

International standards

The OECD Council, meeting at Ministerial level on 27-28 April 1998, called upon the OECD to develop, in conjunction with national governments, other relevant international organisations and the private sector, a set of corporate governance standards and guidelines. In order to fulfil this mission, the OECD established an Ad-Hoc Task Force on Corporate Governance to develop a set of non-binding principles that embody the views of OECD member countries on this issue. The EBRD participated in the meetings of the Task Force on Corporate Governance as an observer and in the process when the *Principles of Corporate Governance* were drafted.

There are five main headings under which the OECD *Principles of Corporate Governance* are organised:

- The rights of shareholders;
- The equitable treatment of shareholders;
- The role of stakeholders in corporate governance;
- Disclosure and transparency; and
- The responsibilities of the board.

The principles enumerated under each of the headings are intended to represent a guideline for use in investigating the relationships between a company's management, its board, its shareholders and other stakeholders. The OECD *Principles of Corporate Governance* have been incorporated into the Checklist. By setting out the corporate governance principle first, followed by a question or set of questions, which relate to the particular principle, the user is assisted in understanding, in the context of the principle, the rationale for the questions being asked.

The EBRD checklist

Questions in the Checklist are designed to be clear and simple, using commonly recognisable concepts and terminology. The responses to the questions and the information provided have been made as concise as possible, in order to support the assessment and evaluation process.

In completing the Checklist for a country of operations, where a specific reference to the relevant law is required, the title or name of the actual law (including its dates of first promulgation and amendments) applicable in the country have also been stated. Although detailed provisions of the law are not always provided, certain questions have contained a clarification in the answer with some explanations. These clarifications, however, have been kept to a minimum.

The following specific objectives have been taken into consideration when completing the Checklist:

- The goal of the CG Assessment Project is an **objective assessment of the existing laws and regulations** addressing the corporate governance issues highlighted by the OECD *Principles of Corporate Governance*. The emphasis of the assessment conducted is therefore on the respective legal framework (i.e., the law "on the books" or "**extensiveness**" of the law) in the countries rather than the practice of individual companies or the actual implementation of the law (i.e., "**effectiveness**" of the law promulgated).

- The scope of the CG Assessment Project is mainly focused on the legal framework of joint stock companies, whose shares are publicly traded.
- Information provided in the Checklist is expected to be used at a later stage to develop a rating system for each country in accordance with its level of corporate governance.
- The Checklist intends to form the basis for a relatively detailed assessment of the corporate governance legal framework of each country.

Assessment results

Results of the CG Assessment Project were completed in November 2002. Therefore, the validity of the assessment results is as of November 2002. While subsequent revisions or updates may be incorporated after that date when necessary, major updates to the assessment for each country are expected to be made on a yearly basis, by taking into account the level of development of corporate governance reforms in the interim.

NOTES

1 Albania, Armenia, Azerbaijan, Belarus, Bosnia & Herzegovina, Bulgaria, Croatia, Czech Republic, Estonia, Georgia, Hungary, Kazakhstan, Kyrgyz Republic, Latvia, Lithuania, FYR Macedonia, Moldova, Poland, Romania, Russian Federation, Serbia and Montenegro, Slovak Republic, Slovenia, Tajikistan, Turkmenistan, Ukraine, Uzbekistan.

2 For a fuller description about the Bank's activities that foster good corporate governance, please refer to the Autumn 1999 issue of the Bank's legal journal, <Law in Transition.>

3 The full text of the OECD *Principles of Corporate Governance* is also available on the website of the OECD at <www.oecd.org>.

DISCUSSION

RENé VAN ROOIJ: Is there a link between your subject and the subject of previous speakers? For instance, is it correct to say that in some countries in Eastern Europe corruption, or human rights, is a big issue? Do you see the work you are doing in the bank as a tool for dealing with these issues? And, more specifically, do you think that well-developed principles of corporate law will help in that regard?

MICHEL NUSSBAUMER: You mentioned corruption, and indeed it is very big issue. Each time we develop a strategy for one of these countries this issue is mentioned. If you look through reports of different organisations, such as Transparency International, you can see that these countries score very low. The issue how to tackle this issue is a very difficult one and good corporate governance is a very important step here. The general condition of the judiciary is of one of the main problems in that region. When the judges are not paid well enough, how can you expect them to be fully objective and impartial? We are also working on the realisation of various programs for judges to help to overcome this problem, but at the end of the day it is very often an economic question. If these people do not have the money, the good corporate governance is not enough.

René van Rooij: Professor Jaap Winter is a partner in the law firm of De Brauw Blackstone Westbroek. He is a chairman of the high level group of company experts, which is advising the European Commission on modernising company law. In this context his name appeared quite regularly in the papers over the last years. He is also a member of a high level think-tank (the Tabaksblat group) which has recently published a corporate governance code for the Netherlands.

Remarks by Jaap Winter*

Ladies and Gentlemen, in my presentation I will also speak about more earthly things, the corporate governance in a more strict way – the relationship between the board and shareholders. I will not speak about the contents of that. Basically how to deal with it, and that area had little to do with human rights.

Although a recommendation to the European Commission was launched last year on how to deal with hostile takeover bids, the initial reaction from the Wallenberg family in Sweden was that this was clearly in violation of their human rights. I have been told by all professors when I was studying law, that when in company law relationships people base their arguments on human rights, then there is something wrong with the real arguments. And I told Mr Wallenberg, that he was successful at least in stopping this recommendation to appear in a form of a legal directive in the EU.

I will speak about the regulation of corporate governance, the relationship between the board and the shareholders. When I am thinking about it, I am always reminded of the remark that the archbishop of Honduras made to me a year ago in a dinner during the World Economic Forum in Davos about the value of science. It was about the benefits that science can bring and about the problems which science can pose if you let it go on and on and develop the products, the ideas and technology, that for instance may violate human dignity. The archbishop said: "Science is like a river. It is a powerful tool to become very beneficial. But that only works, if the river has banks. If we let it flow freely, it starts to destruct, to destroy. So, we must have banks." He than added that the lawyers have to deal with such problems, to deal with the expectations, which the society has. The matter that the river needs banks is also true for corporate governance. Corporate governance is the way how the shareholders and boards of companies direct themselves, control themselves and account how they behave in their own internal relationships. And we need banks, i.e. regulation to make sure that the river flows in the right direction. We can make mistakes if the regulation is too wide, because then people go on and on and destroy value or also if you make regulation too tight, because then we stop entrepreneurial incentives aimed to create wealth. We therefore have to be very careful about the regulation of corporate governance. We have to think very carefully about these banks. And there are three specific reasons for corporate governance in particular you must be really modest in what the legal regulation can really achieve.

* Professor Jaap Winter, De Brauw Blackstone Westbroek, Amsterdam.

In the first place the companies you are going to regulate are not identical. They are not the same – they operate in different product markets, they have different sizes, they have different ages, they have different share ownership structures. All of that determines how they operate, how they function, how they behave. And certainly national original cultures are very influential on corporate behaviour. Secondly, the idea what types of rules work, what types of regulation we should have. These ideas change very fast, because the societies in which companies work change very fast. One example, is that in the last decade from 1991 - 2001, there was an incredibly increased importance of capital markets for financing of companies. Enormous transactions between the companies took place because there were stock markets. The deals were financed because new shares were issued in the stock market.

This has created a completely different environment, in which the companies operate, than it was ten years ago. The whole discussion about corporate governance is because we wish the capital markets to be productive. We suddenly have the rise of institutional shareholders, insurance and pension funds massively investing in shares. They have become a different type of shareholders with a different position within the company. We are suddenly allying the interests of shareholders with the interests of management by giving them stock options and shares and other equity-based compensation forms.

We did not have this situation ten or twelve years ago, and now we have to think how to deal with it. If the only mechanism how to deal with it is strict legal rules, it means that we only can solve the problem once there is new legislation. But this new legislation will always come late and will probably always get it wrong to some extent. So there must be an ability of companies to adapt to situations themselves, without first changes in law having occurred. Law will follow, but cannot lead this type of changes in the corporate environment. And, finally, regulation by law is always imperfect. It will not regulate all human behaviour.

The prime examples of crises, which we have seen in the financial markets was Enron. What has happened in Enron was in breach of existing rules at that time. We do not need new rules to deal with Enron, even the old rules were breached. People go to prison, because they violated the old rules. So the standard political reaction – let us create new rules does not make sense. They were already in breach of old rules, which means if people committed fraud, they will do it whatever the rules are. So, rules are not the solution to many of the problems that we have seen.

For all of these reasons, what we have seen over the last few years is that the way we try to rule or to regulate in a different way what actually happens within boards and in relationships between boards and shareholders is by developing corporate governance codes, which are not individual company codes, but usually are national codes, and sometimes supranational codes, which include a number of elements, which constitute best practices of behaviour. They try to regulate the river within the banks, rather than the banks itself. They do not set banks or the new banks. The banks are the rules that are already there. They try to steer the river in between the banks, to ensure that people as much as possible behave properly.

So that is what these codes do. The key feature of this, that the private sector – the people, who actually swim in this river they make these codes; because it is their river. They have to find for themselves what actually are best practices. Which means that the companies themselves, as well as their investors, which are two key players –

they have to invent these rules. It is not for legislators to dream up codes of corporate governance. It is for business and investors themselves to make them. And it is also important that these codes are renewed and reviewed every few years, to ensure that what is in the code is still valid, is still the best practice after three or four years. Because, as I said, the views can change.

The new thing, which we have seen over the last few years, is that this element of self-regulation is not living in a free space. It is not completely voluntary anymore. The legislators somehow regulate the process of developing these codes and the way they are applied in practice by the rule, which is called "comply and explain rule". Legislators put forward the obligations to comply with these rules, or at least to publicly explain why they deviate and to what extent they deviate. The good thing in this mechanism is that it allows for flexibility, so that the companies can still deviate from these rules, because they are slightly different and act in different circumstances. But they must explain then, they must be transparent. And the result is that they will become accountable for how they behave, how they structure themselves, because they have to explain. And it would allow the market itself to enforce, rather than any public actors. The result is a strange new type of regulation – semi-public, semi-private. At the EU level, the EU Commission endorsed the recommendation that my group sent to the Commission last year to require all Member States of the EU to have such a code of corporate governance and to oblige all the companies to comply with the code or at least to publicly explain why they are different and to what extent. This is going to happen and to influence corporate governance to a large extent in Europe.

The Tabaksblat group is an example how we do this now in the Netherlands. We developed a code of corporate governance, it is now up for consultation and at the end of the year the committee will formally adopt it. And the Minister of Justice of the Netherlands, whom you have heard this morning mentioned that he would introduce this requirement of "comply or explain". It will be completely new for Dutch legislation, certainly in the corporate law area.

We also said that there should not be a European code on corporate governance, because the underlying corporate laws in Member States are rather different. But we agreed to build up a more or less common view on what is the corporate government from the bottom up, rather than the EU imposing it from the top down.

It is very difficult to agree on corporate law issues within the EU. It is very difficult to harmonise the very details of corporate law. The example is the statute of European company, which took forty-three years to agree on the European Company Statute. In the area of corporate law our group and the European Commission came to a conclusion that we have to respond more quickly to the crisis in the capital markets. What do you do if the regulatory progress takes 20, 30 or even 43 years? That does not sound like a quick response. So what we recommended to the Commission, is that rather than going into the process of adopting new directives, taking such a long time, the Commission itself should come up with a recommendation to Member States, telling Member States – we expect you to have in your laws certain sets of rules. The Commission can issue such a recommendation very quickly. It has ideas, at least we gave our ideas, may be they are not good enough, but anyway that is a set of ideas. And then they require Member States either to comply with this recommendation, or at least to explain why they are different – why in the Netherlands or in Scandinavia we do not have to have these rules in our company laws of corporate governance codes.

I have been working in Unilever, so I was involved in discussions on corporate social responsibility from a corporate point of view. Companies are citizens, not regulators. They are citizens, like we are. We are subject to rules, we do not make rules. And companies are not supposed to make rules. They are not supposed by rule-making to change the world. The best they can do is to change the world by behaving. I do not think that we will be able to get clear directions for the companies, what they are supposed to do. This river has very wide banks, if any banks at all. And they do not give clear directions, where the river should flow. People have these directions, people who swim. The cooperation of NGOs, companies and governments is the most fruitful way. The discussion is necessary but the important question remains – what can we enforce, if the legal standards are not clear?

Discussion

Ms. A. Shemberg*: I am working for Amnesty International. If we go to the host government agreement contracts, we can see that countries are making agreements with companies. These contracts tell the governments to refrain from action in certain contacts. And my question is: there are two major obstacles which are dealt with in the presentations to corporate codes of conduct being effective and also making them accountable for this.

The two obstacles are: one is lack of specification about what human rights are and two: the lack of recognition that human rights law is law. Companies are not really aware of what the human rights are. They recognize them in the security context. They do not recognize that there are also economic, social or cultural rights, which are legally binding, especially in Europe, where there is the European convention of human rights. The companies when they make the contracts with governments actually conflict with a country's human rights obligations under international law and European law. We have a lot of jurisprudence to refer to. Is there a problem there – a lack of sophistication, or a lack of understanding. Actually, what you are doing, you are following your corporate codes of conduct, but you understand what you have asked the country to do, is contrary to their human rights obligations. And then there is the lack of resonance of human rights obligations for international lenders. Does the EBRD look at these contracts, and say we have human rights law – is this contract asking the country not to follow its human rights obligations?

René van Rooij: Could you please give one specific example of such a contractual clause?

Ms. A. Shemberg: I refer to something, which Michel knows about – the agreement between Turkey and BP. They are building an oil pipeline. One of the clauses is Turkey cannot intervene in the project, unless there is an imminent material threat. The actions that the country can take to intervene are only to remove that threat. Under the European Convention of Human Rights, especially Article 3 and under Article

* Amnesty International.

8, there is jurisprudence that says that the State has more exacting positive obligations. In fact, when there is a serious risk, or a slow accumulating risk, which will not be an eminent threat, they have a positive obligation to act, to protect lives, to warn and to take actions to protect human rights in this context.

MICHEL NUSSBAUMER: All I can say is that we would not ask a country normally to go against human rights obligations. We look very carefully into human rights records of countries where we operate, our main role though is to promote economic transition to market economy. So, these human rights are not our main focus.

J.P. VAN IERSEL*: My question is to Prof. Winter. Having created the internal market and all those sophisticated rules and procedures within the European Union, why can't we create harmonized corporate law? Common attitudes? Why is it so scarcely connected with national cultures, legal systems? And do you see any progressive developments in this field in Europe, and from Europe to the rest of the world?

JAAP WINTER: I am not sure I know why it is, I know that this is the case. May be the prime reason is that those people, who are interested in no change have such a strong influence in every Member State, that the situation has been like this for many decades. We see the result of these forty years of struggle for the European Company statute. But we are not happy about the result, and we are not sure that we will do the rest. So, the important thing I see is that rather than trying to proclaim everywhere that we have to be the same, we have to allow ourselves to be different in Europe. And may the best man win, and this will help us to compete with others. A better system will survive in an integrated market more easily than other systems. We can see the conversion from the bottom up. That is the only result we can achieve. And in some areas we will be able to set the rules. A crisis helps. And this can be illustrated by the crises in Europe with regard to the payments to senior executives.

RENé VAN ROOIJ: Thank you very much. Your last words show that the organizers of this Conference have been extremely ambitious on this particular session. We have talked about remuneration of executives, human rights, environmental law, about the situation in Nigeria, Turkey, Eastern Europe. We have talked about shareholders' rights; we have talked about social responsibility. And Professor van Genugten has tackled a very difficult issue of what is or is not a rule of law. I find it very difficult to summarize our discussions, and to reach any conclusions. Personally, I feel it was very worthwhile to have this discussion. I feel it is quite interesting that all speakers talked about companies. I seem to be the only representative of an actual company here. And if there is a conclusion, we should draw, it is this: any fruitful discussion on these issues requires involvement of representatives of all relevant groups who are prepared not only to talk but also to listen!

Reporter: Y. Kryvoi, Munchen.

* J.P. van Iersel (The Netherlands).

Corporate Responsibility for Human Rights and Environmental Damage – Issues of Transnational Litigations Including International Jurisdiction

The panel was convened by its Chair, Dr. Georg Berrisch*.

Introductory remarks by Dr Georg Berrisch

Dr. Georg Berrisch welcomed the participants to the session. He briefly introduced the topic of the session which pertained to the enforcement of human rights against corporations, and, more specifically, dealt with the question as to what extent national courts were a proper forum for such enforcement. He stressed the topicality of the issues by pointing out some interferences of the US government on several occasions. In May 2003, the US government submitted an *amicus curiae* brief in the *Doe* v. *Unocal* case under the Alien Tort Claims Act (ATCA), in which it argued for a more restrictive approach of the ATCA. The ATCA allowed private citizens to enforce human rights violations committed anywhere in the world in US courts. Furthermore, Mr Rumsfeld, the US Secretary of Defense, has questioned whether Brussels was still an appropriate place for the headquarters of NATO. Mr Rumsfeld has argued that since the new Belgian genocide legislation, heads of government were no longer secure when they travel to Belgium.

Remarks by Malgosia Fitzmaurice**

Case Study: Wiwa and Royal Dutch Petroleum and Shell Transport and Trading Company before the US Court of Appeals for the Second Circuit (the Alien Tort Claims Act and the doctrine of *forum non conveniens*)

This paper will examine a case involving alleged human rights violations and environmental damage based on the US Alien Tort Claims Act (the 'ATCA').[1] This presentation will address as well the possibility of bringing a claim on the basis of the general law of tort.

The case arose in the context of the well-known crisis in the Niger Delta and relates to the violation of human rights of the Ogoni people. Their opposition both to the then Government of Nigeria and to the oil companies resulted in the execution of nine members of the Movement for the Survival of the Ogoni People (the 'MOSOP')

* Covington & Burling.

** Queen Mary & Westfield College, London.

including Ken Saro-Wiwa, the leader of the Movement, and Kpuinen, the leader of the MOSOP's young movement, in 1995, following their conviction for murder by a special military tribunal based upon fabricated evidence. Before the execution, they were repeatedly arrested, detained and tortured by the Nigerian Government, only because they led the opposition.

The MOSOP accused the company of complicity in what it alleged was the genocide of the Ogoni people. It was clamed that Shell coercively appropriated Ogoni land for oil development without adequate compensation, and caused substantial pollution of the air and water in the region of the Ogoni people. It was alleged that the abuses of human rights carried out by the Nigerian Government and military were instigated, orchestrated, planned and facilitated by Shell Nigeria, as reprisal for the opposition of the MOSOP against its oil development plans. It was alleged that the Royal Dutch/Shell Group provided money, weapons and logistical support to the Nigerian military, including equipment used in raids on villages, that Shell procured at least some of these attacks, that it participated in the fabrication of murder charges against Saro-Wiwa and Kpuinen and bribed witnesses to give false testimony against them.[2]

The case was complex and gave rise to a number of judgments. The Plaintiffs' initial action was brought under the ATCA and also alleged violations of the Racketeer Influenced and Corrupt Organisations Act (RICO) before the United States District Court.

The Defendants moved to dismiss both the initial and the amended complaints on the grounds of lack of personal jurisdiction over Royal Dutch/Shell and *forum non conveniens* (the Defendants argued that the case should be heard either in the Netherlands or in England). The Defendants also argued that the ATCA did not apply to a corporation and that the claim was precluded due to its political nature and the Act of State doctrine, as well on the grounds of Nigerian law on corporate liability. The United States District Court of New York (Judge Wood), found that there was personal jurisdiction but dismissed the action on the grounds of *forum non conveniens,*[3] and found the United Kingdom to be the adequate alternative forum. The reasoning of the Court was based primarily on the fact that although two of the plaintiffs were residents of the United States none of them was a resident of the Southern District of New York where the case was filed. Newell observes that "[t]he common law doctrine of *forum non conveniens* has been the principal means by which transnational cases against companies have been stalled. Whilst choice of forum is normally the prerogative of the plaintiff, the defendant can invoke the principle to claim that the proposed forum is inconvenient, where there is another 'clearly and distinctly more appropriate forum'..."[4] The present case is an example of such an instance, since it is the Defendants in this case who relied on the doctrine of *forum non conveniens.*

In 1999 Ken Wiwa, appealed on behalf *inter alia,* of her father, Ken Saro-Wiwa, and her husband, John Kpuinen, before the Court of Appeals, Second Circuit against Royal Dutch Petroleum Company and Shell Transport and Trading Company PLC[5] under the ATCA and other laws, alleging the above-mentioned violations of human rights by the Appellees in retaliation for the Appellants' political opposition to the Appellee Companies' oil exploration activities in Nigeria. The Court held as follows: 1. The New York Investors Relations Office of Appellee Companies subsidiary was an "agent" of the Appellees for the purposes of New York's personal jurisdiction Statute; 2. The Appellees, through such office, were "doing business" in New York, as required to confer jurisdiction under the Statute; 3. subjecting the Appellees to personal jurisdiction in New York did not violate the due process clause; 4. The District Court failed to weigh all relevant considerations in arriving at its decision on the *forum non conveniens* issue.

The holdings of the Court are very important, since they elucidated the state of law concerning suits based on the ATCA and elaborated on the controversial doctrine of *forum non conveniens.*

First of all, the Court observed that the doctrine of *forum non conveniens* is a discretionary device permitting a court in rare instances to dismiss a claim even if the court is a permissible venue with proper jurisdiction over the claim. In assessing whether dismissal on the grounds of *forum non conveniens* is appropriate, courts engage in a two-step process. The first step is to determine if an adequate alternative *forum* exists.[6] The court's inquiry is focused on the issue whether the defendant is amenable to service of process in a foreign forum. If not, the case cannot be dismissed under the doctrine of *forum non-conveniens.*[7] If an adequate alternative *forum* exists, the Court must then go on to a second step involving the balancing of a series of factors involving the private interests of the parties in maintaining the litigation in the competing *fora* and any public interest at stake.[8] A defendant seeking dismissal under this doctrine has the burden of establishing that an adequate alternative forum exists, and then of demonstrating that the pertinent factors (the "*Gilbert* factors") tilt strongly in favour of trial in the foreign forum. The plaintiff's choice of forum in a federal civil case should rarely be disregarded – only, that is, if the factors favouring the alternative forum are compelling.

According to the *Gilbert* factors, District Courts can only act against the plaintiff's choice of forum when the balance of interests is "strongly in favour of the defendant",[9] and therefore "strongly in favour of trial in the foreign forum".[10] In another case,[11] the Court found that the District Courts "should begin with the assumption that the plaintiff's choice of forum will stand unless the defendant meets the burden of demonstrating "that the plaintiff's choice of forum is not entitled to deference."[12]

Under the *Gilbert* case, the private interests factors include, but are not limited to, the access to evidence, the availability of compulsory process for the attendance of witnesses, the possibility of viewing the premises and all factors that might make the trial less time consuming or expensive.[13] The *Gilbert* factors also include the enforceability of a judgment in the competing *fora.*[14] The US Supreme Court, in the *Piper Aircraft* case, expressly held that courts should offer a greater deference to the selection of the US *forum* by US resident plaintiffs than to non-US resident plaintiffs, when evaluating a motion to dismiss on the ground of *forum non conveniens.*[15]

The public interest under the test of the *Gilbert* case, includes the local interests in adjudicating the dispute, the administrative burden on Courts and juries, knowledge of law and choice of law issues and US policy interests.[16]

The Court in the *Wiwa* case made further important observations concerning the doctrine of *forum non conveniens* and the Alien Tort Claims Act. It said that in determining whether a case alleging human rights violations under the ATCA should be dismissed on the ground of *forum non conveniens* in favour of a British Court, the District Court's failure to weigh the fact that two of the plaintiffs were residents of the United States constituted an error, even though none of the plaintiffs was a resident of the Southern district of New York, where the case was filed. Furthermore, the District

Court's failure to consider the interests of the United States in denying a forum to litigate alleged violations of international human rights law constituted an error. The ATCA, as supplemented by the Torture Victim Protection Act (the "TVPA"),[17] reflects a US policy interest in providing a forum for the adjudication of international human rights abuses. Finally, the district Court failed to balance the substantial expenses and inconvenience imposed on the Plaintiffs by dismissal as against minimal inconvenience for the Companies if the case was retained.[18]

The most interesting part of the Court's Judgment is devoted to the application of the *forum non conveniens* doctrine to ATCA cases, in the present case supplemented by the Plaintiffs through invocation of the TVPA. According to the Court, the Plaintiffs made a strong argument that the present law, in addition to merely permitting the US District Courts to entertain suits alleging violations of international law, express a policy in favour of receptivity by the US Courts to such suits. There are evident difficulties that face torture victims in bringing suits based on such abuses. They often cannot come back to the country where the abuses took place without endangering themselves, and courts of other countries are not willing to entertain such suits, which are "time consuming, burdensome, and difficult to administer."[19] These suits may be embarrassing to Governments and since they concern plaintiffs not protected or governed by domestic law of an alternative jurisdiction, may be considered by the foreign Courts not to be their concern. The Court expressed its views in very persuasive language: "[t]he new formulations of the Torture Victim Protection Act [the "TVPA"] convey the message that torture committed under color of law of a foreign nation in violation of international law is 'our business,' as such conduct not only violates the standards of international law but also as a consequence violates our domestic law."[20] The District Court failed to take into account in favour of retention of the case, the interest of the USA, as enshrined in the TVPA, in providing a forum for the adjudication of claims of torture in breach of the standards of international law.

The Magistrate Judge, whose findings were accepted by the district Court did not consider the financial aspect of the case, i.e. considerable expense and inconvenience, as the Court phrased it "perhaps fatal for the suit" for impecunious Plaintiffs that would be caused by moving the case to the British forum.[21] In addition, the Defendants did not offer a persuasive argument in support of an English forum, such as that costs of shipping of documents from England or flying a Nigerian witness New York rather than to London were excessively burdensome.

The other factors submitted by Defendants, such as the British character of the corporation, so that the UK might have an interest in adjudicating on the matter (an argument which disregarded the fact that the second Defendant was Dutch), or Nigeria's membership of the Commonwealth of Nations, were not of an overriding character.

In summary, the Court balanced public and private factors (as spelled out in the *Gilbert* case) and came to the conclusion that the district Court failed to give weight to three significant considerations that favour retaining jurisdiction for trial: 1 a United States resident plaintiff's choice of forum; 2. the interests of the United States in furnishing a forum to litigate claims of violations of the international standards of the law of human rights, and 3. the factors that led the district Court to dismiss in favour of a British forum were not particularly compelling. [22]

One author observed of the Court's decision, "[o]ne surprising aspect of *Wiwa* is that the proposed alternative forum to the US Courts was not the *situs* State of Nigeria but rather British Courts, which the Second Circuit described as "exemplary in their fairness and commitment to the rule of law". The *Wiwa* Court rejected England as an alternative forum not because it was inadequate but because the district Court did not give proper weight to the US interest, expressed in ATCA and reaffirmed in the TVPA, in adjudicating violations of international human rights law in the US Courts."[23]

In conclusion it may be said that this very important judgment elucidated several pertinent questions concerning the relationship between the *forum non conveniens* doctrine and the litigation based on the ATCA in conjunction with the TVPA. The fundamental question arises whether these two acts nullify, override or diminish the working of this doctrine. It appears that this is not the case. In the opinion of the present author the judgment in this case answers this question fully in the following quotation:

> "[t]his is not to suggest, that the TVPA has nullified, or even significantly diminished, the doctrine of *forum non conveniens.* The statute has, however, communicated a policy that such suits should not be facilely dismissed on the assumption that the ostensibly foreign controversy is not our business. The TVPA in our view expresses the policy favoring our Court's exercise of jurisdiction conferred by the ATCA in cases of torture unless the defendant has fully met the burden of showing the *Gilbert* factors 'tilt strongly in favor of trial in the foreign forum'".[24]

From the above it appears that in each and every case involving the ATCA or TVPA and the doctrine of *forum non conveniens*, the Court has to apply a balancing test between, on one hand, acts "favouring the exercise of Court's jurisdiction conferred by the ATCA"; and, on the other hand, the extent to which the Defendant has met the burden of showing that the *Gilbert* factors favour the alternative jurisdiction. It may be argued that full evidence of the fulfillment of the *Gilbert* factors would still tilt the case in favour of trial in the foreign forum, notwithstanding that the jurisdiction was conferred upon by the ATCA, however, the *Wiwa* case demonstrated that "adjudicating human rights claims in US Courts is in the interest of justice. This argument by the Second Circuit in *Wiwa* is the one likely to have the most precedential value."[25] This view is fully supported by the findings of the Court in this case. The Court stated that: "... in passing the TVPA, Congress has expressed the policy of US law favoring the adjudication of such suits in US Courts. If in cases of torture in violation of international law our Courts exercise their jurisdiction conferred by the 1789 Act only for as long as it takes to dismiss the case for *forum non conveniens,* we will have done little to enforce the standards of the law of nations."[26] From the above pronouncement, it also follows that Courts have at least the obligation to review cases of such a kind and that Courts should not routinely dismiss them.[27]

Notes

1 28 U.S.C. &1350 (1994). The Alien Tort Act was adopted in 1789 as part of the original Judiciary Act. Originally, it did not make any pronouncements as to legal rights. It stated that "[t]he district Courts shall have original jurisdiction of any civil action by an alien for a tort only, committed in violation of the law of nations or a treaty of the United States", 28 U.S.C. &1350. This statute was inactive for about two centuries. The

most important case brought under it was *Filartiga* v. *Pena-Irala* (630 F.2d876 (2nd Cir.1980). However, as a result the increasing international focus on human rights issues, more cases have recently been filed under it. e.g., *Kadić* v. *Karadić*, 70 F.3d 232 (2d Cir.1995, alleging torture, rape and other abuses instigated by Karadić. (survey of the relevant case law, see: B.Stephens and M.Ratner, *International Human Rights Litigation in US Courts* (1996). These cases resulted in several decisions that contributed to the interpretation of the meaning and scope of the 1789 Act. (e.g., in the *Filartiga* case (see above, pp. 880, 884-86) it was held that deliberate torture done under official authority violates universally accepted norms of international human rights law and that such violation of the norms of international law constitutes as well a violation of the US domestic law, giving rise to a claim under the ATCA whenever the perpetrator is properly served within US borders. In the *Kadić* case (see above, pp. 239-40 and 245) it was decided that the ATCA is also applicable in relation to private parties provided that their conduct is undertaken under the authority of a State or violates a norm of international law that is recognized as extending to the conduct of private parties (see the Judgment, paragraph 26). Except in a few narrowly defined situations, plaintiffs must allege facts that satisfy the ATCA's State action requirement. Hence, plaintiffs must usually demonstrate that the Defendant was a government actor or committed the violation while acting "under color of law," 96 Civ. 8386 (KMV), 96 8386 (KMV), 2002, (Judge K. Wood). This case was brought by Ken Wiwa against Royal Dutch Petroleum Company and Shell Transport and Trading Company PLC, and against B. Anderson, 28 February 2002. It was explained in the *Kadić* case that "[a] private individual acts under the color of law within the meaning of section 1983 when he acts together with State officials or with significant State aid".

Also relevant is the "joint action" test, under which private actors are considered State actors if they willfully participated in joint action with the State or its agents. (*Dennis* v. *Sparks*, 449 U.S. 24, 27, 66 L.Ed.2d 185, 101, S.Ct. 183 (1980). In a substantial number of cases of cooperation between the State and private actors in effecting deprivation of rights, a State action is present as well. It must be also proved by plaintiffs whether a particular alleged violation of human rights has been adequately characterized under international customary law, so that it is actionable under the ATCA. This Act is not subject to the Statute of Limitations. When a federal cause of action is not subject to the Stature of Limitations, federal law borrows the limitation period of the closest analogous cause of action under the law of the Forum State. *Ken Wiwa and Jane Doe, plaintiffs against Royal Dutch Petroleum Company and Shell Transport and Trading Company PLC, Defendants, Ken Wiwa et al, Plaintiffs against Brian Anderson, Defendant*, 96 Civ US 8386 (KMW), 96 Civ. 8396 (KMW), United States District Court for the Southern District of New York, 2002 U.S. Dist., LEXIS 3293, 28 February 2002.

2 See in depth on the crisis Human Rights Watch <http://www.hrw.org/reports/1999/nigeria/Nigew991-01.htm>; and see also P. Newell, 'Managing Multinationals: The Governance of Investment for the Environment,' in *J.Int.Dev.* 13, 907-919 (2001). He writes that Shell Transport and Trading, the UK arm of Shell International had an embarrassing confrontation with institutional shareholders in April-May 1997 over its environmental and human rights record in Nigeria, p. 912. quoting W. Lewis, 'Shell to Face Shareholder Vote on Ethics,' *Financial Times*, 12 April (1997).

3 M. Anderson, 'Transnational Corporations and Environmental Damage: Is Tort Law the Answer ?' *Washburn Law Journal*, Vol. 41(2002), pp. 399-425. Anderson explains that this doctrine was initially invoked to protect the Defendant against a plaintiff's choice of an awkward forum. However, it developed into a device for parent companies to avoid liability for tortious acts committed abroad. He gives an example of the most notorious case before the US federal Courts where the proceedings were stayed in the *Bohpal* case gas leak litigation against Union Carbide Corporation, forcing the Indian litigants to sue in Indian Courts. The same author observes that the 1950 European Convention on Human Rights, Article 6, includes the right to "effective access" to national courts in respect to civil claims. It was recognized in jurisprudence of this Court that the right to institute proceedings in respect of civil matters is a universally recognized principle of law, and that denial of this right constitutes a denial of justice. He says that "[t]his human rights argument has received considerable support among lawyers in European civil law systems, for whom the doctrine of *forum non conveniens* often appears to be arbitrary and unjust.," p. 413. a similar view is expressed by Newell, "[t]he current popularity of *forum non conveniens* as grounds for not hearing cases in foreign Courts, the difficulty of using the *Alien Tort Act* and, in many cases, the impenetrability of the corporate veil, means that companies looking to exploit lower environmental and social standards in developing countries can often do so without fear of meaningful legal redress." Newell, *supra*, note 2, p. 916. See also P.T. Muchlinski, 'The Bhopal Case: Controlling Ultra-hazardous Industrial Activities Undertaken by Foreign Investors', 50 *Mod.L.Rev.* 545, 545 (1987); M. Anderson, 'Public Interest Perspectives on the Bhopal Case: Tort, Crime and Violation of Human Rights?', in *Public Interest Perspectives in Environmental Law* 154 (J. Dunkley and D. Robinson, eds., 1995). See also, A.K. Short, 'Is the Alien Tort Statute Sacrosanct? Retaining Forum Non Conveniens in Human Rights Litigation', *Interna-*

tional Law and Politics, Vol. 33 (2001), p. 1001; M.R. Skolnik, ' The Forum Non Conveniens Doctrine in Alien Tort Act Cases: A *Shell* of its Former Self After *Wiwa*,' *Emory International Law Review*, Vol. 16 (2002), p. 187.

4 Newell, *supra*, note 2, p. 915.

5 226 F.3d 88 (2nd Cir. 2000).

6 *Gulf Oil Company* v. *Gilbert*, 330 U.S. 501, (1947), pp. 506-507.

7 *Piper Aircraft*, 454, U.S., pp. 254-255, and n. 22.

8 *Gilbert*, 330 U.S., *supra* note 6, pp. 508-509.

9 *Supra*, at p. 508.

10 *R. Maganlal & Co.* v. *M.G.Chem.Co.*, 942 F.2d. 164, 167 (2nd.Cir. 1991).

11 *Iragorri United Techns.Corp*, 274 F.3d 65 (2nd Cir.2001).

12 *Supra*, at p. 71.

13 *Gilbert*, 330 U.S., *supra* note 6, at p. 508.

14 *Supra*, at p. 508.

15 *Piper Aircraft*, 454, U.S. at p. 249.

16 *Gilbert*, 330 U.S, *supra* note 6, pp. 508-509.

17 28 U.S.C. & 1350 App. 1991. In enacting of this Act, Congress expressly ratified the holding in the *Filartiga* case, to the effect that the United States Courts have jurisdiction over suits brought by aliens alleging torture under the law of a foreign nation, and carried it further. The 1789 Act granted jurisdiction to the district Courts. The 1991 Act expressly states that it creates liability under the US law where "under the color of law of any foreign nation an individual is subject to torture "or "extra judicial killing", and extends its remedy not only to aliens but to any "individual". In that manner this Act covers "United States citizens as well", 28 U.S.C. &1350 App. What the TVPA recognized explicitly was only hinted at in the Act of 1789, namely, that international law is incorporated in the law of the United States and that a violation of international law of human rights – at least in regard to torture – amounts to a violation of municipal law of the US Judgment paragraph 26. The TVPA requires first the exhaustion of local remedies. The Burden is on the defendant, not plaintiff, to demonstrate that the plaintiffs did not exhaust all local remedies. See *supra*, note 1, LEXIS 3293.

18 Paragraphs 15-27 of the Operative part of the Judgment.

19 Paragraph 26 of Reasons for the Judgment (Judge Leval).

20 *Supra* paragraph 26.

21 *Supra* paragraph 27.

22 *Supra* paragraph 21.

23 Skolnik, *supra* note 3, p. 211.

24 *Supra* note 19, paragraph 26, *in fine.*

25 Skolnik, *supra* note 3, p. 211.

26 *Supra*, paragraph 26. However, in relying on the TVPA, the Second Circuit, took into consideration its legislative history in "seeking to justify its novel interpretation of forum non conveniens in ATS [Alien Tort Statute] cases … . Recourse to the TVPA's legislative history to justify curtailment of *forum non conveniens* in ATS litigation proves unconvincing." Short, *supra* note 3, pp. 1041-1042.

27 The Defendants in this case filed a Writ of Certiorari before the Supreme Court which was denied. *cert. denied*, 532 U.S. 941 (2001). In March 2001, the plaintiffs sued B. Anderson, the former Managing Director of the Royal Dutch/ Shell subsidiary Shell Nigeria. Royal Dutch/Shell and Anderson made motions to dismiss the case, arguing that the plaintiffs had no claim. On 24 February 2002, the district Court denied the motions to dismiss on all but two claims: O.Wiwa's Alien Torts Claim Act claims on alleged allegations of his right to life, liberty, and security of persons and under the same Act a claim for arbitrary arrest and detention. The Court held that Anderson could be sued under the Alien Tort Claims Act, in that the actions of the Company and Anderson constituted participation in crimes against humanity, torture, summary execution, arbitrary detention, cruel, inhuman and degrading treatment, and other violations of international law. Anderson was found by the Court to be eligible to be sued under the TVPA which allows victims of torture to sue perpetrators in federal Court. The Court also found that the plaintiffs' RICO claims could proceed, because the Royal Dutch/Shell actions in concert with Nigeria military satisfied the racketeering requirements of the act and because they engaged in these acts in order to facilitate the export of cheap oil to the USA. The case is still pending, see *supra* note 1, LEXIS 3293.

This case also raised interesting issues of the legal status of corporations. The Court raised the questions of personal jurisdiction over foreign corporations in New York, the question of what is "doing business" by a foreign corporation in New York and the position of an agent or representative as conferring personal jurisdiction over a corporation under the New York Statute. Neither Defendant Company maintained a branch office in the USA; and none of the alleged conduct occurred in the USA. The 2nd Circuit nevertheless held that the Defendants were subject to the personal jurisdiction of the US Courts on the basis of the activities of an Investors Relations Office that was operated by a Delaware subsidiary (Shell Oil Co.) of a first tier US subsidiary (Shell Petroleum Inc.) of Royal Dutch and Shell Transport. The Court based its holding on two findings: that the office was an "agent" of the parent companies, and that the activities of the office were quantitatively and qualitatively sufficient to be held to be "continuous and systematic general business contacts" of the parents in New York (at p. 96). As to the agency problem, the Court held that the Defendants "fully funded" the office expenses, that the sole function of the office manager was "to perform investor relations services on the Defendants' behalf" and that they gave "[a]ll of their time to the Defendants' business" and sought the Defendants' approval on important decisions (at p. 96). The Court held further that the activities of the Shell Group's office were wider than required for such support and resulted from a "discretionary determination to invest substantial sums of money in cultivating their relationship with the New York capital markets", (at p. 97). The Court also found that the office evidenced every one of the characteristics that have been held to constitute a substantial "physical corporate presence" in New York attributable to parent companies, including having and maintaining an office, bank accounts, phone listings, public relations work and employees.

Remarks by Dr. Pieter H.F. Bekker*

Corporate aiding and abetting and conspiracy liability under international law

1. Introduction

This paper addresses the question whether contemporary international law recognizes "aiding and abetting" or conspiracy liability of private companies for environmental damage and human rights violations in the light of recent decisions of the courts of the United States pursuant to the "Alien Tort Statute" or "ATS,"[1] a prominent instrument of transnational litigation and jurisdiction in the areas concerned. One may observe the growing use of the ATS, and especially the aiding and abetting and conspiracy theories, by plaintiffs attempting to hold US and foreign companies vicariously liable for wrongs allegedly committed by sovereign entities (who are often protected by immunity or by defenses like the Act of State doctrine). Recent ATS decisions raise the specter of plaintiffs using the liberal pleading standards of the Federal Rules of Civil Procedure to sue private companies based simply on their participation in the global economic system. The complaints argue that corporate defendants must, in effect, police the activities of foreign sovereigns with whom they do business – something not even other sovereigns generally can do. Such cases affect the ability of companies to conduct their global businesses. US rulings have held in this context that a corporation must be viewed the same as a natural person.

It will be shown, however, that regardless the area of application (the environment or human rights), aiding and abetting or conspiracy liability of private companies – a theory resorted to when it is recognized that the defendants did not commit the alleged crimes themselves – has not been universally accepted as a discrete violation of international law and is, therefore, not part of the contemporary body of general international law. Neither treaty nor customary international law has any standards to apply for such notions. With the possible exception of a limited number of

* White & Case LLP, New York.

treaties addressing oil and nuclear pollution, there currently is no concept or regime of corporate liability, criminal or civil, in general international law. This is not surprising, as international law does not recognize the international legal personality of private companies established under domestic law.

Although the international law relating to crimes against humanity constitutes an exception to the rule that non-sovereigns cannot incur liability under international law, it imposes obligations upon individuals only, the violation of which triggers criminal, not civil (tort), liability.

The fundamental problem underlying various ATS complaints and rulings is that they lack a complete and consistent discussion of the sources of international law. A remedy lies in the continued education of the US Bar and Judiciary, as recently undertaken through the judicial outreach program of The American Society of International Law.

2. Lex lata or de lege ferenda: does contemporary international law recognize aiding and abetting or conspiracy liability of juridical persons (private companies)?

By allowing certain claims against the US company Unocal Corp. to proceed, a Panel of the US Court of Appeals for the Ninth Circuit held in September 2002 that aiding and abetting liability for violations of international law may be imposed upon non-sovereign corporate persons.[2] In so holding, it found that the ATS provides a right of action "as long as plaintiffs ... allege a violation of specific, universal, and obligatory international norms as part of" their claim.[3]

An examination of international law shows, however, that it is not at all clear that any private rights of action have been universally recognized as existing against private companies for violations of international law, let alone the aiding and abetting liability posited by the Panel Decision for such violations. As US courts have recognized, without international agreements and other indicia of a concrete and substantial consensus, no right of action can be found under international law.[4] Such indicia may lie in the sources of international law. Article 38 of the Statute of the International Court of Justice (ICJ) is generally recognized to state these sources. It identifies three principal sources: (a) international conventions (treaty law); (b) international custom, as evidence of a general State practice accepted as law; and (c) the general principles of law recognized by civilized nations. In addition, Article 38 *sub* (*d*) refers to judicial decisions (to which category ATS decisions of the US courts belong) and the teachings of the most highly qualified publicists as *subsidiary* means for determining rules of international law.[5]

Historically, international law has been addressed exclusively to the conduct of States, not individuals or private companies.[6] The post-World War II development of international law relating to crimes committed during war and crimes against humanity has altered this understanding, but only with respect to the criminal liability of *individuals*. Treaties defining international crimes envisage that only *individuals* may be prosecuted for the crimes defined in those treaties. Examples are the Convention on the Prevention and Punishment of the Crime of Genocide,[7] the International Convention on the Suppression and Punishment of the Crime of Apartheid,[8] and the Convention Against Torture and Other Cruel, Inhuman or Degrading Treatment or Punishment.[9]

None of the international criminal tribunals, including the International Military Tribunals at Nuremberg and Tokyo or the more recent International Criminal Tribunals for the Former Yugoslavia and Rwanda, has ever applied this developing international law to private companies. The constituent instruments of none of these tribunals provide for corporate criminal responsibility.[10] Article 5 of the Statute of the International Criminal Tribunal for the former Yugoslavia (ICTY) – which has jurisdiction only over "natural persons" (Art. 6) – requires discriminatory intent for all crimes against humanity, including for aiding and abetting by a "person" under Article 7(1).[11] The same applies to Article 3 of the Statute of the International Criminal Tribunal for Rwanda (ICTR), which also has jurisdiction only over "natural persons" (Art. 5).

The Rome Statute establishing the International Criminal Court (ICC), one of the more recent enactments in this area, was meant to include only crimes already established under customary international law. It does not provide for corporate liability. The ICC has jurisdiction only over "natural persons" (Art. 25).[12] The ICC Statute requires "intent and knowledge" (Art. 30), concepts which are limited to natural persons. The ICC's "Elements of Crime" refer to "a person," require "intent and knowledge" and nowhere mention corporate liability.[13]

The Tokyo and US Military Tribunals imposed the stringent requirement of being in a position to determine or influence the making of policy for individual criminal responsibility through conspiracy to commit crimes against the peace.[14] Conspiracy is recognized only with respect to the crime of genocide by Article 4(3)(b) of the ICTY Statute and Article 2(3)(b) of the ICTR Statute. But according to Article IV of the Genocide Convention, genocide can be committed only by individuals. This demonstrates that international criminal law does not recognize a general offence of conspiracy and that such offence does not extend to private companies. Moreover, in none of the reported cases before international criminal tribunals has there been any suggestion that individuals, let alone private companies, might be held civilly liable under general international law.[15]

There is no agreement among national legal systems on corporate liability sufficient to point to a universal custom.

Commentators have observed the inherent limitations of international law, noting that general international law does not impose obligations – civil or criminal – on private companies.[16]

Highlighting the absence of any consensus on corporate liability under general international law are the unsuccessful efforts by the United Nations to frame a Draft Code of Conduct on Transnational Corporations, that would have – for the first time – codified by international agreement the duties of corporations under international human rights law. The draft code was not adopted, and after almost twenty years was abandoned in favor of voluntary guidelines published by the UN Secretary-General.[17]

As such, it cannot be said that a private right of action against private companies for aiding and abetting, or conspiring to commit, violations of international law is a universally accepted norm of international law existing *de lege lata*.

3. The evidentiary and educational deficit in ATS cases

In a recent statement, US Supreme Court Justice Sandra Day O'Connor said that "American judges are becoming more aware of their responsibilities to respect not only domestic law but also the law of nations,"[18] but she also noted that "[m]ore is needed." Various ATS decisions underscore the fundamental problem of the lack of a solid international law foundation, even though the ATS explicitly makes "the law of nations" the only applicable law in ATS cases.

In most ATS cases, the courts are called upon to determine customary international law absent applicable treaties. The ICJ has stated that evidence of custom can be found in two elements, namely, (1) the uniformity of State practice and (2) *opinio juris sive necessitatis.*[19] This rigorous standard for ascertaining custom has been applied consistently by the ICJ, and also by the US Supreme Court.[20] However, many ATS decisions do not include a thorough analysis of international law based on Article 38 of the ICJ Statute. For support under international law some decisions rely almost exclusively on a book or law review article, which are subsidiary sources at best.[21] Despite the lack of evidence of corporate aiding and abetting or conspiracy liability *de lege lata,* a lower court held in a recent ATS case that companies may be liable under international law, citing Nuremberg Tribunal cases that were only directed against *individuals* with respect to wrongs committed by companies,[22] and a limited number of treaties relating to oil and nuclear pollution.[23] None of the Nuremberg cases, however, ever held that private companies could be liable under international law, and none of the cited treaties has been ratified by the US Congress or been held to be self-executing (at most, they appear to allow States to pursue certain remedies). This undercuts the notion that there is a universal and obligatory norm supporting corporate liability and demonstrates that there is a troubling evidentiary and educational deficit in ATS cases.[24]

4. Is the "long arm" of domestic law too long in the case of the ATS?

Alarmed by the growing number of ATS cases against private companies, both US and foreign, the International Chamber of Commerce has appealed to the US authorities to prevent abuse of the ATS, calling it "an unacceptable extraterritorial extension of US jurisdiction."[25]

The *Unocal* court held that aiding and abetting could be asserted based on a showing of "knowing practical assistance or encouragement which has a substantial effect on the perpetration of the crime."[26] This holding would allow claims against virtually any company that carries on substantial commerce with any government that allegedly commits human rights violations, as virtually any commercial conduct could be characterized as "foreseeably" "encouraging" or "assisting" a regime to stay in power such that it could continue to harm its people. Indeed, these are precisely the claims being made in the cases styled *In re South African Apartheid Litigation* (MDL No. 1499) pending in the Southern District of New York. In those cases, involving a large number of US and foreign companies, plaintiffs allege that by doing business in, or even with, South Africa while the South African government maintained the apartheid system, the defendant-companies (including some of the world's largest banks) violated international law so as to be liable to all South Africans who suffered injuries at the hands of the South African government during the apartheid era. The complaint in each case premises jurisdiction on UN resolutions that either are non-binding or are not addressed to private companies.

The two cases relied upon by the *Unocal* court drew from a much narrower context than the transaction of business and so do not directly support the standards of liability adopted. Both involved criminal defendants who were at the scene of the offenses and were among those who could direct events.[27] Moreover, in citing these cases, the court ignored more direct international law authority, including a case in which the Nuremberg Tribunal categorically rejected claims that sought to premise aiding and abetting liability on a defendant having done business with those who committed crimes under international law. The Tribunal held that loaning money did not violate international law, even where a bank's senior executive knew that the loaned funds were being used by government officials in connection with war crimes (e.g., the building of concentration camps).[28]

The broad standard of aiding and abetting liability enunciated by the *Unocal* court potentially puts every multi-national company at risk to the extent they do business in a host of nations where investment by US companies is actively encouraged by the US government. There can be no doubt that the Panel Decision, if upheld on appeal, will be used as a template for lawsuits challenging business activities in a host of places, with the allegation being that by "participating" in business activity a company made it possible (or more likely) that a foreign government could engage in human rights violations against its own people.[29] Prudential considerations require that domestic courts not create this type of risk absent express legislative action regarding the shape and scope of such liability in the context of a company's activities outside such courts' territory.

5. Conclusion

While the ICC's charge that the US judicial system is in danger of becoming the world's civil court of first resort may be exaggerated, it is true that the lack of international law education of domestic judges sitting in international law cases may lead to potentially far-reaching decisions that are at odds with contemporary international law. Even though these suits have not resulted in enforceable judgments, they entail considerable costs for the defendants.

The ATS case law, which continues to divide the various US circuit courts, underscores that the ATS is in dire need of guidance from the US Supreme Court or, better still, the US Congress. At the same time, there are encouraging signs that US courts will not allow abuse. Thus, in the most recent ATS decision, a lower court dismissed a complaint by members of a Colombian labor union against The Coca-Cola Company and its Colombian subsidiary alleging that these corporate defendants conspired with and aided and abetted Colombian right-wing paramilitary groups in violation of international law under the ATS.[30] As is increasingly the case, the plaintiffs had used the allegations in the complaint to mount a public relations campaign against the defendant-companies in hopes of reaching a favorable settlement. Still, the court left open the possibility of corporate liability with regard to another corporate defendant in connection with the Torture Victim Protection Act, often pleaded in tandem with the ATS, reasoning that "the term 'individual' is consistently viewed in the law as including corporations" and that "the legislative history does not reveal an intent to exempt private corporations from liability."[31]

Even if one accepts the outcome of these recent ATS rulings, they are but one small element of State practice and as domestic decisions by themselves cannot establish, let alone alter, international law under Article 38(1) of the ICJ Statute. Corporate liability, in the sense of the kind of aiding and abetting or conspiracy liability featured in recent ATS cases, currently does not exist *de lege lata*. The question of legal liability must be distinguished from accountability or "moral" responsibility. While private companies may not be legally liable under general international law, they remain accountable for their global activities and in this sense have a certain responsibility in the global society, as recognized by recent UN initiatives.[32] Perhaps one day such accountability will lead to corporate liability under general international law. In this regard there currently is more of an emerging rule in the environmental field (oil and nuclear pollution), based on specific treaties, than in the human rights field.

NOTES

1 The ATS, 28 U.S.C. § 1350, vests a US district court with "original jurisdiction of any civil action by an alien for a tort only, committed in violation of the law of nations or a treaty of the United States."

2 *John Doe I* v. *Unocal Corp*., Nos. 00-56603, 00-57197, 00-56628, 00-57195, 2002 WL 31063976, at *9 (9th Cir. 18 September 2002) [hereinafter *Panel Decision*]. References to "Panel Decision at *__" refer to the star-pagination of the Panel Decision available on Westlaw.

3 *Id.* at 8 (quotation and citation omitted).

4 See *Marcos II*, 25 F.3d at 1475 ("Actionable violations of international law must be of a norm that is specific, universal, and obligatory.").

5 In other words, while these subsidiary means (including also UN resolutions) do not themselves qualify as sources of international law, they may be *evidence of* primary sources or rules of international law.

6 Jennings & Watts, 1 *Oppenheim's International Law* 4, 16 (9th edn. 1992).

7 Art. IV ("Persons committing genocide or any of the other acts enumerated in Article III shall be punished, whether they are constitutionally responsible rulers, public officials or private individuals").

8 Art. III (citing as criminally culpable those individuals who "participate in, directly incite, or conspire in[, or] … [d]irectly abet, encourage or cooperate in the commission of the crime").

9 Arts. 1 (referring to "official or other person"), 4(1) (using the phrase "complicity or participation in torture"). While it is true that Article 5 of the 1999 Convention for the Suppression of the Financing of Terrorism provides that States may impose corporate responsibility for terrorist financing under their national laws, that treaty is not yet in force.

10 Although the Charter of the International Military Tribunal ("Nuremberg Tribunal") provided for certain legal consequences to be attached to membership of certain prescribed "criminal organizations," only political and military entities (e.g., the Nazi party and the SS) were declared "criminal organizations." No corporation was so declared. The "Industrialists" (Krupp, Flick, Krauch) cases concerned trials of individual directors and officers of corporations. The issue whether the corporations themselves could incur criminal liability was not raised.

11 The 1993 report of the UN Secretary-General forming the basis of the ICTY Statute (UN Doc. S/25704) states that the conferring of jurisdiction over "natural persons" by Article 6 was "to the exclusion of juridical persons" (Para. 50). It expressly rejected the Nuremberg concept of labeling an organization "criminal" (Para. 51). The relevant cases all impose strict conditions for criminal liability. See Jones, *The Practice of the International Criminal Tribunals for the Former Yugoslavia and Rwanda* 126-29 (2000).

12 See UN Doc. A/CONF.183/9, Part 3, Art. 25(1) (1998).

13 Art. 7 of the Rome Statute includes a reference to apartheid (not found in the constituent instruments of any other international criminal tribunal)). Element 5 of Art. 7(1)(j) (apartheid) requires proof that the perpetrator had *specific intent* to maintain the apartheid regime by his or her conduct.

14 See Brownlie, *International Law and the Use of Force by States* 203-04 (1963).

15 The application by analogy of the law of State responsibility is questionable and, in any event, would im-

pose very strict conditions for vicarious liability.

16 See, e.g., Demian Betz, 'Holding Multinational Corporations Responsible for Human Rights Abuses Committed by Security Forces in Conflict-Ridden Nations: An Argument Against Exporting Federal Jurisdiction For The Purpose Of Regulating Corporate Behavior Abroad', 14 *DePaul Bus. L.J.* 163, 188 (2001); 'Corporate Liability for Violations of International Human Rights Law', 114 *Harv. L. Rev.* 2025, 2030-31 (2001); Curtis A. Bradley, 'The Alien Tort Statute and Article III', 42 *Va. J. Int'l L.* 587, 587, 592 (2002).

17 See 'Corporate Liability for Violations of International Human Rights Law', 114 *Harv. L. Rev.* at 2030-31 and n. 31.

18 Justice Sandra Day O'Connor, Keynote Address, American Society of International Law Annual Meeting, April 2000, available at <www.asil.org/newsletter/news.pdf> (last visited 28 May 2003).

19 I.e., the conviction by States that, in following a certain practice, they are conforming to what amounts to a legal obligation. See *North Sea Continental Shelf*, International Court of Justice, Judgment, *I.C.J. Reports 1969*, 3, 44, §77 (Feb. 20).

20 See, e.g., *The Paquete Habana*, 175 US 677 (1900) (containing over 20 pages of analysis on custom).

21 See *Presbyterian Church of Sudan* v. *Talisman Energy, Inc.*, No. 01 Civ. 9882 (AGS), 2003 WL 1339181, *19 n.27 (S.D.N.Y. 19 March 2003) [hereinafter *Talisman*], citing Steven Ratner, 'Corporations and Human Rights: A Theory of Legal Responsibility', 111 *Yale L.J.* 443 (2001); *Beanal* v. *Freeport-McMoran, Inc.*, 197 F.3d 161 (5th Cir. 1999) (affirming dismissal) citing Philippe Sands (ed.), *Principles of International Environmental Law I: Frameworks, Standards and Implementation* (1995).

22 *Talisman* at *13, *20.

23 *Id.* at *21-23.

24 The *Talisman* court misinterpreted Art. 38(1)(d) of the ICJ Statute by stating that "this Court, as an inferior court, is obligated to accept the law as it has been interpreted by the Supreme Court and Second Circuit. This is no less true with respect to questions of international law than any other question of law. Therefore, in addition to the sources of international law listed [in Article 38 of the ICJ Statute], another must be added – interpretations of international law of superior courts." *Id.* at *18-19. The court refused to dismiss the case because the foreign corporate defendant "fails to cite a single Supreme Court, Second Circuit, or even Southern District case holding that a corporation is 'legally incapable of violating the law of nations.'" *Id.* at *24.

25 Statement of the ICC's American Chairman, Richard D. McCormick, available at_<www.uscib.org/index.asp?documentID=2385> (last visited 6 December 2002).

26 *Panel Decision* at *13 & n. 28. Such "assistance" or "encouragement" only has to be "foreseeable" to satisfy the element of proximate causation. *Id.* at *15 n. 32.

27 See *Prosecutor* v. *Furundzija*, Case No. IT-95-17/1-T (ICTY) (10 December 1998) (Croatian official intimately involved in the commission of human rights violations); *Prosecutor* v. *Musema*, Case No. ICTR-96-13-T (ICTR) (27 January 2000) (government-appointed director who personally raped and murdered ethnic Tutsis, as well as directed and encouraged others to do the same). The *Furundzija* case also relied on two sources of international law that have not been accepted by the United States, a draft UN code and the Statute of the International Criminal Court, which the USA has expressly refused to join. See *Panel Decision* at *12 n. 26.

28 *United States* v. *von Weizsaecker*, reprinted in 14 *Trials of War Criminals Before the Nuremberg Military Tribunals* 622, 854 (1949) ("We cannot go so far as to enunciate the proposition that the official of a loaning bank is chargeable with the illegal operations alleged to have resulted from loans or which may have been contemplated by the borrower."). By making a loan a bank "did not thereby become a criminal partner" with the German government agencies that were committing crimes against humanity. *Id.* at 854-55. These principles remain the governing standards of international law. For example, the ICJ applied these principles when Nicaragua attempted to hold the United States liable for violations of international law committed by the *contras* during their efforts to overthrow the then Nicaraguan government. Although it was established that the United States had provided the *contras* with financial support, as well as logistical support, the ICJ held that the United States had not created the *contras* nor had it provided "direct and critical combat support" to them. Accordingly, the United States was not liable under international law for any violations of humanitarian law committed by the *contras* in Nicaragua. See 'Military and Paramilitary Activities In and Against Nicaragua'_(*Nicaragua* v. *United States*), Judgment, *I.C.J. Reports 1986*, 14, 61-63, 65 (27 June).

29 There are good reasons, other than the absence of a rule of general international law regulating aiding and abetting or conspiracy liability of corporations, why the Panel Decision should not stand. The ATS only defines a jurisdictional class of cases federal courts may hear. It does not create or imply a private right of action for violations of international law. Moreover, under the Supreme Court's reasoning in a recent case, it could be argued that ATS jurisdiction is limited to tort claims in violation of international law as it stood in 1789, the

year the Judiciary Act was adopted. See *Grupo Mexicano de Desarrollo, S.A.* v. *Alliance Bond Fund, Inc.*, 527 US 308 (1999).

30 *Sinaltrainal et al.* v. *The Coca-Cola Company et al.*, Nos. 01-3208, 02-20258, 02-20259, 02-20260 Civ.-Martinez/Dubé (S.D.Fl. 28 March 2003). The author's law firm represented The Coca-Cola Company and its Colombian subsidiary.

31 *Id.* at * 17. See also *Talisman* (including further references to recent ATS decisions involving corporations).

32 See, e.g., the Secretary-General's "Global Compact" initiative and General Assembly Resolution 55/215 of 21 December 2000 ("Towards global partnerships").

Remarks by Harold Hongju Koh*

Four myths about corporate responsibility litigation

My remarks are inspired by an e-mail I recently received announcing a report that bears the striking title of "Awakening the Monster: the Alien Tort Statute of 1789."[1] The report echoes the brief just filed by the Bush Administration in *Doe v. Unocal*, which argues that Alien Tort Claims Act litigation against corporate defendants threatens US foreign policy, endangers corporations, will discourage trade and foreign investment in dozens of developing countries, and undermine the war against terrorism.[2]

What this underscores is how much overreaction and hysteria are developing about this kind of litigation against corporations for environmental injury and human rights abuse. I come to this subject wearing three hats: as a law professor, as a human rights litigator who has been involved in many of these cases, and as a policymaker who helped develop US policy toward corporate responsibility in human rights during the Clinton Administration. Each of these perspectives tells me that we need to separate the reality from the myth: in particular, four major myths about Corporate Responsibility Litigation, many of which run through the presentation that you have just heard from Pieter Bekker.[3]

MYTH #1: Domestic courts cannot hold private corporations civilly liable for torts in violations of international law. This is plainly false, particularly with respect to jus cogens *violations.*

The reasons usually given for this myth are found in Mr. Bekker's paper, which tries to apply highly formal distinctions to make corporate civil liability in domestic courts fall through the cracks in the doctrine. But on reflection, I would argue, none of these distinctions makes any logical sense.

Mr. Bekker argues first that only States and individuals, not corporations, can be held directly liable under international law. But as he admits, many treaties do in fact impose substantive duties upon corporations. The International Labor Organization (ILO) conventions, for example, oblige corporations not to interfere with employees'

* Harold Hongju Koh is Gerard C. and Bernice Latrobe Smith Professor International Law at Yale Law School. He served as Assistant Secretary of State for Democracy, Human Rights and Labor in the Clinton Administration.

rights to form unions and not to use child or slave labor. Nuclear treaties, such as the Paris Convention,[4] and oil spill treaties hold shipowners and operators of nuclear facilities liable for damage or loss of life to persons and property from private nuclear accidents or oil spills. Hazardous waste conventions, such as those concluded at Bamako and Basel,[5] impose strict liability on corporate generators of hazardous waste. The OECD Bribery Convention holds corporations liable for bribery. So how can it be that corporations can be held liable for their complicity in oil spills, but not for their complicity in genocide? How can corporations be held liable under European law for anticompetitive behavior, but not for slavery?

The commonsense fact remains that if States and individuals can be held liable under international law, then so too should corporations, for the simple reason that both States and individuals *act through* corporations. Given that reality, what legal sense would it make to let State and individuals immunize themselves from liability for gross violations through the mere artifice of corporate formation?

If corporations have rights under international law, by parity of reasoning, they must have duties as well. As history and precedent make clear, corporations can be held liable in two ways, particularly when they are involved in *jus cogens* violations.[6] First, corporations can be held liable as agents of the State committing what Andrew Clapham calls "complicity offenses," namely, acting under color of State law or in concert with State actors.[7] Second, it has always been true that a corporation can be held liable under international law if it commits certain "transnational offenses" – namely, a heinous offense that can be committed by either a public or a private entity. For example, if a corporation committed piracy or slave trade or fostered an attack on an ambassador, it would be considered *hostis humani generis* even if it acted in a purely private capacity. Even Judge Bork acknowledged this point in his concurring opinion in *Tel-Oren v. Libyan Arab Republic*.[8] On this basis, the Nuremberg Tribunal held private German industrialists – Flick, I.G. Farben and Krupp – criminally liable for their support of and participation in the Holocaust, finding that the Nuremberg Charter permitted prosecution of a private group or organization and stating that the action of the company and its representatives "under these circumstances cannot be differentiated from acts of plunder or pillage committed by officers … or …officials of the Third Reich."[9] Moreover, under Article 4 of Genocide Convention, a private corporation can commit or aid and abet in genocide, for example, by producing lethal toxic gas for use in a concentration camp.[10] The same goes for Common Article 3 of the Geneva Conventions, which binds all parties to an armed conflict, including those who may be non-State actors.

There is no serious argument that corporations cannot have specific intent to commit crimes. After all, under many US federal laws, such as the antitrust statutes or the Racketeer Influenced and Corrupt Organizations (RICO) statutes, corporations have long been held criminally liable for their specific intent to commit a crime.

Nor does it make sense to argue, as Pieter Bekker does, that international law may impose criminal liability on corporations but not civil liability. Congress passed two statutes – the Alien Tort Claims Act (ATCA) and the Torture Victim Protection Act (TVPA) – precisely to provide civil remedies for international law violations.[11] These statutes constitute a form of domestic legislative internalization of an international norm. Finally, even if for some reason international law did not impose civil liability directly, there is nothing to prevent domestic law (e.g. the ATCA) from supplementing international criminal law remedies with civil remedies arising out of domestic law. Indeed, in *Kadić v. Karadić*, and its progeny, the Second Circuit and other Circuits have held that the ATCA provides domestic civil remedies against non-State actors who violate international law.[12]

As Andrew Clapham notes, corporations are surely liable not just for direct, transnational offenses – which can be committed by private or public actors – but also for their indirect offenses in complicity with gross human rights abuses. Thus, corporations can be held liable for the small class of cases that arise out of a claim of violation of obligatory, definable, and universal norms of international law (direct offenses) as well as from their complicity in a public actor's violation of international law. Indeed, it was precisely the theory of the recent Holocaust Assets deal that private companies, banks, and officials were part of a common plan or conspiracy to commit war crimes or crimes against humanity. To constitute a "complicity offense," the corporate conduct must meet a high threshold. As the International Criminal Tribunal for the Former Yugoslavia specified in the *Tadić* case, the assistance must be direct and substantial,[13] and as the Tribunal noted in the *Furundzija* case in December 1998, the corporate conduct must constitute "practical assistance, encouragement, or moral support which has a substantial effect on the perpetration of a crime;"[14] The International Law Commission's rules of State responsibility suggest that complicity constitutes provision of "aid or assistance to another ... facilitating the commission of the wrongful act by the latter"[15]

Similarly, Art. 7(1) of the ICTY statute[16] and Article 25 of the International Criminal Court treaty hold private citizens criminally liable for committing crimes jointly with or through another person.[17] So all of this would appear to rebut the first myth: that private corporations cannot be held liable in the first place for their direct acts or acts in complicity with State human rights violations.

MYTH # 2: There is a flood of ATCA litigation in US courts that would impose liability on a corporation simply for its presence in a country where bad things happen, or as Pieter Bekker puts it: plantiffs are using the liberal provisions of the Federal Rules of Civil Procedure to sue private companies "based simply on their participation in the global economic system"[18] *Again, this is a gross overstatement.*

First, there is scarcely a flood of cases. Slightly more than twenty cases in more than 214 years of the ATCA's history does not constitute a flood. Of these only three or four have survived a motion to dismiss, and only one, the *Unocal* case, is past the stage of a summary judgment motion.[19] Under current law, the reason why seems clear. There are currently very high, multiple barriers to recovery under the ATCA. To be actionable, the acts committed by a private corporation:

(a) Must be brought in a proper forum with personal jurisdiction and venue
(b) Must not be barred by statute of limitations
(c) Must state a claim upon which relief can be granted, which means alleging either a transnational offense that either a State or private individual could commit, for example, a violation of an obligatory, definable, and universal norm of international law, or an act of actionable complicity in violation of international law in the *Furundzija* sense of practical assistance, encouragement, or moral support

which has a substantial effect on the perpetration of a State crime, and
(d) the claim must be proven, not just pleaded – the plaintiff has the burden of proving the link between cause and effect.

Understandably, these are hard standards to prove. What all this means is that the plaintiff needs to show much, much more than simply that the multinational enterprise has chosen to invest in a "troublesome country." Small wonder that since 1993, there have been more than twenty ATCA cases against private corporations, but the courts have dismissed most of these cases for lack of subject matter jurisdiction, *forum non conveniens* and the like. At this writing, no court has rendered any final judgment against any US company under the ATCA, and no US corporation has yet paid any ATCA damages. It is hard to see where the litigation "crisis" is, when no corporate defendant has yet paid an ATCA plaintiff a penny.

MYTH # 3: To limit the flood of Alien Tort Claims Act litigation, we need to either amend the statute or repeal it, or reject the line of ATCA cases starting with Filartiga. *In fact, no one has made the case that any fix – legislative or judicial – is really necessary.*

As I speak, two "fixes" are being discussed to address this "crisis." The first is legislative reform: amendment of the ATCA or its repeal. But these suggestions bring to mind the old adage "If it ain't broke, don't fix it." Given the relative paucity of litigation, legislative reform would be a massive overreaction. As I suggested more than a decade ago, if frivolous ATCA suits are brought, the best way to deal with them is for judges to manage their dockets wisely and to dismiss insubstantial suits by applying ordinary rules of jurisdiction, pleading, and proof and invoking the sanctions provisions of Federal Rule of Civil Procedure 11 if necessary to prevent frivolous suits.[20]

An even more radical approach has been taken by the Bush Administration in both the *Unocal* case[21] and the *Exxon Mobil* case,[22] in which it has filed *amicus curiae* briefs essentially urging the overruling of the line of Alien Tort Claims litigation since *Filartiga v. Pena-Irala.* In the lawsuit involving *Unocal,* the lower courts initially ruled that the case could proceed, and the full appeals court reheard the case in June 2003 with its decision likely by the end of 2003.

The Bush Administration's Justice Department under John Ashcroft faced four choices. First, in landmark briefs filed in the New York federal courts in 1980 and 1995, the Carter and Clinton Administrations had supported the foreign plaintiffs' right to sue gross violators under the ATCA. Thus, the Bush Administration, like prior administrations, could have simply maintained the position of its predecessors and supported the plaintiffs, citing the need to maintain a consistent governmental interpretation of an unchanging statute. Second, it could have supported the defendants on case-specific grounds; or third, it could have taken a neutral position (as it did, for example, in *Lawrence v. Texas,* the Supreme Court's recent Texas sodomy case). Instead the Administration chose a fourth, radical option, urging a position that would wipe out nearly twenty-five years of appellate precedent. The Administration dramatically changed the US government's interpretation of the two-hundred year-old statute. Opposing victims of the Burmese military junta, the government's brief insisted that victims of gross abuse cannot sue any foreign defendants under the ATCA for fundamental violations of international human rights norms. Even if the victims could prove that defendants shared responsibility for the abuses, the government argued, no ATCA recovery should be available because the claimed abuses occured outside of the United States and a ruling against the corporation would endanger American interests in the war on terror.[23]

The Bush Administration's approach is singularly misguided. In the first place, there has been no congressional change in the wording of either the Alien Tort Claims Act (ATCA) or the Torture Victim Protection Act (TVPA), and thus, no apparent legal reason why the United States should suddenly depart from the positions of the Carter and Clinton Administrations supporting the use of US courts under these two statutes. In addition, the Department's position violates a long line of established legal precedent. In 1795, only seven years after the ATCA first became law, the then-Attorney General opined that "there can be no doubt" that the law affords aliens injured by torts committed in violation of the law of nations "a remedy by a civil suit in the courts of the United States."[24] In the Torture Victim Protection Act of 1992, Congress reaffirmed the ATCA by enacting a modern statute along the same lines.[25] The federal courts of appeals have unanimously held that corporations can be sued under the Alien Tort Claims Act so long as it can be proved that they knowingly committed or collaborated in the commission of crimes against humanity.[26]

Moreover, as a matter of human rights policy, the Administration's position toward the ATCA and TVPA is perverse in five ways. First, it would virtually repeal these laws, without congressional participation, by granting immunity to all human rights abusers, whether official or corporate, so long as they commit their violations abroad. Second, the Administration's approach does not help, but rather undermines, the war against terrorism, for it would immunize from suit not just corporate defendants, but also Fidel Castro, Kim Jong Il, Saddam Hussein or any State sponsor of terrorism. Third, if under this theory "private enterprises" such as corporations cannot be held liable for gross human rights abuse overseas, then it is unclear how Al Qaeda, terrorist groups like Hizbollah and Hamas, and or any other private terrorist organization could be so held liable. Fourth, a California state judge has recently ruled that the *Unocal* case could be heard in state court if necessary, thus making the government's assault on federal jurisdiction sufficient only to shift venue, not to remove these cases from United States court altogether.[27] Fifth and finally, if fully adopted, the Administration's position would perversely push similar lawsuits against US companies into foreign courts, where they would lack the protections of US law. Surely, it is a strange way to fight a war against terrorism to deprive victims of terrorism of a well-tested tool of accountability.

MYTH # 4: Domestic litigation is a bad way to promote higher corporate standards in human rights and environment. In fact, litigation is not a bad way, but it should not be the only way.

My answer: litigation is not a bad way, but neither should it be the only way to promote higher corporate standards with respect to the environment and human rights. One can imagine a host of other ways to promote the same outcome, for example: voluntarism, which is discussed in Michael Addo's paper for this panel,[28] and exemplified by British Petroleum's 2002 human rights code of conduct to govern its operations abroad; domestic legal regulation; promulgation of industry codes of conduct, and the creation of private-public regimes.

With respect to the last, there are many recent efforts worth examining. In the Clinton Administration, for example, Stuart Eizenstat helped to negotiate a private-public deal in which foreign corporations that had profited from the Holocaust paid survivors billions of dollars in compensation for their losses.[29] In 1994, the White House announced Model Business Principles for corporations seeking to maintain high human rights standards and many leading corporations have subscribed to both the Global Sullivan Principles and U.N. Secretary-General Kofi Annan's Global Compact. In 2000, several major oil companies and then-Secretary of State Madeleine Albright announced a code of conduct – which had been negotiated under the auspices of the United States and United Kingdom governments – to regulate human rights abuses for security forces in the extractive industries.[30]

But in my opinion, the most promising avenue is neither statute nor judicial doctrine, but treaty. Corporations do not need immunity so much as they need a safe harbor: certainty that conduct in which they self-consciously and thoughtfully engage will not automatically expose them to domestic human rights lawsuit. The United States and British Governments have been seeking to develop common standards to clarify when a corporation illegally aids and abets official human rights abuse and work has been proceeding to draft an international convention on the subject under OECD auspices.

I agree with André Nollkaemper that what we need most are international legislative developments: draft norms of responsibility for transnational corporations and other business enterprises with regard to rights.[31] Mr. Nollkaemper points in particular to the promising efforts of the Working Group of the Subcommission on Human Rights to develop such norms.

Those of you familiar with my other writings know that I favor a transnational legal process approach: whereby techniques of process are used to internalize into transnational actors – here multinational corporations – standards of right and wrong behavior.[32] Precisely such an approach has been applied for the past quarter century with regard to bribery. In 1977, following the Lockheed scandal, Congress passed a Foreign Corrupt Practices Act, which imposed certain standards on US corporations through domestic civil and criminal legislation. The fact that US corporations were subjected to these constraints made them advocates for an OECD Bribery Convention, which is now functioning and becoming internalized into the law of the member nations. With luck, the same strategy that has been applied to counter corporate bribery practices can be applied to counter corporate complicity in human rights abuses.

In conclusion, let me say that the characterization by the Bush Administration and certain corporate defendants of Alien Tort Claims litigation as an "awakening monster" is wrong, as a matter of both law and policy. It credits these four myths over reality, and marks a gross overreaction to a litigation trend that the US courts are in fact properly managing with existing judicial tools. Furthermore, as a policy matter, efforts to repeal or reform the ATCA undermine meaningful efforts to promote corporate responsibility abroad. These efforts would be far better approached by international treaty drafting aimed at providing safe harbors for responsible corporations and clarifying what does or does not constitute actionable complicity in human rights abuse. If we genuinely care about corporate responsibility, we should put our efforts into developing these kinds of standards and encouraging responsible companies to meet them, not attacking a venerable law that has been used to call terrorists and human rights abusers to account.

So in closing, let me say to corporate counsel: you have nothing to fear but fear itself. If you are sued under ATCA, do not panic, litigate. If you are a good litigator and your clients are responsible actors, you should carry the day. But if not, and your client finds itself in trouble, then it is worth asking whether perhaps that trouble was of the client's own making in the first place.

NOTES

1 Gary Clyde Hufbauer and Nicholas K. Mitrokostas, *Awakening the Monster: The Alien Tort Statute of 1789* (2003).

2 *Doe I et al* v *Unocal Corporation et al*, Brief for the United Sates of America as *amicus curiae*, (9th Cir. May 8, 2003), argued en banc 17 June 2003.

3 Dr. Pieter H.F. Bekker, Provisional Report on "Corporate Aiding & Abetting and Conspiracy Liability Under International Law," see p. 209 *supra*.

4 Paris Convention on Third Party Liability in the Field of Nuclear Energy, done 29 July 1960, 956 U.N.T.S. 251.

5 Basel Convention on the Control of Transboundary Movements of Hazardous Wastes and Their Disposal, done 22 March 1989, Arts. 4(3), 9(5), 1673 U.N.T.S. 57, 132, 137.

6 For an excellent review, see Steven R. Ratner, *Corporations and Human Rights: A Theory of Legal Responsibility*, 111 Yale L.J. 443 (2001).

7 Andrew Clapham, *On Complicity*, M M. Henzelin and R. Roth, eds *Le droit pénal à l'épreuve de l'internationalisation*. Paris: LGDJ, Genève: Georg, Bruxelles: Brulant (2002) 241-275.

8 776 F.2d 774, 798 (D.C. Cir. 1984) (Bork, J., concurring).

9 *United States v. Krauch*, 8 CCL No. 10 Trials, at 1081, 1140 (1952) (U.S. Mil. Trib. VI 1948). In three cases decided by American courts sitting in occupied Germany under Control Council Law No. 10 – *United States v. Flick, United States v. Krauch (*the *I.G. Farben Case),* and *United States v. Krupp* – leading German industrialists were prosecuted for crimes against peace (i.e., initiating World War II), war crimes, and crimes against humanity. See 1 Trials of War Criminals Before the Nuremberg Military Tribunals, at xvi (photo. reprint 1998), vols. 6-9 (1950-1953) (1949). These trials led to convictions of the industrialists not only for slave labor, but also, in the case of *Flick,* for financial contributions to the SS.

10 *Cf.* The Zyklon B Case: Trial of Bruno Tesch and Two Others, 1 Law Reports of Trials of War Criminals 93 (1997) (Brit. Mil. Ct. 1946) (holding individuals liable for producing and supplying lethal case to concentration camp).

11 28 U.S.C. § 1350 & 1350a.

12 70 F. 3d 232, 239 (2d Cir. 1995) ("certain acts violate the law of nations whether undertaken by those acting under the auspices of a State or only as private individuals").

13 See *Prosecutor v. Tadić*, Case No. IT-94-I-T, para. 674 (Int'l Crim. Trib. for Former Yugoslavia Trial Chamber II May 7, 1997), http://www.un.org/icty/tadic/trialc2/judgement/ index.htm:

The most relevant sources for such a determination are the Nuremberg war crimes trials, which resulted in several convictions for complicitous conduct. While the judgments generally failed to discuss in detail the criteria upon which guilt was determined, a clear pattern does emerge upon an examination of the relevant cases. First, there is a requirement of intent, which involves awareness of the act of participation coupled with a conscious decision to participate by planning, instigating, ordering, committing, or otherwise aiding and abetting in the commission of a crime. Second, the prosecution must prove that there was participation in that the conduct of the accused contributed to the commission of the illegal act.

14 See *Prosecutor v. Furundzija*, Case No. IT-95-17/1 "Lasva Valley," (Int'l Crim. Trib. for Former Yugoslavia Trial Chamber II) (10 December 1998) (ICFTY Chamber), available at http://www.un.org/icty/furundzija/trialc2/judgement/index.htm para 249 ("the legal ingredients of aiding and abetting in international criminal law ... consists of practical assistance, encouragement, or moral support which has a substantial effect on the perpetration of the crime").

15 James Crawford, International Law Commission, 'Second Report on State Responsibility' UN Doc. A/

CN.4/498/Add.1, 1 April, 1999, at para. 159.

16 This provision specifies that persons accused of planning, ordering, or committing certain crimes will be held individually responsible for their acts.

17 See Clapham, *supra* note 7 at 10 ("Because the complicity concept in the [ICC] Statute is designed to cover those who act 'for the purpose of facilitating' crimes, rather than those who make a direct and essential contribution to the commission of crime, we can conclude that the assistance provided only has to meet a very low threshold for there to be the objective element for accomplice liability under the ICC Statute.").

18 Bekker, *supra* note 3, at p. 214 *supra*.

19 The cases to date are summarized in the appendices to Hufbauer and Mitrokostas, *supra* note 1.

20 Harold Hongju Koh, *Transnational Public Law Litigation*, 100 Yale L.J. 2347 2382-94 (1991).

21 The *Unocal* case was brought in California federal court by Burmese citizens, who alleged that a California corporation, Unocal, had aided and abetted the Burmese military junta's use of forced labor and other human rights abuses during the construction of a gas pipeline. The last Administration vociferously condemned Burmese human rights abuses, which in recent days led to the brutal arrest of Burma's rightful leader, Nobel Peace Prizewinner Aung San Suu Kyi, and the killing and imprisonment of many of her supporters. The Burmese plaintiffs filed their suit under the Alien Tort Claims Act (ATCA), which permits aliens to seek civil damages in US courts from defendants who commit gross violations of international law. The plaintiffs cited precedents from seven different federal circuits over the last two decades which have upheld the rights of victims of human rights abuse residing in the USA to seek recovery from such perpetrators as torturers from Paraguay, officials of Castro's government, State sponsors of terrorism like Iran, and indicted Bosnian Serb war criminal Radovan Karadić and former Philippine president Ferdinand Marcos.

22 Brief *Amicus Curiae* of the United States in *Doe v. Exxon Mobil Corp.*, Civ. No. 01-1357 (LFO) (D.C.D.C. 2002) (suit alleging corporate complicity in human rights abuses in Aceh).

23 Similarly, in *Doe v. Exxon Mobil*, which is currently pending before Judge Oberdorfer in the US District Court for the District of Columbia, the Legal Adviser of the State Department filed another *amicus* brief, as well as an affidavit asserting that adjudication of an ATCA lawsuit against a US corporation operating in Aceh, Indonesia would "risk a potentially serious adverse impact on significant interests of the United States, including interests related directly to the on-going struggle against international terrorism". Letter of 29 July 2002 written to Judge Louis F. Oberdorfer by William H. Taft IV, The Legal Adviser of the Department of State, in *Doe v. Exxon Mobil Corp.*, Civ. No. 01-1357 (LFO) (DCDC 2002). But see Affidavit of Harold Hongju Koh in *Doe v. Exxon Mobil Corp.*, Civ. No. 01-1357 (LFO) (DCDC 2002) (challenging those assertions).

24 *See* 1 Op. Att'y Gen. 57, 58 (1795) ("there can be no doubt" that the victims "have a remedy" under the ATCA for a civil claims despite its foreign origin). See also 26 Op. Att'y Gen. 250, 253 (1907) ("I repeat that the statute thus provide a forum and a right of action.").

25 According to the House Report, "[t]he TVPA would establish an unambiguous and modern basis for a cause of action that has been successfully maintained under an existing law, section 1350 of the Judiciary Act of 1789…" H.R. Rep. No. 367, 102d Cong., 1st Sess., pt. 1 (1991). Significantly, the House Report referred to *Filartiga* with approval, affirmed the importance of ATCA, and indicated that it "should not be replaced." Id. *See also* S. Rep. No. 249, 102d Cong., 1st Sess. (1991) (virtually identical language in Senate report).

26 See generally *Presbyterian Church of Sudan v. Talisman Energy, Inc.*, 244 F. Supp. 2d 289 (S.D.N.Y. 2003) (reviewing cases).

27 *Judge rules Unocal can be tried in US for alleged Myanmar rights abuses*, available at <story.news.yahoo.com/news?tmpl=story&cid=1519&e=18&u=/afp/us_myanmar_unocal>.

28 See Michael K. Addo, The Poverty of Voluntarism in Corporate Human Rights Responsibility, p. 238.

29 *See generally* Stuart E. Eizenstat, *Imperfect Justice: Looted Assets, Slave Labor, and the Unfinished Business of World War II* (2003).

30 *See* U.S. Department of State, Bureau of Democracy, Human Rights and Labor, Voluntary Principles on Security and Human Rights (released December 20, 2000), *available at* <http://www.state.gov/www/ global/human_rights/001220_fsdrl_principles.html>. For a summary of these principles, see Sean D. Murphy, *Voluntary Human Rights Principles for Extractive and Energy Companies, in* 95 Am. J. Int'l L. 636 (2001).

31 *See* Andre Nollkaemper, Translating Principles of Public International Law into Principles of Corporate Liability (2003), p. 224 *infra*.

32 For elaboration of this argument, see Harold Hongju Koh, *Bringing International Law Home*, 35 Hous. L. Rev. 623 (1998); Harold Hongju Koh, *Why Do Nations Obey International Law?*, 106 Yale L.J. 2599 (1997); Harold Hongju Koh, *How is International Human Rights Law Enforced?*, 74 Ind. L. J. 1397 (1999).

Remarks by André Nollkaemper*

Translating Public International Law into Corporate Liability

In this presentation I will address the question under what circumstances public international law can be translated into corporate liability. My main argument is that since, except for a small category of norms, present international law does not contain rules imposing duties and liability on corporations, such translation can only be achieved through a combined application of international law and national law.

Prima facie the translation of public international law into corporate liability presents fundamental problems. The nature and purpose of State authority is widely different from the nature and purpose of authority exercised by corporations. As a consequence, also the principles and underpinnings of public international law and corporate liability are widely different.

The need to translate principles of public international into principles of corporate liability arises only in a relatively narrow category of cases. Often it may not be necessary to apply public international law in transnational litigation against corporations. National law often will be sufficient. In some cases, however, public international law can and indeed should be relevant to corporate liability. The increase in the power of transnational corporations and the range of their activities has the potential of undermining the protection of public international values. The applicable national law may be inadequate or may even violate international law. In these situations, plaintiffs, but also the international legal order as such, have an interest that public international law is translated into the private domain of corporate liability.

Present international law does not provide for a general principle of civil liability of corporations. Human rights violations and environmental damage may result in public wrongs by the State. But international law leaves the question of whether they also result in private wrongs to the national sphere. There is no reason why this could not be otherwise. International law has provided for criminal responsibility. It could well provide for civil liability, and indeed such liability has been created for a narrow category of cases of environmental harm. However, there is no treaty or State practice that allows us to identify a general principle to that effect. I also do not believe that international law contains a general principle on corporate complicity with wrongs under public international law.

In these circumstances, any translation from public international law to corporate liability can only be achieved through a combined application of international law and national law.

The Alien Tort Claims Act of the United States shows us that the absence of a general international law principle may well be overcome on the national level. Through application of national tort law, combined with a liberal reading of international law, corporations can be held liable for human rights violations and environmental damage. The Alien Tort Statute may achieve a double translation: from the international to the national and from the public to the private.

* Professor of Public International Law and Director of the Amsterdam Center for International Law, University of Amsterdam.

However, in a comparative perspective, the US approach appears to be isolated. It may be helpful to contrast the practice of the United States with that of the Netherlands. Assume that a case would be brought in a Dutch court against a multinational that is incorporated in the Netherlands and that engages in human rights violations and environmental damage in Nigeria, forced labor in Birma or logging in protected forests in Cameroon. These are true scenarios that have been considered by possible plaintiffs. The Netherlands ranks high on the list of States most receptive toward international law. Yet, the number of cases in which public international law norms are applied in the private sphere is limited. Dutch courts have generally found that most of the international norms concerning labor rights, social and economic rights and environmental protection are inapplicable in litigation between injured individuals and corporations. That is: these norms do not directly apply to corporations, thus cannot be breached by them and therefore cannot provide a basis for liability.

This position appears to be more in common with the worldwide situation than the approach of the US Alien Tort Claims Act.

This does mean that norms that cannot be used to determine a violation of international law are necessarily irrelevant for civil liability. A middle way is available. Where public international law norms are sufficiently clear, it seems proper to use them at least as a background for private law determinations. That need not go all the way in the direction of the US courts, which construe acts by corporations to be direct violations of public international law. Courts can also let public international law influence interpretations of reasonableness, due care and so on, that in most States will govern corporate liability. In several States, including the Netherlands and Germany, courts have been prepared to use human rights obligations in the construction of open provisions of civil liability.

This may not be possible for all norms, however. Open ended norms of, say, the Biodiversity Convention, that require acts by public authorities, may be too general to determine corporate liability – even by way of interpretation. In the Netherlands, courts have been reluctant to apply international law norms that are not directly binding on private parties as a decisive element in the construction of the due care norm of civil liability.

The general problem for the translation of public international law into corporate liability, then, appears to be that a large number of public international law norms that may be relevant to corporations, are drafted as public law norms applying to public authorities. The step toward a translation to the private sphere may prove to be too big of a step to be made by the courts.

In this situation, the translation of public international law norms to corporate responsibility in the national legal sphere is dependent on international legislative developments. The most relevant development in this respect is the development of the *Draft Norms of Responsibilities of Transnational Corporations and Other Business Enterprises with Regard to Human Rights*, prepared by a Working Group of the Sub-commission on the Promotion and Protection of Human Rights (hereafter: *Draft Norms of Responsibilities*).[1] This document will be discussed at the Sub-Commission's 55th session in July and August 2003.

The document has much potential to contribute to a shift of public law norms to the private domain. It considers that transnational corporations are obligated to respect generally recognized responsibilities and norms in a long list of over 30 treaties and other instruments. This includes some treaties that pertain to private actors, including civil liability treaties (such as the Convention on Civil Liability for Damage Resulting from Activities Dangerous to the Environment) and criminal law treaties (such as the torture convention). But it also includes a wide variety of treaties that only can be characterized as public law instruments: the addressees are States, and they require State action for their application.

The document does not contain liability rules, but its substantive norms may be connected to national liability principles. Certain norms contained in the document, for instance those on forced labor, may be specific enough to flesh out private law standards in the national sphere and thus may assist national courts in determinations of transnational litigation. The fact that the document is not legally binding does not necessarily prevent this, as there are ample examples of judicial decisions that considered non-binding (international) texts relevant to determinations of civil liability.

However, the document also reveals that the translation of public international law into corporate liability presents fundamental dilemmas. As noted, the principles and underpinnings of public international law and corporate liability are widely different. A drafting exercise as the one that the Sub-Commission is presently engaged in reveals some of the problems caused by these differences.

One question is whether the legal problems created by shift in authority from the public to the private sphere, can be solved by a wholesale and non-discriminate transfer of public international law norms to the private sphere. The *Draft Norms of Responsibilities* appear so assume so. They oblige transnational corporations to "carry out their activities in accordance with relevant international agreements, principles, objectives, responsibilities, and standards with regard to the environment". However, many of these agreements, principles, objectives, responsibilities, and standards require political decisions, a reordering of governmental priorities and legislation. Such standards will provide insufficient guidance to the courts and will be of little or no use in determinations of corporate liability. More fundamentally, such a blanket transfer of public norms to the private sphere may fail to recognize that while public law norms may need to be translated to the private sphere, they cannot simply be transplanted without adjustment.

The answer to the question whether public international law can be transferred to the private sphere depends in part on the question what role one envisages for national courts in fleshing out open-ended principles of public international law. International norms on labour rights, social and economic rights and environmental protection often require further governmental action. Are courts the proper agents to make the choices of public policy and to determine that corporations that do not conform to the court's choices are liable? Or are such choices best left to the national legislator or to the international 'legislator'. The *Draft Norms of Responsibilities* could reduce the leeway of courts by specifying the contents of the relevant norms and thereby provide the public policy choices with a certain degree of international legitimacy.

And finally, the *Draft Norms of Responsibilities* raise the question whether one set of public international law principles can without discrimination be applied to all corporations. As they are presently formulated, they apply to all 'transnational corporations and other business enterprises'. That may not be a problem for principles that require corporations to refrain from ordering killings. But is it possible to apply principles that require more positive action, for instance in the sphere of labour rights or environmental protection, without discrimination to all corporations? In comments made to the Working Group, it has been suggested to confine the application of the *Draft Norms of Responsibilities* to "transnational corporations and other business enterprises employing more than 100 people."[2] A quantitative standard may not be enough, though. As the possibility to comply with certain norms may be dependent on power, resources, capabilities and also factual situations, these norms will have to be subject to some form of due diligence standard. As long as that is not provided for in the primary norms themselves, the due diligence test will have to be brought in by national tort law. Also in this respect the translation from principles of public international law to corporate liability can only be achieved through a combined application of international law and national law.

In conclusion, as long as we do not have a convention on corporate liability, the necessary injection of public law norms in matters of corporate liability will best be served in two ways. First, by a more courageous approach by national courts to use sufficiently specific public law norms as a background for private law determinations. Second, by a somewhat less ambitious UN Sub-Commission that now has no opportunity to specify what public norms are relevant to the private sphere and to what extent principles or public international law indeed can be meaningfully applied to private actors.

NOTES

1 The draft norms are annexed to UN Doc. E/CN.4/Sub.2/2002/13 of 15 August 2002.
2 *Id.*, par. 20.

REMARKS BY ANDREW CLAPHAM*

CORPORATE COMPLICITY IN VIOLATIONS OF INTERNATIONAL LAW: BEYOND UNOCAL

1. THE ALIEN TORT CLAIMS ACT

The US Justice Department has filed an *amicus* brief in the US Court of Appeals for the Ninth Circuit arguing that that Court's precedents concerning the application of the Alien Tort Claims Act (ATCA) be overruled.[1] The brief suggests that the current application of the ATCA disrupts the foreign relations of the US and could undermine the war on terrorism. Harold Koh has in this Conference addressed some of the counter-arguments which have been raised in this context. Apart from pointing out that the ATCA could be used to sue for terrorist acts committed abroad he highlights the fact that the actual case against Unocal regarding its operations in Myanmar/Burma turns on the law of aiding and abetting. Not every commercial contact with a foreign government will result in corporate complicity in violations of international law. The fear in some sectors of the business community is that companies will be simply

* Professor of Public International Law, Graduate Institute of International Studies, Geneva.

tarred by association and that the costs of litigation will prohibit investment is certain developing countries. *The Economist* put the issue as follows: 'Nobody claims that Unocal committed atrocities. But there is some evidence (the muddy part of the case) that it was aware of what was going on. The appeals court held that awareness could be enough to make Unocal in part responsible for the crimes. But even in the Nuremberg war-crime trials, arguments of aiding and abetting largely failed.'[2] This short note looks in a bit more detail at the arguments concerning aiding and abetting, in other words accomplice liability or complicity.

The US government does not really dispute that the Myanmar government is responsible for international human rights violations including forced labour. But the crucial issue is whether a company can be liable for its association with an abusive government. Of course if the ATCA precedents are reversed in the way the Justice department desires these questions may become academic. The Justice Department argues that ATCA is jurisdictional and does not create a cause of action for non-self-executing international law rights, and they argue that it should be interpreted to cover acts outside the US. But some of us are academics and the issues are worth exploring: the theory of corporate complicity is important even outside the context of the US Federal Jurisdiction and the Alien Tort Claims Act. Corporate complicity is important for understanding how the issue might be dealt with in other jurisdictions, and, stepping outside the strictly legal sphere for a moment, it is a crucial concept in contexts such as the UN Secretary-General's Global Compact and the UN Sub Commission on Human Rights' Draft Norms on the Responsibilities of Transnational Corporations and Other Business Enterprises with Regard to Human Rights.

2. Corporate complicity

We will focus on the difficult area of corporate complicity in violations of international law committed by others. Some international crimes could give rise to direct responsibilities under international law for the corporations themselves. This kind of direct responsibility need not be discussed here. Let us turn to the trickier issue of corporate complicity in violations committed by others. We shall have to confront the question as to what sort of intention is required for responsibility in this context. Is it enough that the corporate executives should have known that participation in a certain government project would likely lead to human rights abuses? Do they, and the company, come within our evolving notion of command responsibility? Are they responsible for what they should have known, and for what they failed to halt when they did know about it?

3. The Alien Tort Claims Act litigation concerning corporate complicity

We have recently seen an interesting string of cases before the US courts under the Alien Tort Statute 1789. The origins of this piece of legislation are hazy and have been the subject of conjecture as legal scholars have applied their imagination to events over 200 years ago. (Burley 1989). Nevertheless the effects of the Act today are very real as corporations find themselves as defendants facing multi-million dollar suits. The Alien Tort Claims Act confers upon the federal district courts original jurisdiction over 'any civil action by an alien for a tort only, committed in violation of the law of nations.' 28 USC § 1350. There are currently a number of claims pending or on appeal regarding various oil companies accused of among other things: forced labour, torture and rape. (Zia-Zarifi 1999.) The application of this Statute to the activities of multinational corporations abroad is not without its critics (Thadani 2000). But the judicial decisions on the application of the Alien Tort Claims Act are not only generating interventions from the US Government, they are developing ways of understanding the parameters of legal liability in this area. These decisions in turn affect the way that corporations and non-governmental organizations are determining the meanings to be given to promises and undertakings (such as those found in the UN Global Compact) to 1. respect and protect human rights, and to 2. avoid complicity in human rights abuses. It would be wrong to see the development of the law as hinging solely on the evolving interpretation of the Alien Tort Claims Act and the issue of whether it can create causes of action in the US Federal Courts and whether it can apply to extraterritorial acts. In any event, other jurisdictional statutes include the Torture Victim Protection Act 28 USC § 1350 and the Racketeer Influenced and Corrupt Organizations Act 18 USC § 1961. Both these Acts are also being used in the US courts against multinationals accused of participating in human rights violations outside the United States.

3.1 Corporate complicity in the Unocal ruling

There are various cases and rulings regarding the litigation concerning Unocal and its activity in Myanmar. The most important for present purposes is the ruling of the US Court of Appeals for the Ninth Circuit filed 18 September 2002.

> We hold that the standard for aiding and abetting under the ATCA is, as discussed below, knowing practical assistance or encouragement that has a substantial effect on the perpetration of the crime. We further hold that a reasonable factfinder could find that Unocal's conduct met this standard. (at para. 4).

On this point they disagreed with the Court below which had demanded a higher test, that of 'active participation' in the forced labour. What makes the case particularly interesting from an international perspective is that the tests have mostly been derived from the prosecutions for international crimes which followed the Second World War and the more recent international prosecutions by the *ad hoc* International Tribunals, established by the UN Security Council, with responsibility for prosecuting crimes committed in the former Yugoslavia and Rwanda.[3]

3.2 The *actus reus* of complicity in the Unocal case

The ruling gives an indication of the sort of *practical assistance* which will be evidence of the material element of the crime:

> The evidence also supports the conclusion that Unocal gave practical assistance to the Myanmar Military in subjecting Plaintiffs to forced labor.[[4]] The practical assistance took the form of hiring the Myanmar Military to provide security and build infrastructure along the pipeline route in exchange for money or food. The practical assistance also took the form of using photos, sur-

veys, and maps in daily meetings to show the Myanmar Military where to provide security and build infrastructure. (at para. 11)

The Court found that this assistance had a *substantial effect* on the perpetration of the forced labour, and that the forced labour would most probably not have occurred in the same way 'without someone hiring the Myanmar Military to provide security, and without someone showing them where to do it.' (at para. 12) The Court paid particular attention to evidence from a Representative of Unocal:

> This assistance, moreover, had a "substantial effect" on the perpetration of forced labor, which "most probably would not have occurred in the same way" without someone hiring the Myanmar Military to provide security, and without someone showing them where to do it. *Tadic* at § 688. This conclusion is supported by the admission of Unocal Representative Robinson that "[o]ur assertion that [the Myanmar Military] has not *expanded and amplified its usual methods* around the pipeline *on our behalf* may not withstand much scrutiny," and by the admission of Unocal President Imle that "[i]f forced labor goes hand and glove with the military yes there will be *more forced labor.*" [Emphasis added (in original)] (at para. 12)

The Court applied a variation on a causation test. The participation by the company need not actually cause the violation of international law, but the assistance or encouragement has to be such that without such participation the violations *most probably* would not have occurred *in the same way.*

3.3 The US Court of Appeals and the *mens rea* (subjective or mental element) required for complicity in the Unocal case

The US Court of Appeals examined the evidence and applied a reasonable knowledge test. The requisite mental element for corporate complicity in these circumstances seems to be that the company knew or should have known that its acts assisted in the crime. The fact that a company benefits from the principal perpetrator's human rights violations has been emphasized and creates and important nexus.

> As for the *mens rea* of aiding and abetting, the International Criminal Tribunal for the former Yugoslavia held that what is required is actual or constructive (i.e., "reasonabl[e]") "knowledge that [the accomplice's] actions will assist the perpetrator in the commission of the crime." *Furundzija* at § 245. Thus, "it is not necessary for the accomplice to share the *mens rea* of the perpetrator, in the sense of positive intention to commit the crime." *Id.* In fact, it is not even necessary that the aider and abettor knows the precise crime that the principal intends to commit. *See id.* Rather, if the accused "is aware that one of a number of crimes will probably be committed, and one of those crimes is in fact committed, he has intended to facilitate the commission of that crime, and is guilty as an aider and abettor." *Id.* [fn omitted]
>
> Similarly, for the *mens rea* of aiding and abetting, the International Criminal Tribunal for Rwanda required that "the accomplice knew of the assistance he was providing in the commission of the principal offence." *Musema* at § 180. The accomplice does not have to have had the intent to commit the principal offense. *See id.* at § 181. It is sufficient that the accomplice "knew or had reason to know" that the principal had the intent to commit the offense. *Id.* at § 182. (para. 7)
>
> ....
>
> a reasonable factfinder could also conclude that Unocal's conduct met the *mens rea* requirement

of aiding and abetting as we define it today, namely, actual or constructive (i.e., reasonable) knowledge that the accomplice's actions will assist the perpetrator in the commission of the crime. The District Court found that "[t]he evidence does suggest that Unocal knew that forced labor was being utilized and that the Joint Venturers benefitted from the practice." *Doe/Roe II*, 110 F. Supp. 2d at 1310. Moreover, Unocal knew or should reasonably have known that its conduct — including the payments and the instructions where to provide security and build infrastructure — would assist or encourage the Myanmar Military to subject Plaintiffs to forced labor. (at para. 13)

3.4 The application in Unocal of a non-criminal law test for third part liability for violations of international law

In a concurring opinion Judge Reinhardt spelt out an alternative set of tests for determining the liability of Unocal in such a situation. Responding to the alternative pleadings of the plaintiffs he examined three tests under US tort law. As we shall see below, this examination of tort law is important, even if in the present case the majority opinion relied purely on international criminal law.

We need not enter the debate as to which test a US Federal Court should use under US law. Suffice it to say that whatever the situation in US law, other jurisdictions are likely to use the international criminal law tests for accomplice liability when the same issues come up under their criminal jurisdictions.[5]

The concurring opinion refers to three principles: joint venture, agency and reckless disregard. In considering these principles we should bear in mind the extent that such principles are common to major legal systems and therefore possibly applicable in international law as general principles of law.

With regard to joint venture, Judge Reinhardt concludes, on the basis of an examination of a number of treaties and commentaries that this principle is 'well established in international law and in other national legal systems.'[6] The opinion includes a footnote to the federal common law requirements for joint venture:

It is well-accepted that joint liability will exist where (1) parties intended to form a joint venture; (2) parties share a common interest in the subject matter of the venture; (3) the parties share the profits and losses of the venture; and (4) the parties have joint control or the joint right of control over the venture. W. Keeton, *Prosser and Keeton on Torts*, § 72 at 518 (5th ed. 1984).[7]

Although in the *Unocal* case there is a factual dispute as to whether the Unocal subsidiary was independent of the joint venture and the Military, the Judge pointed to 'evidence in the record states that Unocal would share revenues and costs of both the drilling and transportation components of the Yadana project. In view of the above, I believe that plaintiffs ought to proceed to trial on their claim of joint venture liability.'[8]

Turning to the question of agency liability, the opinion states that 'an agency relationship may be express or implied; in addition, a jury may infer from the factual circumstances that apparent agency authority exists.... As is true of joint liability principles, agency liability principles are well-established in international law. ... Principal-agent liability is also widely adopted by civil law and other common law systems.'[9]

Considering the evidence the Judge considers that it is suggested that such a relationship exists:

> For instance, plaintiffs cite an internal Unocal briefing document regarding the Yadana Project, discussed by the majority, which states that "[a]ccording to our contract, the government of Myanmar is responsible for protecting the pipeline. There is military protection for the pipeline and, when we have work to do along the pipeline that requires security, the military people will, as a matter of course, be nearby." They also point to memoranda by various Total and Unocal employees recounting that oil company officials requested specific battalions to perform various tasks, including the construction of helipads for the convenience of corporate executives. Plaintiffs argue that the record supports either an implied or express agency relationship, based on the conduct of the parties. As the majority has also pointed out, the record contains evidence of daily meetings between Total and Unocal executives and Myanmar military commanders, so that the corporations could instruct the military leaders regarding specific security or infrastructure projects that were required for the pipeline construction. Moreover, Unocal stated publicly on several occasions that it controlled the Myanmar military's actions in connection with the pipeline project. In response to accusations of human rights abuses occurring by the Myanmar military with respect to the Yadana project, Unocal denied the existence of such abuses, and stressed its ability to prevent any wrongdoing due to its control of the military. Unocal's alleged actions directing the Myanmar military create a triable question of fact as to whether an agency relationship existed between Unocal and the Myanmar armed forces.[10]

These passages are important, as they demonstrate that it is not any relationship with an abusive government that will give rise to agency liability for a company. There will have to be an employment situation whereby the company becomes responsible for the acts of its (government) agents. Where a company hires, or is in a position to influence the actual operations which are known to lead to human rights violations, the company will be liable for the acts of those agents who are the principal perpetrators. The opinion is clear that there is no need to show a contractual relationship:

> It is not essential that a formal contract have existed between Unocal and the Myanmar military in order for Unocal to be held liable for the government's actions under an agency theory. Nevertheless, should plaintiffs prove their allegation that such a contract existed, a jury might have considerable difficulty in accepting Unocal's denial of an agency relationship.[11]

Lastly, we should look at the principle of reckless disregard. Judge Reinhardt decided to apply the principle, not only to acts that cause *direct* harm, but also to the situation where a company uses the services of an entity, which in turn, causes harm:

> I see no reason why the general principle that liability arises for one party's conscious disregard of unreasonable risks to another should not apply when a defendant consciously disregards the risks that arise from its decision to use the services of an entity that it knows or ought to know is likely to cause harm to another party.[12]

Under this common law theory the plaintiffs would have to prove that 'Unocal had actual knowledge that the Myanmar military would likely engage in human rights abuses, including forced labor, if it undertook the functions Unocal and the other private parties desired it to perform in connection with the Yadana Pipeline Project. Nevertheless, according to plaintiffs, Unocal recklessly disregarded that known risk, determined to use and in fact did use the services of that military to perform pipeline-related tasks, and thereby set in motion international law abuses that were foreseeable to Unocal.'[13]

3.5 Which tests to use for corporate complicity: criminal law or civil (tort) law?

Not every claim regarding corporate complicity in governmental violations of human rights will involve international crimes. In such cases it seems inappropriate to use international criminal law or even national criminal law principles. For example if the corporation is accused of assisting a government in restricting freedom of expression, neither the violation by the government, nor the aid given by the company, is, on its own, an international crime. International law has not yet criminalized violations of freedom of expression as international crimes. Such a violation is rather an international tort or delict. Such a concept is underdeveloped, but the issues are not totally academic. In the *Wiwa* v. *Shell* case several of the complicity complaints against Shell concern Shell's involvement in such international torts. Let us now turn to that case.

3.6 Wiwa v. Shell and the issue of complicity in international torts

In *Wiwa* v. *Royal Dutch Petroleum (Shell)*[14] the plaintiffs alleged violations of international law in connection with the Nigerian Government's activities in the Ogoni region of Nigeria. The complaint was brought against the oil companies and a named managing director for directing and aiding the Nigerian government in violating the human rights of the complainants. The allegations focus on the suppression of the Movement for the Survival of the Ogoni people (MOSOP). It is alleged that Shell, operating through Shell Nigeria, recruited the Nigerian police and military to suppress MOSOP. The company is said to have:

> provided logistical support, transportation, and weapons to Nigerian authorities to attack Ogoni villages and stifle opposition to Shell's oil-excavation activities. Ogoni residents, including plaintiffs, were beaten, raped, shot, and/or killed during these raids. Jane Doe was beaten and shot during one raid in 1993, and Owens Wiwa was illegally detained.
>
> In 1995, Ken Saro-Wiwa and John Kpuinen were hanged after being convicted of murder by a special tribunal. Defendants bribed witnesses to testify falsely at the trial, conspired with Nigerian authorities in meetings in Nigeria and the Netherlands to orchestrate the trial, and offered to free Ken Saro-Wiwa in return for an end to MOSOP's international protests against defendants. During the trial, members of Ken Saro-Wiwa's family, including his elderly mother, were beaten.[15]

Although the claims include allegations that Shell's conduct violated international law, including the law on crimes against humanity and torture, part of the claims concern violations 'of the right to life, liberty and security of the person and peaceful assembly and association'.[16] To the extent that the complaint relies on the ratification by Shell of such violations of customary international law by Nigeria we should be aware that such violations of international law would not all be international crimes but might nevertheless be violations of international law by Nigeria. Assisting in such violations would not therefore be addressed by international criminal law, as no international crime has been committed. Nevertheless the claims suggest that the corporate activity could involve individual or corporate 'civil responsibility' under international law.[17]

Because international law has focused so far on individual criminal responsibility and State 'civil' responsibility, guidance on the international rules regarding 'civil' responsibility may have to be sought in the developing law of State complicity as elaborated in the ILC's Articles on State Responsibility.

3.7 **State responsibility for State complicity**

In the law of State responsibility the UN International Law Commission (ILC) has recently redefined the scope of complicity as it relates to assistance by one State in the violation of international law by another State. In the articles adopted by the ILC in 2001 relevant article reads as follows:

> *Article 16*
> *Aid or assistance in the commission of an internationally wrongful act*
> A State which aids or assists another State in the commission of an internationally wrongful act by the latter is internationally responsible for doing so if:
> (a) That State does so with knowledge of the circumstances of the internationally wrongful act; and
> (b) The act would be internationally wrongful if committed by that State.

The required connection between the aid and the wrongful act is explained in the final commentary on Article 16. The Commentary states that it will be sufficient for the purposes of this complicity article if the aid or assistance 'contributed *significantly* to that act.'[18]

With regard to knowledge of the unlawfulness of acts committed by the assisted State the situation becomes complicated due to the nature of State obligations. Starting from the point that not all national legal systems make it a civil wrong for someone to assist someone else to breach their contractual obligations, the Rapporteur pointed out that any reading which would suggest State complicity for assisting in the breach of any internationally unlawful act would cover third party assistance to a party to breach a bilateral treaty. This would mean that bilateral treaties could in effect be enforced on the rest of the world who would be under an obligation not to assist the relevant States in breaching them. The Rapporteur also concluded that problems would arise as to proof of the awareness of a State of another State's full range of bilateral and multilateral obligations.

As soon as we admit that the violations of customary international law we are discussing are violations of human rights law, and that the sorts of violations that are alleged represent actions that are clearly wrong, the defence of ignorance of the law seems less viable. The human rights abuses which companies are accused of assisting in all relate to the fundamental human rights principles contained in the Universal Declaration of Human Rights. In the context of corporate social responsibility, the case has been made that all actors have to respect the Universal Declaration of Human Rights (Robinson 1999: 14). The Universal Declaration of Human Rights is now regularly referred to by companies as part of the human rights policy statements. Chris Avery, who maintains a website on business and human rights, has collected the company human rights policy statements that include explicit reference to the Universal Declaration of Human Rights. As of 28 November 2002 he included: ABB, Ahold,

Balfour Beatty, BG Group, The Body Shop, BP, BT Group, CGNU Group, Conoco, Co-operative Bank, Diageo, Freport-McMoRan, Ikea, National Grid, Norsk Hydro, Novo Group, Premier Oil, Reebok, Rio Tinto, Shell, Skanska, Stora Enso, Storebrand Group, Talisman Energy, TotalFinaElf, and Unocal.[19]

In sum, returning to the three limits regarding State complicity, first, one does not have to show that the assisting State shared the intention of the assisted State. What is required is knowledge of the circumstances of the internationally wrongful act. If we apply this rule, by analogy to companies, one would not have to prove the intent of a company (a difficult and perplexing task in national criminal law, (Forcese 1999)), one need merely show that the company knows the circumstances of the wrongful act. Second, to invoke the complicity of States in the wrongful acts of other States one has to show that the aid actually facilitates the wrongful act and was given with a view to that purpose. But one does not need to show that the aid was an essential contribution to a wrongful act. By analogy one does not have to show that *but for* the corporate contribution the wrongful act would not have been committed. The corporate contribution need only *actually facilitate the wrongful act.* And third, under the rules of State responsibility, the accomplice State must be bound by the same obligation to be held responsible in international law for State complicity.

In this context, it is also of interest that the revised OECD Guidelines for Multinational Enterprises have added a human rights obligation in the context of general policies. They now state that enterprises should: 'Respect the human rights of those affected by their activities consistent with the host government's obligations and commitments.' (General Policies II.2.) This guideline simply enjoins enterprises to act consistently with the host States' international human rights obligations and here we can include their obligations under the Universal Declaration of Human Rights. The official commentary states that:

> while promoting and upholding human rights is primarily the responsibility of governments, where corporate conduct and human rights intersect enterprises do play a role, and thus MNEs are encouraged to respect human rights, not only in their dealings with employees, but also with respect to others affected by their activities, in a manner that is consistent with host governments' international obligations and commitments. The Universal Declaration of Human Rights and other human rights obligations of the government concerned are of particular relevance in this regard. (OECD 2001: 12)

It is suggested that where the allegations of corporate complicity concern assistance to States in the violation of the principles contained in the Universal Declaration of Human Rights, and these abuses can not be described as crimes under international law, then it may be appropriate to apply the international State complicity or international civil responsibility test just described. The elements for responsibility are similar. It would seem that for civil wrongs one may actually have to show a greater degree of knowledge and purpose than for most criminal wrongs as international criminal law has a 'knew or should have known' test due to the seriousness of the crimes at issue. There is no need to make too much of this difference. The important point is that international law has complicity tests for crimes and for torts.

There is a second, and separate reason, why it may make sense to focus, not only on criminal law, but also on tort law. Complaints of corporate complicity are aimed at achieving compensation rather that retributive criminal justice. In order to apportion damages it will be essential in some circumstances to consider tort responsibility principles. The ILC Commentary states that 'in cases where the internationally wrongful act would clearly have occurred in any event, the responsibility of the assisting State will not extend to compensating for the act itself.' (Commentary art. 16 para. 1). The drive to hold corporations accountable for complicity in human rights abuses stems in part from the need to claim reparations from the accomplice company in situations where it is difficult, if not impossible, to claim reparations from the offending government. Should the victims be able to hold a corporation responsible for the acts of the offending State?

3.8 Summary on corporate complicity in human rights abuses under international law

- Where a corporation assists another entity, whether it be a State, a rebel group, another company or an individual to commit an international crime, the rules for determining responsibility under international law will be the rules developed in international criminal law. The corporation will be responsible as an accomplice, whether or not it intended for a crime to be committed, if it can be shown that (a) The corporation carries out acts specifically directed to assist, encourage or lend moral support to the perpetration of a certain specific international crime and this support has a substantial effect upon the perpetration of the crime. (b) The corporation had the knowledge that its acts would assist the commission of a specific crime by the principal.
- Where a corporation is alleged to have assisted a government in violating customary international law rights in circumstances which do not amount to international crimes, but rather to international delicts or torts, the international rules for responsibility suggest that the corporations must be (a) aware of the circumstances making the activity of the assisted State a violation of international human rights law (b) the assistance must be given with a view to facilitating the commission of such a violation and actually contribute significantly to the violation. (c) The company itself should have an obligation not to violate the right in question, such obligations stem for example from the principles in the Universal Declaration of Human Rights.

Bibliography

Burley, A.-M. (1989) 'The Alien Tort Statute and the Judiciary Act of 1789: A Badge of Honor', Vol. 83 *AJIL* 3, 461-493.

Clapham, A. (2000) 'The Question of Jurisdiction Under International Criminal Law Over Legal Persons: Lessons from the Rome Conference on an International Criminal Court' in M. Kamminga and S. Zia-Zarifi, eds., *Liability of Multinational Corporations Under International Law*. The Hague: Kluwer , 139-195.

Clapham, A. (2002) 'On Complicity', M. Henzelin and R. Roth, eds., *Le droit pénal à l'épreuve de l'internationalisation*. Genève: Georg (2002) , 241-275.

Crawford, J. (1999) International Law Commission, 'Second Report on State Responsibility' UN Doc. A/CN.4/498/Add.1, 1 April 1999.

Crawford, J. (2002) *The International Law Commission's Articles on State Responsibility: Introduction, Text and Commentaries*. Cambridge: Cambridge University Press.

FORCESE, C. (1999) 'Deterring "Militarized Commerce": The Prospect of Liability for "Privatized" Human Rights Abuses', Vol. 31 *Ottawa Law Review* , 171-221.

GRAEFRATH, B. (1996) 'Complicity in the Law of International Responsibility', 2 *Revue Belge de Droit International* , 370-80.

INTERNATIONAL LAW COMMISSION (1999) *Report of 51st Session.* 1999, Supp. No.10 A/54/10.

INTERNATIONAL LAW COMMISSION (2001) *Report of 53rd Session.* 2001, Supp. No. 10 A/56/10.

KUTZ, CHRISTOPHER (2000) *Complicity: ethics and law for a collective age.* Cambridge: Cambridge University Press.

ORGANISATION FOR ECONOMIC COOPERATION AND DEVELOPMENT *The OECD Guidelines for Multinational Enterprises: Text, Guidelines, Commentary.*

PAUST, J. J. 'Human Rights Responsibilities of Private Corporations', Vol. 35 *Vanderbilt Journal of Transnational Law* 3, (2002) , 801-825.

RAMASASTRY, A. 'Corporate Complicity: From Nuremberg to Rangoon An Examination of Forced Labor Cases and Their Impact on the Liability of Multinational Corporations', Vol. 20 *Berkeley Journal of International Law* (2002) , 91-159.

RATNER, S.R. 'Corporations and Human Rights: A Theory of Legal Responsibility', Vol. 111 *Yale Law Journal* (2001) , 443-545.

ROBINSON, MARY (1998) 'Visions of ethical business', Financial Times Management , London: Financial Times management , 14-17.

THADANI, P.Z. (2002) 'Regulating Corporate Human Rights Abuses: Is *UNOCAL* The Answer?', Vol. 42 *William and Mary Law Review* 2, 619-646.

VAN GENUGTEN, W.J.M. (2000) 'The Status of Transnational Corporations in International Public law: with special reference to the case of Shell', A. Eide, H.O. Bergesen and P.R. Goyer, eds., *Human Rights and the Oil Industry.* Antwerp: Intersentia, 71-89.

WELLS, C. (2001) *Corporations and Criminal Responsibility* 2nd edn. Oxford: Oxford University Press.

ZIA-ZARIFI, S. (1999) 'Suing Multinational Corporations in the U.S. for Violating International Law', Vol. 4 *UCLA J. Int'l L. & For. Aff.* pp. 81-147.

NOTES

1 *Doe I et al* v. *Unocal Corporation et al,* brief for the United Sates of America as *amicus curiae,* May 2003.

2 'The alien problem' 21 June 2003, at 63.

3 Some of this case law on aiding and abetting is discussed in detail in Clapham (2002).

4 Footnote 29 in original reads: 'The evidence further supports the conclusion that Unocal gave "encouragement" to the Myanmar Military in subjecting Plaintiffs to forced labor. The daily meetings with the Myanmar Military to show it where to provide security and build infrastructure, despite Unocal's knowledge that the Myanmar Military would probably use forced labor to provide these services, may have encouraged the Myanmar Military to actually use forced labor for the benefit of the Project. Similarly, the payments to the Myanmar Military for providing these services, despite Unocal's knowledge that the Myanmar Military had actually used forced labor to provide them, may have encouraged the Myanmar Military to continue to use forced labor in connection with the Project.'

5 There are some cases pending in Belgium with similar allegations of complicity in international crimes. By contrast in Belgium the cases are filed as criminal cases see 'Elf est poursuivie pour son soutien au président congolais Sassou Nguesso, Une palinte a été déposée à Bruxelles pour complicité de crimes' *Le Monde,* 18 October 2001 and 'Myanmar refugees seek Belgium trial for TotalFinaElf', *AFP* 8 May 2002.

6 Unocal 2002, *supra* at 14257.

7 Ibid., at 14257 fn 11, and see for another formulation ICHRP (2002) 130 esp fn 349.

8 Ibid., at 14259.

9 Ibid., at 14261.

10 Ibid., at 14262.

11 Ibid., at 14263.

12 Ibid., at 14265.

13 Ibid., at 14263.

14 US District Court for the Southern District of New York, Decided 22 February 2002, filed 28 February 2002.

15 From the ruling at Part IB. Available at <http://www.derechos.org/nizkor/econ/shell28feb02.html>.

16 At I.C.2 of the ruling, for the actual claims see paras. 121-126 of the Statement of Claim available at <www.ccr-ny.org>.

17 The Commentary to Article 58 of the International Law Commission's Articles on State Responsibility deliberately leaves open the possibility that international law, having developed to encompass individual responsibility in the context of the Nuremberg and subsequent international criminal trials, might similarly develop in the field of 'individual civil responsibility.' At para. 2 of the Commentary to Article 58. (*supra*): So far this principle has operated in the field of criminal responsibility, but it is not excluded that developments may occur in the field of individual civil responsibility. As a saving clause Article 58 is not intended to exclude that possibility; hence the use of the general term "individual responsibility"'. Article 58 reads: 'These articles are without prejudice to any question of the individual responsibility under international law of any person acting on behalf of a State'. Because the Articles concern State Responsibility the focus is on individuals acting on behalf of the State, however the commentary is quite clear that all individuals may incur individual responsibility under international law. See paras. 2 and 4 of the Commentary to Article 58 which refer to the principle that individual persons 'including State officials' may be responsible under international law for conduct such as genocide, war crimes and crimes against humanity.

18 At para. 5 of the Commentary to Article 16, [emphasis added].

19 <http://business-humanrights.org/Company-policies-Examples.htm>, last visited 28 November 2002.

Remarks by Michael K. Addo*

The poverty of voluntarism in corporate human rights responsibility

Summary

The debate about the nature and basis for the responsibility of non-governmental actors especially private corporations for human rights is set on two parallel courses. The voluntarism route and the route of legal regulation. In truth, the two routes are complementary but then the advocates of either direction do not necessarily always see the point of the other so clearly. I fully endorse the complementarity of the two approaches in order to give corporate human rights responsibility a decent chance of credible success. However, it is my firm conviction that voluntarism as a basis for corporate human rights responsibility can only carry the management of change so far and not further and that ultimately the future of corporate responsibility for human rights rests in the law.

The idea that the real task for identifying the human rights responsibility of private corporations lies in the law is neither new nor radical. Many others have argued this point either expressly or by implication. The missing piece in this jigsaw is the assessment of the true potential (normatively and practically) of the voluntarism arguments. The value of such an exercise (i.e. assessing the potential of voluntarism as the basis of corporate human rights responsibility) does not lie merely in the effort to prop the legal regulation agenda but also to confront the increasing attraction of the voluntarism school. Above all else, the subject (of human rights responsibility of private corporations) needs direction and vision. This lies with the law.

It is the gist of this presentation that

* University of Exeter.

1. the main premises on which ideas and policies of voluntarism in corporate human rights responsibility are based are flawed; and that
2. the practical potential of the voluntarism approach is extremely limited.

The premise of voluntary initiatives

(a) that the law is an inadequate basis for the regulation of corporate behaviour and hence the refrain of social responsibility 'beyond compliance'
(b) that human rights restrain political power
(c) that human rights are valuable in so far as they can be good for business
(d) human rights as part of charitable initiatives

The limited practical value of voluntary initiatives

(a) the basis of co-operation
(b) complementarity – the reliance on legal standards to define the framework of voluntary action

The legal basis

(a) No need for a radical overhaul of the law
(b) the functional framework [of law and of corporate entities]
(c) the dynamic character of the law [especially through interpretation]
(d) Human rights law [universality of standards; victim-centred focus and the principle of effectiveness].

Discussion

Dr Georg Berrisch invited the participants and panellists for questions and comments.

Mr Sven Koopmans* stated that the presentation of Pieter Bekker had raised some misunderstandings. Dr Bekker had argued that there currently was no rule of general international law holding companies liable for conspiring to commit or aid and abet in human rights abuses. Mr Koopmans asserted that various US courts had misapplied the ATCA. The ATCA required judges to investigate whether companies violated present rules of international law, but did not allow them to judge whether such rules of international law should exist and proceed to hold companies liable under US law. He disagreed with Professor Koh's assertions, in which he, according to Mr Koopmans, failed to differentiate between the *lex lata* and *lex ferenda*.

Professor Harold Hongju Koh reacted to the presentation of Pieter Bekker and criticized his line of reasoning for perpetuating four myths about corporate responsibility litigation in US courts. First, Professor Koh explained that according to Dr Bekker's reasoning, only States and individuals were liable under international law,

* Clifford Chance Amsterdam.

and corporations were not. Individuals could be held criminally liable but not civilly liable, so consequently, corporations were not liable either. Professor Koh argued that this view was wrong. First of all, corporations were responsible for their direct actions and certain transnational crimes, such as piracy, genocide, attacks on ambassadors, slave trade, which were *jus cogens* violations, were also violations of US law if done by a private party at the urging of a public official. Neither States nor individuals who commit international criminal acts should be able to escape liability by creating a corporate form. Furthermore, when corporations aided and abetted acts of the State to the point that those acts were being tantamount to the action of the official, they should also be liable. He further reasoned that if corporations were not liable directly under international law, domestic legislators had the authority to create domestic civil remedies for international crimes, as the US Congress had done in 1789 and had reaffirmed in 1992 in the Alien Tort Claims Act (ATCA) and in the Torture Victim Protection Act (TVPA). Professor Koh distinguished two kinds of offences: direct offences and complicity offences. Concerning complicity offences, the question was what standard of liability we should apply. He argued that this standard should be very high. He referred to the presentation of Andrew Clapham contending that a plaintiff would have to demonstrate a very high degree of substantial assistance. Second, there was no "flood" of litigation in US courts; to date, no corporate defendant had yet paid an ATCA plaintiff a penny. Third, there was no need for legislative or judicial reform to address this "problem"; the best way was for judges to manage their caseload wisely. Fourth and finally, Professor Koh maintained that litigation was not a bad way to promote higher corporate standards, but it should not be the only way. This issue was best regulated by an international treaty, but he did not expect such treaty to be negotiated very soon.

PROFESSOR ANDRÉ NOLLKAEMPER had two comments on the presentation by Pieter Bekker. The first point concerned the ATCA cases and the statement that the complaint in the US *Apartheid* case relied on 7 UNGA Resolutions only in pleading apartheid as a crime against humanity. Professor Nollkaemper explained that there were many other, binding sources, which stated that apartheid was a crime against humanity. His second point related to the fact that there was no general principle on complicity in international law. Professor Nollkaemper argued that for prosecution purposes this norm could be derived from national law.

MS OLIVIA SWAAK-GOLDMAN* observed that on the one hand there were very interesting and progressive developments concerning the ATCA. At the same time, the Bush Administration reacted extensively on the Belgian genocide law. As the ATCA was civil and the Belgian law criminal, she invited the panellists to comment on this dichotomy.

Ms Swaak-Goldman further referred to the assertion of André Nollkaemper in his presentation that Dutch courts had been unwilling to hold corporations civilly liable. She asked him whether he could discuss the recent developments concerning the Dutch International Crimes Act. She highlighted that this regime did not exclude application to legal persons, as penalties included jail time as well as monetary fines. To what extent could this act fill in the gap?

* Ministry of Foreign Affairs, the Netherlands.

PROFESSOR ANDRÉ NOLLKAEMPER explained that the Dutch International Crimes Act implemented the ICC Statute. As far as acts of corporations would fall within the ambit of the act, and thus would fall within the ambit of the ICC Statute, corporations could be held liable in Dutch courts either adjacent to a criminal proceeding or as a separate tort case. He stated that the problem arose when corporations committed acts that were not included in the ICC Statute, namely acts other than genocide, crimes against humanity and war crimes. Cases in Dutch courts included logging in protected forest, environmental damage and forced labour. Professor Nollkaemper argued that no Dutch court was willing to accept that these norms applied in a tort case against a corporation. So the real problem was not genocide and war crimes, but the other, more vaguely circumscribed breaches of international law.

PROFESSOR ANDREW CLAPHAM addressed in response to Ms Swaak-Goldman the issue about the Belgian legislation. Indeed, the ATCA concerned civil law and the Belgian act dealt with criminal law, but Professor Clapham was not convinced that that was why there was more attention regarding corporate accountability on the ATCA. A case had recently been brought under the Belgian legislation against Total Elf Fina alleging war crimes. Professor Clapham reasoned that as soon as an American corporation has been investigated under the Belgian legislation, the USA would criticize the Belgian legislation in the same way that it has criticized the ATCA. It was not just the fact that the Belgians under this legislation could indict Mr Bush or Mr Rumsfeld, but the USA would try to preclude that a Belgian prosecutor could indict an American corporation. Professor Clapham explained that the scope of most of the legislation that had been introduced on the national level to give effect to the Rome Statute included "persons". In the first phase the word "person" either in the common law or the civil law system, would have to be determined whether "person" includes natural as well as legal persons. Professor Clapham argued that it was just a question of time before these cases came through. The Belgian case was the first, and he understood that Belgian multinationals were already lobbying to get the law changed.

PROFESSOR HAROLD HONGJU KOH discussed the recent developments in the USA. He distinguished two positions concerning liability issues. The first implied that "if there is any chance we could be caught up in a system of liability, we should destroy it." The other view considered that there were more benefits from having such a system than there were losses, and therefore we should engage with that system and try to make it a just system. Professor Koh found the first view a shortsighted approach. Nevertheless, he explained, it was the Bush Administration posture towards the International Criminal Court. Professor Koh illustrated his view with the *Radovan Karadzić* case. Karadzić was indicted by the Yugoslavia Tribunal, but not apprehended. Imagine he came to the USA, would he be allowed to raise money and have assets in the USA, which could potentially be held in US corporations? The Second Circuit Court of Appeals of the USA, by recognizing that he could be held liable, had essentially prevented him from holding money in the USA or himself travelling to the USA. The case clearly supported the accountability agenda, which explained why the Clinton Administration had supported the ATCA jurisdiction in the *Karadzić* case. Professor Koh stated that that was a far cry from what was going on now. The Bush Administration would undermine a system of judicial liability even if that system could hold Saddam Hussein, Osama bin Laden, Kim Jong Ill, Fidel Castro or anybody else liable.

DR PIETER BEKKER stated that he felt misunderstood. Indeed, corporations in his view could and should be held liable if and when they violated primary rules of international law. However, national courts should adhere strictly to the framework of Article 38 of the ICJ Statute, and uphold the sanctity of international law.

MS BETTE SHIFMAN* drew attention to the possibilities of alternative dispute resolution in this particular area. She highlighted the arbitration rules for disputes relating to natural resources and/or the environment, adopted by the PCA in 2001. Unlike other rules of the PCA and the general perception of the PCA, there was nothing in these rules that would prevent their use by private individuals, NGOs and States. They could be used by anybody in any combination. Ms Shifman claimed that despite hurdles such as party consent, certain issues of arbitration and other forms of dispute resolution might be more palatable to corporations and States, such as appointment of arbitrators and deciding on applicable law. She further mentioned non-binding forms of dispute resolution like conciliation and fact-finding. Although these forms could not provide for reparations, Ms Shifman argued that victims often simply wanted recognition and someone to listen to them. Moreover, she emphasized the value of voluntary codes of conduct.

PROFESSOR MALGOSIA FITZMAURICE made a comment, which related indirectly to this call for alternative ways to address these kinds of issues. She drew attention to the European Court of Human Rights. Its catalogue of human rights did not include a right to a clean environment. However, recently, the European Court made several interesting pronouncements on violations of environmental rights by companies as well. First of all, the cases were basically brought on the basis of Article 8 of European Convention of Human Rights, which set forth the right to privacy. The most crucial case was *Lopez-Ostra* v. *Spain* in 1995. While the pollution was caused by a private company, the European Court held that States had a duty of due care for the interests of their citizens. Professor Fitzmaurice argued that this very interesting line of reasoning was confirmed by the Court's decision in the *Hatton* case in 2001. The *Hatton* case concerned noise pollution by night flights over Heathrow Airport, which was not governmentally owned. The European Court found that the UK did not exercise enough care to realize the right to privacy for its citizens, and that private interests, those of citizens living adjacent of Heathrow, prevailed over public, economic, interests. Professor Fitzmaurice reasoned that this was another way to address this kind of issues. In these cases the balance of interests was crucial and the European Court showed its capability of balancing public and private interests.

PROFESSOR MAURICE ANDEM** complimented the panel for the enlightening presentations. He argued that multinational corporations were closely connected to the domestic legal system, and therefore States of registration had a duty to control and monitor the activities of their companies, including activities abroad. In Western countries, activities of corporations were well regulated. However, in many countries, especially in Third World countries, Professor Andem stated, recalling the case of the Ogoni people in Nigeria, people did not enjoy protection from their government and they did not have rights to defend themselves against corporations.

* Permanent Court of Arbitration.

** University of Lapland.

MR YARASLAU KRYVOI* asked the panel for comments on the *Asbestos* case in the UK, in which a multinational corporation was held liable for human rights violations in South Africa.

PROFESSOR ANDREW CLAPHAM explained that the parties in the *Asbestos* case had settled and that the court had to approve the settlement.

DR MICHAEL ADDO confirmed that no fair trial could be safeguarded in South Africa.

PROFESSOR HAROLD HONGJU KOH concluded that domestic litigation had a role to play in holding corporations liable, but that it required high standards of proof and strict procedural rules. He denied that corporate voluntarism alone, without litigation, could succeed in raising human rights standards, citing the infamous words of Al Capone: "You get further with a kind word and a gun, than with a kind word alone."

DR GEORG BERRISCH thanked the panellists and participants and closed the session.

Reporter: Esther Kentin**

* Utrecht University.

** Vrije Universiteit, Amsterdam

Using Treaty Cooperation To Improve Capital Flows: The Hague Conference Convention On Securitization

The panel was convened by its Chair, Christophe Bernasconi*.

Remarks by Roy Goode**

Interests in securities held with an intermediary

Introduction: the background

Over the past two decades there has been a marked change in the way in which shares, bonds and other investment securities are held. Two developments merit particular attention: dematerialisation, by which securities are held and transferred by computer entry rather than by paper certificates and transfers; and a move from direct holdings, in which the investor has a direct relationship with the issuer, to holdings through a securities account with a custodian or other securities intermediary. The effect of these changes, together with the trend towards globalisation, is that the overnight turnover of securities is vast, and that security interests in such securities greatly exceed in value security interests in tangible property.

The attached diagram shows a possible chain of holdings where an issuer in country A issues a single global note which is intended to be permanently immobilised with a common depository for the two international central securities depositories, Euroclear in country B and Clearstream in country L. These do not hold the note for their own account but hold interests in it for their participants-account holders. Euroclear and Clearstream are thus first-tier intermediaries. Investors in the global note hold their entitlements through their accounts with the ICSDs. Such investors will typically hold both on their own account and for their customers, who may be national central securities depositories (as in the diagram), central banks, other banks or large corporates. Thus in the diagram CSD1, a customer of Euroclear, is a second-tier intermediary who holds for Bank 1 in country D and Bank 2 in country E. Private investor 1 in country D has an account with Bank 1, private investor 2 in country E with Bank 2. Bank 1, which is a third-tier intermediary as regards its holding from CSD1, also holds directly from ICSD1, and as to this holding Bank 1 is a second-tier intermediary. If private investor 1 wished to make a security transfer of title to private investor 2, this would have to be effected first by a debit of its securities account with Bank 1 and secondly by an in-house transfer in the books of CSD1, the common intermediary of Bank 1 and 2, from Bank 1's securities account to Bank 2's securities account, Bank 2 then crediting the account of private investor 2. On the other side, CSD2 in country D, holding from the first-tier intermediary Clearstream, has a broker-dealer in

* Hague Conference on Private International Law.

** Emeritus, Oxford University.

country F as one of its customers. The CSD is the second-tier intermediary and Broker-Dealer the third-tier intermediary, two of whose customers are private investor 3 and private investor 4. Since both private investors hold their accounts with the same intermediary, Broker-Dealer, a security transfer of title from private investor 3 to private investor 4 is relatively simply, involving merely an in-house transfer in the books of Broker-Dealer.

Typically, securities of a particular issue are not separately earmarked for each customer but are held by the relevant intermediary for all its customers in a fungible, or omnibus, account with its own (higher-tier) intermediary which does not identify any customer of the relevant intermediary.

The issue of a permanently immobilised global note has the effect that, except where an investor's interest is exchangeable for definitive certificates, it never acquires a direct relationship with the issuer. But an investor may also start with a direct holding and then decide to deposit his securities with its intermediary, who then arranges to have the securities transferred into its own name or in turn deposits them with a higher-tier intermediary. In such cases the investor can always demand the return of its securities and re-establish its relationship with the issuer.

It will be apparent that there can be a long chain between the ultimate investor and the issuer, that in the example given no fewer than six countries are involved and that it may be difficult, if not impossible, to show through which links the investor's interest is derived. In the first place, each intermediary's accounts will identify only its own customers, not its customer's customers. Secondly, it is unlikely that securities obtained from multiple sources, with dealings netted out in a clearing system, will be identifiable to a particular investor's purchase.

Several legal issues arise from this typical set of dealings. First, what is the nature of the investor's entitlement under the account agreement? Is it a purely personal right to delivery, a right of ownership separate from that of other investors in the particular issue, or a right of co-ownership? Secondly, what is the investor's position if the intermediary becomes insolvent? Thirdly, is it possible for the investor or its attachment creditor to look through the investor's own intermediary and claim or attach the interest held by a higher-tier intermediary? Fourthly, what law governs (1) the investor's entitlement, (2) pledges and security transfers by the investor, and (3) priorities between competing secured creditors, particularly where a pledge is created in favour of the first creditor in State A and a security transfer of title is granted to a second creditor whose intermediary is in State B? It will be seen from these questions (and there are others that could be raised) that they involve both substantive law and conflict of laws rules. Prior to The Hague Convention, referred to below, there was no uniform conflict rule, and even within a given national legal system there was uncertainty as to the rule to be applied. In consequence determination of the applicable law depended on the choice of forum and the vagaries of whatever law might be found to apply. The resulting uncertainties caused serious problems. Indeed, the European Community was so concerned about systematic risk that it introduced two separate Directives, on settlement finality[1] and collateral arrangements[2] respectively.

The traditional conflict rule applicable to investment securities is that *vis-à-vis* the issuer their characterisation is determined by the law of the issuer's incorporation and that entitlements to registered securities are governed by the same law or alternatively the law of the place where the register is kept, while the effect of a transfer of negotiable securities is determined by the law of the place of the certificates at the time of the transfer. But this rule does not fit easily into the indirect holding system, where the investor's rights are considered to be derived exclusively from its own intermediary, not from the issuer, with whom the investor has no relationship. Modern thinking, therefore, is that the law applicable should be the law of the place of the relevant intermediary, that is, the intermediary with whom the particular investor has an account. This approach, known as PRIMA (place of the relevant intermediary approach), has the effect that a different law may be applicable at different levels and even at the same level as regards intermediaries located in different countries.

The 2002 Hague Convention

In December 2002 there was concluded at a Diplomatic Conference at The Hague a convention on the law applicable to certain rights in respect of securities held with an intermediary. The convention, which is becoming known as the PRIMA Convention, was produced in a remarkably short time, a mere 2½ years after work first began. The convention is a pure conflict of laws convention, albeit with unusual features and one or two highly counter-intuitive rules.

The Convention is in principle confined to the law applicable to proprietary aspects of holdings and transfers of securities held with an intermediary. Thus it does not apply to purely contractual or other purely personal rights but it does apply to dispositions of contractual rights, for these constitute transfers of property. The Convention also determines the law which governs the question whether the securities entitlement is purely contractual or is proprietary. Though for the most part confined to the proprietary effects of consensual arrangements it also extends to a lien by operation of law in favour of the account holder's intermediary in respect of any claim arising in connection with the maintenance and operation of a securities account.[3]

Article 2 sets out the scope of the Convention; Article 4 prescribes the conflict rule. The primary rule is that the applicable law is the law agreed between the parties as governing the account agreement or such other law as they agree shall apply to the issues specified in Article 2(1). But the parties to the account agreement do not have complete freedom of choice; it is also necessary that the intermediary has at the time of the agreement an office in the State whose law is selected where the intermediary is engaged in the business of maintaining securities accounts. If this "reality test" is not satisfied, the selection of the law is ineffective. There are then three fall-back rules, contained in Article 5. If the primary rule does not apply, because the parties have not chosen the governing law or their choice is ineffective, the first fall-back rule is to the law in force in the State of location of the office which is expressly and unambiguously stated in a written account agreement as the office through which the account agreement was entered into by the relevant intermediary. Where that fall-back rule does not apply, there is an intermediate fall-back rule by which the applicable law is the law of the intermediary's place of incorporation. It was recognized that this rule may well produce artificial results but it is likely to operate only in a very small percentage of cases and for these it has the merit of certainty. If the intermediary is not an incorporated body, then the ultimate fall-back rule comes into play, under which the applicable law is the intermediary's place of business or, if more than one, its principal place of business.

A number of key issues had to be addressed before and at the Diplomatic Conference which we can discuss:

(1) Who is to be regarded as an intermediary? See Article 1(3)-(5).
(2) What issues should fall within the scope of the Convention? See Article 2.
(3) Why was the original PRIMA rule (place of the relevant intermediary) not adopted and reference made instead to the agreement of the parties to the account agreement?
(4) What led to the formulation of the so-called black list in Article 6?
(5) How should third-party interests be protected if an account agreement is amended to change the applicable law?
(6) What should be the impact of insolvency? See Article 8.
(7) How should the Convention deal with pre-Convention interests? See Article 15.

No doubt there will be other issues which the group will wish to discuss.

The Hague Convention will undoubtedly necessitate amendment to the two EC Directives referred to above. And, of course, it is only a conflict of laws convention, albeit an extremely important one. Preliminary work is now underway to see if it is possible to harmonise the substantive law relating to indirectly held securities. UNIDROIT has set up a Study Group to examine security interests in investment securities as part of a wider capital markets project. The European Commission is likely to undertake work in this field. And in London a working group set up by the Financial Markets Law Committee of the Bank of England is working on a set of legal principles governing interests in such securities. So far only one country has a fully developed set of rules designed to be responsible to market needs and practices, namely the United States, which in 1994 substantially revised Article 8 of the Uniform Commercial Code. This needs to be read in conjunction with the revised Article 9 on security interests in personal property.

NOTES

1 Directive on settlement finality in payment and securities settlement systems, 98/26/EC dated 19 May 1998.

2 Directive on financial collateral arrangements, 2002/47/EC dated 6 June 2002.

3 Art. 1(2)(c).

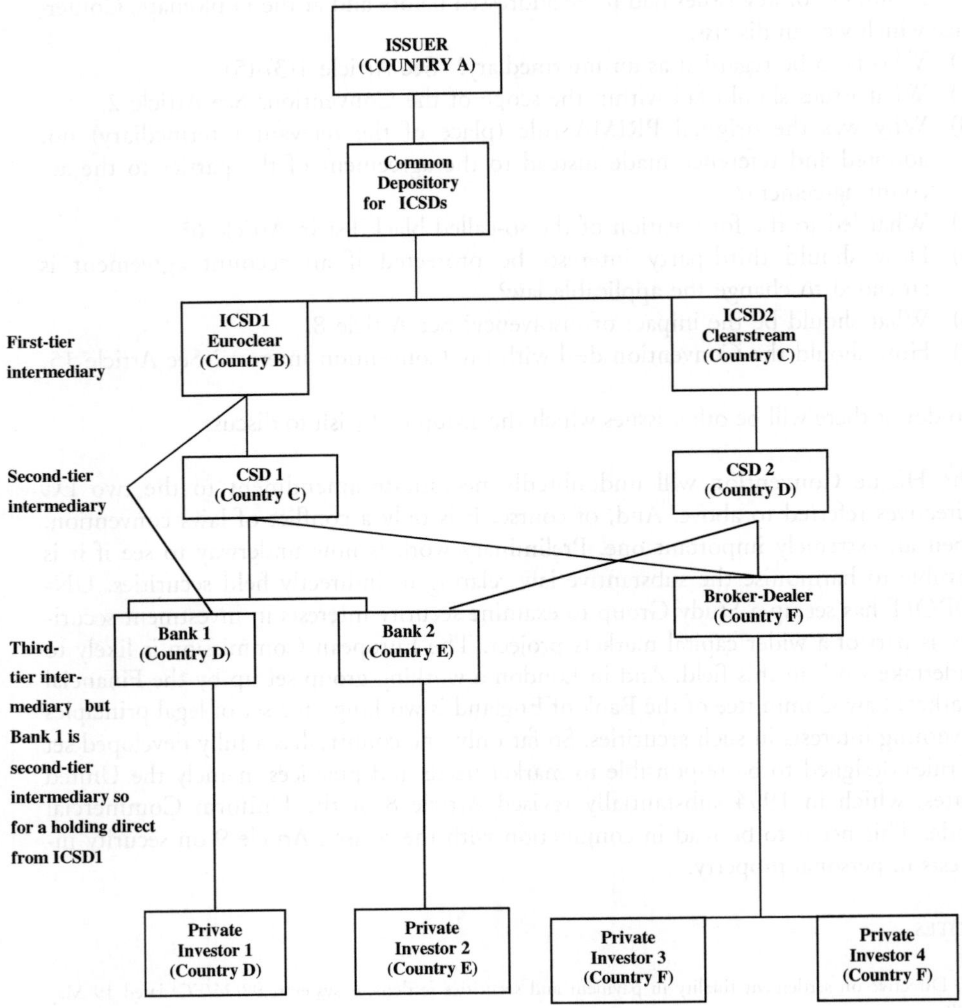

1. The diagram shows a possible chain of relationships set up by the issue of a permanent global note by an issuer in country A which is deposited with a common depository for the two international central securities depositories, who are the first-tier intermediaries.
2. The second-tier intermediaries are CSD1 (a national central securities depository), CSD2 and Bank 1 so far as it holds direct from ICSD1 rather than through CSD1.
3. It will be seen that each private investor may acquire its interest through different chains which in practice it may not be possible to unravel.
4. Private investor 1 may pledge its account entitlement to private investor 2 by having the latter recorded in Bank 1's books as controlling investor 1's account, in which case everything remains in-house in the books of Bank 1, located in country D. Alternatively investor 1 may effect a security transfer of title to investor 2 by procuring a credit to investor 2's account with its own intermediary, Bank 2, in country E. This involves an in-house transfer higher up the chain in the books of CSD1, the common intermediary for Bank 1 and Bank 2.
5. If private investor 3 transfers its securities entitlement to private investor 4, this is effected by an in-house transfer in the books of their common intermediary, Broker-Dealer.

Remarks by Joyce Hansen*

Hague Convention on the Law Applicable to Certain Rights in Respect of Securities Held with an Intermediary

This presentation discusses recent developments in the international securities markets creating the need for the Hague Convention on the law applicable to certain rights in respect of securities held with an intermediary (the "Convention"), describes the similarity of the Convention's choice of law rule with relevant United States "US" choice of law rules and notes the requirements of implementation of the Convention in US law.

Need for the Convention – the Environment

Surveys by a number of international industry trade associations show that the collateralized transaction market is growing substantially across borders. For example, the 2003 International Swaps and Derivatives Association margin survey reported $491 billion of collateral in circulation securing over-the-counter derivatives trades, an increase of 70% over the reported amount in the 2002. Most collateral still consists of cash. However, government securities are the second most common collateral asset, and bonds and equities are also used as collateral. The cross-border nature of collateralised transactions is shown by the fact that 55% of the respondents are based in Europe or South Africa, 21% in North America, 16% in Japan, and 8% in Australia or Asia. Moreover, respondents reported their counterparties by country of incorporation or organization. These responses showed that 54% of the counterparties were in North America, 25% in Western Europe, and 10% in the Caribbean.

The International Securities Market Association surveys its members every six months regarding the European repurchase agreement ("repo") market.[1] Its December 2002 survey shows that 50.4% of outstanding repo contracts were with cross-border counterparties. In addition, transactions were against collateral from 16 countries in Europe and the USA, and other accession, OECD, and emerging market countries.

Linkages and mergers of domestic and international securities clearing and settlement systems support the growth of cross-border trading. The Group of Thirty Report on Global Clearance and Settlement reported (based on surveys by the Securities Industry Association) that US gross activity (both purchases and sales) in foreign securities grew from $53 billion in 1980 to $5.1 trillion in 2001. Foreign gross activity in US securities grew from $198 billion to $20 trillion in the same period, each over a 100 fold increase.

Even central banks are expanding the range of acceptable securities collateral. In the USA, the Federal Reserve Banks accept certain foreign sovereign debt for discount window borrowings, subject to appropriate and satisfactory legal opinions.

In addition to the expansion of cross-border securities business, a key market development is the change in the way securities are held and traded. In the modern secu-

* Joyce Hansen, Deputy General Counsel and Senior Vice President, Federal Reserve Bank of New York. The views and opinions expressed herein are those soley of the author and do not reflect and should not be attributed to the Federal Reserve Bank of New York or any other component of the Federal Reserve System.

rities holding system, large players no longer hold securities in paper form but in dematerialised or immobilised form through accounts maintained with depositories. The depositories may themselves be account-holders at other intermediaries creating a chain of linked intermediaries crossing national borders and legal systems. In many countries, it is not clear what law applies to securities held through accounts with securities depositories. That uncertainty is compounded when you consider that securities are held through tiers of intermediaries.

Objectives of the Convention

In light of the market environment, it was of paramount importance that the private international rules adopted by the Convention reduce risk and promote commercial transactions, investment, and the creation of economic value to the greatest extent reasonably possible. This objective was achieved by adopting a rule that would permit transacting parties to readily determine with a sufficient degree of *ex ante* legal certainty the applicable law for the largest number of important transactions. Thus, the rule had to be a practical and efficient rule that takes account of existing and foreseeable business practice, and enables parties to obtain legal opinions that the transaction is legally sound at its inception. The economic value of the Convention lies in the extent to which it achieves *ex ante* predictability.

Comparison of the choice of law rule of Article 8 and Article 9 with the Convention

Articles 8 and 9 of the Uniform Commercial Code ("UCC") constitute the comprehensive substantive commercial law governing securities transfers and secured transactions. In particular, UCC Article 8, Part 5 applies to securities entitlements that arise from a credit of financial assets (which include securities) to a securities account held with a securities intermediary. In a similar fashion, the Convention determines the law applicable to the rights of an account holder resulting from the credit of securities to a securities account maintained with an intermediary. However, Article 8 is a substantive law and it comprehensively defines the relationship of the account holder and intermediary and the rights and duties between them as well as providing the choice of law applicable to those issues. In contrast, the Convention determines applicable law but does not further define the substantive law rights and duties between the account holder and the intermediary.

A comparison of Articles 8 and 9 can be made on a few different dimensions. This paper compares the choice of law rules in UCC Article 8-110(e) and UCC Article 9-305(a)(3)[2] with the Convention. Those relevant sections provide a choice of law rule similar in concept to the rule adopted in the Convention. The differences between the UCC and the Convention are matters of detail, not fundamental approach. Articles 8 and 9 look to the local law of the securities intermediary's jurisdiction. How is the securities intermediary's jurisdiction determined? A "cascade" approach is used in 8-110(e). See Figure 1. The rule ensures that a single body of law will govern the rights of holders of securities entitlements with securities intermediaries and the issues of priority and perfection.

There are five elements to the cascade. See figure 1. The first three elements in particular look to the agreement between the securities intermediary and its customer. The first element permits the parties to expressly select the securities intermediary's jurisdiction in the agreement governing the securities account. In the absence of such a selection, the law expressly selected to govern the agreement determines the securities intermediary's jurisdiction. If neither the first or second element applies, but the parties have expressly provided in their agreement that the securities account is maintained at a particular office of the securities intermediary, the jurisdiction in which that office is located is the securities intermediary's jurisdiction. There is no nexus test or "reasonable relationship" test that must be met in connection with the parties selection of the securities intermediary's jurisdiction or governing law. As referred to below, under the Convention there is a condition that must be met in order to give effect to the parties selection of applicable law in the account agreement. Under Article 8 there is also no requirement that the account agreement be written. However, in practice, most account agreements are in writing. The last two elements of 8-110(e) are additional default rules.

Figure 1 **Section 8-110. Applicability – Choice of Law**

(e) The following rules determine a "securities intermediary's jurisdiction" for purposes of this section:

(1) If an agreement between the securities intermediary and its entitlement holder governing the securities account expressly provides that a particular jurisdiction is the securities intermediary's jurisdiction for purpose of this part, this article, or this act, that jurisdiction is the securities intermediary's jurisdiction.
(2) If paragraph (1) does not apply and an agreement between the securities intermediary and its entitlement holder governing the securities account expressly provides that the agreement is governed by the law of a particular jurisdiction, that jurisdiction is the securities intermediary's jurisdiction.
(3) If neither paragraph (1) nor paragraph (2) apply and an agreement between the securities intermediary and its entitlement holder governing the securities account expressly provides that the securities account is maintained at an office in a particular jurisdiction, that jurisdiction is the securities intermediary's jurisdiction.
(4) If none of the preceding paragraphs apply, the securities intermediary's jurisdiction is the jurisdiction in which the office identified in an account statement as the office serving the entitlement holder's account is located.
(5) If none of the preceding paragraphs apply, the securities intermediary's jurisdiction is the jurisdiction in which the chief executive office of the securities intermediary is located.

The primary choice of law rule in Article 4 of the Convention also refers to the account agreement between the intermediary and its account holder. The primary rule is most similar to the first two elements in 8-110(e). See figure 2.

Figure 2 **Comparison of Article 8-110(e) and Article 4 Primary Rule**

(e) The following rules determine a "securities intermediary's jurisdiction" for purposes of this section: (1) If an agreement between the securities intermediary and its entitlement holder governing the securities account expressly provides that a particular jurisdiction is the securities intermediary's jurisdiction for purpose of this part, this article, or this act, that jurisdiction is the securities intermediary's jurisdiction. (2) If paragraph (1) does not apply and an agreement between the securities intermediary and its entitlement holder governing the securities account expressly provides that the agreement is governed by the law of a particular jurisdiction, that jurisdiction is the securities intermediary's jurisdiction. …	(1) The law applicable to all the issues specified Article 2 (1) is the law in force in the State expressly agreed in the account agreement as the State whose law governs the account agreement or, if the account agreement expressly provides that another law is applicable to all such issues, that other law. (See second sentence for important proviso).

In accordance with the primary rule of the Convention in Article 4, one looks to the law in force in the State (or territorial unit of a Multi-unit State)[3] whose law governs the account agreement. The selection of this law must be express. If however, the parties expressly select the law of another State (or territorial unit of a Multi-unit State) to govern the issues specified in Article 2(1) (i.e. the scope issues of the Convention),[4] the law in force in that State (or territorial unit) is the law that governs those issues. Thus, both 8-110(e) and the primary rule in Article 4 look to the law expressly chosen to govern the account agreement unless the parties have expressly chosen another law. Consequently, both 8-110(e) and Article 4 of the Convention permit the parties to choose one law to govern the contractual aspects of the account agreement and a different law to govern the proprietary or other *sui generis* rights arising out of the intermediary-account holder relationship. For example, it may be common in certain markets to choose English or New York law to govern financial contracts. For example, the intermediary and its customer might choose English law to govern the account agreement and designate Spanish law to govern the issues specified in Article 2(1) of the Convention. As is the case with 8-110(b), under the Convention there is no requirement that the account agreement be in writing; however, the Article 5 fall-back rules refer to a written account agreement. See below.

Unlike Article 8, the parties' designation of applicable law under the Convention is effective only if the intermediary had, at the time the account agreement was entered into, an office in the State whose law is designated which engages in certain activities associated with maintaining securities accounts, otherwise engages in a "securities account maintenance business", or is identified by some specific means as maintaining securities accounts. This has been referred to as the "office test" or so-called "reality test". See Figure 3.

Figure 3 Article 4(1), Second Sentence

The law designated in accordance with this provision applies only if the relevant intermediary has, at the time of the agreement, an office in that State, which –

a) alone or together with other offices of the relevant intermediary or with other persons acting for the relevant intermediary in that or another State –

i) effects or monitors entries to securities accounts;
ii) administers payments or corporate actions relating to securities held with the intermediary; or
iii) is otherwise engaged in business or other regular activity of maintaining securities accounts; or

b) is identified by an account number, bank code, or other specific means of identification as maintaining securities accounts in that State.

In addition, Article 4(2) lists activities none of which standing alone constitutes the business or regular activity of maintaining securities accounts. See Figure 4. There is no equivalent of the office test in the relevant sections of Article 8 or 9 of the UCC. However, this condition made the consensual approach adopted by both the equivalent US law and the Convention acceptable in an international setting.

Figure 4 Article 4(2)

For the purposes of paragraph (1)(a), an office is not engaged in a business or other regular activity of maintaining securities accounts –

(a) merely because it is a place where the technology supporting the bookkeeping or data processing for securities accounts is located;

(b) merely because it is a place where call centres for communication with account holders are located or operated;

(c) merely because it is a place where the mailing relating to securities accounts is organized or files or archives are located; or

(d) if it engages solely in representational functions or administrative functions, other than those related to the opening or maintenance of securities accounts, and does not have authority to make any binding decision to enter into any account agreement.

Fall-back rule

The Convention's fall-back rule applies if there is no express choice of law, or if the choice is not given effect because of a failure to satisfy the "office test". See Figure 5. It is expected to apply to a very small number of cases. The first fallback rule refers to a written account agreement. If a written account agreement expressly and unambiguously states that it was entered into through a particular office, the applicable law is the law in force in the State in which that office was then located. There are certain account agreement provisions that are not considered in determining whether the agreement is express and unambiguous, such as notice provisions and provisions concerning consent to jurisdiction and legal process. Articles 8 and 9 do not provide an exactly equivalent default rule. However, the third element of the Article 8-110(e) cascade provides a choice of law pointer keyed to the express identification in the account agreement of the office of the intermediary at which the securities account is maintained. This could be considered as similar in concept to the intermediate default rule. The Convention's intermediate default rule was important in the international context where many participants in the negotiations believed that the final default rule, discussed below, might produce a result that was not in accordance with party expectations.

Figure 5 **Article 5 Fall-back Rules**

Article 5 Fall-back rules

(1) If the applicable law is not determined under Article 4, but it is expressly and unambiguously stated in a written account agreement that the relevant intermediary entered into the account agreement through a particular office, the law applicable to all the issues specified in Article 2(1) is the law in force in the State, or the territorial unit of a Multi-unit State, in which that office was then located, provided that such office then satisfied the conditions specified in the second sentence of Article 4(1). In determining whether an account agreement expressly and unambiguously states that the relevant intermediary entered into the account agreement through a particular office, none of the following shall be considered –

(a) a provision that notices or other documents shall or may be served on the relevant intermediary at that office;
(b) a provision that legal proceedings shall or may be instituted against the relevant intermediary in a particular State or in a particular territorial unit of a Multi-unit State;
(c) a provision that any statement or other document shall or may be provided by the relevant intermediary from that office;
(d) a provision that any service shall or may be provided by the relevant intermediary from that office;
(e) a provision that any operation or function shall or may be carried on or performed by the relevant intermediary at that office.

In Article 8, the final default rule is closer in concept to the second paragraph of Article 5 of the Convention, which provides the final default rule under the Convention.

Article 8-110(e)(5) provides that "If none of the preceding paragraphs apply, the securities intermediary's jurisdiction is the jurisdiction in which the chief executive office of the securities intermediary is located". The commentary to Article 9 of the UCC states that the chief executive office, which is not defined, is the place where the main part of the business operations or other affairs are managed. Thus, it is similar in concept to the principal place of business, which is used in the final default rule under the Convention for certain intermediaries.

By comparison to 8-110(e)(5), the second paragraph of Article 5 of the Convention provides that if the applicable law is not determined under paragraph (1) (i.e. the rule that directs one to an express and unambiguous statement in the account agreement that the account agreement was entered into through a particular office) one looks to the law in force in the State of incorporation or organisation of the intermediary at the time the written account agreement was entered into, or at the time the securities account was opened, if there is no written account agreement. For intermediaries that do not have legal personality and for intermediaries that are incorporated or organised under Federal law, one looks to the law in force in the State where the intermediary has its place of business or principal place of business if there is more than one place of business.

Because the chief executive office may differ from the place of incorporation or organisation, it is possible that the final default rule in 8-110(e)(5) may produce a different result than the final default rule under the Convention in some circumstances. This should not be of significant consequence as it is expected that knowledgeable and well advised intermediaries would be able to avail themselves of the primary rule.

Figure 6 Article 5 Fall-back Rules (cont.)

2. If the applicable law is not determined under paragraph (1) that law is the law in force in the State, or the territorial unit of a Multi-unit State, under whose law the relevant intermediary is incorporated or otherwise organised at the time the written account agreement is entered into or, if there is no such agreement, at the time the securities account was opened; if, however, the relevant intermediary is incorporated or otherwise organised under the law of a Multi-unit State and not that of one of its territorial units, the applicable law is the law in force in the territorial unit of that Multi-unit State in which the relevant intermediary has its place of business, or, if the relevant intermediary has more than one place of business, its principal place of business, at the time the written account agreement is entered into or, if there is not such agreement, at the time the securities account was opened.

If the applicable law is not determined under either paragraph (1) or paragraph (2), the law is the law in force in the State, or the territorial unit of a Multi-unit State, in which the relevant intermediary has its place of business, or, if the relevant intermediary has more than one place of business, its principal place of business, at the time the written account agreement is entered into or, if there is no such agreement, at the time the securities account was opened.

Both the primary rule and the fall-back rule in the Convention have temporal elements that are not present in 8-110(e). Whether the intermediary has satisfied the office test specified in the second sentence of Article 4 is determined at the time of the account agreement. Under Article 5 one determines the jurisdiction of the location of the office through which the account agreement expressly expressly and unambiguously states it was entered into at that time. Similarly one determines the place of incorporation or organisation, place of business or principal place of business at the time a written account agreement was entered into or at the time the securities account was opened if there is no written account agreement. This temporal element may affect the due diligence that parties undertake. A party might want to determine whether the intermediary previously maintained other offices engaged in the business of maintaining securities accounts or has changed its place of incorporation, organisation, place of business or principal place of business.

Factors to be disregarded

Both the Article 8 and the Convention identify factors that are not to be considered in determining the applicable law. In both cases these factors were intended to reject the "look-through" approach that had in the past been applied to determination of applicable law for securities held with intermediaries.

Article 8 provides factors that are not to be considered in determining the securities intermediary's jurisdiction. Section 8-110(f) provides that:

"A securities intermediary's jurisdiction is not determined by the physical location of certificates representing financial assets, or by the jurisdiction in which is organised the issuer of the financial asset with respect to which an entitlement holder has a security entitlement, or by the location of facilities for data processing or other record keeping concerning the account."

Those factors are comparable to "factors to be disregarded" in determining applicable law in Article 6 of the Convention. Under the Convention, no account is to be given to factors such as the place of incorporation or organisation, of the issuer, the place where certificates are located, the place where a securities register is located, or the place of any intermediary other than the relevant intermediary.

Pre-Convention account agreements

The Convention applies to existing account agreements and to existing securities accounts. Article 16 of the Convention has interpretive rules for existing account agreements. This Article ensures that parties need not renegotiate or replace existing account agreements to gain the benefits of the Convention. This was very important to market participants in light of the enormous costs that would have been imposed on them if the hundreds of thousands of existing agreements had to be renegotiated. Even though the Convention does not require any particular language formulation or "magic words", existing agreements have been drafted under different legal traditions. Subject to certain qualifications, paragraph 3 of Article 16 states that any express terms of an account agreement that would have the effect under the agreement's governing law of applying a particular law to the any of the issues specified in Article 2(1) of the Convention, shall have the effect of applying that law to all of the issues specified in Article 2(1). Current US style account documentation might say: "securities intermediary's jurisdiction is New York" or "governing law is New York". Those terms have the effect of applying New York law under relevant sections of Article 8 and 9 of the UCC to, for example, the issues of perfection and priority of a security interest in securities held with an intermediary. Thus, the Convention will apply New York law to all the issues specified in Article 2(1) provided the other qualifications of Article 16 are met. Other paragraphs of Article 16 address the existing practice in other jurisdictions.

US IMPLEMENTATION

Adoption of the Convention by the USA involves signature and then ratification. Signature by the USA would typically be a strong indication of the intent to seek ratification of the Convention. The US Senate must vote by a 2/3rds majority to advise and consent to the ratification of the Convention by the President. Once the Convention is signed and ratified by the President and it has become effective, it will become US law without further legislative action and it will not be necessary to amend any Federal or State commercial or corporate law.

NOTES

1 A repurchase agreement is an agreement by a person to sell an asset, usually securities, to a counterparty with the corresponding agreement of the counterparty to resell securities of like amount and type to the person at a particular date or on demand. A repurchase agreement transaction is a widely used means of financing securities and is usually transacted pursuant to an industry master agreement.

2 This section refers back to 8-110(e).

3 Article 12 of the Convention defines the application of Article 4 to a Multi-unit State.

4 The equivalent of the scope issues in the relevant sections of United States law are in 8-110(b) and 9-305.

DISCUSSION

BART PUNT*: Could you go into the question raised by professor Kessedjian, i.e. that Article 11 (3) seems to be in contradiction with the paragraphs 1 and 2 of Article 11?

SIR ROY GOODE: Without paragraph 3 the perfection requirements of States could totally undermine the basic rule of the Convention. The Convention says what law governs the perfection of an interest. If you are then going to allow a State to treat its own perfection requirements as mandatory then effectively what is being allowed to a contracting State is to totally destroy the primary rule of the Convention and that is what we are not prepared to allow, because otherwise you might not as well have the primary rule. To allow by the backdoor the perfection requirement of another State to come in under the guise of public policy or international mandatory rule is not desirable, while other international mandatory rules can be given full respect.

* The Netherlands.

DINNER SPEECH BY JUDGE THOMAS BUERGENTHAL**

Since we are here in The Hague, proudly known as the judicial capital of the world, it is only appropriate that I speak about matters judicial – in the tradition of after-dinner speeches.

As you know, the ICJ has been here in The Hague for more than 50 years, actually some 80 years, if you add the PCIJ to the count, which is as it should be. That does not mean, however, that people in The Hague know what the Court does or even where, in this city, it sits. A Hague taxi driver is more likely to take you to the ICTY, if you ask to be taken to the ICJ. But because the ICJ has that imposing building – the Peace Palace – CNN and broadcasters from other channels are likely to stand in front of the Peace Palace to report on the Milosević trial. It is all very confusing.

That explains no doubt why acquaintances I have not seen or heard from in years are moved to send me emails, congratulating me on the great work I am doing with those terrible war criminals. It is hard to know how to reply to these emails.

Things are going to get even more complicated as soon as the International Criminal Court begins to hear cases. ICC and ICJ – acronyms not easily distinguished by the uninitiated. I have already been asked the other day how it is possible for me, as an American, to sit on a court that the US is so violently opposed to, to the point that it threatens to invade the Netherlands to rescue any American whom that court might decide to try.

Of course, we also have the Iran/US Tribunal here in town. That institution has proved that if you want to create a truly permanent international court, all you need to do is to establish an *ad hoc* tribunal and expect it to finish its work in less than two years. George Aldrich has served on that Tribunal almost as long as Judge Oda on the ICJ. As you know, Oda just retired from the ICJ after 27 years – a record.

ICJ judges drive cars with CDJ license plates, which stands for corps diplomatique judiciaire, but the judges of the ICTY have CD plates. That is intended to confuse potential terrorists who might be tempted to avenge their convicted war criminal friends. To make things even harder for these individuals, the Dutch authorities have designated the private parking spaces assigned to Tribunal judges as reserved for "International Organization". Since there are other non-judicial international organizations in town, these signs are intended to provide a cover for the Tribunal judges. The private parking spaces of ICJ judges are said to be "Reserved for the International Court of Justice". These signs appear sometimes in Dutch, French or English. I have not been able to come up with a good explanation why these signs are not all written in one and the same language. It is so random that I am guessing that it depends on the linguistic skills of individual sign painters. I must have gotten that rare Dutch person who is monolingual, since the sign in front of my house is in Dutch. That will confuse foreign terrorists even more, I hope.

A colleague from the ICTY used to live a few houses down from me, and his space was marked with the bland "International Organization". When the ICTY began to try and convict important war criminals, I started to worry that potential terrorists might confuse his home with mine and toyed with the idea of putting up a sign

** Judge, International Court of Justice; Honorary President, American Society of International Law.

on my door, reading "The judge you really want lives two houses further down the street". After all, you cannot expect potential terrorists to be linguists or familiar with the niceties of diplomatic discourse.

I forgot to mention that The Hague is also the seat of the Permanent Court of Arbitration, which shares the Peace Palace with the ICJ. Of course, the PCA is not a court and it is only permanent in the sense that it has a permanent secretariat. But then, as you will already have noticed, we do not take names very seriously here at The Hague.

You probably also know that, pursuant to an agreement signed long ago by the Dutch Government and the ICJ, the President of the Court has precedence over the Dean of the Diplomatic Corps, and the remaining judges over individual ambassadors in order of seniority. It would appear that these protocol issues have been posing problems for the Dutch Government, which has resolved them in a typical practical Dutch way: we judges, with the exception of the President of the Court, are simply not invited to diplomatic functions. Some of us like it that way, but that may be sour grapes.

So much for life in the judicial capital of the world. You should know, however, that it is a wonderful city and country in which to live. Peggy and I love it here. Also, I cannot really complain about the job.

* *

When you live in this city and serve on an international court, it is natural to wonder about the impact the increase in the number of international courts and tribunals is having or is likely to have on international law. Much has been written on the subject in recent years. A few commentators have suggested that the proliferation of international tribunals, if proliferation is the right word, might in the long run have a negative effect on the unity or universality of international law, the so-called risk of fragmentation factor. I do not believe that this view is shared by a majority of commentators or even many of my ICJ colleagues, and I certainly do not share it myself.

While the need to preserve the unity of international law is an important concern, I doubt that the threat is very significant. The evidence collected thus far on the subject, including the thorough Hague Academy study by our late colleague and friend, Jonathan Charney, supports that conclusion. I believe, moreover, that the increase in the number of international courts and tribunals can have a beneficial effect on the development of international law. Apart from the resulting growth in the sheer volume of international jurisprudence, which can be expected to add greater substance or depth to the corpus of existing international law, it is a reasonable assumption that the expansion of international judicial institutions will lead quite naturally to creative interaction between the different courts and cross-fertilization of innovative judicial solutions. This, in turn, should enable an ever wider group of judges to contribute to and learn from the growing body of international jurisprudence. The resulting intellectual ferment cannot but make the system more dynamic than it has been in the past. It is also likely to encourage greater creativity in the judicial lawmaking process. The experience of the United States with its more than 50 different jurisdictions provides a telling example of the benefits of judicial cross-fertilization.

This is not the time or place to address the more controversial question whether the proliferation of international courts, if it continues, will in the long run require some form of vertical or hierarchic integration of these institutions. Besides, I do not believe that the international community is at this point ready to deal seriously with this problem, nor do I believe that the problem is acute enough to justify it. There is simply not enough evidence at this time of a risk of fragmentation of international law that would justify spending much time on this subject. Of course, if there is to be hierarchical integration, we on the ICJ know which court should have the last authoritative word.

Still on the subject of the proliferation of international courts, it should be asked whether there is a need for yet more courts or whether at some point we will have reached a saturation point. You probably will not be surprised to hear me say that we could use a few more regional international human rights courts and possibly also a UN Human Rights Court with jurisdiction to interpret UN human rights treaties, either as part of an ICJ Chamber or an independent body. While Europe, the Americas and now Africa have such regional courts, Asia has none, and could benefit from two or more sub-regional tribunals. I doubt that we need more specialized international law courts on the model of the Law of the Sea Tribunal, but the perceived need for such additional institutions may well depend upon the ability and willingness of the ICJ to speed up its adjudicatory process. That, at least is a view we hear from time to time.

Of course, some changes calculated to speed up the ICJ process can be implemented by the Court itself. For example, despite likely objections from the Parties, our lengthy oral hearings could be significantly shortened. The Court has made some progress in that regard, but there is room for further improvement. The time limits for the filing of memorials could also be reduced, although here there will be even stronger opposition from the Parties, but they cannot have it both ways – complain about our slow process and ask for unreasonably long time limits. The Court's Note-writing practice, requiring each judge to prepare a lengthy analysis of the case, which in fact amounts to an individual opinion, consumes a great deal of the judges' time and Registry resources. While the Note practice has recently been modified and is now applied only with regard to judgments on the merits, further changes could be instituted to reduce the burden that this exercise imposes on judges and the Registry.

It is clear, moreover, that if the Court is to be able to hear an increasing number of cases in the future, its judges will have to be provided with individual law clerks. Working with a third or half a law clerk, as we currently do, is not very satisfactory or calculated to improve our productivity. Many of our cases are very fact-intensive, making it difficult for judges without the assistance of law clerks to organize and reduce to manageable size the many volumes of documents that are submitted to us with the memorials.

Some more dramatic changes would require amendments of the Court's Statute, which is not an easy process, nor necessarily one that I would favor at this point, if only because it is always dangerous to open Pandora's box. In this connection, it is worth noting that the greater use of chambers under the current system, even if States were willing to resort to them more frequently than they have thus far, would not necessarily lead to greater productivity under the current Statute and Rules of Court. This is so because judges serving on different chambers would for quorum and related reasons not be excused from sitting in concurrent non-chamber cases, and that would produce further delays. This problem could be overcome in part by a lowering of the quorum requirement, but that would again require an amendment of the Statute. A more drastic solution would increase the number of permanent judges and limit the type of cases that would go to the Court sitting in plenary while imposing mandatory chambers for the other types of cases, possibly along the model of the European Court of Human Rights. This solution would, of course, also require an amendment of the Statute. I would be reluctant to support it because it would adversely affect the principle of universality reflected in the plenary Court's hearing of cases, which is worth preserving given the Court's role as principal judicial organ of the United Nations. The solution might, however, have to be adopted if a substantial increase in the Court's docket and ever greater delays were to make it necessary. Fortunately, we are not there yet by a long shot.

We should not overlook the fact that the most exciting aspect of serving on the Court at this time is directly related to the significant increase in the number of cases being referred to it. That States are becoming ever more willing to submit their disputes to be decided by us, is evidence of the Court's growing legitimacy and acceptance. This development indicates that for an increasing number of States international law and the judicial settlement of inter-State disputes are coming to have a practical relevance that belies the frequently heard contention that international law and the work of international courts are irrelevant to contemporary international relations. I have the sense, moreover, that the more international law is under attack from some quarters, the more likely it is that it will be resorted to and deemed worthy of support by States that view these attacks as serious threats to the existing international legal order. I hope that this assumption is correct and that it is not the wishful thinking of an ICJ judge dreaming happy dreams in the Peace Palace.

RESPONDING TO INTERNATIONAL TERRORISM

Challenge of International Terrorism to the International Security System – Designing Responses within the UN Charter and Treaty Frameworks for Regional Security

The panel was convened by its Chair, Jan Wouters*.

Introductory remarks by Jan Wouters

Wouters excused the absence of Ruth Wedgwood. Moving on to the order of speaking of the panelists, Wouters informed the audience that it was in accordance with their approach to the issue to be discussed, from specific to broad, with O'Connell on the US invasion of Iraq and actions in Yemen, Gowlland-Debbas on the response to counterterrorism measures taken in general, Kohen on the legal argument of self-defense as a means of reacting to terrorism, Byers on possible responses to the counterterrorism approach advocated by the US administration within the current international security system, and Packer on the OSCE's approach to terrorism.

Remarks by Michael Byers**

Terrorism, weapons of mass destruction, and the (d)evolution of international law

Evolution: (1) the process by which different kinds of living organism are believed to have developed from earlier forms, especially by natural selection; (2) gradual development …

Devolution: (1) the devolving of power by central government to local or regional administration; (2) descent or degeneration to a lower or worse state …[1]

Introduction

The threats posed by terrorists and weapons of mass destruction have prompted reconsideration of the legal constraints on the use of force in international affairs. Does a system that allows military action only in response to an "armed attack", or if the Security Council has given express authorization, provide sufficient scope for dealing with contemporary security challenges?

* University of Leuven.

** Professor of Law, Duke University, Durham. E-mail: byers@law.duke.edu.

The UN Charter was designed to prevent inter-State wars involving conventional weapons. Today, some of the most serious threats are from non-State actors, which by definition are distinct from (and not necessarily supported by) the States in which they are found. In addition, the technology to produce and deliver chemical, biological and nuclear weapons – which can be used with little if any warning – has become widely available. Yet the existence and severity of these threats are often difficult to determine, as indeed are the appropriate responses to them. As a result, the Security Council can find itself in profound disagreement on matters of such considerable importance that one or more of its permanent members feel compelled to use force without either express authorization or an "armed attack". The collective security mechanisms agreed in 1945 are robust enough to survive a few unilateral actions of this kind. However, a pattern of non-compliance would seriously undermine and eventually destroy them.

The 2002 National Security Strategy and the 2003 invasion of Iraq both indicate that President George W. Bush and his administration are willing to bypass the Council in their efforts to minimize the threats posed by terrorists and weapons of mass destruction. As they do so, they place enormous demands on other States, for military assistance and access to airspace, and for political and economic support of various kinds. This creates a profound dilemma for other governments. What should they do? What, indeed, are their options?

This paper argues that there is only one realistic option: that States should accept the inevitability of some informal, evolutionary changes to the law governing the use of force. The challenge, however, is to ensure that any such changes are both necessary and tightly constrained, that evolution (which by definition is a progressive, strengthening process) does not collapse into devolution (a degenerative process which, on one definition, involves the transfer of decision-making power to a subsidiary authority, in this case the United States).

Option 1: Formal amendment

Formal amendments to the UN Charter might seem to be one option for States grappling with the combined challenges of terrorists, weapons of mass destruction, and the forceful tendencies of the United States. Such amendments could include removing or limiting the veto-power of the permanent members, broadening the right of self-defense so as to explicitly allow preemptive action, or according a formal authorizing or oversight role to the General Assembly in matters of peace and security. Yet formal amendments require the consent of each permanent member. Amendments are therefore rare, and politically unrealistic if their consequence would be to diminish the procedural powers that accompany permanent membership.

Option 2: Informal, evolutionary change

A second option would be to trust in the ability of the Charter, as a quasi-constitutional instrument, to evolve in response to geopolitical change. Such an approach involves accepting that the ordinary meanings of the terms used in the Charter are not necessarily determinative of the law. The practice of States is also important, both on their own and within UN organs. But this raises the question of whether any evolutionary changes to the Charter are precluded. It may be one thing to accept that a permanent member's abstention does not count as an opposing vote for the purposes of a Resolution, and a very different thing to argue that the "armed attack" language of Article 51 does not preclude the unilateral waging of precautionary wars. Where does one draw the line between, on the one hand, evolutionary change that accommodates new realities without sacrificing legal constraints, and, on the other hand, more extensive changes that fatally undermine the entire concept of legal constraint – at least as it applies to the most powerful actor? And how does one prevent that actor from wielding a disproportionate influence in the drawing of the line, and in its application to specific situations? In other words, how does one avoid the result that the United States ends up entitled to do what it wants, while other, less powerful States remain legally constrained?

Option 3: Legal nihilism

There is a third option, whereby States would recognize that legal constraints on the use of force are a chimera – that when it comes to national security, as they perceive and define it, States, or at least powerful States, do not refrain from military action because of international rules.

The United States, with its disproportionate military power, could certainly use force as and when it chose regardless of international law. And it could conceivably do so at little cost to its dominant position, it being unlikely that any government would help to defend a country under attack from the United States. One might even argue that accepting the absence of legal constraints on the use of force would benefit less powerful States, by creating greater transparency in international affairs. Powerful States, no longer able to hide behind dubious legal justifications unequally and opportunistically deployed, might become more easily subject to moral and other non-legal pressures. If the alternative is evolutionary change that perverts the law into a servile instrument of the powerful, then a system that excludes arguments about legality and focuses on legitimacy might actually provide greater protection to the weak.

There are two problems with this third option. First, it is inefficient and perhaps dangerous, even for the United States, since an absence of rules on the use of force would constitute a state of anarchy in this area of international affairs. Anarchy is not necessarily chaotic, but it is not very efficient either, even for disproportionately powerful actors. Although an absence of rules can benefit the powerful in discrete situations, it also requires constant vigilance and an ongoing readiness to threaten and use force. In virtually every society, powerful actors have rejected anarchy in favor of legal rules, which can be designed and manipulated so as to constrain the weak more than they do the powerful.

Second, to adopt a stance of legal nihilism, even if only with regard to the use of force, would be to abandon all hope for a globalized system of participatory involvement in the ordering of international relations. International law, in addition to imposing constraints, also provides entitlements. At the most basic level, these include the right of States, imperfect though they may be as popular representatives, to participate in the making and shaping of international law. Seen from this perspective, the existence of legal constraints on the use of force – a reality supported by the practice and opinions of most States – is a necessary reflection of a rough form of international democracy. Accordingly, the preferences of the powerful cannot easily be imposed upon the weak, but must instead be subject to argument and persuasion. Just as 18th century Americans regarded "taxation without representation" as the most objectionable aspect of British imperialism, the most objectionable aspect of the third option is that it would allow the policy preferences of today's most powerful country to be levied upon the rest of the world, without even the pretense of debate.

Option 2 plus (as chosen by the United States)

The United States is not in fact pursuing the third option of legal nihilism. It is instead focusing on the second, evolutionary option (which, as we have seen, is the only realistic one). But rather than placing their trust in the ability of the evolutionary process to generate the appropriate rules on its own, international lawyers in the US government deliberately seek to direct that evolution – to the long-term benefit of the United States. Of course, most States sometimes behave with a view to influencing legal evolution. But recent US attempts to direct the evolution of the rules governing the use of force have been particularly bold and sophisticated.

Case Study 1: Self-defense against State sponsors of terrorism

Following the terrorist attacks of 11 September 2001, the Bush administration decided to intervene in Afghanistan. This policy decision was probably made without regard to international law. Yet the legal justification advanced was not simply a cynical effort to secure the cooperation of other countries; it constituted a deliberate effort to change a rule of customary international law.[2]

At least four possible legal justifications were available: (1) an invitation from the Northern Alliance (which could have been cast as the legitimate government of Afghanistan), since invitation is widely accepted as a basis for intervention under customary international law; (2) an explicit authorization from the UN Security Council, which had it been requested would have been forthcoming; (3) unilateral humanitarian intervention (based in part on the 1999 Kosovo precedent), since millions of Afghan lives were at risk from famine; (4) a claim of self-defense extended to include action against State sponsors of terrorism.

Rather than advancing two or more of these justifications (as it would normally have done), the United States focused entirely on self-defense. And while the claim of self-defense against State sponsors of terrorism was not new, it had not – as of 11 September 2001 – received sufficiently widespread acceptance to become customary international law. In 1986, Secretary of State George Shultz had said:

> It is absurd to argue that international law prohibits us from capturing terrorists in international waters or airspace; from attacking them on the soil of other nations, even for the purpose of rescuing hostages; or from using force against States that support, train, and harbor terrorists or guerrillas.[3]

Yet when the United States bombed Libya later that year, following a terrorist attack on a Berlin nightclub frequented by US servicemen, the action was widely criticized. Even France and Spain, both NATO allies, denied the use of their airspace for the raid.

Following the 11 September terrorist attacks, the global political environment was more conducive to essentially the same claim. Worldwide concern about terrorism and widespread sympathy for the United States presented an opportunity for international lawyers in the US government, who took several steps to ensure the claim's widespread acceptance. First, they tightened its focus, asserting only a right to use force against State-sponsors of terrorism, such as the Taliban government of Afghanistan, in situations where the terrorists had already attacked the responding State. This made it possible for others to support (or acquiesce in) the claim without necessarily supporting a right to use force against terrorists anywhere, including within States that had neither actively supported nor willingly harbored them.

Second, support for the claim was sought in advance of military action. Collective self-defense provisions in the 1949 North Atlantic Treaty and 1947 Inter-American Treaty of Reciprocal Assistance were invoked even though neither NATO nor the Member States of the Organization of American States were called upon to engage in military action. Similarly, UN Security Council Resolutions adopted unanimously on 12 and 28 September 2001 were carefully worded to affirm, within the context of a broader response to terrorism, the right of self-defense in customary international law.

Again, although the United States did not intervene in Afghanistan because of international law, the decision to intervene nevertheless presented an opportunity for directing the evolutionary change of rules in a manner that worked to its long-term benefit. For while the now-extended right of self-defense is in principle available to all States, it is of use only to those with the ability and will to project military force. The effect is that a handful of powerful States – none of which has any reason to worry about the extended right being used against them – have acquired a somewhat greater sphere of legality within which to intervene abroad.

Case Study 2: Preemptive self-defense

Another effort at provoking and directing evolutionary change has been mounted with regard to preemptive self-defense. Here the United States seeks, first to secure a preexisting claim, and then to stretch the resulting rule so as to render it more ambiguous – which in turn facilitates the application of power and influence to determine when and where the rule applies.[4]

Today, there are three readily discernable positions on the law governing preemptive military action. First, there is Article 51 of the UN Charter and its reference to "if an armed attack occurs". When read according to traditional rules of treaty interpretation, this provision precludes any right of preemptive self-defense.

Second, it is sometimes argued that preemptive action is justified if there is a "necessity of self-defense, instant, overwhelming, leaving no choice of means, and no moment of deliberation". These words were written by US Secretary of State Daniel Webster following the 1837 *Caroline* incident in which British forces seized an American steamboat, torched it and sent it over Niagara Falls. Until the adoption of the Charter in 1945, these criteria were widely accepted as delimiting a narrow right of preemptive self-defense in customary international law.

Third, on 1 June 2002, in a speech at West Point, President Bush announced: "We must take the battle to the enemy, disrupt his plans, and confront the worst threats before they emerge". There is an important difference between this statement and the criteria articulated by Webster – a difference that goes beyond the fact that the president was speaking of the threat posed by chemical, biological and nuclear weapons, and the possibility that such weapons might fall into terrorist hands. Bush made no suggestion of waiting for a "necessity of self-defense" that is "instant, overwhelming, leaving no choice of means, and no moment of deliberation". He was advocating *precautionary* rather than preemptive self-defense – on its face a radical departure from any understanding of the preexisting law.

The president's words conveyed a policy decision that would have been made with little if any reference to international law. Yet international lawyers working in the US government had the task of justifying the policy in legal terms. They would soon have realized that, as expressed, the policy was not only unprecedented but also had little chance of becoming customary international law. Simply put, most countries do not stand to benefit from a right of precautionary self-defense that would give all States – including every State's potential enemies – wide discretion to use force. The absence of a widely reciprocal benefit is usually fatal to the development of customary law, which requires not only a claim but also widespread support or acquiescence.

The policy was therefore reformulated to make it more acceptable, and thus more effective in promoting legal change. The National Security Strategy of the United States, released in September 2002, explicitly adopted – and then sought to extend – the *Caroline* criteria:

> For centuries, international law recognized that nations need not suffer an attack before they can lawfully take action to defend themselves against forces that present an imminent danger of attack. Legal scholars and international jurists often conditioned the legitimacy of preemption on the existence of an imminent threat – most often a visible mobilization of armies, navies, and air forces preparing to attack.
>
> We must adapt the concept of imminent threat to the capabilities and objectives of today's adversaries.[5]

The security strategy makes no mention of the UN Charter, thus implicitly asserting that the pre-1945 customary right of self-defense remains the applicable law. By glossing over this normally contentious issue, it seeks to establish a new baseline for the discussion. It then goes further, asserting that the criterion of imminence now extends beyond threats which are "instant, overwhelming, leaving no choice of means, and no moment of deliberation", so as to include more distant and uncertain challenges.

The claim is made against a policy backdrop that suggests the need for legal change: terrorism and weapons of mass destruction are clearly serious problems. As significantly, States are not actually being asked to agree on a change to the rule. All that is proposed is an adaptation of how the (supposed) existing rule is applied in practice. This apparently reasonable claim is well suited for generating support and acquiescence, which, when combined with military actions justified by the claim, could rapidly lead to a change in the law.

Yet the reformulated claim is hardly innocuous. By adopting and stretching the pre-1945 criterion of imminence, the advocated approach would introduce more ambiguity into the law. This ambiguity would, in turn, enable power and influence to play a greater role in the application of the law to particular situations. In future, whether the criterion of imminence is fulfilled would depend in large part on the factual circumstances – as assessed by individual States and groups of States. And the ability of the powerful to influence these assessments could be considerable, given the various forms of political, economic and military pressure that might be brought to bear. Moreover (and as we saw with regard to Iraq), powerful States will sometimes have special knowledge based on secret intelligence – or at least claim such knowledge in an attempt to augment their influence even more. As a result, it is more likely that the criterion of imminence would be fulfilled when the United States wished to act, than when others wished to do the same. The legal constraints on self-defense would remain generally applicable – and thus available as a tool to be deployed against others – while the most powerful State would have increased freedom to act as it chose. Here again, by provoking and directing the evolution of international law, the United States is deliberately seeking rules that work to its benefit.

Evolution or devolution: A question of degree

The threats of terrorism and weapons of mass destruction cannot be ignored, and changes to the Charter and customary international law may be required before they can be dealt with effectively. If so, informal, evolutionary change is the only realistic way forward, since formal Charter amendments are unlikely and an absence of rules would be contrary to every State's interests.

But evolutionary change could easily be taken too far, especially if the principal instigator of change is a single superpower that desires more freedom to act than most States think necessary and desirable. Evolution, by definition, is a progressive, strengthening process that, within the context of the law on the use of force, should advance the interests of the vast majority of States by improving the ability of existing rules and institutions to prevent armed conflict. If pushed too far, however, informal change could weaken those rules, divest the Council of much of its authority, and "devolve" that authority to the United States. Such a development, while perhaps more conducive than legal nihilism to the interests of the single superpower, would create the same kind of anti-democratic problems for others – and thus constitute a degenerative rather than progressive development.

Responding to US efforts at directed evolution

Efforts by the United States to provoke and direct informal legal change are not necessarily a bad thing. When aimed at widely acknowledged problems such as terrorism and weapons of mass destruction, such efforts could close or do away with dangerous gaps and harmful restrictions in the normative framework of international affairs. The question for today's statesmen, however, is how to respond to US efforts at informal legal change in a manner that facilitates and supports the progressive developments that only the power and influence of the United States can bring, while at the same time blocking or limiting those legal changes that would make it easier for the single superpower to act contrary to the interests of most other States.

Response 1: Close cooperation

One possible response is to cooperate fully with every US effort at informal legal change, on the theory that such cooperation buys a degree of influence. But such a response involves risks, including outright cooption, the loss of independence in foreign policy, and less rather than more influence once full cooperation becomes taken for granted. Moreover, since informal legal change is impossible to reverse except through the same evolutionary process, and since that process today almost necessarily requires the support or acquiescence of the United States, close cooperation is a one-way street: if and when it fails as a strategy, irreparable normative damage will already have been done.

Response 2: Outright opposition

Another possible response is outright opposition, at least to any efforts at informal legal change that are particularly bold or demanding. Such a response, one might argue, is necessary to prevent US governments from assuming that they can secure such changes at will, regardless of the opinions or interests of others. And yet such a response also carries risks, including antagonizing a military and economic superpower, provoking it into preferring legal nihilism, and, perhaps most importantly, preventing the achievement of other, common goals – both in terms of legal change and more broadly.

Response 3: Constructive opposition

Not surprisingly, the most attractive response is some combination of the above, an approach that may be referred to as "constructive opposition". Such an approach entails closely examining the merits of any US effort at legal change, supporting those that are desirable, opposing those that are not, and using that preparedness to either support or oppose as a persuasive tool for influencing the direction of US policy (at least insofar as it concerns international law).

Given the overwhelming power and influence of the United States, no individual State can make constructive opposition work on its own. States adopting such an approach need to identify common interests and goals and then coordinate closely and consistently with one another. This is not as easy as it sounds. The United States is well aware of the problems that "collective bargaining" by others could pose for its efforts, and thus has a longstanding preference for bilateral negotiations, one-on-one tradeoffs, and "special relationships" (of which it has many). It consciously applies "game theory" by seeking to create "prisoners' dilemmas", whereby individual States are forced into concessions precisely because they have been denied the opportunity to coordinate with others.

Finally, the advisability of constructive opposition is strengthened by the fact that the current US administration is something of an historical aberration. No administration governs forever; another, more diplomatic and less ruthless government will appear eventually. Constructive opposition may thus legitimately be directed at damage control, slowing the speed of legal evolution if and when the status quo is not a practical option. One way in which this might be done is by encouraging forms of cooperation that do not contribute, or at least contribute less to the opposed legal change. For example, the adoption of Security Council Resolution 1441 in November 2002, although perhaps not intended for this purpose, has, by providing a more credible legal justification for the intervention in Iraq, "absorbed" much of the impact of that intervention as a precedent for an extended right of preemptive self-defense in customary international law. Another way to slow legal evolution is to promote clarifications and limitations to the changing rules. For example, a collective effort to elaborate new, detailed, *Caroline*-like criteria for a right of preemptive self-defense could help to limit any legal change here, and thus constrain the United States (and other powerful countries) from using any changed rule in undue or abusive ways.

Conclusion

Terrorism and weapons of mass destruction have, together with the Bush administration's efforts to change the international rules governing the use of force, created a situation where at least some informal, evolutionary legal changes are now inevitable. At the same time, these changes must be tightly controlled, lest progressive, evolutionary change be pushed to the point where it collapses into degenerative devolution. The best way to accomplish this is through a global policy of constructive opposition to US efforts at provoking and directing informal legal change. The United States can still be (and should be) a force for global good, but this can only happen if governments around the world ensure that international legal change remains a widely deliberative, truly participatory process.

Notes

1 *Concise Oxford English Dictionary*, 10th edn., (Oxford University Press 1999).

2 For a more detailed analysis, see Michael Byers, 'Terrorism, the Use of Force and International Law after 11 September', 51 *International & Comparative Law Quarterly* (2002) 401; reprinted in 16 *International Relations* (2002) 155.

3 'Address to the National Defense University, Washington, D.C., January 15, 1986', 25 *International Legal Materials* (1986) 204 at 206.

4 For a more detailed analysis, see Michael Byers, 'Preemptive Self-defense: Hegemony, Equality and Strategies of Legal Change', 11 *Journal of Political Philosophy* (2003) 171

5 The National Security Strategy of the United States, at 15, <http://www.whitehouse.gov/nsc/nss.pdf>. See also 'From the Document: A Stress on Disrupting Terrorism', *N.Y. Times*, 20 September 2002, at A14.

Remarks by Vera Gowlland-Debbas*

What responses to counter-terrorism? Or the problem of accountability

I. Introduction: the paradoxes of terrorism

The theme of the panel in which this contribution was presented was how to respond to terrorism. In my view, however, one of the most urgent questions on the international agenda today is how to devise responses to *counter-terrorism* – how to constrain

* Professor of Public International Law, Graduate Institute of International Studies, Geneva.

and hold States accountable for measures adopted in the name of the so-called "war against terror".

The international community is mesmerized by the discourse on terrorism. Yet, unilateral military operations carried out on the pretext of eradicating terrorism have had far-reaching consequences and have probably caused more civilian deaths than 9/11 – I say "probably" because while every single death in the World Trade Center was accounted for and mourned for the world over, we will never know with any precision the number of men, women and children who died under "Operation Enduring Freedom" in Afghanistan or "Operation Iraqi Freedom".

The United Nations has been and still is central to the devising of responses to terrorism and Member States have indeed recognised that the United Nations is uniquely placed to respond to such a scourge.[1] In the normative field, twelve agreements have been negotiated within the scope of the United Nations and Specialized Agencies, the latest being the 1997 International Convention for the Suppression of Terrorist Bombings, and the 1999 International Convention for the Suppression of the Financing of Terrorism. The General Assembly has adopted numerous declarations on terrorism.[2] Its Ad Hoc Committee established in December 1996 is currently working on a comprehensive Convention on international terrorism which aims, *inter alia*, to provide a definition of terrorism, as well as a Convention for the suppression of acts of nuclear terrorism. A high-level UN conference to formulate a joint organized response of the international community to terrorism in all its forms and manifestations is being planned for.

Apart from encouraging States to become parties to the relevant international conventions,[3] the Security Council has also determined that international terrorism is a threat to international peace, thus opening the way to action under Chapter VII. While in the past it was concerned with issues of State responsibility for terrorist acts (for example in the well-known *Lockerbie* case), leading to the adoption of sanctions against the States concerned, more recently, its action has been directed towards penalisation of acts of international terrorism, as well as suppression of its financing, in relation to Al Qaeda and associated Taliban members, and more generally, as set out below.

No Security Council resolution on terrorism provides anything like an unequivocal authorization to use 'all necessary measures', the standard euphemism for use of force, against terrorist acts. The reference to combating terrorist acts "by all means" in the preamble to Security Council Resolution 1373 cannot be seen as providing such an authorisation, in light of its context and the following operative paragraphs of the resolution. At most there is an ambiguous reference to the inherent right of individual or collective self-defence *in accordance with the Charter*, in both the preambles of Resolutions 1368 and 1373, which cannot be taken as an express endorsement of a right of *pre-emptive* self-defence, nor a widening of that right to include responses to armed attacks from non-State actors.

The action of United Nations organs in the general fight against terrorism has thus been situated in the framework of international criminal responsibility, requiring effective interstate and inter-organisational cooperation across borders to bring to justice the perpetrators of such acts. The UN has consistently insisted, moreover, that measures adopted by States comply with international law, including human rights and the stringent requirements of international and domestic criminal procedures.

This UN approach to terrorism is in keeping with the evolution of international law away from the State-centric model, and with recent developments in the field of international criminal responsibility. It is also reflected in the theme of this Joint Conference which is centered on global governance and non-State actors.

Yet paradoxically, the actions of non-State actors have triggered responses which have impeded the move toward what the International Criminal Tribunal on Former Yugoslavia, in the *Tadić* case, referred to as a "human-being-oriented approach".

Firstly, the "war on terrorism" has challenged the regime of international protection of the individual through a reassertion of State sovereignty. The move since 1945 to make States accountable for the treatment of individuals on their territory or within their jurisdiction, principally through the limitations of human rights law, refugee law and humanitarian law, has been stalled, as legal black-holes – legal limbos – have emerged in which none of these regimes appear to apply and individual remedies are slim or non-existent. This has led us back to a world dominated by States in which the rights of individuals in their various capacities as nationals, aliens, peoples, ethnic minorities, refugees, civilians and non-combatants, have been superseded by the imperatives of State security.

Secondly, in contrast to the terrorism discourse, and particularly to United States rhetoric regarding a "war on terrorism" waged against *non-State actors*, the military operations waged in Afghanistan and Iraq have, paradoxically, both been engagements of a traditional interstate kind, based on broad interpretations of the right of self-defence against *State* threats, as well as of the rules of *State* responsibility, alleging, in the case of Afghanistan, a broadening of the criteria for attribution to States which merely *harbour* terrorists. The "war on terrorism" has thus been used as justification for undermining the current rules constraining the freedom of States to use military force in international relations, and for alleging new approaches to humanitarian law. The invasion and occupation of Iraq, for example, takes us back to a pre-1945 world of international relations with its ultimatums, fabricated evidence and massive bombardment of towns.[4] The outcome of this operation is an indefinite military occupation in Iraq, in which the occupiers claim a unilateral right to reshape the political, economic and social set-up of another country and dispose of its natural resources, while unable or unwilling to ensure the obligations of occupying powers – in particular, maintenance of law and order and of infrastructures, and protection of cultural property. We have again departed from the framework of individual criminal responsibility – which is where terrorism belongs – to State responsibility, in which the State is once again a black box confounded with its people.

The revival of the inter-State model on the ground, a consequence of alleged responses to terrorist acts, thus stands in stark opposition to the terrorism discourse which proceeds from a model based on the relationship between the State and non-State actors.

The problem thus faced by the United Nations is not the absence of a significant role in the fight against terrorism, but its limited role in constraining counter-terrorism and in holding States accountable for their related actions. The Policy Working Group on the United Nations and Terrorism established by the Secretary-General in October 2001,[5] has warned United Nations organs that "counter-terrorism can be used to justify acts in support of political agendas............Labelling opponents or adversaries as terrorists offers a time-tested technique to de-legitimize and demonize them. The United Nations should beware of offering, or be perceived to be offering, a blanket or automatic endorsement of all measures taken in the name of counter-terrorism."

I will centre on these two types of challenges to international law posed by counter-terrorism – the challenge to human rights law and to the rules prohibiting the threat or use of force in international relations – in order to underline the problems of accountability which may arise.

II. Counter-terrorism and human rights

A. Security Council resolutions on terrorism and the problem of accountability

The threat that international terrorism poses to human rights has been consistently underlined.[6] However, there is the increasing danger that counter-terrorism poses a similar challenge.

First, Security Council resolutions relating to terrorism and their implementation by Member States have raised important human rights issues. Security Council Resolution 1373 (2001) on the prevention and suppression of the financing of terrorist acts has been central to States' counter-terrorism legislation. It calls, *inter alia*, for the freezing of all funds, financial assets and economic resources of persons or entities who not only commit or participate in terrorist acts, but also who "facilitate the commission" of such acts. This resolution departs from traditional sanctions resolutions in a number of ways. While it does not define terrorism, it imposes on Member States an open-ended obligation with no temporal limitation, to adopt legislation criminalizing specified conduct which up to now may not have been penalized in their domestic law. The target is individuals, as opposed to States, but it is also general and impersonal. The legislative nature of the resolution is evident from the fact that States are called on to implement provisions similar to those found in conventional instruments. The provisions on financial measures leave a wide margin of appreciation to implementing authorities in individual States, including in the identification of targeted persons and entities.

But individually targeted sanctions in the context of the fight against terrorism were introduced by the Security Council even before the events of 11 September 2001 in respect of Afghanistan (in particular, Resolutions 1267 (1999), 1333 (2000), measures which were re-oriented in Resolution 1390 (2002)); these relate, *inter alia*, to the freezing of funds and other financial assets of Osama bin Laden, the Al Qaeda network and the Taliban. The Afghanistan Sanctions Committee was entrusted with the drawing up of lists of designated individuals and entities targeted by these resolutions which were subsequently consolidated, as the sanctions against the *de facto* regime in Afghanistan melted into the broader framework of the response to terrorism, and as cooperation between the Afghanistan Committee and the newly established Counter-terrorism Committee was reinforced. These lists of individual targets of sanctions measures, which are based on designations by the intelligence services of particular Member States, lack transparency and raise serious questions regarding the safeguard and protection of individual rights, such as the right to a fair and public hearing for those listed and the lack of legal procedures for de-listing which at present depends on political and diplomatic processes.

The exemptions from the freezing measures pursuant to Resolutions 1267, 1333 and 1390 which are provided for in Security Council Resolution 1452(2002) – and which also apply to implementation of Resolution 1373 – relating to funds and other financial assets that are "necessary for basic expenses" or for certain extraordinary expenses, may mitigate the hardship but in a sense have eroded the platform for individual complaints.

Such resolutions have therefore fueled the on-going debate surrounding the accountability of the Security Council. Moreover, apart from these lists, implementing States have been left to designate the entities that are targeted and, in the absence of a definition of terrorist acts, to improvise around their own favoured brands of local terrorism. Such targeted measures, while overcoming the indiscriminate effects of comprehensive sanctions, have created their own set of problems.

What recourse is offered to individuals when implementation of such resolutions encroaches on their basic rights?

At the international level, while there is no doubt concerning the Charter and international law limits to the activities of the Security Council, there appears to be little possibility of judicial or other forms of review of either Security Council resolutions, or States' implementing legislation.

The need to protect human rights in the struggle against terrorism has been highlighted by the UN Secretary-General and the UN High Commissioner for Human Rights.[7] The human rights bodies at the United Nations have also drawn attention to the dangers inherent in the indiscriminate use of the term "terrorism" and expressed alarm at the consequent threats that anti-terrorism legislation and policies pose to the enjoyment of virtually all human rights – civil, cultural, economic, political and social.[8] The Human Rights Committee, in reviewing individual State reports under the Covenant, has stressed that legislation enacted pursuant to Security Council Resolution 1373 must be in conformity with the International Covenant on Civil and Political Rights.

The problems arising under the pretext of combating terrorism that have been identified by United Nations bodies include:

- The targeting and discrimination of vulnerable groups on the basis of origin and socio-economic status, in particular migrants, refugees and asylum-seekers, indigenous peoples and people fighting for their land rights.
- The infringement of non-derogable rights and the non-respect of the conditions for measures of derogation.
- The extradition of terrorist suspects to countries where they might be subject to torture or capital punishment.
- Legislation based on designations made by foreign countries of organizations as terrorist organizations, without examining that designation on its merits.

The particular rights identified as being particularly under threat[9] include:

- liberty and security of the person;
- freedom from torture and other inhuman or degrading treatment;
- freedom of expression and of peaceful assembly and association;
- a fair trial and right to a judicial determination on the lawfulness of detention;

- to seek and to enjoy asylum and not to be forcibly returned to countries where people are at risk of suffering serious human rights abuses.

However, while the Security Council is conscious of the human rights and humanitarian law constraints (see, for example, the preamble to Resolution 1373 and the Ministerial Declaration annexed to Security Council Resolution 1456 (2003)),[10] it has divested itself of responsibility. As Sir Jeremy Greenstock put it in a session of the Security Council devoted to threats to international peace and security and terrorist acts,[11] the CTC is not "a tribunal for judging States. It will not trespass onto areas of competence of other parts of the United Nations system. It is not going to define terrorism in a legal sense, although we will have a fair idea of what is blatant terrorism; where necessary, we will decide by consensus whether an act is terrorism."

Moreover, it has been stated that most of the issues concerning the root causes of terrorism – including "poverty, lack of human rights and other forms of deprivation" – did not fall within the mandate of the Security Council.

At the same time, there is little opportunity under human rights mechanisms, to review Member States' efforts in implementing Resolution 1373. It has been pointed out that only three-fourths of the States reporting to the CTC on their implementation of Resolution 1373 (and there has been quasi-universal reporting) are parties to the International Covenant of Civil and Political Rights (CCPR), and only one tenth of those members appear before the Human Rights Committee each year.

At the domestic level, individuals are also left with little recourse for adequate and effective remedies. Resolution 1373 which is binding under Article 25 of the UN Charter must be made operative within States' domestic frameworks. Moreover, such obligations supersede, under Article 103 of the Charter, other international agreements. There is also an increasing perception by regional and national courts, that Security Council resolutions are aspects of international public policy in fulfilment of community objectives – and this may be strengthening as a result of community interest in fighting terrorism –, although this perception contrasts with the more modest place and formal ranking given to these resolutions in domestic law, as at best non-self-executing treaty obligations.[12]

National courts do not always have the competence to review national implementing measures, particularly where the domestic basis of such legislation is tied to questions of national security and where they draw their legitimacy from Security Council resolutions. The following cases relating to measures adopted by the Security Council under Article 41 of the Charter herald a trend in future rulings by domestic and regional courts in the case of challenges to Resolution 1373. In its decision in the case of *Milošević*[13] relating to a request that he be released unconditionally on the grounds that the Netherlands was acting unlawfully in cooperating with the ICTY, the District Court of the Hague ruled that under the Headquarters Agreement the Netherlands had lawfully transferred its jurisdiction over the ICTY's indictees to that Tribunal, that the Statute of the ICTY gave it primacy over national courts and that UN Charter obligations prevailed over the obligations of Member States; the Dutch court thus argued that it had no competence to consider the request. The Court also relied on the case of *Naletilić* v. *Croatia*[14] to argue that the ICTY offered sufficient procedural guarantees. In consequence, it rejected as manifestly unfounded the argument that the surrender of an accused person to the ICTY would violate the right to a fair trial under Article 6(1) of the ECHR.

The problem is that remedies may also not be available at the regional level. In the subsequent case of Milošević against the Netherlands[15] the ECtHR declared inadmissible the complaint brought by Milošević under several provisions of the ECHR, precisely for failure to exhaust local remedies... even though it was plain that there were none that were adequate and effective.

As for the freezing of funds (seen as both property confiscation and penal sanction), regional courts have reiterated that property rights are not absolute and that their exercise may be subject to restrictions.[16] In assessing the proportionality of the measures taken, they have argued that the importance of the general interests embodied in Security Council resolutions – the maintenance of international peace – justified their negative consequences,[17] even of a substantial nature. Accordingly, those consequences could not be regarded as manifestly disproportionate in relation to the aims pursued. In matters of compensation, they have passed the buck to the Security Council, where of course no such remedy is available.[18]

It will be noted that these cases involved individuals affected by sanctions as third parties, not the targeted entities themselves. Undoubtedly, the conflict between fundamental rights and targeting of sanctions following on measures such as the freezing of assets undertaken in response to alleged involvement of the individual in international terrorism will also continue to raise questions in EU and other UN Member States. In the case of *Aden* before the European Court of First Instance,[19] the three Swedish nationals targeted by Resolution 1333, argued, *inter alia*, that their right to a fair hearing had been violated, since they had no possibility of domestic judicial review and hence of verification of the evidence, and that the penal sanction imposed was not the legal consequence of a precise charge filed against them. In its decision of 7 May 2002, however, in which the Court of First Instance refused to grant the requested provisional measures, i.e. the suspension of the EU Regulations implementing the Security Council's resolution, the Court made reference to Articles 25 and 103 of the Charter, which makes it improbable that an eventual decision on the merits would challenge the decisions of the Sanctions Committee. There is also the case of Jose Maria Sison,[20] a recognised refugee in the Netherlands, who was included on lists of targeted individuals and now seeks the annulment of Council Regulations and Decisions. The complaint relates, *inter alia,* to a violation of the obligation to state reasons, of the principle of proportionality and the freedom of circulation of capital. The applicant also invokes the violation of several general principles of Community Law, enshrined in the European Convention on Human Rights, as well as the lack of competence of the EU to adopt Regulation 2580/2001.

This shows how Security Council Resolution 1373 by making the link between asylum-seekers, refugees and terrorism, also has a potentially serious impact on asylum. Moreover, it underlines the possibility of conflicts between Security Council resolutions and human rights which are considered non-derogable or *jus cogens* rights, where deportation of individuals suspected of terrorist activities to countries where they may face torture may infringe the prohibitions under Article 3 of ECHR or Article 3 of the UN Convention on Torture.

B. Unilateral measures to counter terrorism and problems of accountability

Quite apart from the implementation of Resolution 1373, grave issues of accountability have arisen from unilateral measures adopted in the name of the war on terrorism. I refer, for example, to the legal limbo of Guantanamo, where detained aliens are subject to indefinite detention in a territory which is purportedly "outside the jurisdiction" of the United States, with no possibility of access to a court to review the legality of their detentions. Their only other recourse is diplomatic protection by the State of nationality of the detainees which, under international law, remains discretionary, as the case of *Abbasi* in the UK Court of Appeals has underlined.[21] It has been shown that by selectively combining the war model (under which the detainees lack the usual rights of criminal suspects) and the criminal law model (under which the detainees lack the rights of prisoners of war), these individuals are "neither criminal suspects nor POWs, neither fish nor fowl, they inhabit a limbo of rightlessness".[22] As for the detainees imprisoned since September 11 in the United States itself, their situation has been compared to the plight of those "disappeared" under Latin America's past dictatorships.[23]

The building of a wall in Palestine which will turn the West Bank into "the largest prison in the world" also fulfils the worst nightmare scenario of counter-terrorism. According to its statement made before the General Assembly on 20 October 2003, Israel has justified the construction of this wall on the basis of Article 51 of the Charter and Security Council Resolutions 1368 and 1373. According to the Secretary-General's report pursuant to General Assembly Resolution ES-10/248,[24] the wall and all its supporting roads, fences, trenches and watchtowers, is planned to form one continuous line stretching to over 720 kilometers along the West Bank, while deviating in certain places more than 7.5 kilometres from the Green line, encircling Palestinian populated areas. It has been estimated that nearly 400,000 Palestinians will thus live in enclaves between the Wall and the Green Line, effectively cut off from their farmlands and workplaces, schools, health clinics and other social services.

General Assembly Resolution ES-10/13 demanded that Israel stop and reverse the construction of the wall. The General Assembly has also finally succeeded in adopting a long-awaited request to the International Court of Justice for an advisory opinion on whether Israel, the occupying Power, is under legal obligation under Security Council and General Assembly resolutions, to cease its construction of the wall in the Occupied Palestinian Territory, including East Jerusalem, and to dismantle the existing sections.

Nevertheless, the discourse on terrorism continues to obscure the questions arising from Israeli occupation of Palestinian territory and, although Israel can be seen to be in "material breach" of numerous Security Council resolutions,[25] this has prevented it from being held accountable before the Security Council. This despite the fact that Palestine has been the responsibility of the UN ever since the UK abandoned this former mandate and that the United Nations had laid down its own road map for the Territory since 1948.

III. Counter-terrorism, the prohibition of the threat or use of force and problems of accountability

A. The framework of analysis of the military intervention in Iraq

The unauthorised invasion and occupation of Iraq by the US and UK led-coalition on 20 March 2003, has posed even more monumental challenges to the international system than 9/11. At the same time, the devastating attack on the UN headquarters in Baghdad, which came as the after shock, served to underline, in retrospect, how vital the United Nations role and its function of legitimisation is perceived to be in this affair.

I will not dwell on the justifications and counter-justifications which have been the subject of so much debate. I share the view of an overwhelming majority of legal scholars, spanning a large spectrum of legal opinion, that the war against Iraq was a grave violation of one of the most fundamental provisions of the UN Charter.[26] If taken to its logical conclusion, it can only be characterised as an act of aggression within the meaning of Resolution 3314, as one eminent French international lawyer, Alain Pellet, wrote in *Le Monde* of 22 March 2003.

The claim to a very broad notion of pre-emptive self-defence generally against political regimes considered to be hostile, and more particularly against alleged threats from Iraqi weapons of mass destruction and links with Al Qaeda – for the war against Iraq has been justified in the context of the "war" on terrorism – is in my view unsubstantiated, generally unaccepted and would open a dangerous Pandora's box in a war without end.

However, one has to view this intervention more from the perspective of claims to unilateral enforcement of collective decisions, i.e. place it within the framework of the evolving collective security regime of Chapter VII of the Charter. We are faced here with a new brand of unilateralism which claims to operate in pursuit of community objectives, and which is packaged in between United Nations Security Council action which both precedes and follows it.

Despite the disdain which many members of the US administration showed towards the United Nations, both the USA and UK clearly acknowledged the importance of working through that Organization, falling back to arguing, as the main justification of their actions, that the war had been conducted "with international (UN) authority", on the basis of implied or continuing authorization which could be unilaterally deduced from the cumulative effects of two Security Council resolutions – Resolutions 678 and 687 – as somehow revived by Resolution 1441.[27]

I will not go into details on the legal niceties of the arguments used by the Coalition, the grounds of which have already been reviewed abundantly by the literature. I would just like to underline, as have done numerous other commentators, that this unilateral interpretation of international obligations by the coalition is clearly contradicted by the wording and context of Resolutions 678, 687 and 1441, as well as contrary to their object and purpose. The UK/US position is also inconsistent with their representatives' express statements in the Security Council following the adoption of Resolution 1441 that this resolution did not contain a "hidden trigger" for unilateral recourse to force. It is contradicted by the express statements made by other Security Council members and States participating in the debates, including statements by three permanent members – China, France and Russia – issued after the vote on 1441. Nor is this the first time that Security Council members have explicitly rejected any automatic right for members to use force (see, e.g., debates surrounding Operation Desert Fox, the airstrikes against Iraq, in December 1998). Finally, even if adopted, the US-UK-Spanish draft resolution would not have provided a proper authorisation, nor were its implicit objectives in line with those of the Council or the UN Charter, so that the accountability of the Security Council would also have been engaged.

At any rate, implied or continuing authorisations are not compatible with the functions performed by such resolutions. Such authorisations serve as delegations of the Council's enforcement powers under Chapter VII, hence placed under its authority and concurrent responsibility, and they act as a "circumstance precluding wrongfulness" in the framework of State responsibility. Enough concern has been expressed by Member States over the ambiguous and open-textured nature of the resolutions to underline the fact that *even where authorised by the Council* such delegations of power require placing serious checks on unilateral action. It is generally agreed, moreover, that the Council does not have an unfettered right under the Charter to dispose of its powers. In short, resort to unilateral action in the absence of express Council authorisation remains an act of usurpation of Council powers and a resort to force which is prohibited under international law.

This is certainly not to argue for a static approach to Charter interpretation. It is, however, to underline the *raison d'être* of a dynamic and teleological approach which up to now has served the purpose of expanding the collective competence of the United Nations in the face of restrictive and regressive assertions of sovereignty and unilateralism by Member States.

In terms of accountability, however, the fact must be faced that we cannot draw here the usual legal consequences of aggression – non-recognition of the ensuing legal situation and a claim for reparations – in the same way as was spelled out in Security Council Resolutions 662 (1990) in respect of non-recognition of Iraq's annexation of Kuwait, and 687(1991) in respect of Iraqi "liability under international law for any direct loss, damage – including environmental damage and depletion of natural resources .... arising from the unlawful invasion and occupation of Kuwait", regarding which the United States had played a major role. How different from these resolutions is the euphemism used in the current situation of "Iraqi reconstruction", which means that all the destruction and havoc wrought on Iraq, including under the long haul of economic sanctions, is to be paid for largely from Iraq's own oil resources and in part from "donations" from the international community.

That the legal consequences of the unauthorised invasion and occupation cannot be drawn in this case is partly for obvious reasons of *Realpolitik*. But it may also be the case that in an international legal environment which purports to be increasingly more people-oriented, the traditional effectiveness/legitimacy debate may have to be reconsidered in the light of the rights of the Iraqi people and the need to establish a framework for rebuilding a stable and viable Iraq.

While post-war Security Council Resolutions (1472, 1483, 1500 and 1511 (2003)) may be perceived as *ex post facto* legitimisation of unilateralist actions, similar to the alleged *ex post facto* legitimation by Resolution 1244(1999) of the NATO operation in Kosovo, I would like to argue that they serve both to replace the question of Iraq's invasion and occupation within the framework of the primary and collective responsibility of the Security Council in the field of international peace and security, as well as to introduce a thin wedge of international accountability for the actions of the current occupiers of Iraq.

B. The function of legitimisation and the problem of accountability

It must be said that the Iraq crisis has raised the question of the collective legitimization function of the United Nations, and its corollary, collective illegitimization, a function already identified by Inis Claude in 1966 when he pointed to the political and moral impact of the UN's role as the "dispenser of approval or disapproval" of certain situations.[28] But this in the past has also assumed an important legal function, the UN using non-recognition and nullity as a tool in the collective defense of certain fundamental norms.

In my view, while none of the resolutions adopted after the war clearly condemn the occupation, they do not legitimise it either. This is clear from the Security Council debates on Iraq in the immediate aftermath of hostilities. An overwhelming majority of speakers emphasized that the war, carried out without Council authorization, was a violation of international law and the United Nations Charter and thus did not meet the criteria of international legitimacy. The debate underlined the legal and financial responsibility of the coalition for the war, including under the Fourth Geneva Convention. Many members called for a Council reaction demanding the immediate and unconditional withdrawal of UK and US forces from Iraq and called on the Council to ensure that in its resolution (Resolution 1472 (2003)), it did not provide tacit or implied approval for the military operations.[29]

But even those countries opposing the military operation considered that the humanitarian situation of the civilian population and the need to end the foreign occupation made it imperative for the international community to participate in the reconstruction of the country and in the establishment of a viable and representative government. They thus saw no contradiction in their positions of both endorsing community involvement in Iraq under the auspices of the United Nations and insisting on the illegality of the invasion and occupation. It will be recalled that in its Namibia Opinion, the International Court of Justice did indeed hold that the duty of non-recognition imposed by SC Resolution 276 of South Africa's administration of the territory should not result in depriving the people of Namibia of any advantage derived from international cooperation.[30] In short, the need for humanitarian action and the interests of the Iraqi people appear to have been the overriding concern.[31]

The reference to the United States and United Kingdom as occupying powers under unified Command ("the Provisional Authority") in Resolution 1483 and subsequent resolutions, has no legal effects in respect of the position under the *jus ad bellum*. On the contrary, it is required in order to assert their "specific responsibilities, authorities, and obligations under applicable international law". The resolutions insist on the temporary nature of the Authority and on the rapid restoration of the sovereignty of Iraq.

The fact that Security Council Resolutions (1500 and 1511) clearly appear to support the formation of an interim administration run by Iraqis, even if it is appointed by the United States, is only a *de facto* acknowledgement that this can realistically be the only way forward to ending the occupation and to the formation of a duly constituted government. Thus Resolution 1511:

> "(4) Determines that the Governing Council and its ministers are the principal bodies of the Iraqi interim administration, which, without prejudice to its further evolution, embodies the sovereignty of the State of Iraq during the transitional period until an internationally recognized, representative government is established and assumes the responsibilities of the Authority."

What these resolutions provide is, rather, a platform for the assertion of international accountability for the occupation of Iraq, however thin and precarious, which once again highlights the collective responsibility of the United Nations for Iraq and its importance as a legitimizing force.

The actions of the occupying powers are to be "consistent with the Charter of the United Nations and other relevant international law." The resolutions are thus declaratory of the obligations of the occupying powers under international law, including those imposed by the Geneva Conventions of 1949 and the Hague Regulations of 1907, which include the effective administration of the territory and the creation of conditions in which the Iraqi people may freely determine their political future and attempt to regain control over their own natural resources. The resolutions must therefore be interpreted in the light of, and applied consistently with, existing international law, that is interpreted restrictively.

Although it proved impossible to introduce a timetable for the ending of the occupation, some form of international supervisory regime and strategy has been established. This includes the requirement of transparency in the activities of the Development Fund for Iraq, the conditioning of the disposal of Iraq's natural resources to the exclusive use and benefit of the Iraqi people, with a modicum of international supervision by the establishment (long delayed) of an International Advisory and Monitoring Board over the sale and expenditures of oil resources, a UN Assistance Mission to ensure a presence for the coordination of humanitarian and reconstruction activities and promotion of human rights, and a role for the Secretary-General in the constitutional and electoral processes, although the question of the security of the UN staff in Baghdad has been a grave setback to such a presence. The Security Council has arraigned upon itself the right to review the implementation of the resolutions through the establishment of timetables, and presentation of periodic reports, and it will consider further steps that might be necessary.

Finally, authorisation has been granted for the establishment of a multinational force under unified US Command, to take "all necessary measures to contribute to the maintenance of security and stability in Iraq". While that may appear as a concession to the Occupying Powers, it is, on the one hand, a reflection of the failure of the Coalition to obtain troops from other States without UN blessing (the joint statement by France, Germany and Russia indicates the refusal of these countries to contribute troops *even with* such blessing), and on the other, the realisation that the United Nations cannot operate on the ground without ensuring the necessary conditions for implementation of the programme it has established.

The Council has therefore not relinquished its primary responsibility in this matter and its practice in the matter of authorisations is therefore far from terminated.

Moreover, there is an indication that it intends in the future to give explicit and temporary mandates. Resolution 1500 reflects the authorisations previously granted in February and May 2003 in respect of Côte d'Ivoire and the Democratic Republic of the Congo (Resolutions 1464 and 1484 respectively) which were granted on a strictly temporary basis – six and three months respectively – allowing for Council assessment of the situation and some measure of regular reporting.

One can be cynical about these resolutions, the outcome of the political wheeling and dealing that has taken place behind the scenes. The resolutions also provide many loopholes for the protection of the interests of the Occupying Powers. For example, Executive Order 13303 would appear to go further than Resolution 1483, paragraph 22 which provided for immunity for Iraqi petroleum in domestic courts as well as for the Iraqi Development Fund; it has the effect of providing protection from legal proceedings of all foreign – mainly US – corporate oil operations in Iraq without including the Resolution's exception for environmental damages.

In legal terms, however, the insertion of unilateral action within a collective framework serves to provide a platform for accountability and a standard against which may be set the way the occupation is being carried out, whether or not there exists the political will to carry out that accountability in practice.

On the other hand, while the unilateral use of force by powerful States is certainly not a novel feature of international relations – this not the first time the UN has been faced with unilateral military action on the part of one of its Member States – this new type of unilateralism which intermingles with collective action raises major problems, arising from the fact that the unilateral claims to speak in the name of the collective and the collective is perceived to act in the name of the unilateral. This confusion in perceptions has surely been responsible for the recent tragedy in Baghdad. But it does underline the centrality of the role of the United Nations in the fight against terrorism and the importance of its legitimising process.

Concluding remarks

The acts of non-State actors have paradoxically repositioned the State in central position of the international legal system and thus reinforced notions of State sovereignty.

I was asked to address the question of whether the Security Council has become dysfunctional. If it is dysfunctional, it is not because it cannot address terrorism, but because it cannot satisfactorily address counter-terrorism. Security Council resolutions which target individuals have the effect of eroding the protection of individual rights under international human rights instruments. The fact that they override other international obligations, the control by certain permanent members of the Security Council over such decisions and the lack of other than diplomatic channels to review them, results in contradictions and tensions in the purposes and principles of the United Nations – the maintenance of peace and security, and human rights.

Moreover, States under cover of this legitimisation of counter-terrorism measures have assumed an unfettered unilateral right to assert security concerns over fundamental rights in a development which would have been considered untenable in the last decade.

The discourse over terrorism has thus prioritized the reactive provisions of the Charter to maintain and restore peace to the detriment of its peacebuilding clauses, while at the same time, obstructing venues for peaceful settlement of disputes and for the venting of frustrations, whether in the form of political negotiations, international criminal court, advisory opinions of the International Court of Justice or independent action by the General Assembly of the United Nations, the only existing forum that can accommodate and protect the diversity of cultures and claims. It may sound trite to say that a "war" to diminish – it is impossible to eradicate such an old historical phenomenon – the possibilities of terrorist attacks cannot be successful unless it addresses the political root causes of terrorism, but triteness can be self-evidence – one has only to look at the Palestinian problem.

Surely, to echo the ICJ in the *Nicaragua* case, the values of the so-called "civilised world" should not be promoted through methods which undermine the acquis in the fields of regulation of the use of force, human rights, humanitarian law and refugee law. Nor will we succeed in doing so by reducing our complex world, for manipulative purposes, to the reductionist view of "four legs good, two legs bad" of George Orwell's *Animal Farm.*

Notes

1 See Security Council meeting at the level of Ministers for Foreign Affairs on 20 January 2003 (S/PV 4688); the Declaration on the Issue of Combating Terrorism subsequently adopted; and statements made in S/PV 4734 and 4752.

2 See, for example, GA Res. 49/60, Declaration on Measures to Eliminate International Terrorism; GA Res. 51/210; GA Res. 54/164; and GA Res. 56/261, Plan of Action against Terrorism.

3 See e.g. SC Res. 1269 (1999) and SC Res. 1377 (2001), Declaration on the Global Effort to Combat Terrorism.

4 It is telling in this context that the planned initial military operation in Iraq, though ultimately abandoned, had as its title "Shock and Awe". The concept of "Shock and Awe" was first developed by the Pentagon's National Defense University (NDU) in 1996 as part of the "Rapid Dominance" strategy (document on <http: // www. dodccrp. org/ shockIndex.html>). It claimed to produce the effect of a Hiroshima with conventional weapons "through delivery of instant, nearly incomprehensible levels of massive destruction directed at influencing society writ large, meaning its leadership and public, rather than targeting directly against military or strategic objectives…striking directly at the public will of the adversary to resist… the object being 'to convince an adversary to accept our will in the Clausewitzian sense'" (…) "While there are surely humanitarian considerations that cannot or should not be ignored, the ability to Shock and Awe ultimately rests in the ability to frighten, scare, intimidate and disarm".

5 UN Doc. A/57/273; S/2002/875.

6 See e.g. Commission on Human Rights, SubComission on the Promotion and Protection of Human Rights, *Terrorism and Human Rights,* Preliminary report prepared by Ms. Kalliopi K. Koufa, Special Rapporteur (E/CN.4/Sub.2/2001/31, 27 June 2001).

7 See UNHCHR, *Digest of Jurisprudence of the UN and Regional Organizations on the Protection of Human Rights while Countering Terrorism,* 2003, <http://www.unhchr.ch/html/menu6/2/digest.doc>.

8 See *supra,* note 5; Report of the chairpersons of the human rights treaty bodies on their fifteenth meeting at Geneva, 23-27 June 2003, *Effective Implementation of International Instruments on Human Rights, including reporting obligations,* <http://www.unhchr.ch/html/menu2/finalreport15th>; Report of the Secretary-General on *Protection of Human Rights and Fundamental Freedoms while countering terrorism* (UN Doc. A/58/266, 8 August 2003).

9 See 'A Human Rights Framework for Responding to Terrorism', Open statement to the 2002 Commission on Human Rights, by, *inter alia,* Amnesty International and the International Commission of Jurists, <http://www.fidh.org/justice/lettres/2002/opnstat2703a.htm >.

10 See also GA Resolution A/RES/57/219 which specifically focuses on the need to protect human rights and fundamental freedoms while countering terrorism; and Commission on Human Rights, Resolution E/CN.4/RES/2003/68. OHCHR has also exchanged views with the CTC, briefing it three times since its in-

ception in 2001 (see, for example, Note by the High Commissioner for Human Rights submitted to the Chair of the Counter-Terrorism Committee on: 'A Human Rights Perspective On Counter-Terrorist Measures' (<http://www.un.org/Docs/sc/committees/1373/>). Briefings were also arranged between the CTC and the Human Rights Committee in March and June 2003.

11 S/PV 4453rd meeting, 18 January 2002.

12 See V. Gowlland-Debbas (ed.), *National Implementation of Non-Military Security Council Sanctions: A Comparative Approach,* Leiden, Boston, Martinus Nijhoff Publishers, 2004 (forthcoming) and, by the same author, 'The Domestic Implementation of UN Sanctions', in Erika de Wet and André Nollkaemper (eds.), *Review of the Security Council by Member States*, Intersentia, 2003, pp. 63-76.

13 *Slobodan Milošević* v. *The State of the Netherlands* (Judgment in interlocutory injunction), 31 August 2001, President of the Hague Distr. Ct, *Kort Geding* 2001/258, p. 688.

14 Application No. 51891/99, *Naletilić* v. *Croatia* (Decision as to Admissibility), ECtHR, 4 May 2000.

15 See Application no. 77631/01, *Slobodan Milošević* v. *the Netherlands* (Judgment), ECtHR, 19 March 2002.

16 See Case C-317/00 P(R) *"Invest" Import und Export GmbH and Invest Commerce SARL* v. *Commission,* [2000] *ECR* 2000, p. I-09541, 13 November 2002 (Order of the President of the Court on the Appeal against the Order of the President of the Second Chamber of the Court of First Instance of the EC of 2 August 2000).

17 See Case C-84/95, *Bosphorus Hava Yollari Turizm ve Tiçaret AS* v. *Minister for Transport, Energy and Communications, Ireland and others* [1996] *ECR* 1996, p. I-03953.

18 See Case T-184/95, *Dorsch Consult Ingenieurgesellschaft mbH* v. *Council of the European Union and Commission of the European Communities* (Judgment), *ECR* 1998, p. II-00667.

19 Case T-306/01R, *Aden and others* v. *Council of the European Union and Commission of the European Communities [2002] (Order of the President of First Instance of the EC of 7 May 2002*). For the United Kingdom, see also *R. (on the application of Othman)* v. *Secretary of State for Work and Pensions,* [2001], EWCH Admin 1022 (Q.B.2001).

20 Case T-47/03 *Jose Maria Sison against the Council of the European Union and the Commission of the European Community* [2003].

21 *R (Abbasi and another)* v. *Secretary of State for Foreign and Commonwealth Affairs and another* [2002] EWCA Civ159, in which the Court recognised the breach of fundamental human rights constituted by the denial to all detainees of access to a court to challenge the legality of their detention, although it was solely concerned with Abbasi's rights under UK domestic law.

22 David Luban, 'The War on Terrorism and the End of Human Rights', *Philosophy and Public Policy Quarterly*, Vol. 22, Summer 2002, pp. 9-14, at pp. 9-10. See also the seizure by SFOR forces of six "terrorists" sent to Guantanamo who had been released for lack of evidence by the Bosnian Supreme Court. In April 2002, the Human Rights Chamber established under the Dayton Accords ruled to no avail, that the rights of four of the men had been contravened, and ordered their return to Bosnia. See Madeleine Rees (Chief of Mission, Office of the UN High Commissioner for Human Rights (OHCHR), Bosnia, 'Protection in conflict and peacebuilding: some lessons from Bosnia-Herzegovina' (available at: <http://www.odihpn.org/report.asp?ID=2517>).

23 See Nadine Strossen (President of the American Civil Liberties Union), 'Maintaining Human Rights in a Time of Terrorism: A Case study in the value of legal scholarship in shaping law and public policy', *NYL School Journal of International and Comparative Law,* Vol. 22, 2003, pp. 3-23.

24 See Report of the Secretary-General prepared pursuant to General Assembly Resolution ES-10/13, of 24 November 2003 (A/ES-10/248). See also Report of the Special Rapporteur of the Commission on Human Rights, John Dugard, on the situation of human rights in the Palestinian territories occupied by Israel since 1967 (E/CN.4/2004/6) of 8 September 2003 and Report submitted by Jean Ziegler, United Nations Special Rapporteur on the Right to Food, Addendum, Mission to the Occupied Palestinian Territories.

25 Even if not adopted under Chapter VII, many of the Council's resolutions on Palestine have undoubted legal effects as declaratory and quasi-judicial resolutions which reaffirm Israel's obligations under international law and the Charter. See the case of *Namibia, ICJ Rep.*1971.

26 See numerous letters and protests from such well-known legal scholars as Georges Abi-Saab, Gaetano Arangio-Ruiz, Yadh Ben Achour, Paolo Benvenuti, Ian Brownlie, Christine Chinkin, Luigi Condorelli, James Crawford, Pierre-Marie Dupuy, Richard Falk, Thomas Franck, Vaughan Lowe, Jean Salmon, Philippe Sands, Eric Suy … the list can be extended.

27 See, *inter alia*, letter dated 20 March 2003 from the Permanent Representative of the United States to the United Nations, John Negroponte, addressed to the President of the Security Council and legal opinion from Lord Goldsmith, the UK Attorney General, addressed to the Prime Minister on 17 March 2003.

28 See Inis Claude, 'Collective Legitimization as a Political Function of the United Nations', 20 *International Organization* (1966) 367-79.

29 See S/PV 4726, 26 March 2003.

30 *Legal Consequences for States of the Continued Presence of South Africa in Namibia (South-West Africa) Notwithstanding Security Council Resolution 276 (1970)*, advisory opinion, *ICJ Rep.* 1971, pp. 55-56.

31 See in particular, S/PV 4761, 22 May 2003 surrounding the adoption of Resolution 1483 (2003).

REMARKS BY MARCELO G. KOHEN*

IS THE LEGAL ARGUMENT FOR SELF-DEFENCE AGAINST TERRORISM CORRECT?

If there is one point on which all of our epistemic community agrees, it is that international law must play a role in the fight against terrorism. The author of these words has always been convinced that terrorism is an inhuman, unjust and cowardly means of political or religious struggle, no matter the goals invoked. States and peoples belonging to all regions and systems of the world have been the victim of this scourge. Terrorism in all its forms, wherever and by whomever committed,[1] must be condemned and combated. The main question remains however, as to the appropriate means of doing so.

I will limit the scope of this presentation to the analysis of the legal argument of self-defence as a means of reacting to terrorism. What is, in last resort, at stake is the relevance of either unilateral or collective action in the field of the use of force. In fact, the main point at issue is the case of transnational terrorist groups whose activity cannot be attributed to a State. Indeed, if this activity can be attributed to a State, then the situation becomes the traditional one of inter-State relations.

Until now, much of the scrutiny undertaken with regard to this question has focused on the issue of harboring terrorists, the existence or not of direct control by States of terrorist groups and the possibility of terrorist groups conducting an armed attack, falling under Article 51 of the UN Charter and customary law. Another debate arising after September 11 has been whether SC resolutions and State practice can be seen as evidence of a change either of the rules governing the use of force or of the interpretation of these rules. Since I have dealt with these questions elsewhere,[2] it is not my purpose to repeat them here. Therefore, the point I will address here is whether the international legal argument of self-defence is either necessary or relevant in the fight against terrorism, from the point of view of international law.

States and authors that rely on the view that terrorist attacks open the way for self-defence, confine themselves to the analysis of whether they meet the requirements of armed attacks, answering in the affirmative, even if they cannot be attributed to a State. They focus on the forcible character of the action, irrespective of the subject that commits it. They do not elaborate upon this important assertion: if terrorists are able to accomplish armed attacks on their own, without any final attribution of their acts to a State or to another recognized subject of international law, it means that they are able to violate the customary rule of the prohibition on the use of force in international relations, that they are party to an armed conflict, and finally, or as a conse-

* Professor of International Law, The Graduate Institute of International Studies, Geneva.

quence of these previous points, that they enjoy a certain kind of international personality.

There is no need whatsoever to consider that there is an armed conflict in order to "accommodate" international law to the new realities of terrorism. On the contrary: terrorist organizations would be delighted if their actions were considered as being part of an armed conflict, either internal or international. Their members could then lay claim to being considered as "combatants". Nevertheless, a terrorist is not a combatant, in the sense of Humanitarian Law, he/she is simply a criminal. As a result, he/she cannot claim to be treated as a "prisoner of war". Hence, the blatant contradiction of the US Government's treatment of the suspected Al Qaeda members imprisoned in Guantanamo.

As a matter of course, States are not the only subjects of international law able to become parties to an armed conflict. National liberation movements, rebels within a State, are also candidates, amongst others. When two or more States, or one State and a national liberation movement, or rebels and the central government, are parties to an armed conflict, they cannot resort to terrorist methods. International humanitarian law, both the law of Geneva of 1949 and of 1977 are very clear on this point. Terrorist activities can constitute armed attacks when we face these kinds of conflicts.

Some people assert that terrorism is the new type of war of contemporary times. Therefore, to try to apply the old rules of *jus in bello* would simply be nonsensical. The argument is anything but new. It was advanced by the military dictatorships in Latin America during the 1970s, in order to justify their violations of human rights, arguing that the Third World War had already begun in the form of terrorism and that they were the vanguard in this struggle for freedom.

It is not my purpose to scrutinize here the political aspects of this new so-called "war" against terrorism or, viewed from the opposite angle, the war that terrorist organizations are making against the "civilized" world. I would just state that, were it true that the old rules of international law are not useful to deal with this new phenomenon, then there would be a contradiction when the same people attempt to include military reactions against terrorist attacks under the "old" rules of *jus ad bellum*, including self-defence.

The first question that emerges is why terrorist acts ought to be considered as a particular case of armed attack or aggression. Is it their violence, their targets, their aims, the number of casualties or the level of destruction that provides the clue? As we have seen, force may be the common element shared by terrorist acts and traditional military actions engaged in by one State against another. However, this is not the distinctive criterion. For it is clear that a government fighting against its "own" terrorist groups within the State will not invoke self-defence to justify its action. For some scholars, it is the magnitude of the terrorist attack that would allow one to qualify it as an armed attack in the sense of Article 51 of the Charter.[3] They invoke a distinction made by the Court in the *Nicaragua* case in order to justify the invocation of self-defence. In fact, the Court considered that the sending of armed bands amounts to an armed attack authorising self-defence only if, "because of its scale and effects", it would be more than a mere frontier incident.[4] This ICJ finding can be read as assuming that there are two different kinds of armed attacks, and only a *qualified armed attack* authorises the recourse to self-defence.[5] Another way of reading it is by noting that not any sending of armed bands to foreign territory constitutes an armed attack.

Despite the debatable nature of this assertion by the Court, no matter how one interprets it (a State that sends armed bands to a foreign territory could be considered an aggressor irrespective of the gravity of the actions performed by those bands), it presupposes a clear act of a State: the sending of armed bands. It is not simply the gravity of the conduct of armed groups that constitutes an armed attack, but the fact that a State has sent them in order to accomplish the attack. It would be preposterous to consider that a State that commandeered an armed band to commit a terrorist attack would only be responsible for the armed attack if it led e.g. to a significant number of victims but not if there were none. This means that a criterion other than gravity needs to be found. One turns naturally to the external character of the terrorist group. Transnational terrorism would then open the possibility for the plea of self-defence.

Here we have to distinguish two different situations: within and beyond the victim's territory. There is no need to use the category of "self-defence" when dealing with the repression of terrorism internally. Assume that during the tragic events of 11 September an American agent had been present on one of the aircraft and had been able to stop the terrorists by killing them. Or that one of the aircraft had been intercepted by the US Air Force. These acts would not then have been qualified as acts of self-defence, irrespective of whether the terrorists came from abroad or not. One can also take the cases in various countries in which State agents (police or armed forces) have killed terrorists having hijacked aircraft, because this was the only way to obtain the release of their hostages. These kinds of acts can be justified on the basis of municipal law without any need for recourse to self-defence. There simply are cases of legitimate use of violence by the entity having the monopoly over it within its territory: the State.

Rightly, the United Kingdom, when ratifying Additional Protocol I of 1977 to the Geneva Conventions of 1949, made an interpretative declaration regarding Article 1, paragraph 4 and Article 96, paragraph 3, according to which

> "It is the understanding of the United Kingdom that the term "armed conflict" of itself and in its context denotes a situation of a kind which is not constituted by the commission of ordinary crimes including acts of terrorism whether concerted or in isolation".[6]

From the outset, let me be clear on one point: if the terrorist attack *is being* perpetrated from abroad, there is no doubt that the victim State can repel it, even in the foreign territory from which the attack emanates, irrespective of a direct or indirect participation of that foreign State. This is a case of self-defence in the sense of Article 51 of the UN Charter and customary law. A State can defend itself against an ongoing transboundary attack without any need to know beforehand whether the attack is directly committed by the regular armed forces of the other State or by irregular groups. This act of self-defence would, however, finish once the State from which the attack comes took the measures necessary to stop it. But this is not the main hypothesis under consideration in the general discussion engaged in after September 11.

There is increasing evidence that practice goes further than the direct control requirement described by the ICJ in the *Nicaragua case*,[7] in order to attribute terrorist acts to a State. The overall control theory described by the ICTY in the *Tadić case*,[8] means that a higher degree of diligence is required of States in order not to allow, for instance, their territories to be used to launch terrorist attacks or indeed, to organize them. This interpretation of a factual situation with regard to the attribution to States of acts committed by non-State agents, in no way changes either the scope or the conditions of self-defence.

The situation is different if the foreign territory is simply used as a shelter and if the terrorist attack is already over. Is it possible to resort to force in order to capture or kill the terrorists, to destroy their camps or to prevent further attacks by invoking self-defence? If the words have any sense, this is not possible. The expression "self-defence", both in domestic and in international law, refers to a situation in which an individual or a State is aggressed. In order to face this aggression, the victim – individual or State – tries to repel it using in turn similar means, i.e. violence. In domestic criminal law, it is a cause of justification for the violent conduct of the victim. In international law, it is used essentially as an exception to the prohibition on the use of force by a State (or, as preferred by the ILC and the majority of authors, a "circumstance precluding wrongfulness").

The main idea of self-defence implies that the attack is underway and that the aim is to repel it. Once the attack is over, the use of force can at the most be invoked on the basis of other reasons and the legal justifications must be different. One cannot call "defence" the use of force that aims at other goals, unless one believes in the popular expression according to which "the best defence is an attack", applicable to some sports such as soccer but not taken seriously in the field of law. Hence, one could call the use of force in order to capture or kill terrorists, to destroy their bases and thus to prevent them committing further terrorist action a "legitimate attack" (a parody of the French "légitime défense"), but not "self-defence". One could also refer to this forcible action as being armed or forcible countermeasures, but not "self-defence".[9] In fact, the best candidate for this action would be the expression "taking justice into one's own hands". None of these alternative categories are recognised as lawful uses of force under contemporary international law.[10]

Some authors believe that action in self-defence can be undertaken many months after the armed attack. They mention as an example the case of the action against Iraq in 1991 after its invasion of Kuwait more than six months earlier.[11] Assuming that self-defence was the correct justification for the "Gulf War", this idea fails to distinguish between instant and continuing situations. Iraqi aggression was still ongoing in January 1991, since the territory of Kuwait was under military occupation.

By definition, the so-called "war against terrorism" is an indefinite one. One cannot know where and when terrorists will strike next. A war whose battlefield is the whole planet, against an enemy who does not constitute an army –even an irregular one– and without any foreseeable end cannot be called self-defence.

It emerges as a consequence that under the heading of self-defence, one is not justified in pursuing extraterritorial repression of terrorist groups. *For what is mainly at stake with the argument of self-defense is whether the victim State could claim to forcibly act against these terrorist groups, no matter where they are and irrespective of any consent from the State whose territory becomes the battlefield. It would then be a "new war without borders".*

The response is collective security

If a State does not comply with its legal obligations regarding terrorism, either because it is unable or because it is not willing to do so, the unilateral use of force by the victim State is not the appropriate answer. At any rate, self-defence does not help as a legal justification of what is nothing more than the use of force to face problems in the realm of international relations.

Like many other acts not involving the use of force by States, terrorism constitutes a threat to international peace and security. As such, it might be that the response of the international community – through the system of collective security set up by the UN Charter – requires the use of force, amongst other relevant measures.

With the nearly unanimous position taken by States after the terrorist attacks of 11 September 2001, the United States had a unique opportunity to obtain the adoption of a bundle of collective measures, including some forcible action undertaken with Security Council approval. The American government made considerable steps towards multilateralism in different fields of international cooperation against terrorism, with one, but none the less remarkable, exception: the field of the use of force. It preferred not to alter its doctrine of self-defence, in order to keep its liberty to use force unilaterally whenever it considers it necessary.

The Security Council has already shown its readiness to take appropriate measures in fighting terrorism. It began to do so long before September 11. It did so even under legally controversial circumstances, such as when it required of Libya the extradition of its nationals whilst the ICJ was at the same time dealing with the *Lockerbie* cases.[12] It is probably a topic with respect to which the excuse of SC incapacity to act because of the veto of the permanent members, does not work. It is for the collective security regime enshrined in the Charter to effect decisions and to implement such uses of force in the field of international relations.

States have assumed important conventional obligations in the struggle against terrorism, requiring concrete action in different fields, ranging from financial control to extradition. A rigid approach regarding the follow-up of these engagements would also play a decisive role.

Collective responses can be also developed at a regional level. However, if they imply the use of force, there must be an authorization from the Security Council, as stipulated by Article 53 of the Charter.

In relation to individuals, acts such as the terrorist attack against the World Trade Center can be considered as crimes against humanity, without any need to consider them as forming a part of an armed conflict. Still another way to improve the legal arsenal for fighting against terrorism would be the extension of the jurisdiction of the International Criminal Court in order to include this crime.[13] Regrettably, the United States opposed the inclusion of this category of crimes at the Rome Conference of 1998.

Concluding remarks

To sum up, the aim of the fight against terrorism should essentially be twofold: to bring terrorists before the courts and to prevent further terrorist activities. Self-defence is not the legal tool to tackle either of these goals. As a term of art, self-defence is a legitimate use of force to stop an armed attack. Only in the limited circumstance of repelling an ongoing terrorist attack coming from abroad, can self-defence play a role.

Terrorists place themselves beyond law and life, including their very own lives and even those which their cause pretends to defend. The worst punishment for a terrorist is not to be killed in a bombing or in an ambush, or to be kept in detention under inhuman conditions. It is to be seated before a tribunal.

Terrorism must be combated in the field of repression and security as well as by addressing the causes from which it originates or that are invoked as an excuse. To focus upon only one of these fields is to adopt a narrow view of the problem. If repression is necessary, the worst that could happen to terrorist organizations would be that the conflicts they use as an excuse for their actions would be solved.

The triumph of Civilization against Barbary requires a response to terrorism with the weapons of the law and not simply with brutal force. The temptation of all governments to bypass the law in order to struggle more efficiently against terrorism is great. They do not have to loose sight of the fact that by giving in to this temptation, they are adopting the logic of the opponent. Terrorist logic is the logic of violence. The vicious circle of endless violence in which the Israeli-Palestinian conflict has sunk these last years should be taken as a lesson. One cannot fight against terrorism by betraying the essential values of justice and the rule of law. To bypass international law in order to combat terrorism at the international level would lead to the same disastrous results that arose from the infringement of the rule of law in some domestic societies.

At best, the argument of self-defence in fighting against terrorism reflects atavism, a return to the practices of the private wars of Middle Age times. It is just another example of the undermining of one of the major legal conquests achieved in 1945: the prohibition on the threat or the use of force in international relations. It shows the will to return to a period in which war was just another legal means of conducting foreign policy. At worst, the argument of self-defence is simply one intended to conceal other goals carried out under that banner. At the end of the day, self-defence would be the name adopted by today's just war theory.

Notes

1 Cf. GA Resolution 51/210 of 16 January 1997, SC Resolutions 731 (1992) and 748 (1992) of 21 January and 31 March 1992.

2 'The Use of Force by the United States after the End of the Cold War, and Its Impact on International Law', in Michel Byers and Georg Nolte, eds., *United States Hegemony and the Foundations of International Law* (Cambridge, Cambridge University Press 2003) pp. 197-231.

3 See J.A. Frowein, in ibid., at 274.

4 *Military and Paramilitary Activities against and in Nicaragua (Nicaragua* v. *United States of America), Merits, 1986 ICJ Reports*, 14, at 103.

5 It should be recalled that the French text of Article 51 refers to "*agression* armée" and not to "armed *attack*".

6 Ratification by the UK on 28 January 1998. France adopted the same stance on its ratification of 11 April 2001. Texts available in: <http://www.cicr.org>.

7 *1986 ICJ Reports*, paras. 86-93.

8 *The Prosecutor* v. *Dusko Tadić - Case No. IT-94-1-A*, Appeals Chamber, 1999, 38 *ILM* 1518 (1999), at 1545.

9 See W. M. Reisman, 'Self-Defence or Reprisals? The Raid on Baghdad: some Reflections on Its Lawfulness and Implications', 5 *EJIL* 120 (1994), at 125. As a matter of course, he considers that there is a trend towards the acceptance of forceful countermeasures.

10 With regard to forcible countermeasures, see the Friendly Relations Declaration of 1970 embodied in GA

Resolution 2625(XXV), the *Nicaragua* Judgment of June 27, 1986 (*ICJ Reports 1986*, 127, para. 249), the Advisory Opinion on the *Legality of the Threat or Use of Nuclear Weapons* (*ICJ Reports 1996*, 246, para. 46) and the draft article. Moreover, in a study prepared by Julia W. Willis, Deputy Assistant Legal Adviser for European Affairs at the Department of State, about the US position and practice in regard to acts of reprisals, the conclusion was that "the United States has taken the categorical position that reprisals involving the use of force are illegal under international law". 'Contemporary Practice of the United States', 73 *AJIL* 491 (1979).

11 This is the view developed by Yoram Dinstein, *War, Aggression and Self-Defence*, 3rd edn. (Cambridge, University Press 2001) at 212-213.

12 Cf. Resolutions 731 (1992) and 748 (1992).

13 Cf. G. Abi-Saab, 'The Proper Role of International Law in Combating Terrorism', 1 *Chinese JIL* 305 (2002), at 311-312.

Remarks by Mary Ellen O'Connell*

Unlawful responses to terrorism

Our panel is devoted to responses to the challenge of terrorism within the UN Charter and regional treaties. My remarks address two responses to terrorism that *do not* fit within the parameters of international law:

First, the Bush Administration's policy of using preemptive force against perceived threats, and

Second, the policy embedded in the slogan: 'Global War on Terrorism,' namely, the policy of targeting to kill anywhere, anytime individuals suspected of being members of Al Qaeda or other terror groups.

These policies are not mere rhetorical devices, but rather policies the USA has already exercised. In my view the invasion of Iraq was more an exercise of preemptive self-defense than anything else, and the killing in November 2002 by the CIA of six persons in remote Yemen was an exercise of the global war policy.

Neither of these policies can be squared with existing international law. And, of course, if we wish to keep the existing law in place we will have to state the case against these policies clearly and forthrightly. If we fail to do so, if we equivocate, we will be complicit in what José Alvarez warned against at this conference: allowing hegemonic breach to become the seed of new custom.

I. Preemptive force

Let us begin with the use of preemptive force, what is becoming known as the 'Bush Doctrine.' Recall these key terms from page 13 of the September 2002 US National Security Strategy: '[E]ven if uncertainty remains as to the time and place of the enemy's attack[,] to forestall or prevent such hostile acts by our own adversaries, the United States will, if necessary, act preemptively.'[1]

The use of force in Iraq, 'Operation Iraqi Freedom', was justified in part as an act of preemptive self-defense. Ambassador Negroponte's letter to the Security Council

* William B. Saxbe Designated Professor of Law, The Ohio State University

dated 20 March 2003 set out three legal bases for invading Iraq: (1) enforce disarmament, (2) because the ceasefire in the war to liberate Kuwait had lapsed, and (3) – unique to the US letter – the defense of the USA and the international community.[2] From all we know regarding President Bush's decision-making respecting Iraq, invading out of a sense that this will protect America had to be the primary basis for the decision.[3] However, neither the UN Charter nor subsequent developments in custom allow the use of force except in self-defense to an armed attack or with the authorization of the Security Council.[4]

US authors have tried to find arguments for the right to use force more widely in self-defense: Michael Reisman argues that the term 'inherent' right of self-defense in Article 51 allows force if an attack is imminent, as determined by the potential victim.[5] Reisman does not explain how the word 'inherent' can override the other words of Article 51 allowing self-defense 'if an armed attack occurs.'

Ruth Wedgwood has argued that weapons of mass destruction and terrorists willing to use them have changed international life so fundamentally as to make the law obsolete.[6] She fails to explain why the USA before 2002 supported the rules on the use of force; it is true that September 11 was an unprecedented event for the USA, but neither weapons of mass destruction nor terrorists appeared for the first time in this world on that day.

Finally, Michael Glennon has written that due to the many breaches of the rules on force, those rules no longer exist so that no force is unlawful. We simply have no rules any longer prohibiting the use of force.[7] Glennon fails to grapple with the teaching of the International Court of Justice on this point: If breaches of the law lack *opinio juris*, they cannot amount to practice that changes the law.[8] This is true of all international law.

Thus, we can only conclude that the Charter established a workable system of law to restrain force that was still in effect on 19 March 2003 when Operation Iraqi Freedom was launched. That law did not support a US claim of self-defense because the force used did not respond to an armed attack by Iraq.[9]

II. Targeting suspects anytime, anywhere

The case of Iraq and the policy of using preemptive force have received a good deal of attention. We have heard much less about the Yemen strike. On 3 November 2002, the CIA launched a Hellfire missile from an unmanned Predator drone, operating out of Djibouti. The missile hit a car and killed its six passengers. Yemen knew about the strike in advance.[10] The Deputy General Counsel for International Affairs in the US Department of Defense said afterward: the USA can target 'Al Qaeda and other international terrorists around the world and those who support such terrorists, *without warning*.'[11]

This policy of targeting persons anywhere anytime is related to the policy of preemptive force, but different. The USA considers Al Qaeda and other terrorists to be combatants because of the September 11 attacks. Killing them is seen as part of ongoing hostilities and not merely to prevent future attacks. Thus, if the Bush Administration had found any link between Al Qaeda and Iraq, they would very likely have argued the war in Iraq was part of the global war on terrorism.[12] Failing to find any credible link, they based the war on future threats.

The Administration argues that it may treat members of Al Qaeda as combatants regardless of where they are found. As combatants they may be killed by other combatants, per the combatant's privilege within the law of armed conflict. The fatal weakness of this argument is that the law of armed conflict and the combatant's privilege are triggered by the existence of an armed conflict, not by the presence of individuals, who may be combatants in an armed conflict. Certainly the USA does not argue that its own military, for example, are lawful targets wherever they are because the USA is fighting in Afghanistan and Iraq.

Yemen is experiencing a level of lawlessness, but does not apparently recognize an armed conflict, nor does the lawlessness there meet the threshold for the application of the Geneva Conventions. In order for the Conventions to apply, 'There is no need for a formal declaration of war, or for recognition of the existence of a state of war, as preliminaries to the application of the Convention. The occurrence of *de facto* hostilities is sufficient . . ..'[13] But there must be hostilities – something more than 'situations of internal disturbances and tensions such as riots and isolated and sporadic acts of violence.'[14]

In the absence of armed conflict, the peacetime regime of human rights prevails. Under human rights law, suspects may not be killed extra-judicially. At the very least, law enforcement officials must attempt to arrest individuals. Under national and international criminal law, the Predator strike was an extrajudicial execution prohibited by the International Covenant on Civil and Political Rights,[15] to which the United States is a party. Rather than sending an unmanned drone, the USA and Yemen needed to pursue the suspects in a way that allowed authorities to communicate a demand that the suspects surrender.

Amnesty International protested the strike,[16] but I have found no media reports that any State protested. Other countries noted that Yemen consented and seemed to consider that sufficient condition for the strike to be lawful. Yemen's consent meant the United States did not violate Yemen's territorial integrity, but Yemen cannot consent to extra-judicial killing. It may not violate the human rights of persons on its territory and has not authority to consent to other States doing so.

To conclude, this paper describes two US policies respecting terrorism that violate fundamental law, but if States and other international actors do not protest, the policies could effect changes in the law. The fact that the occupation of Iraq is going badly for the coalition as of early July 2003 may provide an opportunity to impress on US policymakers a reconsideration of some of its counter-terrorism tactics. Despite the recent dominance of neo-conservative thinking in US foreign policy, thinking that supports the use of military force to maintain US predominance, the USA was founded on beliefs opposed to imperialism, beliefs that substituted the rule of law for rule by emperors and kings.

Notes

1 White House, The National Security Strategy of the United States of America (2002), at <http://www.whitehouse.gov/nsc/nss.pdf>.

2 Letter dated 20 March 2003 from the Permanent Representative of the United States of America to the United Nations addressed to the President of the Security Council, UN Doc. S/2003/351 (21 March 2003).

3 See, e.g., Joseph Cirincione, *Can Preventive War Cure Proliferation?*, <http://www.ceip.org/files/nonprolif/templates/Publications.asp?p=8&PublicationID=1308> (excerpt from July/August 2003 Foreign Policy)('The

Iraq war was the first application of the new theory that preventive war can be an effective instrument against the spread of nuclear, biological, and chemical weapons'.)

4 Mary Ellen O'Connell, *The Myth of Preemptive Self-Defense* (2002), at <http://www.asil.org/taskforce/oconnell.pdf>.

5 W. Michael Reisman, *International Legal Responses to Terrorism*, 22 HOUSTON J. INT'L L. 4, 17 - 18 (1999).

6 Attacking Iraq: Is Preemptive Self-Defense Lawful?, A Debate between Mary Ellen O'Connell and Ruth Wedgwood, 29 October 2002, co-sponsored by the American Society of International Law and the Johns Hopkins University, Nitze School of Advanced International Studies. Audiocast: <http://www.sais-jhu.edu/mediastream/deb1.ram> (available on 8 July 2003).

7 Michael Glennon, 'The Fog of Law: Self-Defense, Inherence, and Incoherence in Article 51 of the United Nations Charter' 25 HARV. J. L. & PUB. POL'Y 539, 546 (2002); see also, Michael J. Glennon, 'Pre-empting Terrorism; The Case for Anticipatory Self-Defense', WKLY STANDARD, 28 January 2002, at 24.

8 Military and Paramilitary Activities in and Against Nicaragua (*Nicaragua* v. *US*), 1986 *ICJ REP.* 14, para. 186 (27 June).

9 The United States made two other arguments to justify using force against Iraq: to enforce Security Council resolutions on disarmament and because the ceasefire declared by the Security Council had lapsed and the fighting that ended in 1991 could resume. Both justifications require a decision by the Security Council, not a unilateral determination by one or a few members of the UN. See, Mary Ellen O'Connell, Addendum to Armed Force in Iraq: Issues of Legality (April 2003), available at <http://www.asil.org/insights/insigh99a.htm>.

10 Jack Kelly, *US Kills Al Qaeda Suspects in Yemen; One planned Attack on USS Cole, Officials Say*, USA TODAY, 5 November 2002, at A01.

11 Anthony Dworkin, *Pentagon Official Examines Legal Aspects of Terror War*, at <http://hsm.intellibridge.com/summary?view_id=117201800> [on file with author, emphasis added].

12 'UN Panel Finds No Iraq Link to Al Qaeda; The Committee Says that Despite the Allegation by Powell of a Connection, the US Never Provided any Evidence to Back Up the Charge', L.A. Times, 27 June 2003, at A10.

13 III COMMENTARY, GENEVA CONVENTION RELATIVE TO THE TREATMENT OF PRISONERS OF WAR 22-23 (Jean S. Pictet, ed., 1960).

14 IV COMMENTARY TO THE 1949 GENEVA CONVENTION RELATIVE TO THE PROTECTION OF CIVILIAN PERSONS IN TIME OF WAR 3- 9 (Jean Pictet ed., 1958). See also *Prosecutor* v. *Tadić*, Judgment, No. IT-94-1-T, para. 71 (7 May 1997), which defined 'armed conflict' as existing 'whenever there is a resort to armed force between States or protracted armed violence between governmental authorities and organized armed groups or between such groups within a State.' In *Hamdi* v. *Rumsfeld*, 316 F.3d 450 (4th Cir. 2003), a US circuit court recently decided that the law of war applied – and not US (or presumably Afghan) criminal law – because a suspect was apprehended in a 'zone of active military operations,' *id.* at 462, or 'active hostilities,' *id.* at 476.

15 16 December 1966, 999 UNTS 171. Article 6 permits the use of the death penalty 'pursuant to a final judgement rendered by a competent court.'

16 Amnesty International Press Release, 'Yemen/USA: Government Must not Sanction Extra-Judicial Executions', available at <http://web.amnesy.org/library/print/ENGAMR511682002>.

DISCUSSION

JOSÉ E. ALVAREZ:* I would like the panel to consider whether Security Council Resolution 1441 is repeatable. It seems likely to me that this is not so given the opposite reactions engendered by it. In addition, I would like to hear panelists address Resolution 1373's affirmation of collective and individual self-defense and whether that is more likely to be the future role of the Council either in anticipation of US action or in response to it.

* Columbia Law School, USA.

PATRICIA HEWITSON:* On the role of international lawyers:

– How should international lawyers use the media, when airspace available (especially given the disproportionate influence of the "use of force" issue on public perceptions of international law)?

– In the opening session of this Hague Joint Conference Mr. Theo van Boven quoted Madeleine Albright's response to Robin Cook about him having trouble with his lawyer on the legality of action in Kosovo in 1999: "Get new lawyers". Any thoughts on government legal advisers and ethics?

On terrorism and weapons of mass destruction:

There is a contrast between US rhetoric drawing a nexus between terrorism and weapons of mass destruction. However, this contrasts for example with the US approach to nuclear issues where the USA is maintaining US flexibility in nuclear options (e.g. by signaling development of nuclear weapons and refusing to renounce nuclear testing), despite the weakening effect this has on the global legal and political norm against proliferation.

JORDAN PAUST:** Is there a difference of opinion between Professor Kohen and O'Connell concerning armed attacks by non-State actors under Article 51of the Charter, for example in the case of US selective targeting of Al Qaeda in Yemen, persons directly involved in ongoing processes of attack on US Embassies, the USS Cole, and September 11th?

VADIM SAVELYEV:*** I would like to ask your opinion about the concept of the term 'State terrorism'. To the best of my knowledge, it was used only once in one of the UN General Assembly Resolutions which was passed in the early 1980s. It was not used in subsequent resolutions and was never used in international treaties.

Do you think that if this term existed in conventional international law it would be easier then from a legal point of view to take measures against States that sponsor terrorism? It could be used as some moral and legal ground for taking actions against such States.

HARRY POST****: (from tape) After the 9-11 atrocities US President Bush declared 'war'. A war that would be there for a while. Mrs. O'Connell mentioned the drone-launched attack in Yemen. If you take the approach that the USA is in a state of war, taking into account the fact that we look differently upon the concepts of war and peace these days, does not that change the way we classify events like these, since in the context of war they are considered attacks? In other words, are we in a prolonged state of war, which brings us to a completely different approach to legal thinking about war and peace, armed conflict and peace?

JAN WOUTERS: restructured the questions, and first asked the speakers whether 'State terrorism' is to be distinguished from other forms of terrorism (with reference to the question posed by Savelyev), and whether qualifying State terrorism in treaties would enhance effectiveness in combating State terrorism.

MARCELO KOHEN: Responded that the answer to this question depended on one's definition of terrorism. Although no definition has been adopted at the conventional level, if one considered terrorism as the use of indiscriminate violence in order to pro-

* University of California at Berkeley, USA.

** University of Houston Law Center, USA.

*** State Duma, Moscow, Russian Federation.

**** University of Exeter, U.K.

voke terror for the achievement of political goals one could speak about State terrorism as a species of terrorism. Many instruments mentioned terrorism in all its forms and in all its manifestations. He named the forcible disappearance of persons as an example of State terrorism on which a convention already exists.

On ethics and the struggle against terrorism, he stated that all governments had the temptation to bypass the law in order to more effectively fight terrorism. Thereby they were adopting the logic of their opponent. One could not fight terrorism by doing away with the rule of law. With reference to his Argentinian nationality he warned that disrespecting the rule of law at an international level could lead to the same disastrous results it has led to in some domestic societies.

MARY ELLEN O'CONNELL: Responding to the question posed by Post, she cautioned for describing things as fundamental new developments in human society. She mentioned the distinction between war and peace as Hugo Grotius described it in a systematic way. She saw no reason for no longer respecting the fundamental distinction between war and peace in the current context. She argued the laws of war and peace were divided by factual context. The Geneva Conventions applied after a threshold had been crossed, not by who the individuals were, but by the factual situation on the ground.

Only then did we leave the realm of peace to enter into a state of war allowing the belligerent to kill enemy combatants. There was no basis for the use of force in Yemen, since it was no active zone of combat. She made reference to the US 4th Circuit Court, which stipulated in the *Hamdi* case, that Hamdi could be treated as an enemy combatant, since he was arrested in an active zone of combat.

She saw a fundamental distinction between Resolutions 1373 and 1441. She classified Al Qaeda's activities in Afghanistan as State terrorism, which occurred when individuals worked together so closely with a government, that they had the advantage of controlling State territory. The USA had a right under traditional international law to act in self-defense. Resolution 1441 did not accommodate (unlawful) use of force by the USA in Iraq. It was an example of constructive opposition, but not in the sense Byers described it, as Resolution 1441 obliged the USA to return to the Security Council, and therefore left no room for unilateral action.

She stated part of the role of international lawyers was analyzing facts and describing what the problem was, not unlike their counterparts dealing with domestic issues. The problem of terrorism was almost never a problem of war. It was crime and should be addressed as such.

MICHAEL BYERS: On the question posed by Alvarez, he stated he was not sure whether 1441 would be repeated, but indicated a repeat would probably cause more damage to the international security system. The most powerful nation in the world made it very clear that is was prepared to strike with or without the support of the United Nations Security Council. He stressed the practical nature of international diplomacy, in which the result to be obtained often weighed heavier than the legal principle.

Responding to Hewitson's question on the nexus between the US War on Terrorism and Weapons of Mass Destruction, he elaborated on the plans some 'hawks' within the US and UK government had concerning missile defense, leading to development of nuclear weapons to fight nuclear weapons, bringing more danger into the world. He stated constructive opposition could still halt these developments.

VERA GOWLLAND-DEBBAS: On the questions posed by Hewitson she stated that if we took a formalist view on international law it was made by States. If we saw law as a process, however, various sources could be identified. She favored a move towards a more people-oriented law, in which other voices, voices excluded from formal international law-making, would be included. She said she was not in a position to comment on the media, but felt within a context of big business and global media one had to be weary of some medias more than others.

On the nexus between the US War on Terrorism and Weapons of Mass Destruction she pointed out that Security Council Resolution 687 not only spoke of the disarmament of Iraq, but also about nuclear disarmament of the Middle East as a whole. The USA had opposed to this reference.

She cautioned international lawyers for too much ambition in describing the War on Terrorism as an Orwellian nightmare of perpetual war. The reactive clauses in the UN Charter had been prioritized to the expense of conflict-prevention and peace-building provisions.

JOHN PACKER: * Responding to the question of Hewitson on the role of legal advisors, in stressing he spoke on a personal basis, Packer stated that as a legal advisor he basically was asked three types of questions:

1. What is something as a legal matter;
2. What would you advise about something as a legal matter; and
3. I need this, give me an argument.

He advised to always be honest, and be clear on whose behalf one was speaking. He did not agree with the view that international law had been disturbed by the War on Terrorism. In his experience international law had worked well, though he stressed the need to find a people-centered, multilateral approach to terrorism.

He agreed with Kohen that we needed to apply the rule of law in addressing the challenges of international terrorism. He criticized the human rights community for only stressing the need for courts and truth and reconciliation committees. The work needed to start at an earlier stage, addressing material and spiritual needs of people.

JAN WOUTERS: The panelists brought the discussion back to the following question: 'Are we going back to a pre-1945, or even pre-renaissance era state of affairs or can the international legal system adjust to the increased security threats?', thereby deepening the discussion.

*Reporter: Wouter F.W. van Ballegooij***

* OSCE, The Hague.

** Researcher at the T.M.C. Asser Institute for Private and Public International Law, International Commercial Arbitration and European Law, The Hague, The Netherlands.

Concerted Actions to Combat Terrorism and the International Financial and Economic Legal System

The panel was convened by its Chair, August Reinisch*.

Remarks by Axel Marschik**

The United Nations' response to international terrorism

1. Point of departure

Before 2001, operative international counter-terrorism work was primarily police and security cooperation. The United Nations (UN) had, over the period of several years, adopted resolutions against terrorism and concluded conventions on various aspects of terrorism prevention. The Security Council (SC) had condemned specific acts of terrorism and, in 1999, established a sanctions regime dealing with the terrorist threat emanating from Afghanistan.[1] Though terrorism was perceived as an increasing threat, it was no priority issue for the UN.

The terrorist attacks in September 2001 transformed the international focus on terrorism in three significant ways:

- Terrorism was allotted the highest priority on the political agenda.
- The global dimension of terrorism, as demonstrated by Al Qaeda, required immediate and substantial international cooperation and coordination.
- Economic and financial countermeasures requiring direct involvement of the private sector were recognized as essential tools for the prevention of terrorist acts.

Considering the scale of the terrorist acts in September 2001, as well as the political and local implications, it was clear that the UN would react immediately and maintain the fight against terrorism high on its political agenda. Once it became evident, however, that the operative multilateral measures would be concentrated in the economic and financial field, many expected the focus to shift to technical or regional organizations. A Policy Working Group on the United Nations and Terrorism established by the UN Secretary-General in October 2001 recommended in its report that the UN should merely play a supporting role.[2]

Within the last two years, however, the UN has evolved into the principal coordinating organization and a driving force in the fight against terrorism. In the words of

* University of Vienna.

** The author is Legal and Political Counselor at the Austrian Mission to the United Nations. The views expressed in this article are his alone and cannot be attributed to the Austrian Foreign Ministry.

UK-Ambassador Sir Jeremy Greenstock, counter-terrorism had "now gone global, with the United Nations at the center".[3] Ambassador Sergei Lavrov of Russia stated that the SC's counter-terrorism-committee "remains the leading element in the global anti-terrorist architecture".[4]

This report examines the reasons why the UN ended up in this role and how it tries to fulfill its tasks. Due to limitations in scope, the report will focus on the counter-terrorism work of the SC. An attempt will be made to establish the impact, if any, of the Iraq-crisis in 2003 and, in that light, examine the possibilities for the future UN-role in the field.

2. Why the United Nations?

Clearly, the UN is not *per se* an inappropriate body to lead the world in the efforts against terrorism. The General Assembly (GA) has demonstrated its usefulness as a forum to condemn terrorism and negotiate international treaties against various aspects of terrorism. The UN is also well suited to examine the root causes, debate means to address them and propose strategies to combat terrorism,[5] including in the context of crime prevention.[6] It is also in a position to offer assistance to States in the implementation of countermeasures.

As regards technical anti-terrorism competence, however, especially in the economic and financial field, the UN does not come to mind. Though the SC has some experience with economic sanctions, several specialized or regional organizations seem better suited to coordinate counter-terrorism measures in the international economic and financial system.

One reason the international community resorted to the UN was sheer momentum. The adoption of SC-Res. 1368[7] the day after the terror attacks in September 2001 activated the SC. The resolution politically endorsed countermeasures and could have marked the end of further UN-involvement.[8] The USA considered SC-Res. 1368 sufficient for its immediate goals. Other UN-Members, however, saw a need for a much broader international counter-terrorism campaign and argued successfully to take advantage of the UN's unique attributes:

- Universality: Fighting sophisticated, globally active terrorist networks required optimal international cooperation. With 191 States the UN has a unique global membership.
- Visibility: Resorting to the SC demonstrated the political priority attached to the project and ensured appropriate international attention.
- Legitimacy: The UN is accepted – in particular by world public opinion – as a forum that can legitimize international coercive action. With UN-approval, intrusive measures are harder to reject or criticize by governments.
- Binding force and enforceability: SC-resolutions under Chapter VII of the UN-Charter are immediately binding on all States and can be enforced, including by the use of force.
- Speed, practicality and flexibility: Though the UN is not known for speed and flexibility, the SC's procedural rules and structure can facilitate quick decisions.
- Experience: The SC's experience in setting up and running sanctions committees and the – though sparse – existing infrastructure enabled the work to begin fairly quickly.

- Expertise: The UN had been dealing with counter-terrorism in the SC's 1267-Committee and, to certain degree, in the GA's Legal Committee, which had just recently negotiated a convention against terrorist financing. The UN's Crime Commission also had experience in dealing with international organized crime, including money laundering.

As so often, the decisive factor was whether the permanent five members of the SC (P5) could agree on a meaningful role for the UN. Though the Kosovo conflict in 1999 had strengthened antagonistic trends in the Council, terrorism turned out to be a uniting issue. Every one of the P5 had suffered terror attacks. Creating a stringent counter-terrorism regime was in the interest of each of them. At the same time, a novel regime with far-reaching obligations also meant considerable uncertainty. The world's major powers would, in any event, only accept a regime in which they retain full control. No international body gives them more control than the SC. The veto-right, with all its implications of inequality, was thus also a factor in the decision to give the UN, and in particular the SC, a central role.

3. Two regimes

The SC currently relies on two counter-terrorism regimes: In 1999, the SC adopted sanctions against the Taliban and members of Al Qaeda, which have since been substantially amended and enhanced. After the terror attacks in September 2001, the SC established an abstract counter-terrorism regime with particular focus on terrorist financing. The implementation of each regime has been entrusted to a Sanctions-Committee.

UN-sanctions have not always been successful. In some cases, the sanctions led to considerable suffering of the general population while the State's leadership – usually the cause for the sanctions – exploited the system and strengthened its position. Inadequate implementation by States and the reluctance of the SC to enforce the obligations sometimes resulted in highly profitable circumvention schemes and loss of authority of the Council. Both counter-terrorism regimes have adopted novel means to address these problems and to mitigate unintended consequences.

a) **Security Council Resolution 1373**

On 24 September 2001, the SC unanimously adopted SC-Res. 1373.[9] Relying on Chapter VII of the UN-Charter, the resolution contains wide-ranging obligations to prevent and combat terrorism. It obliges States, *inter alia*, to:

- criminalize the provision or collection of funds destined to support terrorism, prohibit persons from doing so, and bring any perpetrator to justice;
- freeze funds and other financial assets or economic resources of terrorists or of persons or entities that attempt, participate or facilitate acts of terrorism, including funds generated from property owned or controlled by them;
- refrain from supporting – also passively – terrorists in any way;
- prevent the commission of terrorist acts;
- cooperate in criminal investigations and proceedings.

Compliance is monitored by the Counter-Terrorism-Committee (CTC), to which States report on their implementation. As customary, all States on the SC are members of the CTC. The UK Ambassador to the UN, Sir Jeremy Greenstock, was appointed first Chairman of the CTC. In April 2003 the Spanish Ambassador, Inocencio Arias, succeeded him.

At the adoption of the resolution, concern was expressed regarding the lack of a "sunset clause" (the regime is in force until terminated by the SC) and of a definition of terrorism. Though the regime is abstract and could potentially affect a large number of individuals, it was generally regarded as adequately focused. In general, the initial reaction to the resolution was quite positive. This was due, on the one hand, to the fact that the resolution relied on language of existing UN-Conventions on terrorism, and, on the other, to the sincere commitment to counter-terrorism worldwide shortly after September 2001.

Since the adoption of the resolution, the main point of concern is the possibility to misuse the resolution to justify measures against individuals for political reasons unrelated to terrorism, including violations of human rights. In the past 18 months, some governments have been accused of manipulating the fight against terrorism to fit their political agenda. SG Kofi Annan has repeatedly warned about the grave consequences of such misuse. The SC and the CTC, however, have so far not suggested any remedies to address this problem.

b) Security Council Resolution 1267

Instituted in late 1999 by SC-Res. 1267,[10] the sanctions regime against Afghanistan was amended several times by SC-Res. 1333,[11] 1363,[12] 1388,[13] 1390,[14] 1452[15] and 1455.[16] Originally consisting of a limited air-travel ban and a limited freeze of funds of the Taliban, SC-Res. 1333 added an arms embargo, a travel ban against senior Taliban officials, the closure of Taliban representations and Ariana Afghan Airlines offices and a freeze of all financial and economic assets of Osama bin Laden and Al Qaeda. After the positive reaction to SC-Res. 1373, the regime was amended again to extend the arms embargo and refine the sanctions against high-ranking Taliban and members of Al Qaeda and their supporters.

Today, the main operative tool is the Committee's regularly updated "comprehensive list" of persons or entities. Every SC-Member can request the addition of a person or an entity to the list. In May 2003 the list comprised 355 names of individuals and entities.

Compliance with the 1267-regime is monitored by a special group of experts, the "Monitoring Group" established by SC-Res. 1363. In the past two years the Group has entered into contact with the authorities of many UN-Members to directly discuss the implementation of the sanctions. The Group also established close relations with the international institutions active in the field. It regularly reports to the 1267-Committee on the status of implementation and makes recommendations to strengthen the regime. States are also required to report on their efforts to implement the resolutions. Recently, SC-Res. 1455 renewed this reporting requirement and requested the Committee to identify uncooperative States to the SC.

The transformation of the 1267-regime mirrors the difficult efforts of the SC to address criticism related to UN-sanctions. After the initial sanctions were considered too broad, they were refined to a degree that they are now directed against individual persons or entities. Never before had the SC adopted such precisely targeted sanctions. Ironically, the efforts to avoid targeting innocent individuals resulted in new grave legal and humanitarian problems.

The most worrisome aspect of the 1267-regime is undoubtedly the lack of legal remedies for the individuals concerned. In implementing sanctions against individuals and entities, States rely on the Committee's list. The 1267-Committee does not give reasons for the inclusion on the list and does not foresee a right to appeal the decision. Under the absolute obligation to implement the resolutions, States are domestically unable to guarantee due process and procedural rights to the persons and entities affected. Protests by States and human rights organizations lead to the adoption of new Guidelines for the 1267-Committee on 7 November 2002 that foresee a de-listing procedure. This enables States of residence or citizenship to request review of the case in the Committee: The requesting State is invited to consult with the State that had originally designated the inclusion in the list and, ideally, submit a joint de-listing request to the Committee. It can also submit a request alone. The Committee decides by no-objection procedure. If that fails, it passes the case on to the SC. Though an improvement, it is clear that the de-listing procedure does not change the legal position of the individuals and entities concerned.

A second problem has now been largely resolved. The original regime had required States to freeze all financial assets of the individuals on the list without exception. As a consequence, the individuals were unable to meet their primary needs and States were obliged to provide humanitarian assistance to them. This could be interpreted as assisting the individuals – an act prohibited by the resolutions. With SC-Res. 1452 States can now exempt financial assets and economic resources deemed necessary for basic expenses after prior notification to the 1267-Committee and in the absence of a negative decision by the Committee within 48 hours.

4. The regimes in practice

Implementation of SC-resolutions has been a central concern at the UN for years. The SC-committees lack financial resources, personnel and technical equipment. The working methods, which require adoption of decisions by consensus, translation in 6 UN-languages and a cumbersome documentation process, are tedious and inflexible. In most cases the Committees rely on States to submit reports on the implementation. Often States do not submit a report or merely state that they have fulfilled the resolution. Both counter-terrorism-regimes are equipped with mechanisms to examine the reports and follow up on the States' claims. Their practice so far indicates a superior performance in comparison to other sanctions regimes.

a) **Security Council Resolution 1373**

In its first 18 months the CTC received 343 reports and sent out 243 detailed letters with follow-up questions.[17] Mid-May 2003, with the submission of the report of Sao Tomé and Príncipe, all 191 UN-Member States had submitted a first, 141 a second and 29 a third report. No sanctions regime in the history of the UN has had such a high rate of response.

The number of reports obviously says little about their content. But the CTC has developed a meticulous approach, in which every report is examined by independent experts and is subject to follow-up questions. To avoid an early classification in complying and non-complying States, the CTC conducts a continuous dialogue with each State on improving the latter's counter-terrorism capacity. Even a State that cooperates dutifully is never deemed to be "fully compliant". On the other hand, a State that does not cooperate is publicly reported to the SC ("name and shame"-procedure).

Due to their sensitive nature, there is little information on acts of national authorities. Reliable data is mainly available in the form of legislative acts: Almost all States have reported initiatives to adopt or amend national legislation and to accede to terrorism-treaties. In September 2001 only 2 States were party to all 12 UN Terrorism Conventions. In early May 2003 there were 31. The number of parties to the Convention for the Suppression of the Financing of Terrorism has risen from 4 States to 84.[18]

Among the reasons for the CTC's impressive results are the highly appreciated policy of maximum transparency, the serious work of the CTC-experts, the unrelenting pressure by the CTC-chairman and the recognition that some States may require assistance in implementing SC-Res. 1373.[19] The UN itself offers assistance through the Office on Drugs and Crime (ODC) in Vienna, which launched its Global Programme against Terrorism in October 2002 to support the work of the CTC. As a result, no State can justify non-compliance by inability.

The main reason for the CTC's success, however, is the real willingness to cooperate on the part of the vast majority of States. Terrorism is still seen as a menacing threat and the CTC with its cautious, non-confrontational approach and its avoidance of controversial issues, such as human rights, defining terrorism and listing "terrorist groups", which, in any case, could not be resolved by the committee, is considered an efficient instrument. By mid 2003, the CTC managed to establish itself as the global coordinating body in multilateral counter-terrorism. It organized meetings with all specialized institutions in the field to promote best practices, codes and standards and to improve international cooperation.[20] The importance of the CTC was stressed by SC-Res. 1377[21] and 1456,[22] both adopted at SC-meetings on ministerial level. This overwhelming support is certainly remarkable, considering that SC-Res. 1373 is, to date, the UN's most comprehensive intrusion into the domestic affairs of its Member States.

b) Security Council Resolution 1267

While the CTC has – so far – concentrated on its continuing dialogue with the States, the 1267-Committee has entrusted its Monitoring Group to visit and consult directly with relevant national authorities and international institutions. The Group has so far produced three reports, which extensively document the attempts of States to implement the resolutions, instances of non-compliance, inadequacies of the resolutions and the impact on Al Qaeda.[23] The 3rd report of the Group indicates that more than 160 States had adopted new measures to combat the financing of terrorism by 2002. In May 2003, the USA declared that the 1267-regime had resulted in a freeze of $ 134 million, $ 98 million of these outside the US.[24] The reports also show the extent of international cooperation in various fora around the world.

On the whole, the Monitoring Group's reports have reflected the impact of the 1267-regime in terms of reducing the operational capability of Al Qaeda. The freeze on financial and economic assets has disrupted Al Qaeda's financial support and forced it to move its finances and find alternative funding methods. On the other hand, the Group also identified a number of inadequacies and problems of the 1267-regime:

- States are not proactive enough in submitting information to the 1267-Committee.
- Al Qaeda has developed new financing methods that are difficult to identify.
- The travel ban is not configured to counter a global terrorist network. Lacking the minimum required identifiers, the 1267-list is not being fully applied by some States.
- The arms embargo is ineffective because national authorities have technical difficulties in implementing an embargo against individuals and entities.

On the whole, the Monitoring Group's activities and reports are effective because direct contact between national authorities and the Group's experts permits clearer evaluation of the implementation of the resolutions. Due to the limited resources of the Group, the regime, however, becomes dependent on the proactive cooperation of all States, especially by the States not directly contacted by the Group. Reporting requirements, introduced by SC-Res. 1390, were initially not very effective.[25] Recently, after SC-Res. 1455 renewed and enhanced the obligations and guidelines were issued by the 1267-Committee, States are beginning to report in a more satisfactory manner.

5. The future

As the regimes evolve, the question of the SC's reaction to qualitative differences in implementation arises. If non-compliance is not sanctioned, States will not invest in cooperation. In the past, the SC has shown profound hesitancy towards enforcement of sanctions, either for political or conceptual reasons. In the long term, inertia by the SC could significantly weaken the counter-terrorism regimes.

On the other hand, it is necessary to bear in mind the unity and resolve among the P5 on counter-terrorism, which enabled the establishment of the regimes in the first place. In cases of sustained non-compliance, this environment could eventually lead to coercive enforcement measures. Obviously, however, "unity and resolve" in international relations are early casualties of political developments. The discord in the SC in 2003 on how to proceed with the Iraq-issue severely undermined the unity in the Council. For both sides of the dispute, as well as for world public opinion, the SC had failed – either to endorse the military operation or to prevent war. For some, the Iraq crisis even marked the end of the UN's system of international security, with dire consequences also for technical issues such as terrorism.[26]

It is true that, in March and April 2003, the deterioration of relations between SC-Members threatened to affect other areas of work at the UN. An examination of the SC's work on the various regional and technical items on its agenda from January to June 2003 did not, however, identify any significant cases of lasting negative consequences. According to experts in the SC and the UN-Secretariat, even during the height of the military conflict in Iraq, the bilateral and multilateral work in the Council, including the counter-terrorism work in both committees, was not negatively affected. In early May 2003, US Ambassador Negroponte stated in a public SC-debate on the CTC: "Clearly, with resolution 1373 (2001) the Security Council got something right."[27]

It appears therefore, that the Iraq-crisis, at least in the short term, has not negatively affected the SC's counter-terrorism work. In the current climate of desperate harmony in the SC, it is likely that the P5 will continue their cooperation on terrorism: Few issues are equally not contentious among them. It remains to be seen, however, whether the unity on the issue in principle is strong enough to enable effective, fair and unpoliticized enforcement. Though the general political climate may not have affected the counter-terrorism work at the UN, it does not seem to favor a breakthrough in the field of enforcement of resolutions.

The current discussions in the SC on how to increase the monitoring capabilities of the counter-terrorism regimes show the difficulties involved. Regarding the 1373-regime, some Members on the SC have begun pressing for inspections ("site visits") by CTC experts to the Member States. Reluctance on the part of some SC-Members could result in a first phase in which States are only inspected if they agree. The 1267-Chairman is studying possibilities to visit a large number of States himself to promote implementation and cooperation. While these measures can induce States to address the various issues, it is doubtful whether they are adequate to ensure full compliance with the regimes.

Other means to improve the regime's effectivity and long-term viability should be explored. Considering the limited resources at the UN, fusing the two regimes into a large, central counter-terrorism body could be advantageous. The result could be an "UNMOVIC-like" commission of the SC with independent experts competent to investigate compliance in each State. To ensure acceptance at the UN, such an intrusive regime would presumably have to be complemented by a political and a technical process: political, by providing for a possibility to discuss the issue of armed struggle for self-determination, for example in the GA or at an international conference; technical, by substantially strengthening the UN's ability to assist States in implementing the obligations, for instance by making best use of the ODC's Global Programme against Terrorism.

6. Conclusion

To a large extent, the UN has justified its central role in the international fight against terrorism. It has been successful in initiating the multilateral process and keeping the issue high on the international agenda. The UN brought – what few other organizations could do – a sense of legitimacy and urgency to the multilateral efforts. The past two years have witnessed a substantial increase in national counter-terrorism activity, international cooperation and the recognition of the central coordinating role of the UN.

The global acceptance of the SC's counter-terrorism work has also benefited the UN itself. By UN standards, the regimes perform well. They demonstrate that the SC can act quickly and effectively when the P5 agree and that disagreement on other issues does not impede cooperation on terrorism. The counter-terrorism resolutions have also invigorated the sanctions-debate at the UN. They have undoubtedly reinforced the shift from general to targeted sanctions. The Council, though still only rudimentarily, has begun taking note of the effects of sanctions on the rights of individuals. All the more, NGOs and States have to continue confronting the Council Members with the negative consequences of the regimes.

A series of problems, however, need to be addressed. The SC deals with terrorism without a definition of the term. The ensuing legal uncertainty can be exploited for political reasons. In the GA, the broad efforts to address the root causes for terrorism must be brought into clearer focus. In particular, tolerance, the value of human life and good representative governance must be promoted more effectively. The SC should review whether the continuation of two regimes is still warranted. It must soon address the question of enforcement or risk losing the existing momentum as well as the broad international support.

Notes

1 SC-Res. 1267 (1999); S/RES/1267 (1999) of 15 October 1999.

2 The UN should dissuade potential terrorists from embracing terrorism, deny them the means to commit terrorist acts and sustain international cooperation. Report of the Policy Working Group; A/57/273, S/2002/875, para. 9.

3 4734th Meeting of the Security Council, on 4 April 2003; S/PV.4734 (provisional), p. 3. Referring to the global coalition that had been established Greenstock emphasized a month later "how uniquely placed the United Nations is to support and facilitate a global approach of that kind."; 4752nd Meeting of the SC on 6 May 2003; S/PV.4752 (provisional), p. 5.

4 4752nd Meeting of the SC on 6 May 2003; S/PV.4752 (provisional), p. 9.

5 GA-Res. 49/60 adopted a Declaration on Measures to Eliminate International Terrorism; A/RES/49/60 of 17 February 1995. The Declaration was reaffirmed and supplemented by GA-Res. 51/210; A/RES/51/210 of 16 January 1997.

6 The Vienna UN Office on Drugs and Crime (ODC) has been dealing with terrorism since 1999. In 2001 the Commission on Crime Prevention and Criminal Justice elaborated a Plan of Action against Terrorism subsequently adopted by the GA; A/RES/56/261 of 15 April 2002.

7 S/RES/1368 (2001) of 12 September 2001.

8 SC-Res. 1368 was not formally based on Chapter VII of the UN Charter and it contained no explicit authorization of force. However, it qualified the attacks as a "threat to international peace" and contained a reference to Chapter VII and to the "inherent right to individual or collective self-defense". Understood by many as political authorization of countermeasures including force, the resolution was lauded as both pragmatic and novel: Pragmatic, because it was obvious that the USA would resort to countermeasures and it was preferable from the UN-point of view that the USA did so with UN-backing. It was novel because the right to self-defense had so far only been recognized in cases of an attack from a State or with involvement by a State.

9 S/RES/1373 (2001) of 28 September 2001.

10 S/RES/1267 (1999) of 15 October 1999.

11 S/RES/1333 (2000) of 19 December 2000.

12 S/RES/1363 (2001) of 30 July 2001.

13 S/RES/1388 (2002) of 15 January 2002.

14 S/RES/1390 (2002) of 28 January 2002.

15 S/RES/1452 (2002) of 20 December 2002.

16 S/RES/1455 (2003) of 17 January 2003.

17 Briefing by CTC Chairman Ambassador Greenstock at the 4734th Meeting of the Security Council, on 4 April 2003; S/PV.4734 (provisional), p. 3.

18 Other counter-terrorism conventions also benefited from a surge in ratifications: The number of parties to the Terrorist Bombings Convention rose from 29 to 96.

19 The CTC currently has two experts devoted entirely to helping States find appropriate organizations to assist implementing SC-Res. 1373.

20 The conference on 6 March 2003 adopted a provisional action plan clearly according the central coordinating role to the CTC; S/AC.40/2003/SM.1/6/Rev.1 of 3 April 2003.

21 S/RES/1377 (2001) of 12 November 2001.

22 S/RES/1456 (2003) of 20 January 2003.

23 First Report: S/2002/541 of 29 April 2002; Second Report: S/2002/1050 Rev. 1 of 8 January 2003, Third Report: S/2002/1338 of 4 December 2002.

24 4752nd Meeting of the SC on 6 May 2003; S/PV.4752 (provisional), p. 5.

25 Almost one year after the adoption SC-Res. 1390 only 80 States had submitted a report, many of which were not detailed; see the Report of the 1267-Committee, S/2002/1423 of 26 December 2002, p. 10.

26 Glennon, 'Why the Security Council Failed', *Foreign Affairs* 82 (2003), Number 3 (May/June), 16-35 at 34.

27 4752nd Meeting of the SC on 6 May 2003; S/PV.4752, provisional, p. 5.

Remarks by Albert Straver*

The fight against terrorism and its financing: freezing measures imposed by the European Community

The terrorist attacks of 11 September 2001 on targets in New York and Washington, DC, shocked the world and elicited a particularly strong expression of sympathy on the EU side. On 21 September 2001, the European Council stated:

> "The European Council is totally supportive of the American people in the face of the deadly terrorist attacks. These attacks are an assault on our open, democratic, tolerant and multi-cultural societies. They are a challenge to the conscience of each human being. The European Union will co-operate with the United States in bringing to justice and punishing the perpetrators, sponsors and accomplices of such barbaric acts. On the basis of Security Council Resolution 1368, a riposte by the US is legitimate."

These attacks also provoked a more policy-oriented reaction: on 28 September 2001, the UN Security Council adopted its Resolution 1373(2001), which foresees a large number of measures and is based on Chapter VII of the UN Charter, a chapter which grants special powers to the Security Council to preserve and restore international peace. The EU Member States have implemented it, both at EU level and at national level.

This report analyses the implementation of the freezing measures foreseen by paragraph 1 – and in particular by points (c) and (d) thereof – of Resolution 1373 (2001) and addresses some of the issues that have arisen. It does not address the implementation of other measures foreseen by Resolution 1373, even if at EU level some activity has taken place to co-ordinate or promote implementation.[1]

CFSP and freezing measures

Resolutions 1368 (2001), which condemns the terrorist attacks of 11 September 2001, and 1373 (2001) were not the first UN Security Council Resolutions on terrorism[2] but their impact on the EU has been considerably greater than that of their pre-

* The author works in Unit A.2 "Legal and institutional matters for external relations. Sanctions" of DG External Relations of the European Commission as Administrator responsible for sanctions legislation. The views expressed are purely those of the author and may not in any circumstances be regarded as stating an official position of the European Commission.

decessors. As Resolution 1373 formally characterises terrorism as a threat to international peace, the EU could rely on it to take new initiatives in the framework of the Common Foreign and Security Policy (CFSP). The freezing measures were discussed and developed in that framework, at the instigation of the Commission, which made a first proposal for such measures on 2 October 2001.[3]

For several years freezing measures have been used as an instrument to attain the objectives of the CFSP. The creation of CFSP, which took place by means of the 1992 Treaty of Maastricht, coincided in time with the liberalisation of capital movements and of payments. For this reason, the EC Treaty makes, in its Article 60, specific provision for (urgent) restrictions on the movement of capital and on payments as regards third countries, while, in its Article 301, providing for general powers to interrupt or to reduce economic relations with third countries, if such action is provided for in a CFSP Common Position or Joint Action. On the basis of these Articles freezing measures were imposed on the leadership of the Federal Republic of Yugoslavia[4] (now Serbia-Montenegro), Myanmar,[5] Afghanistan (Taliban regime)[6] and Zimbabwe,[7] as well as on UNITA of Angola.[8] The recent freezing measures targeting the former regime of Iraq[9] also fall in this category.

The Commission initiative concerning the implementation of UN Security Council Resolution 1373(2001), which was a proposal to use similar measures in the fight against terrorism, was discussed in Council. The proposal to have the Community implement the freezing measures foreseen by Resolution 1373(2001) soon proved one that was not without problems. A major hurdle was the legal base for Community action. Some argued that Articles 60 and 301 of the EC Treaty were not sufficient as a legal base, because the Community's powers were limited to interrupting or to reducing economic relations with one or more third countries. Indeed, if construed in a restrictive manner, terrorist groups can not be assimilated with a country, and hence an additional legal base had to be added. On this basis, agreement was reached on a Regulation based on Articles 60, 301 and 308.[10]

Common Position 2001/931/CFSP of 27 December 2001 provides a basis for action under Articles 60 and 301 of the EC Treaty. Further to this CFSP act, Council Regulation (EC) No 2580/2001 of the same date, implements the freezing measures foreseen by paragraph 1 of Resolution 1373(2001). Together with the more recent Regulation (EC) No 881/2002, which has the same, triple legal base and implements freezing measures targeting the Al Qaeda network and the Taliban, this Regulation provides a basis for action against the financing of terrorism and financial operations of terrorist persons, groups and entities.

However, the legal base of these Regulations imposes certain restrictions on the range of persons, groups and entities that may be hit by the freezing measures. In fact, the Council has reached the conclusion that the freezing measures of Regulation (EC) No 2580/2001 should only target groups which are either linked or related to third countries, or otherwise the focus of the CFSP. This means that freezing measures targeting entirely internal groups and their members cannot be imposed by the Community. This important restriction does not mean that the EU is unable to present a list of such internal groups to third countries. Within the EU, Member States such as Spain and the UK have had to deal with terrorist groups for quite some time. Common Position 2001/931/CFSP not only foresees freezing measures, but also police and judicial co-operation with other Member States. To that end, the Council identifies both external and internal groups in the list attached to this Common Position.[11]

THE MAIN FEATURES OF THE FREEZING MEASURES

The Regulations contain a far-reaching order to freeze the funds and economic resources of a number of persons, groups and entities. Although intended to curtail the financing of terrorism and the financial operations of terrorist groups, the definitions of funds and economic resources cover all assets, i.e. all property. As the Regulations are directly applicable in all Member States of the EU, the statutory obligation to freeze certain funds and economic resources and to abstain from making funds and economic resources available to certain persons, groups and entities requires action by financial institutions, companies and citizens of the EU. Since the freezing measures do not affect relations with only one or two specific countries, these obligations represent a considerable burden: after all, in order to apply them correctly, all transactions should be checked, whatever the country of destination.

For some time the European credit sector has asked for a consolidated list of all persons, groups and entities whose funds and economic resources have to be frozen. They have also given their views on other aspects of the Regulations, such as the absence of liability for freezing in good faith, and the exceptions that should be foreseen. This feedback is most welcome, since it can be drawn upon to improve the wording of the Regulations so as to make them more effective and clearer.

Of course, the application of the Regulations is not the sole responsibility of the private sector. As is usual in the Community, national authorities have a major role to play in overseeing the application of the Regulations and in taking action against breaches of the freezing measures. The Commission and each of the Member States have the possibility to take a Member State to Court, if it fails to take the necessary actions to enforce the Regulations. This possibility makes the freezing measures enacted by the Community somewhat more robust than measures merely enacted at national level. Member States also have to decide on requests for exceptions or, where Regulation (EC) No 881/2002 applies, present them to the UN.

Another positive element is that Member States undertake to exchange information with each other and with the Commission. The Regulations foresee that the private sector must provide "any information which would facilitate compliance" with the Regulations to the authorities. If correctly applied, the exchanges of information will facilitate the application of the freezing measures by all concerned.

A major element of the Regulations are the lists of persons, groups and entities whose funds or economic resources have to be frozen. Regulation (EC) No 881/2002 applies to a list established by a Committee of the UN Security Council and targets the Al Qaeda network. Regulation (EC) No 2580/2001, however, applies to a list established by the EU further to Common Position 2001/931/CFSP. In both cases, the listing process falls outside the area of activity of the Community. Indeed, Common Position 2001/931/CFSP uses the definition of terrorist act agreed for the purpose of police and judicial co-operation[12] and comprises references to prosecution and condemnation for terrorist acts. The list is established by Council on the basis of input from the Member States and third countries. Decisions are made by unanimity of the Member States.

The EU list constitutes a tool with tremendous potential, but the number of entries continues to be rather small. This could be attributed to the rather strict criteria applied by the Council and to the existence of a UN list concerning the Al Qaeda network.

Some legal issues

(a) relationship with judicial and police action

Where freezing measures are imposed against the leadership of a third country, the police and judicial authorities will normally not be engaged in criminal procedures against the persons concerned. In relation to terrorism and its financing criminal procedures are clearly more likely, especially if the persons concerned are living in the EU. Common Position 2001/931/CFSP explicitly recognises that such procedures provide a basis for listing which results in application of freezing measures and police and judicial co-operation between Member States.

The freezing measures have less of an impact than confiscation in the framework of a criminal procedure. In this regard they go less far than orders of judicial authorities, which may also comprise confiscation[13]. As the freezing measures imposed by means of an EC Regulation are directly applicable in all Member States and are obligatory for the private sector, these measures constitute a powerful tool in the fight against the financing of terrorism.

Unlike what is usual in criminal procedures, the listing process does not provide the persons, groups and entities concerned with any particular role. In order for freezing measures to have the largest possible impact, it is not suitable to hear these persons prior to the imposition of the measures. More often than not they will not be present in the territory of the EU when the decision is made, which renders it not practicable to hear them before the decision is made.

Of course, the interrelationship between freezing measures and criminal procedures was addressed, but not in great detail, when the freezing measures were imposed. The Regulations, which take precedence over conflicting national laws and regulations are not explicit on this point, but it is self-evident that the freezing measures are not intended to impair the execution of confiscation orders issued in criminal procedures of the Member States against persons whose funds and economic resources are frozen pursuant to the Regulations. As criminal procedures provide a basis for decisions concerning listing of persons, groups and entities whose funds and economic resources have to be frozen, the freezing measures merely constitute an additional, essentially administrative tool. As a result, they should not be invoked as an excuse for not using or not developing traditional criminal law instruments, such as recognition and execution of judicial freezing orders.

(b) limitations of freezing measures

As stated above, the Regulations imposing freezing measures do not apply to any person, group or entity thought to engage in acts of terrorism which is deemed to be internal to the EU or the financing of such terrorism. Only persons and groups which are linked or related to third countries are targets of the freezing measures. This result must be attributed in its entirety to the interpretation of Articles 60 and 301 of the EC Treaty.

The provisions of the Treaty reflect that a foreign policy is not a policy regulating relations between the constituent parts of the EU. In the fight against terrorism this approach proved an impediment to action by the Community against most of the terrorist persons, groups and entities in its own territory. One may conclude from this that the fight against terrorism is as such not a task for the Community.

However, if it is deemed desirable that the Community imposes freezing measures targeting persons, groups and entities engaging in terrorism which is deemed to be internal to the EU, this can only be obtained by an amendment of the EC Treaty.

(c) protection of fundamental rights

When discussing freezing measures in Autumn 2001, the Council reached the conclusion that exceptions to the freezing measures were appropriate in certain cases. The exceptions should in particular ensure that natural persons in the Community whose funds and economic resources are frozen, are still able to satisfy their essential human needs and those of their family.

In its Articles 5 and 6 Regulation (EC) No 2580/2001 makes explicit provision for exceptions on this point. The subsequent Regulation (EC) No 881/2002, adopted in May 2002 and targeting the Al Qaeda network, did not do so, since the exceptions foreseen by Regulation (EC) No 2580/2001 were not found in the UN Security Council Resolution 1390(2002) which constitutes the basis of the freezing measures targeting Al Qaeda. The non-inclusion of exceptions in the Regulation confirms that, in the EU, Resolutions imposing sanctions based on Chapter VII of the UN Charter are considered mandatory instructions to the Member States.

Subsequently, the Council has made provision for certain exceptions to the freezing measures in March 2003. Regulation (EC) No 561/2003[14] amends Regulation (EC) No 881/2002 to that end. The amendment brings Regulation (EC) No 881/2002 in line with Resolution 1452 (2002) of the UN Security Council. That Resolution was adopted at the instigation of the EU working in close concertation with the USA.

Some may wonder why the EU attaches so much importance to this issue. It would be too simple to attribute this to general concerns about protection of human rights only, since there is another major factor. In October 2001, some persons living in Sweden were put on the UN list of Taliban and Al Qaeda related targets. This decision was implemented by means of a Commission Regulation amending the list of targeted persons, groups and entities attached to Regulation (EC) No 467/2001. This UN decision and the subsequent freezing measure are reported to have caused a very negative reaction among the Swedish public. This reaction was also taken up in the European Parliament, which reminded that the right to life had to be respected in all circumstances, in its opinion on the draft text of Regulation (EC) No 881/2002.

The persons living in Sweden have lodged appeals in the Court of First Instance. Some other persons included in the lists of persons, groups and entities have also done so.[15] The right to lodge an appeal against freezing measures should be granted to persons, groups and entities whose funds and economic resources have to be frozen pursuant to Regulations (EC) No 2580/2001 and No 881/2002, since they are clearly directly and individually concerned.[16] However, since listing is a process that takes place in the UN or the CFSP framework, it should be noted that the Court's jurisdiction does not extend to the UN and the CFSP. Therefore, it remains to be seen to what extent the Court will review whether the listing process meets the criteria laid down in a CFSP Common Position or whether that process respects e.g. the rights of defence. The Court of First Instance has rejected the requests for interim measures made in the case of the persons living in Sweden (7 May 2002 [17]) and in the case of a person living in the Netherlands (15 May 2003 [18]). The Court's judgement on the main submissions in all cases before it is still being awaited. The appeals touch upon a number of questions, including respect for the rights of defence and other fundamental rights.

(d) Impact on EC procedures

As stated above, the legal base for the imposition of freezing measures to fight international terrorism and its financing proved somewhat problematic. The triple legal base – Articles 60, 301 and 308 of the EC Treaty – guarantees the European Parliament a role in this matter. Contrary to what is usual for CFSP-related restrictive measures, the EP has to be consulted on any amendment of the Regulations (except where the Commission or the Council is empowered to enact the amendment as is the case of amendments to the list of persons, groups and entities whose funds and economic resources have to be frozen). Article III-219 of the draft Constitution shows that in future the European Parliament will be informed of restrictive measures, but need not be consulted on them.

Another feature of the freezing measures concerns the role of the Commission. In fact, the Council has decided that, in view of the specific circumstances, it should reserve the right to make decisions on the list of persons, groups and entities whose funds and economic resources have to be frozen pursuant to Regulation (EC) No 2580/2001. As a result, the list is decided in the framework of the CFSP and, contrary to what is usual for Community legislation, decision-making on that list does not require any intervention of the Commission.

Concluding remarks

The attacks on US interests of 11 September 2001 and the subsequent adoption of Resolutions 1373(2001) and 1390(2002) have prompted new activity within the framework of the EU's Common Foreign and Security Policy. The fight against terrorism and against the financing of terrorism has become part of this policy and as a result the Community was able to adopt legislation on the freezing of funds and economic resources, which makes an exception to the freedom of capital movements and payments guaranteed by Article 56 of the EC Treaty. The procedure foreseen by Articles 60 and 301 of the Treaty allows expeditious adoption of the necessary Regulations, but in the present case an additional legal base and a less expeditious procedure had to be used since terrorists and terrorist groups do not qualify as countries. The mere fact that this proved necessary, illustrates that, back in 1992 when these Articles were inserted in the EC Treaty, nobody foresaw that a Common Foreign and Security Policy should also include restrictive measures targeting international terrorism.

The new activity in the CFSP framework should not, of course, preclude further development of traditional instruments in the field of criminal law. The mere impossibility of imposing freezing measures on terrorist groups that are deemed internal to the EU, confirms that action by the Community needs to be supplemented by action at national level. In addition, criminal investigations by the authorities, judicial and police co-operation, including extradition arrangements, will continue to be necessary to bring terrorists to trial and have them sentenced. At European level, work in the area of what is known as Justice and Home Affairs has increased considerably since 11 September 2001. Most of the work concerns co-operation between Member States of the EU. However, the conclusion of an agreement with the USA may well mark the beginning of a new phase in this regard, consisting of making EU arrangements with third countries for judicial and police co-operation.

The use of instruments designed to deal with the leadership of third countries and CFSP-related procedures has given rise to discussion about protection of fundamental rights of those subject to freezing measures. Like the Council of the EU, the Security Council of the United Nations is, of course, not meant to be a court of law and, therefore, its procedures are not those of a court of law. Both Councils have, nevertheless, taken up the task of establishing a list of persons, groups and entities suspected of involvement in terrorism and its financing.

In the EU, a number of cases are pending in the Court of First Instance and a decision on the procedural safeguards that should apply and the extent to which fundamental rights have to be respected will be made in a not too distant future. Since international treaties guarantee a number of rights, such as the right to life and the right to a fair trial (or due process), further reflection on the procedures that should apply could also be appropriate at UN level, even if the Court of First Instance lacks jurisdiction to review the validity of acts of the UN Security Council.

In this regard, one should also take into account that the freezing of funds and economic resources – which constitutes an exception to the freedom of capital movement and payments – is often presented as a tool for administrative control. Of course, such administrative controls need not be equated by default with charging a person with a criminal offence or imposition of a punishment for committing a criminal offence.

Notes

1 See e.g. Common Position 2001/930/CFSP (OJ L 344, 28.12.2001, p. 90) and Commission Staff Working Paper on Actions to combat the Financing of Terrorism adopted on 28 March 2003, reference No SEC (2003)414.

2 See e.g. Resolutions 1189 (1998) and 1269 (1999).

3 Proposal COM (2001) 569. See also amended proposal COM (2001)713 of 30 November 2001.

4 Regulation (EC) No 2488/2000, OJ L 287, 14 November 2000, p. 19, as amended.

5 Regulation (EC) No 1081/2000, OJ L 122, 24 May 2000, p. 29, as amended.

6 Regulation (EC) No 467/2001, OJ L 67, 9 March 2001, p. 1. Repealed by Regulation (EC) No 881/2002 (OJ L 139, 29 May 2002, p. 9).

7 Regulation (EC) No 310/2002, OJ L 50, 21 February 2002, p. 4, as amended.

8 Regulation (EC) No 1705/1998, OJ L 215 of 1 August 1998, p. 1. Repealed by Regulation (EC) No 146/2003 (OJ L 24 , 29 January 2003, p. 1).

9 Regulation (EC) No 1210/2003, OJ L 169, 8 July 2003, p. 6.

10 The draft Constitution prepared by the European Convention on the Future of Europe, makes explicit provision for this situation in Article III-219(2).

11 See for the latest list Common Position 2003/482/CFSP, OJ L 160, 28 June 2003, p. 100.

12 See Council Framework Decision 2002/475/JHA, OJ L 164, 22 June 2002, p. 3.

13 Council Framework Decision 2003/577/JHA, OJ L 196, 2 August 2003, p. 45, establishes the rules on recognition and execution of freezing orders issued by a judicial authority of any of the Member States in other EU Member States.

14 OJ L 82, 29 March 2003, p. 1.

15 See e.g. Cases T-306/01, *A. Aden et al.* v. *Council*, T-315/01, *Y.A. Kadi* v. *Council and Commission*, T-253/02, *Chafiq Ayadi* v. *Council*, and, as regards the EU list, T-338/02, *SEGI et al.* v. *Council* and T-47/03, *J.M. Sison* v. *Council*.

16 This requirement is laid down in Article 230 of the EC Treaty.

17 Case T-306/01 R, *A. Aden et al.* v. *Council*.

18 Case T-47/03 R, *J.M. Sison* v. *Council*.

Remarks by Himamuali Das*

Challenges of US domestic implementation: to list or not to list? Summary

1. UN framework to curb terrorist financing

The UN Security Council established a Sanctions Committee ('1267 Committee') under UN Security Council Resolution 1267 as a subsidiary organ to the Security Council to oversee certain aspects of implementation of the sanctions against the Taliban and to designate individuals and entities ('persons') whose assets UN Member States are required to freeze. A series of resolutions – UNSCRs 1333, 1390, 1452, and 1455 – expanded the 1267 Committee's mandate and broadened the scope of the sanctions to include members of the Al Qaeda organization and Osama bin Laden, and other individuals, groups, undertakings and entities associated with them, as well as the measures to which those persons are subject. Once an individual or entity has been included on the 1267 Committee's consolidated list, each Member State has an obligation under Chapter VII of the UN Charter to take certain steps with respect to that person, including by freezing its funds and other financial assets or economic resources.

The Guidelines of the 1267 Committee provide that the Committee will 'update regularly' its consolidated list.[1] A proposal submitted to the Committee to request an addition to the list 'should … include, to the extent possible, a narrative description of the information that forms the basis or justification for taking action' under the relevant resolutions, as well as adequate information to 'facilitate their identification by competent authorities.' The Committee is required to consider 'expeditiously requests to update the list' on the basis of relevant information received by the Committee. The Committee reaches decisions by consensus of its members, based on bilateral exchanges between interested Member States to clarify any issues prior to a decision, under a 48-hour no-objection procedures. Members of the committee are permitted to

* The author is currently an attorney-adviser for economic and business affairs in the Office of the Legal Adviser, US Department of State. The views expressed herein are the author's own and are not necessarily the views of the United States government or the Department of State.

indicate any objection they might have to a proposed decision within two working days. Under this process, as amended, the 1267 Committee has designated 335 individuals and entities since its inception.

The Security Council has also adopted UN Security Council Resolution 1373 on 28 September 2001. A far-reaching measure that aims at limiting the ability of terrorists and terrorist organizations to operate internationally, UNSCR 1373 requires Member States to prevent and suppress the financing of terrorism and to criminalize the willful provision or collection of funds with the intention that the funds should be used, or in the knowledge that they are to be used, in order to carry out terrorist acts. The Resolution also requires that Member States freeze the funds and other financial assets and economic resources of persons who commit, or attempt to commit, terrorist acts or participate in or facilitate the commission of terrorist acts. Unlike UNSCRs 1267, 1390, and 1455, the Counter-Terrorism Committee established by UNSCR 1373 does not have the authority to create a list of persons to which the measures imposed by that Resolution apply.

To facilitate the implementation of these resolutions, the Security Council also excluded from the scope of those provisions of UNSCRs 1267 and 1390 that froze the assets of Taliban-, Al Qaeda-, Osama bin Laden-linked entities assets necessary for basic expenses or for the payment of reasonable professional fees, as well as extraordinary expenses if notified and approved by the 1267 Committee. UN Security Council 1452 also urged UN Member States to take full account of the considerations set forth in that Resolution in States' implementation of UNSCR 1373.

2. US IMPLEMENTATION OF TERRORIST FINANCING DESIGNATIONS

Against this backdrop, the United States has worked to 'combat and destroy' the 'financial underpinnings of global terrorism'[2] and has encouraged other countries to be full partners in the international efforts to combat terrorist financing by both freezing the assets of persons included on the 1267 Committee's consolidated list, as well as by requesting that the Committee include additional names on its list.

The designation of persons under US domestic laws, in accordance with either the UNSCR 1267/1390/1455 or 1373 regimes, serves purposes well beyond the narrower goal of freezing the assets of terrorists and terrorist supporters and making those assets unavailable to terrorists. In addition to disrupting the flow of terrorism-linked funds, the designation of terrorism-linked persons under either US law or multilateral mechanisms fosters coalition building, encourages other governments to take action, provides a vehicle for focusing legal regimes on issues relating to combating terrorist financing, and serves an important public diplomacy tool. These designations also further law enforcement efforts, since under US law, criminal and civil penalties may be imposed against those persons subject to US jurisdiction that violate either the applicable domestic laws.

Three legal instruments are available under US law to designate and freeze the assets of persons that fall within the scope of UNSCRs 1267/1390/1455 and 1373: (1) Executive Order 12947 of 25 January 1995, as amended; (2) Executive Order 13224 of 23 September 2001, as amended; and, (3) section 219 of the Antiterrorism and Effective Death Penalty Act of 1996 (AEDPA), as amended. Both Executive Orders have similar consequences – i.e., they block the assets of persons designated in or pursuant to those orders and prohibit US persons or persons within the United States from engaging in any transaction or dealing in those assets – whereas section 219, or the Foreign Terrorist Organization (FTO) statute, has additional criminal prohibitions and visa restrictions. This paper will focus on Executive Order 13224, which is the primary vehicle used to combat terrorist financing and to fulfill its obligations to freeze the assets of persons included on the 1267 Committee's consolidated list, and some of the legal issues and judicial challenges that have arisen in the implementation of these authorities.

President Bush issued E.O. 13224 on 23 September 2001 pursuant to his authorities under the International Emergency Economic Powers Act (IEEPA) and the United Nations Participation Act (UNPA). IEEPA gives the President 'broad authority' to 'investigate, block during the pendency of investigation, regulate … prevent or prohibit …' transactions upon the declaration of a national emergency.[3] The President may declare a national emergency with respect to an unusual and extraordinary threat to the national security, foreign policy or economy of the United States.[4] Such a national emergency was declared with respect to 'grave acts of terrorism and threats of terrorism committed by foreign terrorists … and the continuing and immediate threat of further attacks on United States nationals or the United States.' Section 5 of the UNPA, 22 U.S.C. § 287c, separately authorizes the President to take 'necessary measures' to implement mandatory measures that the UN Security Council has decided pursuant to Article 41 of the UN Charter. The Executive Order, as amended, blocks the 'property and interests in property' of 29 individuals and entities listed in the Annex to the Executive Order, as well as persons designated by either the Secretary of State or the Secretary of the Treasury, as authorized by section 1 of the Executive Order.

The Secretary of State may designate, in consultation with the Secretary of the Treasury, the Attorney General, and the Secretary of Homeland Security, foreign persons that have committed, or pose a significant risk of committing, acts of terrorism that threaten the security of US nationals or the national security, foreign policy or economy of the United States.' The Secretary of the Treasury may target, in consultation with the Secretary of State, the Attorney General and the Secretary of Homeland Security, additional persons because they 'act for or on behalf of' or are 'owned or controlled by' designated terrorists or their supporters, 'assist in, sponsor, or provide … support for,' or are 'associated with' them. The Department of the Treasury's Office of Foreign Assets Control (OFAC) administers the measures imposed on persons designated under E.O. 13224 (referred to by OFAC as 'Specially Designated Global Terrorists'), including by promulgating regulations to implement the Order. Regulations promulgated by OFAC generally provide individuals or entities that have been designated by OFAC, or that have had their assets blocked by operation of the Order, to seek 'administrative reconsideration' of the decision, as well as for limited exceptions to the Order, e.g., for basic expenses or legal fees.

Notably, Executive Order 13224 does not allow for the Secretaries of State or the Treasury to designate persons on the Order solely based on the inclusion of a person on the Committee's consolidated list.[5] Rather, the designation of any person requires a decision by the appropriate Secretary that the relevant criteria specified in the Order are satisfied. The US government process for recommending that the appropriate Secretary designate a terrorist and terrorist supporter under the Order normally involves the close cooperation of the agencies specified in the Order, along with the intelligence community, the Federal Bureau of Investigation (FBI), and other agencies, with each agency bringing its separate expertise to the table. This interagency process makes every effort to ensure that individuals or entities are not designated without sufficient evidence to support the designations under the relevant criteria specified in the Executive Order and that adequate identifying information is available to ensure that US financial institutions are able to implement the blocking measures in a reasonable manner. The same review is applied for both designations initiated by the United States and for individuals and entities that other countries request the 1267 Committee to include on its consolidated list. More than 200 individuals and entities have been designated by the President in the Annex to the Order, the Secretary of State or the Secretary of the Treasury, and one person has been designated by both Secretaries.

In particular, the designation of persons under the Order potentially faces at least three different types of judicial challenges[6]: (1) whether the President or the relevant agency head has acted within his statutory authority in designating or freezing the assets of a person under IEEPA[7]; (2) a challenge to the sufficiency of the evidence; and (3) challenges based on the US Constitution.

The Administrative Procedure Act ('APA'), 5 U.S.C. § 706(2)(A), requires that an agency's action must not be 'arbitrary, capricious, an abuse of discretion, or otherwise not in accordance with the law.' The courts have generally held that the actions of the President are generally not reviewable under the APA, but that the actions of the government agencies, such as the Departments of State or the Treasury, are subject to APA review.[8] In effect, US courts review such actions to ensure that the 'agency's reasons and policy choices ... conform to certain minimal standards of rationality.' Courts, however, do not undertake their own factfinding, but rather 'must review the administrative record assembled by the agency to determine whether its decision was supported by a rational basis.' This administrative record may include both unclassified, or open source, information as well as classified intelligence materials, which may be reviewed by the court on an ex parte and in camera basis under recent amendments to the IEEPA.

In two recent cases, after reviewing the administrative records compiled through the interagency process based on an ex parte and in camera review, federal appellate courts have affirmed district court decisions that have held that the evidence in the administrative record provides sufficient evidence for the agency conclusion that the designated person fell within the scope of the criteria set forth in the Order. However, given the potential for legal challenges based on the sufficiency of the evidence, the process for designating persons under the Order can be lengthy, based on the adequacy and availability of the evidence to provide the relevant agency with a reasonable basis to designate a person under the criteria specified in the Order.

Similarly, plaintiffs could argue that their designation violates several provisions of the US Constitution. These challenges have included or could include, among others, those relating to the:

- *Bill of Attainder Clause:* A bill of attainder is 'a law that legislatively determines guilt and inflicts punishment upon an identifiable individual without provision of the protections of a judicial trial.'

- *Ex Post Facto Clause:* The Ex Post Facto clause prohibits four types of laws related to criminal action: laws that denominate an action as criminal even though the action was taken before the passing of the law and was innocent when taken; laws that change the punishment, and inflict a greater punishment; laws that aggravate a crime or make it greater than it was when committed; and laws that alter legal rules of evidence.
- *Taking without just compensation.* The Fifth Amendment prohibits the government from taking private property for public use without just compensation.
- *Unconstitutional vagueness.* Is Executive Order 13224 unconstitutionally vague because it neither defines 'associated with' nor gives sufficient notice of the type of conduct that is prohibited by the Order.
- *Due Process.* The due process clause of the 5th Amendment generally requires the government to afford notice and a meaningful opportunity to be heard before depriving a person of certain property interests.
- *Fourth Amendment.* The Fourth Amendment prohibits the unreasonable search and seizure of a person's house and effects.
- *Sixth Amendment:* The Confrontation Clause of the Sixth Amendment guarantees a defendant in a criminal prosecution the right to confront witnesses against him. Plaintiffs have argued that the government's reliance on ex parte, in camera evidence violate both the Confrontation Clause and due process rights.

To date, a number of these constitutional challenges have been rejected by the courts, either on final consideration on the merits of the case or upon a motion for a temporary or mandatory injunction.

3. Conclusion

The designation of terrorists and their supporters under Executive Order 13224 and other US domestic legal authorities, and those associated with the Taliban, members of the Al Qaeda organization, or Osama bin Laden by the 1267 Committee, provides several critical tools to combat terrorism and terrorist financing, in the freezing of assets and disrupting terrorism-linked financial flows, as well as from a law enforcement and public diplomacy perspective. In moving forward on further designations, both multilaterally and domestically, it is critical that all UN Member States, and in particular, the 1267 Committee, work bilaterally to exchange relevant information regarding requests for addition to that Committee's consolidated list, and to ensure that the appropriate legal regimes are in place to designate and freeze assets linked to persons included in that list on a timely basis.

Notes

1 Guidelines of the Committee for the Conduct of Its Work (adopted on 7 November 2002, amended on 10 April 2003), <http://www.un.org/Docs/sc/committees/1267/1267_guidelines.pdf>.

2 President Declares National Emergency, To the Congress of the United States (24 September 2001) at <http://www.whitehouse.gov/news/releases/2002/09/20010924.htm>.

3 The President may 'investigate, block during the pendency of an investigation, regulate, direct and compel, nullify, void, regulate, direct and compel, nullify, void, prevent or prohibit, any acquisition, holding, withholding, use, transfer, withdrawal, transportation, importation or exportation of, or dealing in, or exercising

any right, power, or privilege with respect to, or transactions involving, any property in which any foreign country or a national thereof has any interest by any person, or with respect to any property, subject to the jurisdiction of the United States . . .' 50 U.S.C. § 1702(a)(1)(B).

4 The President has utilized IEEPA to impose sanctions on certain other foreign countries or foreign nationals, including Zimbabwean leaders, western Balkans extremists, Burma, Iran, and Sudan. A similar – but not identical – provision, the Trading with the Enemy Act, has been used to impose sanctions on Cuba and Libya.

5 It is not clear under US law whether a person may be designated solely because of its inclusion on the 1267 Committee's consolidated list. While several possible legal theories might be advanced to do so, the dearth of judicial precedent on this subject, that might provide some guidance on critical issues relating to constitutional issues and the Administrative Procedure Act involving such a designation, leaves this an open issue.

6 See, e.g., *Holy Land Foundation for Relief and Development* v. *Ashcroft*, 219 F. Supp.2d 57 (D.D.C. 2002), aff'd, __ F.3d __, 2003 WL 21414301 (D.C. Cir. June 20, 2003); *Global Relief Foundation* v. *O'Neill*, 207 F. Supp.2d 779 (N.D.Ill. 2002); *Benevolence International Foundation* v. *Ashcroft*, 200 F. Supp.2d 935 (N.D.Ill. 2002).

7 A number of statutory issues have arisen, including whether IEEPA grants the defendants the power to block domestic assets, whether IEEPA's humanitarian exemption applies to terrorism-linked assets, and whether the President legally delegated certain authorities to US agency heads. However, these issues are primarily those of statutory interpretation and will not be discussed here.

8 Courts, however, have often permitted the indirect challenge of a Presidential action under the Administrative Procedure Act by allowing plaintiffs to challenge the implementation of the action by a government agency. This legal theory has not arisen in the context of a designation by the President in the Annex to E.O. 13224, or other Executive Orders that target individuals or entities. See *Youngstown Sheet & Tube Co.* v. *Sawyer*, 343 US 579, 610-611 (1952).

Remarks by Willy Bruggeman*

Co-ordinated Actions to Combat Terrorism and the International Financial and Economic Legal System

1. The current terrorism threat

Assessing terrorist risk has become a hot topic in the wake of 11 September 2001. Risk modelers and brokers have stepped into the knowledge breach with products, but their accuracy and value remain untested.

Intelligence services and law enforcement agencies try continuously to assess the situation and the actual threat. Recent history has shown how difficult this is and the quality of the analysis done are regularly subject of severe criticism.

Also other organizations, such as Jane's and the Rand Corporation try to test best ways for terrorism modeling.

The hardest fact is predicting when, where and how terrorists will attack. The ability to foresee the tragic events in New York and Washington was admittedly as meager in Europe as in the United States. We cannot use historical data only, because we are in a different geo-political climate than in the past. The frequency and severity of attacks certainly have varied over time. Also the way terrorists behave is that, if they think you can find a pattern, they will try to do something different. So forecasting is extremely difficult.

In general it can be stated that the offensive potential of Al Qaeda and its affiliat-

* Deputy Director Europol, The Hague.

ed groups is still great. The threat of attacks in Spain, as ETA still keeps its operational capability, remains high. The same goes for the threat from Northern-Irish terrorism, particularly from Real IRA and Continuity IRA. The Red Brigades cause threat in Italy. The Revolutionary Organization 17 November, while its operational potential remains limited, is still active.

It is difficult to further specify the threat posed by these organizations. Therefore it is worthwhile to analyze the roots of terrorism in Europe.

The terrorists' commitment to violence raises important questions. Given that terrorist movements have arisen throughout the world, it is only reasonable to assume that the motive for any individual to become terrorist are complex and will be found in that individual's personal experiences with the political system of the society in which he or she lives.

When one looks at the rationalizations that terrorists employ for their violence, a common set of themes emerges which clearly exposes some common psychological origins of terrorism. These origins appear to be rooted in feelings of vulnerability and frustration. With respect to vulnerability, terrorists generally express a belief that they are members of a population that is being unfairly exploited by more powerful individuals. The population the terrorists believe to be exploited can be human, as in the case of terrorists who are and/or act for the Palestinian people. Or, the alleged victims can be non-human, as in the case of terrorist groups who claim they are acting to protect animals and/or all of nature. In either case, it is likely that terrorists experience emotional reinforcement by creating a self-image that presents them as the strongest members of an oppressed population who have constituted themselves as protectors of that supposedly defenseless population. This ability to define themselves as protectors of those in their group who are more helpless than they are, provides the terrorists with psychological compensation to combat their inherent feelings of vulnerability.

The frustration and impatience experienced by members of terrorist organizations may have a genuine basis in the reality of the societies in which they live. They may have experienced exploitation and powerlessness to the point where they can no longer tolerate this. On the other hand, they may have simply been very unsuccessful at employing the economic and political mechanisms available in their society for attaining the success achieved by their peers. Regardless of whether their anger is caused by the unfair acts of others or their own failures, once terrorists have responded to their inability to succeed by projecting responsibility for their condition on a target group, once they have rationalized the violent consequences of their anger against that group and once they have identified with each other and with an exploited entity, it is clear what the result of violence can be.

Violence can become an obsession that frequently follows a path of escalation. Once the pattern of psychological defense is established, violence offers a tremendous outlet for previously repressed anger. The emotional gain experienced by the release of psychological energy through violence can easily lead to an obsession with violence. In addition, careful planning of terrorist violence is necessary to prevent capture and harsh punishment. So it is easy to understand how obsession can also originate from the necessity for caution. Furthermore, obsessive planning may function somewhat like the fantasies of serial sexual killers who ruminate about their future crimes. As such, obsessive planning may further energize the impulse for violent political action.

The elaborateness of these obsessions is this description of how the terrorists study the technology of the target group in order to use it as a weapon against them.

Five sequential objectives that terrorist organizations use to achieve political influence and control through the planned use of violence have been identified. They are: attention (of the public and media), acknowledgement (of the group and its cause), recognition (of the group as a representative of their cause), authority (legitimate political influence) and governance (autonomy and political control).

There are significant differences between groups that are based on variations in culture and on variations in the personal and collective histories of their members. We can divide terrorist groups into three general categories. The first includes secular terrorist groups like right and left wing terrorists and animal rights/eco-terrorist organizations in Europe, America and/or Asia. The second includes ethnic terrorist groups such as those that have operated in the Balkans and the Ku Klux Klan in America. And the third includes religious terrorists like Al Qaeda.

Each of these groups defines its target population differently based on the personal and cultural history of the terrorist organization and the narcissistic injury/act of exploitation that the terrorist group believes that the target group has inflicted upon them. The perceived injury/exploitation will directly affect the terrorists' political agenda, the definition of the target group, the symbolic value to the terrorists of taking action against various members and/or properties of the target group and the rationalization used for the attacks. For example, an animal rights terrorist group may choose to target conservative politicians and corporate officers whose actions promote development of rural areas. They would probably rationalize their violence against these groups and/or their properties as a protection for endangered species whose plight represents the endangerment of all species, including mankind. This scenario presents a rather restricted target group, a highly specific rationalization and a concrete political agenda aimed at stopping development.

Religious terrorists represent the other end of the spectrum. Al Qaeda generally espouses the belief that all who do not believe in Islam and all Muslims who do not specifically adhere to the Wahabbist Islamic philosophy are an insult to God, and must ultimately either accept Wahabbist Islam or be eliminated. They see any contemporary Western presence in any land that has ever been occupied by Muslims as being intrusive and exploitive, symbolizing an intrusion of evil. Buildings and individuals who symbolize Western culture to the Al Qaeda leadership are high priority targets. These would include the World Trade Center, the Eiffel Tower, and Parliament, the President of the United States and the Prime Minister of England.

This indicates that terrorist organizations and terrorism are evolving phenomena, regardless of the psychological origins of a terrorist behaviour; influences exerted upon it over time can produce profound changes in a terrorist group's beliefs, values, mode of operation and psychological adaptation. The lifespan of most terrorist organizations is less than a year, and given the fact that the process of psychological development is on-going throughout adulthood, it is reasonable to propose that the psychology of terrorist organizations is inherently unstable and is subject to change due to outside pressures. On the one hand, this makes it very difficult to develop an integrated theory of terrorist psychology. On the other hand, it means that terrorist organizations are vulnerable to psychological pressure. If they can be subverted to become instruments of State policy, they may also be subject to pressures that challenge their emotional defenses to the point where they cannot maintain their adaptation. Such pressure could therefore compel them to disband.

However, despite sharing these psychological processes and traits, the culture-history of each terrorist group can be seen to have a profound impact on the membership of a terrorist organization, the content of its specific political and/or religious philosophy, its espoused goals, the size and definition of its target group, the methods and nature of the violence perpetrated against the target, and the definition of the constituency which the terrorists claim to be protecting. Finally, State-sponsorship and a variety of other outside influences may exert pressures that alter the psychology of terrorist groups and may make it difficult to sustain itself.

2. European Union initiatives and combating terrorism

In the extraordinary European Summit on 21 September 2001, the EU leaders presented a seven-point anti-terrorism plan. The main measures to be taken included the strengthening of the legislative arsenal, the increased co-operation of magistrates, the increased co-operation and co-ordination of the operational services responsible for combating terrorism, the broadening of co-operation with the USA and the fight against the funding of terrorism.

It is noteworthy that the co-operation has established firm links between the police and the security services throughout the EU. The European Council made it clear that the policy adopted is in line with international conventions. It called for all existing international conventions on the fight against terrorism (UN, OECD, etc.) to be implemented as quickly as possible. Moreover, the MS were encouraged to ratify, as a matter of urgency, the UN Convention for the Suppression of the Financing of Terrorism. In the Ghent European Summit on 22 October 2001, the Council again unequivocally stated its full support for the action being taken against terrorism in all its aspects within the framework defined by the UN and reaffirmed its total solidarity with the USA. The Council formally approved the framework decision on the definition of and penalty for terrorism of 13 June 2002. The discussion on the general harmonization of criminal sanctions at the EU level is still ongoing.[1]

On 13 June 2002, the Council reached a political agreement on the initiative taken by the Spanish Presidency to create points of contact in the police and justice services to co-ordinate the fight against terrorism. Despite, or rather because of, the criticism presented for instance by the Commission, the Council decided to make a Council decision instead of a simple recommendation as anticipated.[2]

The Council adopted, on 27 December 2001, a Regulation in respect of the freezing of funds and a prohibition to provide funds, assets, economic resources or financial services to terrorists (individuals, groups or entities) linked to terrorist organizations. Estimates of the assets frozen throughout the EU since September 11 vary between €40 million to over €100 million.[3]

Although these initiatives are primarily focusing on the fight against terrorism, they will have a long-term effect on the fight against OC as well. Most of the issues cover such subjects that are also relevant in the fight against OC, for instance the discussion about the harmonization of criminal sanctions and the freezing of assets which could also be extended to OC.

European arrest warrant

In the Laeken European Summit on 15 December 2001, the EU leaders agreed upon an ambitious pan-EU arrest warrant. In principle the warrant covers all crimes, but for 32 listed crimes, the EU has abolished a requirement that the offence must be recognized in both Member States. The 32 crimes to be covered by the warrant go well beyond terrorism. The list includes

- murder;
- terrorism;
- participation in a criminal organization;
- sexual exploitation of children and child pornography;
- cyber crime;
- illicit trafficking in people;
- arms and explosives;
- nuclear material and drugs;
- illicit trade in endangered species;
- kidnapping;
- hostage taking;
- organized and/or armed robbery;
- illicit trade in art and other cultural treasures;
- rape;
- arson;
- sabotage;
- racism and xenophobia;
- corruption and fraud.

From 2004 on,[4] when the legislation should be in place across the EU, any competent authority of an EU Member State would be able to ask another, on the basis of an arrest warrant, to transfer a person it suspects of having committed any crime included in the list. In order to extradite a suspect for a crime not on the list, the office would have to carry a minimum jail sentence of 12 months for the suspect to be handed over. For crimes on the list, it would have to carry a minimum of three years.

The EU initiatives cannot be seen in isolation. Especially not when being confronted with so-called 'wandering terrorists', who form unstable groups that are very difficult to monitor. Together with T. Delpech we can state that the attacks, which prompted unanimous resolutions of support within both the General Assembly and the Security Council of the United Nations, had started a new era in international co-operation and alliances, but it quickly became apparent that such was not the case. To a great extent they had the opposite effect. In reality the crisis had initiated a period of deep disagreement on how to jointly prevent and combat terrorism activities.
So even when many co-ordinating initiatives were taken within the EU, the global reaction was subject to deep disagreement and isolated actions.

3. Specific initiatives related to terrorism based financial crimes

Combating the financing of terrorism remains an extremely difficult task.

Only enhanced co-ordination and multi-agency integration at national and international level, across governments working in close partnership with financial sources, may offer a real added value.

It is increasingly evident that terrorists and their organizations need to raise significant amounts of cash for a wide variety of purposes, for recruitment, training, travel and materials as well as often making payments for safe haven protection. US authorities estimate that Osama bin Laden paid over US$100 million to the Taliban during his five year stay in Afghanistan.

Tracking, intercepting and strangling the flow of funds is a vital element in the widening global effort against terrorism. Also the intelligence into terrorist networks, provided by widening knowledge about their financial transactions, proves to be notably important.

It also becomes clear that the amount of frozen assets, seized or forfeited around the world, is only a narrow measure of success.

Measures are necessary to enable the agencies to track financial movements, because:

- the consequences of allowing the financial system to facilitate the movement of terrorist money, are horrendous;
- tracking terrorist money flows, and when possible, freezing it or disrupting its transfer, makes it harder for terrorists to operate and thus deter them from seeking to base their operations;
- tracking these flows provides information on links, profiles and movements which help build up an intelligence picture of the way terrorists and terrorist organizations operate.

Worthwhile instruments to be mentioned are:

- key anti-terrorist UN Security Council Resolutions 1373 of 28 September 2001 (terrorism in general) and 1390 of 16 January 2002 (regarding Bin Laden and Taliban);
- the UN Convention of suppression of financing of terrorism (February 2000);
- IMF and FATF initiatives;
- EC regulations which require all EU members to freeze the assets listed by the UN Sanctions Committee and those listed as associated with Bin Laden, Al Qaeda and the Taliban.

In reality sometimes ratification is still lacking, and more often the lists are *not* of sufficient quality or not adequately used, which hampers the expected operational results.

Notes

1 On 17 November 2001, the Council discussed on harmonizing criminal sanctions, but the views on how much harmonization is necessary and how it should be done were divergent.

[2] Agence Europe, 13 June 2002. About the criticism presented by the Commission see European Report, 1 May 2002. For expectations before the 13 June meeting see for instance Agence Europe, 10 June 2002

[3] See European Commission News Release (MEMO/02/53) and *Financial Times*, 8 April 2002 (an interview of the US Treasury Secretary).

[4] The entry in force of the framework decision is on 1 January 2004. The Member States agreed that each Member State would have the choice of making it retroactive, but only as far back as 1993. This was when the Maastricht Treaty came into force setting up the EU's third pillar of justice and home affairs. On 15 February 2002, France, Belgium, Spain, Portugal, the UK and Luxembourg unexpectedly agreed to introduce the new European arrest warrant a year ahead of schedule, in the first three months of 2003, saying their decision was a clear sign of Europe's commitment to cracking down on terrorism and OC. *Financial Times*, 15 February 2002.

REMARKS BY M.M.T.A. BRUS*

THE SUPPRESSION OF THE FINANCING OF TERRORISM AND THE CHALLENGE OF MULTILEVEL JURISDICTION

1. INTRODUCTION

In this report I will try to link the overall theme of the Conference: *From Government to Governance? The Growing Impact of Non-State Actors on the International and European Legal System* to the specific topic of this panel: the coordinated efforts to combat terrorism, and in particular, efforts to suppress terrorist financing. Is it possible to identify trends and issues that are relevant for fundamental developments in the international legal system? This report will not focus on a description or analysis of the various initiatives taken, but will present these in the context of the debate on developing global or international governance. More details on the various initiatives are being presented by other panelists. I will start with making some remarks on the two central elements in the theme of this conference, non-State actors and governance, followed by an analysis what effect international anti-terrorist action may have on the international legal system. It will conclude that developing international governance in this area confronts us with the challenge of multilevel jurisdiction that is rapidly developing in our present-day international society.

2. THE IMPACT OF NON-STATE ACTORS

When speaking about terrorism and international actions to combat this it will be clear that non-State actors play a dominant role. Terrorism is, with some possible exceptions of State-sponsored terrorism, undertaken by individuals and groups of individuals. The objectives of the individuals or groups may vary, but they have in common that they use violence in an indiscriminate manner in order to intimidate a population or to compel public authorities to do or to abstain from doing any act.[1] It would be possible at this place to make a distinction between acts of terrorism that are exclusively used within a particular State and international terrorism where there is an international element either with regard to the place where the act is performed or the target against which the act is directed. However, making this distinction for the pur-

* Leiden University.

pose of combating terrorism is no longer of great relevance as most, if not all, terrorist organizations will have international links for their financing, supply of arms, etc.[2]

Not only non-State actors dominate with regard to performing acts of terrorism, also the actions against terrorism increasingly are being coordinated and undertaken at non-State level. The United Nations, in particular in Resolution 1373(2001), has assumed a responsibility that earlier clearly rested with the States, as expressed in the anti-terrorist conventions that have been concluded over the past decades. States individually may have adopted in the past anti-terrorist legislation, but international cooperation with regard to the prevention and suppression of terrorism remained, with the exception of cooperation in criminal procedures, quite undeveloped. If one takes a look at the various anti-terrorism conventions it is clear that they almost entirely focus on the establishment of jurisdiction at the national level and that any form of developing an international institutional framework for the cooperation in this area is kept out of these instruments. The UN General Assembly has never been able to reach sufficient consensus on the issue of a definition of terrorism and also did not establish any efficient framework for international cooperation.

How much has changed since the terrorist attacks of 9/11! Existing systems for international collaboration were adapted to include the suppression of terrorism and new roads were opened for a frontal attack on international terrorism. From being predominantly at the State level, the actions moved to the international level. Main examples of this development are:

- The adoption of Resolution 1373(2001) by the Security Council and the creation of the Counter-Terrorism Committee (CTC);
- The strengthening of the Resolution 1267-regime by the Security Council;
- Expanding the mission of the Financial Action Task Force on Money Laundering (FATF) to include action against terrorist financing, in particularly by adoption of 8 Special Recommendations on Terrorist Financing and efforts to ensure implementation of these guidelines;
- Action in the context of IMF and World Bank to include the FATF Recommendations, including those on terrorist financing, in the list standards and codes which are the basis for country-specific assessments;
- Efforts within regional organizations to suppress terrorist financing, with the EU as prominent example.

Besides these actions at the international level, much has been done at the State level. Many States have adopted legislation and strengthened procedures to suppress the financing of terrorism, as they were compelled to do as a result of the initiatives mentioned above. Among the domestic actions, the Patriot Act, adopted by the United States legislation in October 2001, deserves special attention for its strong extra-territorial effects. It exerts great pressure on private parties, in particular financial institutions both within the USA and outside, to adhere to the US standards.

The main point I want to make here is not about the particularities of the various initiatives, but the fact that also with regard to responding to the terrorist threat non-State actors have taken a central role. The non-State actors in the area of terrorism are more than entities that have an impact on the international legal system. They have become part of the international system and international law has to find ways to deal with this fact. Terrorism and the efforts to prevent and combat it are prime examples of the development of the international legal system from being predominantly focused on inter-State relations into a system that governs the international community that includes States, but also non-State actors.

3. From governments to governance

Are we capable of effectively promoting the prevention of serious acts of international terrorism without the development of some form of international governance? For me the answer is a clear no. The problem is a truly global one. It is undeniably closely related to the process of globalization. Terrorists, but also those who are instrumental in suppressing the financing of terrorism, in particular the private financial institutions, are players in a global society. Inter-State cooperation on the basis of existing doctrines of international law will continue to prove ineffective in addressing the problem of the prevention, and to a lesser degree the punishment, of terrorist acts. That this is fully realized is underlined by the fact that the Security Council has adopted Resolution 1373(2001) in which it accepted a new role, namely as quasi-legislator for the world community. Moreover, the creation of a regime for the implementation of this Resolution and other resolutions focusing on particular groups (the 1267-regime) did not lead to strong opposition and shows a considerable degree of compliance so far. It is perfectly possible to challenge the power of the UN Security Council to adopt such measures on the basis of the UN Charter, but this will not be considered here. What is at issue here, is that on behalf of the entire community standards are set that all actors in the legal system will have to comply with. Non-compliance by a particular State, or non-State actor, is no longer a legitimate alternative. States may still violate the standards, but they then can and will be held accountable for this.

International terrorism is not a threat to individual States, but to the international community as such. The destabilizing effects of major terrorist threats or acts will be felt everywhere. It is a common interest to take action against it. International terrorism is certainly not the only problem of this kind and perhaps not even the most serious one. However, at present it are the terrorists who have managed to push the international community into the direction of international governance, whereas pressures on the international system in other areas have been less effective.

International governance is more than effective inter-State cooperation. One can define international governance as 'a process by which the international community on the basis of shared values and interests collectively manages resources, issues and conflicts in a world that is increasingly a "global neighbourhood"'.[3] I think that the *collective* effort undertaken after the 9/11 attacks can be regarded as largely in line with this definition. It is clear that the measures taken are part of a process. Both the implementation of Resolution 1373 and the initiatives by the FATF/IMF/World Bank are not a response to a particular situation, but try to address the issue at a fundamental level. The process aspect is also visible in the attempts to establish a better coordination between the 1373 and 1267-regimes. It is part of a learning process. Furthermore, part of the process is also the fact that States are being offered assistance in the implementation of the various standards. This last aspect is also of importance for the legitimacy of the collective measures. They should be inclusive rather than exclusive.

A major problem with developing international governance in a manner as we see now with regard to terrorism, is to ensure that the actions are indeed based on shared values. 'Values' is a rather vague term. In my view values can and should be related to, on the one hand, the purpose of collective action, e.g. combating terrorism, protecting the environment, or respect for human rights. However, on the content of these values and the modalities of the international actions to promote these, international conflict can easily arise. Therefore, it is of equal importance to ensure that the values that are related to the decision-making procedures are also shared by the participants in the legal community. It is at this point that the development of international governance poses a major challenge to the international legal system. A first step to address this is to recognize that an international legal system that supports international governance will be a system that can be characterized by the exercise of multilevel jurisdiction.

4. The reality of multilevel jurisdiction

In this paper the analysis of the issue of multilevel jurisdiction will be limited to the attempts to suppress financing of terrorism. With this in mind it is possible to identify four general levels of jurisdiction.

First, we have the jurisdiction exercised by the Security Council at supranational level by the adoption of the relevant resolutions taken under Chapter VII of the Charter of the UN. As said before, one may contest whether these decisions are ultra vires or not, fact is that in the present state of international law, we have to assume that these resolutions are binding. Moreover, although States may be reluctant in complying with them, there seem to be no major challenges from their side to the legality or legitimacy of the Security Council's action. The main problem here is that the Security Council by exercising its functions in this area combines the legislative, executive and even the judicial function in one organ. It is difficult to maintain that that will provide a solid basis for international governance on the long term.

The second level is the level of inter-State cooperation in the context of international governmental organizations. At this level there is no supranational exercise of jurisdiction, but we can distinguish a clear trend towards the adoption of certain standards. The FATF, now in close cooperation with the IMF and World Bank are instrumental in harmonizing standards which have to be implemented at State level in order to enable action against the financing of terrorism. In this context it must be mentioned that these activities are not restricted to anti-terrorist practices, but extend to other areas, such as money laundering. Here we see the broader problem of how to respond to international organized crime in the globalizing society. However, terrorism remains a special case, as attempts are increasingly focussed on the prevention of terrorist acts, rather than on dealing with criminal behavior that already has taken place. At this level one cannot properly speak of the exercise of jurisdiction by the mentioned international organizations. However, it is undeniable that the standards that are being developed in this context are difficult for States to ignore. The listing of States and territories that are non-cooperative in the implementation of these standards proves effective, but also leads to questions related to the legitimacy of standards and the process of their adoption. As it is not unlikely that the longer-term role of these organizations in 'managing' the standards related to the financing international terrorism – and for that matter also other financial aspect of suppressing international crime – will increase, further investigation is needed to identify and discuss questions about the legality and legitimacy of the 'jurisdiction' exercised at this level.

Thirdly, we have to take into account the role of regional organizations. The EU is a notable example here. The way the EU exercises its jurisdiction with regard to the suppression of (financing of) terrorism and some problems, both internal and in relation to the UN Security Council, have been discussed by Straver in his contribution; this will not be further pursued here.

Finally there is the exercise of jurisdiction at the State level. In developing its responses to international terrorism States are not free but have to take into account the measures that have been undertaken at the above-mentioned levels. Sometimes these are straightforward legal obligations, and in other instances it is related to the application of codes and standards. Moreover, through bilateral and multilateral conventions, in particular the anti-terrorist conventions, States may have accepted specific commitments, e.g. to create jurisdiction with regard to certain acts of terrorism or the financing of terrorism.

Aspects of the exercise of jurisdiction at the State level that deserves further attention are 1) the use of domestic legislation with a strong extra-territorial effect and 2) the misuse that may be made by some States of the international measures for the purpose of suppressing their opponents or limiting human rights. The first point is of importance in particular if the domestic measures are inconsistent with the ones adopted at the international level, but also because they undermine the efforts to establish an effective regime on the basis of international cooperation. The second issue relates predominantly to the relatively primitive stage of developing international governance. Although States become subject to ever more regimes that can be seen as elements of a developing system of international governance, it is still not more than a trend that may be disrupted by other international developments (or rather is being disrupted at the very moment; see remarks in the concluding part). For the time being States that want to make misuse of international measures can only be held accountable through the traditional not particularly efficient inter-State based mechanisms.

5. The challenge of multilevel jurisdiction

The exercise of jurisdiction with regard to a particular issue at different levels may and probably will lead to conflict. Any legal system that incorporates forms of multilevel jurisdiction will need mechanisms and principles that form the basis for solving such conflicts. The international community and its legal system are increasingly being confronted with the issue of multilevel jurisdiction. This requires a rethinking of the international legal system with respect to at least three basic issues fundamental to a proper system of law:

The first aspect relates to the contents of the obligations. What is required of the participants in the legal system and can they comply with one set of rules or standards without coming into conflict with a set of rules or standards formulated at another jurisdictional level? In a legal community, coherence between the applicable norms is an essential feature. The first question with regard to investigating multilevel jurisdiction in the context of international governance is therefore related to possible mechanisms that can be used to ensure coherence of the normative framework. The traditional rules that would solve a conflict between inconsistent international obligations may not always be adequate, as reliance on the traditional sources of international law may not always be possible. New forms and new fora for decision-making develop which may lead to new problems related to the coherence of norms.

Secondly, it will be necessary to engage in a debate on what institutional principles govern the international community. A clear example of the lack of fundamental institutional principles is the fact that there is no possibility to subject decisions of the Security Council to some form of control, neither for States that are directly affected by a decision, nor for individuals or entities that in the context of suppressing terrorism are placed on a list. The issue of creating an international legal system that incorporates at least some fundamental institutional principles is a difficult one, as it requires acknowledgement that the sovereign equality of States and the principle of consent can no longer serve as the main institutional principles of the international legal system.

A final issue that will have to be addressed in the context of the multilevel jurisdiction in the international community is the issue of fundamental rights and obligations of its participants. Fundamental human rights and other fundamental norms usually referred to as *jus cogens* norms will certainly form a core of rights and obligations, but other fundamental rights or obligations, in particular those related to the common interest of the international community may arise. Core values and norms characterize a community. An international community that is characterized by multilevel jurisdiction, and therefore comprises sub-communities at various levels, has to define which core values represent the common identity without negating the identity of the sub-communities. This is again a major challenge.

6. Conclusion

This is not the place to further enter into a debate on the challenges identified here. The purpose of this paper was to investigate how the topic of the suppression of financing terrorist activities is related to the general topic of this conference. Is there a trend that suggests a move from governments to governance? My answer is clearly affirmative on the basis of an analysis of the various actions undertaken. Is there a growing impact of non-State actors? My thesis goes even further: non-State actors have become part of the international legal system and this requires a rethinking of the basic structure and principles of international law. The emerging international community, in which States will continue to play an important, but not exclusive role, can be increasingly characterized by a system of multilevel governance. Even though in this paper only a rather preliminary investigation has been made with respect to the exercise of jurisdiction at various levels, a trend is visible. Some fundamental issues with regard to multilevel jurisdiction have been touched upon here.

A final remark must be made at the end of this paper. The developments with regard to the suppression of financing of terrorism have been looked upon here in a perspective that is optimistic about the chances of the creation of a world community governed by law. This view can be easily challenged on the basis of the very confused situation in world affairs at the present moment. In particular the attitude of the present US administration towards international cooperation and international law makes the outlook for the realization of the community-oriented perspective extremely bleak. Fundamentals of the current imperfect legal system are being challenged as well as the role of international institutions like the United Nations in governing international affairs. One cannot and should not close his eyes for these worrying developments, but at the same time it cannot distract from the fact that the international society continues to develop into one world society. The fundamental problems that are inherent in a world society cannot be solved on the basis of individual state power. The need to think about the evolution of the international legal system remains relevant, even though there are many obstacles on the way forward.

NOTES

1 See Art. 2.1.b of the International Convention for the Suppression of the Financing of Terrorism.

2 But see the remarks by Straver for this panel on the limitations of the EU in taking action against terrorist acts that are deemed internal to the EU.

3 M. Brus, in Kreijen, et al., *States, Sovereignty and International Governance,* (OUP 2002) p. 5.

DISCUSSION

BIBI VAN GINKEL:* asked Albert Straver whether he could give a prediction of the outcome of cases currently pending before the European Court of Justice (ECJ) concerning listing procedures, like the *Aden* case? She further invited him to explain whether he considered these cases different from previous cases before the European Court of Justice, such as the case regarding the embargo on transactions with Yugoslavia, which resulted in the impounding of a Yugoslavian aeroplane? In this latter case, the freezing measure was generally addressed. In contrast, the listings are personalised which, in her view, called for more guarantees in the process.

She agreed with the remarks made by Marcel Brus as regards the role governance should play in the process of combating terrorism; especially since that would guarantee more of a long-term solution. In this light, she found it striking that most procedures dealing with anti-terrorism measures were administrative measures, while the outcome of these measures on the individuals had a punitive effect. She submitted that criminal procedures would provide more guarantees for the individual during the process. Since it seemed that human rights guarantees were missing in anti-terrorism measures altogether, she considered it advisable that if a fusion took place between the Counter-Terrorism Committee (CTC) and the Sanctions Committee, as mentioned by Axel Marschik, a human rights supervision mechanism should be incorporated as well.

MICHAEL BYERS:** noted that Security Council Resolution 1373 took the provisions of a not-widely-ratified multilateral treaty (UN Convention for the Suppression of the Financing of Terrorism) and made it binding law for all 191 Member States of the UN. He asked Marcel Brus and Axel Marschik whether this did not raise questions of governance, in terms of the lack of widespread participatory, democratic involvement in law-making? Or, he inquired, could it be justified as a more or less temporary measure that was necessary in a time of crisis?

* Utrecht University.
** Duke University School of Law.

ALBERT STRAVER: In reply to Bibi van Ginkel, explained that he had worked on sanctions, like Mr. Das, before working on terrorist-related freezing measures. He was thus aware of some of the case law of the ECJ regarding sanctions issues. He pointed out that the case that Ms. Van Ginkel referred to concerned the impounding of an aircraft. He believed this measure was taken in furtherance to a UN Security Council resolution concerning the former Yugoslavia. He indicated that such a measure could not be compared to the freezing measures that were currently imposed, simply because the impact on individuals was very different. He noted that, unfortunately, there was no real case law on freezing measures, because the 'normal target' of such measures was the leader of a foreign regime. He explained that these people are normally not even thinking of accepting the jurisdiction of the ECJ and taking their case there. They rather react by means of political statements and by means of counter-sanctions if they think fit. They do not bring a case to the jurisdiction where the sanctions have been decided. Nevertheless, he recalled one example of a legal appeal against freezing measures, namely the *Invest-Import* case. This case concerned Serbia-Montenegro, but there was no final judgment of the ECJ, because meanwhile the sanctions were repealed as the Milošević regime was overthrown.

He added that the freezing measures should be assessed in the particular framework of free movement of capital and the possibility for the authorities to reinstate certain controls there. He did not perceive these measures as criminal sanctions, even though people themselves may perceive their listing as an act of name and shame. An order to the banks to look whether they have an account with a particular name was not really the same as a judgment of the kind sentencing to three years imprisonment, in his point of view. Therefore, he argued it was probably justified that the procedure had a more administrative character. He indicated that, finally, it would be up to the Court to decide what guarantees and safeguards are necessary in our legal system. He pointed out that this case would cause 'Luxembourg' a hard time, since they had no jurisdiction for CFSP measures and they certainly could not state that the UN measure was not valid since the Council decided by unanimity that the resolution would be implemented. Hence, he indicated, it would be an interesting judgment.

AUGUST REINISCH: added that the European Court of Human Rights has repeatedly held with regard to Italian freezing measures against Mafia suspects that the freezing itself was not a criminal charge and did not trigger the criminal law guarantees. Such a measure only had to be tested against the due process, fair trial guarantees of Article 6 ECHR. This also showed and supported Mr. Straver's point of view that such a measure could not be compared to a criminal charge. Nevertheless the question concerning human rights had its value. In this respect, he noted that the Council of Ministers of the Council of Europe issued a statement on fighting terrorism and human rights, where it specifically called for judicial review in the context of freezing measures.

MARCEL BRUS agreed with Michael Byers that from an international law point of view, all what happened in the Security Council was completely overstepping the boundaries of the Security Council's powers. Yet, he emphasised that, even though the Security Council may not be a legislative body, it *has* taken this approach at this moment. He found it important to distinguish between the general approach of 1373 and the more specific freezing and listing process, and stressed that in case of the general approach, there has not been so much opposition from States. So, even though the legislative process itself has not been very democratic – there has not been a vote from all States in the world, or from all participants of the international legal system –, within the Security Council, where the permanent five have taken the lead, the other States could have stopped it, and did not do so. Hence, there is support for the current approach.

In his view, the main question was whether this approach was a good start to create global governance that could address global challenges, or whether better alternatives should be discovered. He acknowledged that the current approach was imperfect. He submitted that one should inquire whether there were possibilities to improve it and how more guarantees could be built in to ensure that the decisions reflected core interests and values of the international community, without having to fall back to the traditional mechanisms.

AXEL MARSCHIK: In response to Bibi van Ginkel, cautioned that a fusion of the two regimes was still light-years away. He submitted that the model for such a fusion could be the UNMOVIC-type commission. However, he noted that UNMOVIC was not necessarily an example of enormous success within the UN in recent years, unfortunately so. Therefore, one should wait and see whether such an intrusive regime with the possibility of inspecting onsite would go through the Council. He did not think so. He acknowledged that there were some States voicing this idea in and around the Council, but still he argued, it would take a long process. As regards human rights, an aspect that Ms. Van Ginkel missed, he remarked that he missed it too. He indicated that this was something that experts in the UN were very worried about, and pointed out that currently, neither regime devoted adequate attention to human rights, although the CTC was trying to take human rights considerations on board somehow. So far, the CTC only agreed to have human rights experts present material, but it had not been able yet to appoint a human rights expert from a pool of eight or nine experts for various subjects. This showed how much difficulty some members in the Security Council have and how worried they are to have the Council deal with human rights.

He observed that the listing procedure was indeed an incredibly dangerous process, since the Council puts names on a list without any kind of process, and without giving reasons. He explained that a State may suggest a name for the list. If this name passes through the 48-hours-rule and is on the list, there is no real way to appeal. The de-listing procedure for the 1267-regime foresees merely that a State that wants a name or an agency de-listed can consult the State that originally put the name on the list, and then try to get a joint de-listing request. If that does not work, it can still submit a request to the Committee, and that can only pass if there is no objection. The question is who would take up the interests of individuals who are not in favour of the State. He stressed that this group of persons has no representation within this system of small representation.

In response to Michael Byers' comment on law-making, he recalled the night of the September 24th after the adoption of the Resolution. The people present said 'this is incredible, a completely new phase; after the First Iraq War, the UN is getting active, this is the real thing. Because now we have a legislative Security Council, automatic rights, so what about parliamentary democracy and all these values, where do they fit in?' But there was no reaction. And of course there was no reaction from any State, because this was only 13 days after the September 11th attacks. Everything that the UN wanted to do, and all the Member States that were there, was to show sympathy to the victims of the United States, to do something and to show that they could really contribute in the fight against terrorism. However, he inquired why today, two years later, there was still no appeal and a bigger discussion? He indicated that in May 2003, there were 225 entities on that list, and if one looked at the names and where the individuals were from, one would find that there was no country that would want to represent them. Hence, no State would come out and say this is a problem for us, this whole regime and the way people are being putting on the list, the way 1373 was adopted, its results and effects. In sum, he submitted that the targeted individuals and entities do not have any strong brokers.

Finally, he noted that the developments of the last months, law-making in the Security Council, have now reached a completely different stage. Although the focus has completely shifted, we are still in the midst of law-making. In the case of Iraq, the administration of Iraq is no law-making organ of the Security Council, but there is Resolution 1483, which tries to condone what is happening there. Hence, he stressed, we are in a different phase altogether.

PIETER H.F. BEKKER:* pointed to the French High Court's finding that the President of Libya cannot be held liable for terrorist acts in France, and he recalled that in the *Arrest Warrant* Case, the International Court of Justice held that 'any act of authority' against a high-ranking official (in that case, a foreign minister) was at odds with international law. He further noted that last year, the European Union and the United States froze the assets of the president of Zimbabwe. Subsequently, he asked the panellists how the freezing of assets of Heads of States of rogue or terrorist nations could be reconciled with the international law on immunity?

ALBERT STRAVER replied that he did not perceive immunity as an impediment in this regard. In his view, that was quite obviously based on the outcome of the Council of the European Union. He explained that the freezing measures were normally limited in scope, and did not have extraterritorial effect. In this respect, he noted that the Community, the European Union, did not accept extraterritoriality. Therefore, all sanctions regulations included a jurisdiction clause, which stated very explicitly that the measure had to be applied within the territory and to nationals. Hence, immunity did not play a role. He specified that a personal account related to personal property, and could not be the account in the name of the State where the person has official office. Seen from that angle, he did not consider there to be any real conflict.

AXEL MARSCHIK added that from a UN point of view, the question was irrelevant, since Article 103 UN Charter provides for overriding effect to any other obligations that exist. He indicated that if the Security Council decided to put a Head of State on the list, such would override any other forms of immunity. He recalled that in fact this had happened already, since the 1267-list included the whole former government of Afghanistan.

AUGUST REINISCH agreed with Mr. Marschik, but indicated that the real problem remained as regards the other examples given which concerned not the Security Coun-

* White & Case LLP, New York.

cil, but autonomous decisions of certain States in this area. That problem could, however, not be solved today. With that note, he concluded the session.

*Reporter: W.N. Ferdinandusse**

* University of Amsterdam.

International Terrorism and International and European Criminal Law

The panel was convened by its Chair, Harry Post*

Introductory remarks by Harry Post

Professor Post introduced the panellists and stressed that the subject matter of this panel was international terrorism, in contrast to the kind of terrorism that has been known before. Since a few years the world has been confronted with these new forms of terrorism and it seems that the international community, on the one hand, and the United States of America, on the other hand, are dealing with this issue in a different manner. This differing approach regarding the way in which international terrorism should be dealt with was the crucial topic for the present discussion, as well as the question whether the applicable laws in these situations are the laws of war or the laws applicable to peacetime situations.

Remarks by Andrea Gioia**

The definition of terrorism in international criminal law

Introduction

The term "terrorism" was apparently first employed in order to designate the methods of repression and bloodshed used during the period of the French Revolution from Spring 1793 to July 1794: initially, therefore, the concept principally covered governmental action. However, from the second half of the XIX century, the term has come to apply mainly to the employment of violence or intimidation by individuals, or groups of individuals, against a State, government or community, usually for political purposes.

The increase in terrorist activity following the First World War gave rise to concerted efforts at an international level to develop treaty rules designed to oblige States to criminalize terrorist acts and to exercise their criminal jurisdiction over them or, alternatively, to extradite the alleged offender, thus reducing the risk that terrorists might escape arrest and criminal prosecution abroad. However, the definition of terrorist acts for purposes of international criminal law has proved to be extremely difficult.

Attempting to define international terrorism has been a popular activity among

* University of Exeter.

** Professor of International Law, Faculty of Law, University of Modena and Reggio Emilia.

academics and other interested persons, and a surprisingly high number of definitions has been advanced in the relevant literature. However, precisely because of the difficulty of agreeing on a general definition within the community of States, no comprehensive treaty on the suppression of terrorism has yet been adopted at a world level.

My objective today is not to propose yet another definition of terrorism, but rather to examine past and present attempts to define terrorist acts for purposes of international criminal law, and to ascertain if acts commonly perceived as terrorist acts can sometimes qualify as war crimes or as crimes against humanity.

Existing treaties on the suppression of terrorism

After an abortive attempt to adopt a comprehensive convention on the prevention and punishment of terrorism made in 1937 on the initiative of the League of Nations,[1] States have preferred to follow a "sectoral" approach, consisting in identifying categories of offences which were seen as belonging to the activities of terrorists, and negotiating treaties specifically dealing with each of them. As a result, there are now several treaties dealing with acts endangering the safety of civil aviation,[2] maritime navigation[3] or nuclear materials,[4] crimes against heads of State or government, diplomats and other "internationally protected persons";[5] the taking of hostages;[6] attacks by means of explosives and other lethal devices.[7] These acts are considered to be offences of international concern irrespective of whether or not they are committed for a specific "terrorist" purpose.

In the context of these treaties, and, more generally, so long as a "sectoral" approach is followed, there is clearly no need to define the meaning of expressions such as "terrorism" or "terrorist acts": on the one hand, simply labelling certain offences of international concern as "terrorist" offences would serve no particular legal purpose; on the other, making them punishable only if committed with a specific "terrorist" intent would be counterproductive, inasmuch as by their very nature these offences are such as to cause concern to the international community as a whole.

As soon as the "sectoral" approach is abandoned, however, the definition of such expressions becomes inevitable. A number of existing regional treaties already contain general definitions of "terrorism" or of "terrorist acts" in order to fill the gaps perceived as inherent in the "sectoral" approach: the purpose of these definitions is the criminalization – or "de-politicization" for extradition purposes – of acts not already covered by "sectoral" treaties.[8] A definition having the same purpose is currently being discussed within the United Nations Organization,[9] but an indirect definition already exists at a world level: this can be found in the 1999 UN Convention on the financing of terrorism,[10] although its immediate purpose is the definition of this ancillary offence. In other cases, notably that of a 2002 EU Framework Decision,[11] the purpose of the definition is rather the punishment of acts which in most cases already constitute offences under national law by heavier penalties than those otherwise applicable.

Whatever the purpose of existing definitions, all of them appear to consider as terrorist offences acts which would in most cases already constitute "common" offences under national criminal law. Apart from the international element of such offences, which, given the limited space available, is outside the scope of this report,[12] what is considered to turn them into "terrorist" offences is their purpose. Those writers who have advocated the irrelevance of the purpose of terrorism fail to take into account that, whereas purpose may (and, indeed, probably should) be disregarded so long as a "sectoral" approach is followed, a general, residual, definition of terrorist acts is not easy to conceive without a reference to a specific "terrorist" purpose.

The terrorist purpose *par excellence* is often considered to be the creation of "a state of terror in the minds of particular persons, or groups of persons, or the general public": there is widespread agreement in the relevant literature that the essence of terrorism is in fact the use of unlawful violence in order to inspire fear. Indeed, the 1937 League of Nations Convention appeared to consider that as the only relevant purpose. Significantly, however, the 1937 LN Convention only considered as acts of terrorism those acts "directed against a State". Although it is now generally agreed that acts of terrorism need not necessarily be directed against a State, it may well be argued that the spreading of terror is in fact a method intended to attain a more specific objective.

More modern definitions do not even expressly refer to the spreading of terror, and consider as "terrorist" offences certain violent acts whose purpose is to "intimidate a population" or to "compel a government or an international organization to do or to abstain from doing any act". The 1999 UN Convention on the financing of terrorism indirectly defines as terrorist acts all acts intended to cause death or serious bodily injury to civilians when they have that purpose. The definition which is expected to be adopted in the comprehensive convention on terrorism currently being negotiated within the UN is not very different, except that it also includes acts causing damage to property, including the environment.[13]

On the other hand, certain regional definitions seem to unduly enlarge the concept of terrorism by including among terrorist offences acts committed with the aim of imperilling people's "lives, honour, freedoms, security or rights", of "exposing the environment or any facility or public or private property to hazards or seizing them", of "endangering a national resource, or international facilities."[14] These are not necessarily "terrorist" purposes: all that can be said is that acts committed with those immediate aims may be resorted to by terrorists in order to bring about a "state of terror" and create pressure for the fulfilment of their purposes.

The search for a comprehensive definition at a world level

There can be no doubt that what distinguishes terrorists, as they are usually perceived by the general public, from common criminals is the fact that their acts are, in most cases, not motivated by the pursuit of private ends, but are rather politically, religiously, or otherwise ideologically motivated. Indeed, this is precisely what has made it so difficult to achieve a generally acceptable definition at a world level: acts regarded by some States as "terrorist acts" are sometimes more or less openly supported by other States, who are unwilling to punish, or extradite, the alleged offenders.

It may be significant that, unlike acts intended or calculated to "intimidate a population" or to "compel a government, or an international organization, to do or abstain from doing something", acts designed to "threaten the stability, territorial integrity, political unity or sovereignty of independent States",[15] or to "create a general insurrection in a State",[16] have not been specifically considered as terrorist acts at a world level. The aim of "seriously destabilising or destroying the fundamental political, constitutional, economic or social structures of a country or an international organization" is also considered to be a terrorist aim by the 2002 EU Framework Decision, but the failure to adopt a similar definition at a world level, notably in order to enlarge the scope of the obligation to punish or extradite the alleged offender, could be explained by the reluctance on the part of some States, including some European States, to apply international remedies against individuals or groups who attempt to bring about political changes abroad, notably if the targeted State or government does not abide by minimal standards of democracy and respect for human rights. On the other hand, it could be argued that if "to compel a government to do or abstain from doing something" is always considered to be a "terrorist" purpose, at least some acts designed to bring about political or social change within a State would be covered anyway.

Be that as it may, the difficulties inherent in the adoption of a comprehensive definition of terrorist acts at a world level are made apparent by the fact that the same regional conventions which appear to consider almost any act as constituting a terrorist offence, and most notably one designed to "threaten the stability, territorial integrity, political unity or sovereignty of independent States", are ready, at the same time, to exclude the possibility that terrorist offences can ever be committed in the context of "struggles" waged by peoples for their "liberation or self-determination".[17]

In fact, one of the principal difficulties which stand in the way of the adoption of a general definition of terrorist acts at a world level is the legal assessment of so-called "wars of national liberation". Another difficulty is the assessment of so-called "State terrorism", *i.e.* terrorism in its original meaning of "government by intimidation". Generally speaking, the legitimacy of "wars of national liberation" should not entail a generalized liberty on the part of "freedom-fighters" to resort to *any* means, including terrorist acts, in order to achieve their objectives. At the same time, the legitimacy of a State's reaction to insurgency and, more generally, of its activities designed to enforce law and order should not entail the liberty to give birth to a regime of "terror", such as the French régime of 1793-94.

The events of 11 September 2001 have tragically reminded world public opinion that international terrorism imperils the entire fabric of the international community. It is important to recall that, since the adoption of the Declaration on Measures to Eliminate International Terrorism in Resolution 49/60 of 9 December1994, and most recently in Resolution 57/27 of 19 November 2002, which was adopted by "consensus", the UN General Assembly has reiterated that "criminal acts intended or calculated to provoke a state of terror in the general public, a group of persons, or particular persons for political purposes, are in any circumstances unjustifiable, whatever the considerations of a political, philosophical, ideological, racial, ethnic, religious or other nature that may be invoked to justify them". However, as has been pointed out by Professor Hafner, it still seems to be easier to reach agreement on the text of resolutions than on treaty language.[18]

Terrorist acts as war crimes

Reference to international humanitarian law could prove to be one way out of the stalemate. Indeed, Article 19 of the 1999 UN Convention on terrorist bombings already excludes from the scope of the convention "the activities of armed forces during an armed conflict, as those terms are understood under international humanitarian law, which are governed by that law", and a similar exclusion clause is currently being examined in the context of negotiations for the adoption of a comprehensive UN convention on the suppression of terrorism.[19] The implication seems to be that wherever the use of violence for political purposes actually amounts to an armed conflict, the conventional rules on the repression of terrorist acts do not apply and the laws of armed conflict apply instead.

In situations of armed conflict governed by international humanitarian law, there is no doubt that *some* acts commonly perceived as acts of terrorism are prohibited and that, in some cases, they constitute war crimes. Broadly speaking, these are the use or threat of violence against innocent persons (wounded, sick, shipwrecked, prisoners of war, civilians), or in an indiscriminate or particularly cruel fashion, or with means prohibited by the law.[20] On the other hand, attacks on military targets with weapons that are not prohibited do not normally constitute violations of international humanitarian law. In other words, only what has been described as the "inner core" of terrorism is proscribed by international humanitarian law. In this respect, however, the 1977 Additional Protocols have tightened the prohibition of "terrorist" conduct, since, in particular, even attacks directed at a legitimate military target are prohibited if their "primary purpose" is the spreading of terror among the civilian population.[21]

International humanitarian law has recently evolved so that similar rules apply irrespective of the international or internal character of an armed conflict. From this point of view, therefore, the controversial question of the internal or international nature of "wars of national liberation" is becoming increasingly less relevant. On the other hand, it is important to point out that, whereas international customary law gives all States the faculty to punish war criminals under the universality principle, clear-cut treaty obligations to search for war criminals and to prosecute or extradite them at present exist in respect of international armed conflicts only.

Irrespective of their internal or international character, in order for "wars of national liberation" to be governed by international humanitarian law, they must amount to "armed conflicts": in this respect, I would like to recall an already famous finding by the appeals chamber of the ICTY, in a decision of 2 October 1995 relating to the *Tadić* case, to the effect that "an armed conflict exists whenever there is a resort to armed force between States or *protracted* armed violence between governmental authorities and organized armed groups or between such groups within a State".[22] As is confirmed by several conventional provisions, international humanitarian law does not apply to "situations of internal disturbances and tensions, such as riots, isolated and sporadic acts of violence and other acts of a similar nature, as not being armed conflicts".[23]

Of course, in an internal conflict, insurgents are not considered as "lawful" combatants, *i.e.* persons who have "the right to participate directly in hostilities": on the contrary, they can be punished for their acts of insurgency irrespective of whether or not they also constitute war crimes. Therefore, if "wars of national liberation" are considered to be internal conflicts, acts conforming to international humanitarian law could still be punished by the opposing party. But even if such "wars" are considered as international conflicts, "liberation fighters" have to abide by certain requirements before they can be deemed to be "lawful" combatants.[24] In my opinion, the real question then is this: does the exclusion clause included in the 1999 UN Convention on terrorist bombings (and the identical clause proposed by the Coordinator of informal consultations for inclusion in the future UN comprehensive convention on terrorism) only cover activities carried out by "lawful" combatants? I believe the answer to this question is in the negative.

As mentioned above, the exclusion clause refers to the activities of "armed forces during an armed conflict" which are governed by international humanitarian law. If the clause were intended to apply to international armed conflicts only, it could be argued that it exclusively refers to the "lawful" combatants. But, inasmuch as the clause is meant to apply to both international and non-international conflicts, the expression "armed forces" must necessarily be interpreted broadly to include, in principle, all members of the armed forces of a party to the conflict, irrespective of whether or not they qualify as "lawful" combatants: if that were not the case, it would inevitably follow that in the context of an internal conflict only the activities of the armed forces of the "legitimate" government resisting insurgency would be excluded. Whereas I have no doubt that some people would regard this as a desirable situation, I doubt that it was the one intended by the drafters of the exclusion clause.

Terrorist acts as crimes against humanity

Another exclusion clause included in both the 1999 UN Convention on terrorist bombings and the Coordinator's text of the draft UN comprehensive convention on terrorism applies precisely to the "activities undertaken by the military forces of a State in the exercise of their official duties". But this clause is clearly intended to apply to situations not amounting to armed conflicts and, therefore, not governed by international humanitarian law. Moreover, the exclusion is expressly justified by the fact that the activities in question are "governed by other rules of international law", and the preamble of the 1998 Convention on terrorist bombings makes it clear that it does not "condone or make lawful otherwise unlawful acts, or preclude prosecution under other laws".

There is no doubt that the activities undertaken in time of "peace" by a State's military forces in the exercise of their official duties are "governed" by customary and treaty rules relating to the protection of foreign nationals and their property, to the protection of human rights and, if undertaken abroad, to the protection of other States' territorial sovereignty. But the violation of these rules, while constituting an international wrongful act of the State, does not necessarily entail the individual criminal responsibility of the perpetrator, let alone a duty on the part of the State where the perpetrator is found to prosecute or extradite him or her. Individual criminal responsibility is entailed only in so far as these activities qualify as crimes under a particular treaty or as "crimes against humanity". In this latter respect, there can be no doubt, in my opinion, that acts of "State terrorism" can qualify as crimes against humanity, at least when they are "part of a widespread or systematic attack", *i.e.* they are committed in a systematic or widespread manner pursuant to a State's policy.

Quite apart from acts of "State terrorism", acts committed by members of a terrorist organization could also qualify as crimes against humanity: in fact, as was pointed out by a trial chamber of the ICTY in a decision of 7 May 1997 relating to the *Tadić* case, a "widespread or systematic attack" does not necessarily have to be the result of a State's policy, but can also result from the policy of an "organization", irrespective of whether or not that organization is in *de facto* control of a particular territory.[25] Moreover, whereas under the Statutes of the ICTY, the ICTR and the ICC crimes against humanity must be part of a widespread or systematic attack against civilians, a good case can be made that, under customary international law, the category of crimes against humanity encompasses acts perpetrated against military people or installations also.[26] Finally, as was also pointed out by the trial chamber of the ICTY in the 1997 decision quoted above, a single act by a perpetrator taken within the context of a widespread or systematic attack entails individual criminal responsibility and "an individual perpetrator need not commit numerous offences to be held liable": it is sufficient that he or she knows, or has reason to know, of the broader context in which the act occurs, and that he or she does not act for purely personal reasons.[27]

Consequently, the category of crimes against humanity could in some cases serve as a basis for prosecuting persons belonging to a terrorist organization if no specific treaty is applicable to the offence, and even to "State terrorists" whose activities might be excluded from conventional definitions of terrorism: the category includes murder, extermination, enslavement, deportation, imprisonment, torture, rape, persecution on political, racial or religious grounds, as well as other "inhumane" acts. But, whereas international customary law permits all States to establish their jurisdiction over crimes against humanity on the basis of the "universality" principle, an obligation to prosecute or extradite the alleged criminals cannot easily be derived from customary law.

Concluding remarks

Given that existing treaties following the "sectoral" approach have already given birth to a world network of legal obligations covering the most important aspects of international terrorism, and that acts of terrorism can sometimes qualify as war crimes or as crimes against humanity, the final question remains whether a general definition of terrorist acts is really needed.

The adoption of a residual comprehensive treaty at a world level would, of course, fill all possible gaps, thus further reducing the risk that some States may serve as safe havens or shelters for terrorist activities. Obligations to deny safe haven to terrorists, to ensure that they are brought to justice, and to ensure that "terrorist acts" are established as "serious criminal offences" in domestic law and punished in a way that reflects their "seriousness" have already been imposed upon all UN Member States by Security Council Resolution 1373 of 28 September 2001, which was adopted under Chapter VII of the UN Charter. But this Resolution does not give a general definition of terrorist acts: it could be argued that, until such a definition is agreed in a comprehensive treaty on the suppression of terrorism, the Resolution only refers to acts covered by existing international conventions. On the other hand, inasmuch as the Resolution also applies to the financing of terrorist acts, it could also be argued that a residual definition of such acts can already be derived from the 1999 UN Convention on the Financing of Terrorism.

Secondly, the adoption of an agreed definition at a world level would serve as a basis for the development of a customary rule for the prosecution of terrorist acts under the principle of "universal jurisdiction". The view that terrorism per se *does* amount to a discrete crime under customary international law and that a customary definition of terrorism already exists has been authoritatively put forward in the legal literature.[28] But a recent decision of the US Court of Appeals for the Second Circuit held that "customary international law currently does not provide for the prosecution of 'terrorist' acts under the universality principle, in part due to the failure of States to achieve anything like consensus on the definition of terrorism".[29]

The same decision recognized that "the universality principle permits a State to prosecute an offender of any nationality for an offense committed outside that State and without contacts to that State, but only for the few, near-unique offenses uniformly recognized by the 'civilized nations' as an offense against the 'Law of Nations'", *i.e.* piracy, war crimes and crimes against humanity.[30] The Court seemed thus implicitly to deny that acts of terrorism can ever qualify as international crimes under the customary principle of universal jurisdiction. But, leaving aside the "sectoral" question of whether acts of terrorism can sometimes qualify as "piracy", I have already pointed out that, if certain conditions are met, at least some acts commonly perceived as acts of terrorism can indeed qualify as war crimes or as crimes against humanity.

On the other hand, I have also pointed out that an obligation to exercise "universal" jurisdiction – more specifically, an obligation to prosecute or extradite the alleged offender – is difficult to derive from customary law. A conventional obligation to this effect only exists in respect of "grave breaches" of the 1949 Geneva Conventions and of 1977 Additional Protocol I. No similar obligation exists in respect of war crimes committed in internal conflicts or of crimes against humanity: all that can be said is that, in so far as these crimes fall within the "complementary" jurisdiction of the International Criminal Court, the alleged criminals can be prosecuted at the international level if no satisfactory prosecution takes place at national level.

Given the difficulty of reaching a generally acceptable definition at a world level, a good case could be made that measures to enhance compliance with existing treaties are more urgently needed than a new comprehensive treaty on terrorism. One such measure could be the adoption of a mechanism for the international prosecution of terrorist offences, irrespective of whether or not they qualify as war crimes or as crimes against humanity. It may be interesting to recall in this respect that, when the 1937 LN Convention on the Prevention and Punishment of Terrorism was adopted, another convention designed to establish an International Criminal Court was adopted at the same time, precisely in order to provide for the international prosecution of terrorists. But, of course, that convention, like the Convention on terrorism, never entered into force.

I personally share the view that, despite its flaws, the recent adoption and entry into force of the Rome Statute of the ICC represents a major step forward in the effort to bring international criminals to justice. It is a well-known fact that the inclusion of treaty crimes, including those covered by the "sectoral" treaties dealing with terrorist acts, among the crimes falling within the Court's "complementary" jurisdiction had been envisaged by some States, but, because of opposition on the part of a majority of States, it was eventually left for future decisions by a review conference. A decision to this effect would constitute a further step in the right direction.

Notes

1 Convention on the Prevention and Punishment of Terrorism, adopted in Geneva on 16 November 1937. The 1937 convention never entered into force.

2 Under the auspices of the International Civil Aviation Organization, four important conventions have been adopted: the 1963 Tokyo Convention on Offences and Certain Other Acts Committed on Board Air-

craft; the 1970 Hague Convention for the Suppression of the Unlawful Seizure of Aircraft; the 1971 Montreal Convention for the Suppression of Acts Against the Safety of Civil Aviation; and the 1988 Montreal Protocol for the Suppression of Unlawful Acts of Violence at Airports Serving International Civil Aviation.

[3] Under the auspices of the International Maritime Organization, two conventions were adopted in 1988: the Rome Convention for the Suppression of Unlawful Acts Against the Safety of Maritime Navigation, and the Rome Protocol for the Suppression of Unlawful Acts Against the Safety of Fixed Platforms Located on the Continental Shelf.

[4] Under the auspices of the International Atomic Energy Agency, the Vienna Convention on the Physical Protection of Nuclear Material was adopted in 1980.

[5] Convention on the Prevention and Punishment of Crimes against Internationally Protected Persons, including Diplomatic Agents, adopted by the General Assembly of the United Nations on 14 December 1973.

[6] International Convention against the Taking of Hostages, adopted by the General Assembly of the United Nations on 17 December 1979.

[7] International Convention for the Suppression of Terrorist Bombings, adopted by the General Assembly of the United Nations on 15 December 1997, opened for signature on 12 January 1998.

[8] The latest report on "Measures to eliminate international terrorism" prepared by the Secretary-General of the United Nations (UN Doc. A/57/183, 2 July 2002) lists the following regional treaties: the Arab Convention on the Suppression of the Financing of Terrorism, signed at a meeting held at the General Secretariat of the League of Arab States in Cairo on 22 April 1998; the Convention of the Organization of the Islamic Conference on Combating International Terrorism, adopted at Ouagadougou on 1 July 1999; the European Convention on the Suppression of Terrorism, concluded at Strasbourg on 27 January 1977; the OAS Convention to Prevent and Punish Acts of Terrorism Taking the Form of Crimes against Persons and Related Extortion that are of International Significance, concluded at Washington on 2 February 1971; the OAU Convention on the Prevention and Combating of Terrorism, adopted at Algiers on 14 July 1999; The SAARC Regional Convention on Suppression of Terrorism, signed at Kathmandu on 4 November 1987; and the Treaty on Cooperation among States Members of the Commonwealth of Independent States in Combating Terrorism, done at Minsk on 4 June 1999. Of these, the 1971 OAS Convention is a "sectoral" treaty, and the 1977 European Convention does not contain a comprehensive definition of terrorist acts.

[9] Following General Assembly Resolution 51/210 of 17 December 1996, work on a draft comprehensive convention on the suppression of terrorism, together with work on a draft convention for the suppression of acts of nuclear terrorism, has been going on within an Ad Hoc Committee established by that resolution and within a Working Group of the Sixth Committee. The latest report of the Ad Hoc Committee can be found in UN Doc. A/57/37 of 11 February 2002. The latest report of the Working Group can be found in UN Doc. A/C.6/57/L.9.

[10] International Convention for the Suppression of the Financing of Terrorism, adopted by the General Assembly of the United Nations on 9 December 1999, opened for signature on 10 January 2000.

[11] Council Framework Decision of 13 June 2002 on combating terrorism (2002/475/JHA). EU Framework Decisions are, of course, not regional treaties, but rather acts adopted by the Council of the European Union, which, under Article 34 of the EU Treaty, are binding on EU Member States although they have no direct effect, *i.e.* are not self-executing within their national legal orders.

[12] Suffice it to say, in this respect, that, whereas it is often argued in the relevant literature that terrorism is international when the criminal act occurs in at least two States, or its consequences cross the boundary of a State, or there are persons of different nationalities among the perpetrators, instigators, accomplices, or victims, existing treaties often apply whenever the perpetrator has fled to another country, even if all other elements of the crime are strictly internal.

[13] See the informal text of Article 2 of the convention, prepared by the Coordinator of informal consultations: UN Doc. A/57/37, op. cit. n. 9, Annex II.

[14] See, in particular, Article 1 of the 1999 OIC Convention. But see also Article 1 of the 1998 Arab Convention and Article 1 of the 1999 OAU Convention.

[15] See Article 1 of the 1999 OIC Convention. See also Article 2 of the 1998 Arab Convention.

[16] See Article 1 of the 1999 OAU Convention.

[17] See Article 2 of the 1998 Arab Convention, Article 2 of the 1999 OIC Convention, and Article 3 of the OAU Convention.

[18] See G. Hafner, 'Certain Issues of the Work of the Sixth Committee at the Fifty-sixth General Assembly', 97 *American Journal of International Law* (2003) p. 147 at p. 160.

[19] See the text relating to Article 18 of the draft comprehensive convention circulated for discussion by the

Coordinator of informal consultations: UN Doc. A/57/37, op. cit. n. 9, Annex IV. An alternative text has, however, been proposed by Member States of the Organization of the Islamic Conference: this text would exclude "the activities of the parties during an armed conflict, including in situations of foreign occupation, as those terms are understood under international humanitarian law, which are governed by that law".

[20] A specific prohibition on "terrorism" against "protected persons" can only be found in Article 33 of 1949 Geneva Convention IV: this prohibition covers acts perpetrated by the armed forces of a belligerent against persons who find themselves in the belligerent's territory as internees, or in occupied territory. But, inasmuch as the use of violence for political ends or to coerce a government is the very essence of war, it may well be argued that all serious violations of the laws of war are equivalent to acts of terrorism.

[21] See Article 51, paragraph 2, of Protocol I and Article 13, paragraph 2, of Protocol II.

[22] *The Prosecutor* v. *Dusko Tadić, Decision on the Defence Motion for Interlocutory Appeal on Jurisdiction,* Case No. IT-94-1-AR72, 35 *International Legal Materials*, 1996, 32 ff, paragraph 70. See also Article 8, paragraph 2(f), of the 1998 Rome Statute of the International Criminal Court.

[23] See Article 1, paragraph 2, of 1977 Additional Protocol I (which, however, has a much higher threshold for its application: see Article 1, paragraph 1); Article 1, paragraph 2, of the 1996 amended text of the mines protocol (Protocol II to the 1980 UN Convention on Prohibitions or Restrictions on the Use of Certain Conventional Weapons); Article 8, paragraph 2(d) and (f), of the 1998 Rome Statute of the International Criminal Court. See also Article 22, paragraph 2, of the 1999 Second Protocol to the 1954 Hague Convention on the Protection of Cultural Property in the Event of Armed Conflict (not yet in force).

[24] The traditional requirements for "lawful" belligerency can be found in Article 1 of the Regulations annexed to the 1907 Hague Convention IV Respecting the Laws and Customs of War on Land. The four 1949 Geneva Conventions do not define the notion of "lawful" combatant and concentrate rather on the persons who enjoy the status of prisoners of war in case of capture: see, in particular, Article 4 of Geneva Convention III. For its part, 1977 Additional Protocol I has adopted new and, to some extent, controversial rules on "combatant and prisoner-of-war status" in Section II (Articles 43-47), which are designed to apply to members of national liberation movements engaged in a war of national liberation.

[25] *Prosecutor v. Dusko Tadić a.k.a "Dule", Opinion and Judgment,* Case No. IT-94-1-T, paragraphs 653-655.

[26] See, for example, A. Cassese, *International Criminal Law,* Oxford, 2003, at p. 128.

[27] *Prosecutor v. Dusko Tadić a.k.a "Dule"*, op. cit. n. 25, paragraphs 656-659.

[28] See most recently: A. Cassese, op. cit. n. 26, at pp. 120-125.

[29] See *United States* v. *Yousef et al.*, Nos. 98-1041, 98-1197, 98-1355, 98-1544, 98-1554, 4 April 2003, available through ASIL's *International Law in Brief,* 21 May 2003, at p. 44. It may be interesting to point out that the decision contains some sobering remarks on the importance of "formal lawmaking and official actions of States", as opposed to "the unfounded claim to legal suzerainty by the international law professoriate", in determining customary international law (pp. 47-52).

[30] See: ibidem, at pp. 53-60.

Remarks by Leila Nadya Sadat*

International criminal law, the use of force and 11 September 2001: making the rule of law count

It is the premise of this paper that international criminal law, and not the law of armed conflict, provides the appropriate legal framework through which to view acts of terrorism, even those as heinous as the mass murders of 11 September 2001. Viewing the attacks through the lens of armed conflict distorts their magnitude and exacerbates their effects, and appears ill-suited to combating international terrorism both in the short and long term. In the first part of this paper, I will discuss the growth of international criminal law norms and suggest how they may be properly and creatively

* Professor of Law, Washington University in St. Louis.

applied to the struggle against international terrorism. In the second part, I will examine the 11 September attacks in this context, and suggest how they fit the rubric of international crime. Finally, I conclude with some reflections on both the legality and desirability of current US policy, and particularly the Bush doctrine of preemptive force.

1. The steady accretion of international criminal law norms

The second half of the Twentieth Century witnessed tremendous growth in the normative content of international criminal law with the adoption of several important counter-terrorism treaties, including a series of treaties relating to air safety and airplane hijacking, maritime navigation, fixed platforms on the continental shelf, hostage taking, and the safety of internationally protected persons, the international community was, nonetheless, not united in its condemnation of international terrorism. Persistent debates remained whether there was any uniform definition of the crime. In particular, members of the Non-Aligned group of countries argued for the exclusion of violent actions undertaken by groups fighting in the struggle for national liberation.

Yet, in spite of the significant progress made in criminalizing particular offenses through the adoption of international treaties, there is little doubt that enforcement of those treaties has been problematic. Most anti-terrorism conventions impose a form of "universal jurisdiction by treaty",[1] which grants any State to which the alleged terrorist travels jurisdiction to prosecute him or her. Additionally, these treaties generally impose upon States the duty to try or extradite international terrorists (*aut dedere aut judicare*), and in this manner attempt to create a net through which the terrorist has difficulty in escaping. Yet these instruments notwithstanding, legal experts vigorously debated whether terrorism could generally be considered a universal jurisdiction crime, due in part to the difficulties concerning its definition. Additionally, the crucial enforcement mechanism of the counter-terrorism treaties, *aut dedere, aut judicare,* was generally not believed to be a norm of customary international law, although certain prominent scholars argued to the contrary.[2] Thus, to the extent a terrorist remained on the territory of a "friendly" or incompetent State, that is, a State that was either powerless or not inclined to investigate and punish the criminal in question, the terrorist could largely avoid the application of international law.

Many of these difficulties have been ameliorated in recent times, due to the tremendous progress not only with regard to the enforcement of international norms condemning terrorism, but in parallel areas of international criminal law. In 1993 and 1994 the Security Council took the unprecedented step of establishing the two *ad hoc* tribunals for the Former Yugoslavia and Rwanda. Although there was initial scepticism whether those tribunals would be able to indict and apprehend those thought most culpable in the wars and atrocities committed in Rwanda and the former Yugoslavia, they have been effective and successful, even if not perfect, institutions. Building upon those precedents, the International Criminal Court Treaty was proposed, negotiated and adopted, and has entered into force decades sooner than most would have thought possible. Those institutions do not have the crime of terrorism in their jurisdiction, except to the extent that acts of terrorism could be considered crimes against humanity and potentially the ICC after 2009. But the *Lockerbie* trial, which did address acts of terrorism, is an example of international enforcement that was successfully undertaken by the international community.

The last decade also brought progress in achieving an international consensus on the *per se* illegality of widespread attacks on civilian populations. In 1994 the General Assembly took the position that "criminal acts intended or calculated to provoke a state of terror in the general public, a group of persons or particular persons for political purposes are in any circumstance unjustifiable."[3] The Declaration also required States to "refrain from organizing, instigating, assisting or participating in terrorist acts in territories of other States, or from acquiescing in or encouraging activities within their territories directed towards the commission of such acts."[4] The 1994 Declaration was followed two years later by a second Declaration along the same lines, suggesting the general willingness of the international community to address the problem of terrorism and terrorist havens.[5]

2. The 11 September attacks as international crimes

The attacks of 11 September like the tragic wars in the Former Yugoslavia, the Rwandan genocide, and the horrific bombing of Pan Am 103, presented the world with yet another opportunity to further strengthen the enforcement of international criminal law norms, and fill the gap in enforcement that has plagued efforts to control international terrorists. Indeed, if we leave aside the question whether the acts of 11 September were armed attacks or war crimes, they could clearly be characterized as acts of international terrorism,[6] and crimes against humanity.[7] They involved the intentional killing (murder) of several thousand civilians[8] and attempted murder of thousands more, and appear to have been carried out pursuant to a widespread and arguably systematic attack against a civilian population pursuant to the policy of the Al Qaeda criminal organization. This would fulfill the definition of crimes against humanity in the Rome statute for the International Criminal Court.[9] Moreover, there is no doubt that the attacks violated several of the international terrorism conventions referred to earlier, and that the perpetrators could be prosecuted in US courts under several different federal statutes.

The US government and the international community generally characterized the attacks of 11 September as criminal acts, as evidenced by the Security Council Resolutions adopted after the fact. Security Council Resolution 1373 is extraordinary in this regard. First, building upon the experience of the past decade, the Council assumed that the offenses were crimes of universal international jurisdiction that could be defined by the international community (and presumably could be the subject of adjudication by an international tribunal) and followed by international enforcement action. That is, the Security Council, invoking its Chapter VII authority, has suggested, through its pronouncements after the fact, that the acts of 11 September amounted to international crimes over which the international community (and presumably States, a subject beyond the scope of the present essay) may assert universal international jurisdiction.[10] Although this is consistent with the position the Council has taken in asserting jurisdiction over the crimes committed in the Former Yugoslavia and Rwanda, it is a dramatic extension of those precedents because it suggests that they now apply to acts of international terrorism.

Moreover, as alluded to above, there was substantial debate prior to 11 September 2001, whether terrorism was a universal jurisdiction crime at all. Many national tribunals had opined that it was not, and the *Princeton Principles of Universal Jurisdiction*, adopted in January 2001, only a few months prior to the attack, omitted terrorism from the list of crimes over which States could presumptively exercise universal jurisdiction.[11] Whether Resolution 1373 is the codification of custom, instant custom, or a new form of Security Council "legislation",[12] its adoption suggests a sea change in *opinio juris* on the issue of terrorism as a universal jurisdiction crime, enacted, to be sure, against the backdrop of a custom that had been evolving in that direction already.

In addition, Resolution 1373 appears to suggest that the principle *aut dedere, aut judicare* is also a matter of customary international law. That is, to the extent a crime is a universal jurisdiction crime, this principle appears to apply as a matter of customary international law. This would represent a tremendous advance in the enforcement of international criminal law norms by national legal systems. Resolution 1373 also provides in paragraph 28) that States must "deny safe haven to those who finance, plan, support, or commit terrorist acts", suggesting, like General Assembly Resolutions 49/60 and 51/210, that States may not serve as safe havens for terrorists without running afoul of international law. The question remains, of course, what consequences flow from a State's breach of this obligation.

Given the general prohibition in the Charter against the unilateral use of force by States in resolving international disputes, the course of action that appears most consistent with the existing framework of international law is to request the Security Council to intervene in cases involving terrorist attacks launched from one State against the territory of another. Although some have made the case for the legality of the 7 October military response of the USA in the absence of any explicit authorization of the Council, as we have seen earlier, the facts of that case are quite unique, involving not only attacks significant both in scale and symbolism, prior demands from the Security Council to the Taliban to turn over the individuals suspected of their organization, evidence of complicity between the terrorist organization and the *de facto* government of Afghanistan, virtually universal and worldwide condemnation of the attacks themselves, and few questions as to their source. In other cases, the responsibility of a State may be much less evident, and the unanimity of the international community much less sure. In the case of 11 September, the USA could have obtained a third Security Council Resolution to enforce Resolution 1373: this final Resolution, like the famous Resolution 678 that authorized operation Desert Storm, would have required the Taliban regime of Afghanistan to turn over Osama bin Laden and his accomplices, based upon evidence establishing the equivalent of "probable cause"[13] that he and the Al Qaeda network were responsible for the attacks of 11 September. The resolution could have set a deadline for doing so, and authorized States to use "all necessary means" to effectuate his capture if the Taliban refused to surrender him, just as Resolution 678 did in 1990 with regard to the Iraqi invasion of Kuwait.[14] There is no doubt that this hypothetical international 'arrest warrant" would have been issued by the Council at US urging; the world expressed both its sorrow and solidarity with the United States in the wake of the 11 September attacks, and at the time Resolutions 1368 and 1373 were adopted, bin Laden was threatening the United Nations as a future target of his terrorist network. In this way, the US-led military action and response to international terrorism would have set an important precedent and would have reinforced the normative content and institutional framework of international law. The USA, however, specifically chose not to return to the Council and to keep its use of force solely under its control, thereby rejecting the precedent set largely by the first President Bush in responding to the Iraqi invasion of Kuwait in 1990.

3. Conclusion

The temptation to jettison legal constraints is understandable when faced with a hostile enemy that does not itself obey the law. And there are perhaps times when law fails, or when civil disobedience is appropriate if law itself becomes illegal or immoral. But the attacks of 11 September did not present such a case. Indeed, the hideousness of the acts themselves so shocked the international community that they provided a unique opportunity to strengthen a growing international consensus condemning attacks on civilians whatever the motivation.[15] This is not to suggest that a military response was necessarily illegal under the circumstances, only that any military actions taken must, to be effective in the long term, employ force in service of the rule of law. The ultimate test of America's strength will not be its ability to respond militarily to threats all over the world, threats that are by definition random, designed to inflict terror, and carried out by very small numbers of individuals willing to die in the process of carrying out their criminal design. Instead, America's strength will lie in its ability to persuade others to join its cause against international terrorism, and establish international institutions and international norms to do so, norms which States are willing to enforce domestically.[16]

The attacks of 11 September presented the United States with an extraordinary opportunity to reshape the norms of international law to promote their effective enforcement. International conventions against terrorism that proved ineffective to the extent terrorists could take refuge in States that had either unwillingly or willingly become accomplices to their action were to be enforced by Security Council action to the extent that other means proved ineffective, and the terrorists' activities threatened the maintenance of international peace and security. Moreover, international military action, guided by law and explicitly authorized by a Resolution of the Security Council, would seemingly have proven no less effective than a military campaign launched on more ambiguous terms. Viewing the anti-terrorism campaign in Afghanistan as an international criminal law enforcement operation, rather than an act of retribution would have created a positive precedent for future cases. The present unilateralist approach provides States wishing to do so the opportunity to eliminate dissidents and those otherwise opposed to their rule (including governments or rebels in neighbouring States) by labeling them terrorists, and not therefore subject to the normal legal constraints that govern the use of force.[17] This erosion of the rule of law is in the interest of no State in the world, not even the world's only superpower. While the terrorists of 11 September may have been self-styled warriors, they and their ilk are not combatants engaged in international armed conflict, but seemingly pathological criminals that require arrest and deterrence. Although it is now fashionable to suggest that we must abandon liberal regimes in favor of a new Hobbesian reality when faced with the menace of ruthless international criminals, Hobbes himself did not suggest that "going it alone" was the solution to survival in the state of nature. Indeed, because even the strongest man must sleep, and can be felled by the weakest, with a knife in the back as he sleeps, cooperation and trust are prerequisites for survival in a world where life is, otherwise, nasty, brutish and short.[18]

Notes

1 Jordan J. Paust, et al., *International Criminal Law: Cases and Materials* 157 (2nd edn. 2000).

2 See generally, M. Cherif Bassiouni & Edward M. Wise, *Aut Dedere, Aut Judicare: The Duty to Extradite or Prosecute in International Law* (1995).

3 Declaration on Measures to Eliminate International Terrorism, GA Res. 49/60, UN GAOR 6th Comm., 49th Sess., 84th plen. Mtg., UN Doc. A/49/743 (1994).

4 *Id.*

5 Declaration to Supplement the 1994 Declaration on Measures to Eliminate International Terrorism, GA Res. 51/210, UN GAOR 6th Comm., 51st Sess., 88th plen. mtg., UN Doc. A/51/631 (1996).

6 This essay, admittedly, does not address the often difficult question of terrorism's definition. For a discussion of this question, see, e.g., James A.R. Nafziger, 'The Grave New World of Terrorism: A Lawyer's View', *31 Denv. J. Int'l. L. & Pol'y* 101 (2003).

7 To the extent that the Al Qaeda movement indiscriminately targets persons of particular nationalities for extermination, its actions could even be considered genocidal in character. See also *id.* at 109.

8 It might be possible to consider the attack on the Pentagon an attack on a military object, perhaps bringing it outside the prohibition against widespread attacks on civilian populations. There is insufficient space in this essay to address this question fully.

9 Rome Statute for the International Criminal Court, Art. 7(1)(a).

10 Leila Nadya Sadat, *The International Criminal Court and the Transformation of International Law: Justice for the New Millennium* (Transnational, 2002) at ch. 5.

11 The Princeton Principles on Universal Jurisdiction, Principle 2(1) (Princeton Program in Law and Public Affairs, 2001). The Restatement of Foreign Relations Law (Third) suggests that certain acts of terrorism are increasingly accepted as universal jurisdiction crimes, such as "assaults on the life or physical integrity of diplomatic personnel, kidnapping, and indiscriminate violent assaults on people at large." Restatement of Foreign Relations Law (Third), par. 404, Comment a.

12 Paul Szasz, 'The Security Council Starts Legislating', 96 *Am. J. Int'l L.* 901 (2002).

13 For the argument that "clear and convincing evidence" of a State's complicity should be the standard for a unilateral action based on self-defense in response to a terrorist attack launched from the territory of that State see Mary Ellen O'Connell, 'Evidence of Terror', 7 J. *Conflict & Security L.* 19 (2002). This is not quite the same issue as what evidence should be required in order for the Security Council to issue the equivalent of an "arrest warrant" for the capture of a suspect in a case of international terrorism.

14 UN SC Res. 678 (29 November 1990). For an excellent treatment of recent Security Council practice involving Chapter VII see Mary Ellen O'Connell, 'The UN, NATO, and International Law after Kosovo', 22 *Human Rts. Q.* 57, 67-70 (2000).

15 Anne-Marie Slaughter, *The Future of International Law: Ending the U.S.-Europe Divide, in* A Defining Moment B International Law Since September 11, Crimes of War Project (visited 23 January 2003) <http://www.crimesofwar.org/sept-mag/sept-contrib.html>.

16 Cf. Joseph Nye, *The Paradox of American Power* (2002).

17 This has occurred in Russia, in China, in Israel, and in Uzbekistan, to name a few.

18 Of course, under Hobbes' scheme, for cooperation to work there must be some power of enforcement, which is why he has often been cited for the proposition that the state of nature is preferable to cooperation in international affairs, unless it can be argued that the current collective security mechanism of the UN or the new International Criminal Court can provide such an enforcement mechanism. Thanks to Professor Larry May for bringing his wonderful analysis of Hobbes to my attention. See Larry May, *Crime and Humanity: Philosophical Reflections on International Criminal Law* (forthcoming).

REMARKS BY W.J. FENRICK*

INTERNATIONAL TERRORISM AND INTERNATIONAL LAW: THE ICTY EXPERIENCE

The International Criminal Tribunal for the former Yugoslavia (ICTY) has jurisdiction over serious violations of international humanitarian law (specifically grave breaches of the Geneva Conventions, violations of the laws or customs of war, genocide, and crimes against humanity) committed by natural persons in the territory of the former Yugoslavia since 1 January 1991. All of our offences except genocide must have some linkage with armed conflict. Many of the incidents concerning trials which we have had have been terrifying and horrifying. For that matter, much of what happens in armed conflict can be so described. Our experience at the ICTY might, however, have relevance to this panel discussion in two areas, first, our use of unlawfully inflicting terror upon civilians as a criminal charge and, second, our experience with doctrines of individual criminal responsibility in terrorist-type situations.

In the Office of the Prosecutor (OTP), our interest in using terror as a charge was first generated by reflecting on words written by Sir Hersch Lauterpacht in the bleak aftermath of World War II, a period in which many doubted that limits could be imposed on war:

> [I]t is in [the] prohibition, which is a clear rule of law, of intentional terrorization – or destruction – of the civilian population as an avowed or obvious object of attack that lies the last vestige of the claim that war can be legally regulated at all. Without that irreducible principle of restraint there is no limit to the licence and depravity of force.[1]

As Myres McDougal, the American legal theorist, subsequently observed: "The essentially modest character of this 'absolute rule' needs no underlining".[2]

It appeared to us that the concept of the intentional infliction of terror was an accurate characterization of what was done to the civilian population of Sarajevo over a several years' period. We identified a firm legal basis for a terror charge in common sentences in Article 51(2) of Additional Protocol I and Article 13(2) of Additional Protocol II thereby ensuring the offence was applicable to all armed conflicts. These sentences state: "Acts or threats of violence the primary purpose of which is to spread terror among the civilian population are prohibited." To date, the single use of this offence is in the Galić indictment as follows:

> COUNT 1
> (INFLICTION OF TERROR)
> From about 10 September 1992 to about 10 August 1994, **STANISLAV GALIĆ**, as Commander of Bosnian Serb forces comprising or attached to the Sarajevo Romanija Corps, conducted a protracted campaign of shelling and sniping upon civilian areas of Sarajevo and upon the civilian population thereby inflicting terror and mental suffering upon its civilian population.

* Senior Legal Adviser, Office of the Prosecutor, International Criminal Tribunal for the Former Yugoslavia. These comments are made in a personal capacity and do not necessarily reflect the views of either the Office of the Prosecutor or of the United Nations.

By his acts and omissions, STANISLAV GALIĆ, is responsible for:

COUNT 1: Violations of the Laws or Customs of War (unlawfully inflicting terror upon civilians as set forth in Article 51 of Additional Protocol I and Article 13 of Additional Protocol II to the Geneva Conventions of 1949) punishable under Article 3 of the Statute of the Tribunal.

In its Pre-Trial Brief (para. 142), the OTP submitted that the offence of unlawfully inflicting terror contained the following elements:

(1) unlawful acts or threats of violence;
(2) which caused terror to spread among the civilian population;
(3) the acts or threats of violence were carried out with the primary purpose of spreading terror among the civilian population;
(4) there is a nexus between the acts or threats and an armed conflict, whether international or internal in character; and
(5) the Accused bears individual criminal responsibility for the acts or threats under either Article 7(1) or 7(3) of the Statute.

It also submitted that the elements of infliction of terror upon civilians are primarily distinguished from unlawful attack charges by element (1), which encompasses acts or *threats* of violence, and element (3) which required that the *actus reus* be executed with the "primary purpose of spreading terror among the civilian population." This special intent requirement is the key distinguishing feature of this crime. It is distinguished also by its effect, which in the present case was the profound psychological impact on the population.

As Articles 51 and 13 encompass "threats" as well as "acts" of violence, the scope of the *actus reus* of the offence of unlawfully inflicting terror upon civilians is accordingly broad. The *acts* of violence in *Galić* consisted of deliberate and systematic shelling and sniping at civilians. The nature of the acts and manner in which they were carried out represented a constant *threat* to civilians that, at any moment, they too could be subject to such violence.

The Galić indictment was confirmed and Count 1 has withstood all challenges to date, including a Defence Motion for acquittal under our Rule 98 bis at the close of the Prosecution phase of the case. The *Galić* Trial ended in May but we are awaiting the judgment of the Trial Chamber.

The ICRC has addressed the terror issue in Article 51(2) of API and Article 13(2) of APII as follows:

"In the second sentence the Conference wished to indicate that the prohibition covers acts intended to spread terror; there is no doubt that acts of violence related to a state of war almost always give rise to some degree of terror among the population and sometimes also among the armed forces. It also happens that attacks on armed forces are purposely conducted brutally in order to intimidate the enemy soldiers and persuade them to surrender. This is not the sort of terror envisaged here. This provision is intended to prohibit acts of violence the primary purpose of which is to spread terror among the civilian population without offering substantial military advantage. It is interesting to note that threats of such acts are also prohibited. This calls to mind some of the proclamations made in the past threatening the annihilation of civilian populations."[3].

> "Attacks aimed at terrorizing are just one type of attack, but they are particularly reprehensible. Attempts have been made for a long time to prohibit such attacks, for they are frequent and inflict particularly cruel suffering upon the civilian population. Thus the Draft Rules of Aerial Warfare, prepared in The Hague in 1922, already prohibited such attacks. Air raids have often been used as a means of terrorizing the population, but these are not the only methods. For this reason the text contains a much broader expression, namely "acts or threats of violence" so as to cover all possible circumstances.
> Any attack is likely to intimidate the civilian population. The attacks or threats concerned here are therefore those, the primary purpose of which is to spread terror, as one delegate stated during the debates at the Conference."[4]

The OTP submitted that the spreading of terror among the civilian population of Sarajevo was an intended consequence of the acts and threats of violence referred to above. There was a climate of extreme psychological fear in Sarajevo during the Indictment period, generated by the unlawful shelling and sniping campaigns, with the result that much of the civilian population lived in a state of terror. Whether or not unlawful acts do in fact spread terror among the civilian population could be proved either directly of inferentially. It can be demonstrated by evidence of the psychological state of civilians at the relevant time, including the civilian population's way of life during the period, and the short and long-term psychological impact of these acts and threats. Although the acts or threats may have been directed against particular persons, the consequence, namely terror, was directed against and felt by the "civilian population" in general. The requirement that terror be spread among the civilian population is satisfied even if certain civilians, or sectors of the population, were not so affected.

The prohibition in Articles 51(2) and 13(2) of Additional Protocols I and II refers to unlawful acts or threats of violence, the *primary purpose* of which is to spread extreme fear among the civilian population. Although attacks upon legitimate military objectives may in fact cause terror among the civilian population, this would not suffice to make such attacks unlawful. Rather, the OTP submitted that acts or threats fall within the prohibition against deliberately inflicting terror only if they are unlawful and if the *principal purpose* of the acts or threats is to terrorise civilians. Thus, the prohibition against terror is distinguishable, first and foremost, for this special intent requirement.

We look forward with considerable interest to the ruling of the Trial Chamber on this important count.

Although the *Galić* case has been the only one including a terror count, issues relevant to terror have been raised in connection with a variety of cases. In Galić itself, the Defence in its opening statement raised the argument that Bosnia under Muslim control could be a gateway to Europe for the mujahedin and emphasized the horror of this prospect by putting a picture of Osama bin Laden on the courtroom TV monitors. In the *Hadzihazanović* case, expected to start in the near future, Bosnian Muslim commanders are charged on the basis of the doctrine of command responsibility because, allegedly, mujahedin from the Muslim Brigade killed Bosnian Croat civilians and soldiers who had surrendered. In the *Blaskić* case, relying on the approach of the Israeli Kahan Report into events in the Beirut Refugee Camps in 1983[5] the court held in paragraph 474:

"[....] any person who, in ordering an act, knows that there is a risk of crimes being committed and accepts that risk, shows the degree of intention necessary (recklessness) so as to incur responsibility for having ordered, planned or incited the commitment of the crimes. In this case, the accused knew that the troops which he had used to carry out the order of attack of 16 April had previously been guilty of many crimes against the Muslim population of Bosnia".

The Trial Chamber's approach to the meaning of "had reason to know", its willingness to draw an inference that offences had been ordered because of their widespread and systematic nature, and its willingness to assign criminal responsibility to superiors for the subsequent activities of their troops who are known to have been guilty of offences in the past, may well be relevant to terrorism cases.

The concept of Joint Criminal Enterprise (JCE) or Common Criminal Purpose may be of particular importance in terrorism cases. It is not explicitly referred to in the ICTY Statute. It is referred to in passing in the *Tadić* Trial Chamber[6] decision (para. 685). The concept was argued by the Prosecution in the *Tadić* Appeal and then focused on at considerable length in the *Tadić* Appeal Chamber decision. JCE has since been applied to senior persons in the *Kordić/Čerkez* Trial Chamber decision,[7] the *Krstić* Trial Chamber decision,[8] and the *Kvočka* decision.[9] The doctrine has also been discussed at length in the *Prosecutor* v. *Brdanin and Talić* Decision on Form of Indictment.[10]

The *Tadić* Appeals Chamber has emphasized that JCE is, by implication, a necessary component of Article 7(1) and firmly rooted in customary international law. One might observe, however, that:

a) the International Military Tribunal (IMT) Charter[11] contained the following provision in Article 6: "Leaders, organizers, instigators and accomplices participating in the formulation or execution of a common plan or conspiracy to commit any of the foregoing crimes are responsible for all acts performed by any persons in execution of such plan."
b) IMT and IMTFE[12] (which had a similar provision in its charter) confined application of JCE to crimes against peace,
c) Control Council Law No. 10[13] had an even broader explicit JCE provision,
d) although the ICC Statute[14] has a "JCE" provision, it is narrower than the ICTY JCE doctrine and states:
   Article 25 (3) In accordance with this Statute, a person shall be criminally responsible and liable for punishment for a crime within the jurisdiction of the Court if that person:.....
e) in any other way contributes to the commission or attempted commission of such a crime by a group of persons acting with a common purpose. Such contribution shall be intentional and shall either:
   (i) Be made with the aim of furthering the criminal activity or criminal purpose of the group, where such activity or purpose involves the commission of a crime within the jurisdiction of the Court: or
   (ii) Be made in the knowledge of the intention of the group to commit the crime; ...

As opposed to the ICTY JCE doctrine, the ICC Statute has an explicit JCE provision and it does not extend to crimes beyond the scope of the enterprise.

The basic features of JCE before the ICTY and its distinction from aiding and abetting are set out in the Tadić Appeals Chamber decision:

220. … the notion of common design as a form of accomplice liability is firmly established in customary international law and in addition is upheld, albeit implicitly, in the Statute of the International Tribunal. As for the objective and subjective elements of the crime, the case law shows that the notion has been applied to three distinct categories of cases. First, in cases of co-perpetration, where all participants in the common design possess the same criminal intent to commit a crime (and one or more of them actually perpetrate the crime, with intent). Secondly, in the so-called "concentration camp" cases, where the requisite *mens rea* comprises knowledge of the nature of the system of ill-treatment and intent to further the common design of ill-treatment. Such intent may be proved either directly or as a matter of inference from the nature of the accused's authority within the camp or organisational hierarchy. With regard to the third category of cases, it is appropriate to apply the notion of "common purpose" only where the following requirements concerning *mens rea* are fulfilled: (i) the intention to take part in a joint criminal enterprise and to further – individually and jointly – the criminal purposes of that enterprise; and (ii) the foreseeability of the possible commission by other members of the group of offences that do not constitute the object of the common criminal purpose.

227. In sum, the objective elements (*actus reus*) of this mode of participation in one of the crimes provided for in the Statute (with regard to each of the three categories of cases) are as follows:

i. *A plurality of persons.* They need not be organised in a military, political or administrative structure…

ii. *The existence of a common plan, design or purpose which amounts to or involves the commission of a crime provided for in the Statute.* There is no necessity for this plan, design or purpose to have been previously arranged or formulated…

iii. *Participation of the accused in the common design* involving the perpetration of one of the crimes provided for in the Statute. This participation need not involve commission of a specific crime under one of those provisions (for example, murder, extermination, torture, rape, etc.), but may take the form of assistance in, or contribution to, the execution of the common plan or purpose.

228. By contrast, the *mens rea* element differs according to the category of common design under consideration. With regard to the first category, what is required is the intent to perpetrate a certain crime (this being the shared intent on the part of all co-perpetrators). With regard to the second category (which, as noted above, is really a variant of the first), personal knowledge of the system of ill-treatment is required (whether proved by express testimony or a matter of reasonable inference from the accused's position of authority), as well as the intent to further this common concerted system of ill-treatment. With regard to the third category, what is required is the *intention* to participate in and further the criminal activity or the criminal purpose of a group and to contribute to the joint criminal enterprise or in any event to the commission of a crime by the group. In addition, responsibility for a crime other than the one agreed upon in the common plan arises only if, under the circumstances of the case, (i) it was *foreseeable* that such a crime might be perpetrated by one or other members of the group and (ii) the accused *willingly took that risk*.

229. In light of the preceding propositions it is now appropriate to distinguish between acting in pursuance of a common purpose or design to commit a crime, and aiding and abetting.

(i) The aider and abettor is always an accessory to a crime perpetrated by another person, the principal.

(ii) In the case of aiding and abetting no proof is required of the existence of a common concerted plan…
(iii) The aider and abettor carries out acts specifically directed to assist, encourage or lend moral support to the perpetration of a certain specific crime (murder, extermination, rape, torture, wanton destruction of civilian property, etc.), and this support has a substantial effect upon the perpetration of the crime. By contrast, in the case of acting in pursuance of a common purpose or design, it is sufficient for the participant to perform acts that in some way are directed to the furthering of the common plan or purpose.
(iv) In the case of aiding and abetting, the requisite mental element is knowledge that the acts performed by the aider and abettor assist the commission of a specific crime by the principal. By contrast, in the case of common purpose or design more is required (i.e., either intent to perpetrate the crime or intent to pursue the common criminal design plus foresight that those crimes outside the criminal common purpose were likely to be committed), as stated above.

It must be emphasized that before an accused can be convicted on the basis of JCE it must be established that another member of the JCE, with the requisite intent, perpetrated the crime. Article 7(3) responsibility of one JCE member does not, of itself, provide a basis for imposing 7(1) responsibility on another member of the JCE. Although JCE may be a useful tool for terrorism cases, one must draw the line far before making all persons on one side criminally culpable.

"The country's planted thick with laws from coast to coast – Man's laws, not God's – and if you cut them down – d'you really think you could stand upright in the winds that would blow then? Yes, I'd give the Devil benefit of law, for my own safety's sake." (Robert Bolt, *A Man for All Seasons*)

Notes

1 Hersch Lauterpacht, 'The Problem of the Revision of the Law of War', 29 *Brit.Y.B. Int'l L.* 360, 369 (1952).
2 M.S. McDougal & F.P. Feliciano, *The International Law of War: Transnational Coercion and World Public Order* 80 (1994)
3 Y. Sandoz, C. Swinarski, B. Zimmerman, eds., *Commentary on the Additional Protocols* (1987) para. 1940.
4 Ibid., paras. 4785-86.
5 Final Report of the Commission of Inquiry into the Events at the Refugee Camps in Beirut, 7 February 1983, reproduced in 22 *ILM* 473-520 (1983).
6 *Prosecutor* v. *Tadić*, Trial Judgment 7 May 1997, Appeals Judgment 15 July 1999, ICTY Case No. IT-94-1-T&A.
7 *Prosecutor* v. *Kordić & Čerkez*, Trial Judgment 26 February 2001, ICTY Case No. IT-95-14/2-T.
8 *Prosecutor* v. *Krstić*, Trial Judgment 1 August 2001, ICTY Case No. IT-98-33-T.
9 *Prosecutor* v. *Kvočka et al*, Trial Judgment 2 November 2001 ICTY Case No. IT-98-30/1-T.
10 *Prosecutor* v. *Brdanin & Talić*, Decision on Form of Further Amended Indictment 26 June 2001 ICTY Case No. IT-99-36-PT.
11 Charter of the International Military Tribunal, in H.S. Levie, *Terrorism in War – The Law of War Crimes* 549 (1993).
12 Charter of the International Military Tribunal for the Far East, in ibid., 571.
13 Control Council Law No. 10, in ibid., 558.
14 Rome Statute of the International Criminal Tribunal adopted on 17 July 1998 in W.A. Schabas, *An Introduction to the International Criminal Court* 167 (2001).

Remarks by Jordan J. Paust*

International law concerning domestic prosecutions of Al Qaeda attacks

I. Introduction

It is widely expected that Al Qaeda, a non-State entity headed by Osama bin Laden, has been engaged in terroristic attacks against the United States and other countries and their nationals. Prominent examples include the attack on the housing compounds in Saudi Arabia in 2003; of 11 September 2001, in the USA on the World Trade Center and the Pentagon; the attack on the USS Cole in 2000; the attack on US Embassies in Kenya and Tanzania in 1998; and the attack on the World Trade Center in 1993. Would any of those attacks attributed to members of Al Qaeda constitute international crimes under customary or treaty-based law? Is terrorism such a crime? If so, would there be extraterritorial jurisdiction under principles of international law in countries such as the United States over perpetrators of such crimes?

II. Al Qaeda and international crimes

A. **Generally not war crimes**

1. *States cannot be at war with Al Qaeda as such*

Al Qaeda is not a State, nation, belligerent, or insurgent under international law.[1] Thus, outside some context of war the United States cannot be at war with Al Qaeda as such (or with "terrorism" generally). For this reason, outside a wartime context to which the laws of war apply, the laws of war do not apply to US operations directed merely against Al Qaeda (or vice versa) and members of Al Qaeda cannot be "enemy combatants," prisoners of war, unlawful combatants,[2] or war criminals prosecutable for violations of the laws of war.

2. *The 7 October 2001 war in Afghanistan*

However, when the United States used military force in Afghanistan on 7 October 2001 against the Taliban, the United States upgraded a belligerency between the Taliban and the Northern Alliance and was engaged in an international armed conflict to which, at least, all of the customary laws of war apply.[3] Any violations of the laws of war engaged in by members of Al Qaeda within the theater of the Afghan war would be prosecutable as war crimes.[4] However, other conduct by members of Al Qaeda outside the theater of war would not qualify as acts of war or war crimes. Thus, Al Qaeda attacks on the USA or its nationals outside Afghanistan or prior to 7 October 2001 would not qualify as war crimes.

* Law Foundation Professor, University of Houston, Houston, Texas.

B. Terrorism

1. *International proscription of terrorism*

Are terrorist acts engaged in by Al Qaeda international crimes? At least since 1985, the international community has recognized that terrorism is criminally proscribed. For example, in 1985 in sweeping, unlimited language, the UN General Assembly "[u]nequivocally" condemned, "as criminal, all acts, methods and practices of terrorism wherever and by whomever committed."[5] Also in 1985, the UN Security Council "resolutely" condemned "'all acts of terrorism' ... in all its forms, wherever and by whomever committed."[6] However, the international community has not been able to provide a definition of that which is so unequivocally and resolutely condemned as criminal. Nonetheless, there has been widespread condemnation of 11 September, Cole, and US embassy attacks as impermissible terrorism.

2. *An objective definition*

If terrorism is proscribed as criminal under international law, what is "terrorism"? In prior writings, I have suggested that a definition of terrorism should not confuse issues concerning permissibility of an overall struggle with permissibility of the use of terroristic tactics during such a struggle.[7] Moreover, one should try to identify objectively what the tactic of terrorism involves and, as the international community seems to stress in UN Resolutions, one should not exclude certain actors or contexts by definitional orientation. An objective definition of "terrorism" should involve the following elements: (1) an intentional use of the tactic by a human perpetrator, (2) violence or a weapon, (3) a political purpose, and (4) creation of intense fear or anxiety (i.e., a "terror" outcome).[8] If there is no terror outcome, use of the word "terrorism" would be highly inappropriate, although attempted terrorism might fit.

With these and other points in mind, it was suggested that an objective definition will recognize that terrorism involves the intentional use of violence, or the threat of violence, by a precipitator against an instrumental target (e.g., property or human) in order to communicate to a primary target a threat of future violence, so as to coerce the primary target through intense fear or anxiety in connection with a demanded political outcome.[9] Since such writings, it is evident that violence is not absolutely necessary. For example, use of bacteriologic or biologic weapons in order to produce terror should suffice even if they are not delivered by violent means. Thus, the phrase "intentional use of violence or a weapon" seems preferable. Additionally, there may be a question whether groups like Al Qaeda intend to produce political outcomes. Do they intend to produce merely religious outcomes or, in context, is there a significant difference? Perhaps Al Qaeda primarily engages in religiously motivated terrorism that is intended to produce certain political outcomes, which would be covered by the definition.

C. Hague and Montreal aircraft hijacking and sabotage conventions

The 11 September attacks on the World Trade Center and Pentagon by members of Al Qaeda engaged in non-State actor aircraft hijacking and sabotage are covered by treaty-based international crimes that are also most likely criminal under customary international law. The attacks fit easily within criminal conduct outlined in Article 1 of the Hague Convention on the Suppression of Unlawful Seizure of Aircraft[10] and Article 1 of the Montreal Convention for the Suppression of Unlawful Acts Against the Safety of Civil Aviation.[11] However, Article 3(3) of the Hague Convention excludes coverage if the place of take-off is not outside US territory. Yet, Article 3(5) allows coverage if the offender is found in territory of a State other than the State of registration of the aircraft (i.e., other than the USA, since American Airlines and United Airlines are US registered). Similarly, Article 4(2) of the Montreal Convention would exclude coverage when the aircraft took off and were scheduled to land in the USA (which is the case) and the offenses were committed in US territory. Yet, Article 4(3) allows application of the treaty if an offender is found in the territory of a State other than the United States. Thus, Article 3(5) of the Hague Convention and Article 4(3) of the Montreal Convention would allow prosecution of members of Al Qaeda who were perpetrators of the attacks (e.g., by giving orders) or an "accomplice"[12] if they are found outside the USA. Since the primary acts occurred within the United States, the USA would clearly have territorial jurisdiction and even objective territorial jurisdiction with respect to perpetrators, conspirators or accomplices located outside the USA[13]. As noted in Part III, the USA would also have protective and universal jurisdiction.

D. **Crimes against internationally protected persons**

Quite clearly, Al Qaeda attacks on US Embassies in Kenya and Tanzania involved attacks on internationally protected persons within the meaning of Articles 1(1)(b) and 2(1) of the Convention on the Prevention and Punishment of Crimes Against Internationally Protected Persons, Including Diplomatic Agents.[14]

E. **Crimes against humanity**

Al Qaeda attacks on civilians or civilian groups as such, as opposed to the attacks on the Pentagon and the USS Cole, can also constitute crimes against humanity under customary international law over which there is universal jurisdiction. The attacks involved unlawful killing of civilians, or "murder," and under customary instruments addressing crimes against humanity this should suffice whether or not particular attacks were also "widespread" or "systematic."[15] The attacks on the housing compounds in Saudi Arabia, the World Trade Center, and the US Embassies in Kenya and Tanzania, or their combination, may have even been both widespread and systematic.

As noted in another writing, prosecution of Mr. bin Laden and others acting outside the United States in connection with the 11 September terroristic attacks on the United States and on US nationals is possible under the US Antiterrorism Act.[16] Section 2332(a) of the Act is not applicable to homicide as such arising from the 11 September attacks because, although the section applies to "[w]hoever kills a national of the United States," it adds the limiting phrase "while such national is outside the United States." Yet, such language would cover prosecution of homicide against US nationals abroad involving the bombings in Saudi Arabia, of US Embassies in Kenya and Tanzania, and the attack on the USS Cole. Section 2332(b) does not contain the limiting phrase noted above regarding the location of US victims and can cover attempts and conspiracy in connection with the killing of a national of the United States (apparently anywhere) although the accused must be "outside the United States" at the time of the attempt or the engagement in a conspiracy to kill. Section 2332(c) should also be applicable, since it reaches an accused "outside the United States" who "engages in physical violence – (1) with intent to cause serious bodily injury to a national of the United States; or (2) with the result that serious bodily injury is caused to a national of the United States." Section 2332(d) requires written certification by the US Attorney-General "or the highest ranking subordinate" that offenses under Section 2332 were "intended to coerce, intimidate, or retaliate against a government or a civilian population" – a certification that would likely be forthcoming and appropriate. Other provisions of the legislation would also be applicable.[17] Jurisdiction under international law supporting prosecution could involve objective territorial, protective, and universal jurisdiction, the latter especially with respect to crimes against humanity and underlying violations of customary human rights law (e.g., the right to life).

III. Jurisdiction under international law

A. Protective jurisdiction

Various principles of customary international law exist concerning jurisdictional competence of a State to prescribe rules attempting to reach conduct outside the State's borders, although such laws are usually enforced within the State. One such principle is the protective principle. It provides a useful basis for criminal and civil prescriptive jurisdiction over extraterritorial conduct implicating responsibility for certain acts of terrorism. Even though all relevant acts occur outside the territory of a State, jurisdiction is possible under the protective principle if a significant national interest is at stake and it is not otherwise impermissible under international law to exercise jurisdiction.[18] As US cases recognize, if protective jurisdiction exists, no contacts or nexus between proscribed conduct and the territory of the United States are needed.[19]

Relevant protective interests can involve significant threats to national security, territorial integrity, or political independence[20] and acts triggering the right of self-defense.[21] Thus, one can recognize that armed attacks by Al Qaeda on targets within the United States or on US Embassies, US military, and other US nationals abroad can trigger both the right of self-defense[22] and protective jurisdictional competence.[23] In light of the increase in the number of terroristic threats against US citizens abroad, there can be no doubt that the United States has significant security and protective interests at stake, at least when demands are made upon the US government or the security of the United States is seriously threatened.[24]

There is a danger in pushing the protective theory too far, however, and the better view is that actual effects should be felt, or be likely to be felt, before the protective principle could properly apply.[25] Additionally, the national interests at stake, when viewed in context, should be of real significance.

B. Universal jurisdiction

1. *Regarding violations of customary international law*

Another basis for jurisdiction recognized in international law is universal jurisdiction.[26] With respect to criminal sanctions, the universality principle provides for jurisdiction both to prescribe domestic laws and to enforce sanctions against crimes or violations that have an independent basis in international law. At a minimum, the principle applies to crimes that are of interest to the international community or "to crimes that affect the international community and are against customary international law."[27] Universal jurisdiction is thus technically jurisdiction to enforce customary international law, and enforcement is actually made on behalf of the international community by any State that has an accused within its control.[28]

US criminal prosecutions and extradition of aircraft hijackers, hostage-takers, terrorists, and others have rested in whole or in part on universal jurisdiction.[29] Specific contacts with the forum (i.e., the State seeking to enforce jurisdiction) are not required.[30] Thus, nationality of the victims or perpetrators and the location where the alleged crimes took place are not relevant. For example, during a civil suit in *Daliberti* v. *Republic of Iraq*,[31] the district court rejected a due process - minimum contacts claim by Iraq with respect to alleged State sponsored terrorism, since "States are on notice that State sponsorship of terrorism is condemned by the international community," "nations that operate in a manner inconsistent with international norms should not expect to be granted the privilege of immunity from suit," States that sponsor terrorism have "adequate warning" of possible US sanctions, including lawsuits in US courts, and it is "reasonable that foreign States be held accountable in the courts of the United States for terrorist actions perpetrated against US citizens anywhere."[32]

From the dawn of USA, universal enforcement jurisdiction has been recognized over "crimes against mankind"[33] and the "enemies of the whole human family,"[34] or those persons who are "hostes humani generis."[35] It was also recognized more generally that violations of international law were subject to criminal sanction,[36] and the US government has been successful in numerous instances in enforcing criminal sanctions against individuals for violations of international law.[37] It has also been recognized that civil or criminal sanctions for private violations of international law were often interchangeable, depending on whether an individual or government was seeking enforcement.[38]

More generally, as the US Supreme Court recognized in 1795, the customary "law of nations" is part of "our law" and "*all...trespasses committed against the general law of nations, are enquirable, and may be proceeded against, in any nation* where no special exemption can be maintained, either by the general law of nations, or by some treaty which forbids or restrains it."[39] Justice Iredell thus affirmed as well the related principle that domestic law or limits are no bar to prosecution abroad.[40] In 1820, it was also recognized that piracy "is an offense against all. It is punishable in the Courts of all.... [Our courts] are authorized and bound to punish".[41] Similarly, in another case the Court recognized that piracy "is against all, and punished by all...within this universal jurisdiction."[42] As noted in 1821 in *La Jeune Eugenie*[43] with respect to "an offence against the universal law of society," "no nation can rightfully permit its subjects to carry it on, or exempt them... [and] no nation can privilege itself to commit a crime against the law of nations."[44] In 1859, an opinion of the Attorney General provided a strikingly similar affirmation: "A sovereign who tramples upon the public law of the world cannot excuse himself by pointing to a provision in his own municipal code… public law must be paramount to local law in every question where local laws are in conflict."[45] Non-immunity of a head of State with respect to violations of international law had also been affirmed earlier by the Supreme Court: "If…he [a foreign sovereign] comes personally within our limits, although he generally enjoys a personal immunity, he may become liable to judicial process in the same way, and under the same circumstances, as public ships of the nation" that violate international law.[46]

Importantly, as the early cases recognized, the reach of universal jurisdiction is also universal with respect to the status of perpetrators. For example, with respect to international crimes, there is absolutely no head of State, diplomatic, or public official immunity under customary international law or any international criminal law treaty or instrument.[47] As the I.M.T. at Nuremberg affirmed: "The principle of international law, which under certain circumstances protects the representatives of a State, cannot be applied to acts which are condemned as criminal by international law. The authors of these acts cannot shelter themselves behind their official position," and one "cannot claim immunity while acting in pursuance of the authority of the State if the State in authorizing action moves outside its competence under international law."[48] Similarly, domestic amnesties, pardons, immunities, statutes of limitation, and limiting laws or orders are not valid internationally or binding in other States.[49] Indeed, the mandatory duty to initiate prosecution of or to extradite those reasonably accused of international crime requires recognition of such a principle.

2. *Regarding certain treaty-based crimes*

There is a new type of related jurisdictional competence termed "universal by treaty"[50] or universal by consent. Such a competence exists only among signatories (and their nationals)[51] to a multilateral treaty establishing a new offense and competence to prosecute, for example, whenever an accused is found within a signatory State – at least until such an offense or competence becomes part of customary international law (at which time there will exist universal jurisdiction among all nation-States, reaching the nationals of any State).[52] Universal by treaty is actually a form of consensual jurisdiction among the signatories. Thus, if treaties creating a duty to initiate prosecution of or to extradite all persons found within a State's territory who are reasonably accused of hostage-taking, torture, aircraft hijacking, aircraft sabotage, attacks on internationally protected persons, forced disappearance, financing of terrorism, or terrorist bombings do not reflect customary international law, the consensual jurisdiction over all accused reflected in such treaties is applicable only to nationals of the signatories to such treaties. There may be disagreement, but in my opinion the proscriptions in the first six treaties are now customary.

IV. Conclusion

In conclusion, there are several types of international crime that have been committed by Al Qaeda attacks on the United States and its embassies, military, and other nationals. Terrorism is such a crime, but the international community should adopt an objective definition of terrorism. Extraterritorial jurisdiction under international law is possible over several such crimes, especially under the protective and universal principles.

Notes

1 *See, e.g.*, Paust, *Antiterrorism Military Commissions: Courting Illegality*, 23 Mich. J. Int'l L. 1, 8 n. 16 (2001) [hereinafter *Courting Illegality*]; Paust, *War and Enemy Status after 9/11: Attacks on the Laws of War*, 28 Yale J. Int'l L. 325 (2003) [hereinafter *Status after 9/11*].

2 *See, e.g.*, Paust, *Judicial Power to Determine the Status and Rights of Persons Detained Without Trial*, 44 Harv. Int'l L.J. n. 30 (2003); Paust, *Status after 9/11*, *supra* note 1.

3 *See, e.g.*, Paust, *Status after 9/11*, *supra* note 1; Paust, *Courting Illegality*, *supra* note 1, at 5-7 & n. 15.

4 War crimes can be engaged in by civilians and non-state actors. *See, e.g.*, US Army Field Manual 27-10, The Law of Land warfare 178, paras. 498 ("Any person, whether a member of the armed forces or a civilian"), 499 ("by any person or persons, military or civilian") (1956). "Every violation of the law of war is a war crime." *Id.* at para. 499. Thus, violations of the laws of war engaged in by members of Al Qaeda, regardless of personal status, would be war crimes. Further, there is universal jurisdiction over war crimes. *Id.* at 182, para. 507.

5 GA Res. 40/61, 40 UN GAOR, Supp. No. 53, at 301, UN Doc. A/RES/40/61 (1985). Similar Resolutions appeared in 1989, 1991, and 1993. *See, e.g.*, Paust, Bassiouni, *et al.*, *International Criminal Law* 1005 (2nd edn. 2000). In the Declaration on Measures to Eliminate International Terrorism, UNGA Res. 49/60 (9 December 1994), the members reaffirmed their unequivocal condemnation of all acts, methods and practices of terrorism as criminal and unjustifiable, wherever and by whomever committed. See also International Convention for the Suppression of Terrorist Bombings, preamble, adopted by UNGA Res. 52/164 (9 January 1998) (same); International Convention for the Suppression of the Financing of Terrorism, preamble, adopted by UNGA Res. 54/109 (9 December 1999) (same).

6 Note by the President of the Security Council, UN Doc. S/17554 (1985) (acting "on behalf of the members of the Council" and endorsing the Secretary-General's statement of 8 October 1985); see also UNSC Res. 1373, UN SCOR, 4385th mtg., UN Doc. S/RES/1373 (2001) (also reaffirming "its unequivocal condemnation of the terrorist attacks which took place in New York, Washington, D.C. and Pennsylvania on 11 September 2001....").

7 *See, e.g.*, Paust, *An Introduction to and Commentary on Terrorism and the Law*, 19 Conn. L. Rev. 697, 700 (1987).

8 See Paust, Bassiouni, *et al.*, *supra* note 5, at 997-99, 1002-05.

9 Paust, *supra* note 7, at 701.

10 860 UNTS 105, 22 U.S.T. 1641 (1970).

11 974 UNTS 177, 24 U.S.T. 564 (1971).

12 *Id.* Art. 1(2).

13 Concerning objective territorial jurisdiction, *see, e.g.*, Jordan J. Paust, *International Law as Law of the United States* 417-19 (2nd edn. 2003); Paust, Bassiouni, *et al.*, *supra* note 5, at 181-86, 209-16.

14 1035 UNTS 167, 28 U.S.T. 1975 (1973).

15 *See generally* Paust, Bassiouni, *et al.*, *supra* note 5, at 857-75, 905-07. I do not believe that requirements of "widespread" or "systematic" conduct placed in statutes of particular tribunals, like the ICTR and ICC, or found in French judicial opinions create new customary international law for the international community. *See, e.g.*, *id.* at 905-07, 915-16; *but see id.* at 911, setting forth *The Prosecutor* v. *Rutaganda*, ICTR-96-3-T, para. 66 (6 December 1999).

16 18 U.S.C. §§2331 *et seq.* See Paust, *Sanctions Against Non-State Actors for Violations of International Law*, 8 ILSA J. Int'l & Comp. L. 417, 418-19 (2002). *See also Smith* v. *The Islamic Emirate of Afghanistan, The Taliban, and Al Qaeda, bin Laden, et al.*, 2003 US Dist. Lexis 7629 (S.D.N.Y. 7 May 2003) (civil suit under 18 U.S.C. § 2333 and 20 U.S.C. § 1605(a)(7)).

17 *See, e.g.*, Paust, *supra* note 16, at 819, addressing §2332(b).

18 *See, e.g.*, *United States* v. *Yousef*, 327 F.3d 56, 93-94 (2d Cir. 2003) (terroristic aircraft sabotage and threats to US national security); *United States* v. *Pizzarusso*, 388 F.2d 8, 10 (2d Cir. 1968) (false visa application threatened US govt.), *cert. denied*, 392 U.S. 936 (1968); *Rivard* v. *United States*, 375 F.2d 882, 885-87 (5th Cir. 1967) (drug smuggling), *cert. denied*, *sub nom.*, *Groleau* v. *United States*, 389 U.S. 884 (1967); *Rocha*

v. *United States*, 288 F.2d 545, 549 (9th Cir.), *cert. denied*, 366 U.S. 948 (1961); *United States* v. *Zehe*, 601 F. Supp. 196, 196-98 (D. Mass. 1985); *United States* v. *Layton*, 509 F. Supp. 212, 215-16 (N.D. Cal. 1981); *United States* v. *Keller*, 451 F. Supp. 631, 635 (D.P.R. 1978); *United States* v. *Archer*, 51 F. Supp. 708, 711 (S.D. Cal. 1943); Paust, *supra* note 13, at 420, and references cited; Paust, *Federal Jurisdiction Over Extraterritorial Acts of Terrorism and Nonimmunity for Foreign Violators of International Law Under the FSIA and the Act of State Doctrine*, 23 Va. J. Int'l L. 191, 209-11 (1983).

19 *See, e.g.*, *United States* v. *Yousef*, 327 F.3d at 79; *United States* v. *Tinoco*, 304 F.3d 1088, 1110 n.21 (11th Cir. 2003) (drug smuggling case), *citing*, *United States* v. *Gonzalez*, 776 F.2d 931, 938-41 (11th Cir. 1985); *United States* v. *Peterson*, 812 F.2d 486, 493-94 (9th Cir. 1987); *United States* v. *Osama bin Laden, et al.*, 92 F. Supp.2d 189, 194, 220 (S.D.N.Y. 2000) (indictments re: 1993 World Trade Center bombing); *United States* v. *Zehe*, 601 F. Supp. at 196-98 (espionage).

20 *See, e.g.*, *United States* v. *Yousef*, 327 F.3d at 93-94 (threats to national security posed by terroristic aircraft sabotage); *United States* v. *bin Laden*, 92 F. Supp.2d at 194, 198, 215 n.42, 221(terroristic attacks); *United States* v. *Zehe*, 601 F. Supp. at 196-98 (espionage); *United States* v. *Layton*, 509 F. Supp. at 215-16 (threat to national security posed by complicity re: murder of congressman); *United States* v. *Keller*, 451 F. Supp. at 635 (invasion of territory); Paust, *supra* note 13, at 420 & n. 37.

21 *See, e.g.*, Paust, *supra* note 13, at 420 & n. 38.

22 *See, e.g.*, Paust, *Use of Armed Force against Terrorists in Afghanistan, Iraq, and Beyond*, 35 Cornell Int'l L.J. 533, 534-35 (2002).

23 *See, e.g.*, *United States* v. *bin Laden*, 92 F. Supp.2d at 194, 220; see also *United States* v. *Yousef*, 327 F.3d at 79.

24 *See, e.g.*, Paust, *supra* note 13, at 420 & n. 39. While quoting the author, the court in *Yunis* rightly conditioned protective jurisdiction on *the existence of demands against the US government or threats to US security. See United States v. Yunis*, 681 F. Supp. 909, 903 n.14 (D.D.C. 1988) (adding a requirement that the threats be direct and directed to the US government as such). *See* also *United States* v. *bin Laden*, 92 F. Supp.2d 189, 215 n. 42, 221-22.

25 *But see United States* v. *Keller*, 451 F. Supp. at 635 (stating that no actual effect is necessary under the protective principle).

26 For evidence of the content and application of the universality principle, *see, e.g.*, Paust, *supra* note 13, at 420-22, and numerous references cited [which forms a basis for most of this portion]; Paust, Bassiouni, *et al.*, *supra* note 5, at 157-76, and references cited.

27 *Demjanjuk* v. *Petrovsky*, 776 F.2d 571, 582 (6th Cir. 1985), *quoting* Restatement of the Foreign Relations Law of the United States §404 (3 ed. 1987).

28 *See, e.g.*, *Demjanjuk* v. *Petrovsky*, 776 F.2d at 582.

29 *See, e.g.*, *United States* v. *Rezaq*, 134 F.3d 1121, 1131, 1133 (D.C. Cir. 1998), *cert. denied*, 525 U.S. 834 (1998); *Demjanjuk* v. *Petrovsky*, 776 F.2d 571, 581-83 (6th Cir. 1985), *cert. denied*, 475 U.S. 1016 (1986); *United States* v. *bin Laden, et al.*, 92 F. Supp.2d 189, 215 n.42, 221-22 (S.D.N.Y. 2000); *United States* v. *Yousef*, 927 F. Supp. 673, 681-82 (S.D.N.Y. 1996); *United States* v. *Yunis*, 681 F. Supp. at 900-01, *aff'd*, 924 F.2d 1086 (D.C. Cir. 1991); *infra* notes 39, 41-42; *but see United States* v. *Yousef*, 327 F.3d at 79 (universal by treaty exists (under the Montreal Sabotage Convention), *id.* at 88-89, 96; but concluding "the indefinite category of 'terrorism' is not subject to universal jurisdiction." *Id.* at 79, see also *id.* at 86-87 - not addressing *opinio juris* evidenced in UN Resolutions since the 1980s and misreading the 1970 Declaration on Principles of International Law, UNGA Res. 2625 (1970), as if it excludes terroristic tactics during a self-determination struggle).

30 *See, e.g.*, *In re* Estate of Marcos, 978 F.2d 493, 499-500 (9th Cir. 1992); *Demjanjuk* v. *Petrovsky*, 776 F.2d at 582; *Daliberti* v. *Republic of Iraq*, 97 F. Supp.2d 38, 52-54 (D.D.C. 2000); *United States* v. *bin Laden*, 92 F. Supp.2d at 194, 220; Restatement, *supra* note 27, §404, cmt. a; Paust, Bassiouni, *et al.*, *supra* note 5, at 157, 161-64, *passim*; I.L.A., Final Report on the Exercise of Universal Jurisdiction in Respect of Gross Human Rights Violations 2, 4, 7-8 (London 2000); 18 Op. O.L.C. 148, n.9 (1994); *see also Kadić* v. *Karadzić*, 70 F.3d 232, 236, 240 (2d Cir. 1995), *cert. denied*, 518 U.S. 1005 (1996); *United States* v. *Yunis*, 681 F. Supp. at 900-01.

31 97 F. Supp.2d 38 (D.D.C. 2000).

32 *Id.* at 52-54, quoting *Flatow* v. *Islamic Republic of Iran*, 999 F. Supp. 1, 23 (D.D.C. 1998). Other cases recognizing universal jurisdiction over customary human rights violations (including torture, forced disappearance, summary execution, arbitrary detention, and cruel and inhumane treatment) include: *Kadić* v. *Karadzić*, 70 F.3d at 236, 240; *Linder* v. *Portocarrero*, 963 F.2d 332, 336-37 (11th Cir. 1992); *Peterson* v. *Islamic Republic*

of Iran, (D.D.C. 2003) ("international terrorism is subject to universal jurisdiction," extrajudicial killing at Marine barracks in Beirut and FSIA §1605(a)(7)); *Presbyterian Church of Sudan* v. *Talisman Energy, Inc.*, 244 F. Supp.2d 289, 306 (S.D.N.Y. 2003); *Xuncax* v. *Gramajo*, 886 F. Supp. 162, 183 n.25, 193 (D. Mass. 1995); *see also Abebe-Jira* v. *Negewo*, 72 F.3d 844 (11th Cir. 1996), *cert. denied*, 519 U.S. 830 (1996); *In re* Estate of Ferdinand Marcos, 25 F.3d 1467 (9th Cir. 1994); *Filartiga* v. *Pena-Irala*, 630 F.2d 876 (2d Cir. 1980); *Iwanowa* v. *Ford Motor Co.*, 67 F. Supp.2d 424 (D.N.J. 1999); *Doe* v. *Islamic Salvation Front (FIS)*, 993 F. Supp. 3 (D.D.C. 1998); *Hirsh* v. *State of Israel*, 962 F. Supp. 377, 381 (S.D.N.Y. 1997); *Paul* v. *Avril*, 812 F. Supp. 207, 211-12 (S.D. Fla. 1993); *Forti* v. *Suarez-Mason*, 672 F. Supp. 1531 (N.D. Cal. 1987), 694 F. Supp. 707 (N.D. Cal. 1988).

33 1 Op. Att'y Gen. 509, 513 (1821) (citing Grotius). See also *Respublica* v. *De Longchamps*, 1 U.S. (1 Dall.) 109, 116 (1784) (assault on foreign consul is "crime against the whole world"); 1 Op. Att'y Gen. 515 (1821) (universal jurisdiction recognized in cases concerning "crimes against the human family"); E. de Vattel, *Law of Nations* 464-65 (J. Chitty ed. 1883) (recognizing violence against a foreign ambassador as a "crime against mankind" and an "offence against the law of nations").

34 1 Op. Att'y Gen. at 515; *see also id.* (quoting Vattel, who referred to pirates and "poisoners, assassins, and incendiaries by profession," as those particularly subject to universal jurisdiction "because they attack and outrage all nations, in trampling under foot the foundations of their common safety"); 11 Op. Att'y Gen. 297, 306 (1865) (quoting Patrick Henry in his discussion of banditti as "an enemy to the human name"); Cowles, *Universality of Jurisdiction Over War Crimes*, 33 Cal. L. Rev. 177, 188-90 (1945) (quoting Ayala's statement that brigands are the "common enemy of all" and Gentili's statement that brigands had "broken the treaty of the human race").

35 *Demjanjuk* v. *Petrovsky*, 776 F.2d at 582.

36 See *Lopes* v. *Reederei Richard Schroder*, 225 F. Supp. 292, 297 (E.D. Pa. 1963) (*citing* 1 Kent, Commentaries 181 (1st ed. 1826)) (violation of passports, violation of ambassadors, piracy, and slave trade are offenses against the law of nations); 1 Op. Att'y Gen. 68, 69 (1797); *id.* at 62 (1796); *id.* at 58-59 (1795); *id.* at 27-28 (1792); 4 W. Blackstone, *Commentaries* 68 (1769) (principal offenses against the law of nations included violations of safe-conducts, infringement of the rights of ambassadors, and piracy).

37 *See, e.g., Ex parte* Quirin, 317 U.S. 1, 27-36 (1942); *United States* v. *Arjona*, 120 U.S. 479 (1887); *United States* v. *Smith*, 18 U.S. (5 Wheat.) 153 (1820); *Talbot* v. *Janson*, 3 U.S. (3 Dall.) 133, 159-61 (1795) (Iredell, J., concurring); *United States* v. *Ravara*, 2 U.S. (2 Dall.) 297, 298-99 (1793); *Respublica* v. *De Longchamps*, 1 U.S. (1 Dall.) 111, 116-17 (1784); Henfield's Case, 11 F. Cas. 1099, 1107-08 (C.C.D. Pa. 1793) (No. 6,360) (charge of Wilson, J.); *see also United States* v. *White*, 27 F. 200, 201-03 (C.C.E.D. Mo. 1886); *United States* v. *Baker*, 24 F. Cas. 962, 965 (C.C.S.D.N.Y. 1861) (No. 14,501); *United States* v. *Jones*, 26 F. Cas. 653 (C.C.D. Pa. 1813) (No. 15,494); *supra* notes 29, 36.

38 *See, e.g.*, 26 Op. Att'y Gen. 250, 252-54 (1907); 1 Op. Att'y Gen. 57, 58-59 (1795); Paust, *supra* note 13, at 421.

39 *Talbot* v. *Janson*, 3 U.S. (3 Dall.) at 156 (Paterson, J.), 159-61 (Iredell, J.), quoted in The Divina Pastora, 17 U.S. (4 Wheat.) 52, 65 (1819) (Marshall, C.J.). *See also* 1 Op. Att'y Gen. 68, 69 (1797) ("violation of territorial rights…[is] an offence against the law of nations… [and] it is the interest as well as the duty of every government to punish….").

40 *See also infra* notes 44-45, 49. Universal jurisdiction under customary international law is not limited by domestic notions of jurisdictional priority, competing interests, or connections with a forum; double jeopardy regarding different sovereigns; or the concept of *non bis in idem* (the latter being only rarely extended by special treaties that also contain broad exceptions and not extended in numerous international criminal law treaties reflecting the customary duty to extradite or initiate prosecution (*aut dedere aut judicare*) and addressing specific crimes such as hostage-taking, torture, aircraft hijacking, aircraft sabotage, attacks on internationally protected persons, forced disappearance, financing of terrorism, and terrorist bombings, or in older international criminal law treaties reflecting the same customary duty, such as the 1949 Geneva Conventions). *See, e.g.*, Paust, *supra* note 13, at 421, and numerous references cited.

41 *United States* v. *Klintock*, 18 U.S. (5 Wheat.) 144, 147-48 (1820). *See also United States* v. *Smith*, 18 U.S. (5 Wheat.) 153, 161, 163 (1820) (piracy is "an offence against the universal law of society"); *Ross* v. *Rittenhouse*, 2 U.S. (2 Dall.) 160, 162 (Pa. 1792) (courts enforce "universal law" re: prize); *Respublica* v. *De Longchamps*, 1 U.S. (1 Dall.) 111, 113, 115 (Pa. 1784) (assault on consul is "crime against the whole world," "crime against...all other nations"); *United States* v. *La Jeune Eugenie*, 26 F. Cas. 832, 847-51 (C.C.D. Mass. 1821) (No. 15,551) (slave trade violates "universal law").

42 *United States* v. *Furlong*, 18 U.S. (5 Wheat.) 184, 197 (1820).

43 26 F. Cas. 832 (C.C.D. Mass 1821).

43 *Id.* at 846. See also *supra* note 40; *infra* notes 45, 49.

44 9 Op. Att'y Gen. 356, 362-63 (1859).

45 The Santissima Trinidad, 20 U.S. (7 Wheat.) 283, 350-55 (1822).

46 *See, e.g.*, Paust, *supra* note 13, at 422 & n.69, and numerous references cited; Paust, Bassiouni, *et al.*, *supra* note 5, at 27-34, 38, 132-34, 136, 170-71; *The Prosecutor* v. *Furundzija*, ICTY-95-17/1, at para. 140 (10 December 1998); *The Prosecutor* v. *Milošević*, ICTY-99-37-PT, at paras. 26-34 (8 November 2001); *but see* Case Concerning the Arrest Warrant of 11 April 2000 (*Democratic Republic of the Congo* v. *Belgium*), 2000 I.C.J. paras. 58-59 (tragically finding diplomatic immunity).

47 Opinion and Judgement of the International Military Tribunal at Nuremberg (1 October 1946).

48 *See, e.g.*, Paust, *supra* note 13, at 422 & n.71; Paust, Bassiouni, *et al.*, *supra* note 5, at 133-36, 140, 170-71.

49 *See, e.g.*, Paust, *Suing Saddam: Private Remedies for War Crimes and Hostage-Taking*, 31 Va. J. Int'l L. 351, 372-73 & nn.99-100 (1991); *Extradition and United States Prosecution of the* Achille Lauro *Hostage-Takers: Navigating the Hazards*, 20 Vand. J. Transnat'l L. 235, 249-50 (1987).

50 It might also reach aliens with a significant nexus to the signatory State, but it is not clear whether a State can thereby bind non-nationals otherwise subject to its control.

51 See Restatement, *supra* note 27, §404, Comment a and Reporters' Note 1.

Remarks by Christopher C. Joyner*

International extradition and UN counter-terrorism conventions

I. Introduction

Terrorism today is a global phenomenon that threatens civil society.[1] Despite the currently popular law-of-armed conflict approach, the law-enforcement approach remains the principal means for dealing with global terrorism. The strategic key to combating transnational terrorist activities turns on the apprehension, prosecution, and punishment of persons who perpetrate or conspire to commit such criminal offenses. To that end, close international cooperation and collaboration is required, as are the open diplomatic channels and feasible legal means to accomplish those ends. The chief forum for coordinating multilateral responses to the worldwide terror threat is the United Nations.[2] Preeminent among the UN's international legal contributions is the adoption and promotion of twelve international instruments that codify and criminalize certain terrorist acts as unlawful offences against the peace and security of humankind.[3] This study examines the international extradition process that operates through these UN multilateral counter-terrorism instruments.

II. Terrorism and the extradition process

The politically sensitive, subjective nature of what constitutes "terrorism" and how terrorists should be punished has fostered reluctance among certain States to harmonize their national criminal codes on such unlawful activities. Municipal laws tend to concentrate on the intentions and targets of terrorists. Hence unlawful activity in one State may be regarded as lawful acts in another. This conundrum has precluded some governments from asserting jurisdiction over terrorist acts. The consequence through-

* Georgetown University, Washington DC

out most of the last century was often the failure to prosecute. One strategy for States in meeting this challenge is for governments to adopt and implement special extradition procedures, usually through bilateral treaties, for accused criminal offenders.

Historical experience, however, demonstrated that a treaty agreement providing for the extradition process between States, while necessary, might not be sufficient. Under contemporary international law, no universal rule obligates governments to extradite, or even prosecute, alleged offenders who hide in their territory.[4] Indeed, the international extradition process today operates almost entirely through bilateral treaties, and certain conditions such as the nationality of the offender, concern over the fairness of a foreign trial, or the supposed political nature of the offense can obstruct the extradition process. Of defects in the extradition process, perhaps most problematic for extradition cases involving acts of terrorism is the political offense exception. Many modern extradition treaties specifically exempt political offenses from extradition, since liberal and democratic governments developed a strong antipathy toward the idea of surrendering dissidents into the hands of a despotic government.[5] There are, however, no recognized criteria as to what constitutes "a political" offense, or rule of international law prohibiting the extradition of political offenders.

In recent decades, certain events gave rise to harmful activities that prompted the international community to take law-making action to prohibit those activities and punish the offenders. The forums for creating and instituting these new international legal rules were special organs and agencies within the United Nations system. In this regard, since 1960 four specific issue-areas tended to dominate international concern over global terrorism: crimes against the safety of international aviation; crimes against the safety of individual persons; crimes against the safety of maritime navigation; and crimes associated with violent terrorist activities. As the need to deal with these concerns arose, UN agencies became the organizers for instigating legal action.

Crimes against the safety of international aviation

The first UN effort to internationally criminalize terrorist activities dealt with threats to safe international aviation. During the 1960s, the international community became seriously concerned over the unlawful seizure of aircraft flying international routes. To suppress these dangerous activities, the principal United Nations specialized agency concerned with safe and secure global air transportation, the International Civil Aviation Organization (ICAO), sponsored the promulgation of four prominent international legal instruments. First, in 1963, ICAO sponsored negotiation of the Tokyo Convention on Offences and Certain Other Acts Committed on Board Aircraft.[6] This instrument deals with offenses committed on board aircraft, but is not specifically directed against terrorist offenses.[7] The prominent focus of the Tokyo Convention falls on establishing jurisdiction over offenders.

The watershed legal development for extraditing terrorist skyjack offenders came in 1970 with the adoption of the Hague Convention for the Suppression of Unlawful Seizure of Aircraft.[8] This instrument specifically deals with aircraft hijacking. The Convention defines the act of unlawful seizure of aircraft, and contracting States were obliged to make such an offense punishable by severe penalties.

The extradition process assumes a critical role within the 1970 Hague Convention. The convention contains a lengthy provision on the extradition of alleged offenders in Article 8. Importantly, this provision obligates parties to treat the offenses defined in the convention as extraditable offenses in present and future extradition treaties. It permits a State party which conditions extradition of an offender on the existence of an extradition treaty to regard the convention itself as the basis for extradition to a State with which it has no extradition treaty. For parties which do not insist on a treaty as the basis for extradition, it requires that the offense defined in the convention be regarded as an extraditable offense.

The Hague Convention, unlike its Tokyo predecessor, puts considerable emphasis on enforcement. Under the Hague instrument, a State is obliged to take such measures as may be necessary to establish its jurisdiction over the offense in the case where the alleged offender is present in its territory and it does not extradite him. If no extradition treaty exists between the States concerned, and an offender is in the territory of a contracting State and that State refuses to extradite that offender, then it must submit the case to its domestic authorities for the purpose of prosecuting that offender under its criminal law.

It is important to realize that Article 8 of the Hague Convention is used as the model extradition provision in several subsequent UN counter-terrorism conventions. No less significant, if a government decides not to extradite an accused offender, under the Hague instrument it is obligated to prosecute him. The key provision here is Article 7, which provides for the legal principle of *aut dedere aut judicare*—the duty to extradite or prosecute accused offenders.[9] Subsequent UN counter-terror agreements mirror the language of the Hague Convention's Article 7 in the formulation of their extradite-or-prosecute obligations. This prescription requires the State party in which an alleged offender is discovered either to extradite that person to a State which is acknowledged to have jurisdiction over the offense, or alternatively if it opts not to extradite, "to submit the case to its competent authorities for the purposes of prosecution."

During the late 1960s, the threat of terrorists destroying international airliners became of serious concern to ICAO members. During 1967-1970, terrorists destroyed several airplanes by placing bombs on board. To address these crimes of aircraft sabotage, the Convention for the Suppression of Unlawful Acts of Violence Against the Safety of Civil Aviation was negotiated in 1971.[10] The Montreal Convention defines a broad spectrum of unlawful acts against the safety of civil aviation, and contracting States should make these offenses punishable by severe penalties. The convention contains detailed provisions on jurisdiction, custody, prosecution and extradition of an alleged offender similar to those in the Hague Convention.

In February 1988, ICAO sponsored negotiation of a Protocol on the Suppression of Unlawful Acts of Violence at Airports Serving International Civil Aviation, supplementary to the Convention for the Suppression of Unlawful Acts against the Safety of Civil Aviation.[11] The Protocol adds to the definition of "offence" given in the Montreal Convention of 1971 by including unlawful and intentional acts of violence against persons at an airport serving international civil aviation.

Crimes against the safety of individual persons

In the early 1970s, the international community became acutely alarmed over threats that serious harm or injury might be inflicted on diplomats and individual persons taken hostage by groups of terrorists. A major catalyst for this apprehension came in March 1973, when US Ambassador Cleo Noel and Chargé d'Affaires George Curtis Moore, along with Belgian diplomat Guy Eid, were kidnapped and murdered in Khartoum, Sudan, by Palestinians terrorists.[12] This tragic event prompted the United States to introduce to the General Assembly the Convention on the Prevention and Punishment of Crimes against Internationally Protected Persons, including Diplomatic Agents, New York.[13] The convention applies to the crimes of direct involvement or complicity in the actual or threatened murder, kidnapping, or attack on the person, official premises, private accommodation, or transportation services of diplomatic agents and other "internationally protected persons."[14]

Universal jurisdiction appears essential for ensuring the performance of the two key provisions relating to extradition of offenders. As with other UN counter-terrorism conventions, the Internationally Protected Persons Convention mandates in Article 6 that a State party which discovers an alleged offender in its territory, "...shall, if it does not extradite him, submit, without exception whatsoever and without undue delay, the case to its competent authorities for the purpose of prosecution, through proceedings in accordance with the laws of that State."[15]

Articles 7 and 8 of the Internationally Protected Persons Convention closely resemble companion provisions in the 1970 Hague and 1971 Montreal Conventions. The State where an alleged offender is found retains the option of either instituting proceedings aimed at prosecution of that person or, assuming that a request for extradition has been received, of complying with that request. If no request for extradition is received, the requisite proceedings for prosecution must go forward. If one or more requests for extradition are received, but the decision is made not to extradite the alleged offender, the holding government must proceed to prosecute. Nonetheless, the obligation is for the State to institute proceedings against an accused offender. It is not duty-bound to complete trial proceedings or to convict and punish him.

Hostage-taking became a grave international concern in the immediate aftermath of the Islamic Revolution in Iran. On 4 November 1979, Iranian students seized the US embassy complex in Teheran, Iran, and took hostage more than one hundred persons, most of them American citizens.[16] While all the hostages eventually were released unharmed, this incident prompted the United States in December 1979 to introduce to the United Nations the International Convention against the Taking of Hostages,[17] which defines the peacetime taking of hostages as a separate international crime. Each contracting party is required to make this offense punishable by appropriate penalties and to cooperate in preventing such offenses.[18] Where hostages are held in the territory of a State party, that government is obligated to take all measures it considers appropriate to ease the situation of the hostages and secure their release. Each State party is further obligated to take such actions as may be necessary to establish jurisdiction over the offence of taking of hostages.[19]

The Hostages Convention relies heavily on extradition for the apprehension of suspected offenders. States parties are obligated to take alleged offenders into custody, prosecute or extradite them, and exchange information and evidence needed in related criminal proceedings. Article 10, which in the main replicates language in the 1970 Hague Convention, assigns extradition a salient role in the enforcement process. The provision stipulates that the offenses in the convention are deemed to be extraditable offenses between States parties under existing and future extradition treaties, as well as under the convention itself. The convention may also be used as the legal basis for the extradition of alleged offenders, subject to the law of the requested State. Finally, to facilitate the lawful execution of the extradition process, offenses associated with hostage-taking will be treated as if they occurred not only in the territory of actual commission, but also in the territories required of States who seek to establish legal jurisdiction over an offender. In this manner, the Hostages Convention directly applies the universality and passive personality principles.

Yet, unlike other active UN counter-terrorism conventions, the 1979 Hostages Convention also sets out specific reasons for which extradition might be refused. An extradition request can be denied by a State party if that government has "substantial grounds" for believing that the request has been made by another government "for the purposes of prosecuting or punishing a person on account of his race, religion, nationality, ethnic origin or political opinion."[20] Such criteria are normally reserved for persons seeking asylum as refugees in a foreign State. Nonetheless, insertion of this language into the convention gives to the holding State considerable discretion in determining whether to extradite an accused offender.

Crimes against the safety of international maritime navigation

Over the last two decades, terrorist threats to maritime security became a serious international concern. On 5 October 1985, five Palestinian gunmen seized the Italian-flagged *Achille Lauro* cruise ship while it was sailing offshore Egypt in the Mediterranean Sea. During the episode, the perpetrators deliberately murdered an invalid, wheelchair-bound American passenger. This horrific act, erroneously branded an act of piracy in the international media, was in fact crime distinct in international law.[21] As such, it became the catalyst for the International Maritime Organization (IMO) to sponsor negotiation in March 1988 of a special legal instrument, the Convention for the Suppression of Unlawful Acts Against the Safety of International Maritime Navigation,[22] to address such unlawful terrorist acts against ocean vessels.

The IMO Convention provides in Article 11 for the extradition of offenders in language that essentially replicates Article 8 in the 1970 Hague Convention. The offenses in question are deemed extraditable in cases where extradition treaties are concluded between parties. If no treaty is available, the Convention may serve as the legal basis for the extradition of alleged offenders. Finally, for purposes of extradition, the pertinent offenses may be treated as if they were committed within the jurisdiction of a requesting State.[23]

Intimately associated with the 1988 IMO SUA Convention is its Protocol for the Suppression of Unlawful Acts against the Safety of Fixed Platforms located on the Continental Shelf.[24] This Protocol applies to the offenses described in the Convention for the Suppression of Unlawful Acts against the Safety of Maritime Navigation when they are committed relative to a "fixed platform," which is defined as an artificial island, installation, or structure permanently attached to the sea-bed for the purpose of exploration or exploitation of resources or for other economic purposes.[25]

Crimes associated with violent terrorist activities

Four special UN conventions were negotiated to deal with particular activities associated with destructive terror violence. The first of these was negotiated under the auspices of the International Atomic Energy Agency (IAEA) to prevent international smuggling of nuclear materials. Presently, the international legal system has few institutional defenses, with the most salient being the 1979 Convention on the Physical Protection of Nuclear Material.[26] Significantly, the Physical Protection Convention functions mainly as an anti-terrorism agreement, not a non-proliferation measure. In this respect, it presents two objectives. First, the convention aims to establish levels of physical protection needed for the safe international transportation of nuclear material used for peaceful purposes. Second, it provides for measures to take against unlawful acts that affect such nuclear materials when they are being transported internationally, as well as while they are in domestic use, storage and transport. Once again, extradition emerges as the critical legal ingredient underpinning the international enforcement process.

The second instrument, the Convention on the Marking of Plastic Explosives for the Purpose of Detection,[27] was sponsored by ICAO in 1991 to suppress the use of plastic explosive explosives for bombing aircraft in flight. The Convention requires each State party to prohibit and prevent the manufacture in its territory of unmarked plastic explosives. Plastic explosives must be marked during the manufacturing process by special detection agents that are defined in the Technical Annex to the convention.

Unlike other post-1970 UN counter-terrorism instruments, the Plastics Convention omits provisions for extradition or prosecution of offenders. The focus of this instrument is not on the prosecution and punishment of persons who use these plastic explosives. Rather, the convention aims at imposing obligations for strict authoritative control and destruction of such explosives in States parties. Consequently, no specific mention is made within the convention for extradition, prosecution, or means of direct inter-State enforcement of provisions.

A third violent activity intimately associated with terrorism is the act of bombing public buildings and private property. To suppress this grave concern, in 1997 the UN General Assembly adopted the International Convention for the Suppression of Terrorist Bombings.[28] Under the convention, an offense is committed when any person engages in the intentional and unlawful delivery, placement, discharge or detonation of an explosive or other lethal device in a place of public use, a State or government facility, a public transportation system, or an infrastructure facility.[29]

States parties are obliged to establish jurisdiction over and make punishable under their domestic laws the offenses specified in the convention. As provided for in Article 8, governments are also required to extradite or submit for prosecution persons accused of committing or aiding in the commission of the offenses.

In contrast to previous UN counter-terrorism instruments, the Terrorist Bombings Convention explicitly recognizes the problematic nature of the political offenses exception. Accordingly, Article 11 rejects the political offenses exception. But at the same time the convention contains a caveat that governments could use to refuse extradition of alleged offenders to another State. Like the 1979 Hostages Convention, the Terrorist Bombing Convention asserts that no government is obligated to extradite if it has "substantial grounds" to believe that an extradition request is being made "for the purpose of prosecuting or punishing a person on account of that person's race, religion, nationality, ethnic origin or political opinion or that compliance with the request would cause prejudice to that person's position for any of these reasons."[30]

Such conditions normally are reserved for governments to consider in grants of political asylum to persons seeking refugee status. While this provision preserves that protection for refugees, it seems critical that governments must not abuse these conditions as loopholes or rationales to protect terrorist offenders.

The final UN counter-terrorism convention strives to curtail financial support for terrorist activities. In late 1999 the General Assembly adopted the International Convention for the Suppression of the Financing of Terrorism.[31] This convention provides for a legal regime prohibiting the unlawful activities by individuals or groups that are ancillary to terrorist acts.

The convention defines an offense as the direct involvement or complicity in the intentional and unlawful provision or collection of funds with the intention or knowledge that any part of the funds may be used to perpetrate: (1) any of the offenses described in the eleven UN conventions enumerated in the Annex; or (2) an act intended to cause death or serious bodily injury to any person not actively involved in armed conflict in order to intimidate a population or to compel a government or an international organization to do or abstain from doing any act. The offenses referred to in the convention are deemed to be extraditable offenses.[32] Accordingly, States parties are mandated to establish their jurisdiction over these offenses, make them punishable by appropriate penalties, take alleged offenders into custody, prosecute or extradite alleged offenders, cooperate in preventive measures and countermeasures, and exchange information and evidence needed in related criminal proceedings.

III. The comprehensive convention on terrorism

The United Nations' most recent initiative against terrorist activities deals with negotiating a draft comprehensive convention on international terrorism. The text for such an instrument first was proposed by India in 1996,[33] and in 1999 the General Assembly entrusted its Ad Hoc Committee with elaboration of such a convention. Those negotiations began in 2000, in the Working Group of the Sixth Committee and have progressively continued since then.

To a considerable degree, this draft anti-terrorism convention represents a synthesis of provisions from earlier UN conventions. Of twenty-seven proposed articles in the Terrorism Convention's text (the final five of which are procedural clauses), fifteen directly relate to extradition or jurisdictional considerations for exercising that process.[34] For purposes of prosecution or extradition, this convention's jurisdictional scope over the offenses is broader than any other UN counter-terrorism instrument.

Article 10 initiates the convention's extradition procedures. Parties are obligated to investigate and apprehend alleged offenders. Accused offenders are accorded rights to communicate with the "nearest appropriate Representative" of the State of which they are a national, as well as to be visited by that representative. A State party is also directed to notify the Secretary-General of the United Nations that is has take a person into custody.[35] Article 11 reaffirms for States parties the extradite-or-prosecute principle, in language virtually identical to similar provisions in earlier UN counter-terrorism conventions. Significantly, the draft Terrorist Convention contains an explicit prohibition on the use of the political offense exclusion as the "sole ground" for denying a request for extradition or mutual legal assistance.[36] That proscription, however, subsequently is qualified by a mandate stating that no obligation exists for a requested State party to extradite "if it has substantial grounds for believing that the request for extradition for offences … has been made for the purpose of prosecuting or punishing a person on account of that person's race, religion, nationality, ethnic origin or political opinion or that compliance with the request would cause prejudice to that person's position for any of these reasons."[37] Such preemptive protections are welcome on human rights grounds. Yet, the highly subjective nature of this exclusionary clause might make it possible for governments to deny the extradition of alleged offenders to other States on evidence that is merely interpretative, which could obfuscate bringing offenders to justice.

Article 17, the core extradition provision, draws its language from obligations in similar provisions in earlier counter-terrorism instruments:

1. The offences set forth in Article 2 shall be deemed to be included as extraditable offences in any extradition treaty existing between any of the States Parties before the entry into force of the Convention. States Parties undertake to include such offences as extraditable offences in every extradition treaty to be subsequently concluded between them.
2. When a State Party which makes extradition conditional on the existence of a treaty receives a request for extradition from another State Party with which it has no extradition treaty, the requested State may, at its option, consider this Convention as a legal basis for extradition in respect of the offences set forth in Article 2. Extradition shall be subject to the other conditions provided by the law of the requested State Party.
3. States Parties which do not make extradition conditional on the existence of a treaty shall recognize the offences referred to in Article 2 as extraditable offences between themselves, subject to the conditions provided by the law of the requested State.
4. If necessary, the offences set forth in Article 2 shall be treated, for the purposes of extradition between States Parties, as if they had been committed not only in the place in which they occurred but also the territory of the States that have established jurisdiction in accordance with Article 6, paragraphs 1 and 2.
5. The provisions of all extradition treaties and arrangements between States Parties with regard to offences set forth in Article 2 shall be deemed to be modified as between States Parties to the extent that they are incompatible with this Convention.[38]

In sum, the offenses in the convention are deemed to be extraditable offenses under existing extradition treaties and under future treaties. Should States parties have no extradition agreement with one another, the convention may serve as the legal basis for undertaking extradition between them. Finally, the convention declares that universal jurisdiction may serve as a lawful justification amongst parties for extradition as well.

IV. Conclusion

The internationalization of law enforcement activities remains a vital strategy for governments to combat global terrorism. Key to this law enforcement process is making use of special international instruments that designate certain acts as criminal offenses and provide for and facilitate the extradition of accused offenders to States for trial and prosecution. To fill this need, United Nations agencies since 1963 have sponsored, adopted, and promoted implementation of a constellation of conventions that today criminalize certain terrorist acts as offenses under international law and facilitate extradition and or prosecution of the perpetrators. In this connection, governments now realize that the fight against global terrorism necessitates a multifaceted response that must involve improved law enforcement procedures, including more widespread use of extradition. Governments should be given wider legal scope for bringing alleged terrorist perpetrators to trial, and extradition practice should be reformed such that more restrictions are placed on applying the political offence exception. Along these lines, more effective measures to promote international cooperation in the prevention of terrorist violence and the prosecution of its perpetrators must be developed at the international, regional and bilateral levels. These UN conventions facilitate that process, especially by criminalizing certain offenses and highlighting extradition as an integral means for multilateral law enforcement.

Contemporary global terrorism involves criminal acts usually perpetrated by non-State actors. Accordingly, an appropriate response of a victim State in defense against such acts is to seek law enforcement. Preeminent in this regard is the obligation of States party to UN counter-terrorism instruments to extradite or prosecute. Yet, the legal obligation for governments to extradite or prosecute, while necessary, is not sufficient. The force of legal obligation may motivate governments to move toward enforcing legal rules that punish terrorists. But the critical ingredient for that process is political will. Governments must possess the political resolve to implement obligations fully into policy action, to be willing to make international extradition law function as it is intended. International statesmen crafted and implemented these UN instruments in order to outlaw various acts of global terrorism and to facilitate means for punishing the offenders. But if governmental officials are not willing to convert these laws into actual practice, those legal obligations will be mere words on paper, without the force of law. The bottom line is that legal obligations must be transformed into real policy actions. Given the experience of governments in the past, that prerequisite need will be no easy task to achieve.

Notes

1 On 20 September 2001, in an address to a Joint Session of Congress and the American people, President George W. Bush declared war on terrorism in general and al Qaeda in particular. 37 *Weekly Comp. Pres. Docs.* 1347 (20 September 2001). For international legal implications, see Jack M. Beard, 'America's New War on Terror: The Case for Self Defense', 25 *Harvard J. L. & Pub. Pol'cy* 559 (2001).

2 The United Nations is the principal source of international legal measures to combat global terrorism. The General Assembly's adoption of its 1994 Declaration on Measures to Eliminate Terrorism signaled the UN's formal commitment to condemn and suppress terrorist activities. GA Res. 49/60, 9 December 1994, Annex. In 1996, the General Assembly adopted its Declaration to Supplement the 1994 Declaration on Measures to Eliminate Terrorism, which seeks to restrict granting asylum to possible terrorists, remove the political offenses exception for persons who commit terrorist acts, and promote the extradition of offenders. GA Res. 51/210, 17 December 1996, Annex. Moreover, this resolution created an Ad Hoc Committee to develop a comprehensive legal framework of conventions dealing with terrorism. This committee, in concert with the General Assembly's Sixth (Legal) Committee, is now negotiating texts for a convention for the suppression of acts of nuclear terrorism and a comprehensive convention on the suppression of international terrorism. In addition, the Security Council created a special Counter-Terrorism Committee by its Resolution 1373 (2001) of 28 September 2001. Acting under Chapter VII of the Charter, the Security Council in Resolution 1373 unequivocally

condemns the attacks of September 11 as threats to international peace and security, thus legitimizing an international military response by the United States and other countries in self-defense. SC Res. 1373 (2001), 28 September 2001. It must be said, however, that the principal UN contribution to combating terrorism remains the series of international counter-terrorism instruments adopted between 1963 and 2000. See Report of the Policy Working Group on the United Nations and Terrorism, Annex U.N. Doc. A/57/273, S/2002/875 (2002).

3 The texts of these conventions can be found on the UN website at: <http://www.undcp.org/odccp/terrorism_conventions.html> (Conventions Against Terrorism) (accessed 4 September 2003).

4 Restatement (Third) of Foreign Relations Law of the United States, sect. 401 cmt. B (1987) [Hereinafter Third Restatement].

5 For overviews of the political offense exceptions, see M. Cherif Bassiouni, *International Extradition: United States Law and Practice* 502-83 (2nd edn., 1996) and Christopher L. Blakesley, *Terrorism, Drugs, International Law, and the Protection of Human Liberty* 264-70 (1992).

6 Done 14 September 1963, U.S.T. 2941, 704 U.N.T.S. 219 (entered into force 4 December 1969). On 1 September 2003, 176 States were parties to the Tokyo Convention.

7 The Tokyo Convention applies to "offences against penal law" and "acts which, whether or not they are offences, may or do jeopardize the safety of the aircraft or of persons or property therein or which jeopardize good order and discipline on board." Id. Art. 1.

8 Done 16 December 1970, 22 U.S.T. 1641, 860 U.N.T.S. 105 (entered into force 14 October 1971) In late 2003, at least 177 States are parties to the Hague instrument.

9 The duty to extradite or prosecute stems from the Roman notion of *aut dedere aut judicare.* The term *dedere* means to surrender or extradite, while *judicare* refers to the need to adjudicate or prosecute. For use of this expression, see 1 *Oppenheim's International Law* 953, 971 (R. Jennings & A. Watts, eds., 9th edn. 1992).

10 Convention for the Suppression of Unlawful Acts of Violence Against the Safety of Civil Aviation, 23 September 1971, 24 U.S.T. 564, 974 U.N.T.S. 177 (entered into force 26 January 1973). By 1 September 2003, 179 States had become parties to the Montreal Convention.

11 Done 24 February 1988, ICAO Doc. 9518 (entered into force 6 August 1989). In late 2003, 137 States were parties to this protocol.

12 See Joseph Farah, 'New evidence Arafat killed US diplomats: Nixon historian finds CIA report on Fatah link to 1973 murders', WorldNetDaily.com, 18 March 2002, online at: <http://www.worldnetdaily.com/news/article.asp?ARTICLE_ID=26856> (accessed 8 January 2003).

13 Done 14 December 1973, 28 U.S.T. 1975, 1035 U.N.T.S. 167 (entered into force 20 February 1977). In late 2003, there were 133 parties and 25 signatories to this convention.

14 Id. Art. 2. "Internationally protected persons" are defined as Heads of State or Government, Ministers for Foreign Affairs, State officials and representatives of international organizations entitled to special protection in a foreign State, and their families. Id. Art. 1.

15 Internationally Protected Persons Convention, Art. 7.

16 The Iranian government refused to intervene and allowed 53 Americans to be held hostage by the "students" in the Ministry of Foreign Affairs for 440 days until they were released on 20 January 1981. The United States also brought suit against Iran in the International Court of Justice that this act violated the diplomatic sanctity of the US embassy. See International Court of Justice (179), I.C.J. Case Concerning United States Diplomatic and Consular Staff in Tehran (*United States of America* v. *Iran*) I.C.J. Rep. 3. The decision of the ICJ was unanimous in favor of the US claim.

17 Adopted 17 December 1979, TIAS No. 11,081, 1316 U.N.T.S. 204. (entered into 3 June 1983). In late 2003, at least 123 States were parties and 39 others were signatories to the Hostages Convention.

18 Id. Arts. 2 & 4.

19 Id. Art. 3

20 Id. Art. 9(1)(a)

21 For discussion, see Christopher C. Joyner, 'The 1988 IMO Convention on the Safety of Maritime Navigation: Towards a Legal Remedy for Terrorism at Sea', 31 *German YB Int'l L.* 230 (1989) and Malvina Halberstam, 'Terrorism on the High Seas: The Achille Lauro, Piracy and the IMO Convention on Maritime Safety', 82 *Am. J. Int'l L.* 269 (1988).

22 Convention for the Suppression of Unlawful Acts Against the Safety of International Maritime Navigation, 10 March 1988 (entered into force 1 March 1992). [Hereinafter the 1988 SUA Convention]. In late 2003, 90 States were parties and 58 were signatories to this IMO Convention.

23 Id. Art. 11(1) (2) & (3).

24 Done 10 March 1988, entered into force 1 March 1992. By September 2003, at least 82 States are parties to the IMO SUA Protocol.
25 Id Art. 1(3).
26 Adopted 26 October 1979, TIAS No 11,080, IAEA Reg. No.1533 (entered into force 8 February 1987). In late 2003, there are at least 89 parties and 45 signatories to this convention.
27 Done 1 March 1991, ICAO Doc. 9571 (entered into force 21 June 1998). At least 97 States are party to this instrument in September 2003.
28 Done 15 December 1997, annexed to GA Res. 52/164 (15 December 1997) (entered into force 23 May 2001). In January 2003, 101 States were parties and 58 States were signatories to this convention. The United States initiated negotiation of this convention in the aftermath of the 1996 deadly truck bombing attack on US military personnel at the Khubar Towers housing facility in Dhahran, Saudi Arabia. Nineteen US citizens were killed and some 500 other persons were wounded. See US Dep't of State, Pub. No. 10,433, *Patterns of Global Terrorism: 1996*, at 35 (1997).
29 Id. Art. 2(1).
30 Id. Art. 12.
31 Done 9 December 1999, GA Res. 54/109 (9 December 1999), annex. (entered into force 10 April 2002). As of September 2003, 91 States were parties to the Financing Convention.
32 Id. Art. 11.
33 See UN Doc. A/C.6/51/6 (1996).
34 Viz., Articles 3-17.
35 Id. Art. 10.
36 Id. Art. 14.
37 Id. Art. 15. This language draws from Article 12 in the Terrorist Bombing Convention.
38 Id. Art. 17.

Remarks by Monica den Boer*

Counter-terrorism in the EU: The internationalisation of domestic criminal justice priorities

Introduction

Within the EU, the subject of terrorism has always been inserted under the umbrella of nation State reponsibility, and under the joint competencies of an international political union. Since the mid seventies, when the cooperation against terrorism was initiated because many EC Member States suffered from domestic terrorism, nation States have increasingly experienced external pressure to achieve a balance between the preservation of their own national policies and laws and the progress towards a harmonisation of laws, politics and policies. Within an intergovernmental context of policy-making (Den Boer, 1998; Harlow, 2002: 41) – the governance regime which has hitherto applied onto Justice and Home Affairs (JHA) Cooperation within the European Union - this can only amount to a curious mixture between extreme reluctance and eagerness to move ahead. The result is an arranged marriage between preservation of national State values and the gradual acceptance of foreign influence on sovereign politics. This begs the question whether and to what extent the EU will ever arrive at a fully harmonised legislation against terrorism.

* Managing Director of EULEC (European Institute of Law Enforcement Cooperation). The views expressed in this chapter are strictly those of the author.

Another issue is whether the 11th of September established the basis for a fundamental paradigmatic shift in counter-terrorism in the EU. If one takes into account that prior to this date, the EC/EU Member States had already been cooperating against terrorism for nearly two decades, the answer can only be negative. Several measures had already been adopted in the Trevi-era, and later also by the Council of JHA-ministers. But because terrorism is such a politically sensitive and thus also a potentially divisive issue, many of those measures belong to the domain of soft law, which means that their implementation has remained fuzzy and that their impact on national laws has been limited.

Notwithstanding these critical comments about the hitherto limited effectiveness of EU law against terrorism, the events on the 11th of September 2001 certainly provided a political window of opportunity for legislative hyperactivity, which, to express it in the words of the EU's justice commissioner Vitorino, helped Justice and Home Affairs cooperation to take "a giant leap forward". EU approaches to the fight against crime, in particular terrorism, were suddenly regarded as more feasible and important.

In this chapter, we will analyse the relationship between the internationalisation of domestic counter-terrorism policies within the context of the EU and the opportunity structures that were created by virtue of the terrorist attacks against the USA in September 2001.

Domestic counter-terrorism policies

Although terrorism was considered a major issue by almost all European countries throughout the seventies, it had been moved to the backburner in the seventies and eighties as it lost ground to other prominent agenda items, such as illegal immigration, drug trafficking, and international organised crime. The "obvious reason" for this, as Marianne van Leeuwen writes in the introduction to her recent book on terrorism, is that "most countries, even those like Germany and Italy that had been shaken by repeated terrorist outrages in the 1970s and 1980s, had been spared terrorist attacks for quite some time." (Van Leeuwen, 2003: 1). Spain and the United Kingdom continued to suffer however from (the threat posed by) terrorist groups, which – in the EU context – meant that they remained the staunch advocates of joint policies against terrorism; it was at the request of Spain that terrorism was added to the list of Europol's competencies earlier than agreed when the Europol Convention was adopted and signed (July 1995).[1]

Meanwhile, on the other side of the Atlantic, concern about terrorism and political violence had risen due to some major attacks against American citizens both inside and outside the USA (Van Leeuwen, 2003: 1). In response, the Clinton Administration allocated substantial funds to the management of terrorist crises and American scholars devoted many of their publications to terrorist policies and catastrophic threats.

Certain European countries remained active on the domestic front to enact counter-terrorism legislation. In the UK, for instance, the Terrorism Act 2000 was adopted which established a more uniform regime and which, according to Clive Walker, brought about important modifications, including a greater emphasis on international terrorism. The 11th of September provided the catalyst for a far more strict Anti-terrorism, Crime and Security Act 2001, as it allowed for detention without trial and as it introduced a range of policing and criminal law reforms (Walker, 2003: 11). Particularly new is also the fact that asylum and immigration matters are addressed, which includes detention without trial of foreign persons denied asylum on national security grounds or because of their international crimes (Walker, 2003: 23f). This last measure has notably been the subject of a derogation under the European Convention.

In Spain, legislative responses to the ETA began in the seventies, e.g. with the creation in 1977 of a National Court in Madrid which was to deal with serious organised crime and terrorist offences, and with the proclamation of the first constitutional law to combat terrorism in December 1978. During the eighties, new laws were adopted but in part overturned by the Constitutional Court. And in early 2001, the Penal Code was modified so as to include new provisions that were adapted to changes observed in terrorist *modus operandi* (Reinares, 2003: 64f). No particular domestic legislative response seems to have been propelled by 11/9. Its domestic anti-terrorism laws were compared with the new legislative instruments of the EU, but no additional legislation seemed necessary. Spain welcomed the shift in attitude among other national governments within Europe when they opened themselves up to the achievement of goals that had been pursued by Spain for a long time (Reinares, 2003: 70).

Except these two more striking cases of countries that were a major subject of terrorism, other European countries also experienced serious attacks. The terrorism that was dominant in France was first of the revolutionary and anti-imperialist type (*Organisations Communistes Combattantes, Action Directe*), but as of the early 1980s, increasingly of an international kind. The range of Islamic terrorist attacks in France was both religiously and politically motivated, was organised in the form of networks, and formed an early example of how these networks could penetrate western Europe (Cettina, 2003: 74f). In response, the anti-terrorism system in France was reinforced, for instance in the form of the Vigipirate plan, in which police and gendarmes are supposed to work together and to perform local surveillance on vulnerable points. In 1986, France adopted a law which, for the first time, contained a definition of terrorism. In 1996, a new law complemented the old one, when a specific and separate terrorist charge was created. More recently and relevant to the debate concerning the opportunity structure that was created by 11 September 2001, in response to the New York attacks the legislature added anti-terrorist provisions designed to strengthen the competencies of the police services (law passed on 15 November 2001), which will continue to apply until 31 December 2003 (Cettina, 2003: 87). The fact that France experienced early forms of international (Islamic) terrorism facilitated its authorities to establish working contacts with European counterparts.

Germany responded to 11/9 with the rapid introduction of new police competencies, in particular to stage house searches on buildings belonging to religious organisations. Secret services were given the possibility to intercept telecommunications – including e-mail communication – in a preventive manner. In Belgium, the legislation was not changed after 11/9, but it has become easier to freeze assets.[2]

This selective overview of domestic counter-terrorism policies in the EU shows a rather heterogeneous picture. It seems that European Union Member States have followed their own path and have had different opinions about the need for legislative and organisational reform.[3] Although the UK and Spain have had similar experiences with the persistence of domestic terrorism, their response to participation challenges within the EU and 11/9 has been rather dissimilar. Not in all EU Member States, 11/

9 provided a political window of opportunity for drafting and adopting new anti-terrorist legislation.

The Netherlands are an exception to this, which is marked by an announcement from the Dutch Minister of Justice that a new anti-terrorist law will be enacted, thereby making terrorism a punishable offence for the first time in Dutch history.[4] Moreover, to enhance counter-terrorism efforts in the Netherlands, there have been proposals to facilitate the demand for data from the financial sector, to introduce compulsory identification, and to relax the employment pro-active investigation methods (in particular the employment of criminal informants).

When one looks at it the other way around, European anti-terrorism policies seem to have an increasingly strong influence on domestic criminal justice systems, particularly when one takes into account that some of these measures have a much wider application than terrorism. The implementation of EU measures, such as the (binding) EU Arrest Warrant, is again a matter of domestic politics and is thus subject to variety between and within the Member States. In the UK, for instance, the Anti-terrorism, Crime and Security Act 2001 facilitates rapid implementation of the Council Framework Decision on Combating Terrorism, but the European Arrest Warrant is to be implemented under primary legislation and not under the 2001 Act (Walker, 2003: 24).

The wave of EU measures against terrorism post 11/9

The onset of international networked terrorism,[5] combined with the catastrophic attacks in the United States, provided a substantial window of opportunity for the adoption of a wide range of anti-terrorism measures at EU-level (Den Boer, 2003; Den Boer, forthcoming)[6].

Due to the enhanced political focus on terrorism, decision-making on the European Arrest Warrant[7] was particularly accelerated. In fact, the procedure came down to a "rubber-stamping" of a decision that was already underway. The design for this warrant had already been on the shelves, and even days prior to the terrorist attacks in the USA, the European Parliament had called for the rapid introduction of stronger joint measures against terrorism. Hence, without the terrorist attacks of the 11th of September, the decision-making would have taken its normal snail-pace: in the JHA-domain, it may take years to conclude the adoption of legal instruments, and it often depends on the whim of the EU Presidency whether dossiers are treated with any priority. This time, however, no escape was possible, certainly not once an Extraordinary Council Meeting adopted a Plan of Action announcing an extensive range of measures (21 September 2001).

The EU Arrest Warrant, which is supposed to facilitate the extradition regime between the EU countries and which is applicable to 32 (ill-defined) criminal offences, was part of this wider package. After a fast-track procedure – partly due to the use of the urgency procedure within the European Parliament – the Framework Decision on the European Arrest Warrant had been ready for adoption at the JHA Council meeting on 6 and 7 December 2001. However, it took another six months before controversial matters were ironed out. These related to problems caused by the extradition to countries which practise the death penalty, the application width, the removal of the political offence exception, the removal of the double criminality principle for a substantial number of criminal offences falling under the remit of the Arrest Warrant, the removal of the exemption to extradite one's own nationals, and constitutional problems. The European Arrest Warrant contains highly detailed procedural rules based on a system of instant mutual recognition, which, since the European Council Summit in Tampere in October 1999, has become the cornerstone of police and judicial cooperation in criminal matters between EU countries.

Other legal measures that were subject to rapid adoption included:

- The adoption of the Framework Decision on Terrorism[8]. This instrument was adopted at the JHA Council of 6 and 7 December 2001, but three parliamentary reserves were submitted. The instrument includes a list of offences that are treated as acts of terrorism. Furthermore it establishes minimum rules relating to the constituent elements of criminal acts. As far as the penal sanctions are concerned, the JHA Council chose a maximum penalty with a limit of fifteen years of imprisonment for leading a terrorist organisation, and a maximum sentence of not less than eight years for participating in a terrorist group.
- Similar to the European Arrest Warrant, the draft EU Framework Decision on the Freezing of Assets of Suspects had also been on the shelves before it was adopted. Another similarity is that this instrument is also based on the principle of mutual recognition that amounts to the automatic execution in one State of orders to freeze assets or evidence from another. The draft instrument was overtaken by the Council Regulation (EC) No 2580/2001 of 27 December 2001, which is referred to in the Council Decision on Specific Measures directed against certain persons and entities with a view to combating terrorism, and in the Council Common Position on the Application of Specific Measures to Combat Terrorism. In an annex, this regulation includes a list of organisations and individuals thought to be related to the 11th of September attacks, but it was later extended to several others. The instrument contains no information on which actors are responsible for deciding on the listing of these organisations (except "the Council"), nor do they outline how these organisations can lodge an appeal against that decision. Shortly after the events on 11 September 2001, the European Commission introduced emergency legislation to freeze more than 100 million euros worth of assets of people suspected of terrorism.
- Other avenues towards legal 'approximation' include: the ratification of existing conventions, including the 1995[9] and 1996[10] EU Conventions on Extradition[11] and the 2000 Mutual Legal Assistance Convention;[12] EU-wide standards introduced by the Commission to improve security for air travellers, and measures to reinforce security measures of the common visa;[13] investigations by the Commission into how EU legislation on asylum and financial markets can be made 'terrorism proof'; and tackling illegally obtained profits that are exploited for the benefit of sponsoring terrorist activities, under the 1985 EC Directive on Money-Laundering.

Also institutionally, the 11th of September opened the door for a strengthening of competencies, such as the creation of an anti-terrorism unit within Europol and the exchange of intelligence with US law enforcement authorities through mutual liaison officers (Gregory, 2003). Eurojust was formally launched on the basis of a Council

Decision that was taken on 14 December 2001:[14] its remit includes all crimes and offences for which also Europol is competent. According to the conclusions of the Extraordinary Council on 21 September 2001, Eurojust was mandated to pursue a cooperation between anti-terrorism magistrates.

In addition, the Article 36 Committee, which has the task to monitor and coordinate progress in the Justice and Home Affairs domain, was given the task to ensure the cooperation between Europol, Eurojust and the EU Police Chiefs Operational Task Force. It was also made responsible for the design and co-ordination of a peer evaluation system that allows a mutual evaluation of anti-terrorist measures.[15] The mechanism involves "evaluation teams" and "evaluation subjects" to monitor the effectiveness of national systems and their implementation of anti-terrorism measures. Furthermore, according to a Council Recommendation adopted in April 2002, multinational ad-hoc teams were to be established for gathering and exchanging information on terrorists.[16] Finally, the European profile of national security and intelligence services received a significant boost, as they were requested to second national counter-terrorism experts to the Council Secretariat and as the Heads of Security and Intelligence Services were to meet on a frequent basis. Other inter-institutional relationships include joint meetings between COTER (the CFSP counter-terrorism group) and the JHA Working Party on Terrorism Troikas, to be held four times a year. They have had to report to high-level transatlantic meetings. Other fora to be included in this strengthened institutional set-up include the Forum of Magistrates, the Financial Action Task Force (FATF) and the European Coordinator of Civil Protection (Den Boer, 2003: 202).

Although the surge of EU counter-terrorism legislation and reinforced institutional efforts has gradually come to a halt,[17] there is still some legislation related to visa policy and identity controls which reveal that anti-terrorism efforts have also extended to immigration and border controls.

Critical notes

This avalanche of legal and institutional measures does not leave everyone with a sense of satisfaction. Several aspects deserve a special concern.

First, there are different schools of thought about the desirability and usefulness of legal harmonisation. The EU Arrest Warrant covers a range of 32 different offences – should this be regarded as the beginning of the end? Should it be regarded as the initiation of what some regard as the formalisation of a layer of "federalised" Euro-crimes, for which a European criminal law system will be designed? The school that propagates the spreading of a European "*corpus juris*" is challenged by those who are of the opinion that legal harmonisation will create inconsistencies in national criminal law systems, and will thus harm the balance which has been so cautiously constructed in many EU Member States.

Data protection rights are considered to be under pressure. The terrorist attacks in the USA have contributed to a new frame of mind, which allow a relaxation of the use of personal data. An example is the use of biometrics under immigration law for the purposes of counter-terrorism. Several worries have been expressed about the way in which intelligence is handled by overseas authorities, notably in the USA.

For the same sake, the free movement of persons (especially immigrants) is becoming increasingly restricted. External border control, visa issuing and passport control have all been subjected to more rigorous standards. Moreover, security levels have been raised significantly. These interventions – whether executed by State or private security authorities - have a tangible bearing on travelling EU citizens. Arguing on from that: A more explicit discursive link seems to have been created between terrorism and asylum/immigration; the UNHCR commented for instance that under the new European Arrest Warrant procedures, a refugee could be transferred from one EU Member State to another Member State for prosecution.

Human rights organisations more generally have been dismayed about the speed at which the Council agreed to various measures: academics have pointed at the "fragility of the human rights culture" (Bonner, 2002: 523). Criminal lawyers in particular are worried about the suspension of the presumption of innocence.

In sum, there are plenty of considerations why the legal community ought to be apprehensive about a rapid and unsystematic approach to criminal law harmonisation, especially when propelled by dramatic events such as large-scale catastrophic terrorist attacks, and especially when pursued by means of a "secretive and sub-standard law-making process" (Harlow, 2002: 45). On behalf of civil society, non-governmental organisations monitor these developments critically and submit their opinions in petitions or letters to politicians.

Conclusion

It is still too early to measure the effect(iveness) of EU-wide measures against terrorism, whether they are meant to be employed in a preventive or a repressive manner. Even though some countries have committed themselves to an early implementation of the European Arrest Warrant, the uneven enforcement pattern of European decisions will make it hard to evaluate their impact in first instance. For the moment, however, it seems the existing national counter-terrorism arsenal supplies sufficient space for manoeuvre in order to stage law enforcement interventions and to initiate criminal investigations. Notwithstanding this display of increased effort within the EU, in the eyes of the American authorities, some European countries are seen as behaving irresponsibly because the national proceedings against suspected terrorists end in an acquittal or a conviction for minor facts.

Bibliography

Bonner, David (2002), 'Managing Terrorism While Respecting Human Rights? European Aspects of the Anti-Terrorism Crime and Security Act 2001', *European Public Law*, Volume 8, Issue 4 (December 2002) pp. 497-524.

Cettina, Nathalie (2003), 'The French Approach: Vigour and Vigilance', in Marianne Van Leeuwen, ed., *Confronting Terrorism. European Experiences, Threat Perceptions and Policies* (Kluwer Law International) pp. 71-94.

Chalk, Peter (2000), 'The Third Pillar on Judicial and Home Affairs Cooperation, Anti-Terrorist Collaboration and Liberal Democratic Acceptability', in Fernando Reinares, ed., *European Democracies Against Terrorism. Governmental Policies and Intergovernmental Cooperation'* (Dartmouth, Ashgate) pp. 175-210.

Den Boer, Monica (1998), *Taming the Third Pillar: Management and Decision-making in Justice and Home Affairs*, Current European Issues (Maastricht, European Institute of Public Administration).

Den Boer, Monica (2002), ed., *Organised Crime. A Catalyst in the Europeanisation of National Police and Pros-*

ecution Agencies? (Maastricht, European Institute of Public Administration).

DEN BOER, MONICA (2003), 'The EU Counter-Terrorism Wave: Window of Opportunity of Profound Policy Transformation?', in Marianne Van Leeuwen, ed., *Confronting Terrorism. European Experiences, Threat Perceptions and Policies* (Kluwer Law International) pp. 185-206.

DEN BOER, MONICA (forthcoming), 'Terrorism: A Threat Homogeneous to Europe?', *Notre Europe* (Paris).

GREGORY, FRANK (2003), 'The EU's role in the war on terror', *Jane's Intelligence Review* (January 01).

HARLOW, CAROL (2002), *Accountability in the European Union* (Oxford, Oxford University Press, Academy of European Law European University Institute).

REINARES, FERNANDO (2003), 'Democratization and State Responses to Protracted Terrorism in Spain', in Marianne Van Leeuwen, ed., *Confronting Terrorism. European Experiences, Threat Perceptions and Policies* (Kluwer Law International) pp. 57-70.

VAN LEEUWEN, MARIANNE (2003), 'Confronting Terrorism', in Marianne Van Leeuwen, ed., *Confronting Terrorism. European Experiences, Threat Perceptions and Policies* (Kluwer Law International) pp. 1-9.

WALKER, CLIVE (2003), 'Policy Options and Priorities: British Perspectives', in Marianne van Leeuwen, ed., *Confronting Terrorism. European Experiences, Threat Perceptions and Policies* (Kluwer Law International) pp. 11-35.

NOTES

1 There was initial reluctance to include sensitive terrorist intelligence in the overall ambit of Europol, particularly from the UK, which was afraid that the information would be compromised ('destroyed') in the international exchange by 'untrustworthy' police officers from certain EU Member States (Chalk, 2000: 185, note 15).

2 *NRC Handelsblad*, 9 April 2003.

3 This resembles the response of EU Member States to international organised crime (Den Boer, 2002).

4 *Wetsvoorstel tot uitvoering van het EU-Kaderbesluit terrorismebestrijding* (Wet terroristische misdrijven) (28 463).

5 EU TE-SAT report 2002, p. 20f.

6 See also the report by Willy Bruggeman in this volume.

7 2002/584/JHA: Council Framework Decision of 13 June 2002 on the European Arrest Warrant and the surrender procedures between Member States – Statements made by certain Member States on the adoption of the Framework Decision, *Official Journal* L 190 , 18/07/2002 P. 0001-0020.

8 Council Framework Decision of 13 June 2002 on combating terrorism (2002/475/JHA), 13/06/2002, *Official Journal* L 164 , 22/06/2002 P. 0003-0007.

9 In October 2001, this Convention still had to be ratified by France, the UK, Ireland, Italy and Belgium (Doc. 12759/01).

10 In October 2001, this Convention still had to be ratified by France, the UK, Ireland and Italy (Doc. 12759/01).

11 Convention on Simplified Extradition Procedures between the Member States of the EU, signed 10 March 1995; Convention on Extradition between the Member States of the EU, signed 27 September 1996.

12 Convention on Mutual Assistance in Criminal Matters between the Member States of the EU (*OJ* 2000 C 197/1).

13 Within the EU, there is discussion about a uniform model document for visas in case the travel document of the traveller is not officially recognised (use of biometrics and in the future digitalised versions of the photographs). Moreover, work is carried out concerning the standardization of residence permits for non-EU citizens; see *Brief Tweede Kamer*, 27 October 2001.

14 Council Decision of 28 February 2002 setting up Eurojust with a view to reinforcing the fight against serious crime. *Official Journal* L 063 , 06/03/2002 P. 0001-0013.

15 Council Decision of 28 November 2002 establishing a mechanism for evaluating the legal systems and their implementation at national level in the fight against terrorism (2002/996/JHA), *OJ* L 349/1.

16 5715/6/02 ENFOPOL 19 REV 6.

17 For instance, under the Greek Presidency of the EU, which lasted from January to July 2003, the Council of Justice and Home Affairs Ministers adopted only two documents explicitly related to anti-terrorism. This included the Council Decision concerning the signature of an EU-USA Agreement on Extradition and Mutual Legal Assistance and the Strategic Document on Terrorism (9054/2/03 ENFOPOL 36 REV 2), both adopted on 5 and 6 June 2003.

Discussion

Vadim Savelyev:* noted that several international anti-terrorism treaties include provisions according to which terrorism is an extraditable crime and is not considered as a political offence. On the other hand these treaties provide that extradition can be declined, where the request for extradition has been politically motivated. The conclusion of Mr. Savelyev was that at present the characterisation of terrorism as a political or a non-political offence is of no real importance, as extradition can in practice always be declined. The question to the panellists was whether they find this a weak point in the anti-terrorism treaties and whether it provides a possibility not to extradite an individual accused of committing a terrorist act.

Terry D. Gill:** expressed the opinion that in situations where armed forces are employed in combat operations against terrorist organisations, humanitarian law is applicable, although these situations might be relatively exceptional. While international criminal law and international law enforcement cooperation are the normal legal frameworks for addressing the problem of terrorism, there have been (Afghanistan) and probably will be situations in which armed force is employed in a context of protracted military operations. Under those conditions the law of war is the only comprehensive legal regime, which is applicable.

Bibi van Ginkel:*** asked the panellists to address the relevance of the comprehensive convention on combating terrorism and its relation to the issue-specific conventions. The question was whether the convention should be a truly comprehensive – and therefore a superseding – convention, or an umbrella convention, or whether it should merely fill in some of the gaps left by the issue-specific convention.

Leila Sadat commented by saying that in a situation as that in Afghanistan, there is no doubt that the laws of war apply. However, if you are fighting terrorism in potentially 60 countries, you cannot call this a war on terrorism. She expressed the view that it is in this respect that the United States makes a mistake. Agreeing with Prof. Joyner in his presentation, she stated that it is necessary to have cooperation between States in order to achieve the enforcement of treaties. Government support cannot be won by bombing countries. Accordingly, the present concern is the larger idea that we might end up in a perpetual war against a terrorist organisation.

Jordan Paust stated that there is no such thing as a war on terrorism. The laws of war do not apply to something like that. Furthermore, there are ideological consequences to such a scenario. The laws that are applicable in these situations are human right laws, although this might not be recognised by the United States government. Human rights law applies in peacetime and in times of war. If armed force is being used, at least the customary law principle of proportionality is applicable. In response to the question on the anti-terrorism convention, he expressed a word of caution regarding conventions that have overly broad and limiting foci.

Monica den Boer expressed the view that with regard to political offences, a judge is not the appropriate instance to decide what offences are to be considered po-

* Law Department of the State Duma, Russian Federation.

** Institute of Public International Law, Utrecht University; Department of Criminal Law, University of Amsterdam.

*** Utrecht University.

litical. Such a discussion should be held at the pre-trial stage and not be decided in court. The political offence discussion is, however, a very complex one. Examples of provisions that deal with this issue can be found in the agreements relating to refugees.

CHRISTOPHER JOYNER addressed the problems with regard to an umbrella convention on terrorism. The first problem is the definition of terrorism. Secondly, there is no solution as to the relationship between this comprehensive convention and future undefined terrorist activities. Finally, there is also the problem of the differentiation between terrorism and acts that are part of the exercise of the right to self-determination of peoples. An example of that is the suggestion that resistance to foreign occupation should not be considered terrorism. With regard to the political offences exception, he noted that this exception is in general rejected, but in the case of Article 12 of the Convention on Terrorist Bombings, there is a provision, which allows for applying the political offences exception in certain situations. The question is, thus, laden with political problems.

ANDREA GIOIA added that the United Nations umbrella convention is still a draft and, accordingly, these provisions have not yet been finalised and agreed upon. However, the draft convention says that in a situation where the umbrella convention and another convention apply to the same terrorist act, the provisions of the latter convention shall prevail. The most broadly accepted opinion seems to be that the definition of terrorist acts is a residual definition and applies only where more specific provisions are not applicable to the offence.

WILLIAM FENRICK addressed the situation where you have to make use of legal creativity in relation to crime definitions, which is an important issue for the Office of the Prosecutor (OTP) of the ICTY. This creativity by the OTP has to fall within what might be called a two- or a three-box framework, containing law applicable first to international armed conflicts, secondly to internal armed conflict and finally law applicable to all conflicts. Among these laws, there has to be a pre-existing offence, which provides the basis for stretching the envelope in a certain direction. An example of a crime in relation to which this form of legal creativity has been used is the new crime 'unlawfully inflicting terrorism on the civilian population'. Stretching the envelope is as such not problematic and, in fact, it is something that the OTP has to do, as long as this is done with care. It is, however, also a duty of the tribunal to ensure protection of the rights of the accused.

MR. BUNYAN* mentioned the plan of the European Union to launch multi-national teams to deal with terrorism and laid out his concern that this might lead to torture and assassination. Soft law plays a big role in the planned measures and these are, therefore, not binding on the Member States. However, in this case soft law can be dangerous, as it will allow States to take measures that do not have to comply with any rules relating to criminal procedure. In fact, there are several examples of groups that have acted in this manner already, although that was never thought to happen in Europe.

*Reporter: Maria Nybondas***

* Statewatch, UK.

** T.M.C. Asser Institute, The Hague.

SUMMING UP:
A CONCLUDING DEBATE

and

CLOSING OF THE CONFERENCE

The Structure of the International and European Legal System and Its Values

The concluding debate/summing-up session was convened by its co-chairs, Dorinda Dallmeyer* and Ige F. Dekker**.

Introductory remarks by Ige F. Dekker

As the co-chairs of this concluding debate, we have tried to stretch the upcoming discussion a bit, to generate some debate by formulating a few questions to be put to the panel in front of you. The first question we want to put to the panel is, I think, a rather obvious one. It is about the main title of this conference, in particular of course the question mark behind it. Is there really a transition from government to governance? And can we discern such a transition in international, political and economic relations? In other words, can or will the concept of governance be an autonomous element of the international legal system or is it a notion that will prove no more than a convenient catch phrase in a particular context, which will be replaced sooner or later by a newer, trendier phrase to catch the fluid ideas of politicians and bureaucrats?

Remarks by Sean D. Murphy***

The structure of the international and European legal system and its values

In considering whether non-State actors are fundamentally changing the international legal system – both in the sense of the types of participating actors and in the sense of its core values – I am reminded of the perhaps apocryphal comment made by the Chinese leader Zhou Enlai. Asked in the twentieth century what he thought about the consequences of the French Revolution of the eighteenth century, he reportedly responded that "it's too soon to tell." In the same vein, it may be too soon to tell exactly what we are seeing in the rise of non-State actors in international law, but certainly international lawyers and scholars have a responsibility at least to try to understand the changes we are amidst. And in that spirit, I think we have seen in this conference, broadly speaking, the emergence of four themes.

First, as the many panels of this conference have amply demonstrated, we are in the midst of a period of unprecedented transnational non-State governance. The de-

* University of Georgia School of Law, USA.
** University of Utrecht, The Netherlands.
*** George Washington University Law School, smurphy@law.gwu.edu.

velopment of the European Union is, of course, the preeminent example, of governance by means of a supra-national organization, but the diversity and depth of other international organizations has never been greater, and they have an extraordinary law-generating capacity, not just from the generation of treaties, but also from non-binding measures and techniques of dispute resolution that coordinate transnational behavior. One marvels at the detailed regulations adopted by the International Civil Aviation Organization or the food safety standards issued by the Codex Alimentarius or the global economic sanctions mandated by the Security Council. The emergence in the past decade of institutions such as the World Trade Organization or the NAFTA demonstrates the considerable vitality of international organizations in both norm-generation and norm-interpretation. Mini-international organizations are emerging embedded in multilateral agreements, particularly in the environmental arena. Similarly, non-governmental organizations (NGOs) are playing an extraordinary role in regulating transnational behavior, whether one looks at the codification of the *lex mercatoria* as discussed by Judge Brower or the dispute resolution before the now-numerous transnational arbitral institutions worldwide.

A second, counter-theme of the conference, however, as was reflected in some of the presentations, is that we should be careful not to overstate these developments as signaling a demise of States as the central organizing component of transnational governance. The description of this panel assumes that there is a "transition" to international governance, which I take to imply that we are leaving behind the traditional mode of transnational governance through the acts of States. My own view is that we are not transitioning to a post-sovereign world. In fact, the main components of a liberal view of international society – one that favors democracy, free markets, and peace – can only be provided by the effective functioning of States. Despite the rise of international organizations and non-governmental organizations, it remains the case that only the traditional State can effectively act as the agent of its own and its citizens' interests. Indeed, international organizations are built around the concept of serving the interests of States, whether one looks at how they are formed, how they operate, or the limits of their powers. In his keynote address, Professor Alvarez even cautions us to consider whether the United States is using the United Nations to project hegemonic power; in order words, he worries that the "governance" to which we are transitioning is not that of the "independent" will of the United Nations but, rather, that of a superpower. Europeans can certainly point to an extraordinary relinquishment of sovereign power within the European Union, but must also concede that certain core sovereign attributes remain firmly embedded in European States, and must further concede that the evolution underway in Europe has not caught fire anywhere else in the world to the same degree. Likewise, non-governmental organizations are now playing a significant role in lobbying governments on transnational matters, in participating at multilateral treaty negotiations, and in having their views placed before international dispute fora, but in each of those cases the NGO's role is one of influencing and not supplanting inter-State governance. One of the points made during the panel on the legitimacy of NGOs was that we should not be overly concerned about the lack of "democracy" in NGOs precisely because they are not directly wielding governmental power but, instead, are modes by which segments of global civil society seek to influence those that do wield such power.

Moreover, one need not be a cynic to note that, while there are quite a lot of international organizations today, they are not powerful. They do not enforce international law. They only occasionally adjudicate international law. They fare better in the sense of generating law, but even here, and with some exceptions, international organizations typically coordinate among States general norms of conduct, leaving to national governments the task of detailed implementation of those norms. One way to think about this issue is not just to ask whether we have more international organizations today than we did 50 or 100 years ago (we certainly do), but to ask whether the role of international organizations has increased in relative terms over the past 50 or 100 years *vis-à-vis* the role of national regulation. That is, 100 years ago there were few international organizations, but it is also true that national regulation was far less than it is today. In 1903, most States of the world were still highly agrarian, and national governments simply did not regulate matters of health, environment, consumer protection, business relationships, etc. Today, of course, with the rise of welfare States and their vast administrative structures, national governments are intimately involved in matters affecting our daily lives, and thus it may be of no surprise that there is a spill-over effect to national regulation of transnational activity, which in turn requires greater use of international organizations. In other words, are international organizations gaining in significance *vis-à-vis* national States, or are they just trying to keep pace?

For example, if you focus just on the fact of the creation of the UN Environment Programme in 1972, you might conclude that it signaled a shift from national regulation of environmental matters to international regulation of environmental matters. Yet if you focus on what was happening at the national level, you would see that until the 1960s and early 1970s, there was no systematic regulation of the environment at the national level, and therefore such "governance" was not being transferred to UNEP. Rather, beginning in that time frame, nation States began aggressively regulating the environment at the national level, and UNEP was simply an adjunct to that national regulation, whereby States decided to create a forum for coordination of their activities as they related to transnational issues.

A third theme of the conference concerns whether the rise of non-State actors is having an effect on the values and principles of the international legal system. International organizations, though creatures of States, take on a life of their own; they develop a centralized bureaucracy devoted to advancing core norms of the organization and seek to do so by alliances with certain Member States, even if other Member States would prefer the status quo, since any change would diminish their sovereign power. Similarly, NGOs have brought to the international table concerns and interests that the elites within governments would prefer to set aside. The histories of the human rights movement, the environmental movement, and the movement toward global justice for global crimes cannot be told without taking account of the normative impact of international organizations and NGOs.

To illustrate, let me mention two obvious examples of this normative influence of non-State actors. Looking first at law on the use of force, I think that the recent movement away from a fairly strict interpretation of the UN Charter's prohibition on the use of force to one that contemplates or tolerates humanitarian intervention even in the absence of Security Council authorization is to be attributed in no small part to the aggressive focus of many NGOs and some international organizations on the sanctity of core human rights, the condemnation of genocide, and the rejection of norms of sovereignty in the face of a government's mistreatment of its citizens. Looking at trade law, now that the *Shrimp/turtle* case has run its course at the World Trade Organization, it seems pretty clear that the outcry by non-governmental organizations that the WTO (and that States) be more sensitive to conservation concerns is having an effect. The WTO Appellate Body's most recent decision upholding the US revised guidelines on imports of shrimp reflects a desire to provide meaning to the GATT Article XX environment and conservation exceptions, as do other WTO decisions, such as in the *White Asbestos* case. In the absence of NGO pressure, it seems unlikely that the WTO would seek to become "greener."

By bringing new values to the table, the world has become a better place in many respects, but has also become a more complicated place, and in some respects perhaps a worse place. In this respect, let me return to the issue of humanitarian intervention and the issue of GATT Article XX. As I indicated, the emergence of the doctrine of humanitarian intervention owes much of its existence to the sustained pressure by NGOs and some international organizations to strengthen human rights. On the one hand, you can view this as a highly welcome development, one that refines the use of force paradigm to take account of values insufficiently addressed in the UN Charter. On the other hand, critics of the doctrine of humanitarian intervention worry about whether we are really improving use of force norms or are diminishing them by creating new bases for States, acting on their own authority, to use force ostensibly to protect human rights, but in reality for more prosaic purposes. Intervention in Somalia under UN authority to protect human rights seems like a good idea, but some are less convinced that intervention in Kosovo only under NATO authority was a good idea, and even fewer think that intervention in Iraq to oust a dictator was a good idea. So, at a minimum, introducing new values to the use of force paradigm has made things more complicated, and maybe made things worse.

Similarly, NGOs have forced the WTO to take Article XX of the GATT more seriously, but in doing so they may be going too far. NGOs have managed to promote aggressively concerns with the exports of genetically modified (GM) food from the United States to Europe, so much so that GM exports are virtually non-existent. There is, of course, no credible scientific evidence that consumption of licensed GM food causes adverse health consequences, and, in my view, no credible argument that we cannot regulate GM food to protect human health and the environment in the same way that we regulate numerous other products, including chemicals, pharmaceuticals, and pesticides. I also think that European resistance to GM food has profound consequences for the developing world, in that countries that could benefit from crops engineered to thrive in arid soil or to be pest resistant do not want to invest in such technologies if export markets in Europe are closed to them. There are, of course, serious arguments on the other side of this debate, but I raise the issue simply as an illustration that by bringing human health/environmental issues to the table, we have complicated the issue of trade in GM products and, at least from my perspective, made things a bit worse than they should be.

A final theme of the conference – one that reflects the joint nature of the conference – concerns the US-European dimension to the rise of non-State actors. In thinking about the value and promise of international organizations, some observers think Americans and Europeans are operating on completely different planets. Robert Kagan writes that Americans are from Mars and Europeans are from Venus, by which he means that Americans see the world as a nasty, brutish place of threats and dangers, where survival rests largely on the maintenance of judicious use of military power, while Europeans are living in a "Kantian" postmodern paradise. With the European Union, Europeans have constructed a happy way of life, one predicated on negotiation of disputes, cooperation, and fidelity to rules. Europeans want to civilize the world by making their "happy place" a global phenomenon, using treaties, courts, and international organizations. For Kagan, Americans see Europeans as engaged in a march of folly; having failed to maintain any credible military capability, Europe is impotent to the threats that loom. Consequently, America must bear the burden of protecting not just itself, but Europe as well, and in doing so is vulnerable to the very international treaties, courts, and organizations that Europe is peddling.

This image of America and Europe is a caricature; there are certain truths embedded in it, but neither side is quite so monolithic in its views. Europe has shed its share of blood over the past decade in deploying military forces abroad, just as the United States has championed the creation of path-breaking international organizations, such as the World Trade Organization, NAFTA, and the ad hoc war crimes tribunals. Yet America and Europe, if not on different planets, are certainly on different parts of the same planet, and seem to have differing innate instincts when it comes to the development of international organization. Probing those differences, developing convergence where possible, accepting divergences where necessary, is the challenge ahead of us.

Remarks by Theo Raaijmakers*

Self-regulation of corporate governance issues by non-State actors?

(1) As a member of the Closing Panel of this conference on *government* governance I was asked to reflect on the role that non-State actors play in the regulation of *corporate* governance issues and their influence on the international and European legal systems. It is a broad issue and the ten pages available for the proceedings only allow me to make a few brief remarks. A more detailed analysis will be the subject of a broader paper to be published in 2004.

There can be no doubt that 'non-State actors' have already been influencing the worldwide corporate governance debate for some time. Pension funds, institutional investors, the international securities industry, leading consultancy firms, interest groups of smaller investors, commercial service providers, academics and others have pushed for what is now called the 'standard (shareholder-oriented) model', which is contrasted with the State- and/or employee-oriented model. Shareholder activism usually concentrates on specific firms that perform poorly, although sometimes, like the Californian CalPERS, it has even addressed nations. It is apparently hard to prove firm-specific effectiveness in terms of a firm's pre- and post-action performance. To some extent

* Theo (M.J.G.C.) Raaijmakers is Professor of Corporate Law at Tilburg University, Director of its Center for Company Law and former Legal Advisor of Royal Philips Electronics (The Netherlands).

shareholder activism in the 1980s and 1990s developed as private, non-State action on the part of those market participants. It is tempting to characterize this development as 'self-regulation' (through market forces) in contrast with State intervention. The reality appears to be somewhat more diffuse. There seems little doubt that 'shareholder activism' produced wider results through its influence on the political agenda and, hence, State intervention.

Needless to say, Enron, the *pars pro toto* for a series of scandals in the USA and elsewhere which marked the burst of the Internet- or dotcom-bubble, had an immense impact. It seems to have changed the nature and scope of the corporate governance debate and to have shifted attention to the role of States in regulating the financial markets. The governance of private firms was 'nationalized' in a certain way. Not by undoing privatization, nor by States' taking direct and full control of firms, but by detailed market regulation for issuers and a degree of intrusion into the organizational charter of public corporations. The liberalization of markets and nations seems to have produced a remarkable growth of State intervention under the (political) umbrella of 'restoring the confidence of markets and investors', recently often disguised as 'codes'. This development has itself been significantly influenced by public debate and fuelled by a variety of market players, though some of them now seem to be part of the problem themselves.

So, within the framework of this conference, we shall now turn to the key question: whether the role of non-State actors will grow and, if so, in what direction and in what way. Will the cyclical process that history has produced over time come to a standstill and leave us with the 'standard model', where necessary enforced by States (and thus becoming State-oriented)? And hence with a reallocation of commercial activities, firms and societal wealth in a global economy? And to what extent will 'self-regulation' survive to govern private firms as the expression of the basic freedoms of contract, enterprise, commercial association and incorporation?

The crucial trigger for State intervention seems to reside somewhere between the freedom of enterprise in our 'capitalist' economies and the protection of the integrity of our money and capital markets.

The influence of entrepreneurs and managers on the process of promoting or, conversely, preventing regulation has been the subject of vast research. One of the battlefields has been the regulation of the 'market for corporate control'. Promoted by many as an effective means to trigger and punish poor management and to allow a premium-exit to investors, it is opposed by promoters of new businesses going public to finance their venture with capital from the market, by incumbent management and, for various other reasons, by staff and employees and by host States wishing to preserve their domestic industries. In substance such issues often turn on the basic division of powers in a public corporation.

If we simplify the matters at hand to the issues of ensuring market integrity, protecting the position of investors in the market, and creating and sustaining a general business climate that promotes new businesses and generates societal wealth, what is the clue for regulation in the first place? Where is the dividing line between personal freedom on the one hand and protection of the interests of others by State intervention on the other? How do we achieve global or international solutions for problems that themselves seem to be global and international but are basically regulated by nations in the first place?

(2) The fall-out from major scandals like Maxwell, BCCI and Metalgesellschaft, the pressure to enhance corporate disclosure and, more widely, investor orientation by maximizing shareholder value and to create an effective market for corporate control was already fuelling shareholder activism by pension funds, institutional investors, associations of smaller investors and others in the pre-Enron era. Among other things this resulted in a variety of codes of best practice, guidelines and principles.

The post-Enron burst of the Internet Bubble not only damaged the US market but also had a global effect and resulted in immense losses. Employees not only lost their jobs but also their accrued pension rights. The public outcry for 'action' may have obscured a comprehensive and in-depth analysis of the economic, financial, business, societal, psychological and other factors that caused the Bubble to burst. With hindsight the herd nature of human beings, including market players, may have caused them once again to join the dance around the Golden Calf, neglecting warnings and the conventional wisdom that all that goes up must come down. Even sophisticated US market regulation could not prevent managers, aligned to shareholders' interests to reduce the moral hazard, from cooking the books. Power, wealth and reputation always tempt public officials, agents and fiduciaries to act in their own rather than in the public or private interest with which they have been entrusted. The public investor owned firm is no exception. Though rulers have never been very successful at creating honest and courageous men,[1] the post-Enron outcry activated many interest groups that forced, in turn, politicians and States to act. An avalanche of acts, rules, codes and other regulatory measures followed, promulgated by many different national and international authorities, governments, agencies, and stock exchanges as well as by private initiative, the OECD and IASB.

Covering a variety of issues under the broad umbrella of corporate governance, these initiatives have largely been nation-oriented and do not properly reflect the international causes and problems behind the Bubble's burst. Convergent global solutions have not been sought, neither in scope nor in substance as can be demonstrated by a comparison of the Sarbanes Oxley Act with the Action Plan of the European Commission. A self-regulatory approach seems to diffuse regulatory issues, for example legitimacy in rule-making and the enforcement of these rules by the State judiciary. What room is there for self-regulation in the grey area between corporate and securities law?

(3) The post-Enron State's focus is on the role of States and non-State actors to 'restore market confidence', and enhancing 'corporate governance' has been made instrumental to that end. If the 'standard', the shareholder-oriented model, has been placed centre stage, this is hardly a surprising development: the demarcation lines between corporate and securities law on the one hand and market regulation on the other are then obscured, or simply erased, since they serve the same ultimate objective. However, if regulatory measures focus only on a firm's internal affairs (management, oversight, division of powers), there is a danger that the economic and institutional structure of the market, the organization, role and operations of its players, such as investors, pension funds, the financial industry, merchant bankers, retailers, brokers, analysts, fund managers and auditors will be overlooked. Corporate law is organizational law for business ventures and in one way or another reflects the basic freedom

of enterprise, association, contract and market transactions in our societies. Thus corporate law is part of the broader law on business organizations and, hence, a major element in a nation's business climate, not only for start-up firms but also for firms that go public. This distinguishes corporate law from securities law, even though corporate law has traditionally also focused – as in the EU – on protecting investors and third parties. Securities law, in contrast, focuses primarily on enhancing and sustaining market efficiency and integrity and, because the public interest is directly involved, the role of States will be more evident and include the financial and securities industry at large. This distinction induces different public (political) choices concerning States' responsibilities, their room to manoeuvre and the enforcement mechanisms at their disposal: what State powers are to attain the desired goal. This applies all the more if a problem can be clearly identified as essentially multi-jurisdictional. Constitutional and international (and/or federal) law then come into play. The same analysis has to be made to guide a choice for 'downward delegation' of rule-making and enforcement to the market, private organizations and other non-State actors or 'upward' from States to federal or international authorities. Traditionally, the role of States has differed in the areas of corporate and securities law and market regulation.

History reveals that there is nothing new under the sun. State intervention usually followed scandals and the subsequent public outcry. The South Sea Bubble (1720) ruined the British economy, but the British Parliament's '*corporate* law response' of the Bubbles Act effectively banned the public corporation altogether. Several jurisdictions introduced a strict chartering (concession) system and only over time liberalized their corporate law to principles of free covenant, albeit with minimum standards of protection of shareholders and third parties. The stock market crash of 1929 led to *federalization* of the US *securities* laws (1933 and 1934 Acts) and a powerful federal agency, the SEC, with regulatory, investigative and enforcement powers. Its focus is primarily on the integrity of initial and subsequent disclosure to allow investors to take well-informed decisions to buy, hold or sell. Thus present US law, reflecting the constitutional division of powers, is, or at least has been based upon a fairly clear division between corporate (State) law and (federal) securities law and market regulation. The law on business organizations is thus subject to regulatory competition between the States, resulting in enabling and permissive statutes, though the Model Business Corporation Act, the dominant Delaware law and the ALI Principles of Corporate Governance have had a convergent effect. Securities law and market regulation, in contrast, are based on strict federal statutes under strong State supervision by the SEC.

Regulation in the EU follows a different pattern. Starting with different corporate law systems and aiming to prevent Delaware-like regulatory competition, the EU harmonized certain basic elements of corporate law under the Treaty of Rome, but failed to reach agreement on the Fifth Directive on the basic governance structure of large firms, or on cross-border reorganizations and reincorporations. It adopted a federal statute on the European Company which allows a cross-border merger and conversion, but has so far failed to resolve existing tax and other burdens on cross-border group relationships. The 'petrification' inherent in the system of harmonization has often been criticized, also in the final report of the High Level Group of Company Law Experts. Regulatory competition was intentionally disfavoured, but may be fuelled by case law of the Court of Justice which not only upholds the freedom of primary and secondary settlement but also mutual recognition of 'companies' (*Überseering, Centro and Inspire Art Ltd*).

Similarly, but only quite recently a start has been made with the harmonization (not federalization) of a variety of securities law issues and market regulation. Harmonization directives require adoption by the Council of Ministers but the Lamfalussy procedure allows some degree of delegation as well as acceleration of the process. The European Court of Justice has jurisdiction with respect to the implementation of EU directives as well as on free movement of firms. The EU is therefore pursuing the same harmonization mechanisms for both corporate and securities law.

Even this very brief overview illustrates the different approaches taken by the USA and the EU in responding to the post-Enron pressures for action.

(4) The US Congress responded to "Enron" by sharpening its *federal securities* law through the Sarbanes Oxley Act, which allows the SEC to further rule-making and enforcement. In line with some but not all of the ALI Principles of Corporate Governance, Congress did focus on scrutinizing the integrity of financial and other relevant corporate disclosures. More severe *statutory* rules on market regulation, public oversight and also on corporate governance should enhance the integrity of corporate disclosure through mandatory rules on certification of accounts by the CEO and CFO. They also raise the quality of the underlying business controls, and provide for oversight of financial disclosures by an independent and competent audit committee of the board, and stricter civil and criminal liability and disqualification rules. The Act thereby also intrudes on the issuers' internal affairs and, hence, the State's powers on corporate law, but its focus is on improving the integrity of the disclosure process. Because of the international integration of capital markets, the Act and subsequent rules apply extra-territorially to foreign issuers traded or listed in the US market as well as to auditors and others, irrespective of the checks and balances under their own foreign jurisdictions. Since the larger EU firms have such dual listings/tradings[2] the Act directly influences the evolving standards in the EU and the perception of 'best practices'. It also illustrates the influence of the US system on the international capital market. This should be taken into account in any regulatory action within the EU, which, in turn, must clearly be based on the Member States' own systems with their own checks and balances (following an analysis of how to react and to make choices on regulatory options). Congress and the SEC did not limit their action to 'internal' improvements of the disclosure process. The Act and the rules promulgated under it also address the position and functioning of other parties in the markets besides issuers: auditors, merchant bankers, analysts, rating agencies and stock exchanges. It reflects the concentrated and delegated authority of the SEC in its various capacities. The basic features of corporate governance in the narrow sense, however, were left largely untouched.

(5) The EU approach differs substantially. Recognizing its failure to harmonize governance of public corporations (draft Fifth Directive and related Thirteenth Directive) and applying the Treaty's subsidiarity principle, the Commission essentially followed a corporate law route and built on existing codes that had emerged over the last decade.[3] In its May 2003 Action Plan it refrained from top-down mandatory regulation by leaving it to the Member States to designate a national code of best practices which public companies in their jurisdiction should adhere to (applying the 'comply or explain'

rule). At first sight this approach seems permissive, but it is less so upon closer analysis since it implicitly establishes that it is within the EU's power to impose obligations on Member States by means of a framework directive. It suggests a greater role for non-State actors in drafting and promoting corporate governance principles: the framework directive will require Member States (a) to designate a national ('self-regulatory') code of best practices which public companies under their jurisdiction should apply by the 'comply or explain' rule and (b) to provide means for compliance and enforcement. Whilst 'assigning' enhancement of corporate governance to national codes, the Commission does not provide any guidance as to their purpose, scope, nature, democratic legitimacy, quality standards, enforcement or the more precise meaning of the 'comply or explain' rule, nor on the question how to take account of broader societal aspects and policies, for example the Lisbon Summit's ambitions (2000) and the ultimate objective of restoring economic growth and success of firms. It left unanswered whether and to what extent international and global deficiencies in the financial market should be addressed and how unnecessary costs and burdens to financing in foreign markets should be avoided. That it also obscures the EU policy directions as such is evidenced by the Commission's transatlantic contacts with the USA on such 'post-Enron' topics as recognition of auditors and the convergence of accounting standards (US GAAP and IAS). These are very important, but a clear road map does not seem to be available.

The EU is pursuing its traditional path by harmonizing (rather than federalizing) securities law to further and facilitate market integration and concentration of financial markets, banking, the securities industry and stock exchanges. A Prospectus Directive and a directive on the admission of securities to listing have been followed by others on, for example, market abuse (covering a wider range of issues, including market professionals and insider trading) and continuous disclosure (cf. the US 1934 Act). The Commission now is clearly speeding up. Proposals on the audit profession and accounting standards are under way. A main difference with the USA remains that the mechanism is harmonization rather than federalization and also the lack of a federal agency such as the SEC. This may avoid concentration of bureaucratic power in Brussels, but it also blocks flexible rule-making and consistent enforcement. The latter is now envisaged through close coordination by national authorities in CSER. Over time the European Court of Justice may again play an integrating role.

So the diffuse overlap between corporate and securities laws and market regulation seems to hinder a more coherent EU approach. Part of the problem may be the diffusion of expertise and responsibility and the lack of coordination between national ministries and Brussels DGs.[4] Also important are the different views in our western and 'capitalist' economies on the constitutional freedom of contract, enterprise, association and organization and the related role of the State's power to regulate and oversee compliance.

(6) Thus the EU approach seems to diffuse the fundamental choices that have to be made. The High Level Group advocated a revision of the corporate law harmonization process with a view to enhance entrepreneurship and the business climate, but the European Commission apparently prefers to follow that path rather than concentrating on federalization of basic securities rules and, where necessary, related basic corporate law principles (leaving the law on business organizations to the Member States). The

envisaged framework directive on corporate governance codes now seems to refrain from giving clear guidance as to the scope, nature and enforcement of codes of best practices. This might, and presumably will, result in rather different national approaches to international market principles, also influenced by foreign rules whose background is not always clearly understood. As noted above, the crucial trigger for State intervention lies somewhere between the freedom of enterprise in 'capitalist' economies and the protection of the integrity of their money and capital markets. If we wish to develop global/international answers to similar problems we shall have to take that distinction into account and the different ways they are embedded and function in our systems.

Contract and organizational law governing firms has developed on the basis of freedom of enterprise, association and contract, as well as financing by and/or through market intermediaries. The crossover occurs when a firm goes public to find financing for its activities and investors contract into the firm as 'capital lenders', thereby becoming 'members' and seeking a return on and liquidity of their investments. The modern corporation created a per se separation of ownership from control as early as the chartering of the Dutch East India Company in 1602. Free covenant gradually overthrew chartering. It marked a sort of retreat from State intervention, but corporate law long attempted to encompass the aims of protecting market investors in public corporations. Emerging securities law clearly illustrates the public choice on the periphery of the capital market for finance in tradable shares and 'membership', and reveals the distinction between a 'partnership-like' orientation in corporate law and market regulation for liquid securities such as commodities.

Regulators often balanced between these two approaches and regularly shifted from market regulation (focusing on integrity of and confidence in the markets) to the corporation as such (its nature, organization and ability to cope with the moral hazards of the agency problem). The result was often a mixture.

(7) Now that the EU envisages delegating (undefined) corporate governance issues to national self-regulatory codes, proper analysis is even more indispensable to identify subject matters and avoid isolation of the issues that created the global post-Enron crisis. If we do not exclude the financial markets and its players and include, besides issuers of securities, the structure of the market, the securities industry (underwriters, merchant bankers, brokers, dealers, analysts, auditors, rating agencies, pension funds and institutional investors) and public oversight, we may find that measures and 'regulation' which are not based on such in-depth analysis soon become obsolete and prove to be ineffective and non-cost-efficient. It may result in a further drifting apart where in fact the opposite is indispensable for the future of the EU in the development of its own answers in global markets and competition.

The corporate governance debate goes back to pre-Enron scandals. The Cadbury Code was a response to Maxwell and BCCI. Globalizing capital markets and M&A activities, resulting in numerous cross-border alliances, increased the influence of the US capital market and, consequently, its rules, regulations, deal structure and transaction process. This influence is and seems likely to remain substantial, also in terms of business concepts, strategies and perspectives, including such directions as 'maximizing shareholder value'. It fuelled shareholder activism, but also highlighted the different underlying 'values'.

One of the dangers of 'voluntary/self-regulatory' codes is that they assume, explicitly or implicitly, that systems will converge under the influence of the international markets but overlook the basic differences in the economic, legal and societal background of national systems. Thus US post-Enron regulatory actions may be copied into EU systems based upon incomplete analyses and wrong assumptions about how the new US rules are embedded in their own broader system. Not infrequently, discussions on transatlantic issues are confused by a misconception of each other's systems and rules. I will try to illustrate this with a few examples.

(a) Rules and their creation should not be isolated from the realities they address. First there are differences in market structure and liquidity. Monitoring of public firms by blockholders or banks and institutions controlling blocks is easier in a concentrated market than in one with dispersed ownership: compare the USA and UK with Germany, Japan, Korea and the emerging Chinese market. The US, UK and Netherlands show growth in institutional investment and pension fund holdings, Germany still shows large holdings by banks, often combined with bonds and loans. Italy, France and Belgium have large family holdings controlling large groups *de facto* or *de jure*. Japan still has its *keiretsu*. These realities do matter when discussing 'market for control' concepts and rules (mandatory bids, public offers, but also contacts between issuers and major investors).

(b) There is a striking difference with respect to accounting and disclosure. Going public requires a one-time prospectus disclosure. Once 'public', firms are supposed to allow their investors and the market to take well-informed decisions on the basis of continuous annual and intermediate information. EU law (Fourth Directive and Seventh Directive) is based on the notion that companies account for their policies and actions by presenting annual accounts to the AGM for adoption. Only when the accounts have been adopted can profits be distributed and the Board be discharged for the performance of its duties, unless the accounts were misleading, incorrect or incomplete. US law simply focuses on disclosure to the market and does not require adoption of the annual accounts by the AGM. The Revised Model Business Corporation Act (RMBCA) only requires that the accounts be sent to shareholders for information purposes, not for adoption, and hence dividends may be declared without shareholder approval of the accounts. US securities law does, however, require public corporations to *disclose* their annual and intermediate statements focusing on the integrity of the information as such, under the public oversight of the SEC. The Sarbanes Oxley Act did not change this and rather focuses on enhancing the process to achieve integrity of public disclosure by the Board's Audit Committee and CEO/CFO, including the role of internal and external audits. This difference in vision directly influences important issues of 'corporate governance', including the division of powers and Board accountability.

As noted above, a similar concept of continuous and fair disclosure is being harmonized in the EU for *public* corporations as part of the harmonization of securities laws. Remarkably, the US GAAP address only public corporations, whilst the principles-based directives (the Fourth and Seventh) apply to all corporations, including those that are closely held. The EU elected to adopt IAS principles as the standard and is discussing further alignment with the USA.

(c) As has already been stated, visions on the nature of corporations (and hence the structure of their regulation) also differ. I briefly refer to the development from State concession to free covenant with material substantive rules and, recently, the 'nexus of contracts' which centres on (constitutional) freedom of contract. Regulatory competition in the USA resulted in Delaware corporate law becoming the dominant US system, albeit in a shareholder-oriented model. EU corporate law is more diverse and includes employee-, stakeholder- and State-oriented models with broad discretionary executive board powers. This in itself limits the possibilities for self-regulatory codes of corporate governance within such systems. On the other hand, the harmonization process resulted in rules that explicitly aimed to protect investors by means of corporate law rules.

(d) The EU Action Plan specifically refers to 'shareholder democracy', apparently embracing the standard shareholder-oriented model. It is, however, debatable whether such a vague political and philosophical concept can serve as a clearly defined regulatory principle for corporate and securities law. Even if the concept were clear, which it is not, the mere freedom of enterprise and organization seems to limit any 'automatic' application. Both political and business realities exhibit a great variety of organizational patterns: presidential democracies resembling chairman-CEO governed enterprises, oligarchical and party-based democracies resembling oligarchical organizations led by the original entrepreneur and/or his family and so on. Concepts and realities may also differ: Caesar was murdered because he wanted to be king, Augustus, however, ruled *de facto* as a dictator whilst *de jure* adhering to the Republic's constitutional principles. Life cycles of organizations reveal changes from sole proprietorships to employee- and investor-owned firms and vice versa.

EU directives have made a variety of corporate resolutions subject to shareholder approval and an extension of this regime is proposed in the draft Thirteenth Directive (on takeover bids). In contrast, the RMBCA only empowers shareholders to elect board members and approve extraordinary transactions such as mergers, the sale of assets and dissolution. Shareholders may present proposals of their own but the Board is not obliged to follow these (if indeed they are adopted). The process is regulated by federal proxy rules. Bylaws are separated from the certificate of incorporation and, unless otherwise specified, may be amended by the Board without shareholder approval. Shareholders do not adopt annual accounts. Pre-emptive rights only exist if provided for. Boards may resist hostile takeovers and State law provides for a variety of anti takeover devices. The EU May 2003 Action Plan's intention of a duty to vote shares is no part of Sarbanes Oxley.

(e) Proper Board monitoring, required to cope with the phenomenon that public corporations by their very nature separate ownership from control and hence cause moral hazards for directors and managers as 'agents', has been addressed in EU jurisdictions by assigning oversight to a supervisory board that is separated and independent from the executive board (e.g. in the Netherlands, Germany and the Nordic countries). It is not permitted to combine the position of CEO and chairman of the supervisory board. Accounting to the AGM is part of the monitoring system.

(f) US Boards remain entrusted with wide and discretionary powers to direct the firm, and the use of these powers is protected by the business judgement rule, as well as by indemnification by the corporation and D&O insurance. US securities law provides for liability for misleading and incorrect disclosures, whereas the European pattern of the Fourth and Seventh Directives still focuses on shareholder approval of the annual

accounts. In principle this discharges the members of the board for their reported performance over the preceding fiscal year. Specific liabilities are envisaged in securities and bankruptcy law. Disqualification of directors is not a widespread notion in the EU. Criminal sanctions for corporate misbehaviour are increasing in the EU, but expertise for enforcement has yet to be developed.
(g) US securities law, as amended by the Act, is strict law and enforceable by the SEC or, in case of claims for damages, by private claimants. Corporate law enforcement is in the hands of shareholders and other parties asserting a claim. The EU Action Plan, under which Member States are to designate national codes, only envisages a European joint advisory committee, but no specific enforcement mechanism for the 'comply or explain' rule. This will depend on national choices. To the extent that State action (including action by the judiciary) is required, this will *per se* reduce the self-regulatory character of the national codes. The UK Combined Code is 'enforced' by means of the listing requirements of the London Stock Exchange. Dual listing and/or trading in globalizing markets may result in a cumulation of requirements for the corporations concerned.

However brief and incomplete this overview is, it may nevertheless illustrate the different visions and structures underlying corporate governance issues in the wider sense. What does this signify for the self-regulatory approach envisaged in the EU Action Plan?

(8) It is imperative that we understand these basics when we attempt to find solutions for clearly defined problems in globalizing capital and financial markets in the grey area between corporate and securities law. Misconceptions may point us in the wrong direction. Coming back to this Conference's central theme we may observe that non-State actors do indeed have an increasing influence on the development of corporate governance principles and rules. The ALI Principles of Corporate Governance, combining the character of restatements and of a model law, were the well-drafted and elaborated product of more than a decade's work by non-State actors. The OECD Code under review addresses nations rather than firms. The great variety of 'soft law' codes which have emerged or are being reviewed in the EU – see the Weil Report commissioned by the European Commission – and which Member States will presumably be designating under the forthcoming EU framework directive, vary substantially in the manner of their creation, scope, reach, nature and enforceability. Their effectiveness may differ. Consequently, the final result of the Action Plan will presumably differ from country to country and will not contribute to finding solutions and approaches that fit into the international dimension of the markets in which many public corporations finance their equity. Firms with multiple listing are faced with a cumulation of different rules. Let me – again very briefly – illustrate my concerns.

(a) The **initiators** of 'codes' are of a very different nature. The Sarbanes Oxley Act was initiated by Congress and enacts mandatory federal law, which is enforceable by the SEC and may be litigated. The UK Combined Code (Cadbury, Greenbury, Hampel and Higgs) was initiated by the Financial Reporting Council, the LSE and the accounting profession. The Dutch Peters Code was initiated by the Amsterdam Stock Exchange and the Association of Issuers, the Tabaksblat Code – still under some degree of political threat – was initiated by the Netherlands Association of Employers, though the committee consists of members from different backgrounds. In fact the term 'initiators' conceals the true driving forces. Often these originate in public opinion and pressure from interest groups. This soon involves the political arena. More often than not initiatives for codes are 'forced' upon participants under the **political threat** of introducing strict and binding rules if no such 'code' is produced.

(b) Political threat influences the **nature** of codes. Self-regulation has long been accepted as a way of governing also stock exchanges and other homogeneous 'peer groups' (like auditors, lawyers and doctors). In that case self-regulation is deliberately left to the peer group, both the establishment of the rules and their enforcement. Self-regulation has been considerably reduced in these areas. One of the reasons the Merger Code of the Netherlands Social and Economic Council, comparable to the UK City Code, was replaced by statutory law, was because it could not be enforced against foreign parties in a public offering. Corporate governance issues may also be made part of listing requirements (UK Combined Code: the LSE). This presupposes prior involvement in the drafting process or a later separate decision to adopt the Code (changed or unchanged). The 'comply or explain' rule is consistent with listing requirements, but the draft Dutch Tabaksblat Code seeks the support of a mandatory rule obliging firms to address the comply or explain rule in their report to shareholders, thus incorporating the issue into corporate law enforcement rules on annual accounts and corporate investigation ('*enquêterecht*') rather than securities law.

(c) The **addressees** differ. The Sarbanes Oxley Act addresses public corporations, but also auditors and various market professionals. It applies to domestic and foreign issuers (including more than 40 Dutch companies). The OECD Code addresses nations rather than companies. The draft Dutch Tabaksblat Code addresses not only public corporations, but also directly and indirectly the State legislator. It also requires institutional investors to vote their shares and account to their beneficiaries. It remains a problem of national codes that they are not formally enforceable against foreign parties without the assistance of additional rules. Obviously this does not exclude the force of reputational and other mechanisms.

(d) The **scope** differs. The Sarbanes Oxley Act extended its reach to parties other than issuers and included auditors and market professionals. The Action Plan and the draft Tabaksblat Code extend their aim to voting by institutional investors and the promotion and facilitation of electronic means of voting and proxies (without providing for detailed proxy rules). The latter therefore seem to belong to the domain of State action rather than 'self-regulation'. This again illustrates how internal corporate law and securities law or market rules for auditors, analysts, rating agencies and institutional investors have become mixed up.

(e) As far as they relate to listing and trading in a market, their **reach** may be extraterritorial, like the Sarbanes Oxley Act, which only allows application in domestic practice to a limited extent. This immediately bears on the **enforceability** of the rules and the difficulty of non-binding codes, whose application can be enforced in a soft, reputational way, but not against foreign firms. In the Netherlands the new rules may become 'enforceable' under our very broad investigative rights, which allow for far-reaching interim injunctive sanctions under the broad denominator of 'misconduct of the firm', in which generally accepted principles can be applied. To the extent enforceability *is* provided for (whether explicitly or implicitly) we should start from

the beginning and ask ourselves whether, and to what extent, mandatory rules ought not to be established through the usual democratic legislative process.
(f) The above analysis may already have illustrated the confusion that may arise from mixing up corporate and securities law and market regulation issues.
(g) From an **international perspective** also (EU as well as transatlantic and global) we may and should ask ourselves whether a soft law approach is the right one to cope with the post-Enron questions we have.

(9) Let me try to summarize the above. The post-Enron public outcry produced political pressure on politicians and hence States to take action to repair the deficiencies, perceived and/or real, under the broad but imprecise slogan of restoring market confidence. A variety of non-State actors played an important part in that debate. But proper diagnosis is required if we are to avoid curing only the symptoms or, alternatively, achieving overkill. Securities law and market regulation have, over time, focused on market integrity and investor protection. Self-regulation was reduced and replaced by strict rules and public oversight. Corporate governance focuses primarily on organizational corporate internal affairs as part of corporate law in general. Corporate law, being part of the law on business organizations, is by its very nature based on freedom of enterprise and commercial association and of contract. But it also covers the position of shareholders, including those in a public corporation. The crossover of these two branches of law causes any regulatory action to respond to this distinction: whether any action is needed, which field it should cover, what mechanisms are available or needed, how enforcement is envisaged. These are difficult questions, but they become more complicated in view of the globalization of markets and the securities industry.

In its Action Plan the EU refers part of the problem to self-regulatory codes to be designated by the Member States. Thus the EU and the Member States have to establish how they will address the issues at hand and what responsibility and power they have even if they 'delegate' and enforce the creation of such codes through political threat. Whether the result should be labelled self-regulation will depend on the standards applied with respect to the homogeneity of drafters and addressees, as well as their enforcement by 'peers' rather than State-supported enforcement by the judiciary or public oversight. The comply-or-explain principle promoted by the EU seems to obscure the non-binding character of such codes. If Member States create actionable rights and/or public oversight this would seem to imply that the adoption of rules by non-State actors should meet minimum standards in the first place, for example on representativeness and quality standards.

It is doubtful whether 'codes' can replace State action in the long run, although States are not omnipotent either. The international character of the market issues requires States to cooperate or provide for federal and international rules. But markets are regulated nationally subject to domestic concepts, values and rules. In view of the dominance of the US system misconceptions on that account should be avoided. Corporate law should remain embedded in national law on business organizations reflecting the freedom of enterprise, commercial organization and contract. Regulatory competition in the EU should enhance innovation in the spirit of the Lisbon Summit (March 2000). Only successful entrepreneurship in a global competition, including strong emerging markets like China, will 'restore confidence' in the long run.

NOTES

1 Note that the Roman Corpus Iuris starts: Praecepta iuris sint haec: honeste vivere, alterum non laedere et suum cuique tribuere (The main principles of law are: live honestly, do not damage others and give others what is theirs).

2 This is true of more than 40 major Dutch firms.

3 The earlier Maxwell, BCCI and other British scandals led to a *self-regulatory* approach. The Committees chaired by Sir Adrian Cadbury, and subsequently the Greenbury, Hampel, Turnbull and Higgs Reports resulted in the Combined Code. Listing requirements of the LSE require issuers to comply or explain. Germany got its Codex (Cromme), France its Vienot Code and the Netherlands its Peters Code, which is to be replaced by the Tabaksblat Code. Compare the Weil Report commissioned by the European Commission. I will be returning to these issues and the questions that have to be answered below. Here I note that these answers are typically nationally oriented.

4 Remarkably the High Level Group of Company Law Experts in its final report of 4 November 2002 also focused primarily on corporate rather than securities law.

REMARKS BY ANNE-MARIE SLAUGHTER*

A GRAND EXPERIMENT: THE EU AS A PIONEER FOR GLOBAL GOVERNANCE

The EU has pioneered a new form of governance that is potentially the answer to the globalization paradox. According to Robert Keohane, we need more government on a global and a regional scale, but we don't want the centralization of decision-making power and coercive authority so far from the people actually to be governed.[1] Indeed, Renaud Dehousse has identified precisely this paradox in the EU itself, noting that while "increased uniformity is certainly needed; greater centralization is politically inconceivable, and probably undesirable."[2] In many ways the EU answer to this paradox is still a grand experiment for the peoples of Europe, much less of the world. But even in its experimental phase, and even with all caveats that must be heeded in any effort to extrapolate from Europe to the rest of the world, the distinctive system of governance that is becoming a hallmark of the EU has much to offer not only to EU lawyers and constitutional lawyers, but also to international lawyers.

In response to the challenges of trying to harmonize or at least reconcile the regulations of its diverse and growing membership, the EU has developed a system of "regulation by networks," located in the Council of Ministers and closely connected to the complex process of "comitology" that surrounds Council decision-making.[3] This use of an organized network of national officials is designed to ensure "that the actors in charge of the implementation of Community policies behave in a similar manner."[4] At the same time, on the judicial side, the EU has pioneered the development of "vertical networks," close and mutually interdependent relationships between the European Court of Justice (ECJ) and national courts in EU member countries. These vertical networks ensure that EU law is directly enforced by national courts and that national judges learn to identify EU legal issues; at the same time, these courts can serve as a valuable check on ECJ overreaching if and when necessary. Finally, national legislators in EU countries are increasingly networking with one another regarding EU rules and

* Dean, Woodrow Wilson School of Public and International Affairs, Princeton University; President, American Society of International Law.

policies, even as they are beginning to form vertical networks with their counterparts in the European Parliament.

Each of these phenomena can be understood as a specific response to a specific problem arising in the course of the development of the EU, and often a very *ad hoc* response. Yet taken all together, these networks comprise an extraordinarily comprehensive example of transgovernmentalism: interactions not among States but among their component government institutions – regulators, judges, and even legislators. In the world beyond the EU, all these officials are reaching out beyond national borders in various ways, finding that their once "domestic" jobs have a growing international dimension. As they venture into foreign territory, they encounter their foreign counterparts – regulators, judges, and legislators – and create horizontal networks, concluding memoranda of understanding to govern their relations, instituting regular meetings, and even creating their own transgovernmental organizations. They are also, although much less frequently, encountering their supranational counterparts, judge to judge, regulator to regulator, or legislator to legislator, and establishing vertical networks. In all these areas, the EU experience can provide a beacon, and perhaps often a cautionary tale.

1. Regulatory networks in the EU

In many ways the hallmark of the EU method of integration is lawmaking at the supranational level and implementation at the national level – through government networks. The effort to harmonize national laws within the European Community (EC) involves the passage of regulations at the Community level but depends on national authorities for their implementation.[5] The EU legislative process, involving the Council, the Commission, and the Parliament, issues directives that set forth Community objectives. National authorities must then implement the goals of these directives into their national laws.[6] This process is "slow and cumbersome."[7] But as scholars like Renaud Dehousse point out, it is in many ways the secret of the EU's success. It permits collective action at the supranational level while nevertheless leaving enormous power and discretion in the hands of the national regulatory authorities.[8]

Dehousse's identification of the resulting "regulation by network" thus refers to the functional need for mid-level officials from national ministries in different issue areas to exchange information with one another and with both Commission officials and private actors. Dehousse casts upon these networks a far more favorable eye than many of his fellow EU observers. Even for him, however,

> ad hoc meetings of national officials, no matter how frequent, are not enough to bring about a true 'community of views', let alone a 'community of action" Partnership must be structured by common rules, which lay down the rights and duties of all members. Equally important, the network itself must be given some stability, which generally implies the setting-up of a structure which will manage the interaction among network members.[9]

European regulatory agencies fulfill this function. Eight new agencies were created at the European level between 1990 and 1997 as a way of facilitating further harmonization. Four of these – the European Environmental Agency, the Lisbon Drug Monitoring Centre, the European Agency for Health and Safety at Work, and the European

Agency for the Evaluation of Medicinal Products – are best described as "information agencies."[10] Their job is to collect, coordinate, and disseminate information needed by policymakers. They lack decision-making authority, much less coercive enforcement power.

Dehousse also sees the European information agencies as network creators and coordinators.[11] "Their primary aim is to run networks of national administrations which come into play in the implementation of Community policies."[12] They accomplish this function by setting up a "permanent technical and administrative secretariat," which tries not only to collect and disseminate necessary information but also to encourage "horizontal cross-fertilization" among counterpart national officials.[13] From a more dynamic perspective, it appears that the emergence of transgovernmental networks through the EU method has given rise to the need for a central node, which in turn helps spur more coordinated and effective transgovernmental action.

Giandomenico Majone refers to such networks within the EU as "bearers of reputation," observing that they "facilitate the development of behavioral standards working practices that create shared expectations and enhance the effectiveness of the social mechanisms of reputational enforcement."[14] For example, the European Agency for the Evaluation of Medicinal Products "works closely with the corresponding national authorities," linking together national agencies that have an incentive "to maintain their reputation in the eyes of the other members of the network."[15]

Reputation is particularly important to the extent that specific government networks themselves embody a system of "regulation by information," in which power flows not from coercive capacity but from an ability to exercise influence through knowledge and persuasion.[16] Many countries have experimented with various forms of regulation by information as the deficiencies of traditional command and control regulation have become more apparent. Here more than ever, success in exercising this kind of power requires an agency to establish its credibility and professional reputation.[17]

Within the EU, the shift from direct regulation to regulation by information has been part of a "radical rethinking of the way in which norms are elaborated and applied."[18] Even the EU Commission has had to recognize that the straightforward model of regulation as "the elaboration of norms by legislators followed by their application by administrators or judges" is inadequate in the face of uncertain and complex public policy issues, particularly those involving risk regulation. The response has been what the EU dubs "co-regulation" –the simultaneous decentralization of regulatory authority, so as to shift more power to regulators within the EU Member States, and the creation of a new generation of specialized administrative agencies at the supranational level.[19]

The decentralization of regulatory authority to national officials increases the need to ensure minimum uniformity among them; hence the value of a network. The network can and does emerge on an *ad hoc* basis, but the existence of a supranational agency charged with its coordination strengthens it immeasurably. Thus, according to the Commission, the eight new agencies created at the European level between 1990 and 1997 have broadened the existing government network to include parallel networks of private actors, "with the aim of establishing a 'community of views'."[20] Creating these broader networks has resulted in "wider ownership of the policies in question" and has thereby achieved "better compliance, even where the detailed rules are non-binding."[21]

These developments within the EU regulatory networks – the creation of supranational agencies and ties to parallel networks of private actors – are particularly promising for the global arena. In many cases the equivalent of such agencies already exists in the form of a treaty-based but relatively weak international organization. Networks of both civic and corporate actors also often outpace the formation of government networks in the global arena. In both these cases, the emergence of defined government networks would provide valuable interlocutors to help assure implementation of agreed international rules.

2. Judicial networks in the EU

The legal system of the European Community was built through the decisions of lower national courts to send cases up to the European Court of Justice (ECJ). These lower courts regarded the ECJ not as a Supreme Court, but as a supranational court, often bypassing their own supreme courts and at least in tacit opposition to the views of the executive branch in their respective countries.[22] The ECJ in turn, took the opportunity to lay the foundation of what it originally called "a new legal order," in which the Treaty of Rome and much legislation passed in Brussels was "directly effective" ("self-executing" in US terms) and thus able to be invoked by individuals in national courts.[23] The result was to empower individual litigants and lower national courts to hold governments (executive and legislatures) to their international commitments.

A new generation of scholarship has focused on the motives driving the national courts to ally themselves with the ECJ, noting substantial variation in the willingness both of different courts within the same country and of courts in different countries to send references to the ECJ and to abide by the resulting judgments. What is most striking about these findings is the extent to which specific national courts acted independently not only of other national courts, but also of the executive and legislative branches of their respective governments.[24] For example, a lower German financial court insisted on following an ECJ judgment in the face of strong opposition not only from a higher financial court but also from the German government.[25] The French Court of Cassation accepted the supremacy of EC law, following the dictate of the ECJ, even in the face of threats from the French legislature to strip its jurisdiction amid age-old charges of "gouvernement par juges."[26] British courts overturned the sacrosanct doctrine of parliamentary sovereignty and issued an injunction blocking the effect of a British law pending judicial review at the European level.[27]

Such judicial action might be unremarkable in the domestic context. However, particularly in the early days of the construction of the European Community, steps toward further integrating the Treaty of Rome were considered foreign policy decisions to be made by the executive on the basis of calculations of relative advantage and disadvantage among competing Member States. How then to explain why national courts did not line up behind the executive and await instructions? The motives of these various national courts were multiple: a desire for "empowerment"[28]; competition with other courts for relative prestige and power[29]; a particular view of the law that could be achieved by following EC precedents over national precedent[30]; or the desire to advantage or at least not to disadvantage a particular constituency of litigants.[31]

The German Federal Constitutional Court (*Bundesverfassungsgericht*, or BVerfG) in particular has a long history of engaging and challenging the ECJ as a co-equal rather than a superior court.[32] In its recent decision in *Brunner* v. *The European Union Treaty*[33] – a case that challenged the constitutionality of the Maastricht Treaty – the BVerfG explicitly proposed a "cooperative relationship" with the ECJ, by which the BVerfG would establish a threshold of constitutional guarantees and the ECJ would adjudicate the application of these and additional guarantees on a case by case basis.[34] Within this relationship, both courts are to ensure that both Community law and national law are properly respected by the government institutions most directly within their jurisdiction and to acknowledge their "mutual influence" on one another.[35]

The BVerfG has been the most outspoken and perhaps the most assertive in its relations with the ECJ. But it is not alone, garnering support from the Italian, French, and Belgian high courts in more subtle guises.[36] The tug of war between the ECJ and all national courts, both high and low, will continue, even as their relations and their jurisprudence become increasingly intertwined. But just as the BVerfG declared the European Union to be not a "confederation" but a "community of States,"[37] so too is its legal system best characterized as a community of courts. Within this community, each court is a check on the other, but not a decisive one, asserting their respective claims through dialogue of incremental decisions signaling opposition or cooperation.[38]

Many observers might discount the experience of national courts in the European Union either as a *sui generis* phenomenon or as more analogous to the experience of state courts in the early decades of the United States than of contemporary courts worldwide. It is certainly possible that the European Union is an emerging federal State, but federalism is currently out of fashion among member governments. More important for the argument advanced here, a federalist vision of the Union has been rejected by leading national courts, which see themselves as still interacting with a supranational rather than a federal tribunal. They are engaged in a dialogue of constitutionalism within a recognizably traditional framework of international law, a framework that can be adopted and adapted by courts around the world.[39]

It is noteworthy in this regard that although the relations between the European Court of Justice and national courts in Europe were originally structured by the Treaty of Rome, providing for national courts to refer cases involving questions of EEC law to the ECJ, the actual relations that have evolved between the ECJ and the national courts and the principles governing them are informal. The national courts of the individual members of the EU have no separate status at international law; they are simply bound as organs of the member governments to uphold all international legal obligations incumbent on the nation. Similar obligations apply to the national courts of any nation subject to a treaty establishing an international or supranational tribunal.

Nothing in principle prohibits these national courts from developing relationships with WTO panels or the WTO Dispute Resolution Body, the European Court of Human Rights or other regional human rights courts, or indeed any of the proliferating international tribunals of various types. Cases cannot be formally referred in these instances, but decisions can certainly be exchanged and expertise consulted. The result could be a global community of courts, or, better yet, multiple overlapping communities of courts committed to the national and international rule of law.

3. Legislative networks in the EU

The European Parliament (EP) is in some ways a world of its own. It is an independent legislative body established as one of the governing institutions of the EU; further, it is composed not of national parliamentarians, but of directly elected representatives. Originally, the Treaty of Rome, which established the European Economic Community in 1957, gave the EP only a consultative role in Community decision-making. Subsequent treaties and important rulings by the European Court of Justice have extended the EP's autonomy as an institutional actor within the European system, so that the Parliament and the Council of Ministers now share power in a substantial number of areas. In recent years the EP has become an important and influential player within the EU system.

Notwithstanding this increased power for parliamentarians at the European level, discussions of the "democratic deficit" within the EU in the 1990s still focus on input from national parliamentarians. Shirley Williams, ever an advocate of legislative power, pointed out in 1991 that: "Most national parliaments have until recently lacked effective mechanisms linking them to the EP. They have been suspicious of attempts by the EP to demand greater powers and have been unwilling to work closely with it in establishing a joint structure of parliamentary accountability."[40] She proposed holding occasional "assizes," consisting of specialized parliamentary commissions from national parliaments and the EP, to address specific policy areas in depth.[41]

The powers that be did not see fit to follow her advice. However, the EU is gradually constructing something similar: a set of vertical legislative networks between a genuine supranational parliament and its national counterparts, similar to its vertical judicial networks although less formal and powerful. In 1989, for example, the EP created a body to bring together the committees of national parliaments that specialized in European affairs – the awkwardly named Conference of the Community and European Affairs Committees of the Parliaments of the European Union (COSAC). COSAC convenes twice a year; it has discussed subjects such as internal security and the environment and has done a lot of work on the role of national parliaments in EU decision-making. Partly as a result of this activity, the Treaty of Amsterdam in 1997 included a special Protocol requiring the EP to share information and consult with national parliaments on pending EP legislation.[42]

In sum, the past decade has witnessed many initiatives in EU parliamentary relations that have important implications for other parts of the world. It also highlights the pioneering nature of EU governance, which is heavily dependent on networks of both ministers and regulators. Directly elected legislative assemblies at the regional level may yet have a valuable role to play in the world. Similar bodies on a global scale may also have a future, though it is hard now to imagine any that would be taken seriously. Even at the regional level, however, a directly elected assembly cannot substitute for national parliaments. It is likely to be effective only to the extent that it succeeds in networking with national parliamentarians and helping serve as a catalyst for their interactions with one another.

4. A NEW SYSTEM OF GLOBAL GOVERNANCE

A world of horizontal and vertical government networks composed of different types of government institutions – regulatory, judicial, legislative; performing different functions – information exchange, enforcement cooperation, harmonization, technical assistance and training; with different members; of different degrees of formality; co-existing in different ways with international organizations – is a messy world indeed. It may seem impossibly complex. But the underlying concept is simple. It is a world in which the basic elements of governance – making rules, implementing rules, enforcing rules and resolving disputes arising under the rules – are carried out by networks of the government institutions – national and supranational – responsible for performing those functions.

In many ways the model for this world order is the European Union. Networks of government ministers exercise the most important powers in the EU at the European level; networks of national judges exchange ideas and cooperate in resolving Europe-wide disputes; networks of national parliamentarians are emerging to monitor the European activities of the networks of ministers. At the same time, the EU has genuine supranational institutions – a Court, a Commission, a Parliament – that exercise genuine governmental authority and that increasingly enforce their authority through vertical networks with their national counterparts. Individual EU members can maintain the distinctive character and autonomy of their national institutions, while at the same time reaping the benefits of collective governance through government networks.

The EU itself sits within a broader set of regulatory networks among OECD countries. OECD officials see all OECD Member States, including the USA, all EU Members, Japan, and now South Korea and Mexico, as participating in a "multilayered regulatory system."[43] The infrastructure of this system is government networks. Put these all together, and the world becomes a world of concentric circles of regulatory networks, although with different centers. Ideally, over time, new networks will be created, overlapping with existing ones, with developing countries at their center. The EU itself demonstrates the ways in which it is possible to have different but overlapping networks through its "variable geometry arrangements," in which Schengen or the Eurozone encompass networks of subsets of all EU Members.

The world differs from the EU in critical ways, of course. EU Members share a common region, history, culture, political and economic ideology. These factors all reinforce the founding commitment of the EU treaties toward: "an ever closer union."[44] This commitment provides both impetus and cover for government networks within the EU. They are explicitly charged with cooperation, harmonization, and enforcement of national and EU law. And they operate with a high degree of trust in one another – trust strengthened by the knowledge that they will be interacting with one another for a very long time to come.

Overall, however, the EU has many features that make its distinctive form of government by network exportable to other regions and to the world at large. It remains a collection of distinct nations, even as it works to create the governing power and institutions at the supranational level necessary to solve common problems and advance common interests for all its members. Indeed, it is a vibrant laboratory for how to establish the necessary degree of collective cooperation among a diverse group of States while retaining the dominant locus of political power at the national level. It has limited supranational institutions, albeit more powerful than any that currently exist at the global level, but they cannot function without the active cooperation and participation of national government officials.

Europeans themselves and international lawyers in general have long debated whether the EU itself and its corpus of rules, regulations, and practices can be understood as a specific international legal regime or as a *sui generis* phenomenon. The answer must be a bit of both. In its commitment to an ongoing process of integration, the EU is a project particular to a set of nations bound by geography and history. But as a grand experiment in how to allow a group of States to gain collective governance capacity without relinquishing independent identity, the EU's particular combination of networked horizontal and vertical government institutions may be the shape of things to come in international law.

Notes

1 Robert O. Keohane, 'Governance in a Partially Globalized World – Presidential Address, American Political Science Association, 2000,' *American Political Science Review* 95 (March 2001): 1.

2 Renaud Dehousse, 'Regulation by Networks in the European Community: The Role of European Agencies,' *Journal of European Public Policy* 4 (1997): 246-61, 254.

3 Ibid., 259.

4 Ibid., 254.

5 "Harmonization," which has been the main vector of Community intervention in national policies, is a legislative exercise that strives for a uniformity of substantive rules in EC Member States' laws. Ibid., 247-249.

6 Ibid.

7 Ibid., 249.

8 Ibid., 249-51.

9 Ibid.

10 Giandomenico Majone, 'The New European Agencies: Regulation by Information,' *Journal of European Public Policy* 4 (1997): 262-75, 262-63; Dehousse, 'Regulation by Networks in the European Community,' 255-57. Dehousse quotes the regulation establishing the Lisbon Drug Monitoring Centre as specifying that: "The Centre may not take any measure which in any way goes beyond the sphere of information and the processing thereof." Article 1(4) of Council Regulation EEC 302/93, *OJ* L 36/1, 12 February 1993, quoted in ibid., 256-57. Similarly, Council Regulation No. 1210/90, 7 May 1990, sets forth the task of the European Environmental Agency as follows: "to provide the Member States and the Community with information; to collect, record and assess data on the state of the environment; to encourage harmonization of the methods of measurement; to promote the incorporation of European environmental information into international monitoring programs; to ensure data dissemination; to co-operate with other Community bodies and international institutions." Majone, 'The New European Agencies,' 263.

11 Dehousse, 'Regulation by Networks in the European Community,' 255.

12 Ibid.

13 Ibid.

14 Giandomenico Majone, 'The New European Agencies,' 272.

15 Ibid., 271-272.

16 See Spencer Weber Waller, 'The Internationalization of Antitrust Enforcement,' *Boston University Law Review* 77 (1997): 343, 364.

17 Ibid.

18 Notis Lebessis and John Paterson, 'The Future of European Regulation: A Review of the Workshop,' (Working Paper 1997, European Commission, Forward Studies Unit, 11 June 1997) (summarizing a workshop attended by Giandomenico Majone and Renaud Dehousse), In Europa homepage [cited 2 January 2003]; formerly available at <http://europa.eu.int/comm/cdp/working-paper/nouveaux_modes_gouvernance_en.pdf>.

19 Commission of the European Communities, 'European Governance: A White Paper' 25 July 2001, 21.

20 Lebessis and Paterson, 'The Future of European Regulation'; Dehousse, 'Regulation by Networks,' 255.

21 'European Governance: A White Paper' 21.

22 For the classic accounts of the construction of the EC legal system, often referred to as the "constitutionalization" of the Treaty of Rome, see Eric Stein, 'Lawyers, Judges, and the Making of a Transnational Constitution,' *American Journal of International Law* 75 (1981): 1; Joseph H.H. Weiler, 'The Transformation of Europe,' *Yale Law Journal* 100 (1991): 2403; Gerhard Bebr, *Development of Judicial Control of The European Communities* (Hingham, MA: Kluwer Boston Distributors, 1981). For accounts from ECJ judges themselves, see Ulrich Everling, 'The Member States of the European Community before their Court of Justice,' *European Law Review* 9 (1984): 215; G. Federico Mancini, 'The Making of a Constitution for Europe,' 26 *Common Market Law Review* 26 (1989): 595; and Thijmen Koopmans, 'The Birth of European Law at the Crossroads of Legal Traditions,' *American Journal of Comparative Law* 39 (1991): 493.

23 See Case 26/62, *N.V. Algemene Transp. & Expeditie Onderneming Van Gend & Loos* v. *Nederlandse Administratie der Belastingen*, 1963 E.C.R. 1, 12 (Eur. Ct. of Justice 1962) (landmark decision allowing a private Dutch importer to invoke certain common market provisions of the Treaty of Rome directly against the Dutch government); Case 6/64 , *Flaminio Costa* v. *ENEL* (Ente Nazionale Energia Elettrica) 1964 E.C.R. 588 (asserting that where a treaty term conflicts with a subsequent national statute, the treaty must prevail). For a discussion of "direct effect" jurisprudence, see George Bermann et al., *European Community Law* (St. Paul, Minn.: West Publishing Company, 1993).

24 This view is not uncontroverted. Some political scientists have argued that these national courts were in fact following the wishes of their respective governments, notwithstanding their governments' expressed opposition before the ECJ. The claim is that all Community Member States agreed to economic integration as being in their best interests in 1959. They understood, however, that they needed a mechanism to bind one another to the obligations undertaken in the original treaty. They thus established a court to hold each State to its respective word. See Geoffrey Garrett, 'International Cooperation and Institutional Choice: The European Community's Internal Market,' *International Organization* 46 (1992): 533; Geoffrey Garrett and Barry Weingast, 'Ideas, Interests and Institutions: Constructing the EC's Internal Market,' in *Ideas & Foreign Policy: Beliefs, Institutions and Political Change*, eds. Judith Goldstein and Robert O. Keohane (Ithaca : Cornell University Press, 1993), 173; Geoffrey Garrett, R. Daniel Kelemen and Heiner Schulz, 'The European Court of Justice, National Governments, and Legal Integration in the European Union,' *International Organization* 52 (1998): 149.

This rationalist reconstruction ignores the apparent intent of the Member States to establish a court whose judgments they could all too easily prevent or avoid; it also flies in the face of the actual history recounted above. For a debate on precisely this point, see Walter Mattli and Anne-Marie Slaughter, 'Law and Politics in the European Union: A Reply to Garrett,' *International Organization* 49 (1995): 183; Geoffrey Garrett, 'The Politics of Legal Integration in the European Union,' *International Organization* 49 (1995): 171.

25 Karen Alter, *Establishing the Supremacy of European Law: The Making of an International Rule of Law in Europe* (New York: Oxford University Press, 2001), 80-87; Karen Alter, 'Who Are the "Masters of the Treaty"?: European Governments and the European Court of Justice,' *International Organization* 52 (1998): 121.

26 See Jens Ploetner, 'Report on France: The Reception of the Direct Effect and Supremacy Doctrine by the French Supreme Courts,' in *The European Court and National Courts – Doctrine and Jurisprudence: Legal Change in Its Social Context*, eds. Anne-Marie Slaughter, Alec Stone Sweet, and J. H. H. Weiler (Evanston, Ill.: Northwestern University Press, 1998), 41-75; and Alter, *Establishing the Supremacy*, 145-157, 173 (both discussing the Cour de Cassation's decision in the 1975 case, *Administration des Douanes* v. *Société Cafés Jacques Vabre and J. Weigel et Compagnie S.a.r.l.*, (Cour de Cassation, France 1975) 2 *Common Mrkt. L. Rep.* 343 (1975).

27 *Secretary of State for Transport, ex parte. Factortame Ltd.* Case 213/89, R. V. (UK 1989) 3 Common Market L. R. 867 (1990) (ECJ preliminary ruling that the British courts could grant interim relief to the applicants by setting aside the national law forbidding such relief); *R.* v. *Secretary of State for Transport, ex p. Factortame Ltd.* No. 2, 1 A.C. 603 (UK House of Lords 1991) (House of Lords decision awarding interim relief against the Crown). For a full discussion of these decisions and their implications (dicta of the House of Lords clearly curtails parliamentary sovereignty by stating the duty of courts to resolve conflicts in favor of EC law over national law), see P.P. Craig, 'Report on the United Kingdom,' in *The European Court and National Courts – Doctrine and Jurisprudence: Legal Change in Its Social Context*, eds. Anne-Marie Slaughter, Alec Stone Sweet, and J. H. H. Weiler (Evanston, Ill.: Northwestern University Press, 1998), 195, 200-203.

28 Joseph Weiler was among the first to claim that national judges were motivated by dreams of "judicial empowerment," by which he seems to have meant the heady experience of engaging in judicial review of na-

tional law for conformity with European law. Weiler, 'The Transformation of Europe', 2426; *see also* Anne-Marie Burley and Walter Mattli, 'Europe Before the Court: A Political Theory of Legal Integration,' *International Organization* 47 (1993): 41, 63-4.

29 Karen Alter has pioneered this thesis in several important articles and a forthcoming book. See Alter, *Establishing the Supremacy*, 45-52; Karen Alter, 'Explaining National Court Acceptance of European Court Jurisprudence: A Critical Evaluation of Theories of Legal Integration,' in *The European Court and National Courts – Doctrine and Jurisprudence: Legal Change in Its Social Context*, eds. Anne-Marie Slaughter, Alec Stone Sweet, and J. H. H. Weiler (Evanston, Ill.: Northwestern University Press, 1998), 227-252.

30 See Mattli and Slaughter, 'Law and Politics in the European Union.'

31 See Ploetner, 'Report on France,' 61 (arguing that the Cour de Cassation accepted the supremacy of EC law out of a desire not to disadvantage the French merchants who were a prime constituency).

32 For a concise but thorough account of the principal cases in this dialogue, see Juliane Kokott, 'Report on Germany,' in *The European Court and National Courts – Doctrine and Jurisprudence: Legal Change in Its Social Context,* eds. Anne-Marie Slaughter, Alec Stone Sweet, and J. H. H. Weiler (Evanston, Ill.: Northwestern University Press, 1998), 77-131.

33 *Brunner* v. *The European Union Treaty,* Bundesverfassungsgericht (2. Senat) [Federal Constitutional Court, 2nd Chamber] Oct. 12, 1993, 1 *C.M.L.R.* 57 (F.R.G.).

34 1 *C.M.L.R.* at 79; 89 BVerfGE 155, at 175. The BVerfG also continues to recognize the ECJ's exclusive competence as interpreter of European law, in the sense that the BVerfG will not offer an alternative interpretation of a particular legal provision, but will only decide whether that provision as interpreted is *ultra vires.* The recognition of the ECJ's interpretive competence was laid down in the BVerfG's *Vielleicht-Beschluss* ("Maybe Decision") of 1979. 52 BVerfGE 187 (1979).

35 Kokott, 'Report on Germany,' 109. The most recent event in this saga preserves the *status quo* established by the *Maastricht* decision. In the *Bananas Case,* 2 BvL 1/97 (7 June 2000), the Second Senate of the *Bundesverfassungsgericht* rejected a claim that the *Maastricht* decision stands for the Court's resumption of active, interventionist human rights review in the Community, of the type in which it had engaged prior to the landmark decision in *Solange II,* 73 BVerfGE 339 (22 October 1986).

36 See Joseph H.H. Weiler, 'Epilogue: The European Courts of Justice: Beyond 'Beyond Doctrine' or the Legitimacy Crisis of European Constitutionalism,' in *The European Court and National Courts – Doctrine and Jurisprudence: Legal Change in Its Social Context,* eds. Anne-Marie Slaughter, Alec Stone Sweet, and J. H. H. Weiler (Evanston, Ill.: Northwestern University Press, 1998), 365, 367. The Belgian *Cour d'arbitrage,* for example, was asked to strike down the Law of 26 November 1992, which approved the "Maastricht Treaty," 18 October 1994, Case 76/94. The applicants, who were Belgian nationals, argued that their (national) constitutional right to vote in municipal elections was infringed by the new European citizenship provisions, which extended the franchise to citizens of another EU Member State. In an earlier decision (Case 12/94, 3 February 1994), the Court had held that Article 107 of the Belgian Constitution cannot be read as authorizing the legislator to disregard the Constitution indirectly by virtue of the assent to an international agreement. However, the Belgian High Court took a much more restrictive approach to the challenge against the Maastricht Treaty: While the right to vote is "the fundamental political right of a representative democracy," the dilution of the impact of an individual vote through the enlarged franchise did not create a sufficient interest to grant the applicants standing before the Court. See also Hervé Bibriosa, 'Report on Belgium,' in *The European Court and National Courts – Doctrine and Jurisprudence: Legal Change in Its Social Context* , eds. Anne-Marie Slaughter, Alec Stone Sweet, and J. H. H. Weiler (Evanston, Ill.: Northwestern University Press, 1998), 305, 320-29.

37 The Maastricht decision uses the term community of States to describe the EU (*Staatenverbund*) rather than confederation (*Staatenbund*), 1 *C.M.L.R.*, at paras 36-38; 1993 WL 965303 (BVerfG (Ger)), at 48.

38 See generally, William W. Burke-White, 'A Community of Courts: Toward a System of International Criminal Law Enforcement,' *Michigan Journal of International Law* 24 (2002): 1.

39 See Alec Stone Sweet, 'Constitutional Dialogues in the European Community,' in *The European Court and National Courts – Doctrine and Jurisprudence: Legal Change in Its Social Context*, eds. Anne-Marie Slaughter, Alec Stone Sweet, and J. H. H. Weiler (Evanston, Ill.: Northwestern University Press, 1998), 305-308; Weiler, 'Epilogue: The European Courts of Justice,' 368 ("Constitutionalism . . . constitutes the official vocabulary of the inter-court dialogues . . . .").

40 Shirley Williams, 'Sovereignty and Accountability in the European Union,' in *The New European Community: Decisionmaking and Institutional Change*, eds. Robert O. Keohane and Stanley Hoffmann (Boulder: Westview Press, 1991): 159, 155-176.

41 Ibid., 172-175. The idea of joint commissions or assizes is compatible with the basic framework of the EP.

Most of the Parliament's work is carried out in its 17 standing committees, as well as in additional subcommittees and temporary committees. Joint parliamentary committees maintain ongoing relations with the parliaments of States linked to the European Union by association agreements; and inter-parliamentary delegations do the same with the parliaments of many other countries and international organizations. The model of committees and subcommittees narrows the substantive matters dealt with, and thus allows for better alignment of interests among parliamentarians from different countries.

42 Protocol on the role of national parliaments in the European Union, *OJ* C 340/1, at 113-14 (1997). The Protocol sets a six-week period before the Community institutions make a decision on legislative proposals, to allow for national parliaments' consultation procedures. The protocol also provides for the Conference of European Affairs Committees ("COSAC") to participate in institutional debates whenever the issues debated might have a direct bearing on the rights and freedoms of individuals.

43 Scott H. Jacobs, 'Why Governments Must Work Together,' *The OECD Observer* 186 (February/March 1994): 15, 18. 'Regulatory Co-Operation for an Interdependent World: Issues for Government,' in *Organisation for Economic Co-operation and Development, Regulatory Co-operation for an Interdependent World* (Paris, France: Organisation for Economic Co-operation and Development, 1994), 15-38, 18.

44 Treaty of European Union, Title I, Article A, (7 February 1992).

Discussion

Anne-Marie Slaughter: Well, what I find really surprising about the title of this conference is that we do not have government. We say "from government to governance" as if we had international government. But we do not have anything like international government. What we have is distinct international institutions and yet, interestingly, except for a very small handful of world federalists, what you will generally hear in any international law or international relations forum is "but of course we are not advocating world government". We do not have a world government, so what are we talking about when we say from government to governance? I think what we are referring to is a movement from national government to an international or global "something", meaning that what has changed – and what I think is a durable change – is that national government officials now understand that they cannot perform their national functions alone. There must be something that allows them to cross borders, whether that something is an independent international institution or cooperation with their counterparts around the world in some kind of network relations. But government – islands of national governments alone – is not enough.

I will make two more points on what then we are moving to – what "governance" captures.

One is what Robert Kagan has called the globalization paradox, which says that though we need more governance capacity because of globalization, yet we do not want centralization of power. In other words, we need the power that a world government would give us, but we do not want a world government if that implies some centralized global authority, which is probably not feasible nor for many of us desirable. So that is the paradox. And how do we address it? Well, governance seems to capture that and with governance we seem to bring in just about everyone. Governance is different from government and means government officials and corporations and non-governmental organizations and individuals and charities and churches and everyone you can think of, in some kind of governance networks. But then governance is not going to solve the problem either, because at some point, we will need to move from governance back to government, meaning individuals who can be held politically accountable in ways that all these other non-State actors really cannot be.

IGE F. DEKKER: Thank you. May I invite Mr. Raaijmakers to shed some light, probably on the more economic aspects of this debate?

THEO RAAIJMAKERS: Being here specifically to address corporate governance issues rather than the governmental governance issues, I will approach the question from that perspective. And in this regard, I think the overall question of this conference – will the impact of non-State actors on the international and European legal systems grow? – should be answered in the positive as far as at least Europe is concerned. And to explain briefly what I mean by that, I will first observe that there will always be the tension between State interference or intervention into the economics of the market and public corporations on the one hand, and the borderlines that are created by effectively restoring freedom of enterprise in our Western societies. We all know that the Enron, the shorthand to mark the recent corporate scandals and the burst of the Internet bubble, caused an enormous public outcry for State intervention. US Congress reacted very quickly to the situation by the enactment of the Sarbanes Oxley Act. And what is interesting about that Act is that, as I understand from the American perspective, it intrudes on the one hand into the internal affairs of public corporations – in other words State intervention into the internal organization of corporations, and on the other hand, it is certainly oriented at market regulation. As you know, public auditors and even analysts are within the scope of the Act and the regulations that are now being prepared by the Securities and Exchange Commission.

Looking at the European scene, it is remarkable that in dealing with corporate governance, we are seen to address only the internal affairs of public corporations rather than the broader market elements of stock exchanges, merchant bankers, analysts, auditors and so on. That gives remarkable difference in scope and regulation. There is no doubt in my mind that as far as the principles of the market as such are concerned, the public confidence in the capital and money markets is so crucial and essential for our society that it is a task which has to be assigned to government and governmental agencies. With respect to corporate governance in the more narrow sense, it is remarkable that the Sarbanes Oxley Act directly interferes not only within the USA into state law, but also extraterritorially into corporations that are listed on the chart or which are traded in the USA when they also have their seat in Europe. It influences the debate because at least those corporations have to comply with the US rules directly.

With respect to what the EU itself is going to do, I suppose that Jaap Winter has told you about the very recent action plan of the European Union, which in fact boils down in this respect to recognising that it is impossible to have a federalized system of corporate rules specifically on corporate governance, accepted and assigned to individual Member States to designate voluntary codes based on the comply or explain principle, and supported by a framework directive of the Union itself. That in fact leaves it to States to at least designate codes. But still this initiative is of a voluntary nature and of course there are many questions which will be raised with respect to the enforceability of any such codes afterwards. But essentially, it is shifting the task of preparing rules, principles and codes to non-State actors, and while this can never take away the responsibility of national governments under the European Union for having a proper regulation of the capital and securities market, of course to that extent the answer is 'yes' to the central question of this conference.

DORINDA DALLMEYER: Thank you. Since you bring up issues of enforceability and rules, it also brings up the issue of underlying values. Are values changing? That is part of the question we have here. Also are those changes in values constructive in the sense that they are helping to reach solutions to problems?

SEAN MURPHY: I think that the rise of international organizations or non-governmental organizations is having a very significant effect on the values that are being incorporated into international law. And you can think of a couple of examples of this. Take for instance, the use of force paradigm we have under the UN Charter, which in its classical form does not really take account of human rights as a basis for deploying force. I think what we are seeing is that with the rise of human rights instruments and the role of NGOs and others in pressing for human rights, there is an increasing sentiment that there should be an ability to use force to protect human rights. Some would say that is only to be done under the authority of the Security Council. Others would say that even short of that it should still be possible, such as NATO going into Kosovo. I think though that for something like that, it is the case that we need to worry about where some of these values are taking us. Is it ok for the USA to go into Iraq to, let us say, engage in regime change because there is a totalitarian dictator who is oppressing his people? I think some people, who would feel comfortable with the Security Council authorising an intervention in Somalia, are less comfortable with Kosovo, and certainly very uncomfortable with Iraq. But once you begin introducing new values, you do have to find a way of coordinating views as to how these values should be taken into account.

Another example might be the greening of trade these days. One can point to examples of how NGOs have done a very good job of bringing to the attention of the trade community the need to be more sensitive to the effects on human health and the environment of trade and restrictive trade. The example of the *Shrimp-Turtle* case came up, I think, in one of the panels and there is a terrific example of the USA having a conservation law that was initially being implemented in a manner that the WTO found to be inappropriate under GATT rules. The USA then altered its approach but maintained, nevertheless, restrictions on imports of shrimp so as to protect sea turtles and that was upheld by the WTO Appellate Body and also in the US judicial system. So that is a value brought into the regime which is very good but you can also think of problems. Genetically modified goods comes to my mind. In that regard, I think NGOs have done a very good job of making it very difficult for a country like the United States to export genetically modified products, even though in my view there is no credible scientific evidence that those products cause adverse effects to human health. And I think the fact of chilling of that kind of trade is having some profound consequences on the developing world where I think those sorts of products could actually do quite a bit of good. So in my opinion, it is a rather mixed bag at this point. I do think that the NGOs and international organizations are to some extent bringing new values into international law that would not probably be brought before by States themselves. But I am not sure we are coping entirely well with how we incorporate these values.

NICO SCHRIJVER:* I believe that in the rather confusing political climate after the end of the Cold War, some existing and some new values came to the fore. Some ex-

* Free University, Amsterdam; NVIR.

isting values with more emphasis such as peace and security, humanity; and new values such as, for example, sustainability and public participation. And I do believe that the rise of non-governmental organizations certainly has something to do with it. They have been instrumental in putting these values to the fore and making them really shared international community values. During our discussions in this conference, we have often referred to the important role of NGOs in the making and success of the Rome Statute of the International Criminal Court. But we can also refer to the Ottawa Anti-Landmines campaign resulting in the Convention on banning of landmines. We could refer to the WHO Code on Substitutes for Breast Milk. We could also refer to a very interesting convention here in the context of Europe – the Economic Commission for Europe Convention on Access to Information, Public Participation in Decision-Making and Access to Justice in Environmental Matters. And there, the role of civil society and non-governmental organizations has been very constructive and to be applauded. However, if I may add, that is not to say that non-governmental organizations should get a kind of monopoly over the formation and interpretation of values. I am quite concerned, as quite a few other people during this conference were, that in terms of representativeness, in terms of governance, in terms of accountablity, NGOs are sometimes operating at odds with the values they advocate into our international system. And therefore, I think we cannot say they should replace the role of the old or traditional States and their international organizations.

ANNE-MARIE SLAUGHTER: I will make a short reaction to the question of where we are now. And I am just going to build on a point that Nico Schrijver made about where we are in the sense of values changing. We hear this – and we have heard it a great deal over the past two days – that we are in a particularly fluid time. And I agree with what Nico said about the role of non-governmental organizations and the concerns expressed with regard to their activities. I would like though to insist on a point that Judge Kooijmans made yesterday, which is that the State is very much alive and, I would argue, more important than ever. The problems that we are seeing globally are as much a result of weak States as anything else. States that are either unable or too weak to be able to actually implement their international or national legal obligations, States that are too weak to provide basic security and thus, become sites for all sorts of illegal activity. Having strong States is more important now, certainly as important as or more important than it has ever been. And everything else that we look at – for example we are now talking about non-State actors – ought to be thought about not as an either/or. The State is weakening and we have all these other actors doing what the States have done. It has got to be that the State is absolutely critical, but it now also operates in a world in which many other actors are capable of doing things that States once did.

SEAN MURPHY: Well, I think that is right and I think one way to think about this is that if you go back a hundred years, there were not that many international organizations nor non-governmental organizations operating in a transnational sense. So we have had big changes since then. We need to think also about the differences in national State regulation between then and now. A hundred years ago, you did not have national governments regulating consumer protection, environment, health, business organization, etc. in the very detailed, systematic and intrusive way that they do now. So one way you can think about the explosion in international governance, in the sense of international organizations and NGOs, is really more as an adjunct to this extraordinary increase in the administrative State, the welfare State of countries around the world. It is not that you are transitioning or moving from national regulation to international. It is that there is an increasing amount of regulation generally, of which this international governance is just one part.

THEO RAAIJMAKERS: From a somewhat different perspective, I will make a short reaction on this point. We are all aware of the dichotomy between what is called the so-called Raimond model, which stands for European corporations on a stakeholder basis, as opposed to the Anglo-American model of which the primary value is that it is based on the interests of shareholders. So do values change? I think there is certainly US dominance in the globalizing capital market, but one of the things which might emerge from the European plan on national codes of corporate governance could be that we, per nation, can find an equilibrium between the interests of the capital market and the investors in that market on the one hand, and other stakeholders in the narrow sense, also in the broader sense of NGOs, on the other hand. But I must say that I was a little bit surprised, that the European Commission very clearly put "shareholder's democracy" as the central theme for codes on corporate governance. It may sound somewhat strange for one to be surprised about such a nice word, but the question behind that is that what we are really discussing is organizations from a constitutional point of view. Here, we have been discussing State organizations or international organizations and in this regard, I think there are similarities with the case of private corporations. And I think taking such a very broad denominator as "shareholder's democracy" as the focus for corporate governance conceals the realities behind that. My perception of US corporations is that they are organised and managed on a very centralized basis and that while perhaps you may find some reference to the democracy of shareholders, the realities may be somewhat different. On the other hand, at least in the law of the books, democratic elements and powers are vested in the hands of shareholders in our continental systems in Europe.

DORINDA DALLMEYER: Many of our panelists over the last two days and certainly our panelists in this concluding session have alluded to the feeling that we are on the verge of some sort of fundamental change in the underlying structure of international law. Two questions arise from this observation. First, how do we know that and which way are we going? Some have said it is back to the Dark Ages or whatever was going on before 1945, or something we have never experienced before. Also, how do we cope with our role as international lawyers in either being creative or clinging to Grotius desperately?

NICO SCHRIJVER: "A fundamental change in the underlying structure of international law". These are big words, quite sweeping statements. Yes, we see a greater variety in terms of actors in international relations, and therefore, also in terms of subjects of international law – a widening circle of actors with an increasingly established functional status in international law. Take the example of transnational corporations, now more and more active as we discussed during the past two days, in the field of so-called corporate social responsibility; in formulating and enacting their own business standards, their own codes of conduct. This may amount not only to a widening of the circle of the subjects of international law, but also to a widening of the sources of international law, alongside the ones listed in Article 38 of the Statute of the ICJ. For example, what will be the impact of these self-regulatory business standards and codes of conduct on the formation of customary international law and on treaty-making? It is still early to assess that, but I think it is something to note and it is one of the elements where we move indeed from government to governance involving a wider variety of subjects and a wider variety of sources. As to the big words, I do not think there is really reason for them, and here I may differ with Anne-Marie Slaughter, my colleague from the American Society of International Law. There was a very inspiring article by her, I believe in the *Harvard International Law Journal.* If I am correct, it was titled 'The New International Constitutional Moment' or 'Towards a New International Constitutional Moment'. Also a rather sweeping phrase. I am not quite sure about that. I feel much can be gained by applying and interpreting principles and rules of international law as they are, as living instruments in order to indeed meet new concerns in present-day circumstances. For example, as we discussed yesterday in the terrorism panels, with respect to Charter concepts such as armed attack, threats to peace, breach of the peace. I am sure that further progressive development of international law is called for to meet concerns in the field of international criminal law, counter-terrorism and also as regards international cooperation for development, for sustainability. But to say that that also calls for a fundamental change in international law, I am not quite sure whether that is very helpful because we may move beyond what is realistically possible, we may even push international law more to the margins of international relations.

ANNE-MARIE SLAUGHTER: First, I should note that my co-author on that article, 'A New Constitutional Moment' – William Burke-White – is also here. At the end of these two days, I would argue that we are on the verge of dramatic fundamental change. The article you referred to – 'A New Constitutional Moment' – was talking about changes in the Charter to regulate the use of force against individuals and not simply States. It was talking about a global constitutional norm of civilian inviolability which means that civilians should be protected against the use of force in the same way as States are. That is a broadening of where we have been. I would argue though, much more fundamentally, that we are moving towards an international order in which we will continue to have unitary States and international organizations that are composed of unitary States. But at the same time and often mixed together in ways that José Alvarez discussed yesterday, we will have a world order of networks of parts of States, in other words, horizontal networks – all that you have heard of over the past couple of days. Networks of financial regulators, of intelligence, of police, all the apparatus that is fighting terrorism right now. Those are, for the most part, not international organizations. They are networks of national officials, they are parts of States. Similarly networks of judges who are already cooperating in all sorts of ways, also networks of legislators. Equally as important as the horizontal is the networks of vertical relations between international courts and national courts, international regulators and national regulators, and at some point – at least at the regional level – international legislators like members of the European Parliament and national legislators like members of the national parliaments of Europe. Those vertical networks are every bit as important as the horizontal networks because they will allow international rules to be directly enforced by the national counterparts. So national regulators, judges and legislators will find their responsibility in conjunction with their supranational counterparts to enforce international rules. But at the same time, a great deal of what we as international lawyers would have thought had to be done by some international or supranational institution will be done by networks of national officials instead. So we are going to have a network world order made up of these aggregated State institutions. For those of you who are Americans, who know the globe that Atlas holds above his head at Rockefeller Centre, as you see it is a globe made up of intertwining bands. So, it will be a world order of networks that will coexist with unitary States and international institutions as we know them now.

DORINDA DALLMEYER: Even a concluding debate itself has to conclude, so I will ask Mr Raaijmakers and Sean Murphy to have the last words.

FINAL REMARKS BY THEO RAAIJMAKERS

Taking up this idea with respect to market regulation as such, I foresee particularly in Europe, that there will be more international law. This needs be since markets are globalizing, certainly also on an European scale. With respect to the codes which I referred to earlier, and thinking in terms of networks, I believe there will certainly be a substantial degree of convergence between the different countries and societies within our European Union, certainly influenced by the American standards under the Sarbanes Oxley Act and the underlying rules and regulations of the Securities and Exchange Commission. Taking the thoughts a step further – at least for the purpose of market regulation, an area where as I said before, the State is responsible and certainly should intervene – I would like to promote the idea of an European Securites and Exchange Commission in order to go even further than convergence and bring this process forward to a level of federal rather than harmonized State legislation. Finally, I feel there should be a better understanding on the one hand, and more discussion on the other, between Europe and the United States – in other words, an institutionalized European-American platform for corporate governance.

FINAL REMARKS BY SEAN MURPHY

I would like to throw up what might be a bit of a grenade, which is a good thing to do right at the very end. The grenade is that it is a wonderful vision that Anne-Marie Slaughter has spelt out and thus, discussion of this convergence is something I think pretty much everybody in this room would like to see. And I have read a draft of Anne-Marie's book on that and it is terrific, so I highly encourage everyone to buy a copy when it comes out. But there is a different vision one can imagine and that is significant divergences among different parts of the world. And since we are here in a sort of US-European Joint Conference, it may be worth thinking about the differences between the USA and Europe. There certainly are convergences on some of the economic issues. But some of you may be familiar with the book and article that Robert Kagan of the United States recently wrote, where he talks about the USA as being from Mars and Europe as being from Venus. The idea being that the USA looks out and sees a world that is Hobbesian in nature (there have been many references to Hobbes at this conference) and feels that the way to deal with that is to maintain military power and to use it unilaterally, if necessary, in order to keep the world a safe place. Whereas Europeans, in Kagan's view, have moved into this happy place where they are converging through the European Union and have got such happy things as negotiation of conflict, dispute settlement, rules everyone will follow, etc.

and they want to take that and spread it worldwide so that we will have a big global happy place. And Americans look at that and say: you guys have basically given up on maintaining military power, you are impotent and we have to be the ones to step in and protect you, and we are vulnerable because of your creation of such crazy things as an ICC, which are going to zapp the USA when it is out there trying to protect the planet. I do not know if any one gives too much credence to this kind of a theory, although I think Kagan's views are widely being looked at. My own feeling is that Europeans have shed a lot of blood in the past decade sending forces abroad, and at the same time, the USA has undertaken very important initiatives in creating international institutions like the WTO and the ad-hoc criminal tribunals. So this is a caricature that does not hold up completely. But I think it at least highlights that we should be thinking about ways the different parts of the world do not agree. And that we have to find ways of developing that convergence if we can, and if we cannot, find ways of managing divergences that will not go away.

*Reporter: Nwamaka R. Okany**

* Amsterdam Centre of International Law, University of Amsterdam, The Netherlands.

Closing of the Conference

by Judge Shi Jiuyong*

Excellencies, distinguished participants,

It is a great pleasure and honour to be here today. Let me first of all thank the organizers of this Joint Conference, the American Society of International Law, the Asser Institute and other learned associations of international law of The Netherlands, for their kind invitation for me to speak at such a distinguished gathering.

The theme of your Conference, as I understand, is: *"From Government to Governance: the Growing Impact of Non-State Actors on the International and European Legal System"*. Indeed, a discussion on the involvement of non-State actors in the development of the international legal system is both significant and topical. I regret that I was unable to participate in any of the sessions of the Conference, other than the present concluding debate, but I can well imagine that the papers presented would have been enlightening and thought provoking, and that the ensuing debates were of an in-depth nature. I hope you will excuse me if, for my part, I am only prepared to speak on the subject in very general terms.

There is no doubt that since the end of World War Two international law has progressed to a more inclusive configuration: from a system with strictly defined subjects and limited activities to a more comprehensive structure of governance progressing towards a more cohesive international community sharing common values and ideals. While States are still at the centre of this international political system, non-State actors have an increasingly relevant impact on the development of such an international governance structure.

The term 'non-State actors' comprises diverse organizations curiously united by one negative characteristic, that of "not being States". This designation indirectly recognises that States remain the definitional attribute of the international legal system. Conversely, each group of non-State actors is defined by unique features.

In my presentation, I would like first to consider three such groups, each distinctive and significant, and assess their individual influence on the international legal system. I will then make some brief remarks on the consequences of such impact on the general development of international law.

The first group is of course international organisations. They are probably the most prominent group of non-State actors. The group includes the entire United Nations system, as well as other inter-State and regional organisations. Although intergovernmental organisations are constituted by governments, they are independent from them and have a separate legal personality. The International Court of Justice recognised

* President of the International Court of Justice, The Hague, The Netherlands.

such unique status of the United Nations in its 1949 Advisory Opinion in the *Reparation* case. However, the Court was also explicit in saying that the organization had a separate legal personality which was not the same thing "as saying that it is a State, which it certainly is not, or that its legal personality and rights and duties are the same as those of a State. Still less is it the same thing as saying that it is a 'super-State', whatever that expression may mean." As subjects of international law, international organisations have specific rights and duties, which can be created "under general rules of international law, under their constitutions or under international agreements to which they are parties."

The involvement of the United Nations system in the development of an international legal order is unmatched. As noted by the Court, the functions of the UN include political negotiations, policy decisions and policy implementation in diverse fields including disarmament, peace and security, terrorism, human rights, and economic and social development. The United Nations is the core of development and codification of international law.

International organisations also play a fundamental role in the setting of the agenda of the international community. In many cases they are asked to negotiate and develop common policies and norms on behalf of the international community. They also play a pivotal role in the political arena. Uniquely, the United Nations also retains a mechanism of control over the use of force and can sanction the legality of the use of force in particular circumstances. Furthermore, intergovernmental organisations are in charge of monitoring compliance by States with their international obligations, for example in the human rights arena, and may take measures against a State that does not comply with its treaty obligations.

Among all inter-governmental organizations other than the United Nations system, which deserve special mention here, is the European Union. The European Union retains a particular important position in the development of the international legal system, and specifically of the European legal system. As is well known, this Union of States which began as an economic community has developed to encompass competency over matters including environment, economic development, trade and tariffs, immigration, agriculture, etc. In these and other matters, members of the Union have gone further than members of the United Nations, as they have transferred their powers on these matters to the Union.

However, I barely need to mention to this audience that the system of intergovernmental organizations is based on a dichotomy. As subjects of international law, intergovernmental organisations do not possess a general competence, but are governed by the principle of speciality. Their powers are specifically enumerated in their constitutive instruments, or may arise as implied powers to fulfil their mandates.

A second group of non-State actors, – probably the most visible one – which plays an increasingly relevant role in the development of the international legal system is that encompassing non-governmental organisations (NGOs). NGOs are not only non-State actors, but are also defined by a further negative, that of being non-governmental, i.e. as existing outside and often in opposition to the State. Indeed, NGOs portray themselves as representatives of civil society and as an alternative to the political system represented by States.

NGOs are not a uniform group. They are associated to different constituencies, often with somewhat complicated political backgrounds, and are involved in several different aspects of the international legal systems; they include voluntary organisations, trade unions, cooperatives, religious organisations, research and advocacy institutions, grass-roots groups, and legal centres. NGOs are active in the field of public concern and they vary in size, aims, structure, membership, geographical reach and methods and means of action. Overall, they have three elements in common:

1. they are, as their name indicates, not established by a government, nor by an intergovernmental agreement;
2. they are typically private institutions: associations, foundations, federations or other unions founded on the basis and under the regime of the private law of a State;
3. the concerns, purposes and objects of NGOs are, in contrast to their origins, of a public nature.

NGOs are particularly vocal, and are involved in all the major topics of interest of the international legal system, such as human rights, environmental matters, issues related to peace and security, social and economic development, humanitarian assistance. Often, they add a driving and shaping force of advancement to international governance.

NGOs are the most outspoken supporters of the development of a more inclusive form of governance.

They are involved in numerous sectors of the international arena, including policy and norm development and implementation. NGOs participate in the international community as actors of social change. They influence the agenda of international organs and World Conferences – such as the Rio Conference on environmental matters, the World Conference of Human Rights in Vienna, the Habitat Conference, and the World Women's Conference – and can provide expert and technical advice to delegations during negotiations. NGOs also play an important role in many aspects of treaty law development. Authors, such as Professors Charlesworth and Chinkin have argued that NGOs "have to some limited extent lessened the State monopoly in the treaty-drafting process".[1] Professor Wedgwood noted that "in the campaign against landmines, the NGO community is given credit for accelerating the political process, successfully seeking to transfer the negotiations from the UN Committee on Disarmament in Geneva to the convocation of "like minded" States in Ottawa. This yielded a Treaty on Anti-Personnel Landmines in 1997."[2] Then again, other authors maintain that during the negotiations on the Statute of the ICC, for example, NGOs negotiated transversally among themselves from within delegations, and were able to promote the adoption of some ideas that alienated the support of more conservative States, which eventually decided not to sign the Convention. Of course there are still a number of States which have not yet ratified the Convention.

NGOs participate in negotiations, influence agendas and debates, monitor the implementation of international law and of guiding political principles. They lobby for ratification and execution of obligations. Their importance in shaping the international legal system has grown substantially since the thaw of the Cold War, in particular. However, despite their high profile, the activities of NGOs, as Professor Wedgwood has written, "do not challenge the primacy of States in law-making. However influential their input, the final documents, whether in treaty or soft law form, are agreed on by States."[3] I would add that NGOs are perhaps well aware that, at the present stage of development of the international community, their role in the international arena is dependent on the sanction of States themselves.

The third key group of non-State actors that has an increasingly prominent role in the development of the international legal system is that of 'transnational' or 'multinational' corporations (TNCs). A transnational enterprise, as is well known, operates with or within foreign countries. Contrary to NGOs, TNCs do not fulfil a clearly public purpose but operate in the economic sphere. However, because of their control over immense economic resources they are influential both in their home countries and in the countries where they operate, especially in economically less developed countries and have a substantial leverage on the international and national communities. In the international arena, TNCs influence the development of the international legal system in at least two ways. First, like NGOs, they lobby treaty-making processes to support an outcome that is more favourable to business. This has been especially significant in negotiations of international environmental treaties, for example, in the Climate Change negotiations. Second, by controlling substantial economic resources they may influence agendas and behaviour of States.

Nonetheless, even more so than NGOs, TNCs remain non-State and non-territorial actors in the international community. Only private national law and relevant conflicts-of-law provisions regulate them. All efforts to codify a TNC's code of conduct have yielded no results, and no international treaties or conventions have been negotiated to codify norms applicable to TNCs. TNCs are dependent on States, both within and outside their home country.

To conclude, these few considerations on three such diverse kinds of non-State actors highlight the fact that the relationship between States and non-States is in reality, on the whole, symbiotic, not antagonistic.

The international legal system and structure of governance are reinforced by a mutually supportive relationship between States and non-State actors. Non-State actors have developed a specific role in international governance. The characteristic features of non-State actors, as displayed in negotiations, implementation or lobbying, are essential for the development of an international community based on common values of justice and equality. However, the State remains the only actor capable of fully operating within the international system. Member States guide policies of international organisations. States ultimately sign and ratify international treaties. National legislation regulates trans-national corporations.

The growth of importance of non-State actors in the development of an international legal system is a vital exercise in democracy and pluralism. Yet, on one side it highlights the inability of States to provide for all the needs of the societies they represent; on the other, it also emphasises the strengthened position of States, as keystones of the international legal system. It is within this structure that the impact of non-State actors must be assessed. States are still fundamental, although not the only significant actors in the international arena.

Proponents of a more relevant role of non-State actors in the international community should not lose sight of the importance of State sovereignty. It would be unrealistic and careless to do so. Thus, the international legal community must also not lose sight of the fact that State sovereignty and sovereign equality of States are the very foundation of the Charter of the United Nations. Any legal justification for departure from this principle will serve the interests of strong States against weak States, big States against small States, and rich States against poor States. True, the world should progress steadily and gradually from government to governance. States and non-State actors must build on their mutual advantages and work closely together to develop an international system of governance based on ideals of justice and respect for fundamental rights that are genuinely common to all civilizations, cultures and religions of the world. To entertain, whether consciously or instinctively, any idea of the superiority of any one particular value system, and the resultant attempt to impose on the world that particular system, as a system common to all civilizations, cultures and religions, would only be racism and imperialism in disguise. And I believe that any such attempt would, in the end, lead to international disorder and chaos. In all sincerity, I must say that today these are the real concerns of developing members of the international community of sovereign States.

With this humble presentation of mine, the Joint Conference is drawing to a close. I extend to you, both the organizers and all the distinguished participants, my hearty congratulations. The theme of the Conference is particularly contemporary and of vital significance. I am sure that the fruitful results of three days of discussions will not merely enrich the literature on the study of the topic, but will also have an impact on the progressive development of the international community towards governance.

Thank you for your patience in having listened to me.

Notes

1 H. Charlesworth and C. Chinkin, *The Boundaries of International Law: a feminist analysis* (2000) p. 99.

2 R. Wedgwood, 'Legal Personality and the Role of Non-Governmental Organisation in International Law and the Changing Role of the State', in *Non-State Actors as New Subjects of International Law*, p. 21.

3 Ibid. p. 89.

APPENDIX

ROUND TABLE

GOVERNANCE AND INTERNATIONAL LEGAL THEORY

Utrecht, 1-3 July 2003

Chair: WOUTER G. WERNER

INTRODUCTION

The Round Table on 'Governance and International Legal Theory' was held as special part of the 6th Hague Joint Conference on Contemporary Issues of International Law. It was not organised as one of the regular seminars of the conference, but was held at the University of Utrecht, The Netherlands, *before* the official start of the Hague Joint Conference, namely from 1 July 2003 (evening) until July 3 (afternoon).[1] The Round Table was chaired by dr. Wouter Werner.[2]

The main aim of the Round Table was to stimulate an ongoing discussion between scholars who are interested in theoretical aspects of international law and international politics. Since the aim of the Round Table was to stimulate discussion about (and not to be a forum for presentations) there was only room for a relatively small number of papers and speakers were asked to hold only short introductions to their papers and to send in their position papers in advance.

The common link between the papers discussed at the Round Table is the theoretical perspective on the theme of the conference: From Government to Governance. Change is one of the enduring aspects of international law. In response to cultural, political, technological and economic developments, international law has continuously rethought and reconsidered its sources of normativity, the structures of its argument, its interpretation of the relationship between State, people and territory as well as its interpretation of the nature and basic values of international society. The basic problem of international law, however, seemed to remain relative stable and constant: the problem of order between separate, sovereign authorities.

At least from the end of 19th century, however, this definition of the basic problem of international law has been questioned. Liberal as well as Marxist schools declared the precedence of economics over politics and pointed at the growing importance of non-State actors at the international level. Recently, several authors have argued that the exercise of authority in international life can best be compared with a situation akin to Bull's concept of 'New Medievalism': a situation where several authorities have overlapping and competing competencies, without the existence of clear rules determining which set of rules take precedence of the other. Others have argued that the traditional focus on 'government' (with its connotations of State authority) should be replaced by a focus on 'governance' (with its connotations of informal, multi-level and non-State authority). Yet others, however, have argued that the concept of State sovereignty still constitutes the basic scheme of interpretation for our understanding of international life.

1 A year before, in 2002, a first session of this Round Table was organised, also at the University of Utrecht and also convened by dr. Wouter Werner. The papers discussed at this Round Table are published in: I.F. Dekker and Wouter G. Werner, eds., *Governance and International Legal Theory* (The Hague, Martinus Nijhoff Publishers 2004).

2 Senior Lecturer in International Law, University of Utrecht, The Netherlands.

The alleged change from 'government' to 'governance' raises several interesting questions for the theory of international law and international relations. The aim of the Round Table was to explicate, clarify and discuss these questions with regard to a selected list of topics.

Capitulations of Political Governance in the WTO: An Alternative Narrative of International Judicialization

Tomer Broude*

Competing narratives of judicialization

A constitutional narrative captivates our imaginations and molds our perceptions of the role of judicialization in the evolving structures of international governance. When contemplating the World Trade Organization (WTO), for example, we imagine a domestically analogous separation-of-powers system.[1] We visualize the judicial WTO dispute settlement system (DSS) as constitutional counter-ballast to political power; and we assume that the political and judicial branches of international organizations like the WTO are engaged in an inter-institutional tug-of-war over normative influence, adopting the schema of relations between branches of national government, drawn 'as though legislators and judges always compete for influence over policy outcomes while exercising power'.[2]

Moreover, in an alternative narrative, the international judiciary – in our case the WTO DSS – is not a peer organ, constitutional counterweight to political power, but a subordinate of political organs, enjoying only restricted judicial power.[3] It is a response to a demand, not for control of political fiat, but rather for international norms and policies of systemic importance that the political branch fails to supply. For example, civil society participation in dispute settlement proceedings through *amicus curiae* briefs;[4] the balance between trade and non-trade concerns such as the environment, labour standards and human rights;[5] the access of developing countries to imported pharmaceuticals necessary to combat epidemics threatening public health;[6] and the sequencing problem.[7] In all these issues, the political Ministerial Conference (MC)/ General Council (GC) have failed to produce agreed policy although the demand clearly exists, ultimately leaving the problems to judicial determination.

Finally, the judicial and political branches are not in competition over influence. Rather, the political repeatedly capitulates before the judiciary, consciously entrusting it in many (but not all) systemic issues with the task of norm-creation needed to satisfy the demand for policies.

In this paper I focus on these capitulations of political governance, suggesting some explanations for them, offering a different perspective of the role of judicialization in the shift from government to governance.

* B.A. (International Relations) and L.L.B., Hebrew University of Jerusalem; SJD Candidate, Faculty of Law, University of Toronto; Advisor, International Lawyers and Economists Against Poverty (ILEAP) Initiative.

Explaining failure? The consensus rule

Why do the WTO's political organs fail to satisfy the demand for norm-creation in such important cases? This is puzzling, since the WTO agreement envisions the Membership jointly taking policy decisions and forging rules on a regular basis. The WTO's formal decision-making procedures (far-removed from reality) provide the MC/GC with a broad range of (quasi-)legislative options. Beyond the negotiation of new or amended treaties in periodic negotiation 'rounds', the MC/GC may adopt 'amendments' under Article X, 'interpretations' under Article IX:2, and 'waivers' under Article IX:3-4 WTO. Each of these procedures, allows for rule-making by specialized majority voting. If the constitutional narrative of judicialization held true, the political branch would employ these provisions, and rules would be created politically wherever the demand for them arose. This is not the case in reality.

A superficial response to this puzzle would focus on the persistence of the rule of consensus in WTO decision-making. The procedures of Articles IX and X WTO are very well in theory, but in practice the Membership overtly and obstinately clings to consensus, virtually sanctifying the first sentence of Article IX: 'The WTO shall continue the practice of decision-making by consensus followed under GATT 1947'. This is given absolute priority over the other rule-making provisions; the option of majority-based decision-making thus becomes a dead letter.

The effects of this consensus commitment are real, and illustrations abound. A political overruling of the Appellate Body's procedures on *amicus* briefs was prevented only because consensus was narrowly missed.[8] Progress on an agreement on public health and TRIPS obligations has also, similarly, continuously been forestalled by single-party intransigence, barring consensus.

Extraordinarily, in the sequencing issue, the EC actually proposed to free decision-making procedures from the consensus straitjacket, formally requesting that the GC adopt an authoritative interpretation, adding that 'if consensus cannot be achieved', the majority voting procedure 'could be pursued and undertaken without delay'.[9] This approach was hardly received with sympathy by other Members who were opposed to voting, fearing that it would lead to voting in all areas.

In the alternative narrative, the consensus tradition obstructs effective political policy-making, leaving the demand for it unsatisfied in many important instances. Yet this self-evident finding merely begs the question: why does the Membership adhere to consensus? The political branch is not so much 'plagued' by consensus as it consciously chooses to tie its own hands with it.

Justifying consensus? Sovereign control

One explanation for adherence to consensus is Members' fear of supranational authority and loss of sovereignty. States block the move from consensus to majority decision-making because of the implied loss of Member control over policy formulation. The consensus requirement grants every State an effective veto, allowing it to prevent the adoption of objectionable rules, presumably protecting the balance between international regulation and national sovereignty.

Yet this explanatory hypothesis rings hollow when one acknowledges that the effect of consensus is in many important cases, such the *amicus* briefs, sequencing, and

TRIPS-AIDS/HIV – to produce decisional deadlock. Consensus may prevent some rule-making that a State finds undesirable, but in many other cases, it thwarts rules that it supports. Indeed, the difficulty of consensus-building keeps important policies entirely off the table. For the sovereignty explanation to hold true it is insufficient to note that States attach value to their veto; it must be demonstrated that States perceive their gains from barring objectionable rules as outweighing their costs from the prevention of desirable ones.

The sovereignty excuse for consensus is particularly problematic because the political deadlock it causes inevitably brings the selfsame issues before the judiciary, implying an even greater loss of sovereign control. The demand for international policy does not simply disappear because the political branch has not supplied it. The incapability of the political branch to promulgate rules regarding civil society participation in dispute settlement has left this issue, by default, entirely up to judicial regulation.[10] The inability to reach political agreement on the TRIPS-AIDS/HIV nexus has consciously left it exposed to future judicial intervention;[11] and the sequencing issue continues to be governed by judicial interpretation, unregulated by 'legislative' Membership-based rule, although it is being debated in the Doha talks.

It is therefore illogical to argue that the Members' fear of supranational political authority, alone, establishes their loyalty to consensus, driving them to the arms of judicial authority that transcends the 'supranational'. The sovereignty excuse does not explain the ubiquity of consensus, but rather makes its reasoning even more questionable.

Causes of capitulation

Why, then, do the WTO Membership and political organs – by voluntary adherence to consensus – allow numerous normative questions to be regulated by the judiciary, instead of by political means? Why do they capitulate?

This query in itself illustrates the alternative narrative of judicialization, that rejects the convention of constant inter-institutional competition. In the WTO, the political elements have the power of effective, deliberative, political decision-making, but in many cases, they neglect to employ them. These elements have the authority to make binding rules by special majority voting, but they explicitly abhor its use, viewing consensus decision-making as sacrosanct. They do so while aware that due to their failure, many critical questions will reach the dispute settlement docket and be decided judicially. By default, the Membership practically invites the normative intervention of the judiciary.

This idea – that the political and legislative branches of international governance are sometimes interested in judicial intervention, to the point of actually inviting it – may seem odd because the general perception in domestic affairs is that the legislative branch and its members 'are resigned to the intervention of the courts, but have certainly never invited it'.[12] Moreover, 'many scholars have already noticed that judicial power is sometimes the result of legislative deference to the courts',[13] so even a simple conversion of domestic politics to the international plane – as per the constitutional narrative of judicialization in the WTO – must take this phenomenon into account; the alternative narrative in fact sees these 'political capitulations' as a central part of governance in the WTO.

On the domestic plane, it has been persuasively argued and demonstrated by political scientists that in some cases – termed 'legislative deferrals' – legislators 'strategically use ambiguity in statutory language to shift responsibility for deciding contentious policy issues to judges'.[14] In other analyses, deferrals may also occur where legislators simply abstain from effective positive action.[15] Deferrals of both sorts are explained by the complexity of legislative impetus. The pursuit of public policy and the maximization of influence over policy outcomes is only one of the motivations of legislators; in the domestic arena, other motivations include reelection and career advancement, for example. When a legislative actor is faced with 'conflicting constituencies, particularly when those constituencies are potentially well mobilized on opposite sides of a divisive issue',[16] the pressures of complex motivation mount, and the legislative actor may choose to defer to the judicial branch to avoid offending a segment of the constituency. This deferral will either 'delay final resolution of the controversy, typically long enough to get through the next election cycle', or more importantly, make 'it likely that judges will get at least some (and perhaps all) of the blame from constituents who end up on the losing side'.[17] Thus, in certain issue areas, legislators court judicial intervention, in order to reduce their own political accountability for normative policy results.

The general logic of domestic legislative deferrals may be converted to international governance, taking into account the additional complexities of the systems, actors and 'constituencies' involved. State positions in WTO deliberations are not motivated solely by broad-based public policy choices of States; other motivations exist. Each State has its own complex constituency structure, that is at least divided in each different trade issue along consumer-producer lines. Thus, State positions already reflect the outcome of political debates and compromises at the domestic level. Furthermore, each WTO delegate and policy-maker has an equally complicated personal political base and motivation structure, including the need to placate the competing national constituencies and the requirements of career advancement and political future. This complexity provides the Membership with many incentives to shift responsibility for difficult normative decisions to the judicial branch through political capitulation, just as national legislative actors have cause to defer to judicial decision-making.

When this general observation is applied in detail, the possible reasons for this capitulation are numerous. When taken cumulatively, the effect of these considerations is to lead the political branch to prefer – not merely permit – judicial norm-creation instead of political processes in many cases, particularly in issues that are highly contentious, either internationally or domestically, or both. Rather than provide an all-inclusive theoretical explanation for political capitulation in the WTO, the following is a non-exhaustive list of its possible sources:

– *Political cost to governments*: Majority-based political rule-making would require Members to take unequivocal high-resolution positions on contentious issues. This dynamic has potentially high political costs to national governments, forcing them to choose between competing interests of conflicting segments of their constituencies, and to bear electoral responsibility for the legislative results.

In contrast, maintaining a consensus-based system that allows 'fuzzy' rule-making and reflects international compromises in the mold of the lowest-common-denominator, allows governments to satisfy broader portions of their societies. When the DSS is required to provide a detailed interpretation of ambiguous or vacuous rules, the blame for offending local constituencies is shifted to the judiciary, leaving national governments far less accountable.

– *Political and personal cost to diplomats*: Majority-based rule-making that requires greater specificity and clarity would take its toll on the diplomats in charge of representing national policy, who would ultimately bear the personal cost of political failure. WTO delegates must walk the tightrope between 'external diplomacy' – maintaining working relations with delegates of other nationalities – in order to achieve results – and 'internal diplomacy' – satisfying the domestic political needs of their own governments, that include constituency appeasement. Delegates have little interest in pursuing clear rule-making policies that they would be held personally accountable for if in the mid-term or long-run they offended a domestic political group. It is safer to leave the normative ground less clear, allowing for greater flexibility, and shifting the responsibility for damaging decisions to the judiciary.

– *Reduced transaction costs of judicial decision-making*: Political negotiation of rules highlights the complex linkages of trade law, with each issue affecting other issue areas, entangling normative questions with crude economic bargains.[18] In contrast, judicial decision-makers are expected to neutralize these linkage effects. Given the scope and complexity of WTO law, in difficult cases it may be less costly for Members to reach established long-term normative outcomes by proxy, through delegated third-party 'judicial legislation', even when the cost of loss of control is factored in.

– *The predominance of short-term interests*: Short term interests and specific exigencies have a tendency to prevail over long-term policy thinking in the WTO. Governments and delegates are more concerned with specific disputes or negotiating particular national or sectoral gains than in producing long-lasting normative policy. When faced with pressing demands from national governments and interest groups to achieve results in trade negotiations, diplomats have little time and resources left to devote to long-term thinking, policy-making and structural problem-solving. The tactical thus firmly supplants the strategic in WTO politics.

– *Absense of a culture of politique*: Although formal decision-making procedures have been instated, and majority-based rule-making is permitted, the 'epistemic community'[19] of government officials and trade delegates lacks the political culture of international rule-making. Weiler has described the dissonance between the diplomatic heritage of the GATT/WTO – the 'ethos of diplomats' – and the judicial nature of the WTO DSS – the 'rule of lawyers'.[20] Yet an additional, disharmonious gap exists between the WTO's diplomatic tradition and the burden of political, legislative, rule-forging. The WTO remains in many senses a market place of trade concessions as was the GATT, and has failed to 'connect' to its legislative role. Lacking a legislative identity, the WTO reduces normative issues of tremendous systemic importance to their technical level, preventing normative deliberation,[21] leaving them to judicial determination. Paradoxically, it is thus the 'ethos of diplomats' that brings on the 'rule of lawyers', preferring it to the 'rule of the majority' and the political culture it would necessarily bring.

– *Targeted use of judiciary for domestic political ends*: In certain cases, the DSS is employed by Members in order to relieve domestic political pressure. DSS rulings grant national policies a legitimation that political rule-making cannot. Political legislation is associated with compromise and resignation, that carry little sympathy with national interest groups. When a complainant loses a case, its government can show the domestic interest group involved that it did not compromise and backed it all the way.[22] The judicial element is then conveniently to blame, with little or no fault being allocated to politicians. When a respondent loses, it can then implement remedying national policies under the umbrella of judicial intervention, again having shown its domestic industry that it did its utmost, and that there is no choice. Winning disputes has similar effects. The Membership as a whole appreciates the domestic political gains to be had from this targeted use of the DSS, providing it with another reason to prefer judicial intervention over political rule-making.

THE DIALECTIC OF GOVERNANCE: POLITICAL MASTER, JUDICIAL BONDSMAN

The WTO's Membership and political branch may indeed have powerful motives for preferring at least some important normative decision-making to be done by judicial rather than political means. The main instrument of political capitulation is the rule of consensus, around which WTO Members rally unequivocally. How is the idea of political capitulation consistent with our alternative assertion that the WTO DSS, as international judiciary, is subservient to the political branch, rather than on a par with it?

A nuanced understanding of WTO governance – and perhaps of future models of international governance in general – may be gained by viewing it through Hegel's 'Lordship and Bondage' dialectic. Like Hegel's original self-consciousness, the political elements of the WTO need the DSS in order to confirm the validity of their existence and the efficacy of the rule-based WTO system that defines them. Yet an independent DSS would threaten the political branch's grip on organizational and substantive power. Cancellation of the DSS would call into question the very existence of the WTO as a whole, and so is not an option. Hence, the Membership designed a WTO in which the political organs are deemed independent, 'existing for themselves'; the judicial branch, on the other hand, has been designed as the Bondsman, holding little relative judicial power, bounded by many ties as subservient to the political organs.[23]

The Membership expresses its independence through its dominance of the DSS, employing it in order to satisfy its own needs – first, the successful resolution of disputes; and second, the production of international judicial policy and norms that are necessary to satisfy the demand for them, at reduced costs to the Membership. Moreover, the Membership and political organs of the WTO have developed a dependence on both the dispute-settlement and rule-making services of the DSS, just as the 'Master' self-consciousness became dependent of its 'Bondsman'.

Thus, the alternative narrative of judicialization suggested here sees capitulations of political governance as a dialectical expression of both judicial subservience to the political branch, and of the dependence of the latter on the former.

In sum, I do not argue that this alternative narrative of judicialization is 'right', while the constitutional narrative is 'wrong', but would suggest that a strictly constitutional view of international governance, even in the relatively institutionalized WTO, is premature, at best, misguided, at worst.

NOTES

1 See F. Roessler, 'Are the Judicial Organs of the World Trade Organization Overburdened?' in R.B. Porter, et al. (eds.), *Efficiency, Equity, Legitimacy: The Multilateral Trading System at the Millenium* (Washington, D.C.: Brookings Institution Press, 2001) 308 at 308-9, analogizing the WTO structure to the '*trias politica*' of modern states; and G.E. Evans, *Lawmaking under the Trade Constitution: A Study in Legislating by the World Trade Organization* (The Hague: Kluwer Law International, 2000) at 31-34.

2 See G.I. Lovell, 'Legislative Deference to the Courts in a Separation of Powers System', paper, Annual

Meetings of the American Political Science Association, San Francisco, 2001, online: APSA, <http://pro.harvard.edu/papers/047/047001LovellGeor.pdf>.

3 This is admittedly debatable, but is expressed in many aspects of WTO architecture, e.g., the organizational subordination of the judicial DSS to the political Dispute Settlement Body (DSB); the responsibility of the DSB, rather than the judicial organs, for the administration of the Dispute Settlement Understanding (DSU) (Art. 2 DSU); and the involvement, in monitoring, communicating views and in constitutive decision-making, of the DSB in the initiation, management and conclusion of legal proceedings, including the unique (if unutilized) power of the DSB to prevent the entry into force of DSS Reports (Arts. 16, 17.14 DSU). See T. Broude, 'International Judicial Bodies as Sources of Normativity: The WTO Dispute Settlement System in Comparative Context' in I. Dekker and W. Werner (eds.), ***Challenge of Governance:*** *Collected Papers on the Methodology and Subjects of International Law and International Relations (The Hague: Kluwer Law International, 2003).*

4 This issue has haunted the WTO for years and is deemed critical to the legitimacy of the WTO. See the early contributions of M. Nichols, S. Charnovitz and G.R. Shell, (1996) 17(1) *U. Pa. J. Int'l Econ. L.* 295, 331 and 359 respectively; J.L. Dunoff, 'The Misguided Debate over NGO Participation at the WTO', (1998) 1 *J. Int'l Econ. L.* 433; and G.C. Umbricht, 'An "Amicus Curiae Brief" on *Amicus Curiae* Briefs at the WTO' (2001) 4(4) *J. Int'l. Econ.* L. 773.

5 Much has been written about the 'trade and…' problem. A broad perspective can be gained from the various contributions by J.E. Alvarez, D.W. Leebron, S. Charnovitz, K. Bagwell, P.C. Mavroidis, R.W. Staiger, J.P. Trachtman, R. Howse, J.H. Jackson, J. Baghwati, D.P. Steger in 'Symposium: The Boundaries of the WTO' (2002) 96 *AJIL* 1-158; see also M. Hilf and G.J. Goettsche, 'The Relation of Economic and Non-Economic Principles in International Law', in S. Griller (ed.), *International Economic Governance and Non-Economic Concerns: New Challenges for the International Legal Order* (Vienna: Springer Verlag, 2003) 5.

6 Following the Doha Declaration on the TRIPS Agreement and Public Health (WTO Doc. WT/MIN(01)/DEC/2 (2001)), WTO Members have not reached agreement solving this issue, despite its life threatening urgency, mainly due to the intransigence of one key player – the USA.

7 The DSU does not specify the chronological order – the 'sequencing' – between Art. 21.5 DSU proceedings on the consistency with covered agreements of measures taken to comply with DSS rulings, on one hand, and Art. 22 DSU procedures on retaliation, on the other hand.

8 The question was not brought to a vote at the special meeting of the DSB (WTO, Dispute Settlement Body, *Minutes of Meeting* (held on 17 November 2000), WTO Doc. WT/DSB/M/92), but only three Members were vocally opposed to a decision that would overrule the judicial procedures.

9 WTO, *General Council*, Request for an Authoritative Interpretation Pursuant to Art. IX:2 of the Marrakesh Agreement Establishing the World Trade Organization – Communications from the European Communities (25 January and 5 February 1999), WTO Docs. WT/GC/W/133 and WT/GC/W/143.

10 Indeed, *amicus* briefs were again accepted by the Appellate Body, subject to its own procedure, in *European Communities – Trade Description of Sardines* (2002), WTO Doc. WT/DS231/AB/R (Appellate Body Report)

11 The USA, while blocking agreement on this issue, has pledged – temporarily – 'not to challenge any WTO Member that breaks WTO rules to export drugs produced under compulsory license to a country in need' (USTR, Press Release, December 20, 2002, online: <http://www.ustr.gov/releases/2002/12/02-119.htm>). This declaration ostensibly puts off judicial proceedings, but may also be read as a veiled threat to litigate.

12 Justice Scalia of the US Supreme Court in the hearings of the 2000 Presidential election cases, quoted by Lovell *supra* n. 2. Lovell describes an exchange in which Gore attorney Laurence Tribe suggested that 'the Florida legislature wanted the courts to play an important role creating the boundaries for resolving post-election disputes', prompting this comment from Justice Scalia.

13 Ibid., at 2, referring mainly to the work of M. Graber, 'The Non-Majoritarian Difficulty: Legislative Deference to the Judiciary' (1993) 7 *Studies in American Political Development* 35.

14 Lovell, ibid., at 3.

15 This is one point in which Graber's analysis of legislative deferrals (*supra* n. 13) differs from Lovell's (*supra* n. 2). Lovell focuses on statutory interpretation, confining the term to the strategic use of deliberate ambiguity in legislation; Graber advocates a broader approach, encompassing cases where the legislature defers to the courts by not taking any action at all, as well as cases of deliberate ambiguity in legislative acts.

16 Lovell, ibid., at 12-13.

17 Ibid.

18 K.W. Abbott ('Rule-Making in the WTO: Lessons from the Case of Bribery and Corruption', (2001) 4 *J. Int'l. Econ. L.* 275) describes WTO decision-making as being 'mired in the obsessive quid pro quo thinking that has always dominated tariff negotiations, even when asked to address issues [...] on which international rules could produce significant mutual benefits'.

19 I apply Ruggie's term ('The New Institutionalism in International Relations' in J.G. Ruggie, *Constructing the World Polity: Essays on International Institutionalization* (London: Routledge, 1998) at 45) to the WTO's 'insider network' subject to the same caveats as advanced by R. Howse, 'From Politics to Technocracy – and Back Again: The Fate of the Multilateral Trading Regime' (2002) 96 *AJIL* 94 at note 13.

20 J.H.H. Weiler, 'The Rule of Lawyers and the Ethos of Diplomats: Reflections on the Internal and External Legitimacy of WTO Dispute Settlement' in R.B. Porter, et al. (eds.), *Efficiency, Equity and Legitimacy: The Multilateral Trading System at the Millennium* (Washington, DC: Brookings Institution Press, 2001) 334.

21 See, similarly, Abbot *supra* n. 18 at 294; and Howse *supra* n. 19.

22 This could said to be the case, for example, *Japan – Measures Affecting Consumer Photographic Film and Paper* (1998), WTO Doc. WT/DS44/R (Panel Report).

23 See n. 3 *supra*.

John Rawls on Constitutionalism and the Charter of Fundamental Rights of the European Union

Paul De Hert*[1]

1. Introduction

Churches are half-empty and people are massively turning away from organized religion. Still the Vatican wants a mention of God and Christianity in the new European Union (EU) Constitution, currently under discussion. This future basic European document must create a common identity, make the list of the EU's tasks clearer, guarantee a high quality of political leadership and ensure that a larger Europe will be able to take action in day-to-day politics. Obvious merits of the initiative are the fusion of the present European treaties in a single document and the inclusion of a charter with fundamental rights. This document, the *Charter of fundamental rights of the European Union*, contains chapters on solidarity, dignity, liberty and subsidiarity. Different authors have used John Rawls' theory of constitutionalism to comment on the Charter. Some have rejected his theory as not suitable to explain the rich content of the Charter. Others have amended his theory to account for the multi-layered content of the document.

This contribution does not discuss whether a European Constitution is feasible or desirable. Only one aspect of constitutionalism is touched upon, namely the insertion of human rights and references to values in the Constitution. This contribution holds that the references to certain ethical values in the newly drafted text is a serious matter that may hamper a successful political integration of the Union based on values such as pluralism and State neutrality. Also we criticize the idea that a long list of human rights may be instrumental in achieving the principles of democracy and pluralism. Our handling of the subject will be grounded on a discussion of John Rawls' theory of minimal constitutionalism. We reflect upon Rawls' basic intuition ('the fact of pluralism') and contradict the use of Rawlsian apparatus by some authors who are in favor of the current developments in European constitutionalism. Within the Rawlsian framework there is no reason to see progress in long or ethically inspired bills of rights. A political conception of justice does not imply a bill of substantive rights, certainly not an extensive one. Neither pluralism nor democracy are served by the European Charter in its present form.

* Professor of law at the Free University of Brussels & Associated-Professor at the Leiden University

2. The EU charter of fundamental rights

The drafting process

The 'Charter of fundamental rights of the European Union', that will be incorporated in the new European Constitution, was finished three years before the draft Constitution that is currently under discussion.[2] Although one can come up with many reasons to adopt a Charter,[3] there is not very much in the Preamble of the Charter about the need to adopt a separate bill with rights and liberties. One can induce from certain paragraphs of the Preamble that there was a combined need of bringing existing bills with rights together and of updating them in order to face new challenges such as those created by scientific progress. The Charter itself is a strange mix of values borrowed from worldviews such as Christianity, Protestantism, humanism, and liberalism. It contains chapters on solidarity, dignity, liberty and subsidiarity.

Important to understand the way the debate over an EU Charter of Fundamental Rights has developed has been the importance of reports by independent committees, appointed by the Commission or encouraged by it, in preparing the way for new human rights initiatives.[4] A first committee, the *Comité des Sages,*[5] reported in 1996. A second *Comité des Sages* reported after the Amsterdam Treaty. This committee arising from a project funded by the Commission at the European University Institute in Florence adopted a 'human rights agenda'.[6] The Agenda explicitly refuted the idea of creating new rights and initiatives that are no more than 'legal sophistry'. However, a further Commission-appointed group, led by Professor Simitis of Frankfurt recommended another way forward on the issue in their report 'Affirming fundamental rights in the European Union: Report of the Expert Group on Fundamental Rights' (1999). This time a proposal for a human rights bill was made. Only the last proposal met with political enthusiasm.[7]

The German concern about the relationship between the fundamental rights in the German constitution and EC/EU law is well known. In cases of conflict, European law breaks national law, including parliamentary legislation and constitutional norms. Even the German Constitutional Court had to give up its claim to be the last interpreter of basic rights concerning German citizens and German territory.[8] What better way to answer this concern by using the German constitution as a main source for the drafting of the Charter? For example, the chapter on *Dignity* in the Charter (*infra*) is a clear concession to the German constitutional tradition in view of the German concerns discussed above.[9]

3. The argument for pluralism

Pluralism through a choice for values

We saw that the 'Charter of fundamental rights of the European Union' contains a mix of values. Klink and Klop are very much in favor of the Charter with its rich ethical layers. These authors hold that fundamental texts should reflect the ethical values of societies. Active maintenance of values and moral education are two goals that should be pursued by the conventional convention.[10] These values should be mirrored by constitutional texts. Although Klink and Klop hold that bills with rights and liberties should not be restricted to the uncontroversial, they argue that the current Charter is a good and acceptable compromise between the major European comprehensive worldviews. The extremes are avoided. At the one hand the Charter does not reflect liberal preference for a neutral State and a common political language free from controversial values.[11] At the other hand radical catholic propositions for a Charter, such as those proposed by Cardinal Ratzinger, were not upheld. For Klink and Klop the Charter presents a third way. It is a thoughtful document that reflects a wide consensus within Europe. The Charter cannot be understood as a product of one comprehensive world view, but should be understood as a product of an overlapping consensus, in a sense that is the result of a convergence of the various political, moral and religious views within our society. In this context they introduce the idea of a *dynamic overlapping consensus*.[12] In part this concept is necessary in view of their belief that bills with rights and *liberties* should not be restricted to the uncontroversial.

Pluralism through avoidance of controversial values

With the notion 'dynamic overlapping consensus', Klink and Klop explicitly refer to and amend the Rawlsian theory of political justice. This reading of Rawls, grounded on a subtle perversion of the basic intuitions, does not impress us. It is not difficult to find for most values cherished in Western society some source. This is not what Rawls is about. Rawls' political conception of justice is indeed historically embedded (and constructivist) but the whole Rawlsian question is precisely to pick out those values that are suitable to ground the political institutions of a society upon. Especially when it comes to this selection and the question of incorporating the selected values into a constitution Rawls calls for prudence. It is therefore very unlikely that having to choose between a small common core or a larger common core, he would choose the latter. Let us recall some elements of Rawls' idea of constitutionalism.[13]

Rawls' points of departure are the fundamental differences between citizens in the Western world (the 'fact of pluralism'). Notwithstanding this fact, at the political level a pluralistic and democratic society needs a shared basis to refer upon when taking political decisions. Indeed, people need to live with one another and they exercise power upon each other when taking decisions. But it is important for this common basis to be acceptable for all. When policy would be grounded on values that are not in generally shared by everyone, violence would be called upon to impose them ('the fact of oppression'). To avoid the use of violence, a pluralistic and democratic society must therefore turn to political principles that can be accepted by all, regardless of their (religious or political) world-view. Rawls therefore conceives what he calls a political concept of justice: a model for the political institutions of a society independent of controversial philosophical, moral and religious doctrines. It is not 'metaphysical' but 'political': as far as possible it avoids philosophical questions (e.g., what is the a-historical nature of man?, what is the nature of the human subject?, what motivates moral behavior? and what is the sense of human life?).[14] A political conception tries to draw solely upon basic intuitive ideas (necessary to regulate the basic structure) that are embedded in the political institutions of a constitutional democratic regime and the public traditions of their interpretation.[15] These shared values (such as freedom and equality) are then worked up into more determinate principles to govern society.[16]

These principles, however acceptable, are by themselves insufficient to solve the problem of stability in pluralist societies. That's why the idea of an 'overlapping consensus' is needed. The necessity of an overlapping consensus arises because those with different comprehensive moral views must seek some common ground for reaching consensus about principles of justice. Rawls beliefs that rational people will unanimously adopt his principles of justice if their reasoning is based on general considerations, without knowing anything about their own personal situation, cultural background or belief.[17] For Rawls this consensus about the political model of justice is more than an idea. Such a consensus exists. History shows that there is a convergence of the various moral and religious views, each of which accepts the political conception from within their own comprehensive views.[18] Hence, Rawls' optimism about the existence of a shared basis, especially in his later work where he presents his theory of 'justice as fairness' as a spelling-out of the Western, especially American consensus.[19] The restriction of scope clearly shows the pragmatist nature of Rawls' theory. Is does not come as a surprise that Rawls does not defend a natural law theory of rights, but favors the idea of basic liberties.[20] These *basic liberties* are part of the fundamental ideas that are familiar to all and are drawn from public political culture of a democratic society 'that has worked reasonably well over a considerable period'. Rawls sees the basic liberties as the constitutional essentials of domestic (or Western) justice, since they provide for the central elements of the overlapping consensus between reasonable people with different moral, political and religious backgrounds in Western regimes.

Is pluralism served by an extensive bill of rights?

Rawls would certainly oppose himself to extensive constitutions with a strong ethical footing (for instance, with references to the dignity of the person). This lessens the chances for an overlapping consensus. This consensus, Rawls specifies, is not a consensus simply in accepting a certain authority, or simply as compliance with certain institutional arrangements. In order to better understand the idea of an overlapping consensus Rawls contrasts it with another way of reaching agreement on a political conception, that of a *modus vivendi*. A social consensus based upon a *modus vivendi* occurs when the various parties find it to be in their own self-interests to abide by the conditions of a contract or a treaty.

Our discussion of the drafting process of the Charter *above* suggests that this kind of calculation was at work. In order to overcome German resistance, it was decided to incorporate a full chapter on *human dignity*, a concept central to the German constitutional post-World War II tradition. There are however three problems with this concept. First, it is not firmly rooted in other European constitutional traditions (see *above*). Second, within the Western World there is no consensus about the necessity of this notion, partly because it has no precise meaning and because is potentially a conflicting value with regard to the value of freedom that has a wider recognition.[21] It is difficult to find consensus about an imprecise notion that only thrives because behind it there are conceptions at work behind it of what is of value in human life. *Dignity*, to put it differently, is a very apolitical notion.[22] There is so far no proof that it has worked 'reasonably well' in Europe since it has only worked in one country as a constitutional norm.[23] This brings us to our third point: the concept of *human dignity* is still too much indebted to Christianity. Only Christians seem to know what is meant by it. That by itself is already enough reason to do away with it, if one takes into account the frequent waves of provocation that are launched by defenders of this religion.[24] We recall that the parties to the Rawlsian contract must choose these principles in light of the possibility that they might be anything from religious ascetics to atheistic libertines. A regime of toleration, with strong protection for the freedom of individuals and associations to pursue different ends in life, only becomes possible when we refrain from imposing our own conception of the human good on others against their will, even if we have the political power to do it by voting a text with fundamental rights. Comprehensive values of religion and ultimate ends should be left to voluntary communal and personal pursuit.

Under these conditions, the incorporation in the Charter of *dignity* should be seen as the result of a *modus vivendi* (Germans and Christians 'got' dignity, while social movements 'got' solidarity) and possibly as a fact of oppression. There is no sufficient evidence to suggest an overlapping consensus. Klink and Klop observe that religious people with their idea of man created to the idea of God will recognize themselves in the prohibition of eugenic practices, whereas people adhering to the idea of humanitas will 'recognize' themselves in the requirement of free and informed consent in the fields of medicine and biology.[25] However, they still have to prove that non-religious or atheists can recognize themselves in all the prohibitions and rules laid down in the first Chapter of the Charter.

To understand the kind of evidence we seek one has to turn to the idea of a *normative* conception of the constitution.[26] Menéndez distinguishes two main families of normative conceptions along the procedural/substantial divide.[27] All conceptions of the constitution combine procedural and substantive elements, only they put more or less emphasis on one or the other. If we apply this distinction we notice that, for instance, Article 3 of the Chapter qualifies as such a mix. There is a procedural normative conception behind the rule that free and informed consent is necessary in the fields of medicine and biology, while all the prohibitions in the said Article are inspired by a substantive normative conception of the person. Needless to say that the analysis made by Klink and Klop of the consensus about this Article is flawed. As seen above, they observe that religious people will recognize themselves in the prohibitions, whereas others will 'recognize' themselves in the requirement of free and informed consent. Holding that liberals like procedural norms and religious people prefer substantive norms is hardly new and does not ground the assumption about a readily consensus.[28]

The argument of pluralism can be pushed a little further. What is at stake here is constitutionalism at the European level. Existing national constitutional traditions should be taken seriously and the Charter should respect the need for subsidiarity. Therefore the Charter should recognize the desirability of diverse conceptions of human rights within Europe.[29] It goes to say that this position is difficult to reconcile with a Charter that was drafted on the Constitution of one Member State with opening provisions and key-values that are absent in most other Member States. Perhaps the Charter can be defended on other grounds. The next paragraph contains a discussion of the argument for democracy. Does this justify a Charter with a long list of human rights?

4. The argument for democracy

A thin constitution

Rawls' theory of political justice does not remain solely within the realm of abstract principles, but contains a very concrete constitutional project. Central to this project, that is inspired by the history of American constitutionalism, stands the idea of a legal four-stage sequence. Once the two principles of justice (including the basic liberties that together make up for the first principle) are chosen in the original position, there follow three further stages of implementation, as the parties move to a constitutional convention establishing rights of citizens, then to a legislative stage where the justice of laws and policies are considered, and finally to the stage of judicial interpretation of particular cases.[30] One of the first actions of this convention is to incorporate the basic liberties in a constitution in order to protect them.[31] A closer look reveals that this constitution takes the form of the 1787 American Constitution *before* the Bill of Rights was added two years later.[32]

Indeed, there is in Rawls' work an explicit preference for a thin constitution. He proposes a limited scheme identifying 'truly' basic liberties – consisting exclusively of individual liberty rights – to avoid controversy. Within the Rawlsian framework there is no reason to see progress in long or ethically inspired bills of rights. A political conception of justice does not imply a bill of substantive rights, certainly not an extensive one.[33] Regulating power and setting constraints on the work of the legislator are constitutional requirements.[34] Nowhere in *A Theory of Justice* Rawls is saying that the work of the convention *should* result in the drafting of a bill of rights or a chapter on human rights in the constitution.[35] What he does say is that most issues should be debated and decided upon in the third legislative stage. This follows clearly from Rawls' answer to the question whether the right to property should be regarded as a basic right.[36]

The democratic argument against a thin constitution

Some hold that the idea of a thin constitution shows a lack of respect for democracy and popular sovereignty. Dutch and Belgian authors such as Maurice Adams, Heysse and Goossens, explicitly refute John Rawls' theory of constitutionalism and see in it a model that is not suited to understand the current process of European Constitutionalism. This time the argument relates to the principle of democracy. For these authors, Rawls' preference for a thin constitution is of a conservative nature. Tradition cannot be consulted but has to be re-interrogated. There is no such thing as substance within tradition. Tradition is itself a result of political debate and the lawgiver has therefore the important task of continuing this debate about fundamental values and to intensify it.[37] Thinking ahead, in this perspective, means looking back at the values that have been important for us. In order to discuss new problems, the lawmaker and the society as a whole have to reunite around values by continually debating and reflecting upon them.[38] Democracy, the argument goes, is precisely this. Defining new rights is part of the democratic process. Maurice Adams, professor at the Antwerp University, writing in the context of bio-medical questions, would have no difficulty, so it seems to us, with the current European process of constitutionalism (recalling past history in the

Preamble, bringing existing rights together and updating them in order to face new challenges).

A possible Rawlsian reply to the democratic argument

There is of course no discussion about the fact that the idea of a thin constitution implies that not all interests can be uplifted to the constitutional level. Rawls simply sees no room for such things as third or fourth generation human rights. The constitution should establish a secure common status of equal citizenship and realize political justice. But does the foregoing means that Rawls is not democratic? We believe not. One can question the solidity of the project of thin constitutionalism,[39] but to doubt the democratic nature of it is highly disrespectful of the Rawlsian enterprise.

Take for instance social and economical rights. For Rawls these rights are no less essential for *justice as fairness*, but he simply does not want to insert them in the constitution.[40] This does not make him less democratic, since omission of these rights at the level, makes them the object of the third (legislative) stage where the normal majority rule applies. Social justice is the prime task of the legislator who can develop social and economic policies aimed at maximizing the long-term expectations of the least advantaged under conditions of fair equality of opportunity and is subject to the duty to maintain equal liberties.[41] Reserving societal issues to the legislative stage is making democracy possible, Rawls seems to think. This position shows that Rawls is not far away from Richard Bellamy, a fierce critique of human rights. Incorporating (comprehensive) values into the constitution is detrimental to politics, Bellamy holds, since constitutions have higher legal value and bind the legislator.[42] Technically this implies that in legal systems with no flexible procedures to initiate constitutional amendments, the democratic process is seriously hampered. Practically, Bellamy adds to this, the immunization will seldom work, since constitutional rights often need to be balanced with one another.[43] In this view, one can do away with most civil rights (not the political rights) in the Charter, especially with the prohibitions in Article 3. These prohibitions (of eugenic practices, etc.) have never been the object of a proper democratic discussion.[44] Even when one assumes that they were not part of bargain, the democratic problem remains. Alteration of the principle behind the prohibition by majority rule in the future is simply made impossible, which is difficult to reconcile with the principle of democracy.[45] Also, legislation contradicting this principle will not pass judicial review. Societal issues thus become legal or technical issues. Judges, not popular sovereignty, will determine what is possible in the new Europe within the framework of the Charter.

5. Conclusion

Throughout this contribution we detected several flaws in the contention that current developments in European constitutionalism can be understood and defended within a Rawlsian framework and in the contention that Rawls' theory of constitutionalism is too conservative and thus not fitted to understand constitutionalism in democratic States.

The Charter is the outcome of 'horse-trading-based' negotiations typical for an

Intergovernmental Conference or a Convention. The drafting process and the result do not respect Rawls' concern for keeping metaphysical values out of the constitutional work and his priority for the liberties contained in the first principle of justice. Rawls theory is free from lack of respect for democracy and popular sovereignty. On the contrary, an in-depth analysis of his constitutional idea of a legal four-stage sequence shows that he was well aware of the risks for democracy to overburden a constitution with substantive norms, as is the case in the Charter. Rawls' theory explains us why there is no reason to see progress in long or ethically inspired bills of rights, why there is no absolute or pressing need to spell out 'the rights of man' or 'the rights of humans' in detail and why we should not on a political level identify the shared values of the past, others than those needed for justice as fairness. All these lessons were neglected by the drafters of the Charter. This Charter is not a promising start for the European construction and it is questionable whether the initiative furthers the objectives of European integration, that is bringing our Union closer to its citizens and strengthening our Union's democratic character.[46]

NOTES

1 The author wants to thank Jörg Friedrichs of the University of Bremen and Wouter Werner of the University of Utrecht.

2 It was published in the *Official Journal of the European Communities,* C 364/1, 18 December 2000. On the Charter: Ricardo Alonso García, 'The General Provisions of the Charter of Fundamental Rights of the European Union', Jean Monnet Working Paper 4/02, (36 p.) via <www.jeanmonnetprogram.org>; *E.O.Eriksen, J.E. Fossum and A.J. Menéndez (eds.), The Chartering of Europe. The European Charter of Fundamental Rights and its Constitutional Implications, Nomos Verlag, 2003.*

3 For a 'plethora of justifications' in favor of the Charter brought forwards at various times, but pointing to entirely different models of a human rights Charter, see Christopher McCrudden, *The future of the EU charter of fundamental rights,* Jean Monnet Working Paper No. 10/01, 2001, (27 p.) 8-9., via <www.jeanmonnetprogram.org>.

4 Christopher McCrudden, loc. cit. n. 3, 2-7.

5 *For a Europe of Civic and Social Rights,* Report by the Comité des Sages chaired by Maria de Lourdes Pintasilgo (1996).

6 *Leading by Example: A Human Rights Agenda for the European Union for the Year 2000,* Agenda of the Comité des Sages and Final Project Report (1998). The agenda is reprinted in Annex 1 from Ph. Alston, M. Bustelo & J. Heenan (eds.), *The EU and Human Rights,* Oxford, Oxford University Press, 1999.

7 In fact '[t]he German presidency was decidedly unenthusiastic about many of the substantive suggestions which were made in the first and more detailed of the two reports (for example the setting up of a specific Commission directorate with responsibility for human rights, or the establishment of a human rights monitoring center ...) but was attracted to the theme of the second report, which focused on the perceived need for an EU Bill of Rights'. (Gráinne de Búrca, 'The drafting of the European Union Charter of fundamental rights', *European Law Review,* 2001, Vol. 26, (126), p. 129).

8 Hauke Brunkhorst, 'A Polity without a State? European Constitutionalism between Evolution and Revolution', 2003, Arena Working Paper 14/03, (30 p.), 2 via <http://www.arena.uio.no>.

9 Article 1.1 of the German Constitution states that: 'Die Würde des Menschen ist unantastbar. Sie zu achten und zu schützen ist Verpflichtung aller staatlichen Gewalt'. This orientation may explain why the Charter is more than just a facelifting of the European Convention on Human Rights (ECHR), concluded in 1950. This orientation is not unproblematic, since German constitutionalism contains ingredients that are not typical for other Western constitutional traditions. More 'liberal' constitutions such as the Belgian and Dutch Constitution do not acknowledge values such as human dignity. On the 'communitarian' orientation of German constitutionalism: D. Kommers, 'Can German Constitutionalism Serve as a Model for the United States?', *Zeitschrift für ausländisches öffentliches Recht und Völkerrecht (ZaöRV),* 1998, Vol. 22, 787-798.

10 See A. Klink and C. Klop, 'Het handvest van grondrechten voor de Europese Unie als juridische positi-

vering van morele overtuigingen' [The Charter of fundamental rights of the European Union: legal positivisation of comprehensive world-views], in P. Cliteur, et al. (eds.). *It ain't necessarily so*, Kluwer, Leiden, 2001, 107-126.

11 A. Klink and C. Klop, loc. cit. n. 10, 107.

12 A. Klink and C. Klop, loc. cit. n. 10, 124.

13 John Rawls, 'Justice as Fairness: Political not Metaphysical', *Philosophy and Public Affairs*, Vol. 14 (1985), No. 3, 223-251; John Rawls, *Political Liberalism*, New York: Columbia University Press, 1993; John Rawls, *Justice as Fairness. A Restatement*. Cambridge: Harvard University Press, 2001.

14 Rawls distinguishes political and metaphysical concepts of justice. Both are moral theories, but the latter one refers to a comprehensive, general, substantial and 'naturalistic' world-view, whereas the former is of a more restrained nature. A political concept of justice has three distinctive features. It is a moral conception worked out for a specific subject. This subject can be local justice, domestic justice or global justice. By accepting a political conception of justice, a person does not commit him/herself to a deeper comprehensive theory or doctrine. Thirdly, it is a conception that cannot be found everywhere, since it has its basis in certain fundamental ideas latently present in the public political culture of a democratic society.

15 John Rawls, 'Justice as Fairness: Political not Metaphysical', 225.

16 Our conception of justice, Rawls contends, 'is constituted by principles we would agree to live by under fair conditions, in particular: 1. Each person is to have an equal right to the most extensive basic liberty compatible with a similar liberty for others (the Liberty Principle). 2. Social and economic inequalities are to be arranged so that they are both (a) reasonably expected to be to everyone's advantage, and (b) attached to positions and offices open to all (the Difference Principle)'. Cf., *A Theory of Justice*, para. 46.

17 It is possible and necessary to respond to the 'fact' of pluralism, Rawls holds, for persons with conflicting, but reasonable comprehensive views to agree that the political conception of justice should be the account of justice that is most compatible with their own views. As such the political conception would then be the object of an overlapping consensus about justice. Cf., John Rawls, *Political Liberalism*, 15. Since democracies cannot and may not use State power, with its attendant cruelties and corruptions of civic and cultural life, to eradicate diversity, 'we look for a political conception of justice that can gain the support of a reasonable overlapping consensus to serve as a public basis of justification' (*Justice as Fairness. A Restatement*, para. 11.5.). An overlapping consensus 'consists of all the reasonable opposing religious, philosophical, and moral doctrines likely to persist over generations and to gain a sizable body of adherents in a more or less just constitutional regime, a regime in which the criterion of justice is that political conception itself'. (John Rawls, *Political Liberalism*, 15).

18 'For all those who affirm the political conception start from within their own comprehensive view and draw on the religious, philosophical and moral grounds it provides'. Cf., *Political Liberalism*, 147; *Justice as Fairness. A Restatement*, para. 58.

19 'That there are such ideas in their public culture is taken as a fact about democratic societies' (*Justice as Fairness. A Restatement*, para. 9.1.). Critical of this movement away from Kant's universal conception of public reason: Onora O'Neill, 'Political Liberalism and Public Reason: A Critical Notice of John Rawls' *Polical Liberalism*', *The Philosophical Review*, 1997, Vol. 106, No. 3, 411-428.

20 See more in detail: P. De Hert and S. Gutwirth, 'Rawls' Political Conception of Rights and Liberties. Illiberal but Pragmatic Approach to the Problems of Harmonisation and Globalisation', in M. Van Hoecke (ed.), *Epistemology and Methodology of Comparative Law*, Oxford, Hart Publishers, (The European Academy of Legal Theory Series), 2004, 317-358.

21 We are persons because we are free, not the other way around. Compare Jacques Mourgeon, 'Les droits de l'être humain, destructeurs de sa liberté', in *Territoires Liberté. Mélanges en hommage au Doyen Yves Madiot*, Brussels, Bruylant, 2000, (391-407), 403: 'En voulant remplacer l'initial (la liberté) par le dérivé (la dignité) dont on ne sait ce qui fait la dignité de l'être humain, on me répond: sa qualité d'être humain. Et si je me demande ce qui fait sa qualité d'être humain, on me répond: sa dignité. Le cercle vicieux de la tautologie est parfait'.

22 Rawls regards a moral theory to be comprehensive when it satisfies the following conditions. First it must apply to a wide range of subjects. This is what makes it general. It becomes comprehensive 'when it includes conceptions of what is of value in human life, as well as ideals of personal virtue and character, that are to inform much of our non-political conduct ...' Cf., John Rawls, *Political Liberalism*, New York: Columbia University Press, 1993, 175.

23 See above, n. 9.

24 Cf., Sophie Arie, 'Outrage at Vatican ethics dictionary', *The Guardian*, Tuesday 1 April 2003. In May 2003 the Vatican published an ethical dictionary saying homosexuality has 'no social value', warning against

concepts such as 'safe sex' and 'reproductive health' and insisting that condoms do not protect against sexually transmitted diseases. The book, one of the Vatican's most scathing attacks yet on what it considers deteriorating social values, caused outrage in Italy's gay community, among some Italian politicians and even at certain levels within the Vatican itself.

25 A. Klink and C. Klop, loc. cit. n. 10, 112-113.

26 A.J. Menéndez, 'Three conceptions of the European Constitution', 2002, (40 p.), via <http://www.arena.uio.no>. This author distinguishes between the *formal, material* and a *normative* conception of the constitution. We already discussed the first two concepts above. The normative constitution is composed of those norms that present certain properties which are normatively relevant, Menéndez holds. Neither formal criteria nor material criteria (derived from social practice) can account for the essence of a constitution. The basic insight underlying the normative conception of the Constitution is that 'ideal' standards (in the sense of counterfactual) play a major role. No matter what the vast majority of the people say, a society in which rights are not protected and the powers of the State are not separated has no constitution. This *emancipation* from facts is the key element in the normative conception of the constitution (A.J. Menéndez, loc. cit. n. 26, 8).

27 'The concrete "ideal" standards to be considered vary with different normative conceptions of the Constitution. There could be as many normative conceptions of the constitution as there are normative theories, that is, theories about what is *right*. But one can distinguish two main families of normative conceptions along the usual procedural/substantial divide. A substantive normative conception of the constitution will point to the *intrinsic normative* qualities of constitutional norms. Therefore, the relevant normative properties will be related to a substantial conception of the good. Liberalist conceptions of the constitution consider as constitutional the basic norms protecting the right to private autonomy. (...) In its turn, a procedural normative conception of the constitution will refer to the qualities of the process through which the norms were agreed upon. That is, all norms approved through a given process will be defined as constitutional. Democratic conceptions of the constitution could be said to be standard examples of procedural conceptions of the constitution. But also conceptions, which consider constitutional the norms produced by wise legislators, for example, will qualify as procedural. It goes without saying that the procedural/substantive conception points to basic types' (A.J. Menéndez, loc. cit. n. 26, 9).

28 Below we will argue that the incorporation of a chapter on *Solidarity* is equally hard to define within a Rawlsian political framework grounded on an overlapping consensus. The argument, this time, will not be pluralism, but democracy and the division of labor within the Rawlsian political concept of justice. However, the argument of pluralism should also be investigated. Is it evident for everyone that work is sacred? Are we born to work? Or do we need to work to become human? Again there is a feeling that the drafters of the Charter are imposing a certain conception of the human good on others against their will, while it is very well possible to imagine a society where 'work' has been replaced by other values.

29 Christopher McCrudden, loc. cit. n. 3, 9.

30 See the first Chapter of the second part ('Institutions') of *A Theory of Justice*.

31 *A Theory of Justice*, para. 31.

32 There is no ideal constitution; justice as fairness is not an account of how constitutional conventions actually proceed. However, according to Rawls the idea of a four-stage sequence is suggested by the United States Constitution and its history (cf., the first footnote of the second part of *A Theory of Justice* on political justice). We recall that the original 1787 Constitution contained no bill of rights, although the 1776 Declaration of Independence declared their foundational weight and several important rights, especially with regard to the rule of law, are contained in the various provisions of the Constitution. For example the prohibition of ex-post-facto law in Article 1, section 9. An enumeration is contained in Alexander Hamilton, *The Federalist No. 84*, (1788), included in *The Federalist, A Commentary on the Constitution of the United States*, (1787-1788), introduction by E.M. Earle, New York, The Modern Library, s.d., 556-557. See also: P. Boon *Amerikaans staatsrecht*, Zwolle, W.E.J. Tjeenk Willink, 1992, 125-130.

33 'The reason for this limit on the list of basic liberties is the special status of these liberties. Whenever we enlarge the list of basic liberties we risk weakening the protection of the most essential ones and recreating within the scheme of liberties the indeterminate and unguided balancing problems we had hoped to avoid by a suitably circumscribed notion of priority' (John Rawls, 'The Basic Liberties and Their Priority', loc. cit., 10).

34 More in detail: P. De Hert and S. Gutwirth, loc. cit. n. 20, 336.

35 'A bill of rights *may* remove certain liberties from majority regulation altogether, and the separation of powers with judicial review *may* slow down the pace of legislative change' (*A Theory of Justice*, para. 37). The italics are added. The concept of constitution Rawls has in mind is not formal, but rather material and normative (in the sense of procedural, not substantial). See on these distinctions: A.J. Menéndez, 'Three conceptions

of the European Constitution', 2002, (40 p.), via <http://www.arena.uio.no>. One can even ask the question whether rights form an indispensable part of the Rawls' basic structure. See on this: P. De Hert and S. Gutwirth, loc. cit. n. 20, 336.

36 The right to property forms a basic right, since it allows a sufficient material basis for personal independence and a sense of self-respect, both of which are essential for the adequate development and exercise of the moral powers. Wider conceptions of the right to property are not taken as basic. They may, however, still be justified, Rawls note, depending on existing historical and social conditions, 'the further specification of the rights to property is to be made at the legislative stage, assuming the basic rights and liberties are maintained. As a public political conception, justice as fairness is to provide a shared basis for weighing the case for and against various forms of property, including socialism. To do this, it tries to avoid prejudging, at the fundamental level of basic rights, the question of private property in the means of production. In that way perhaps discussion of this important question can proceed within a political conception of justice that can gain the support of an overlapping consensus' (*Justice as Fairness. A Restatement*, para. 32.6). The demonstration with regard to property is of interest because it shows what kind of work the legislator (still) can do.

37 T. Heysse and W. Goossens, 'Macht en rede in de democratie. Algemene beschouwingen' [Power and reason in the democracy], in T. Heysse and W. Goossens (eds.), *Engelen van de wereld. Hedendaagse filosofen over democratie* [Contemporary philosophers about democracy], Kapellen, Pelckmans, 2001; M. Adams, 'De wetgever en het bio-ethisch pluralisme' [The lawmaker and bio-ethical pluralism], *UVV-Info*, 2003, Vol. 20, No. 2, (20-23), 22-23.

38 M. Adams, loc. cit. n. 37, 20-23; F. De Wachter, 'Politiek en het goede leven [Politics and the good life]', in B.J. De Clercq (ed.) *De burger en zijn staat* [The citizen and his state], Leuven, Davidfonds, 1998, 45.

39 See Richard Bellamy, *Liberalism and Pluralism. Towards a Politics of Compromise*, London, Routledge, 1999, 245 p. Rawls' assumption that a consensus is more likely to emerge with regard to constitutional essentials than to social and economical issues is not realistic, Bellamy holds. For some, social and economical rights are as essential as individual liberty rights. There is little hope that a large majority can be found willing to exclude the question of private property and the means of production from the political agenda.

40 Social and economical rights are the objects of Rawls' second principle of justice, but they are not part of the basic rights that are the object of the first principle and are dealt with at the level of the constitutional convention. Rawls would therefore certainly disapprove of the Chapter on *Solidarity* in the Charter.

41 *A Theory of Justice*, para. 31.

42 Richard Bellamy, *Liberalism and Pluralism. Towards a Politics of Compromise*, London, Routledge, 1999, 245 p. Bellamy sees a 'process of immunization of societal issues' at work by giving these issues the status of human rights. The second part of his work contains an alternative for the traditional Western model based on separation of powers and a bill of rights. The first part contains a critique of Rawls. It is our contention that Rawls, especially the young Rawls, was much closer to Bellamy, than is shown by the analysis of Bellamy.

43 Bellamy discusses the problem of conflicting liberties such as freedom of expression and privacy and sees no solution for it within Rawls' analysis.

44 See our discussion of a modus vivendi, above.

45 Compare with Jeremy Waldron, *The Dignity of Legislation*, Cambridge, Cambridge University Press, 1999, 206 p. This author shows that the democratic principle of the majority-decision is more than a technical device. It is an efficient and respectful decision-procedure that treats individuals with equal respect and takes seriously the reality of their differences of opinion about justice and the common-good. Majority-decision does not require anyone's view to be played down or hushed up because of the *fancied importance of consensus* (p. 158).

46 Cf., 'Thessaloniki European Council 19 and 20 June 2003 Presidency conclusions' via <http://europa.eu.int/rapid>.

Globalization and Global Governance: A Conceptual Analysis

Roland Pierik*

1. Introduction

The concept of globalization, pre-eminently the buzzword of our days, is as much popular as intangible. Not only the concept itself is confusing, also the literature on globalization contributes to the mystification of the idea. For one thing, it is sometimes unclear whether the term is used in a descriptive sense – something that actually happens – or in a normative sense – something that should (not!) happen. Moreover, one could ask whether globalization is a recent phenomenon, or whether it already began with the dawn of history. It is impossible to point to a single moment in time when 'globalization' started. Instead, as James Foreman-Peck argues, the 'globalizing tendencies have lineages stretching far into the mists of time' (1998: xiii). He describes two preceding developments for globalization: the discovery of other oversee continents and the emergence of international trade – which began in the fifth century AD (1998: xiv). These events are very much related to economic activities, and one could therefore conclude that globalization has something to do with international trade. If so, globalization is not a recent phenomenon. However, although international trade is indeed an important forerunner of globalization, the two cannot be equated. Before the Second World War, there was much international trade and international diplomacy but it is something different from globalization as we interpret the term today. National States were preeminently the loci of political power and the dominant actors on the international stage. International relations were seen in terms of the diplomatic and military interactions between States, which were seen as the only truly transnational actors. Of course, there were internationally operating corporations, but these were firmly embedded in the State in which they were headquarted. Therefore the essence of globalization is not situated in the rising international trade. Instead, it is situated in the transition of the focus on national States to a more international orientation, the rise of a 'global consciousness'.

The final source of confusion I want to mention here is that globalization is not a specific *object*, instead, it is a *process*. Or more precisely, globalization is a set of accumulating processes, resulting from and generating a dialectical whole of political, economic, technological, and cultural changes. To concentrate the discussion, I define globalization as a multidimensional phenomenon that embodies a shift in organization of human activity and the deployment of power from a local and national orientation

* Assistant professor in political theory, Faculty of Law, Tilburg University, the Netherlands <r.pierik@uvt.nl>.

towards global patterns, a rising interconnectedness on a global sphere, and a rising awareness of this interconnectedness. (Cf., Held 1999: 7; 2000: 398; Waters 1995: 3).

This paper focuses on the effects of globalization of political and legal systems. In section 2 I shall argue that the shift in organization of human activity takes different forms and follows different routes in different social domains, by describing the effects of globalization for the market, civil society and the political system. These separate descriptions are brought together again in section 3, when I describe the political effects of globalization in terms of the shift from government to global governance. Section 4 wraps up the argument and presents some afterthoughts.

2. Three domains of globalization

In the last section I described globalization as a shift in organization of human activity. In this section I will shortly describe this shift in the three dominant domains of society: the market, government and civil society. How have processes of globalization affected these social domains?

Globalization of markets and the production of goods and services

As argued above, international trade is as old as the hills. The new element of globalization for the economy is the shift from international trade between primarily nation-based corporations to a more internationally organized trade. Especially after the Second World War, the world economy became more and more integrated, dominated by corporate networks and their financial relationships. The whole of national markets, connected though separate, has transformed into one single market, operating on a global scale. The global economy is more open, fluid, volatile, and less controllable for national governments. Capital and stock markets have become cosmopolitan markets: financial and stock markets ignore national borders and are largely operated by electronic devices, which allows trade 24 hours a day.

Moreover, companies operating on the international market have increasingly lost their national bonds and have become 'Stateless' multinational corporations. These 'multinationals' possess sizable economic interests outside the country in which they are (originally) based, through ownership, control, participation or other means. Some MNEs were created by international mergers between former national icons such as DaimlerChrysler and AKZO Nobel. Global brand names and world-wide companies have become increasingly important. Consumers develop a universal taste since goods are promoted internationally via global advertisement campaigns for goods such as clothing, footwear, and food. Technical developments in the ICT-sector have made a global task-specific division possible. Keeping account of transactions such as frequent flyer points and credit-card transactions, and the actual 'manual programming' of software is done in those countries with educated but cheap labor such as India and Ireland. To put it briefly, the consumers market, production processes, and the division of labor has shifted from a local to a global scale. This has resulted in a social convergence on global scale and larger similarities between markets and industries in separate countries.

Globalization of the civil society

Civil society is understood as the arena of organized activity between, on the one hand, the private sphere and family life and, on the other hand, formal political and commercial institutions. This is the whole of civil self-organization in non-governmental organizations (NGOs). The term 'NGO' is an all-embracing concept: everything from a neighborhood organization concerned with the organization of child care through an organization operating globally, such as Oxfam or Amnesty International, are equally labeled 'NGO'. In this paper I concentrate on the larger and more formally organized NGOs. NGOs appeal to values that are shared within the organization and membership of the organization is voluntary. NGOs can concentrate on several goals. Some NGOs provide services and goods, more or less similar to those provided by national governments. For example, the Red Cross provides medical service in places where government is unable (or unwilling) to provide them. Other NGOs such as Greenpeace and Amnesty International concentrate on influencing public debates about specific public goods.

How did NGOs get involved in the process of globalization? Laura MacDonald describes a cumulative development of NGOs that can be interpreted as a development into globalization (1997: 8-13). Her typology is especially designed to describe developmental organizations, but the general thrust applies to NGOs in general. In the first stage, NGOs focused on providing direct action in actual problematic situations. The origin of NGOs is usually civil self-organization, generated by an acute problem and the wish to provide a solution for that problem. In the case of development co-operation, many NGOs important today, such as OXFAM and CARE, were formed in the post-Second World War period to provide material relief, address short-term needs, and assist the reconstruction of Europe. Subsequently they shifted their activities to emergencies in other parts of the world. In the second stage – dominant in the 1960 and 1970s – these acute help activities were supplemented with small-scale community development. NGOs experienced that short-time support in emergencies did not generate long-lasting effects, and therefore did not fundamentally diminish poverty. Therefore they expanded their activities with strategies of institutional change. In the early days, development co-operation was primarily seen as a technical problem, to be solved through a combination of technical skills and financial resources. Over time, they gradually became integrated into the efforts of official development strategies. The third stage emerges from the frustration of NGOs by their inability to attack the root causes of problems in society by help on the spot, since the success of their efforts was frequently undermined by broader national and international forces. The 'third generation' approach is directed more towards attempts to change national politics in favor of their aim. Here we see a development of the interpretation of their role by NGOs from direct on the spot-support to more emphasis on policy influence. In a fourth stage, NGOs not only seek to influence national policies, but also to participate in the international debate. Since more and more problems go beyond the national level, especially (large) international non-governmental organizations (INGOs) not only participate in national debates but also in the international debates, for example in international organizations such as the United Nations and the World Trade Organization.

To conclude, the activities of (I)NGOs have developed gradually from *ad hoc* help on the spot via initiating institutional changes to influencing policy on a national and later on an international level. Other INGOs that have always focused on the influencing of policy, such as Greenpeace and Amnesty International, also have shifted their sphere of activity from a national to an international level. So the civil society, here conceptualized as NGOs, also globalized. INGOs understood that, to achieve their goals effectively, it is necessary to make use of globalized strategies.

Globalization of the political system

During the 20th century, there have been several trends towards more international co-operation between national political systems, especially as a reaction to the horrors of Second World War. Governments sought co-operation to counteract causes for possible new wars. The European Union and its predecessors and NATO are clear examples of such co-operation. The foundation of the United Nations, after the Second World War, was at first a shared attempt to avoid war, later this goal was supplemented with the aim to define and defend universal human rights. More in general, after the Second World War national governments have been confronted with problems with increasingly global dimensions. Examples of problems with trans-boundary dimensions are environmental pollution, international migration, and, as mentioned above, the globalization of the market and the internationalization of corporations. MNEs have become Stateless corporations, and governments are no longer assured of the loyalty of their originally 'national companies' – Royal *Dutch* Shell, *British* Petroleum, etc. Instead, States have to compete with one another, and to concentrate on their national comparative advantage to attract foreign direct investment (FDI) from multinational enterprises within their State borders.

This internationalization of the market and societal and environmental problems has limited the competence, mandate and authority of national States. This can be recognized in connected consequences, for example, the decreasing importance of State borders, national self-determination and State sovereignty and the increasing permeability of national legal and political orders. Globalized social and political problems have forced national governments to change their role, however, they did not made them obsolete by default. Leo Panitch argues that 'today's globalization is authored by States and is primarily about reorganizing rather than bypassing them" (1996: 84-86). Meyer, et al., claim that 'globalization certainly poses new problems for States, but it also strengthens the world cultural principle that nation-States are the primary actors charged with identifying and managing those problems on behalf of their societies' (1997: 157).

Three domains of globalization: a conclusion

I have described the processes of globalization for the three elements within society: market, government and civil society, and argued that these domains had their own path into globalization. Although they can be described separately, it is also clear that these diverse globalization processes did not evolve isolated from one another. For example, the globalization of the market required governments to join forces, while the shift of societal problems and political debates from a national to a global level forced INGOs also to change their strategy.

The arguments in this section confirm the assertions made in section 1. There is no clear starting point for globalization. Instead, the process of globalization – and the public awareness thereof – developed gradually, especially in the post-second World War years. Moreover, it is argued that globalization is not one single process – we can distinguish different globalization-paths for different sectors in national States that have initiated and influenced one another. In the next section I will focus on the new balance of political power in this new globalized constellation.

3. From government to global governance

In pre-globalized times, political and legal analysis was dominated by a State-centric-paradigm, organized in the Westphalian order. This position is clearly recognizable in the 'realist' approach that has dominated the discipline of international relations for a long time. Their assumptions can – oversimplified – be summarized as follows: The land of the world is divided up into clearly demarcated territories, each territory has one single sovereign government and each government is recognized by other governments as having full jurisdiction over all persons and resources within its domain. Therefore, States are seen as sovereign over their citizens and corporations. Only States were seen as truly trans-national actors, and the world was seen as a whole of self-contained and sovereign States with only some links – as States – to other States.

This (fiction of) national sovereignty is now evidently undermined. National sovereignty is decreased by the emerging co-operation of national governments in supranational organizations, since entering these organizations implies transferring discretionary political power to these supranational organizations. Moreover, due to the emerging importance of INGOs and MNEs, the balance of power and the meaning of the concept of political power has changed dramatically. We could characterize this change in terms of the shift from *government to global governance*. These processes have limited the competence, mandate and authority of national States – *the decline of government* – whereas other institutions, such as international and supranational organizations, INGOs and MNEs have filled this power vacuum – *the emergence of global governance*. Where traditional understanding of international politics could be summarized as a *Politics Among Nations*, in our post-Westphalian days, political power has shifted from national governments to the interplay of different actors: local and national governments, international and supranational organizations, INGOs, and MNEs. Global governance can be described as:

> 'The sum of many ways [...] institutions, public and private, manage their common affairs. It is a continuing process through which conflicting or diverse interests may be accommodated and co-operative action may be taken. It includes formal institutions and regimes empowered to enforce compliance, as well as informal arrangements that people and institutions either have agreed to or perceive to be their interest'. (Governance 1995: 2).

This shift from government to global governance has consequences for political and juridical analysis. I will shortly describe three of them.

The shift in political debates from emphasis on actors to issues

The shift from government to global governance marks a shift in politics from emphasis on actors in the political process (especially national governments in the realist's approach) to fluid processes of debating and decision-making about specific issues. We have seen that as a result of globalization, the international debate has changed from a debate between diverse national governments to a fragmented debate between several actors. Dependent on the subject in question, different actors participate. The debate on child labor has different participants than the debate on global warming.

Moreover, the location of the debate is fragmented. We can see a shift of the arena of political debates from only national parliaments to an amalgam of places: supranational organizations and their conferences (for example the UN), the media (for example in the case of the *Brent Spar* affair), boardrooms of MNEs (where the contents of corporate codes were discussed with INGOs), etc. Of course, national parliaments remain an important location, amongst the others. Governments shift from a unitary into a plural sense: they participate in local, regional and national appearance.

For this reason we should alter the perspective from which we analyze the debate. Instead of approaching the debate from the perspective of *actors*, the international debate on social and moral issues is better analyzed from the perspective of *issues*. Each of these issues has its own arena with participants, and its 'international regime', implicit or explicit principles, norms, rules, and decision-making procedures, around which actors' expectations converge in a given issue area (Krasner 1984: 2). The convergence of expectations means that its participants have similar ideas about what rules will govern their mutual participation: everyone expects to play by the same rules. Such international regimes are necessary in the anarchic world of global governance. Examples of such issues are: global warming, child labor, development co-operation, terrorism, etc. Each of these international regimes has its own (set of) actors. (I)NGOs are organized around specific issues, the United Nations has specific branches around specific topics; national governments have a ministry structure which collides often with these subjects, and international enterprise is usually attacked from one or more of these specific angles.

The shift from command to negotiation

The shift from government to global governance also marks a shift in the role national governments play. Take the example of the relation between government and the business community. In pre-globalized times, corporations were strongly nation-based and governments could prescribe who did what within their jurisdiction. Nowadays corporations still have to obey the laws of the States in which they are settled. But at the same time:

> 'It is the firm that is adding the value to the labor and materials and know-how going into the product. States are therefore competing with other States to get the value added done in their territory and not elsewhere' (Strange 1992: 7).

Corporations have an exit option: they can (threaten national governments to) shift their activities from one country to another. This has shifted the balance of power between national governments and corporations dramatically. The latter have obtained more bargaining power and can play national governments off against one another. Developments such as these have changed the role of national governments. They are still important actors in the debate, but not necessarily dominating actors. They cannot 'dictate' policy, but have to negotiate with other national governments, transnational organizations, international organizations, MNEs and INGOs. This implies a reforming of the attitude towards the role of governments:

> 'The new paradigm of government should eschew such negative or emotive sounding words such as "command", "intervention", "regulation", and replace them by words such as "empower", "steer", "cooperative", "coordination" and "systemic". Moreover, not only must governments recognize the need for a much more integrated and holistic system of organizing their responsibilities, which demands a "spider's web" rather than a "hub and spoke" relationship between the various decision taking initiatives and the core of government' (Dunning 1998: 5).

This has altered the background against which national governments, INGOs, MNEs, supranational and international organizations discuss. Sometimes national governments are, relatively, the weak party in a negotiation, for example, when a large multi-national enterprise negotiates with a poor country about possible capital expenditures. Other national governments – e.g., the United States – have so much power that they can solve some issues on their own.

The necessity of a contextual approach

Finally, the shift from government to global governance forces the academic debate to employ a more contextual approach. Due to the decreased sovereignty of national governments, well-known actors in the international debate – States, international and supranational organizations – have to regain their position. At the same time, new actors – especially INGOs and MNEs – have found opportunities to enter this arena and have drawn up their chairs to the 'global negotiating tables'. The shift of emphasis from government to governance indicates a transition of the arena in which the political process is carried out, and a shift in the role of the actors. Some policy issues – for example health care or welfare State redistribution – remain the domain of national politics because States can realize their interests directly through the unilateral application of their political power. Other policy issues cannot be resolved at the national political level and have shifted to the international arena. The solutions for these issues are sought in an international or global context. Here governments do not have a dominant position by default. Their position and power is depending on the context. In some cases, national governments are even absent in international disputes. The 'Brent-Spar controversy' in 1995 was primarily a dispute between a multinational corporation – Shell – and an INGO – Greenpeace.

4. Conclusion

Although globalization is generally seen as an economic phenomenon, in this paper I have focused on its effect on legal and political systems, and described the new political constellation in terms of the shift from national governments to global governance. This balance of power generates new academic questions, and I will conclude by focusing on two of them. Firstly, this debate has been seized by optimists who think that the promise of global governance is to provide the 'global civil society' – a transnational network of good-willed people – with new power that can fill the gap of the retreating governments to control the negative effects of economic globalization. I do not share this optimistic view. For one thing, I am not sure that there is a global civil society. Indeed, there are global policy issues – for example environmental pollution, human rights, or international co-operation – and related 'international regimes.' But these different topics are discussed quite independently and international regimes operate relatively separate. In my view, the term 'global governance' is thus best used as a conceptual device to describe this new equilibrium of power, it should not be seen as a panacea that can set aside all negative (side) effects of economic globalization (cf., Friedrichs 2003).

Secondly, multinational enterprises and international non-governmental organizations have gained significant power, a structural and systematic influence on international debates, and evident impact on people's lives. INGOs participate in public debates, organize protests, boycotts, and campaigns to raise public awareness, they seek to influence political leaders, governments and inter- and supranational organizations via lobbying activities. They also plan and implement concrete action programs, either on their own, or in collaboration with other organizations in the own branch or corporations. Also MNEs have an enormous impact on local and national communities, and sometimes have more (economic) power than national governments.

This raises questions about the legitimacy of the activities of non-State actors. Power implies responsibility, and whenever power is exercised, the issue of accountability and legitimacy is appropriately posed (Spiro 2002: 162). NGOs and MNEs often lack the forms of democratic legitimization and democratic control that are typical for the icons of accountability: liberal-democratic governments, characterized by constitutional checks on power and electoral laws and practices that ensure citizens a voice in the political process. Moreover, NGOs are often single-issue organizations, while MNEs are – by their nature – narrowly focused on making a profit. This one-sidedness of both NGOs and MNEs makes in necessary to discuss their accountability and the legitimacy of their participation in decisions about the (global) common good.

Bibliography

DUNNING, JOHN (1998) *The Changing Nature of Firms and Governments in a Knowledge-Based Globalizing Economy*. Pittsburgh: Carnegie Bosch Institute.

FOREMAN-PECK, JAMES (1998) Introduction: The Historic Foundations of Globalization. In *The Historic Foundations of Globalization*, edited by J. Foreman-Peck. Cheltenham: Edward Edgar.

FRIEDRICHS, JÖRG (2003) The Neomedieval Renaissance: Global Governance and International Law in the New Middle Ages. In *Governance and International Legal Theory*, edited by I. Dekker and W. Werner. Dordrecht: Kluwer.

HELD, DAVID (1999) *Globalization*. London: The Foreign Policy Centre.

— (2000) Regulating Globalization? The Reinvention of Politics. *International Sociology* 15 (2): 394-408.

KRASNER, S.D. (1984) Structural Causes and Regime Consequences: Regimes as Intervening Variables. In *International Regimes*, edited by S. D. Krasner. Ithaca: Cornell University Press.

MACDONALD, LAURA (1997) *Supporting Civil Society. The Political Role of Non-Governmental Organizations in Central America*. Basingstoke [etc,]: Macmillan.

MEYER, JOHN W, JOHN BOLI, GEORGE M. THOMAS, AND FRANCISCO O. RAMIREZ (1997) World Society and the Nation-State. *American Journal of Sociology* 103 (1): 144-181.

PANITCH, LEO (1996) Rethinking the Role of the State. In *Globalization: Critical Reflections*, edited by J. H. Mittelman. Boulder: Lynne Rienner Publishers.

SPIRO, PETER, J. (2002) Accounting for NGO's. *Chicago Journal of International Law* 3: 161-169.

STRANGE, SUSAN (1992) States, Firms and Diplomacy. *International Affairs* 68 (1): 1-15.

THE UN COMMISSION ON GLOBAL GOVERNANCE, (1995) Our Global Neighbourhood. The Report of the Commission on Global Governance. New York: Oxford University Press.

WATERS, MALCOLM (1995) *Globalization*. London and New York: Routledge.

ANYTHING NEW UNDER THE SUN?
THE POLITICAL STRUGGLE BEHIND THE LEGAL DEBATE ON INTERNATIONAL TERRORISM

Jörg Friedrichs* and Raphael Muturi**

Who shall have the power to define terrorism, and who shall distinguish it from other forms of political violence? To answer these questions is an eminently political task. Experience has shown that as long as there is no political consensus among States on these issues, it does not help very much to vest the problem in a legal cloak. At the surface, the definition of terrorism may be a matter of debate among experts in legal bodies like the Sixth Committee of the UN General Assembly, the International Law Commission, or the International Law Association. But when one looks behind the technicalities of such legal debates, it immediately becomes clear that the problem is at the centre of a political maelstrom. In the present paper we examine the political struggles that are behind the legal debate on international terrorism.

It is often presumed that September 11th has completely changed the world. But this is at best a half-truth. Take as an example the two UN debates on international terrorism in the 1970s and in the 2000s. Given that terrorism is now so different from what it used to be, one would probably expect these two debates to be very different as well. At first glance, however, the ongoing UN debate on international terrorism seems to reproduce the same cleavages that were already apparent in the 1970s. But then, on closer inspection, it turns out that not only international terrorism *per se* but also the debate surrounding it has indeed changed very much over the last thirty years. Despite the occasional repetition of some familiar arguments, the main cleavages from the 1970s are now obsolete. Instead, new points of contention loom on the horizon.

On the basis of a comparison between the two debates (1970s v. 2000s), it will be possible to better understand what is new about the present debate and what is not. We start with a general overview of legislative efforts undertaken by the UN against international terrorism. Then we give an outline of the two debates, which are understood as political struggles aiming at a common understanding of the problem.[1] This allows us, in the ensuing section, to assess the similarities and differences between the debates. Having enucleated the political backdrop of the two legal debates, which has changed very much from the 1970s to the 2000s, the paper ends with a daredevil attempt to formulate some policy suggestions. The latter are directed primarily to the

* Jörg Friedrichs is working at the International University Bremen, School of Humanities and Social Science, in a research center about the transformation of statehood <j.friedrichs@iu-bremen.de>.

** Raphael Muturi is a student at the International University Bremen <r.muturi@iu-bremen.de>.

European delegations in the Ad Hoc Committee and in the Working Group on international terrorism of the Sixth Committee of the UN General Assembly.

The UN and International Terrorism

In 1972, the quest to reach a common understanding on international terrorism took centre stage at the United Nations, namely in the Sixth Committee of the General Assembly. It soon became apparent that due to political disagreement no consensus could be reached. During the 1980s and 1990s the quest for a comprehensive convention on terrorism was therefore left aside. Instead a more pragmatic approach held sway. This pragmatic approach has led to the piecemeal construction of more than a dozen conventions against particular manifestations of international terrorism (Bassiouni 2001). It should be appreciated that a legal *acquis* about international terrorism is slowly maturing. Nevertheless, in the absence of an overarching legal framework these conventions do not coagulate into a coherent whole. While affording some help in dealing with international terrorism, they do not insure against the threat of new violence towards new innocent victims. It is thus that around the millennium's turn the issue of a comprehensive convention and the quest for a common understanding of international terrorism has returned onto the agenda of the UN.

In international as well as in domestic politics, combat on terrorism tends to follow the politics of the latest outrage. Conventions are mostly discussed and eventually agreed upon after major events. This pattern can be detected from the very first and inconclusive attempt to set up a comprehensive convention on international terrorism. That attempt was undertaken by the League of Nations between 1934 and 1937, after the assassination of the Yugoslav king Alexander and the French foreign minister Barthou (Dubin 1991). The same pattern could again be observed in 1972. After a series of terrorist attacks, most notably on the Olympic village in Munich, a comprehensive convention on international terrorism became a topic on the UN agenda. Eventually, the debate ended in a failure. Another round is now going on at millennium's turn. It had a difficult start in 2000. But although there has been some progress after September 11th, up until now no final agreement has been reached on a comprehensive anti-terrorist convention.

On the other hand, there are by now more than a dozen UN conventions against particular manifestations of terrorism such as skyjacking, assaults on diplomats, the taking of hostages, etc. Despite the obvious utility of these instruments, they do not lead significantly closer to a shared understanding of international terrorism. Normally the word terrorism is not even used, let alone defined, in these instruments. This is unfortunate since the lack of consensus about the political and legal boundaries of the phenomenon can undermine international coalitions. The predetermined breaking point for anti-terrorist coalitions is disagreement about the scope of the phenomenon itself. This was true in the 1970s when States like Algeria, Libya and Syria struggled to exempt national liberation movements from the definition of terrorism, and it is still true after the terrorist attacks on the World Trade Centre on September 11th 2001. All over these years, there has been a profound disagreement whether international terrorism covers activities by national liberation movements on the one hand, and certain acts of State-committed and State-sponsored political violence on the other.

THE FIRST DEBATE (1972-1979)

As has been already mentioned, in 1972 the world was outraged by the terrorist attacks on the Olympic village in Munich. Immediately after this event, the USA submitted to the General Assembly a draft *Convention for the Prevention and Punishment of Certain Acts of International Terrorism.*[2] The US draft was not intended to be a comprehensive convention on terrorism. It was explicitly and deliberately limited to certain acts of international terrorism and did not suggest any legal definition of the phenomenon. Nevertheless, the US initiative faced stout opposition from the Non-Aligned Group, spearheaded by Algeria. Many Arab and African countries argued that it was appropriate first to discuss the root causes of terrorism before suggesting repressive measures. Moreover, the non-aligned countries suspected that the US draft was intended to outlaw national liberation movements, whereas they perceived State terrorism as the most harmful and deadly form of terrorism. These allegations were not justified if one considers the letter of the US draft, which took a relatively moderate and pragmatic stance. But whether justified or not, the fierce opposition of the non-aligned phalanx ultimately scuttled the US draft in the General Assembly.

Conversely the General Assembly adopted, on instigation by Algeria and other States of the Non-Aligned Group (and against the votes of the USA), a resolution to establish an Ad Hoc Committee on international terrorism.[3] Despite the affinity of this committee with the requests of the non-aligned States, the USA and many other Western countries nevertheless engaged in the deliberations. As could have been expected, the main problem in the Committee was to find a common understanding of international terrorism. At its first round of meetings in 1973, the Ad Hoc Committee did not reach any substantive consensus and could only re-state 'the diversity of existing views on the various aspects of the subject submitted for consideration'.[4] Although the Ad Hoc Committee was twice reconvened in 1977 and 1979, it finally had to be suspended without any tangible results due to a blatant lack of political consensus (cf., Franck and Lockwood 1974; Dugard 1974, 1982; Levitt 1986; Murphy 1975, 1989).[5]

Disagreement among the States represented in the Committee started with the apparently innocuous question if and when concrete measures should be taken against international terrorism. The non-aligned States held that first it was necessary to study the underlying causes of terrorism, and only after understanding the legitimate reasons behind the grievances raised by international terrorists would it make sense to take concrete steps. In this spirit, the Algerian delegation not only pinpointed certain root causes of international terrorism, but also implicitly made the argument for justified terrorism. 'Violence becomes terrorism', as it were, 'when situations which lead to violence are exacerbated'.[6] Accordingly, terrorism was considered as the inevitable consequence of fundamental freedoms being violated, and therefore a cause for sympathy rather than retribution. Against that argument, the USA and other Western States repeatedly protested that in their domestic legislation States did not wait either for the underlying causes of crime to be identified before enacting penal laws.[7]

Another bone of contention was whether international terrorism had to be condemned regardless of motive, or whether certain causes such as national emancipation struggles could justify the political use of violent means. Again on behalf of the Non-Aligned Group, the Algerian delegation was very outspoken on that point: a distinction should be made between 'heinous terrorism' and 'terrorism that was political in origin and purpose'.[8] The Western response to this was somewhat ambiguous. On the one hand most delegations recognized the legitimate claims of liberation movements. On the other hand they insisted that the end could not justify the means, i.e., that violence against innocent people could not be condoned under any circumstances.[9]

Finally, the non-aligned group was adamant on the inclusion of State terrorism under the Committee's mandate. Acts of violence by colonial, racist and alien regimes, they maintained, constituted 'the cruelest and most pernicious form' of international terrorism, and therefore were of the highest priority during any deliberations on that issue.[10] Against this, Western States insisted that there already existed appropriate provisions in international law to restrain State violence, as for example the convention against genocide. While rejecting the inclusion of State-perpetrated terrorism, however, some Western States paradoxically supported the inclusion of State-supported terrorism into the perimeter of the convention.

THE SECOND DEBATE (2000-2003)

The debate of the 1970s was the last attempt to reach a comprehensive convention on international terrorism for many years to come. Only in December 1996 did the General Assembly again establish an Ad Hoc Committee on international terrorism.[11] The Committee, which is supported by a Working Group, has the mandate to draft appropriate instruments against international terrorism. The Ad Hoc Committee and the Working Group are meeting once a year in spring and fall, respectively. Late in 1999, the General Assembly called upon the Ad Hoc Committee and the Working Group to deal with a comprehensive convention on international terrorism.[12] Since 2000, discussions are indeed taking place on the basis of a draft comprehensive convention submitted by India.[13] Article 2 of the draft in its present version contains a definition of international terrorism. According to this definition, serious offences against persons or heavy damage to private or public property qualify as offences within the meaning of the convention 'when the purpose of the conduct, by its nature or context, is to intimidate a population, or to compel a Government or an international organization to do or abstain from doing any act'.[14] Presumably to avoid controversies, the word terrorism is used explicitly only in the title and in the preamble of the draft.

At the beginning, the bargaining positions were very similar to those of the 1970s. Thus, many States of the Third World insisted that terrorism be clearly defined and distinguished from acts of legitimate self-defence.[15] Most notably, the 56 members of the Organization of the Islamic Conference (OIC) demanded the exemption of national liberation movements from the perimeter of the convention.[16] 'People's struggle including armed struggle against foreign occupation, aggression, colonialism, and hegemony, aimed at liberation and self-determination in accordance with the principles of international law shall not be considered a terrorist crime'.[17]

However, despite the apparent similarity with the arguments raised in the 1970s, at a closer look it turns out that there is a significant departure from the traditional view of Arab States that State terrorism is the most harmful and deadly form of terrorism and therefore falls into the perimeter of a comprehensive convention on international terrorism. Of course this view was initially brought to the negotiation table and is still being reiterated in certain contexts, especially with hindsight to Israel.[18] But the exclusion of State terrorism has now become negotiable under the condition that political violence by liberation movements be exempted as well. Specifically, draft Article 18 asserts that *all* parties during an armed conflict, and not just the armed forces of a State, are to be exempt from the provisions of the convention, 'including in situations of foreign occupation'.[19] Thus for the members of the Islamic Group, maintaining the distinction between freedom fighters and terrorists is a strategic objective that now supersedes earlier efforts at de-legitimising State-perpetrated acts of political violence.

A similar development can be observed for the traditional claim that before taking specific measures against international terrorism it is necessary to study the underlying causes. While an OIC resolution from 2000, in re-affirming 'the need for specific and agreed-upon international criteria, to enable the international community to differentiate clearly between terrorism and people's struggles for national liberation' still alluded to the underlying cause argument, this does not any longer seem to pose any serious obstacle to the conclusion of a convention on international terrorism.[20]

All in all, the discussions in the Ad Hoc Committee and in the Working Group illustrate once more how difficult it is to agree on the conceptual boundaries of terrorism, let alone to reach a legal definition. In the first weeks after September 11th a breakthrough seemed in sight. But the attempt to reach a comprehensive convention was once more thwarted by the opposition of certain States of the Third World (Wiesbrock 2002). In January 2002, the OIC Group rejected a proposal to exempt the activities of armed forces during an armed conflict. According to the OIC Group, the exemption should be expanded to *all* parties during an armed conflict, including national liberation movements.[21] The discussions are still going on, and according to the reports issued over the last three years some substantial progress has been made.[22]

CHANGE AND CONTINUITIES

Cynics stick with great relish to the cliché that *your* terrorist may be *my* freedom fighter. And indeed, if one looks at the debate about international terrorism held in the 1970s, this does not seem to be far off the mark. Indeed, States tended to favour those concepts of terrorism that subsumed their political enemies, while opposing concepts that might have labelled their political friends as terrorists. Since it was impossible to reach an agreement on these and similar issues, the international community had to limit itself to conventions against particular manifestations of terrorism. The word terrorism normally does not appear in the main text of these conventions, although it is sometimes used in the title and preamble. In none of these conventions is there any explicit attempt to define terrorism. The focus is on specific criminal acts, and the intent of the perpetrators is set aside. Thereby it is possible to avoid political conflict over basic definitional principles, permitting textual agreement to be reached. New categories of conduct are always subject to coverage in subsequent instruments. Although the crux of reaching a legal definition of terrorism is deliberately left aside, it must be appreciated that the 'piecemeal' approach is slowly contributing to the emergence of a common understanding of terrorism by way of induction.

Since 2000, there is another attempt to reach a comprehensive convention on international terrorism. It seems that the positions are much less erratic now than they were in the 1970s. Despite the inconclusive attempt to reach a comprehensive convention in the immediate aftermath of September 11th, it should be appreciated that the

OIC Group is less adamant on State terrorism now than was the Non-Aligned Group in the 1970s. Whereas the latter had categorically demanded the inclusion of State terrorism into the perimeter of the convention, the OIC Group has come to accept its exemption under Article 18 of the draft. Moreover, the members of the OIC Group do not make a comprehensive convention any longer conditional on a study of the underlying causes of international terrorism. However, they are adamant on the exemption, under Article 18, of *all* parties during an armed conflict, including in situations of foreign occupation. This seems to be the last substantive obstacle to a legal definition of international terrorism under Article 2 and thereby to the conclusion of a comprehensive convention on international terrorism.[23]

Apart from the gradual emergence of an anti-terrorist legal *acquis*, there is another important difference between the two UN debates. This difference concerns political power and the ideological climate. In the 1970s, the Western States played the role of status quo powers challenged by the Third World, with the Communist Bloc somewhere in between (Blishchenko and Zhdanov 1984: 208-231). It was in the perceived interest of many Third World regimes that liberation movements used violence against the status quo powers. Therefore they demanded the exemption of liberation movements from the perimeter of a comprehensive convention on terrorism, and called for the inclusion of State terrorism into the definition of the phenomenon; in any event, they asked for analysing the causes of terror prior to taking measures against it. Unsurprisingly the status quo powers could not accommodate these claims, and the comprehensive convention on international terrorism failed.

In the 1990s and 2000s, by contrast, the situation is different. There is still a broad field of mostly European and Eurasian status quo powers, but the Third World movement is virtually dead. Especially the Arab and Muslim States fear a worsening of their position at the regional and at the international stage. Accordingly, their demands have become significantly more moderate. As we have seen, they have come to accept the exemption of State terrorism from the perimeter of the convention, and they have dropped their demand for analysing the causes of terrorism prior to taking measures against it; however, they still do ask for the exemption under Article 18 of *all* parties during an armed conflict, 'including in situations of foreign occupation'.

The obvious crux is that the United States do not seem to be a status quo power any more. Together with a small number of other States they have created a *fait accompli* in the Gulf Region. Or, in other words, they have created a situation of foreign occupation, and they may even become party to an armed conflict. It is difficult to imagine that they will preclude themselves the possibility of branding their opponents in such a conflict as terrorists. Moreover, combat on terrorism may play an important 'positive' role in a political project where it is important to determine on a case-by-case basis who is a terrorist and who is not. So how could the USA agree to an exemption of *all* parties to an armed conflict, *including in situations of foreign occupation*? In other words, the United States probably would have to become a status quo power again for the comprehensive convention on international terrorism to become a success.

Global governance or realism redux?

It turns out that, despite the obvious similarities between the two debates, there are important differences as well. These differences have to do with the different legal and political context within which either debate was taking place. Let us now place these findings within a broader conceptual framework. One of the authors of this paper is also writing on such lofty issues as 'global governance'. Although this author would insist that global governance is still a valid analytical tool in many other issue areas, it must be admitted that combat against terrorism does not seem to be within the conceptual reach of global governance. Quite to the contrary, combat on terrorism seems to be a threat to the liberal principles enshrined in the very idea of global governance. As is often the case, different theoretical approaches seem to be appropriate in different empirical domains. Concerning terrorism, political realism seems to fare much better than global governance as a framework for analyzing the issue at hand.

Although this may not be a pleasant view, the superior explanatory power of realism can be nicely exemplified by adopting the hyper-realist stance taken by the (in)famous Carl Schmitt (1922, 1932). According to Schmitt, politics is primarily about fighting the public enemy. In such an optic, the person or institution that is able to control the state of emergency holds the ultimate sovereign power. Of course this is not to deny that in the state of normalcy, i.e., most of the time, politics is broadly in line with the civilizing process which de-legitimizes the use of violence from below (Elias 1939). But there is another side to the same coin: Real or perceived challenges to the civilizing process must be constantly suppressed from above. In the final analysis, this is what combat on terrorism seems to be all about.

At present, the USA seems to be in the convenient position to define on a case-by-case basis who the public enemy (read: terrorist) happens to be. It therefore comes hardly as a surprise that, as far as can be seen from the UN documents, the United States is not actively participating in the debates of the Ad Hoc Committee and the Working Group.[24] It simply would limit too much their freedom of action if there was a comprehensive convention on international terrorism stating who is a terrorist and who is not. From the standpoint of the powerful, *omnis definitio in iure periculosa.*

From the standpoint of the less powerful it is quite the contrary. A reasonably clear definition of terrorism would work as an assurance against the tendency of the hegemonic power to define at its own discretion who is a terrorist and who is not. In this context, it is somewhat surprising that the European States and Russia are keeping a relatively low profile in the discussions about a comprehensive convention on terrorism. Maybe this is still due to the experience of the 1970s, when it was rather unpleasant for a Western State to participate in these debates. But the situation has changed, and it might be a gross political mistake to leave the issue to the Arab States.

It is now in the common interest of the Arab States and other status quo powers alike to agree on a binding legal definition of terrorism. The current position of the OIC Group should be acceptable to all those interested in the maintenance of the status quo, especially in Western Europe but possibly also in Eastern Europe, Russia, India and China. At least as far as Western Europe is concerned, national liberation movements have ceased to be an important matter of concern many years ago. The times of colonialism and the Cold War are over, and the Palestinians have ceased to rely on international terrorism. Where liberation movements are still in vigour they should be dealt with in legal frameworks other than terrorism, such as the humanitarian law of conflict. The policy of the hegemonic power defining on a case-by-case basis who the public enemy is and thereby creating a perpetual *Ausnahmezustand* is hardly tolerable to the status quo States. Therefore it is important that a definition of international terrorism shall make sure that, in order to qualify as an international terrorist, one has to be the enemy of all civilized States and not just the enemy of one particular State.

Notes

1 Unless stated otherwise, all primary sources are quoted according to the UN Documentation System.

2 A/C.6/L.850: Draft convention, 25 September 1972.

3 A/RES/3034: GA resolution, 18 December 1972.

4 A/9028: Report of the Ad Hoc Committee, 1973.

5 A/32/37: Report of the Ad Hoc Committee, 28 April 1977; A/34/37: Report of the Ad Hoc Committee, 17 April 1979; A/AC.160/SR.11-19: Ad Hoc Committee, summary records of the meetings, 1979.

6 A/9028: Report of the Ad Hoc Committee, 1973, annex 7b.

7 A/C.6/SR.1355-1374: Verbatim records from the Sixth Committee, November 1972.

8 A/32/37: Report of the Ad Hoc Committee, 1977, p. 14.

9 A/AC.160/1; A/AC.160/1/Add.1: Observations of States submitted in accordance with A/RES/3034, 16 May 1973 and 12 June 1973; A/AC.160/2: Analytical study by the Secretary-General on the basis of that material, 22 June 1973.

10 A/32/37: Report of the Ad Hoc Committee, 1977, p. 14.

11 A/RES/51/210: GA Resolution, 16 January 1997. The ongoing debate is an exception from the rule that debates on terrorism follow major events. Apparently the return of the issue on the agenda of the Sixth Committee was provoked by discussions about whether or not to include terrorism into the mandate of the ICC.

12 A/RES/54/110: GA Resolution, 2 February 2000.

13 A/C.6/55/1: Draft convention, 28 August 2000, which is a revised version of A/C.6/51/6: Draft convention, 11 November 1996.

14 A/57/37: Report of the Ad Hoc Committee, 11 February 2002, p. 6.

15 GA/L/3008: Press release, 4 October 1996.

16 In June 2000, the OIC had launched Res. No. 64/27-P 'On the Convening of an International Conference under the auspices of the U.N. to Define Terrorism and Distinguish it from Peoples' Struggle for National Liberation'.

17 Malaysia on behalf of the OIC Group, A/C.6/55/WG.1/CRP.30, reproduced in A/C.6/55/L.2: Report of the Working Group, 19 October 2000, annex iii.

18 E.g., A/57/730-S/2003/178: Note verbale by Syria, 13 February 2003.

19 A/57/37: Report of the Ad Hoc Committee, 11 February 2002, p. 17.

20 OIC Res. No. 64/27-P (June 2000).

21 L/2993: Press release, 1 February 2002.

22 Reports of the Ad Hoc Committee A/56/37: 27 March 2001; A/57/37: 11 February 2002; A/58/37: 2 April 2003. Reports of the Working Group A/C.6/55/L.2: 19 October 2000; A/C.6/55/L.9: 29 October 2001; A/C.6/57/L.9: 16 October 2002.

23 Cf., Richard Rowe in A/C.6/57/L.9: Report of the Working Group, 16 October 2002, annex ii.

24 To the USA and to the UK, the counter-terrorism committee of the UN Security Council seems to provide a much more attractive platform (Williams, 2002).

Bibliography

BASSIOUNI, M.C. (2001) *International Terrorism: Multilateral Conventions (1937-2001)*, New York: Transnational Publishers.

BLISHCHENKO, I. AND ZHDANOV, N. (1984) *Terrorism and International Law*, Moscow: Progress Publishers.

DUBIN, M.D. (1991) *International Terrorism: Two League of Nations Conventions, 1934-1937*, Millwood (N.Y.): Kraus International Publications [microfiche, accompanied by a monograph].

DUGARD, J. (1974) 'International terrorism: problems of definition', *International Affairs* 50 (1): 67-81.

— (1982) 'International terrorism and the just war', in D.C. Rapoport and Y. Alexander (eds.) *The Morality of Terrorism: Religious and Secular Justifications*, New York: Pergamon, pp. 77-97.

ELIAS, N. (1939) *Über den Prozess der Zivilisation*, Basel: Haus zum Falken; transl. E. Jephcott (1994) *The Civilizing Process*, Oxford: Blackwell.

FRANCK, T.M. AND LOCKWOOD, B.B. (1974) 'Preliminary thoughts towards an international convention on terrorism', *American Journal of International Law* 68 (1): 69-90.

LEVITT, G. (1986) 'Is "terrorism" worth defining?', *Ohio Northern University Law Review* 13: 97-115.

MURPHY, J.F. (1975) 'United Nations proposals on the control and repression of terrorism', in M.C. Bassiouni (ed.) I*nternational Terrorism and Political Crimes*, Springfield (Ill.): Thomas, 493-506.

— (1989) 'Defining international terrorism: a way out of the quagmire', *Israel Yearbook on Human Rights* 19, The Hague: Nijhoff, 13-37.

SCHMITT, C. (1922) *Politische Theologie: Vier Kapitel zur Lehre von der Souveränität*, München and Leipzig: Duncker & Humblot; transl. G. Schwab (1986) *Political Theology: Four Chapters on the Concept of Sovereignty*, Cambridge (Mass.): MIT Press.

— (1932) *Der Begriff des Politischen*, München and Leipzig: Duncker & Humblot; transl. G. Schwab (1995) *The Concept of the Political*, Chicago: University of Chicago Press.

WIESBROCK, K. (2002) 'Wer ist Terrorist', *Vereinte Nationen* 50 (2): 72-73.

WILLIAMS, I. (2002) 'Abbringen, Verweigerung, Zusammenarbeit: Der Ausschuss des Sicherheitsrats zur Bekämpfung des Terrorismus', *Vereinte Nationen* 50 (6): 213-216.

IRRATIONAL GOVERNANCE: THE USE OF FORCE

Nicholas Tsagourias*

INTERNATIONAL GOVERNANCE OF PEACE AND SECURITY: TERRORISM AND SELF-PRESERVATION

Governance in the area of international peace and security is dominated today by two conditions: the threat or reality of terrorism in its multifaceted forms and the reaction thereto in the form of self-preservation. Terrorism is challenging the primordial function of the State which is to protect its citizens, internally and externally. When terrorists strike, the State is de-legitimised not only because it fails to provide effective protection but also because it ceases to be the sole source of legitimate violence at the domestic or the international level. Terrorism introduces alternative sources of violence which have the potential of establishing alternative sources of legitimacy thus defying the primacy of the State. Consequently, States' reactions to terrorism in the form of self-preservation reflect the seriousness of the challenge they face. States re-emphasise their monopoly on violence, even by condoning its more extreme and authoritarian forms, and recast the relation with their citizens, in particular when they demand that their citizens should sacrifice their own self-preservation to facilitate the preservation of their State. Although both terrorism and self-preservation employ and excuse the use of violence, their construction is different. Violence as an aspect of terrorism is irrational and illegitimate whereas in self-preservation it is presented as rational, protective and legitimate. We shall not deal here with the (ir)rationality of terrorism[1] but only with the (ir)rationality of violence as an essential manifestation of the concept of self-preservation.

Self-preservation alludes to the security of a State and any security discourse invokes the concept of threat. We attain security when threats have been annihilated or the capabilities exist to deal with them successfully. What is a threat is, however, circumstantial, time-specific and psychological, founded on empirical calculations or emotions. The diversity and intensity of threats as construed by the referent entity constantly reinterpret self-preservation making it idiosyncratic and elastic. However, on a more general level, self-preservation encompasses the military, political, social, economic and environmental security of the State as well as its moral standing, including its prestige and honour.

Hence, self-preservation is an adjunctive value that envelops the State in its physical or moral expression. As such it is a governing condition for the existence or exercise of all other rights and duties but also a source of rights.[2] One right that derives from self-preservation is that of self-defence. It is a reaction to the injury that a protected sphere has suffered, for example the territorial integrity of the State. If the protected sphere is enlarged, the scope of self-defence becomes broader. When the pro-

* Nicholas Tsagourias, LLM, PhD, Lecturer in Law University of Bristol.

tected sphere becomes abstract and intangible, it becomes even more difficult to legally regulate and control the exercise of any right deriving from self-preservation. In a nutshell, self-preservation is an all-inclusive attribute containing a variety of other individualised and interconnected conditions that to a large extent are specific to the particular subject and cannot be fully demarcated or defined. It is thus an elastic end-value that makes the use of violence for its fulfilment equally erratic.

In the following sections we shall examine the rationality of the use of force (war or violence used here conterminously) in international relations by employing Weber's description of rationality in his *Economy and Society*.[3] Our conclusions convey our scepticism about the viability of a rational order in this field because of the disruptive but central property of individualism in the international system as it is currently expressed in the doctrine of self-preservation.

Rationalisation of the International Governance of Peace and Security: The Regulation of Violence

Modernity is identified with reason and with the rejection of theology, metaphysics, emotion, or tradition. Modern man leads a calculable life reducing his enquiries into reasoned propositions of commensurability between facts and values. Similarly, the use of violence at the domestic or international level has not escaped the process of rationalising the means, conditions and pursued ends.

According to Weber, the rationality of modern civilisation is founded on the distinction between formal and substantive rationality. The formal rationality of a political order is based on agreed general rules underpinned by legal formalism. Legal formalism is based on the distinction between substantive and procedural law; law and fact; and, law-making or law enactment and law finding or law application.[4] These processes differentiate modern rational law from the polymorphous and polysynthetic pre-modern regulations. Modern legal norms are formal and general, describing the general characteristics of the action. As a consequence, law is predictable because it demands the application of general rules to the facts and these general rules are devoid of substantive values, emotions or randomness. This is contrasted with more traditional aspects of adjudication such as by oracle or kadi justice which are either unable to be controlled by intellect or require an individualised and separate sense of justice.[5]

The UN system of collective security corresponds to a system of formal rationality by containing general rules that are value neutral. It contains a regime where the individual use of force is prohibited and where procedures internal to the system exist to regulate the institutional use of force.[6] Thus, the UN Charter exorcises the religious or metaphysical of previous eras as well as randomness and power politics.[7] The only case where unorganised violence is condoned is in self-defence when an armed attack occurs.[8] Condensing self-defence to a preceding armed attack constitutes an important development because it signifies the denunciation of the totalitarianism inherent in the concept of self-preservation. For this reason, the Charter also avoids the term 'aggression' whose meaning is broader and imprecise as the attempts in codification reveal.[9] Thus, although self-defence derives from self-preservation, it becomes a circumscribed right. It does not redeem any injury suffered by the State – be it to its territory, nationals or prestige – but only an armed attack which is a real and substantive act rather than a mere feeling of being threatened. The formulation of self-defence in Article 51 of the UN Charter also signifies the rejection of its customary content. The concurrence between customary and Charter law has been a fraught issue with the former considered to be more permissive. The customary rule on self-defence is considered to be receptive of all ensuing changes, often mute and unconscious, and it is contrasted to the deliberate enactment of Article 51 after a process of negotiations.[10]

There is an additional benefit in using armed attack as a benchmark for self-defence. What constitutes an armed attack or when it takes place can be established through a process of examining the facts whereas this is impossible if aggression or threats become the benchmarks. Consequently, self-defence as formulated in Article 51 becomes a general proposition that applies every time an armed attack occurs, irrespective of the value or the justice of such an attack. However, and particularly after 9/11, the concept of pre-emptive self-defence has been employed to justify the use of force against potential or less immanent threats.[11] The new dogma on pre-emption justifies defensive wars against threats that have not yet materialised or against that that causes fear. Pre-emptive self-defence is integral to self-preservation because it affords protection even before any injury takes place. However, since the relation between the supposed threat and the defensive act is framed on the basis of multiple calculations including psychological or emotional ones, it is difficult to ascertain or verify the conditions under which this right is exercised or assess the intentions of the other party or the probability/possibility of future attacks.[12] As a result, the application of the law to the particular case demands an atomised sense of justice. Consequently, pre-emptive self-defence is incalculable and too individualised to create general rules.

Substantive rationality on the other hand refers to the values of the system and their consistency. The irreconcilability of the multifarious ends and values reveals its limits. What is rational from one point of view, may be irrational from the point of view of another substantive value or observer. It is not only the conflict between the different visions of self-preservation invoked by its subjects but also the conflict between the separate values contained in the concept such as individual or State survival, order, prosperity, justice. These values and ends may be antagonistic or contradictory at the individual level or at the meta-normative level considering the absence of any meta-principle to adjudicate between them. Failing to produce a consistent and general set of rules, subjective rationality remains formally irrational.

A compendium to formal rationality as described above is that of a bureaucratic administration that applies in a technocratic and neutral manner legal rules.[13] In the UN system, this role is confined to the International Court of Justice. Self-defence as we described its content above can become the object of adjudication. For instance, in the *Nicaragua* case the issue before the Court was to establish whether an armed attack had taken place that would give rise to self-defence. Since both the USA and Nicaragua were claiming that they were acting in self-defence, it was for the ICJ to establish, after examining the presented evidence, which action constituted an armed attack. Eventually, the ICJ found that only certain practices, due to their scale and effects, constitute an armed attack justifying self-defence, whereas other practices such as the provision of assistance to rebels constitute lesser uses of force and do not reach the threshold of an armed attack.[14] As a consequence, the USA could not exercise their right to self-defence since Nicaragua's actions did not reach the level of an armed attack.[15] The Court debated at length what constitutes an 'armed attack' as any judge would have done when interpreting the letter of the law under new circumstances.

Moreover, although adjudicating on the basis of customary law, the Court was apprehensive and mindful of the latter's flexible content. Thus it declared that the customary law on self-defence and Article 51 UN Charter are identical, both demanding an armed attack.[16] Its failure to examine the content of customary law as shaped by State practice has been criticised[17] but, on the other hand, it established the Court as the neutral administrator of justice not falling into the trap of politics. Any foray into identifying the content of customary law would have required judicial venturing into the uncharted waters of politics with a strong likelihood that further claims may be registered. To this effect, it is important to note that the ICJ rejected the US contention that its actions were in defence of democracy and human rights. According to the Court, intervention is impermissible irrespective of the political, economic or social development of a State.[18] Thus the Court sided with the value-neutral formal rationality of the system.[19]

Related to the rationality of modern political orders is the rationality of action. Human action can be guided by habits and emotions or be deliberate.[20] The first two imply irrationality, whereas deliberate action either as inherently worthy or commensurable is rational. In effect, all actions gear towards rationality but Weber makes the distinction between two kinds of rational action: objective and subjective.[21] Objective rationality concerns the calculability between ends and means. Subjective rationality is distinguished into *Wertrationalität* and *Zweckrationalität*. For the first, there is an inherent and intrinsic belief in the particular form and mode of action, in our instance violence in its different forms, irrespective of its consequences. Objective rationality does not apply to this type of rationality because it depends on the subjective values of the actor. It fuses the calculus between ends and means, for example in the proposition 'war for the sake of war' or when the *raison d'état* which unleashes violence becomes unmanageable leading to a vicious competition between ends and means. In such cases, the ends usually fade and the means become the end. For example, a show of force or the initiation of war in order to show resolve or power may distort the initial aims and drag onto mindless violence which may also have the opposite result if it is protracted or ends in defeat.

Moreover, if the pursued goals are abstract, multifarious or alternate then violence becomes irrational, not reduced to the objective rationality of ends to means. Self-preservation in the age of terrorism has adopted an absolute character because the terrorist is considered to be *hostis humani generis* and someone that abides by no rules, makes no distinctions, strikes randomly and threatens all the values for which the State stands for.[22] Having said that, the security dilemma that States face cannot be resolved because absolute security is just a chimera. However, by preaching absolute and total security, the State raises the stakes for violence that degenerates into total, uncontrollable and directionless violence with no end.[23] If the enemy is invisible and her means and targets equally unidentifiable, what tangible ends does the war on terrorism satisfy and when does it end? Terrorism and self-preservation engender a vicious circle of total violence where ends and means overlap and become incommensurate. In addition, the used means may provoke certain effects that may be disproportionate and compromise the validity of the specific end but also of many other values. For instance, strict controls may help in keeping potential terrorists under control but may infringe many other rights and affect the political, social and economic fabric of the particular society. Consequently, in those cases where multiple ends are pursued and where means do not measure up to ends or the consequences are not accounted for, there can be no objective rationality.

The second type of subjective rationality distinguishes between ends, means and secondary results.[24] Although still retaining its subjectivity, an objective calculus can be applied to assess their adequacy. If we apply the above categorisation to the use of force, we should begin with Clausewitz's exhortation that war is the continuation of politics (*Zweck*) with other means. What he meant is that war is a means for attaining political goals and, although politics belong to the sphere of the irrational, the politics of Weber's stable and organised system of administration, adjudication and legislation transform irrationality into objective commands performed by the servants of the system. Thus violence as means can measure up to the ends as defined by politics.[25] Such instrumental rationality has two aspects. One is to measure up means as forms of violence to the pursued political ends; the other is to measure up means as instruments to the ends. In order to do this there should be a clearly defined end to calculate the used violence. If the political goal for which violence is the means can be defined, then violence being instrumental is rational to the extent that it is adequate. For instance, if the end is to repel an armed attack, then violence for this purpose (self-defence) is rational to the extent that it is also proportional as standard international law requires and the means used satisfy the requirements of military necessity.[26] If, on the other hand, the threat is quantitatively or qualitatively different, it can justify different forms of violence or different means.[27] In such cases, the means used may be subjectively rational but not objectively, as the ICJ made clear in the *Nicaragua* case. In that case, the ICJ differentiated between actions that justify self-defence and actions that trigger lesser uses of force – in the language of the Court, countermeasures[28] – and in the *Legality of Threat or Use of Nuclear Weapons,* the ICJ also expressed concern about the effects of using nuclear weapons even in self-defence. [29]

Moreover, in international law, instrumental (means/ends) rationality also rests on the distinction between the State of peace and the State of war where means and ends are calculated accordingly, each retaining their distinct character and internal rationality. For instance, combating terrorism in time of peace or war may entail different sanctions whose instrumentality is measured accordingly. Self-preservation obscures such distinctions and the State of war enters the realm of peace. Thus, terrorists are dealt invariably with the weapons of peace and those of war because they are considered to be *hostes generis humani*. As we mentioned above, when the pursued ends are fluctuating in their totality and exert control over the means dispensing with any conceptual or practical distinctions, objective rationality does not apply.

THE GHOST OF IRRATIONALITY: STATE INDIVIDUALISM

The preceding sections described an edifice of rationality in the area of international peace and security that created a paper governance. The ghost behind the erected edifice that steadily devours the construction is that of State individualism which is at the basis of international law.[30] The relation between individualism and rationality is mutually empowering but also mutually defeating. Individualism goes together with rationality because it liberated States from the pre-modern integrated order of rules, values, beliefs and controls, contained for example in the concept of *civitas maxima*. In modernity's fragmented order, it made international rules the object of free individual choice and commitment more than given presets. Having said that, individualism makes international law and any form of organisation conditional upon State subjectivity that challenges the idea of formal and objective rationality as we described it above. Individualism is not asocial or unsocial but its intrinsic value is self-reference and self-determination. That is, the subjective assessment of circumstances and rules is superimposed upon any systemic interpretation; the specific and the individual overrules any general and macroscopic law. Although influences by the system are not discounted, they are filtered by individualism and indeed enfeebled when vital interests are at stake. The UN system is an example of a precarious balance between unfettered and circumscribed individualism when, on the one hand, it promotes State sovereignty and independence whereas, on the other, it erects an organised system that tries to contain its excesses. It is also an example of how the system implodes or falls into disrepute when States feel strongly about their interests. Our present predicament does not come as a surprise. The struggle for primacy between individualism and systematic organisation is not new. It was expressed in the professed exceptions to the UN rules on the non-use of force in the form either of reprisals, liberation wars or pre-emptive/anticipatory self-defence. All these instances were justified on the basis of the particular, the specific, the individual description and assessment of the situation and demonstrated the lack of any consensus or agreement on the underlying order. After 9/11, the retreat to the value of self-preservation has not only destroyed the weak vestiges of rationality that the UN system has provided for but made individualism even more pronounced. States that act on the grounds of self-preservation are the sole judges of whether the conditions justifying such action exist or whether the means are appropriate to achieve their aim. This represents the defining moment of individualism when the international order is seen through the eyes of its members and their needs or interests.[31] In this context, the international order does not represent an ontologically autonomous and imperative order for conditioning States' preferences but it is States' subjective appraisal of social facts that defines this order. In other words, the failure of international law to suppress the irrational is due to the fact that it is defined by the individualism of its constituents that substitute formal and objective rationality with their substantive, subjective and emotive rationality.

This condition has been candidly admitted in the *Legality of Threat or Use of Nuclear Weapons* case where the rational administrators of the law conceded that there is a legal void when issues of State survival are involved.[32] This state of affairs is the result of the unique monadism of international law gyrating around States that react with all the force of individualism when they face existential threats. It is difficult to predict what the future holds but what causes anxiety is the uncertainty as to whether the present condition signals the end of rationalism and the dawn of a new era of passion, emotions, fear, anxiety and hatred or whether the end of the 'war on terrorism' will reinstate the previous regime of formal rationality.

Notes

1 W. Reich (ed.), *Origins of Terrorism: Psychologies, Ideologies, Theologies, States of Mind,* (Washington D.C., Woodrow Wilson Centre Press, 1990).

2 An example of how self-preservation affects the content and exercise of other rights is the detention or trial conditions of the suspected terrorists held at Guantanamo Bay. *The Times* 5 July 2003; *The Guardian* 5 July 2003.

3 Max Weber, *Economy and Society,* Guenther Roth and Claus Wittich (eds.), (Berkeley, University of California Press, 1978) hereinafter refered to as Weber.

4 Weber, pp. 653-654, 809-815; R. Brubaker, *The Limits of Rationality: An Essay on the Social and Moral Thought of Max Weber,* (London, George Allen & Unwin, 1984), pp. 16-17; M. Rheinstein, *Max Weber on Law in Economy and Society,* (Cambridge Mass., Harvard University Press, 1966), pp. xlvii-lvii.

5 Weber, pp. 655-658, 1115-1117.

6 Art. 2(4) and Chapter VII of the UN Charter.

7 *The Corfu Channel case, ICJ Rep.* (1949), p. 4 at p. 35.

8 Art. 51 UN Charter.

9 GA Res. 33314 (XXIX).

10 Weber, pp. 319-321; 753-758.

11 '... we will not hesitate to act alone, if necessary, to exercise our right of self defense by acting pre-emptively against such terrorists, to prevent them from doing harm against our people and our country.' *The National Security Strategy of the United States of America* (September 2002) <www.whitehouse.gov/nsc/nss.pdf>.

12 Hugo Grotius, *De Jure Belli Ac Pacis libri tres*, trans. F.W. Kelsey, A.E.R. Boak, H.A. Sanders, J.S. Reeves and H.F. Wright, *The Classics of International Law,* (Buffalo, N.Y, W.S. Hein & Co. Inc., 1995), Bk. II, ch. I, V. According to Paul Wolfowitz, US Deputy Secretary of Defence: 'the nature of terrorism is that intelligence about terrorism is murky. I think the lesson of 9/11 is that if you are not prepared to act on the basis of murky intelligence, then you are going to have to act after the fact, and after the fact now means after horrendous things have happened to this country'. *The Times,* 28 July 2003.

13 Weber, pp. 244, 956-958, 976.

14 *Case Concerning Military and Paramilitary Activities in and against Nicaragua, ICJ Rep.* (1986), p. 14, paras. 191, 195.

15 Ibid., paras. 228-238.

16 Ibid., paras. 188, 102-106.

17 Ibid., dissenting opinions by Judges Oda, pp. 215-217; Schwebel, pp. 302-306 and Jennings pp. 530-534.

18 Ibid., paras. 258, 263, 268.

19 N. Tsagourias, 'The Nicaragua Case and the Use of Force: The Theoretical Construction of the Decision and Its Deconstruction', 1 *J. Armed Conflict Law,* (1996), p. 81.

20 Weber, pp. 24-26; Rheinstein, *supra,* p. lviii.

21 Brubaker, *supra,* pp. 49-51.

22 *The National Security Strategy of the United States of America* (September 2002) p. 6.

23 Weber, p. 26: '...the more the value to which action is oriented is elevated to the status of an absolute value, the more "irrational" in this sense the corresponding action is'.

24 Weber, p. 26.

25 V. Heiskanen, 'The rationality of the use of force and the evolution of international organisation', in J-M. Coicaud, V. Heiskanen (eds.), *The Legitimacy of International Organisations,* (Tokyo, United Nations University Press, 2001), pp. 157-166.

26 *Caroline* case 29 *BFSP* 1137-1138; *Nicaragua* case, *supra,* para. 176; *Legality of Threat or Use of Nuclear Weapons, ICJ Rep.* (1996), para. 41.

27 P. Weckel, 'L'usage déraisonnable de la force', 107 *RGDIP* (2003), p. 377.

28 *Nicaragua case, supra,* paras. 195, 201, 247-249.

29 In relation to nuclear weapons see *Nuclear Weapons* case, paras. 43, 92-95

30 According to A. Pillet 'la théorie de l'indépendance de l'état, réputée loi fondamentale du droit international public ... est l'erreur la plus grave qui ait jamais été commise dans notre domaine, et que cette erreur à elle seule est responsable de la plupart des imperfections de notre science. ... .[l]a notion de l'indépendance est entièrement subjective et par la même illimitée ... elle conduit fatalement à la négation même de tout droit entre les états aussi bien qu'entre les individus' quoted in S. Séfériadès, 'Principes généraux du droit international de la paix' 34 *RC* (1930 IV), pp. 354-355.

31 *The National Security Strategy of the United States of America* (September 2002), p. 6: 'While the United States will constantly strive to enlist the support of the international community, we will not hesitate to act alone, if necessary, to exercise our right of self defense by acting pre-emptively against such terrorists, to prevent them form doing harm against our people and our country'.

32 *Legality of Threat or Use of Nuclear Weapons, supra,* paras. 96-97.

The World Summit on Sustainable Development: Turning Point in Global Governance

Joyeeta Gupta* and Nicolien van der Grijp**

1. Introduction

In order to manage environmental problems, three competing tendencies are visible.[1] The first calls for addressing issues at the highest political level in the global order, the second for developing policies at the lowest possible level – the so-called principle of subsidiarity, and the third the need to involve third parties, namely business and civil society organisations, in addressing environmental problems. These tendencies ensure that the world of law is neither in line with the billiards ball metaphor where States occasionally come in contact with each other, nor is it quite a global community with an integrated market and disappearing State boundaries. Instead, the new world is more in line with the vision that Perrez presents of an asymmetrical three-dimensional net of complex interactions.[2]

With globalisation, the processes of policy development are reaching velocities never achieved before. States are struggling to cope with the developments that are taking place and inter-State negotiations provide at best a rudimentary framework within which these developments are expected to take place. Increasingly State control of these forces is becoming less and less of a reality. Some even argue that the management processes of the globe are being silently taken over by large corporations whose assets are in excess of some regions in the world and who have power to influence and manage the politicians even in the richest countries.[3] Instead of engaging in a competitive process, the UN system seems to have adopted 'corporatism' as the new way to manage the private sector and the demands of civil society.[4] This corporatism is manifest in bodies like the World Commission on Dams,[5] the Forest Stewardship Council[6] and, *inter alia*, the Secretary-General's Global Compact.[7] The latest innovation is the Type-2 Agreement,[8] promoted actively by the World Summit on Sustainable Development.[9] Such agreements are non-negotiated agreements; in other words they are agreed to by social actors who form a partnership to promote sustainable development. These agreements were registered at the 2002 World Summit on Sustainable Development. The Summit thus both promoted corporate responsibility, responded

* Joyeeta Gupta is UNESCO-IHE Professor of Policy and Law on Water Resources and the Environment at the UNESCO-IHE Institute for Water Education and Head of the Programme on International Environmental Governance at the Institute for Environmental Studies, Vrije Universiteit Amsterdam <e-mail: joyeeta.gupta@ivm.vu.nl; jgu@ihe.nl>.

** Nicolien van der Grijp is senior researcher at the Institute for Environmental Studies <e-mail: nicolien.van.der.grijp@ivm.vu.nl>.

to the demands of civil society, and retained for itself a co-ordinating (and possibly monitoring) role. It thus made deals with the mighty private sector without stepping on its toes or giving it the impression that there is governance from above. Relying on the new wave of self-regulation and accountability in the private sector, the UN hopes to at best sail on the potential benefits that may flow from such partnerships, at a minimum monitor such developments, and at worst have established a bureaucracy to monitor activities that are not much more than public relations activities. It appears to smack of the idea – if you can't beat them, join them.

Against this background, this paper examines the nature of the new forms of environmental governance and legal pluralism. It develops a methodological framework on the basis of existing governance frameworks and then briefly studies three contemporary regimes in the field of environmental governance. These three regimes are the climate change regime, the World Summit on Sustainable Development and the emerging regime on 'sustainability' labelling and certification.

2. New forms of governance

Van Kersbergen and Van Waarden[10] present a literature analysis that shows that five major governance shifts are visible. These are a shift from States to supranational and international governance levels, shifts from governments to courts, from public to private international, from public to private national, and from markets to hierarchies. On the basis of existing literature,[11] we can argue that there are six different types of governance.[12] We have used terms to express these forms of governance that can be visually expressed, i.e., horizontal, vertical, parallel, diagonal, polar and point. But these terms should not be taken too literally.

Horizontal governance refers to the traditional relationship between States. Although horizontal governance can take place at all administrative levels, for the purpose of this paper, we restrict it to inter-State negotiations and relationships – the traditional focus of public international law. Vertical governance refers to the relationships between different administrative levels within the international and national hierarchy. Self-governance initiatives undertaken by the private sector in parallel to or independent of governments are expressed here in terms of parallel governance. For example, efforts by industry to self-regulate their production processes and products through, for example, codes of good practice and labelling and certification schemes fall under this category.[13] Diagonal relationships include relationships of a legal nature between State and non-State actors. We refer to them as diagonal because State and non-State actors are actors with a different legal status. Diagonal relationships can include agreements between State and non-State actors such as the Type 2 Agreements and the Global Compact, or mechanisms such as the Clean Development Mechanism under the Kyoto Protocol to the Climate Change Convention, where private actors can make contracts with each other but such contracts are dependent on the express or implied permission of State or inter-State actors.

All these new types of initiatives are not necessarily outside the boundary of law. Alott argues that all legal phenomena everywhere (whether soft or hard) fall within the framework of (international) law.[14] But nevertheless, it is the contention of this paper that these new phenomena are not tried and tested and as a result their impact both on environmental protection and as new legal instruments needs to be evaluated. For example, while UN think tanks such as the International Law Commission have inherent authority, Commissions such as The World Water Commission, The Brandt Commission, The Commission on Environment and Development, The Commission on Global Governance have less authority, limited mandating authority, no enforcement powers and no compliance pull.[15] Further, the establishment of social contracts with social partners while indicating the need to involve local stakeholders, may not necessarily be effective in that these may not include quantitative commitments or legal penalties. The following sections discuss some regimes as hybrid forms of governance. We refer to these forms of governance as hybrid because these regimes include a combination of different kinds of governance. The following sections are limited to studying only four forms of governance – horizontal, vertical, parallel and point. This analysis can in the future be extended to include the last two forms of governance.

3. Climate change as top-down strong hybrid governance

3.1 The climate change regime

The first case to be studied in this paper is the climate change regime. The climate change regime refers to the United Nations Framework Convention on Climate Change (FCCC) of 1992,[16] the Kyoto Protocol to the FCCC of 1997[17] and the Marrakesh Accords. It also includes the decisions of the parties and all other institutional arrangements.

The purpose of the Convention is to stabilise the global concentrations of greenhouse gases. The Protocol translates this into specific quantitative obligations for the developed countries.[18] In order to facilitate the implementation of these obligations, the Protocol proposes two flexibility mechanisms for involving the private sector. These are Joint Implementation, which allows a developed country industry to invest in another developed country (most likely the Countries with Economies in Transition). These investments are expected to promote the transfer of modern climate friendly technologies to these countries in return for emission reduction units.[19] A similar instrument is the Clean Development Mechanism which allows the private sector from developed countries (and possibly also the developing countries) to invest in developing countries in return for certified emission reductions.[20]

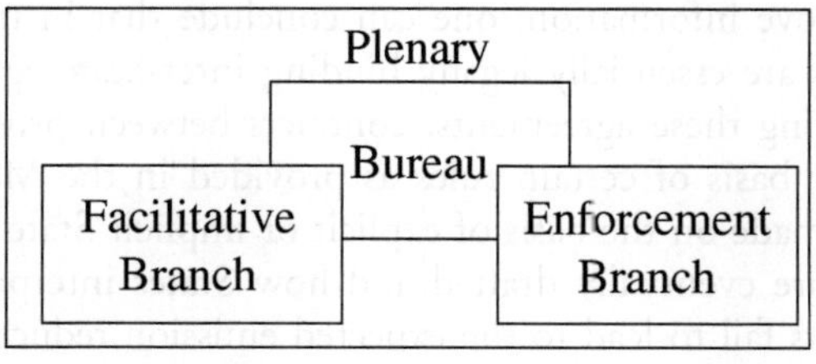

Figure 1. The Compliance Mechanism

The Marrakesh Accords have, *inter alia*, developed a compliance mechanism in response to the call for such a mechanism in the Kyoto Protocol.[21] The Marrakesh Accords prepared a draft decision which is expected to be adopted at the first meeting of the

Parties to the Kyoto Protocol. This draft decision envisages the establishment of a Compliance Committee which includes a plenary, a bureau and two branches. The first branch focuses on facilitation and the second on enforcement. The plenary can signal the implementation problems through reports to the Conference of the Parties and develop advice. It can develop rules of procedure for countries. The Facilitation Branch especially helps developing countries to meet their commitments and the Enforcement Branch can develop criteria to see when a developed country is not in compliance and what sort of action needs to be taken in relation to these countries. It has the power to request a party that is in non-compliance to prepare a plan that analyses why the party is in non-compliance and what measures will be taken to ensure that the party will be in compliance. The eligibility of Parties to participate in the flexibility mechanisms depends on how they comply with their commitments. For example, if a Party does not meet its quantitative commitments, it is subject to a penalty equivalent to a deduction of 1.3 times the number of tonnes of excess emissions in the following commitment period. This implies a lower quota in the follow-up commitment period and is expected to be an effective penalty.

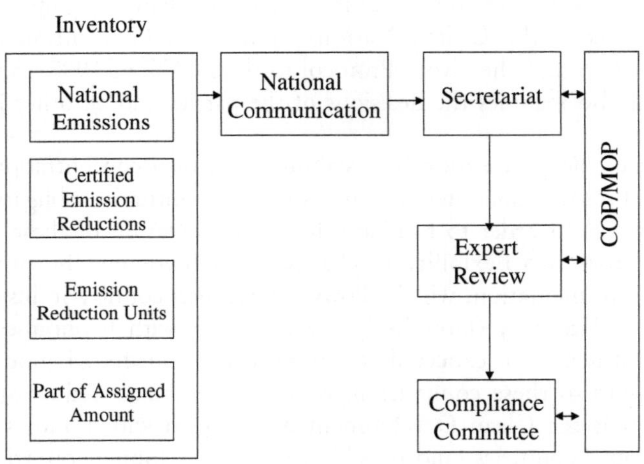

Figure 2. The process of determining non-compliance

On the basis of the above information, one can conclude that in the climate change regime, the agreements are essentially legally binding inter-State agreements. As part of the process of fulfilling these agreements, contracts between private sector entities can be initiated on the basis of certain rules as provided in the Marrakesh Accords. Such contracts can be made on the basis of explicit or implicit State approval depending on how the rules are eventually drafted and how States interpret these rules. If, however, the agreements fail to lead to the expected emission reductions, this may affect the State's ability to meet its quantitative commitment. The State may then become subject to strong non-compliance mechanisms. In other words, the design of the regime includes a horizontal agreement, vertical control through the non-compliance mechanisms, and these two control the effectiveness of the diagonal contracts developed under the regime. One could then argue that in terms of design, the regime exhibits strong hybrid governance. This does not imply that there are no loopholes in the regime. But the loopholes exist more in the detail of the structure than in the general architecture of the regime.

4. World summit on sustainable development as weak hybrid governance

Let us now move to the second example – the World Summit on Sustainable Development (WSSD). During the preparatory process it was more than obvious that the WSSD encouraged participation by non-State actors.[22] There was a huge participation by non-State actors with more than 3000 organizations present with about 8000 representatives. They participated in the multi-stakeholder event, the high-level round tables and the plenaries.

The WSSD led to the adoption of a Type 1 Agreement – i.e., an inter-State agreement which included the Johannesburg Declaration on Sustainable Development and the Plan of Implementation. This document is not legally binding, being of a soft law character. While the agreement makes attempts to create a regulatory framework for the private sector so as to promote corporate accountability[23] and a duty to contribute to the evolution of equitable and sustainable communities and societies,[24] it is unclear if it is likely to have any major impact since most of the recommendations are articulated in vague language and there is no mechanism for monitoring or measuring whether those addressed have taken any action. The Type 1 Agreement included some quantitative goals for the international community in relation to water access, sanitation, etc. However, as is made very clear by the US Government's written reservation to the Type 1 Agreement, the USA does not see the WSSD as creating new international law commitments.[25]

The WSSD also led to the registration of a number of Type 2 Agreements. Over 220 have been formally registered though some counts lead to an estimate of 400 such agreements. These agreements were made between social actors and sometimes between these social actors and governments. According to the Explanatory Note by the Chairman of the Preparatory Committee, these Type 2 outcomes would 'consist of a series of commitments and action-oriented coalitions focused on deliverables and would contribute in translating political commitments into actions'.[26] These agreements are to reflect partnerships that are open and transparent and developed in good faith. The Partnerships are on subjects ranging from changing unsustainable patterns of production and consumption, protecting and managing the natural resource base of economic and social development, health and sustainable development, sustainable tourism, sustainable development of small island developing States, sustainable development initiatives for Africa, capacity building, local authorities and urbanization. Most of these partnerships are led by civil society as opposed to the private sector, where civil society includes 'the major social groups named in Agenda 21 including women, youth, labour, indigenous peoples, farmers, NGOs, and others including, disabled people, the elderly, faith based organisations, peoples of African descent, social movements, people under foreign occupations and other under-represented groups'.[27]

Let us now review the information. The World Summit has quantitative commitments in a soft law inter-State agreement. It then allows social actors to develop partnerships to implement these agreements. A cursory look at the partnerships indicates that few have any quantitative commitments, and that it is very difficult to see precisely how they fit into the Type 1 Agreements and who is to be held responsible if these agreements fail. There is no compliance mechanism. In the final analysis the success of the Type 2 Agreements depends on the good will of civil society, but there is a very strong risk that the new form of governance chosen here may turn out to be a very weak form. The big fear is that Type 2 Agreements instead of complementing Type 1 Agreements may substitute for it.[28] This could lead to a new governance trend where the inter-State agreements were abandoned in favour of more flexible arrangements between those social organisations and governments that were like-minded. This could also allow governments to abdicate their responsibilities in favour of voluntary social initiatives. At the same time, there is some initial anecdotal evidence that shows that while governments may be willing to put money into such agreements, they want the responsibility and accountability for the implementation of the agreement to be left to the social actors and do not want to be held responsible for the failure of such agreements.[29]

Thus, this regime indicates the development of a diagonal form of governance accompanied by relatively weak horizontal governance. The two are poorly linked if at all (e.g., through registration) to the diagonal governance initiatives! This model of governance may be the only practical way forward given that many governments do not wish to assume far-reaching responsibilities at international level. This form of governance builds on the existing constructive forces within the global society. It is too early to say whether this form of governance may be successful or not. One may argue that by focusing on what is possible this form of governance may give momentum to international sustainable development governance. On the other hand, by reducing the momentum for horizontal agreements and by offering countries an alternative route, this form of governance may turn out to be a weak form of hybrid governance.

5. Sustainability labelling and certification as bottom-up hybrid governance

The third regime addressed in this paper is the 'sustainability' labelling and certification regime consisting of private protocols of environmental and/or social standards. As international law is progressing relatively slowly for some social actors and as they are feeling the pressure from consumers, these social actors are adopting voluntary labelling and certification schemes. Such labels serve to differentiate the products on the market and to reach a target clientele that cares for those values that are represented on the label and certification schemes.[30] These schemes are becoming very popular and there is a veritable proliferation of such schemes in the international and national arena.[31] Such schemes help to limit the risk and liability of these companies and enhance their reputation at the international and national level.[32] This is seen as necessary since the modern consumer is becoming more and more aware of global issues and many would like to behave as conscious consumers.[33]

In the meanwhile, the standards adopted by these private parties may set a precedent and may eventually influence any formal standards eventually set by governments.[34] An example of this are the IFOAM[35] basic standards for organic production and processing[36] that have been used as input for the EU regulation on organic production[37] and the FAOs Codex Alimentarius Commission guidelines for the production, processing, labelling and marketing of organically produced food.[38] Furthermore, the EU promotes the use of labelling and certification as an instrument to serve the goals of integrated product policy[39] and its policy on corporate social responsibility.[40]

Thus we see a number of parallel governance initiatives in the form of private sustainability labelling and certification, and some recent attempts of the private sector itself to harmonise national and regional standards by developing overarching international programmes. Moreover, the ISEAL Alliance[41] is preparing a Code of Good Practice for Setting Social and Environmental Standards, that is a further specification of the work done by ISO and the WTO in relation to standardization.[42] This code contains procedural requirements for the development of standards, elaborates on their effectiveness, relevance and international harmonization and gives criteria for participation in the standards development process.[43] Application of the code is mandatory for ISEAL member organizations and voluntary for other standard-setting organizations. The development of this code means that the private sector aims to exercise control over standard-setting by private entities.

6. Analysis

This paper has taken three case studies to show the hybrid nature of new forms of governance. In the case of the climate change regime, the combination of a strong horizontal legally binding inter-State agreement combined with non-compliance mechanisms that ensure domestic enforcement of commitments is in itself a strong hybrid governance form. The use of diagonal governance options involving non-State actors is expected to increase the opportunities for implementation while decreasing the related costs. But these options are also subject to control and are closely linked to the commitments in the agreements and the non-compliance procedures.

In the case of the WSSD, there is a weak inter-State agreement in that it is a soft law rhetorical document. There is a strong initiative in the Type 2 diagonal Agreements. The obligations in the former are general in nature and the quantitative commitments are addressed to the global community in general. In the case of sustainability labelling and certification, there are strong parallel initiatives and weak public efforts at control.

The above comparative analysis can be depicted in the form of a figure. The different forms of governance are shown via the different thick horizontal, vertical, diagonal and parallel lines. In the case of the climate change regime, the close relationship between the three forms of governance is shown by drawing these three thick lines close to each other and thereby forming a triangle. In the case of the WSSD regime, there is a weak horizontal regime depicted by a lightly dotted horizontal line. The Type 2 Agreements are depicted via a diagonal line. The two lines are not joined because there is a very limited link if at all between the inter-State agreement and the Type 2 Agreement. The certification and labelling regime are depicted by strong parallel lines. There are some attempts at creating national schemes and hence a lightly dotted vertical line is also presented. There are some discussions within the WTO on how to deal with such schemes and that is why a weak form of horizontal governance is also depicted. Because all these initiatives are being undertaken often in different arenas of action and are not closely related, the parallel, vertical and horizontal lines do not join.

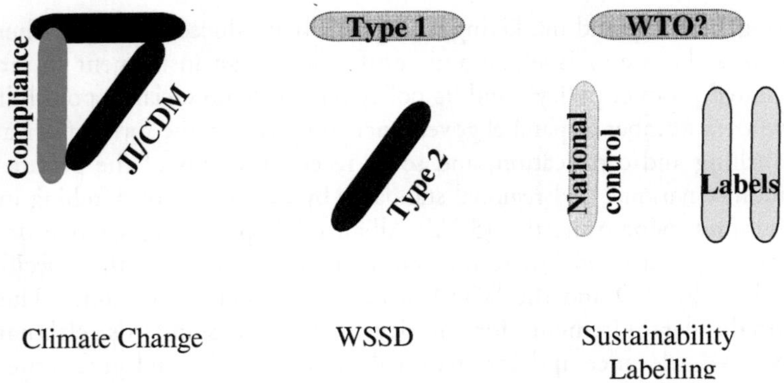

Figure 3. New Hybrid Forms of Governance

The question is: what is the use of such a representation. We would argue that such representation helps to provide an analytical framework for studying these different regimes, and also that such representation is a clear and useful tool for communication and comparative purposes. One could also depict the above information in the two by two figure as shown below.

Horizontal Control \ Vertical Control	Strong	Weak
Strong	Kyoto Protocol	
Weak		WSSD, Sustainability Labelling

Figure 4. Horizontal and Vertical control.

The sustainability labelling and the WSSD regimes are different in that sustainability labelling and certification is essentially a parallel initiative and the WSSD is meant to be a diagonal (and sometimes parallel) initiative (see Figure 3).

Horizontal & Vertical Control	Strong	Weak
Parallel		Sustainability Labelling ?
Diagonal	Kyoto Protocol	WSSD

Figure 5. Diagonal and Parallel governance

7. Conclusion

This paper has argued that based on the new trends in governance, six separate trends can be distinguished. These trends are represented in terms that can also be graphically expressed. It then analyses three different regimes and compares them in terms of their overall architecture.

Following the negotiation of the Kyoto Protocol, there was considerable criticism of the design of the regime. But with hindsight, one can argue that the Kyoto Protocol was a very modern and possibly effective combination of three forms of governance – horizontal, vertical and diagonal. While many had expected that the WSSD would lead to a further development of the development and environmental principles of the last decade, the Summit suffered from the withdrawal symptom of the USA. Given US pressure to reduce intergovernmental obligations and to push instead for voluntary agreements, the World Summit represents a new form of hybrid governance, but a relatively weak form. The regime of private labelling and certification schemes is a hybrid form where the private sector and the non-State actor have the initiative and are also taking the control.

Using the language of Junne,[44] one could argue that although 'sceptics' believe that the UN and the nation State is sticky, hyperglobalists see that new (diagonal) institutions and regimes will become dominant forms of governance in the future. For example, Ruggie argues that the Global Compact and such corporatist ventures are likely to become the most dominant forms of co-operation in the future.[45] It is possible that the above examples show that the hyperglobalists may turn out to be right. At the same time, we believe that although there are fairly refined rules of procedure for ensuring the rule of law and good governance within horizontal and possibly vertical governance, there are less established rules of procedure and good governance approaches for diagonal and parallel forms of governance. This implies that there is a major role for the progressive development of international law to ensure that these forms of governance conform to the norms of good law and good governance and hence have legitimacy within the context of a changing world.

Acknowledgements

This paper is written as part of the projects – Inter-governmental and private environmental regimes and compatibility with good governance – financed by the Netherlands Scientific Organisation- and Sustainability labelling and certification: towards an integrated legal, economic, ecological and social approach' (Contract EVG1-CT-2000-00031),– financed by the European Commission.

Notes

1 J. Gupta, The Role of Non-State Actors in International Environmental Affairs, *Heidelberg Journal of International Affairs*, 2003, forthcoming.

2 See F.X. Perrez (2000), *Cooperative Sovereignty: From Independence to Interdependence in the Structure of International Environmental Law*, Kluwer Law International, The Hague 2; A. Franceschet (2002), 'Justice and International Organization: Two Models of Global Governance', *Global Governance*, 8, No. 1, 19-34.

3 N. Hertz (2001), *The Silent Takeover – Global Capitalism and the Death of Democracy*, William Heinemann, London.

4 See M. Ottaway, Corporatism Goes Global, International Organisations, Nongovernmental Organisation Networks and Transnational Business, *Global Governance*, 7, No. 3, (2001), 265-292.

5 The World Commission on Dams (WCD), established by the World Bank and IUCN, has published a report on international dams; see <www.dams.org>.

6 FSC operates an international labelling and certification programme for forest products; see <www.fsc.org>.

7 See <www.unglobalcompact.org>.

8 At the World Summit on Sustainable Development, the concept of type 1 and type 2 Agreements were launched. Type 1 Agreements are agreements between States. Type 2 Agreements are agreements between social actors including States.

9 Report of the World Summit on Sustainable Development, 2002, A/CONF./199/20.

10 Van Kersbergen, K., and F. van Waarden (2002). *Shifts in governance: problems of legitimacy and accountability*. Paper as part of the Strategic Plan 2002-2005 of the Netherlands Organization for Scientific Research, Social Science Research Council (MaGW), The Hague, The Netherlands.

11 Van Kersbergen, K., and F. van Waarden (2002), see note 10 above; IDGEC (1999), *Science Plan*, Institutional Dimensions of Global Environmental Change, International Human Dimensions Report No. 9, Bonn; Young, O. (2002), *The Institutional Dimensions of Environmental Change*, MIT Press, Boston.

12 Gupta, J. (1997), *The Climate Change Convention and Developing Countries – From Conflict to Consensus?*, Environment and Policy Series, Kluwer Academic Publishers, Dordrecht. Gupta, J. (2003), 'The Role of Non-State Actors in International Environmental Affairs', *Heidelberg Journal of International Law*, forthcoming.

13 Bendell, J. (ed.), (2000), *Terms of Endearment: Business, NGOs and Sustainable Development*, New Academy of Business, London; Gibson, R. (ed.), (1999), *Voluntary Initiatives: The New Politics of Corporate Greening*, Broadview Press, Peterborough, Broadview Press; Manheim, J. (1999), *Corporate Conduct Unbecoming: Codes of Conduct and Anti-Corporate Strategy*, Tred Avon Institute Press, St. Michaels, Maryland; Campins-Eritja, M. and J. Gupta (2002), 'Non-State actors and Sustainability Labelling Schemes: Implications for International Law', *Non-State Actors and International Law*, Vol. 2, No. 3, 213-240.

14 Allott, P. (1999), 'The Concept of International Law', *European Journal of International Law*, Vol. 10, pp. 31-50.

15 See M. Ottaway, note 4 above.

16 The United Nations Framework Convention on Climate Change of 9 May 1992 (text in: *ILM* 31 [1992], 822).

17 The Kyoto Protocol of 10 December 1997 to the 1992 Framework Convention on Climate Change (text in: *ILM* 37 [1998], 22).

18 Article 3 and Annex B of the KPFCCC, note 17 above.

19 Article 6 of the KPFCCC, note 17 above.

20 Article 12 of the KPFCCC, note 17 above.

21 Article 18 of the KPFCCC, note 17 above.

22 UN Doc. A Res/55/199; UN Doc. A Res/56/226.

23 See Report of the WSSD (note 9 above), para. 29.

24 See Report of the WSSD (note 9 above), para. 27.

25 The US reservation states that it does 'not accept any interpretation of Principle 7 of the Rio Declaration that would imply a recognition or acceptance by the United States of any international obligations or liabilities, or any diminution of the responsibilities of developing countries under international law', and that it 'notes that, like other such declarations and related documents, these documents [....] do not create legally binding obligations on States under international law'. This written statement is reported in the Report of the World Summit, (note 9 above), at 145-146.

26 Partnerships/Initiatives to Strengthen the Implementation of Agenda 21; Explanatory Note by the Chairman of the Preparatory Committee, available at <http://www.johannesburgsummit.org/html/documents/prep2final_papers/wssd_description_of_partnerships2.doc>.

27 The Global Peoples Forum: Civil Society Declaration, 24 August-3 September, <http: www.worldsummit.org.za/policies/cs decl.html>.

28 Cited by EcoEquity Submission of 20 August 2002 to the World Summit, prepared by Consumers International, the Danish 92 Group, Greenpeace International, the Northern Alliance for Sustainability (ANPED), OXFAM International, WWF International, available at: <http://archive.greenpeace.org/earthsummit/docs/type2fin.pdf>.

29 Personal notes from people participating in such discussions.

[30] See J. Bendell (ed.), note 13 above; R. Gibson (ed.), note 13 above; V. Haufler, *A Public Role for the Private Sector: Industry Self-Regulation in a Global Economy*, (2001), and J. Manheim, note 13 above.

[31] Haufler, note 30 above, lists the different self-regulatory initiatives of the private sector to the International Labour Organisation and the United Nations Environment Programme; at 13.

[32] Haufler, note 30 above.

[33] See Bendell (ed.) generally, (note 13 above).

[34] See, for details of this argument, M. Campins-Eritja and J. Gupta, note 13 above.

[35] International Federation of Organic Agriculture Movements.

[36] <Http://www.ifoam.org>. First version was published in 1980.

[37] Regulation 2092/91 of 24 June 1991 on organic production of agricultural products and indications referring thereto on agricultural products and foodstuffs, OJ L 198, 22/7/1991, p. 1-15.

[38] Codex Alimentarius Commission, GL 32-1999, Rev. 1-2001.

[39] See, e.g., COM(2001) 68 final.

[40] See, e.g., COM(2001) 366 final.

[41] The International Social and Environmental Accreditation and Labelling (ISEAL) Alliance is a formal association of the leading international voluntary standards, certification and accreditation programs focused on social and environmental issues. Its membership includes: Fairtrade Labelling Organizations (FLO), Forest Stewardship Council (FSC), International Federation of Organic Agriculture Movements (IFOAM), International Organic Accreditation Service (IOAS), Marine Aquarium Council (MAC), Marine Stewardship Council (MSC), Social Accountability International (SAI), Sustainable Agriculture Network (SAN). Associated members are the Global Ecolabelling Network (GEN), and Chemonics International.

[42] The Code draws on ISO/EC Guide 59 Code of good practice for standardization, the WTO Technical Barriers to Trade (TBT) Agreement Annex 3 code of good practice for the preparation, adoption, and application of standards and the TBT Second Triennial Reviiew Annex 4.

[43] Public draft 2 (July 2003), available at <http://www.isealalliance.org>.

[44] See G. Junne, 'International Organisations in a Period of Globalisation: New (Problems of) Legitimacy', in: J-M Coicaud and V. Heiskanen (eds.), *The Legitimacy of International Organizations*, (2001), at 189-220.

[45] J.G. Ruggie, global_governance.net:The Global Compact as Learning Network, *Global Governance*, 7, No. 4, (2001), 371-396.

BINDING DECISIONS OF INTERNATIONAL ORGANIZATIONS AND THEIR LEGITIMACY: NO LOVE AT FIRST SIGHT?*

Nikolaos Lavranos**

1. INTRODUCTION

In this position paper the word governance is understood only in terms of institutional international law, namely, defined as international or global governance[1] through Intergovernmental Organizations (IGOs), which is broadly understood as International Organizations (IOs) or comparable structures established by international treaties.[2] Accordingly, classic IOs such as the UN, EU, WTO, IMF and World Bank are included as well as structures which do not meet the formal criteria of an IO but nevertheless are comparable to them such as the G 7/8, Conference/Meeting of Parties (COP/MOP) established by multilateral environmental agreements (MEAs). These *de facto* IOs can be defined as institutionalized international agreements.[3]

The results of my doctoral thesis[4] illustrate that the organs of those IOs or institutionalized international agreements increasingly adopt far-reaching binding decisions in various different policy areas, such as international trade (WTO), international security (UN), global environment (MEAs), etc. In many cases those decisions are adopted on a non-consensual basis, i.e., by some sort of majority voting and thus can be adopted against the will of a Member State. In addition, these decisions are generally adopted by executive representatives of the IOs and the Member States, meeting behind closed doors, thus adopting decisions with little transparency and hardly any judicial or parliamentary control. Or to put it in the words of *Stein*: 'internationalization almost invariably means a loss of democracy'.[5] Thus, it appears that those decisions are adopted with very little democratic legitimacy, which is understood as parliamentary and judicial control which ultimately should be linked to the will of the electorate.

2. LEGITIMACY OF DECISIONS OF IOs

Legitimacy[6] in international law is based on two fundamental principles: consent of the Member States concerning the decisions adopted by the organs of IOs and representation of the will of the citizens in the decision-making process leading up to the decisions within the organs of IOs.

As to the principle of consent, non-consensual decision-making process becomes increasingly the standard procedure in many IOs. For instance, in the EU most legally

* The title of this position paper is inspired by the article of: Stein, 'International Integration and Democracy: No love at first sight', *American Journal of International Law* 2001, pp. 489-534. The usual disclaimer applies.

** Lecturer EU Law and Senior Researcher International Law, Dep. of EU Law and Amsterdam Center for International Law (ACIL), Law Faculty, University of Amsterdam. contact: <lavranos@jur.uva.nl>.

binding decisions (Regulations and Directives) are adopted by the co-decision procedure which entails qualified majority voting in the Council and full participation of the European Parliament (EP). Moreover, in most COPs/MOPs established by MEAs binding decisions can be adopted by some sort of majority voting (mostly 2/3 or 3/4 majority of members).[7] Finally, as regards the adoption of panel or Appellate Body reports in the WTO Dispute Settlement Body (DSB), a 'reversed' consensus procedure applies, that is, a report is adopted unless all WTO members agree that it should *not* be adopted. As this is highly unlikely and so far has not happened, panel and Appellate Body reports become *de facto* automatically legally binding.

In sum, these examples clearly indicate that the requirement of consensus that used to be a fundamental principle in international law and is still applicable as regards international treaties (Article 34 Vienna Convention on the Law of Treaties) is increasingly substituted by majority voting in the decision-making process of many IOs.

As to the principle of representation of citizens, the research results of my doctoral thesis indicate that representation of citizens through elected members of national parliaments is practically absent with regard to the adoption and implementation of decisions of IOs – at both the international and national level. At the international level, it appears that in practically all IOs – with the exception of the EC – decisions of organs of IOs are adopted by representatives of the members and/or representatives of the IO itself, without any involvement of members of parliaments at the international level. At the national level, most decisions of IOs usually do not need ratification and are adopted by the members by issuing executive regulations which are adopted by the Governments or the responsible Minister of the members of the IOs without requiring approval by national parliaments. Accordingly, there is no parliamentary involvement and thus no representation of the will of the citizens when decisions of IOs are adopted at the international level as well as when they are implemented on the national level. The only element of parliamentary control exists between the executive representative and the national parliament to which he/she is responsible. However, this link is very weak since in many cases the national parliaments are not even aware of what is going on in the numerous IOs.

Accordingly, in most IOs (with the exception of the EC) there is only one executive power and no legislative power and only to limited extent a judicial power. So, the decision-making process within IOs cannot be compared with the decision-making process on the national level, in particular the classic ideas of separation of powers or checks and balances. As a consequence thereof, the usual models of representative democracy are not very useful.[8] Nonetheless, many authors observe that there is a 'democratic deficit' within the decision-making process of IOs.

3. The EU model

The discussion of a 'democratic deficit' within IOs is by no means new. Indeed, the discussion concerning the E(E)C and the EU has been going on for many years.[9] In fact, the author considers the ongoing constitutionalization of the EU as providing useful insights for reducing the democratic deficit of IOs in general.[10]

Two features of the EC system stand out: a) the all-embracing jurisdiction of the ECJ and b) the strong involvement of the European Parliament in the decision-making process. As to a), this leads to a process of judicialization which in turn introduces a process of rule of law in the decision-making process of the EC. As to b), the generally applicable co-decision procedure ensures representation of the European citizens and thus introduces representation. Indeed, both factors contribute to a process of constitutionalization of the EC, which in turn enhances the legitimacy of its decisions. The positive effects concerning the reduction of the democratic deficit is best proved if one compares the situation of the I. pillar (EC) with the situation in the II. and III. pillar (EU). For instance, in both the II. and III. pillar the involvement of the EP is non-existent, while the jurisdiction of the ECJ extends only to the III. pillar and in addition is much more limited than in the I. pillar. It is for that reason that the II. and III. pillar are described as 'intergovernmental' as compared to the 'supranational' I. pillar. Indeed, it is because of the general dissatisfaction with the intergovernmental elements, that the European Convention proposes radical changes in its draft European Constitutional Treaty which will basically 'communitarize' the III. Pillar,[11] thereby substantially improving the position of the EP and the ECJ as regards Justice and Home Affairs. Thus, only the II. pillar (Common Foreign and Security Policy) will still remain under an intergovernmental regime. Thus, the process of 'communitarization' leads to a further constitutionalization of the EU and thus increased representation of the European citizens.

4. The triangular legal interplay

On the basis of these considerations it is now appropriate to turn to the decisions of IOs and the situation of the EU Member States as members of the EU.

The research results of my thesis indicate that since the EU is member of numerous IOs which adopt binding decisions, it is increasingly obliged to implement them. Many – but not all – binding decisions of IOs are implemented by the EC through the adoption of Regulations and Directives on the basis of the co-decision procedure. As a result, the EP is fully involved in the implementation of those decisions and the ECJ obtains comprehensive jurisdiction. Thus, the features of representation and judicialization are introduced by the process of communitarization of those decisions. So, in cases where the EC is competent, the involvement of the EP and in particular the ECJ increases the democratic legitimacy of decisions of IOs.

On the national level, the situation changes for the EU Member States. Whereas without the involvement of the EC, the classic bipolar legal situation 'public international law – national law' remains intact, the involvement of EC law changes that into a triangular legal situation 'public international law – European law – national law'. This effectively means that while the EU Member States and their citizens loose much of their democratic control concerning the implementation of decisions of IOs (at least for those that fall within the competence of the EC), they gain at the same time more legitimacy because of the involvement of the ECJ and EP.

Thus, while the increased law-making activities of IOs, which increasingly lead to a governance through IOs, result clearly in a loss of legitimacy from the point of view of citizens and national parliaments, the situation for the EU Member States is actually improved by this development. That is so because of the increasing involvement of the EC in the adoption and implementation of decisions of IOs, which in turn lead to a communitarization of those decisions. As a result thereof, democratic legitimacy – at least as regards the implementation of decisions of IOs – is improved through the participation of the EP and ECJ. Although, this improvement does not affect the lack of legitimacy that still exists regarding the adoption of decisions within IOs.

Nonetheless, the creation of the triangular legal situation provides the basis for more legitimacy of binding decisions of IOs. In other words, there can be love between decisions of IOs and their legitimacy – perhaps not at first sight but surely at second sight.

Notes

1 See: Held/McGrew, Governing Globalization, Cambridge 2002.

2 See the extensive analysis on International Organizations by: Schermers and Blokker, International Institutional Law, 3rd edn., The Hague 1995.

3 See: Röben, Institutional Dynamics under modern Environmental Agreements, *Max-Planck Yearbook of UN Law* 2000, pp. 363-443; Churchill/Ulfstein, Autonomous Institutional Arrangements and Multilateral Environmental Agreements: A little-noticed phenomenon in International Law, *AJIL* 2000, pp. 623-659; Bodansky, The Legitimacy of International Governance: A coming challenge for International Environmental Law?, *AJIL* 1999, pp. 596-624.

4 *The Interaction between Decisions of IOs, the European and domestic legal order of selected EU Member States*, will be published by Europa Law Publishing in the spring of 2004.

5 Stein, op. cit., p. 490.

6 Stein, op. cit.

7 Lavranos, 'Multilateral Environmental Agreements: Who makes the binding decisions?', *European Environmental Law Review* 2002, pp. 44-50.

8 Held, *Models of Democracy*, 2nd edn. Cambridge 1996.

9 See: Craig/De Búrca, *EU Law*, 3rd edn., Oxford 2003, pp. 167-177; Bankowski/Scott, *The EU and its Order: The Legal Theory of European Integration*, Oxford 2000; MacCormick (ed.), *Constructing Legal Systems "European Union" in Legal Theory*, The Hague 1997.

10 See e.g.: Pernice, Multilevel constitutionalism and the Treaty of Amsterdam: European constitution-making revisited, *Common Market Law Review* 1999, pp. 703-750 and more recently: Multilevel constitutionalism in the EU, *European Law Review* 2002, pp. 511-529; Walker, The idea of constitutional pluralism, *Modern Law Review* 2002, pp. 317-359.

11 Draft Treaty establishing a Constitution for Europe, CONV 850/03, 18.7.2003.

Best Practices Concerning Corporate Governance

Codes of Conduct: An Alternative Instrument for National Legislation and International Treaties?

Herman Voogsgeerd*

1. Introduction

In recent years we have witnessed an enormous proliferation of codes containing best practices on topics related to corporate governance like shareholder primacy and transparency of decision-making in companies. These are national codes, made by working groups of national experts. Academic interest in these types of codes has grown in a decade characterized by a trend from government to governance. Is it possible that these codes will become the instrument 'par excellence' of an area of increased governance by civil society itself?[1]

Only in Europe there are already more than 25 separate national codes concerning this topic. The interesting thing about these national codes is that they can be seen as an alternative for national legislation and as 'surrogate statutes'. Most of these codes were issued as non-binding instruments. During the years, however, some formalization has taken place. In some countries the codes are not completely voluntary any more. By way of obligatory listing rules Stock Exchanges and/or Financial Market Authorities demand that those companies that want to be listed need to comply with the standards in the code, or at least need to explain why they do not comply. This 'comply or explain' technique is now used in some countries.

Notwithstanding the huge internationalization of FDI in the 1990s, the codes of best practices concerning corporate governance are, with some exceptions, national codes. The differences between national company laws are enormous. Therefore it is not an easy thing to make more international codes concerning these topics. The main research question of this paper will be 'Under what conditions can new instruments such as codes of conduct concerning corporate governance be an alternative for traditional instruments like national legislation and international treaties?'. The two aspects, national as well as international, will be dealt with. Because there are so many national codes I will start with the national aspect (section 3) before the international aspect (section 4). In the last section a more substantial question will be asked, in what way does the proliferation of national codes concerning corporate governance lead to a convergence? Is a convergence of corporate governance 'law' (substantial as well as procedural norms) to be expected as a result of the existence and the proliferation of

* Lecturer, University of Groningen, Departments of Commercial Law/Labour Law and International Organizations/International Relations.

codes concerning corporate governance? First I will start in the following section with a short description of this 'proliferation'.

2. The proliferation of codes concerning corporate governance

It is important to stress that codes concerning corporate governance are not in exactly the same category as 'ethics codes'. These are more on topics like corporate social responsibility or child labor. Nonetheless codes concerning best practices of corporate governance and 'ethics codes' do overlap. In some countries corporate governance is interpreted in a broad way in order to include interests of stakeholders. In most corporate governance codes it is for example stated that companies shall 'obey the law'. But corporate governance codes do represent a specific category because these codes treat the internal decision-making mechanisms of the company.

One of the first countries in which a code of conduct concerning corporate governance was created is the United Kingdom. The reasons were diverse. Financial scandals in the late 1980s and the beginning of the 1990s were at the basis of this so-called Cadbury code. Sir Alan Cadbury had the chair of a committee of experts supported by the London Stock Exchange (LSE) and the accountancy branch. This committee issued the code in 1992. This Cadbury Report has been extremely influential, not only in the UK, but also far outside that country. The most influential aspect was the idea of 'comply or explain', companies listed on the stock exchange have the choice to comply with the code of best practices concerning corporate governance or to explain and state the reasons why they did not comply. The LSE made this 'comply or explain' obligatory for listed companies in 1993. After the Cadbury Code several other codes have been issued in the UK. The most important of them is the Combined Code (1998), which combines practices from earlier codes. The UK is not only the country in which the first code concerning corporate governance was created, it is also the country in which codes of corporate governance are very popular and effective. An explanation for this effectiveness is partly cultural. The American company lawyers Bernard Black and John Coffee in their discussions concerning institutional investors in the UK write with some curiosity about 'blue ribbon committees', effective because these consist of persons with high reputations in the business world. Listed companies are not easily inclined to violate norms that have been issued by committees consisting of 'their own people'. In the USA on the other hand, Black and Coffee admit, there is a need of strong legislation including hard sanctions in order to let companies comply with standards.[2]

Nevertheless, the British example was followed immediately in other countries, first of all in other 'Anglo-saxon' countries in which the Cadbury Code had a huge influence.[3] Almost all Member States of the EU do have one or more codes concerning corporate governance.[4] After 1997, continental European countries also started to introduce best practices codes. In France the report of the committee chaired by Viénot appeared in 1995, in the Netherlands the report of the Peters committee in 1997. Many of the codes were prepared by committees with the business community represented in it. There is an explicit or implicit purpose to prevent national legislation. The Asian financial crisis was at the basis of the introduction of codes in countries like Japan, India and South Korea. In Latin America too, some countries introduced best practices codes for corporate governance. In programs like Nepad for

Africa benchmarks of corporate governance do have a big role. From a UK-basis this topic and this instrument is going all over the world. It is becoming one of the instruments of a globalized world.

Experience with the codes has been good in the UK. In other countries the impact of the codes has been less clear-cut. This is because there the codes are not supported by national legislation or because the provisions in the code were too vague. Companies in those countries act slowly in reaction to codes, it is only the threat of legislation that makes the codes more effective. Can the codes become a real alternative for national legislation?

3. Best practices codes as alternatives for national legislation

When we study the relation between the codes and the national legislation of the respective countries we see immediately that the relation between the two instruments is not the same in each European country. This is not surprising, because there are enormous differences between the European countries. The mix between legal and other norms is different in each country. There are big differences between legal norms too. The issues that are dealt with in German national legislation are for a large part the same as those that are dealt with in the British codes! British legislation is in general less detailed than German legislation.

A research concerning alternatives for national legislation has to take into account a number of problems. In the first place there is the problem that legislation and codes sometimes consist of the same standards. Some of the German best practices codes reproduce parts of German company law. These texts can be seen as a marketing instrument of national company law, it is meant to make foreign investors, especially large institutional investors, acquainted with the main elements of German company law. Those elements, like for example codetermination of workers and the two-tier board system,[5] are not present in most of the other European legal systems. It is therefore apparently necessary to convince foreign investors that there is nothing wrong with national law. The argument is that national legislation does not have to be adapted because of globalization, it only has to be better presented to the (foreign) investors. Especially the big institutional investors from the UK and the USA become more active on the European market. National legislation, in so far as it differs from Anglo-American standards, has to be presented more effectively. Maybe codes of conduct are here a better instrument in comparison with national legislation. It is an instrument that big international institutional investors might read earlier than detailed national legislation with all its specific technical vocabulary.

Secondly, there is the problem that the national legislator might react to the discussion brought about by standards in codes. In this context, codes can be seen as paving the way for national legislation. Here codes have the role of *laboratoire* of ideas. This is especially so in case experiments in self-regulation by business have not been successful. An example is the Netherlands where the so-called principles concerning corporate governance of the Peters committee (1997) have been monitored twice. The conclusion of this monitoring process is that the principles did not make much difference. Of course there has been a lot of discussion in boardrooms concerning the principles, but the monitoring process showed that the threat of legislation is far more effective in company boardrooms than pure 100% self-regulation. Without some form of legal sanction it takes a long time before companies change their behavior. In the Netherlands the monitoring process also had another consequence: the installment by the Dutch government this time of a new committee, the committee Tabaksblat. This committee prepared a real Dutch code of corporate governance in May 2003. This code will follow the 'comply or explain' method. It even advises the legislator to insert this method explicitly into national legislation. The final version for the code will be due in December 2003.

The implicit purpose of committees like the Peters committee or the Cadbury committee in the UK has been to preempt national legislation. Corporate governance should be a matter for business itself, and not for national legislators. But low effectiveness of the principles could bring back the threat of national legislation. This has happened for example in the Netherlands where the standards of the Peters committee were not effective enough, therefore the Minister of Finance has threatened more than one time the enactment of legislation. Another problem of these standards was that some of the principles were phrased in very wide terminology and were meant originally only for discussion purposes within the company boardrooms.

Finally there is an opposite deregulatory trend. National legislation has become very detailed in some Member States of the EU. There is also a discussion going on concerning the limits of government-sponsored legislation. In some countries there is talk of deregulation, e.g., in Germany. The creation of codes is in those countries a process simultaneous with deregulation. Sometimes the codes do already exist before the decision which national legislation has to be abolished or deregulated is taken.

Now that these problems and trends in the relation between codes and national legislation have been summed up, it is time to address the main question. Under what conditions can codes be a real alternative for national legislation? First, it is very important to separate the vague and general principles from the detailed standards which are immediately ready for implementation. If codes are for example only meant to stimulate discussion, they can never be an alternative for national legislation. Therefore it is important to separate the principles and the norms from the rules and the decision-making procedures, as these are called in the words of Krasner.[6] Standards designed to stimulate the discussion in a certain body are generally not to be found in a piece of national legislation. Though modernity strikes here as well, in Germany the KontraG introduces so-called *Anregungsnormen*. These are standards that do not prescribe or proscribe but try to stimulate a certain behavior.[7] But this category of norms remains an exception in national legislation.

A peculiar aspect is that the Dutch Tabaksblat-committee was explicitly installed by the government with the order to make principles in stead of rules. The experience with rules in the area of corporate governance is apparently not good. This view is not only the view of the business sector. Even a specialized judge commented in a Dutch newspaper that rules do not work.[8] In case codes are limited to principles and legislation to rules there is not necessarily a clash between both types of instrument. They can be combined perfectly.

A second element of importance is the rule of law, in most of the European countries this principle is still at the basis of the legal order. Governmental power can only be legitimately exercised within the borders of this rule of law. That is why any document containing standards issued by a non-governmental organization is regarded with skepticism or even some alarm. This is for example so in Germany, where there is a strong rule of law tradition. But also in the Netherlands the highest court, the *Hoge Raad*, refuses to accept the standards issued by the Peters-committee as legally binding, because these standards are not based on the law.[9] In order to meet the requirements of the rule of law the creation of a direct relation between a code of conduct and a national law or the national legal system is very essential. In national legislation an explicit reference to a code could be helpful in this respect. In that case the national legislator will legitimize the codes concerning corporate governance. In the introduction I wrote already that codes could be surrogate statutes. To this end the legislator could do a step aside and leave some space for these codes. In the draft of the code issued in May 2003 by the new Dutch Tabaksblat-committee the committee makes some suggestions to the legislator in order to 'facilitate' a specific best practice principle from the code. That means some sections of the Civil Code would have to be changed or withdrawn in order to give a maximum potential to the principles.

However, the legislator will never and should never step permanently aside for codes concerning corporate governance. Even in the UK, where the codes have been quite successful, a complete overhaul of company law has been introduced since 1998. Of course, the legislator keeps full freedom to legislate. But best practices codes containing principles could supplement national legislation containing rules. In order for the codes to have more legitimacy some form of involvement of the government might be necessary. One government representative could participate in the deliberations of the committees that set up the best practices. The British committees were all set up by civil society itself. Professional groups were responsible for the creation of the standards or the 'best practices'. The business community regards the very substance of corporate governance as a prerogative of the big companies themselves. They do not like any involvement of the legislator in matters such as composition of the boards, influence of the shareholders and influence of the stakeholders. But when the business community wants the national legislator to do a step aside involvement of government officials in the committees might be a necessity. It is not necessary for the legislator to deal with every internal aspect of the governance system of firms. Some involvement in the work of the committees for the sake of legitimacy is advisable.

One of the big pros of codes in relation to national legislation is that codes are more flexible. Codes can be changed in a quicker way than legislation. A dynamic topic such as corporate governance is better dealt with in codes, supported by national legislation. The making of formal legislation systems is expensive.[10] Therefore even governments are not against self-regulation by the business community, but self-regulation will have to be more effective in order to be a real alternative for national legislation. Paradoxically legislation could help codes to become more effective. Especially concerning procedures and sanctions legislation could 'back up' codes concerning corporate governance. Of course, 'mobilization of shame' is of importance here as well, but the threat of a legal sanction is very helpful indeed.

In this context the term *procéduralisation du droit* is used.[11] The legislator limits itself to standards and rules of a procedural nature. It guards the effectiveness of the substantive standards and intervenes in case these standards are not longer effective. The legislator limits itself to supervision. The substantive standards concerning corporate governance are, on the other hand, left to the committees mentioned above. This dual system could work.[12] It is necessary though that national legislation refers explicitly to the codes concerning corporate governance for the sake of legitimacy of the codes and for problems concerning the rule of law. And this is also necessary for codes in order to become an alternative or a surrogate for national legislation. The dual system goes hand in hand with a division of tasks. The legislator or specially created market authorities should concentrate on the creation of procedural standards and on supervision.

4. Codes concerning corporate governance as alternatives for traditional instruments such as international treaties and EC Directives

Can national best practices codes or international best practices codes become an alternative for traditional instruments like international treaties and EC Directives? Multinational companies are increasingly active across borders. We have seen an enormous increase in scale and size of those companies. It is almost an established fact that globalization leads to a loss of control for national governments. Their capacity to run the economy has been affected severely. The governments tried to regain some control by the conclusion of international treaties. In the second half of the 1990s a huge number of bilateral investment treaties have been concluded. Until now there are no bilateral treaties concerning corporate governance. This is probably because corporate governance is a matter for companies and national company laws differ enormously.

Intergovernmental organizations are another vehicle through which States or States-parties could regain some influence over the global economy. Some international organizations deal explicitly with the topic of corporate governance. Within the framework of the OECD principles concerning corporate governance were established in 1999. According to commentators these principles were strongly influenced by the UK Combined Code.[13] The OECD principles consist of some aggregate principles, which are sometimes quite vague. This is proof of its character as a compromise text. Its vagueness makes it less useful for the OECD Member States. It is also possible that the OECD code was not created for the Member States at all, but for non-Member States and for States in economic transition. The OECD principles are an example for their efforts to deal with this modern development. In 1998 the Commonwealth Association for Corporate Governance was created, it issued the CACG Principles for Corporate Governance in the Commonwealth. The EU is another international organization that could deal with matters concerning corporate governance. Commissioner Bolkestein is preparing European legislation in order to reach co-ordination between the legal systems of the Member States. Differences between the Member States are high.

International organizations are not always the best positioned to impose sanctions in case of violations of standards. Therefore the sanctioning capacity of national States remains extremely vital for the effectiveness of the international codes. The OECD does have a surveillance mechanism, quite effective are the so-called contact points for companies, trade unions, etc., within the framework of the principles concerning multinational enterprises. But this is another topic to be distinguished from corporate governance. The EU with its different sanctioning mechanism would better fulfill this position, but this international organization does not have yet standards concerning corporate governance.[14]

A third development is the internationalization of private parties themselves. It is not only the big companies here, recently even the national stock exchanges started to co-operate. The stock exchanges of Paris, Brussels and Amsterdam merged: Euronext was created. Later the stock exchange of Lisbon became a party to Euronext. Other stock exchanges are also discussing further co-operation. This merging process could have some implications for corporate governance as well. The listing rules will become internationalized. Pension funds and other big institutional investors will co-operate more across borders. They themselves set standards concerning corporate governance. Famous examples are the standards of CalPERS[15] in the USA and Hermes[16] in the UK. The European Association of Securities Dealers (EASD) has its own recommendation concerning corporate governance. The Confederation of European Shareholders does have corporate governance guidelines of its own. These standards could on their turn influence the national codes.

The picture here is quite similar with that of the previous section. Although the international legal order is becoming more horizontal with all these standard-setting actors, States are still necessary for sanctioning capacity. Enforcement by the market alone would not be enough and lack legitimacy. There is a trend in countries to give surveillance powers to newly created authorities. A network of such bodies co-operating together, could try to get cross-border surveillance power.

In order to deal with the increasingly cross-border activity of big companies another option is to refer to cross-border situations in the national best practices codes. An example is a disposition in a German code: multinational companies should disclose at least the same material that they are required to disclose under other national legal systems. This could bring about more uniformity in disclosure standards worldwide. This might be even in the interest of multinational companies, as they have to disclose only one set of information. I would submit that national codes should at least refer to cross-border situations.

Corporate governance is a new and a dynamic topic, at this very moment it is not dealt with in international treaties. In the future this could change. It is possible though, that corporate governance will remain a completely private regime,[17] where governments do only have a surveillance role and where substantive norms are left to the market. It is in any case up to governments to guard and keep under constant surveillance market parties. Surveillance is certainly something that is of the utmost importance. In case the markets fail in their surveillance there is nobody else than the governments to do the job.

5. Conclusion: Towards a Convergence of the Law and Practice Concerning Corporate Governance Thanks to the Proliferation of the Codes?

Is a convergence of the law and practice concerning corporate governance (substantial as well as procedural norms) to be expected as a result of the existence and proliferation of codes concerning corporate governance? There has been some market-driven convergence. The standards in the national codes concerning corporate governance are already remarkably similar in EU countries. It is the underlying national systems of company law that are different.

Convergence will certainly be strengthened in the long term when the national codes of conduct will influence the underlying national legal systems. This will happen in case the legislator keeps at a distance and intervenes concerning the procedural standards and only periodically concerning the substantive standards. An improvement in transparency and disclosure, more independence within the boards of listed companies, and more ways to influence company strategy for shareholders are the main elements of this convergence. In each national legal system these elements are implemented in a different way. But the elements are the same, world-wide.

In my opinion it is still too early to talk of 'an emergent Common Law or Practice concerning Corporate Governance'.[18] At the heart of 'an emergent Common Law of international trade', according to Weiler, is the convergence in substantive law concerning tax-related and other internal regulations. There is indeed some convergence concerning substantive issues of corporate governance. But the main elements of company law still differ enormously. The role of employee codetermination in companies and the existence of two-tier boards with a separate board responsible for 'supervision' are still far away from the dominant board governance in the Anglo-American system. The world-wide proliferation of national codes concerning the same topics related to corporate governance could however help national legislators to grasp some of the urgent and actual problems of corporate governance and to bring these problems into conformity with their national legislation. The specific mix of legal and other norms will always remain different in each country. Cultural factors are the most difficult ones to change. But a modern updated national legislation is a prerequisite for effective codes concerning corporate governance. In that sense, codes are not a complete alternative to national legislation but have to go hand in hand with that same traditional instrument.

Notes

1 See also the papers on related topics by J. Mifsud Bonnici about non-State actor normativity and R. Pierik about globalization and the legitimacy of actors in international debates of global governance.

2 B.S. Black and J.C. Coffee Jr, 'Hail Britannia?: institutional investor behavior under limited regulation' in: *Michigan Law Review*, Vol. 92, 1994, p. 1997.

3 But differences remain between for example the UK and Australia, as is shown by Fiona Ellett in 'Australia and the UK on the Quest for Best Practices', in: *International Corporate Law Annual*, Vol. 1, 2000, p. 171 at 175/6.

4 An inventory of all these codes can be found in Weil, Gotshal & Manges, *Comparative Study of Corporate Governance Codes relevant to the European Union and its Member States*, on behalf of the European Commission, Internal Market Directorate General, January 2002.

5 This is the system in which the board of a company is split in a managing board and a supervisory board.

6 S.D. Krasner, 'Structural causes and regime consequences: regimes as intervening variables', in: S.D. Krasner (ed.), *International Regimes*, Cornell paperbacks, 1983, p. 2. 'Principles are beliefs of fact, causation, and rectitude. Norms are standards of behaviour defined in terms of rights and obligations. Rules are specific prescriptions or proscriptions for action. Decision-making procedures are prevailing practices for making and implementing collective choice'. The difference between norms on the one hand and rules on the other hand is not that clear. Norms seem to be the more substantive standards of a regime. A change in norms is a regime change, a change in rules is only a change within the regime.

7 KontraG means '*Gesetz zur Kontrolle und Transparenz im Unternehmensbereich*' Law of 27 April 1998, BGBl. I, 786.

8 Interview with Judge Willems, President of the *Ondernemingskamer* of the Appellate Court of Amsterdam, in the Dutch newspaper *NRC*, interview on 4 July 2003.

9 *Hoge Raad*, *HBG*-zaak Rek.nr. OK 101 (Hollandse Beton Groep NV), 21 February 2003, *Jurisprudentie Onderneming en Recht*, 2003, No. 57 p. 428.

10 W. Cragg, 'Ethics Codes: the Regulatory Norms of a Globalized Society?', in: A. Soeteman (ed.), *Plural-*

ism and Law, Kluwer Academic Publishers, Dordrecht, Boston, London, 2001, p. 194.

11 See for example I. Ayres and J. Braithwaite, *Responsive Regulation*, Oxford, 1992, who stress procedural norms to enforce standards created by pure self-regulation. National legislation should help companies to uphold their own sanction mechanisms, p. 44. In this respect the concept of 'reflexive law' is interesting as well. Reflexive law takes as a point of departure the self-regulation of civil society. Legislation should be limited to procedural norms, G.-P. Calliess, *Zeitschrift für Rechtssoziologie*, Vol. 23, 2002, p. 190/1.

12 Compare for example the attitude of the national government towards collective labor agreements between trade unions and employers organizations.

13 A. Dignam, 'Exporting corporate governance: UK regulatory systems in a global economy', in: *The Company Lawyer*, 21, No. 3, 2000, p. 76. He is extremely critical concerning 'the exportation of a UK style negotiated regulation into the international arena is also worrying. While effective regulation needs to bring the regulated along with the regulator, this particular form defers exclusively to one particular interest with little consideration of the public interest in such arrangements'.

14 Plans for EC legislation are already in a far-reaching stadium. A group of company law experts, however, did express reservations on the creation of a European code concerning corporate governance. The underlying national legal systems would have to be co-ordinated better too, see the company law group p. 72.

15 CalPERS is the abbreviation for California Public Employees' Retirement System. It has its own corporate governance principles for its international investments.

16 Hermes is a daughter of the British Telecom Pension Scheme and has its own Statement on Corporate Governance and Voting Policy.

17 Victoria Haufler is of the opinion that private regimes or private corporate regimes do exist. One of the purposes of such a regime is maintaining industry autonomy. See her 'Crossing the Boundary between Public and Private' in: V. Rittberger (ed.), *Regime Theory and International Relations*, Oxford, 1993, p. 103. See also her 'Private sector international regimes' in: R.A. Higgott, G.R.D. Underhill, A. Bieler (eds.), *Non-state actors and authority in the global system*, London, New York, 2000, p. 126.

18 In reference to: J.H.H. Weiler, *The EU, the WTO and the NAFTA: towards a common international trade law*. Oxford, 2000.

TRACING THE SOURCES OF NON-STATE ACTOR REGULATION: THE SETTING OF GLOBAL TECHNICAL STANDARDS IN CYBERSPACE AS AN EXAMPLE

J.P. Mifsud Bonnici* and C.N.J. de Vey Mestdagh**

INTRODUCTION

States are no longer the sole participants in the international normative arena. Multiple players – States, intergovernmental organisations, multinational corporations, individuals, non-governmental organisations, etc.[1] – negotiate the international normative space. Current international relations theory scholars[2] argue that the increased presence of multiple actors is leading a shift from government to governance of the international space.

International lawyers are more reluctant to acknowledge a similar shift in international regulation. Nonetheless, there is a growing literature describing non-State actor involvement in the international law-making process or in the enforcement of international law, especially in the environmental[3] and human rights[4] fields. Others acknowledge that non-State actors create norms complementary to inter-State legislation.[5] Non-State actors also create rules alternative to or, even, in the absence of inter-State legislation.[6]

Part of the reluctance is based on the impression that non-State actor participation and rule creation is largely *ad hoc*, dependent on non-transparent and idiosyncratic reasons.[7] This paper tries to rebut the impression of arbitrariness in the non-State actor rule setting process by tracing a common source of State and non-State actor regulation. In international law the term 'source' has multiple meanings, amongst which: (a) to refer to the origin or causation of a rule. Used in this way, the term source explains the major influences that triggered the making of a rule; (b) to refer to the rule-making process. This is often called 'formal' sources of law;[8] (c) to refer to the factual existence of a given rule of law.[9] 'Material' sources 'provide evidence of the existence of rules which, when proved, have the status of legally binding rules of general application';[10] and (d) to refer to information sources, research sources or bibliographies on international law. The first two interpretations of the term 'source', that is, primarily as a description of causation of rules and of the rule-making process, are used in the discussion below.

This paper argues that the rule-making process followed by non-State actors is not at all arbitrary. In fact, non-State actors adhere to a similar process as is pursued

* Centre for Law & ICT, University of Groningen.
** Centre for Law & ICT, University of Groningen.

by States when creating inter-State law. Both processes are triggered into action by a perceived need for regulation. Subsequently, the actors involved agree on the norm to be followed. The agreed norms are translated into rules having binding effect, which rules are then accepted, adopted and enforced by the rule-making actors. The main difference between State-led processes and non-State actor processes does not lie in the process but specifically in the actors taking part. The paper argues, that it is the attributes of the actors involved that explain the occurrence of non-State actor regulation and make the non-State actor process a better 'fit for purpose' for certain specific areas needing regulation. The making of technical standards in cyberspace by non-State actors in the absence of State regulation is used to illustrate and support the arguments.

The paper is organized in three parts. In the first section, a brief description of cyberspace and technical standards is given. The function of this section is to place the later study of the Internet Domain Names System (DNS) in context. In section two the legal implications of the DNS standards are discussed. The third section compares the State-led law-making processes and non-State actor law-making processes. This section discusses the similarity in the processes and the difference in the attributes of the actors leading the law-making process. In conclusion, the paper provides some comment on relevance of the case-study in a wider context.

1. Cyberspace and standards

Cyberspace is predominantly a-territorial and a ubiquitous presence. Once allowed access a participant can link to other participants sharing common interests, irrespective of their nationality, country of origin or culture. Most activities in cyberspace take place across a number of State territories. This makes it difficult for one State alone to regulate cyberspace. In addition, States alone cannot effectively regulate cyberspace activities since they often lack technical access to the actual activities that require regulation. The governance of activities in cyberspace requires the participation of multiple participants: States, users, Internet service providers, expert communities, industry, etc.

Apart from the international flavour of the activities taking place in cyberspace, cyberspace itself can be viewed as a common shared international resource. Rules regulating who can access, how to access and participate in this resource, have been a matter primarily of non-State actors. Like other areas of international significance, States have been reluctant to participate in this technologically complex area leaving the non-State actors to use their expertise in designing appropriate rules and procedures.[11] The making of technical standards is a typical example of non-State actor rules created in the absence of State or inter-State regulation.

Technical standards may have important legal implications. This can be illustrated by the following example: there is a technical standard in cyberspace that no two domains can be identified by the same domain name. The technology itself does not allow a double entry. The normative consequence of this standard is one of ownership: two competing domain owners cannot own the same domain name.[12]

By conforming to standards participants in an activity accept to behave in a manner that is consistent with the standard set. In a broad sense, standards represent an acceptable behaviour[13] and set the parameters of the acceptable behaviour.

Traditionally, the setting of standards is predominantly entrusted to State authorities, State-set committees and international governmental organisations. For instance, the International Telecommunication Union (ITU) is constituted of representatives of Member States and private sector organisations. An important benefit of State-led systems is that once the particular standard is established it is binding, at least, in the particular jurisdictional territory of the States involved in the process. Another benefit is that the presence of the State can guarantee a degree of fairness in the process of establishing the standard.

The processes in State-led organisations are, however, often slow moving as the setting of a standard is dependent on achieving a consensus between the parties involved. In addition, the process does not always guarantee that the 'best' standard is selected. Consensus on the standard is achieved by a series of compromises between the parties that water down the level of the standard significantly. Furthermore, these organisations do not always reach a consensus and consequently harmonisation of the technical requirements is not accomplished.[14]

Non-State standard-setting initiatives have proliferated in a number of areas: on the one hand, to counteract the cumbersome State processes and on the other to set standards in areas where States are either not involved or have no access to the area in question. The setting of the DNS is discussed in this paper.

2. The legal implications of the internet Domain Name System (DNS)

The DNS is a method to map a user-friendly name to a numeric address.[15] When a person types in a domain name to communicate with or access information on a firm or person, the domain name is converted into a series of numbers know as the machine's Internet Protocol (IP) address. Each computer attached to the Internet has a unique IP address, which may be allocated to it permanently or temporarily.[16] Then one machine communicates with another machine via name servers that identify the location of the other machine and allow (or deny) communication with the other machine on the network. DNS involves the creation of domain names and the administration of the addressing system. Our discussion on the DNS looks at two aspects of the system: (I) the numeric addressing system standard; and (II) the standard for the allocation and organisation of the domain names.

2.1 Main actors in the rule-making process

The development of the DNS standards is largely in the hands of non-State actors. Apart from the United States, which had funded much of the research connected with the development of cyberspace, governments have traditionally taken little interest in regulating cyberspace at code (technical) level. The development of technical standards has been developed 'bottom-up' from research and academic environments.

Two non-State actor organisations took the initiative to set standards in cyberspace: the Internet Engineering Task Force (IETF)[17] and the Internet Assigned Numbers Authority (IANA).[18]

2.2 Need for developing the standards

The technical standards we discuss below were developed to address specific technical needs: primarily a need for computers on a network to communicate with each other and secondarily a need to have a user-friendly way for computers to address each other. To address the former need the numeric addressing system standard was developed. The domain name allocation and organisation standards were developed to address the latter needs.

2.2.1 *The numeric addressing system*

The IETF established the IP addresses standard to meet the need of identification for efficient communication between machines. This numeric addressing system standard is called IPv4.[19] This standard requires that each computer on the Internet is allocated a unique numerical address. This address is used to route packets of information across the network. IP addresses are therefore the technical cornerstone of the Internet's ability to move data from sender to any connected receiver.[20] For the system to work efficiently there is an absolute requirement that each allocated number is unique and follows the prescribed standard. This ensures that a computer on the system can be identified and able to participate on the network. The most important legal aspect of the IP technical standard is that an IP address determines one's access and participation in cyberspace. Unless one is allocated an IP address one cannot participate in cyberspace. IANA manages the allocation of IP addresses to different organisations. Most of the address blocks have been allocated to research, education, government, corporations and Internet Service Providers, who in turn assign them to the individual computers under their control.

Since there are a finite number of IPv4 addresses that can be allocated[21] one can imagine that, for example countries that are still developing infrastructures capable of allowing their citizens to connect to cyberspace would not be allocated any IP addresses because all the IP numbers would have been taken up. To counter the shortage of IPv4 addresses – a new technical need – a new technical standard, the IPv6 is being set by the IETF. Once again IETF has taken the initiative to set a new standard as a result of a need that has arisen.

The numerical standard has been adopted by all users in cyberspace. Unless they follow the standard they are incapable of either having access or to participating in cyberspace.

2.2.2 *The allocation and organisation of the domain names*

As long as the networks belonged to academic research circles, the numerical standard was enough for computers to communicate with each other. The opening of the networks to more people introduced new needs especially the need of user-friendly ways of communicating. To satisfy this need, a standard to map a user-friendly name to a numeric IP address was developed by IETF. The standard involves that each user-friendly name (hereafter called 'domain name') is mapped to one IP address.

The effect of this standard is that each domain name can only be used once. This is understandable from a technical point of view, in that computers can communicate with each other by means of the unique IP address assigned to a computer. The domain name mapped on to the IP address becomes the 'unique' name of the computer and thus can be used only to represent one address.

The technical standard requiring that a domain name can be used only for one address has a number of legal consequences:

(a) Identification and authorisation
By having an IP address (and an associated domain name) a person has a presence in cyberspace. This allows the person to access information and to communicate with others. The parameters of communication and access can be limited or extended simply by blocking or allowing a particular IP address. That is, for example, a person can be disallowed to send e-mails to the rest of the world by blocking that person's IP address. Similarly, as an owner of information on the network one can disallow another person from accessing that information by rejecting access to the person's IP address.

(b) Ownership
Since a domain name is a unique identifier of a web location, a 'good' address has an economic value. This allocation introduced new proprietary parameters to the ownership of the domain name different to the situation in the off-line world of trademarks. Trademark law allows multiple entities to own the same name if they are not in competing businesses and/or not in the same geographical area.

The differences between the position of domain names in cyberspace and trademarks in the off-line world induced a number of legal disputes. These legal disputes were in turn, at times, partially addressed by standards adopted by non-State actors. Government, or States, have traditionally been involved only very sparingly in the way domain names are regulated and assigned.

Generally these disputes can be classified in:

(i) a clash between two persons wanting to register the same name
This was resolved by domain names registrars adopting the 'rule' of 'first come first served', that is, who registers the name first gets the name. This rule was set by IANA. The rule was maintained and is still applied by domain name registries across the world.

(ii) a clash between a domain name and a trade name holder
Conflicts also arise between multiple owners of a trademark in the same string of characters. The owners may be (1) sectorally separate (same country, but different use or different category of goods and services), or (2) geographically separate (same business, but different countries or regions within a country), or (3) both sectorally and geographically separate. Conflicts also arise between domain name holders and persons with some other legitimate interest in a mark not deriving from a trademark.[22]

One technical solution, developed by IETF, to address these clashes is the organisation of the DNS into various classes of domain types. There are two general categories of domain types: generic top-level domain (gTLD)[23] and country top-level domain (ccTLD). In this way the name part of the address without the domain level indicator can be used with multiple domain level indicators.[24]

(iii) a clash between domain names that are similar and are meant to pass off for the other
This is generally a situation of fact that needs to be resolved in a classical way through court action; through the Uniform Domain Name Dispute Resolution (UDRP); or through dispute resolution services offered by some of the local (country) registries.

(iv) situations of cyber squatting
This arises when a domain name is registered by a person before the 'true' owner of the domain name does so. These situations were common when some businesses had failed to recognise the normative and economic consequences of domain names. In order to avoid similar situations of cyber squatting when the new set of gTLDs were added in 2000, IANA set a number of pre-launch procedures to reduce the possibilities of abuse.[25]

3. State and non-State actor international law-making processes

In the preceding section we have seen the legal implications of the setting of technical standards. In this section we look at the similarities and differences in the law making process between State-led and non-State actor-led processes. The section is divided into three parts: section 3.1 describes the State-led process in international law; section 3.2 points to the broad similarities between the State-led process discussed in section 3.1 and the non-State actor process using the DNS standard setting as an example; section 3.3 discusses the differences in the attributes of the main actors in the processes.

3.1 **State-led international law-making process**

From a positive law perspective, laws in a community can be identified as such not so much through their content but rather from the manner in which they were created and adopted.[26] In a national law-making context identifying the procedure followed for the enactment of law is not usually too difficult a task. The national law-making process is, in most States, standardised and centralised.

In comparison to the national law-making process, the law-making process of international law does not seem to follow a standardised procedure. The lack of apparent standardisation has led some authors[27] to claim that looking at the formal sources in international law is unhelpful. Descriptions of international law-making are bound to the area they intend to regulate and to the institutions involved in the law-making process.[28]

However, in spite of the formalities in law-making particular to each institution one can firmly identify, at least for purposes of analysis, a number of steps that are followed in the majority of international law-making processes. There is some commonality in the process followed to enact the thousand or more multilateral treaty instruments that are added to the body of international law each year by a whole variety of institutions. These five basic steps have been abstracted from the particularities that might exist in the different instances of law-making. The abstraction allows us to look at the fundamental steps without the distraction of the particular details belonging to the individual institutions and specific areas. At times, a study of the details may obscure the main features of the process and indicate misleadingly differences or transformations that might not be present.

Taken at an abstract level the making of international law (here being understood as inter-State law) follows these steps:

a. *Recognition of need:* Any law-making process of international law is set in motion to address a need for regulation. Faced with a newly emerged or existing problem States and international organisations recognise the need for regulation and set the law-making process in action. For example, confronted with the need to control the proliferation of child pornography and cybercrime in cyberspace, Member States of the Council of Europe recognised the need to take collective action to regulate the situation.

b. *Valuation of need:* While States and international organisations recognise many needs for regulation they take action only on those that they deem of greater importance. The need for regulation is given a value by the States and international organisations involved in the process. The need for action is measured and justified against the values, often moral values accompanied by financial and political values, of the States and international organisations involved. For example, the need to regulate child pornography is reckoned with the values of the States to protect children and the value of freedom of speech and possible financial considerations of enforcement.

c. *Formulation of norm:* The valued need is translated into a norm, that is, the States and international organisations agree on a shared expectation of desirable behaviour. The making of certain recommendations of behaviour may be one way of expressing the shared expectation. Using the same example of child pornography and cybercrime in the Council of Europe setting – once the Member States agreed that there was an actual need for regulation of child pornography and other cybercrimes, the Council of Ministers issued a Recommendation[29] concerning problems of criminal procedural law connected with information technology. The Recommendation recommended certain norms of behaviour to be followed by the Member States.

d. *Implementation into a law:* The shared expectation is translated into rules having binding effect, for example, a law-making treaty. This is invariably a long process of drafting and negotiating between the States and international organisations involved. The Council of Europe Cybercrime Convention[30] contains rules primarily of criminal procedural law that Member States should follow in case of child pornography and other cybercrime.

e. *Acceptance and enforcement of law:* The binding rules only come to effect when enough States individually accept the binding effect of the rules. The rules then come into force only for the States that have accepted the rules. The Cybercrime Convention (mentioned earlier) has not yet come into force since not enough States have ratified the Convention.[31]

3.2 Non-State actor-led international law-making process

In spite of the impression that non-State actors create rules in an *ad hoc* manner, it is argued that non-State actors follow the same steps described for inter-State law-making. As can be seen in the example in the setting of Internet DNS standards, non-State actors pursue a similar sequence:

a. *Recognition of need:* In our example the actual need is a technical one: a need for machines on the network to be able to identify and communicate with each other and a need for the solution to be intelligible to the user of the machine. As we have seen, the technical need has regulative implications. Similar to the State-led processes, the need is recognised by the actors in the field. Here primarily by the members of the technical community.

b. *Valuation of need:* The expertise and knowledge of the non-State actors in the area enabled the actors to acknowledge the importance of the technical need. The non-State actors recognised further that the need had to be addressed in a collective (international) manner. Similar to State-led processes, the need to take action is balanced against the different values of the technical community. One criticism that can be levelled is that non-State actors may overlook the values and interests of other possible participants in the scene. For example, the IETF establishes standards based on the technical expertise of its participants. One cannot assume that in setting a standard the IETF takes into consideration the interests of a particular industry community or the privacy issues of the users that will be regulated by the standard.

c. *Formulation of norm:* In our example this stage involved drawing up and agreeing on desirable technical specifications. These technical specifications were based on the shared expertise and expectations of the technical actors involved in the process. For example, in the setting of the numerical addressing standard the desirable technical specifications included that the system would allow a large number of computers to participate in the network. Similarly to State-led processes the technical recommendations at this stage are not binding on the participants. They are indicative of desired behaviour and of probable possible future regulatory developments.

d. *Implementation into law:* Following a process of technical and expert discussions and negotiations, the requirements are formalised into a 'standard' – a technical law that has to be followed by the participants in the area. (The nature of these standards is discussed in the next paragraph.) This stage in the process is similar to the State-led process in as much as the process of formalisation is often a process marked with compromised, consensus building, drafting and re-drafting.[32] The end product of this stage is different in both processes, though the effects of the end product are the same (as we see in the next paragraph). State-led processes frequently, but not exclusively, are formalised in treaties or conventions. The form of the implemented rules of non-State actors can be expressed in different instruments, for example, written codes of conduct, technical standards, written contracts, charters, etc.

e. *Acceptance and enforcement of law*: Similar to State-led processes the implemented law needs to be accepted and adopted to come into effect. The standards once accepted by the non-State actors are adopted as the binding standard. In our example two categories of standards were developed by non-State actors into two categories: (i) standards that were developed to meet the needs of communication between participants; and (ii) standards that were developed to reduce claims between domain names and trademark holders. Both categories are binding standards. However, the process of application and enforcement in each category differs.

In the first category, once the standard has been adopted the participants have no actual choice to make whether to follow the standard or not – unless the participants follow the standard they cannot participate in the community. Any deviation from the standard would automatically result in being technically ousted. Once the standard is adopted it becomes the 'law' that has to be followed if the participants want to benefit from, in this case, the use of the cyberspace network. Furthermore, the standard is considered law by the participants even though no State-institutional mechanism is involved neither in the creation and development of the standard nor in its adoption and application. Non-State actor rules have a binding effect independently of the State. In a wider context, this is no different from State laws created to satisfy a communication or co-ordination need.[33] Once adopted the law has an almost self-enforcing quality.

The second category of standards points to other issues then those outlined for co-ordination standards. At the outset, the development and adoption of these standards reflect the flexibility non-State actor law-making processes have to react to new needs. These standards attempt to provide an equitable playing field where domain name and trademark holders can co-habit in cyberspace. The adoption of these standards gives parties the possibility to co-exist in cyberspace without 'losing' too much. Unlike the co-ordination standards, these standards[34] do not have the same self-enforcing character and so enforcement mechanisms have been developed (e.g., domain name registries). This does not, however, impact the binding character of the standards once adopted by the community of users. The difficulty in enforcing certain standards is not limited to non-State actor rules. The same difficulties are faced by State-created rules. In spite of the difficulties in enforcement, however, the binding character of the rules remains undiminished.

3.3 Attributes of non-State actors

As can be seen, the main difference between the two processes is not in the process itself but in the actors participating in the process. In inter-State law-making processes the main actors are States or governmental organisations. In the non-State processes the main actors are private organisations of people. Non-State actors can include professional groupings, like the IETF, industry groupings, business communities or a combination of different groupings involved in a common activity.[35] Non-State actors have a number of attributes that are different from State or governmental organisations. We look here at three of these attributes:

i. Non-State actor expertise and familiarity with the area

The key attribute of non-State actors is that they have the necessary relevant knowledge and expertise in the activity needing regulation. Through their expertise, non-State actors can determine the actual need for regulation, analyse the implications and settle on the most effective way of regulating the need. Non-State actors, contrary to States, are themselves participants in the area needing regulation. Being participants enables them to initiate the rule-making process as soon as the need arises. Non-State actor initiative is sustained by their expertise in the field. In the case of States, once the need for regulation is identified and recognised as necessary, States have to rely on the expertise of specialists in the field in identifying the possible solutions and method of regulation.

In the above description of the numerical addressing system, the non-State actors had an in-depth knowledge of the technological infrastructure and how it works. The standard implemented reflected this knowledge and expertise.

ii. Non-State actor ability to adapt according to needs

Non-State actors are able to create new rules to satisfy needs for regulation as soon as they arise. The standards developed in response to conflicts between domain names and trade marks reflect the flexible attributes of non-State actors. Non-State actors, unlike States, are capable of responding to a need and constructing efficient solutions in a quick manner. One reason why non-State actors can be more flexible is that they are familiar and expert in the area requiring regulation.

iii. Non-State actors have a direct interest in the standard being set

Being participants in the field, non-State actors have often an interest in having required regulation in place. Having the necessary regulation sustains the non-State actor existence in the field, for example, without the numerical addressing standard the whole community using the Internet infrastructure could not exist.

In the discussion on non-State actors, these attributes are often overshadowed by the debate on the legitimacy of non-State actors to participate in the law-making process. While it is usually assumed that States and governmental organisations are 'authorised' to create rules to be followed (at least by the nationals of the States parties to the rules), the legitimacy of non-State actors in international rule making has often been questioned and is discussed at length in the contribution of Pierik in this publication. While the issue of legitimacy has not be looked at in this paper, it is important to note that legitimacy may be given to private actors by governments or can be obtained by reason of their special expertise in the field.[36]

Conclusion

This paper identifies the sources of non-State actor regulation. The term 'sources' is used in this paper to refer to (a) the law-making process of non-State actor regulation; and (b) the causes that initiate non-State actor rules. The setting of technical standards in cyberspace, particularly those related to the numeric addressing system standard;

and the standard for the allocation and organisation of domain names, is used as an example of non-State actor rules. Technical standards have important legal consequences including issues of:
– *Access*: The technological standards determine who can participate in the network: only users with computers following the standards can participate in cyberspace.
– *Identification*: These standards distinguish who participates in the network: since these standards establish a unique identifier for each participant computer on the Internet one can block or allow the participation of a user through the user's computer's unique number.
– *Ownership*: Domain names have introduced a new category of ownership different to the off-line world of trademarks.
–- *Supranational Application*: These technological standards set by non-State actors have world-wide application. Any part of the network that does not follow the standards is automatically unable to communicate with the rest of the network.
– *Alternative to State Regulation*: The standards of the Internet Domain System were created to satisfy a need participants in the early life of the Internet were facing: that for computers to communicate with each other they needed to be identifiable. The initiative to set these standards came from the participants themselves. The technical experts established the standards to be followed. The bottom-up approach in setting the standard has meant that governments have traditionally kept out of this normative process. The setting of standards for computers on a network to communicate with each other is carried out completely by non-State actors.

The paper shows that non-State actor rule-making is not *ad hoc*. The non-State actor rule-making process is similar to that followed in State-led international law-making processes. Both State and non-State actors go through five steps in their law-making process: (a) recognition of a need for regulation; (b) valuation of the need; (c) formulation of norm; (d) implementation into a law; (e) acceptance and enforcement of the law.

The main difference between the State and non-State actor rules is not in the law-making process itself but in the actors participating in the process. The particular attributes of non-State actors, specifically their expertise and familiarity with the field, their flexible approach in arriving towards solutions and their direct interest in satisfying the regulatory need are specific sources (here, used in the sense of 'causes') of non-State actor regulation. One can say that the choice of actors is greatly determined by the area needing regulation. In our case, States have kept back from or have been slow in setting a law-making process in action. The technical need was addressed by non-State actors in a bottom-up manner. The setting of technical standards has normative effects on the behaviour of the same participants as our examination of the setting of standards in the Domain Name System shows. Non-State actors use their expert technical and substantive knowledge to direct their activities with efficient and effective norms especially in areas where States are unable to participate in.

Furthermore, the attributes of non-State actors explain the pertinence and occurrence of non-State actor regulation. Non-State actor rules created are appropriate for the area needing regulation. Having technical and substantive expertise allows non-State actors to set appropriate and effective means of regulation and sanction.[37] The flexible approach of non-State actor allows them to create, as swiftly as necessary, new rules addressing additional needs. The inherent interest of the participants to regulate the area ensures that the most efficient and appropriate rules are created.

In conclusion, given that there is no fundamental procedural distinction between State and non-State actor law-making processes, future studies on issues of non-State actor legitimacy, transparency and accountability as rule-makers would profit by focusing on the actual distinguishing factors in the process – the particular attributes of non-State actors.

NOTES

1 Cassese, Antonio. *International Law.* Oxford University Press 2001, p. 5.

2 See Risse, Thomas. 'Transnational Actors and World Politics'. Chapter 13 in Carlsnaes, Walter, Thomas Risse and Beth A. Simmons (eds.) *Handbook of International Relations.* Sage Publications, London 2002, pp. 255-274.

3 For example Gupta, J. and N. van der Grijp paper in this publication.

4 For example Frost, Mervyn. *Constituting human rights: global civil society and the society of democratic States.* Routledge, London 2002; van Tuijl, Peter. 'NGOs and Human Rights: sources of Justice and Democracy'. *Journal of International Affairs*, Vol. 52 (1999) issue 2 p. 493 and many others.

5 The paper of Voogsgeerd, H. in this publication on codes of corporate governance in the financial sector is such an example.

6 E.g., Spar, Debora L. Lost in '(Cyber)space: the Private Rules of Online Commerce', Chapter 2 in Cutler, A. Claire, Virginia Haufler and Tony Porter (eds.) *Private Authority and International Affairs*, State University of New York 1999, pp. 31-52.

7 Haufler, Virginia. *Beyond Government: Business Self-Regulation in International Affairs.* Working Paper dated 29 September 1998 Carnegie Endowment for International Peace accessed at <http://www.ciaonet.org/conf/cei05/ceio5a.html> on 30 October 2003.

8 Malanczuk, Peter. *Akehurst's Modern Introduction to International Law*, 7th revised edn. Routledge London 1997, p. 35 (and not as in the 'material' sense of the term, that is, the sources that 'provide evidence of the existence of rules which, when proved, have the status of legally binding rules of general application.' Brownlie, Ian. *Principles of Public International Law*, 5th edn., Oxford University Press 2001, p. 1.

9 Malanczuk, Peter. *Akehurst's Modern Introduction to International* Law, 7th revised edn., Routledge London 1997, p. 35.

10 Brownlie, Ian. *Principles of Public International Law*, 5th edn. Oxford University Press 2001, p. 1.

11 Cutler, A. Claire. Virginia Haufler and Tony Porter. 'Private Authority and International Affairs', Chapter 1 in Cutler, A. Claire, Virginia Haufler and Tony Porter (eds.) *Private Authority and International Affairs*, State University of New York 1999, pp. 4-5.

12 Except of course as co-owners of the same one domain name.

13 Cargill, Carl F. (1989) *Information technology standardization: theory, process and organisations.* Digital Press: United States, p. 13.

14 For a thorough description of the formation of standards predominantly by the State lead organizations see Salter, Liora. 'The Standards Regime for Communication and Information Technologies' (Chapter 4) in Cutler, A. Claire, Virginia Haufler and Tony Porter (eds.) *Private Authority and International Affairs*, State University of New York Press 1999.

15 Shaw, op. cit. p. 109.

16 Smith, Graham J.H. (2002) *Internet Law and Regulation*, 3rd edn., Sweet & Maxwell: London, p. 78.

17 The IETF is perhaps the Internet's longest-established technical standardization body. It was formally constituted in 1986. It is open to anyone who wants to attend its meetings or participate in its on-line discussions. The technical standards are developed by expert Working Groups. The standards are not developed by majority vote, but rather by persuasion and consensus building. Those with technical expertise and solid arguments are likely to convince their working group on the best technical standard to satisfy a given problem. See further Mitchell, Don, Scott Bradner and K Claffy (1997) 'In whose Domain? Name Service in Adolescence' in Kahin, Brian and James H. Keller (eds.) *Coordinating the Internet*, MIT press: Cambridge, Massachusetts, at p. 268.

[18] The IANA was originally part of the University of Southern California School of Engineering. It was made up of a small group of people lead by Jon Postel, one of the Internet pioneers. It has, to a certain extent, overall authority for the IP addresses, domain names and other parameters. Standards set by IANA are available as documents entitled 'Requests for Comments' (RFCs). The standards are not formally enforced by a particular entity. However, if a computer on the Internet does not follow these accepted standards, it will be unable to communicate with other machines. See further Shaw, Robert (1997) 'Internet Domain names: Whose Domain is this?' in Kahin, Brian and James H. Keller (eds.) *Coordinating the Internet,* MIT press: Cambridge, Massachusetts, at p. 120 and Zittrain, Jonathan (1999) *ICANN: Between the Public and the Private. Comments before Congress.* Accessed at <http://www.law.berkley.edu/journals/btlj/articles14_3/Zittrain/html/text.html> on 26 September 2001.

[19] An IP address is made up of four bytes of information (totalling 32 bits) expressed as four numbers between 0 and 255 shown separated by periods, for example, 129.125.113.196.

[20] Hoffman, Eric and K. Claffy (1997) 'Address Administration in IPv6' in Kahin, Brian and James H. Keller (eds.) *Coordinating the Internet,* MIT press: Cambridge, Massachusetts, at p. 270.

[21] Each of the four numbers can be any number between zero and 255. Therefore, there are 4,294,967,296 possible IP addresses (256*256*256*"256).

[22] Each potential conflict tends to be aggressively pursued by trademark owners because trademark law punishes owners who fail to police uses of their rights. An owner who fails to take action against a true infringer can soon find that the infringer has established rights of his own, and that the original mark is thus reduced in value. See Froomkin, A. Michael (2000) 'Semi-private international rulemaking: Lessons learned from the WIPO domain name process' in Marsden, Christopher, T. (ed.) *Regulating the Global Information Society.* Routledge: UK.

[23] There were initially a number of gTLD domain categories (.com, .org, .gov, .edu, .mil and .net). These had been provided by IANA. In November 2000 seven new generic top level domain categories were added on (.biz, .info, .name, .pro, .aero, .coop, and .museum). The increase in gTLDs (a) widens the possible number on persons using the same name part in the domain name but with a different domain level indicator; (b) allows certain categories or organisations to use domain level indicators that describe them better. (see Smith, op. cit. n. 16 p. 82).

[24] That is, for example the 'Corner Bar' in Moseley, United Kingdom and in Dublin, Ireland can both use the name Corner Bar as part of their internet address as long as the domain level indicator is different in both, e.g., .uk and .ie respectively.

[25] Smith, op. cit. n. 16 p. 82. For pre-launch procedures see <http://www.icann.org/announcements/icann-pr15may01.htm>.

[26] See Hart, H.L.A. *The Concept of Law.* Oxford Clarendon Press 1994; Dworkin, R.M. 'Is there a System of Rules?' in *The Philosophy of Law.* Oxford University Press, Oxford, 1977 and Thirlway, H., 'Reflections on *Lex Ferenda*', in *Netherlands Yearbook of International Law,* 2001.

[27] Like Brownlie, Ian. *Principles of Public International Law,* 5th edn. Oxford University Press, 2001

[28] Buergenthal, Thomas. *Law-making in the International Civil Aviation Organization.* Syracuse University Press, United States of America, 1969.

[29] Recommendation 13/1995.

[30] Council of Europe Convention on Cybercrime Treaty No. 185 (found at <http://conventions.coe.int/Treaty/en/Treaties/Html/185.htm>).

[31] As of December 2003 only Albania, Croatia, Estonia and Hungary had ratified the Convention while 33 other States had signed the convention. See <http://conventions.coe.int/Treaty/EN/CadreListeTraites.htm>.

[32] For procedure followed in the IETF see <http://www.ietf.org/rfc/rfc3160.txt> this document explains the process followed through RFCs (Requests for Comments) from recommended specifications to standard setting.

[33] For a description of co-ordination norms see Ullmann Margalit, Edna, *The Emergence of Norms,* Oxford, Clarendon Press 1977, pp. 74-132.

[34] In the Ullmann-Margalit terminology these are Prisoner Dilemma Norms – these norms help 'those involved to protect themselves from damaging, even ruining each other'. Ullmann-Margalit, op. cit. n. 33 p. 119.

[35] Gunningham, Neil and Joseph Rees. 'Industry self-regulation: an Institutional Perspective'. '*Law and Policy*', Vol. 19 (Issue 4) 1997, pp. 370-380.

[36] Cutler, A. Claire, Virginia Haufler and Tony Porter. 'Private Authority and International Affairs'. Chapter 1 in Cutler, A. Claire, Virginia Haufler and Tony Porter (eds.) *Private Authority and International Affairs,* State University of New York 1999, p. 4.

37 Poullet, Ives. 'How to regulate Internet: new paradigms for internet governance. Self-regulation: value and limits', in Burkert, H., J.F. Lerouge, F. Pichault, D. Poulin, Y. Poullet, C.D. Raab, J. Reidenberg and M. Vivant (eds.), *Variations sur le droit de la société de l'information*, Cahiers du Centre de Recherches Informatique et Droit. Bruylant: Bruxelles 2002.

Program Committee

The American Society of International Law

Dorinda Dallmeyer, Chair
Ruth Gordon
August Reinisch
Dinah Shelton
Peter Trooboff

Nederlandse Vereniging voor Internationaal Recht

Ige Dekker, Chair
Niels Blokker
Katharina Boele-Woelki
Ellen Hey
Alfred Kellermann
Frans Nelissen
Bette Shifman
Wouter Werner
Ramses Wessel

Conference secretariat

T.M.C. Asser Instituut
R.J. Schimmelpennincklaan 20-22
2517 JN The Hague
The Netherlands

The American Society of International Law
2233 Massachusetts Avenue, N.W.
Washington, D.C. 20008
U.S.A.
Tel.: 1-202-939-6010
Fax: 1-202-797-7133

Nederlandse Vereniging voor Internationaal Recht
Hugo de Grootstraat 27
2311 XK Leiden
The Netherlands
Tel.: 31-71-527-7748

Officers

THE AMERICAN SOCIETY OF INTERNATIONAL LAW

HONORARY PRESIDENT:
JUDGE THOMAS BUERGENTHAL

PRESIDENT:
ANNE-MARIE SLAUGHTER

PRESIDENT-ELECT:
JAMES H. CARTER

VICE PRESIDENTS:
JOSE ALVAREZ
LUCINDA LOW
DAVID MARTIN

EXECUTIVE VICE PRESIDENT AND EXECUTIVE DIRECTOR:
CHARLOTTE KU

SECRETARY:
FREDERIC KIRGIS

TREASURER:
NANCY PERKINS

EXECUTIVE COUNCIL:
ADENO ADDIS, ROGER ALFORD, KARIMA BENNOUNE, DANIEL BETHLEHEM, DANIEL BODANSKY, BARTRAM S. BROWN, ALLISON M. DANNER, KAREN KNOP, ALAN J. KRECZKO, EDWARD KWAKWA, JEFFREY LANG, MARY CATHERINE MALIN, JUDITH MILLER, SEAN D. MURPHY, GERALD I. NEUMAN, LUCY REED, LEILA SADAT, MIRIAM SAPIRO, DAVID SCHEFFER, BETH SIMMONS, CHANTAL THOMAS, DAVID WIPPMAN

NEDERLANDSE VERENIGING VOOR INTERNATIONAAL RECHT

(ACTING) PRESIDENT:
NICO SCHRIJVER

SECRETARY:
JACOMIJN VAN HAERSOLTE-VAN HOF

TREASURER:
MIEKE BOERSMA

EXECUTIVE COUNCIL:
KATHARINA BOELE-WOELKI
NIELS BLOKKER
IGE DEKKER
ASTRID DELISSEN
ELLEN HEY
CARLA JOUSTRA
MARIELLE KOPPENOL-LAFORCE
HANS LAMMERS
FRANS NELISSEN
FONS ORIE
BART PUNT
BETTE SHIFMAN
GUUS STILLE
ELSBETH DE VOS
JAN WOUTERS

List of Abbreviations

ACC	UN Administrative Coordination Committee
ACIL	Amsterdam Center for International Law
AEDPA	Antiterrorism and Effective Death Penalty Act
AGM	Annual General Meeting (of Shareholders)
AI	Amnesty International
AJIL	American Journal of International Law
ALI	The American Law Institute
AP	Additional Protocol
APA	Administrative Procedure Act
ASIL	American Society of International Law
ATCA	Alien Tort Claims Act
ATS	Alien Tort Statute
BFSP	British and Foreign State papers
BGBl.	Bundesgesetzblatt
BVerfG	Bundesverfassungsgericht
BVerfGE	Entscheidungen des Bundesverfassungsgerichts
BWC	1972 Biological Weapons Convention
CACG	Commonwealth Association for Corporate Governance
CC	OPCW Confidentiality Commission
CCF	Country Cooperation Framework
CD	Corps Diplomatique
CDJ	Corps diplomatique judiciaire
CEELI	Central and Eastern European Law Initiative of the American Bar Association
CEO	Chief executive officer
CFI	Court of First Instance of the European Communities
CFO	Chief financial officer
CFSP	Common Foreign and Security Policy (EU)
CG	Corporate Governance
CIA	Central Intelligence Agency
CIME	OECD Committee on International Investment and Multinational Enterprises
CIS	Commonwealth of Independent States
CMLR	Common Market Law Review
CNN	Cable News Network
CNRT	National Council of East Timorese Resistance
COM	European Commission document
Coreper	Comité des Représentants Permanents (EU)
COSAC	Conference of Community and European Affairs Committees
COTER	EU CFSP Working Group on Terrorism
CPA	Coalition Provisional Authority (in Iraq)

CSCE	Commission on Security and Cooperation in Europe
CSD	(national) Central securities depository
CSER	Committee of European Securities Regulators
CSP	OPCW Conference of States Parties
CTC	Counter-Terrorism Committee
CW	Chemical weapons
CWC	1993 Chemical Weapons Convention
CWPF	Chemical weapons production facility
DG	Directorate-General
DNS	Domain Name System
D&O	Directors & Officers
DPI	UN Department of Public Information
DSB	Dispute Settlement Body
DSS	Dispute Settlement System
DSU	Dispute Settlement Understanding (WTO)
EASD	European Association of Securities Dealers
EBRD	European Bank for Reconstruction and Development
EC	European Community
EC	OPCW Executive Council
ECHR	European Convention for the Protection of Human Rights and Fundamental Freedoms
ECJ	European Court of Justice
ECOSOC	UN Economic and Social Council
ED	Executive Director
EEC	European Economic Community
EIFSP	Entry into force of the Convention for the State Party
EJIL	European Journal of International Law
E.O.	Executive Order
EP	European Parliament
EPP	European Public Prosecutor
ESAF	Enhanced Structural Adjustment Facility
ETA	Euskadi Ta Askatasuna, Bask Separatist Movement
EU	European Union
EULEC	European Institute for Law Enforcement Co-operation
Eurojust	EU prosecutions unit
Europol	European Police Force
FAO	Food and Agriculture Organisation
FATF	Financial Action Task Force on Money Laundering
FBI	Federal Bureau of Investigation (USA)
FDI	Foreign direct investment
FLO	Fairtrade Labelling Organizations International
FPÖ	Freiheitliche Partei Österreich
FRY	Federal Republic of Yugoslavia
FSC	Forest Stewardship Council
FTO	Foreign Terrorist Organization
G-7	Canada, France, Germany, Italy, Japan, United Kingdom and the United States of America

G-8	G-7 plus Russia
GA	General Assembly
GAAP	Generally Accepted Accounting Principles
GATT	General Agreement on Tariffs and Trade
GAVI	Global Initiative Alliance for Vaccines and Immunization
GC	General Council
GDP	Gross Domestic Product
GEN	Global Ecolabelling Network
GM	Genetically modified
HDI	Human Development Index
HQ	Headquarters
HR	Human Resources
HURIS	Global Sub-Programme for Human Rights Strenghtening
IAEA	International Atomic Energy Agency
IANA	Internet Assigned Numbers Authority
IAS	International Accounting Standards
IASB	International Accounting Standards Board
IBRD	International Bank for Reconstruction and Development
ICAO	International Civil Aviation Organization
ICC	International Chamber of Commerce
ICC	International Criminal Court
ICCPR	International Covenant on Civil and Political Rights
ICESCR	international Covenant on Economic, Social and Cultural Rights
ICJ	International Court of Justice
ICJ Rep.	International Court of Justice, Reports of Judgments, Advisory Opinions and Orders
ICRC	International Committee of the Red Cross
ICSD	International central securities depository
ICSID	International Centre for the Settlement of Investment Disputes
ICT	Information and Communication Technologies
ICTR	International Criminal Tribunal for Rwanda
ICTY	International Criminal Tribunal for the former Yugoslavia
IDA	International Development Association
IDI	Institut de Droit International
IEEPA	International Emergency Economic Powers Act
IEO	Independent Evaluation Office of the IMF
IETF	Internet Engineering Task Force
IFI	International financial institution
IFOAM	International Federation of Organic Agriculture Movements
IGO	Intergovernmental Organization
ILA	International Law Association
ILC	UN International Law Commission
ILM	International Legal Materials
ILO	International Labor Organization
IMF	International Monetary Fund
IMO	International Maritime Organization
IMT	International Military Tribunal Nuremburg

IMTFE	International Military Tribunal for the Far East
INCADAT	International Child Abduction Database
INGO	International Non-Governmental Organization
Interpol	Commission Internationale de Police Criminelle
Int.l Org.	International Organization
IOs	intergovernmental organizations; international organizations
IOAS	International Organic Accreditation Service
IP	Internet Protocol
IRA	Irish Republican Army
ISEAL	International Social and Environmental Accreditation and Labelling
ISO	International Organization for Standardization
ISP	Inspected State Party
ITA	International Territorial Administration
ITU	International Telecommunication Union
IUCN	International Union for Conservation of Nature and Natural Resources
JCE	Joint Criminal Enterprise
JHA	EU Justice and Home Affairs
KFOR	Kosovo Force
LJ	Law journal
LMG	Like Minded Group (ICC)
LN	League of Nations
LSE	London Stock Exchange
MAC	Marine Aquarium Council
M&A	Mergers & Acquisitions
MC	Ministerial Conference
MCA	Millennium Challenge Account
MEA	Multilateral environmental agreements
MNCs	Multinational corporations
MNE	Multinational enterprise
MOP	Meeting of the parties
MOSOP	Movement for the Survival of the Ogoni People
MS	Member States
MSC	Marine Stewardship Council
MSR	Member State Responsibility
NAFTA	North American Free Trade Agreement
NATO	North Atlantic Treaty Organization
NEPAD	New Partnership for Africa's Development
NGLS	UN Non-Governmental Liaison Service
NGO	Non-governmental Organization
NVIR	Nederlandse Vereniging voor International Recht, Netherlands Branch International Law Association
OAS	Organization of American States
OAU	Organisation of African Unity
OC	Organized crime
ODA	Official development assistance
ODC	UN Office on Drugs and Crime

OECD	Organisation for Economic Co-operation and Development
OFAC	Department of the Treasury's Office of Foreign Assets Control (UK)
OHCHR	Office of the High Commissioner for Human Rights
OHR	Office of the High Representative
OIC	Organization of the Islamic Conference
OJ	Official Journal of the European Communities
OLA	UN Office of Legal Affairs
OPCW	Organisation for the Prohibition of Chemical Weapons
OSCE	Organization for Security and Co-operation in Europe
OTP	ICTY Office of the Prosecutor
P5	The permanent five members of the SC
PCA	Permanent Court of Arbitration
PCIJ	Permanent Court of International Justice
PKF	UN Peacekeeping Force
POEO	National Prosecutor's Office for European Offences
PRGF	Poverty Reduction and Growth Facility (IMF)
PRIMA	Place of the relevant intermediary approach
RC	Recueil des cours
RFCs	Requests for Comments
RGDIP	Revue Générale de Droit International Public
RICO	Racketeer Influenced and Corrupt Organisations Act
RMBCA	Revised Model Business Corporation Act
SAARC	South Asian Association for Regional Cooperation
SAB	OPCW Scientific Advisory Board
SAI	Social Accountability International
SAN	Sustainable Agriculture Network
SC	Security Council
SC Res.	Security Council Resolution
S.D.N.Y.	Southern District of New York
SEC	US Securities and Exchange Commission
SG	Secretary-General
SHD	Sustainable Human Development
SP	State Parties
SRSG	Special Representative of the Secretary-General for Kosovo
SS	(Nazi) Schutzstaffel
SUA	Convention for the Suppression of Unlawful Acts against the Safety of Maritime Navigation
SWOT	Strengths, Weaknesses, Opportunities, Threats Analysis
TA	Transitional Administrator
TBT	Technical Barriers to Trade
TEC	Treaty on the European Community
TEU	Treaty on the European Union
TNC	Transnational or multinational corporation
TNI	Indonesian military
TRIPs	Trade Related Aspects of International Property Rights (WTO)
TS	OPCW Technical Secretariat
TVPA	Torture Victim Protection Act

UCC	Uniform Commercial Code
UDHR	Universal Declaration of Human Rights
UDRP	Uniform Domain-Name Dispute-Resolution Policy
UK	United Kingdom
UN	United Nations
UNCITRAL	United Nations Commission on International Trade Law
UNCTAD	United Nations Conference on Trade and Development
UN Doc.	United Nations document
UNDP	United Nations Development Programme
UNECE	United Nations Economic Commission for Europe
UNEF	United Nations Emergency Force
UNEP	United Nations Environment Programme
UNESCO	United Nations Educational, Scientific and Cultural Organization
UNFCCC	United Nations Framework Convention on Climate Change
UNGA	United Nations General Assembly
UN GAOR	UN General Assembly Official Records
UNHCR	Office of the United Nations High Commissioner for Refugees
UNICEF	United Nations Children's Fund
UNIDROIT	International Institute for the Unification of Private Law
Unitá	Angola's former rebel movement
UNMIK	United Nations Interim Administration Mission in Kosovo
UNMISET	United Nations Mission of Support in East Timor
UNMOVIC	United Nations Monitoring, Verification and Inspection Commission
UNOCAL	Union Oil Company of California
UNOMUR	United Nations Observer Mission in Uganda-Rwanda
UNOSOM	United Nations Operation in Somalia
UNPA	United Nations Participation Act
UNPROFOR	United Nations Protection Force
UNSC	United Nations Security Council
UNSCOR	UN Security Council Official Records
UNSCR	United Nations Security Council Resolution
UNTAC	United Nations Transitional Authority in Cambodia
UNTAES	United Nations Transitional Authority in Eastern Slovania
UNTAET	United Nations Transitional Administration in East Timor
UNTS	United Nations Treaty Series
UNTSO	United Nations Truce Supervision Organization
U. Pa. J. Int'l Econ. L.	University of Pennsylvania journal of international economic law
US	United States
U.S.	United States Reports
USA	United States of America
USAID	US Agency for International Development
U.S.C.	United States Code
USS	United States Ship
USSR	Union of Soviet Socialist Republics
U.S.T.	United States Treaties and Other International Agreements

WCD	World Commission on Dams
WHO	World Health Organization
WMO	World Meteorological Organization
WSSD	World Summit on Sustainable Development
WTO	World Trade Organization
WW II	World War II
ZaöRV	Zeitschrift für ausländisches öffentliches Recht und Völkerrecht

Index of Names

Addo, M.K., 238, 243
Andem, M., 242
Alvarez, J.E., 11, 297

Van Ballegooij, W.F.W., 300
Barnhoorn, B., 58, 93
Bekker, P.H.F., 209, 242, 337
Bernasconi, Chr., 244
Berrisch, G., 202
Blokker, N., 31
Den Boer, ms M., 379, 388
Boisson de Chazournes, L., 76, 94
Bonnici, J.P.M., 503
Van Boven, Th.C., 3, 120
Bradlow, D.D., 73, 94
Broude, T, 435,
Brower, Ch.N., 44, 56
Bruggeman, W., 322
Brus, M.M.T.A., 328, 335
Buergenthal, Th., 258
Bunyan, T., 121, 388
Byers, M., 265, 299, 334
Van Bijsterveld, ms S., 121

Clapham, A., 227, 241, 243
Curtin, ms D.M., 95

Dallmeyer, ms D., 419, 421
Das, H. 317
De Hert, P., 443
Dekker, I.F. 391
Donner, P.H., 7

Eikelboom, A.W., 172
Fegue, C., 121
Fenrick, W.J., 354, 388
Ferdinandusse, W.N., 94, 338
Fife, R.E., 51
Fitzmaurice, ms M., 202, 242
Friedrichs, J., 463

Gamble, J.K., 124
Garry, ms H.R., 176
Gill, T.D., 387
Van Ginkel, ms B., 334, 387
Gioia, A., 339, 388
Goode, R., 57, 244, 257
Gowlland-Debbasch, ms V., 273, 300
Grolemund, ms A., 124

Van Genugten, W., 187, 193
Van der Grijp, ms N., 479
Gupta, ms J., 479

Hansen, ms J., 249
Heere, W.P., 15
Henning, ms W., 58
Hewitson, ms P., 298
Hey, ms E., 121
Hobe, St., 101, 122
Hoekstra, R.J., V

Van Iersel, J.P., 201

Joyner, Chr.C., 369, 388

Kellermann, A.E., 83
Kentin, ms E., 243
Kohen, M.G., 288, 298
Koh, H.H., 216, 239, 241, 243
Koopmans, S., 239
Kooijmans, P.H., 21
Kryvoi, Y., 201, 243
Ku, ms Ch., 66, 94
Kuijper, P.-J., 39-56

Leubuscher, ms S., 121, 192
De Lange, ms F., 120
Lavranos, L., 490
Lawson, R., 130
Lortie, Ph., 134
Lyons, ms C., 120, 121

Marschik, A., 301, 336, 337
Meindersma, ms Chr., 145, 170, 172
Meron, Th., 123
Murphy, S.D., 391, 419, 420, 423
Muturi, R., 463

Nollkaemper, A., 224, 240
Noortmann, M., 113, 121
Nussbaumer, M., 194, 196, 201
Nybondas, ms M., 388

O'Connell, ms M.E., 294, 299
Okany, N.R., 424

Packer, J. 300
Patel, B.N., 60, 94

Paust, J., 56, 57, 298, 360, 387
Pawelski, ms E., 93
Pierik, R., 454
Post, H.F., 298, 339
Punt, B., 257

Raaymakers, Th., 395, 418, 421, 423
Raimondo, F., 122
Rawls, J., 443
Reed, ms L.F., 176, 186, 193
Reinisch, A., 120, 301, 335, 337
Van Rooij, R., 175, 186, 193, 196, 201

Sadat, ms L.N., 348, 387
Savelyev, V., 93, 298, 387
Schrijver, N., XIII, 419, 421
Shi Jiuyong, 425
Shemberg, ms A., 200
Shifman, ms B., 242
Slaughter, ms A.-M., XIII, 60, 94, 407, 420, 422
Smits, R., 93
Spiro, P.J., 108, 122
Straver, A., 310, 335
Swaak-Goldman, ms O., 240

Thoolen, H., 154
Tsagourias, N., 472

Vella, ms T., 57, 172
De Vey Mestdagh, C.N.J., 503
Voogsgeerd, H., 494
Vryonides, D., 186

Werner, W.G., 431
Wessel, R., 31
De Wet, ms H.E., 55, 170
White, N., 57
Wiessner, S., 95, 122
Wilde, R., 164, 171
Winter, J., 197, 201
Wouters, J., 265, 298, 300

Subject Index

Accountability, 76, 95, 96, 99, 104, 105
- counter-terrorism, 274, 276, 280, 284
- EU, 88, 90
- IGOs, 60
- international military operations, 66
- IOs, 60, 76
- NGOs, 108
- self-regulation, 93
- UN, 66, 152

Advisory opinions, 21, 77
- Chemical Weapons Convention, 79
- ILO, 81
- NGOs, 81

Aggression, 473

Al Qaeda
- legal combatants, 295, 296, 360
- war crimes, 360

Amicus briefs
- ICJ, 25
- USA, 202, 219, 227
- WTO, 97, 111, 436

Arbitration, 44
- Ios, 44
- 1985 Model Rules, 44
- PCA 2001, 242
- Unidroit principles, 46

Chemical Weapons Convention
- advisory opinions, 79
- dispute settlement, 65
- good governance, 60
- mandate, 61

Civil aviation
- crimes against -, 370
- extradition, 370, 371
- hijackings, 361, 362
- sabotage, 362, 371

Climate change, 481, 485, 486

Codes of conduct, 175, 176, 187, 397, 404
- corporate governance, 495
- disclosure, 402
- EU, 399, 401, 403, 421, 495
- global compact 2000, 180, 182, 221, 228
- human rights, 177
- ILO, 179
- internal codes, 180, 198
- national codes, 494
- OECD, 179
- self-regulation, 93, 94, 188, 199, 498
- shareholders' democracy, 421
- shareholders v. boards, 197, 402, 403
- Shell, 181
- Sullivan principles, 179, 180, 221
- USA, 399, 403, 404
- *See also* Self-regulation

Codex Alimentarius
- FAO, 40, 484

Constitutionalism
- J.Rawls, 443

Corporate complicity, 217, 227, 235
- corporate liability, 211, 224, 239, 240, 401
- *See also* MNCs

Corporate governance, 194, 197, 395, 401, 494
- EU, 499
- OECD, 499

Counter-terrorism, 273
- accountability, 274, 276, 280, 284
- conventions, 277, 340
- extradition, 349, 369
- EU, 310, 325, 379
- finances, 303, 310, 317, 328, 334, 340, 375
- human rights, 276, 279
- international criminal law, 340
- role of the SC, 285
- war on terrorism, 275

Crimes against humanity, 362
- customary international law, 345
- terrorism, 344
- universal jurisdiction, 362

Customary international law
- ATS cases, 212
- and IOs, 11
- crimes against humanity, 345
- universal jurisdiction, 364
- violations of -, 364

Cyberpace, 503

Data protection, 384

Discrimination, 86, 87
- gender-, 16

Dispute settlement, 12, 21, 44
- Chemical Weapons convention, 65
- non-State actors, 27
- Unidroit principles, 46
- WTO, 97, 435, 491
- *See also* Arbitration

East Timor, 145

ombudsman, 153, 170
UN administration, 165, 171
EBRD
good governance, 92, 194, 200
ECOSOC
and NGOs, 103, 113, 121
EU, 392
accountability, 88, 90
Charter of Fundamental Rights, 444
company statute, 199, 201
constitution, 34, 35, 84, 443, 448
corporate governance, 398, 399, 418, 499
counter-terrorism, 379
decision-making, 490, 491
domestic legislation, 380
EBRD, 92, 194
EU Arrest Warrant, 382, 384, 385
extradition, 383
Framework Decision 2002, 340, 341, 347, 382, 383
financing of terrorism, 310, 312, 325, 383
good governance, IV, 83, 87, 399, 401, 407, 413
human rights, 85, 130
ICC, 54
judicial networks, 410
law-making, 408, 412
legal personality, 41, 43
member of IOs, 39, 57
mixity, 39, 40
networks, 407, 422
responsibility of Member States, 130
sanctions, 334, 335
SC Res. 1373, 310, 311
securities, 400, 403, 423
terrorism, 310, 315, 325, 379
treaty-making power, 41
Extradition
civil aviation, 370, 371
EU, 383
hostages, 372
maritime navigation, 373
political offenses, 370, 374, 387, 388
protected persons, 372
terrorism, 349, 369, 387
UN Convention on Terrorism, 375, 376

Force, use of, 419, 472
against civilians, 419, 472
developments, 266
UN, 393, 426
USA, 267
See also Self-defense
Functional duality of IOs , 464, 467, 468

G 7, 93, 94
no law-making power, 32
G 8, 74
Gender discrimination, 16
Globalization, 101, 107, 417, 454
definition, 454
ICT, 455
Governance (good), 1, 330, 429, 480
accountability, 76, 88, 108
and legal theory, 431
Chemical Weapons convention, 60
codes of conduct, 175, 197
definition, 125, 154, 330
EBRD, 92, 194
elements, 61, 84, 89, 129, 146
EU, IV, 83, 87, 399, 401, 407, 413
global governance, 172, 458, 469, 479
Hague Conference on PIL, 134, 137
human rights, 131, 157
ILA, 126, 127
IMF, 73
IOs, 126, 134, 490
military forces,
OECD, 92, 499
OHCHR, 157
terrorism, 330
UN operations, 66, 145, 165

Hague Conference on PIL, 44, 134
convention on securities, 244, 246, 249
good governance, 137
Hijackings, 361, 362
Human rights
and MNCs, 177, 203, 209, 216, 238, 242
codes of conduct, 177
counter-terrorism, 276
discrimination, 86, 87
Draft Norms of Responsibilities, 225, 226
Europe, 85
freezing measures, 335
good governance, 131, 157
ILO conventions, 190
immigrants, 87
jurisdiction, 333
national minorities, 86
NGOs, 103
OHCHR, 157, 180
refugees, 86
terrorism, 387
Humanitarian intervention, 268, 393, 394, 475

ICC, 51, 54, 95, 211, 214, 218
corporate liability, 211
crimes against humanity, 349, 350
Dutch Act, 240, 241
EU, 54
NGOs, 54, 95
USA, 19, 241

ICJ, 259
advisory opinions, 13, 21, 77
amicus briefs, 25
chambers, 260
non-State actors, 21, 24, 27
ICSID, 24
ICTY, 53, 214, 218, 258, 349, 354
joint criminal enterprise, 357
jurisdiction, 278
NGOs, 103, 211
IGOs, 425
decision-making, 490
good governance, 124
legitimacy, 490
ILO, 111
1977 Declaration, 179, 188
human rights, 190
IMF
accountability, 73, 93
decision-making, 73
governance, 74
political prohibition, 75
Immunities
terrorism, 337, 365
International courts
hierarchy, 260
International criminal law
Afghanistan, 352
terrorism, 339, 348
International humanitarian law, 343
and terrorism, 387
1977 Protocols, 343, 354
wars of national liberation, 343
IOs, 11
accountability, 60, 76
and international customary law, 11
constitutions, 33, 35
decision-making, 490
EU as member, 39
good governance, 126, 134, 490
international legal personality, 31, 32
law-making, 11, 16, 490
separate will, 31, 57
subjects of international law, 31
Iran-US Claims Tribunal, 45, 56
Iraq, 72, 93, 94, 266, 275
1990 Kuwait, 282, 291, 351
2003 intervention, 72, 281, 295

Jurisdiction, 363
multilevel -, 329, 331
protective -, 363
terrorism, 329
universal -, 345, 346, 349, 350, 362, 364
universal - by treaty, 349, 365

Kosovo, 146, 171, 394
ombudsman, 153, 170
UN administration, 165
Kyoto Protocol 1997, 481, 482, 487

Landmines
Ottawa Convention, 96
League of Nations
1937 Convention, 341, 346, 464
NGOs 114, 119

MNCs, 176, 428
and governments, 459, 460
and public international law, 224
application of ATCA, 203
codes of conduct, 176, 183
conspiracy liability, 209, 210, 216, 224
globalization, 457
human rights, 177, 183, 203, 209, 216, 238
See also Codes of conduct
Multilateral environmental agreements
decision-making, 491

National minorities, 86
minority rights, 160
NATO, 35, 68, 69
The Netherlands
code of conduct, 404, 405
corporate governance, 199, 496, 498
terrorism, 240, 382
NGOs, 95, 392, 426, 456
accountability, 95, 96, 99, 104, 105, 108, 112, 120, 420
and ECOSOC, 103, 113, 121
definition, 102
democratic control, 99, 104
globalization, 101, 456
human rights, 103, 106
information, 119
Landmines Convention, 96, 419, 427
legal personality, 120, 122
legitimacy, 95, 97
recognition, 98, 104
subjects of international law, 105
transparency, 99, 104
Non-State actors, 11, 21, 328, 391, 425, 503
armed attacks by -, 298
corporate governance, 395, 404
cyberspace, 504
internet, 504
legal personality, 111, 425
MNCs, 191
rule-making processes, 503, 510

OECD, 111, 195, 413
Bribery Convention, 217, 221

governance principles, 92, 156, 195, 499
Guidelines, 179, 188, 235
human rights, 182
Ogoni case, 203, 233, 242
OHCHR
good governance, 157
OSCE
good governance, 156

Power, 9
legitimacy, 97
Public international law
and IOs, 13
and MNCs, 224
law-making, 508, 509
States, 234
violations of -, 228
See also International customary law

Refugees, 86

Securities
EU, 400, 403
Hague Conference on PIL, 244, 249
intermediaries, 244, 246, 401
law, 398
USA, 250, 399, 404
Security Council, 17
control of decisions, 333
CTC, 17, 278, 304
frozen assets, 17, 303, 312, 317
fusion CTC–Sanctions committee, 308, 334, 336
ICC exemption, 19, 241
listing procedure, 304, 305, 336
sanctions, 17, 304, 306, 317
SC Res. 1267, 17, 277, 304, 306, 308, 317, 336
SC Res. 1373, 20, 274, 278, 303, 305, 310, 318, 335, 345, 351
SC Res. 1422, 19, 20
SC Res. 1441, 297, 299
SC Res. 1452, 305, 314
SC Res. 1483, 18, 283, 285, 337
separate will, 32
Self-defense, 18, 265, 269, 288, 294, 363, 472, 473, 474
against non-State actors, 18, 298
armed attack, 265, 267, 269, 289, 295, 474
Caroline criteria, 269, 270
ICJ, 474
imminent threat, 270
pre-emptive -, 269, 294, 474
terrorism, 288
Self-regulation, 93, 94, 188, 192, 193, 199
Self-preservation, 472, 473, 477

Soft law, 12, 84, 388
State responsibility, 234
Sustainable development
2002 World Summit, 479, 483, 485

Terrorism, 265, 322, 463, 475
1977 Additional Protocols, 343, 354
crimes against humanity, 344, 349, 350, 362
definition, 298, 339, 349, 361, 463
diplomats, 371, 362, 372
EU, 310, 325, 379
European Arrest Warrant, 382, 384, 385
extradition, 369
financing, 303, 310, 317, 328, 334, 340, 341, 375
freedom fighters, 342
good governance, 330
hostages, 371, 372
human rights, 334
humanitarian law, 387
ICTY, 354
immunities, 337, 365
international criminal law, 339, 348
jurisdiction, 329, 331
lawful combatants, 289, 296, 299, 343
1937 LoN convention, 340, 341, 346, 464
PoWs, 289
self-defense, 265, 269, 288, 294
11 September 2001, 292, 295, 303, 350, 352
State -, 268, 298, 299, 344, 364, 466, 468
UN, 301, 464
UN convention, 375, 387, 388, 466
universal jurisdiction, 329, 351
USA, 465
use of armed forces, 387, 467, 468
war crimes, 342
war on terrorism, 275, 281, 387
wars of national liberation, 342, 349, 466
Treaties
contracts v. constitutions, 33, 36

UK
codes of conduct, 404, 495, 496, 498
counter-terrorism legislation, 380
UN
accountability, 66, 152
Charter, 34
constitution,
ECOSOC, 103, 113, 117, 121
functional duality, 164, 167, 168
human rights, 165
legal personality, 425, 426
military forces, 66
NGOs, 103, 113, 117, 121
operations, 68
peace-keepimg operations, 67

terrorism, 301
transitional administrations, 145, 165
UNDP, 155, 158
UNEP, 393
UNESCO, 117, 128
UNMOVIC, 308, 334, 336
See also Security Council
Unidroit
1994 Principles, 45, 58
USA
amicus briefs, 202, 219, 227
ATCA, 176, 202, 217, 218, 224, 227, 240
ATS, 209, 212, 216
conservation law, 419
corporate governance, 399, 418, 500
disclosure, 399, 402
forum non conveniens, 203, 204
ICC, 19, 241
sustainable development, 483
terrorism, 465, 469
terrorist financing, 318
TVPA, 205, 213, 220
UCC, securities law, 250, 399, 404
use of force, 267

War crimes
Al Qaeda, 360
1977 Additional protocols, 343
terrorism, 342
Wars of national liberation, 342, 343, 349, 466
Weapons of mass destruction, 265, 295, 299
WTO, 16, 394
amicus briefs, 97, 111, 436
consensus, 436, 440
decision-making, 436, 491
EU, 40
governance, 440
role of the judiciary, 435
Shrimp-Turtle case, 394, 419

MIX
Papier aus verantwortungsvollen Quellen
Paper from responsible sources
FSC® C105338

If you have any concerns about our products,
you can contact us on
ProductSafety@springernature.com

In case Publisher is established outside the EU,
the EU authorized representative is:
Springer Nature Customer Service Center GmbH
Europaplatz 3, 69115 Heidelberg, Germany

Printed by Libri Plureos GmbH
in Hamburg, Germany